TIME ZONE
5 DAY POWER RESERVE
SWISS
HARRY WINSTON

RICHARD MILLE
RM009
SWISS MADE
CALIBER RM 009
ULTRA LIGHT
Hand-wound movement
Movement plate in Aluminium-Lithium
Variable inertia balance
Frequency 21 600 vph
Inertia 10mg /cm²
Tooth system with corrected involute profile Case
in ALUSIC (Aluminium AS7G-Silicium-Carbon)
Sapphire glass with double-sided anti-glare treatment
Water-resistant to 50 meters

**CALIBER RM 007-1**

AUTOMATIC LADY'S WATCH

Bi-directional automatic winding
18k gold rotor
100 micro balls in 18k gold
Tooth system of barrel
with corrected involute profile
V VS F/C diamond setting
Folding buckle
Available in platinum,
white gold and red gold

THE ORIGINAL ANNUAL OF THE WORLD'S FINEST WRISTWATCHES®

**TOURBILLON INTERNATIONAL, LLC**
ADMINISTRATION, ADVERTISING SALES, EDITORIAL, BOOK SALES

11 West 25th Street, 8th Floor, New York, NY 10010
Tel: +1 (212) 627-7732 Fax: +1 (212) 627-9093
sales@tourbillon-watches.com

CHAIRMAN
Joseph Zerbib

CHIEF EXECUTIVE OFFICER & PUBLISHER
Caroline Childers

U.S. EDITOR
Roberta Naas

MANAGING EDITOR
Elizabeth Kindt

CONTRIBUTING EDITORS
Deborah Cohen, Roland Murphy, Caroline Ruiz

ART DIRECTOR
Mutsumi Hyuga

DIRECTOR PRESS
Maurizio Zinelli

BUSINESS INTELLIGENCE & WEB MASTER
Marcel Choukroun

PRE-PRESS AND COLOR TECHNICIAN
Franca Vitali

TRANSLATIONS
Igino Schraffl

DIRECTOR OF FINANCE
Elliott Elbaz

INTERNATIONAL ADVISOR
John Simonian

WEB DISTRIBUTION
www.amazon.com

PHOTOGRAPHERS
Photographic Archives
Property of Tourbillon International, LLC

# Letter from the Editor

Each year as I walk BaselWorld and the other watch and jewelry exhibitions around the world, I am awed by the number of impressive anniversaries our watch industry celebrates. For some members, it is a century or more doing business. For others, it is the celebration of the first five years of a successful new brand. Sometimes, it is an anniversary commemorating a successful historic or signature watch line. Anniversaries are the source of a wealth of reflection and determination. Every milestone, no matter how small or how big, deserves such reflection.

This said, we welcome you to the sixth English edition of *Watches International*. As *Watches International* makes its sixth foray into the world watch market, the editors here reflect on its beginnings, the growth we have experienced in the past years, and the relationships we have forged with so many watch brands, their leaders and their watchmakers. It has been a wonderful time, and we thank each and every watchmaker and watch brand that has allowed us to enter their hallowed halls and review their techniques and timepieces.

It is interesting to reflect upon how each of us in some way, makes an impact on the world in the time we are here. Watchmakers, however, make an impact on the world and on the world's view of time. The pages of this book are dedicated to this all-encompassing world of time. They pay homage to the men and women who create our visions of time—who toil quietly for hours on end to provide us with new mechanisms, new presentations, new standards. The latest multi-faceted introductions from these geniuses keep us entranced and enthralled year after year.

Today's watches range from complicated masterpieces to breathtaking haute joaillerie beauties and professional sports instruments. They encompass fashion and design, technology and achievement. Now, for the sixth year in a row, *Watches International* is pleased to present this annual must-have tool of the industry, representing the most comprehensive presentation of the world's finest brands and their finest timekeepers.

I take pleasure in inviting you to peruse the pages of this book, indulge in time, and enjoy.

Roberta Naas

©2004 m
wynton marsalis, composer-performer, virtuoso.
eliro®. new tonneau-shaped case. stainless steel.
black dial. swiss made. water resistant.
movado is proud of its long-time association with the arts.
movado.com

MOVADO

# WESTIME
## LOS ANGELES, CA

**Arguably one of the largest retailers** to offer extraordinary watches and jewelry, Westime brings some of the most exclusive brands to the forefront in America. With an elegant setting and some of the most knowledgeable sales associates, Westime caters to its savvy clientele with more than 30 prestigious watch brands.

Indeed, this premiere west coast jeweler is an authorized dealer for the world's finest names: Audemars Piguet, Breguet, Chopard, Girard-Perregaux, Harry Winston, IWC and more. Not only does Westime carry the legendary brands, but also it specializes in offering complex watches created by independent watchmakers. The store also boasts an incredible list of unique, one-of-a-kind watches and limited edition timepieces that are coveted internationally.

Owned and operated by second-generation watchmaker John Simonian, Westime enjoys a rich history that has grown with the brands its carries. Simonian, also a collector with a passion for complicated mechanical timepieces, opened his store in Los Angeles in 1988.

**BRANDS CARRIED**

AUDEMARS PIGUET
BAUME & MERCIER
BLANCPAIN
BREGUET
BREITLING
CHANEL
CHOPARD
CONCORD
CORUM
DE GRISOGONO
EBEL
FRANCK MULLER
GIRARD PERREGAUX
GLASHÜTTE
GREUBEL FORSEY
GUCCI
HAMILTON
HARRY WINSTON
IWC
LE MANS CLASSIC
LONGINES
OMEGA
RADO
RICHARD MILLE
ROGER DUBUIS
TAG HEUER
TISSOT
TUTIMA
UNDERWOOD
URWERK
VACHERON CONSTANTIN
VERTU
ZENITH

Since then, he has cultivated a loyal following of celebrities, sports stores and international business travelers thanks to his store's superior selection and superb service.

In fact, the staff at Westime goes over and above the normal call of duty, by making personal deliveries across town or even across the country. Additionally, Westime hires multi-lingual sales associates to assist its international clientele. Most sales associates speak at least two languages, and some speak more. Like the United Nations, one can enter Westime and hear as many as 10 different languages being spoken.

Education is key at Westime, and watchmakers and executives from the various brands are regularly brought in to the store to train associates. Some associates even travel to Switzerland to become proficient with some of the most complicated watches so that they can more efficiently discuss these pieces with the sophisticated Westime clientele.

To service customers after the sale, Westime's two full-time watchmakers utilize state-of-the-art equipment for watch repairs and other maintenance. In its 6,000-square foot West Pico Boulevard store in Los Angeles, Westime caters to its discerning clientele with expansive showcases, comfortable seating arrangements and Chopard and Audemars Piguet boutiques. Naturally, Westime offers front door valet service, as well.

A second Westime salon is located on famed Rodeo Drive in Beverly Hills, California.

**10800 West Pico Blvd., #197, Los Angeles, CA 90064**
**Tel: 310.470.1388**
**www.westimewatches.com**

MEYERS
SWISS MADE

agence B-T

MEYERS
agence B+T

# DARAKJIAN JEWELERS

## SOUTHFIELD, MI

**Few jewelers can boast** what this Southfield, Michigan retailer has to offer. Darakjian Jewelers recently celebrated 40 years of service-driven business with its founding father still actively at the helm.

John Darakjian first opened his jewelry store door in October 1964 in the once-famed Metropolitan Building in downtown Detroit. Early on, Darakjian built an incredibly loyal following of customers from all walks of life. That clientele has remained steadfast in its commitment to this family-owned firm, and the owners of Darakjian remain faithful to them. At 74 years old, John still enjoys laughing and talking with the customers who first made his business a success four decades ago.

Indeed, John Darakjian, along with his wife Bergy and sons Ara and Armen, are dedicated to offering a three-prong approach to keeping customers and friends happy: service, selection and a comfortable, uplifting atmosphere. Service before, during, and after sales is key. While some stores use the words service-oriented as a marketing buzzword, Darakjian lives by it. Service is the thread that holds the store together. Darakjian guarantees 24-hour repairs and 72-hour appraisals, or they're free. The sales staff is incredibly knowledgeable, with ongoing training and a passion about their products.

### BRANDS CARRIED

| | |
|---|---|
| AUDEMARS PIGUET | MONTBLANC |
| BELL & ROSS | MOVADO |
| BLANCPAIN | PHILIP STEIN |
| CHOPARD | RADO |
| GLYCINE | TECHNOMARINE |
| GUCCI | TISSOT |
| HUBLOT | ULYSSE NARDIN |
| LONGINES | VACHERON CONSTANTIN |

Selection is equally as important. According to Armen Darakjian, "We offer something different, unique, in all price ranges, things the savvy customer can't find anywhere else."

Indeed, in addition to its custom jewelry and elegant lines, Darakjian Jewelers carries approximately 16 watch brands in its store. The brands range in price so that the jeweler is sure to have something for every one of its customers, no matter their profession or spending range. Among the best-selling brands at the store: Audemars Piguet, Blancpain, Chopard, Gucci, Movado, Rado, Ulysse Nardin, Vacheron Constantin. These tried-and-trues are complemented by some high-tech brands including Bell & Ross, Philip Stein and TechnoMarine.

The store's customer-friendly service and selection policy is backed by a champagne and cappuccino bar and its "concierge-on-Saturdays" approach. At any given time, juices, champagne and cappuccino are served to customers in a relaxed setting. On Saturdays, a concierge works the store, happy to help with plans for dinner, events and the like. The store's atmosphere is a superb blend of contemporary and traditional thanks to the colorful, geometric balance and warm wood cases. It is at once comfortable and relaxing. At one end of the store is an elegant boutique area dedicated to three of the more luxurious brands: Audemars Piguet, Ulysse Nardin and Vacheron Constantin.

Even Darakjian's approach to thanking its clients and to marketing and advertising is unique. VIPS were treated to a huge, fabulous party held in honor of the brand's 40 years and special anniversary promotions were offered to members of the community.

Indeed, everything this jeweler embraces—from customers to products, marketing and events—is done with a fervent emphasis on personalized service, to preserving friendships and relationships that can last for decades to come. It is this honest, down-to-earth approach that has earned Darakjian Jeweler its distinguished reputation.

**29333 Northwestern Highway, Southfield, MI 48034**
**Tel: 888.843.6659**
**www.darakjian.com**

# The accuracy of a Lange watch can be measured with great precision.

**Feeler gauge by Lange, ca. 1900.**
The precision of a watch cannot exceed that of the measuring instruments used in its making. That was absolutely clear to Adolph Lange when he, as the first watchmaker in history, decided in 1844 to replace the complicated Parisian ligne system by the metric system. It was a bold step, but also an exemplary one, adopted by Swiss watchmakers a few years thereafter. Concurrently, he developed many new measuring instruments, such as the 1/10-mm feeler gauge shown here. The instruments available to the master watchmakers at Lange today allow them to verify the precision of parts to an accuracy of 1/1000 mm.

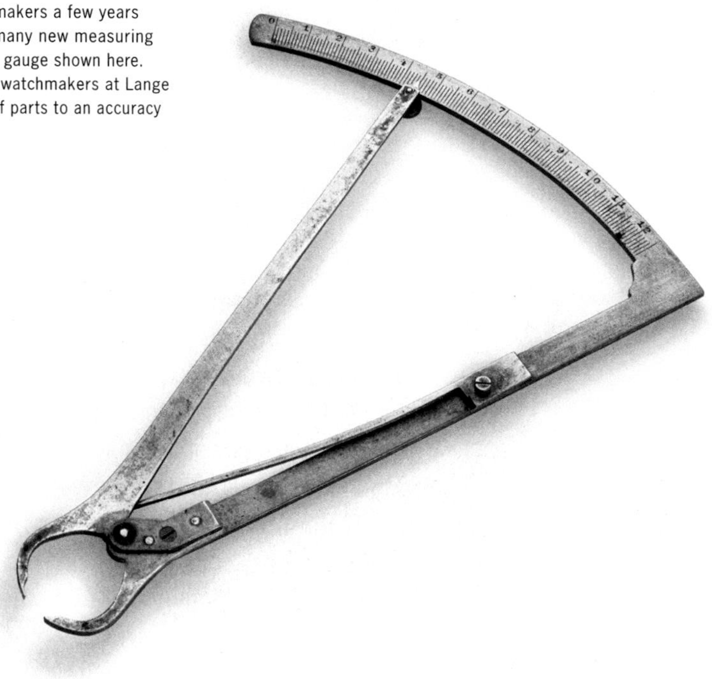

A. LANGE
GLASHÜT

During a period of over 500 years, the art of mechanical timekeeping was developed to stunning perfection. And some of the most important inventions were born in the mind of Adolph Lange. In 1845, he abandoned his privileged position as royal Saxon court watchmaker to establish German fine horology in the Ore Mountains. In Glashütte, he trained young men to become consummate craftspeople, developed totally new precision tools and invented pioneering mechanical devices and manufacturing methods. Subsequently, for 100 years, the watches of "A. Lange & Söhne" were among the most sought-after in the world, until the division of Germany eradicated the proud company's name on timepiece dials. "A. Lange & Söhne" became a legend. But immediately after German reunification,

Or just enjoyed.

**The Lange 1 Moonphase.**
It cannot be detected by acuity, but it can be sensed instinctively: the accuracy with which the Lange 1 Moonphase emulates the motion of the earth's satellite. It takes no less than 122 years of uninterrupted operation before its continuously driven gold moon disc deviates from the actual lunar orbit by one day. Apart from a patented outsize date and a power-reserve indicator, the Lange 1 Moonphase also has luminous hands and hour markers. This masterpiece is available in 18-carat gold or platinum.

Walter Lange, Adolph Lange's great-grandson, returned to Glashütte to once again demonstrate the prowess of Lange watchmaking artistry with the same love of innovation that originally made Lange famous around the globe. And as in the old days, Lange's unique watches are still painstakingly crafted and assembled by hand. Lange watches will always be exclusive, as are the few jewellers in the world that offer "A. Lange & Söhne" masterpieces. There, connoisseurs of watchmaking excellence can find a catalogue documenting the ingenious creations of "A. Lange & Söhne" and the company's legacy – as is only fitting when a legend comes back to life. General Agent for A. Lange & Söhne: Richemont North America Inc., 645 Fifth Avenue, 10022 New York, NY, phone (212) 891 2355. www.lange-soehne.com.

# SUMMARY

de GRISOGONO®
GENEVE

de GRISOGONO
GENEVE
04
SWISS MADE

# Web Site Directory

| | |
|---|---|
| **A. Lange & Söhne** | www.alange-soehne.com |
| **Anonimo:** | www.anonimousa.com |
| **Armand Nicolet:** | www.armandnicolet.com |
| **Arnold & Son:** | www.arnoldandson.com |
| **Audemars Piguet:** | www.audemarspiguet.com |
| **Baume & Mercier:** | www.baume-et-mercier.com |
| **Bertolucci:** | www.bertolucci-watches.com |
| **Blancpain:** | www.blancpain.com |
| **Boucheron:** | www.boucheron.com |
| **Bovet:** | www.bovet-fleurier.ch |
| **Breguet:** | www.breguet.com |
| **Breitling:** | www.breitling.com |
| **Bvlgari:** | www.bulgari.com |
| **Cartier:** | www.cartier.com |
| **Chanel:** | www.chanel.com |
| **Chaumet:** | www.chaumet.com |
| **Chopard:** | www.chopard.com |
| **Clerc:** | www.clercwatches.com |
| **Concord:** | www.concord.ch |
| **Corum:** | www.corum.ch |
| **Cuervo Y Sobrinos:** | www.cuervoysobrinos.com |
| **Daniel Roth:** | www.danielroth.com |
| **David Yurman:** | www.davidyurman.com |
| **De Bethune:** | www.debethune.ch |
| **de GRISOGONO:** | www.degrisogono.com |
| **DeWitt:** | www.dewitt.ch |
| **Dior:** | www.dior.com |
| **Dubey & Schaldenbrand:** | www.dubeywatch.com |
| **Ebel:** | www.ebel.com |
| **Eberhard & Co:** | www.eberhard-co-watches.ch |
| **ECW:** | www.europeancompanywatch.com |
| **F.P. Journe:** | www.fpjourne.com |
| **Franck Muller:** | www.franckmullerusa.com |
| **Georges V:** | www.georges-v.com |
| **Gérald Genta:** | www.geraldgenta.com |
| **Gevril:** | www.gevril.ch |
| **Girard-Perregaux:** | www.girard-perregaux.ch |
| **Glashütte Original:** | www.glashuette.de |
| **Graham:** | www.graham-london.com |
| **Greubel Forsey:** | www.greubelforsey.ch |
| **Gucci:** | www.gucci.com |
| **Guy Ellia:** | www.guyellia.com |
| **Harry Winston:** | www.harry-winston.com |
| **Hermès:** | www.hermes.com |
| **Hublot:** | www.hublot.ch |
| **Invicta:** | www.invictawatch.com |
| **IWC:** | www.iwc.ch |
| **Jacob & Co:** | www. jacobandco.com |
| **Jaeger-LeCoultre:** | www.jaeger-lecoultre.com |
| **Jaquet Droz:** | www.jaquet-droz.com |
| **Jean-Mairet & Gillman:** | www.jean-mairetgillman.com |
| **JeanRichard:** | www.jeanrichard.com |
| **Locman:** | www.locman.it |
| **Longines:** | www.longines.com |
| **LVMH Group:** | www.lvmh.fr |
| **Mauboussin:** | www.mauboussin.com |
| **Maurice Lacroix:** | www.mauricelacroix.com |
| **Meyers:** | www.meyers.fr |
| **Michele Watches:** | www.michelewatches.com |
| **Movado:** | www.movado.ch |
| **Officina del Tempo:** | www.officinadeltempo.com |
| **Omega:** | www.omega.ch |
| **Panerai:** | www.panerai.com |
| **Parmigiani Fleurier:** | www.parmigiani.com |
| **Patek Philippe:** | www.patek-philippe.ch |
| **Paul Picot:** | www.paulpicot.ch |
| **Piaget:** | www.piaget.com |
| **Raymond Weil:** | www.raymond-weil.ch |
| **RGM:** | www.rgmwatches.com |
| **Richemont Group:** | www.richemont.com |
| **Roger Dubuis:** | www.roger-dubuis.com |
| **Rolex:** | www.rolex.com |
| **Rotary:** | www.rotarywatchesdirect.com |
| **S. Coifman:** | www.scoifman.ch |
| **Scatola del Tempo:** | www.scatoladeltempo.com |
| **Swatch Group:** | www.swatchgroup.com |
| **TAG Heuer:** | www.tagheuer.com |
| **TB Buti:** | www.domushora.com |
| **Tutima:** | www.tutima.de |
| **Urwerk:** | www.urwerk.ch |
| **Vacheron Constantin:** | www.vacheron-constantin.com |
| **Zannetti:** | www.zannettiwatches.com |
| **Zenith:** | www.zenith-watches.ch |

## RELATED SITES

| | |
|---|---|
| **Tourbillon International:** | www.tourbillon-watches.com |
| **BaselWorld:** | www.baselworld.com |
| **Auctions:** | www.christies.com<br>www.sothebys.com |

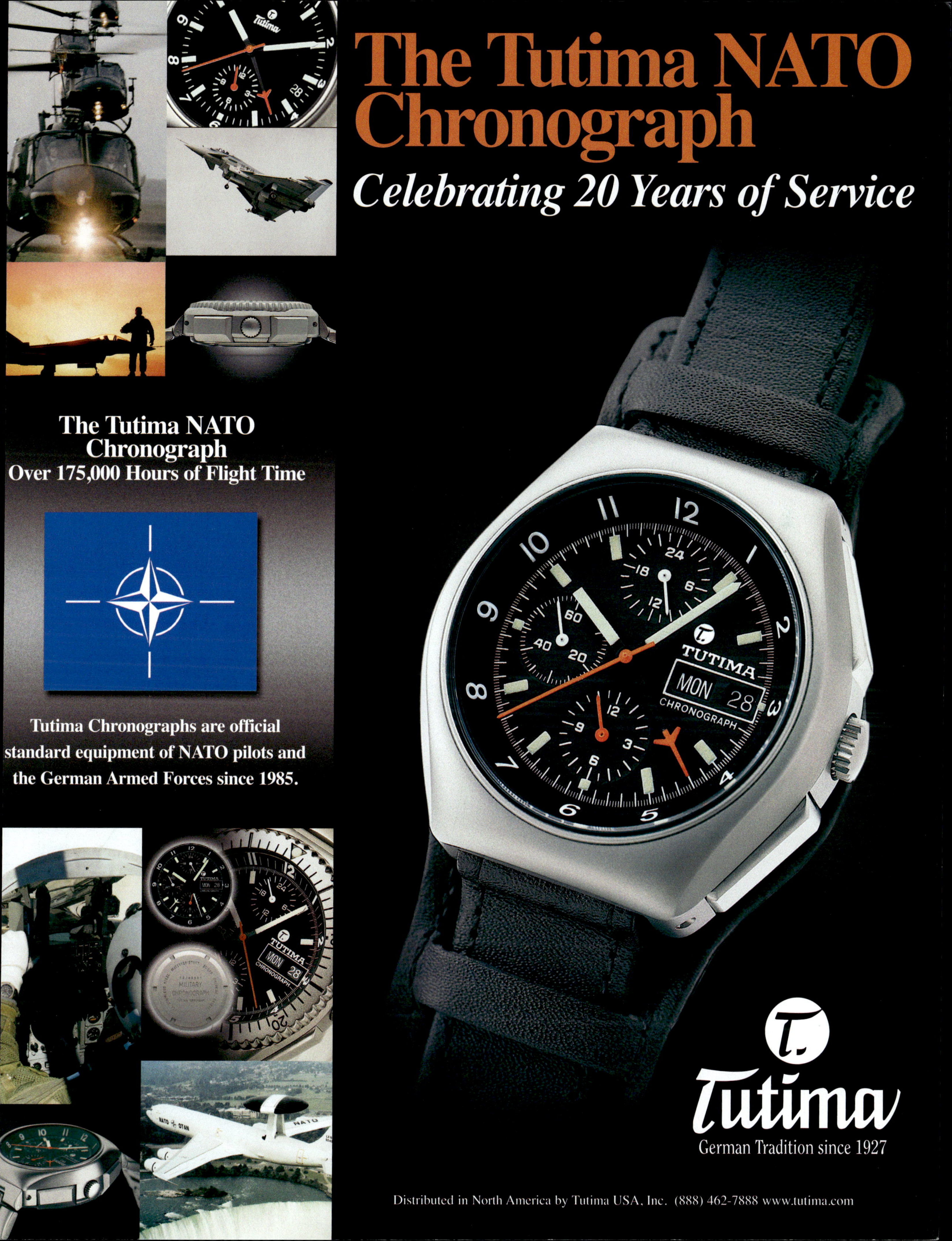
The Tutima NATO Chronograph
Celebrating 20 Years of Service
The Tutima NATO Chronograph
Over 175,000 Hours of Flight Time
Tutima Chronographs are official standard equipment of NATO pilots and the German Armed Forces since 1985.
TUTIMA
MON 28
CHRONOGRAPH
Tutima
German Tradition since 1927
Distributed in North America by Tutima USA, Inc. (888) 462-7888 www.tutima.com

# CINETTE ROBERT

*Few women reign in the world of watchmaking. Cinette Robert is the exception. A lover of timepieces, this patient woman became the first female in history to own a watch company when she purchased the fine Dubey & Schaldenbrand watch brand in 1995. She has since brought the brand to stellar heights.*

Robert spent years collecting retired mechanical movements that had been abandoned by other brands—and created an exceptional collection of limited edition watches for Dubey & Schaldenbrand using the 6,000 movements she had amassed by fitting them in superb retro-styled cases. This unprecedented union of old and new brought her and the brand international recognition.

CENTER
Cinette Robert spent many years in the watch industry before acquiring Dubey & Schaldenbrand.

Robert then went on to augment the vintage movement collection with new Dubey & Schaldenbrand watches—manufacturing only complex mechanical timepieces. To appeal to the discerning collector, Robert insists that every watch feature exquisite detailing and honor the traditions of the past.

Included in the Dubey & Schaldenbrand collection are round, tonneau and carré-shaped timepieces. Robert is most proud, however, of the Gran'Chrono Astro watch with moonphase indicator, day, date and month readings. The prototype for this automatic chronograph took 16 months to build and the making of the case involves 90 operations.

Robert grew up in the 1940s in a canton of Neuchâtel near Le Locle. Home-bound during snowy winters in the mountains, the resourceful Robert learned many arts, including playing the organ, harmonium, guitar and flute—all to no real avail. Says Robert, "I was not able to progress. If you are always at the same level, you are not an artist."

So instead she turned her sights to watches, answering her true artistic calling, which was in her blood anyway. In fact, her great-grandfather was Meylan-LeCoultre. Robert spent endless hours reading about watches and by the time she was 16 she was entranced by split-second chronographs instead of clothes and other trappings typical of young girls.

**TOP LEFT**

Georges Dubey taught watchmaking at the La Chaux-de-Fonds horological school.

**TOP RIGHT**

The original Index Mobile performed the functions of a split-seconds chronograph.

Frowned upon for her boyish interests (mechanical things were not meant for young women), Robert was undeterred. She sought help from Georges Dubey, a professor of watchmaking in La Chaux-de-Fonds and co-founder of Dubey & Schaldenbrand. Frequently, Robert would bring complicated watches to Dubey—who would patiently explain the movements to her, often taking her to the watch school to use the microscopes.

In 1985, with the buzz of quartz in the air, Robert struck out on her own to build and sell mechanical antique watches. Were it not for her intense knowledge of and passion for the watch world, Robert would not have succeeded. However, she built professional relationships based on trust and slowly broke ground. As many other companies were folding under the duress of abundant, inexpensive quartz watches infringing upon their turf, the astute Robert quickly snapped up lots of unused mechanical movements.

"I wanted something nobody wanted," says Robert. "I believe when a lot of handiwork goes into making something, the value goes up. You just have to wait."

When the quartz revolution slowed and mechanical watches regained their command, Robert was in a prime position to move ahead with her mechanical calibers. Additionally, she had been approached about the possibility of buying Dubey & Schaldenbrand—an opportunity in which she was very interested. Everything meshed, and by 1995 Robert was the proud owner of a Swiss brand introducing antique movements in stunning cases based on Dubey & Schaldenbrand's archival designs.

Today, Robert has introduced new lines in classic styles. Dubey & Schaldenbrand sells its exclusive timepieces in 30 countries—moving in a slow-but-steady growth pattern to greater positioning. The watches from Dubey & Schaldenbrand are created according to tradition with carefully chosen components from the movement to the smallest screw. Sapphire crystals and precious metals comprise the outer casing and the inner mechanics demonstrate technical excellence.

To Robert, her watches are her babies, and her goal is to create the most reliable, trustworthy timepiece today that will last for generations to come.

“Le temps
n’a pas la même allure
pour tout le monde.*
WILLIAM SHAKESPEARE
* Time does not have the same appeal for everyone.

# TODAY'S TIME

by Roberta Naas

Life is about time. It's about having enough time to do the things we want to do, the things we have to do, and everything in between. Every second is measured in today's world. For this reason, top watchmakers offer a host of stunning timepieces to track those seconds, those minutes, those hours. In fact, some watchmakers offer us so many additional treasured functions in a watch that sometimes, it can serve as our only guiding instrument. Whether one is on a business trip, vacationing in a far-off corner of the world, diving to deep depths or running a marathon, there is a watch out there designed to accompany him.

ABOVE
Radiomir Black Seal® (Panerai)

CENTER
Microtimer (TAG Heuer)

BOTTOM LEFT
Ladies' Hampton Spirit PM and Hampton Spirit XL Phase de Lune (Baume & Mercier)

BOTTOM RIGHT
GMT (The Longines Master Collection)

**TOP LEFT**

Casablanca 10th Anniversary (Franck Muller)

**TOP RIGHT**

Tank Louis Cartier Skeleton (Cartier)

**CENTER LEFT**

Patrimony Grande Taille ultra-slim (Vacheron Constantin)

**CENTER RIGHT**

Firshire Tonneau 3000 (Paul Picot)

**BOTTOM RIGHT**

L.U.C 4R Quattro Regulateur (Chopard)

**Elegance** reigns supreme in sublimely simple or masterfully complicated timepieces. Clean, classic designs for men include those in steel, gold and platinum, with three hands or even regulator dials. Most of the finest watch companies indulge watch lovers with these stunning beauties, and some brands like Jaquet Droz and Chopard offer meticulously finished regulators that feature off-centered dials or unusual hour and minute readouts. Skeletonized watches are also magnificent beauties that allure and entice collectors with their open-worked movements. Brands such as Piaget, Cartier, Girard-Perregaux and a host of other luxurious watchmakers offer stunning, intricate skeleton watches.

Westime
RODEO
254 RODEO DRIVE
BEVERLY HILLS. CA 90210
T. (310) 271-0000

JAQUET DROZ

**Complicated** watches also offer classic elegance, as many of these complications originated centuries ago and are the specialties of such legendary firms as Patek Philippe, Audemars Piguet, Jaeger-LeCoultre and IWC. Among the most coveted complications are tourbillons from such brands as Blancpain, Chopard, Franck Muller, Girard-Perergaux, Zenith and, of course, Breguet—the grandfather of tourbillons.

**TOP LEFT**
Tourbillon Revolution 3
(Franck Muller)

**CENTER**
Tourbillon with
throo gold Bridges
(Girard-Perregaux)

**TOP RIGHT**
Time Square Z 1 Tourbillon
Magistère (Guy Ellia)

**ABOVE**
Double Tourbillon 30°
(Greubel Forsey)

**BOTTOM LEFT**
Gyrotourbillon
(Jaeger-LeCoultre)

BVLGARI
12
BVLGARI
AUTOMATIC
6
6
BVLGARI
BULGARI.COM
ergon

Elegance
Swiss made - www.longines.com - © Paramount Pictures Corporation
Longines supports the Audrey Hepburn Children's Fund

LONGINES
AUTOMATIC
23
SWISS MADE

**TOP LEFT**

Tourbillon Minute Repeater (Patek Philippe)

**TOP RIGHT**

Forma XL Minute Repeater (Parmigiani)

**ABOVE**

Fleurier (Bovet)

**FAR LEFT**

Grande Complication (IWC)

**BOTTOM RIGHT**

New Emotion Minute Repeater (DeWitt)

# Minute repeaters

and sonneries that chime the time for all to hear are coveted pieces. These works of art are incredibly elegant—especially when the wearer pushes the slide and activates the melodious notes.

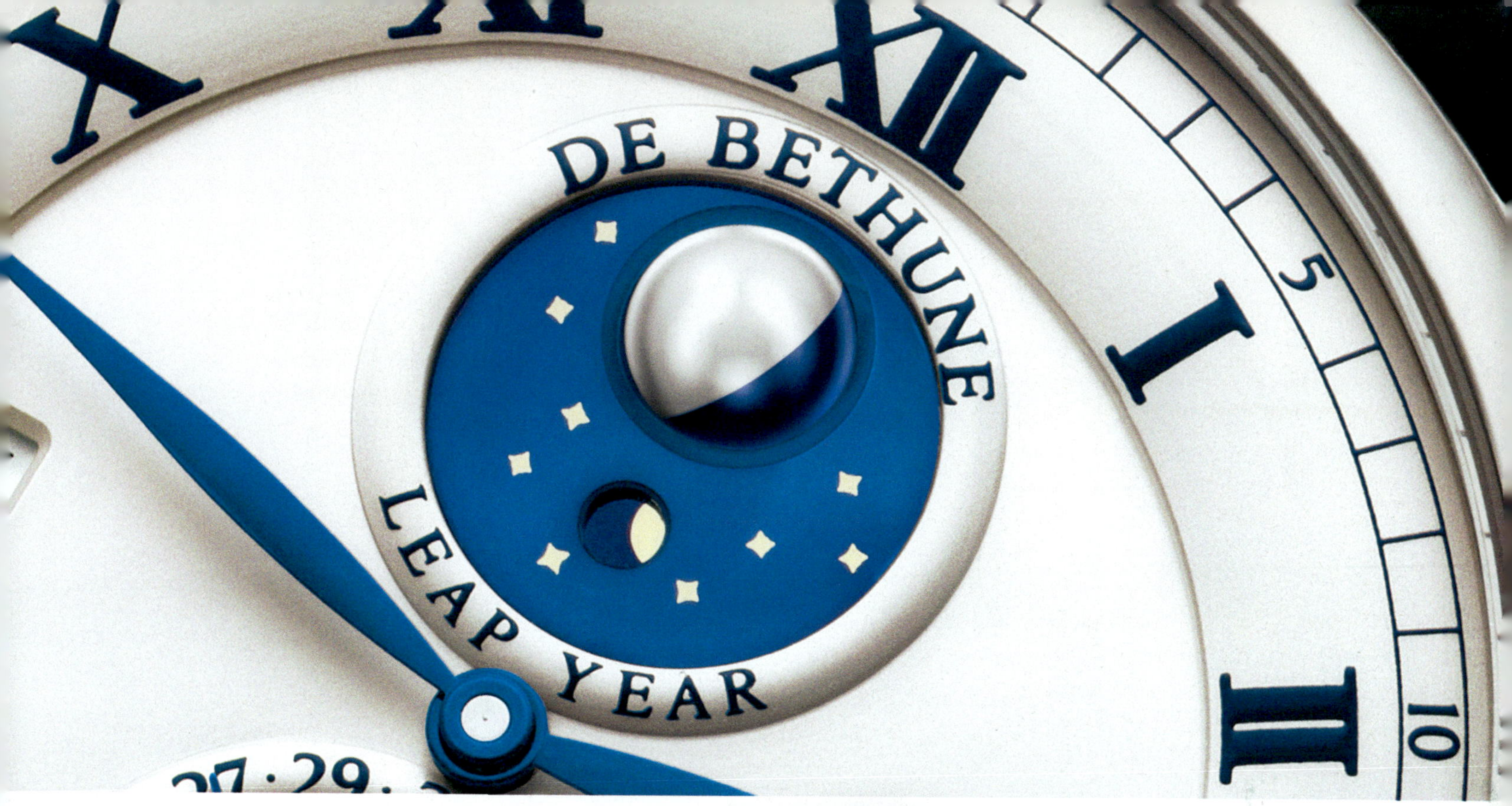

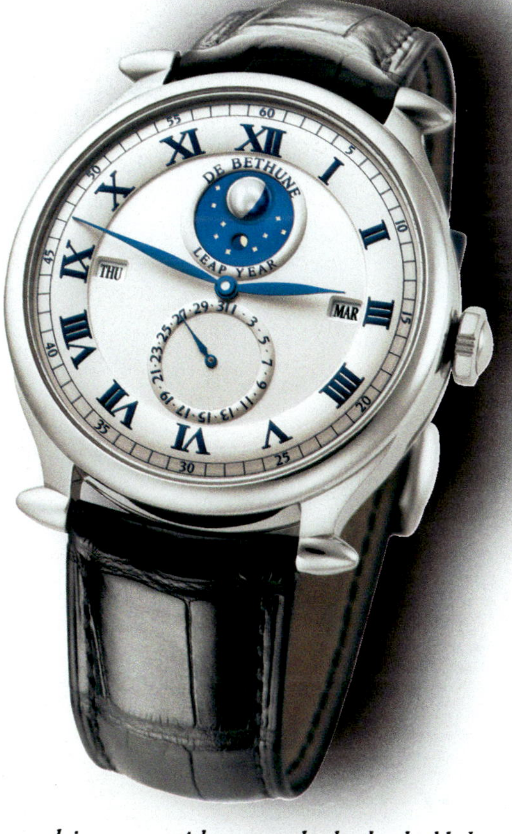

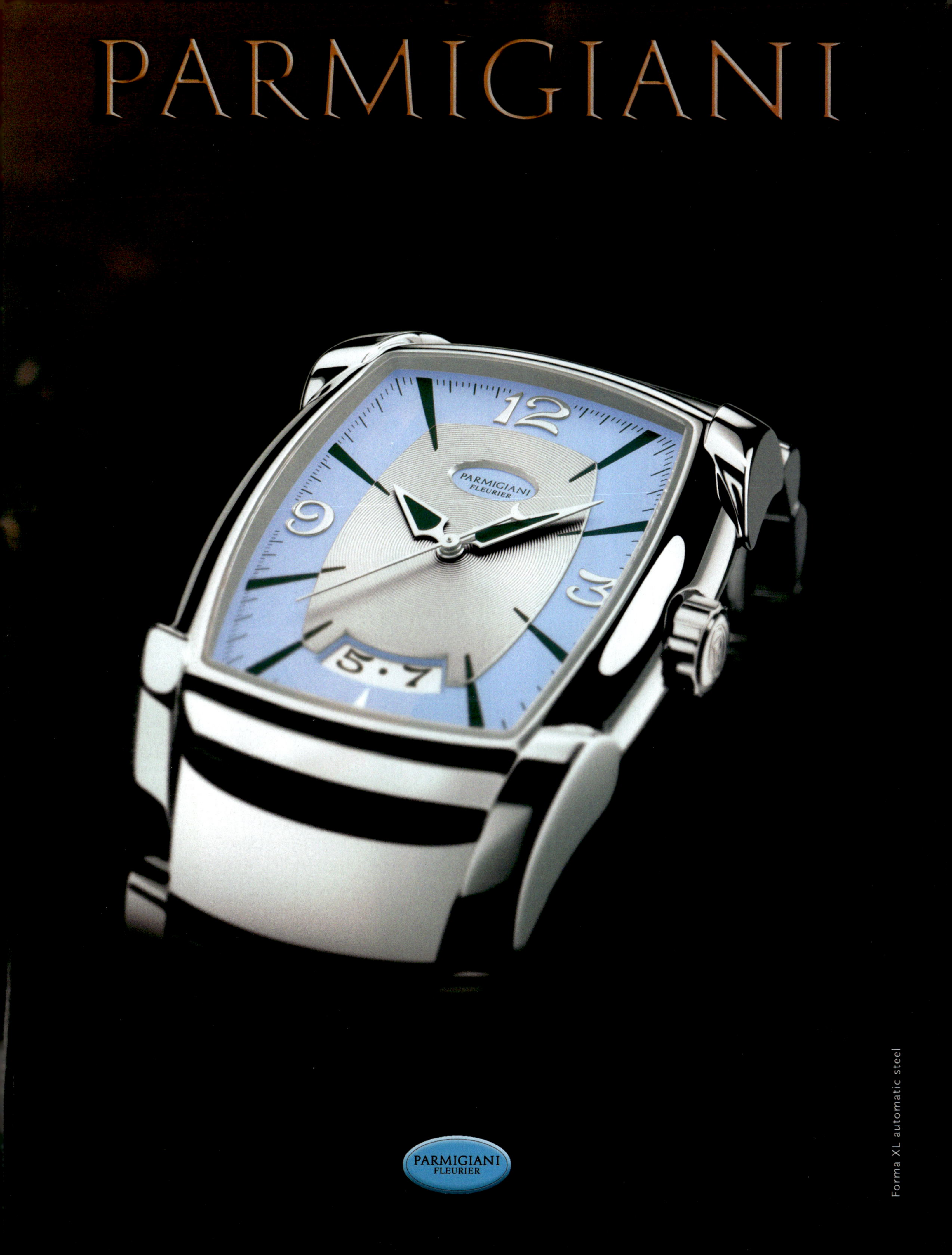
PARMIGIANI
PARMIGIANI FLEURIER
PARMIGIANI FLEURIER
Forma XL automatic steel

**Calendar** watches—annual calendars, perpetual calendars and moonphases—all have something special to offer the busy person who depends on his or her watch to keep the correct time for days, weeks, months, and years without the need for adjustments. Today's perpetual calendars typically track time to the year 2100 before needing manual adjustments and a handful of companies have created watches that will remain accurate beyond this date. Also on the market are annual calendar watches—those that need adjustments on March 1 of every year. The technology of mechanical calendar watches is complex, utilizing a system of levers and wheels intricately interconnected. Many calendar watches include stunning moonphase readouts and some complicated perpetual calendars include astronomical indicators and equations of time.

**TOP LEFT**
Grande ChronoMaster XXT Quantième Perpétuel (Zenith)

**TOP RIGHT**
Complete Calendar M02 (Armand Nicolet)

**CENTER LEFT**
Gondolo Calendario (Patek Philippe)

**CENTER RIGHT**
Da Vinci Perpetual Calendar (IWC)

**BOTTOM LEFT**
De Bethune Perpetual Calendar with Revolving Moon Phase DB15 (De Bethune)

Chopard

# The ultimate reference

**L.U.C Regulator.** The watch-making workshops of yesteryear always had a master clock by which every other timepiece was regulated. From its elevated position, this regulator was an absolute reference that commanded the attention of all the master watchmakers. The hands of this rare precision instrument were eccentrically positioned on separate dials to allow the time to be read as precisely as possible. With their mastery of all the skills of the horological trade, the Chopard Manufacture has now expertly miniaturised this clock into a wristwatch. And it still captures everyone's attention.

A masterpiece within the Chopard collection, the L.U.C Regulator incorporates the chronometer-certified Quattro 1.98 movement. Five eccentric dials in four colours and three guilloché patterns display the hours, minutes, seconds, a more than 8-days power reserve and a second time zone.

**L.U.C**

**MANUFACTURE DE HAUTE HORLOGERIE**
**LOUIS-ULYSSE CHOPARD**

**L.U.C Regulator:** available in yellow, white or rose gold, in a limited and numbered series of 250 pieces per metal (ref. 16/1874). Movement with "Poinçon de Genève".

The L.U.C Regulator has been awarded watch of the year 2004 by Montres Passion - Uhren Welt.

The L.U.C collection is exclusively available at selected watch specialists and Chopard Boutiques worldwide.
For further information: Chopard USA Ltd, 21East 63rd Street, NEW YORK, NY 10021-1.800.CHOPARD - www.chopard.com

For more information call 212 218 7543 or visit www.ebel.com ©2005 Ebel

Ebel Beluga Tonneau
EBEL
THE ARCHITECTS OF TIME
EBEL

**TOP CENTER**

Diagono Professional GMT 40 Flyback (Bvlgari)

**CENTER LEFT**

Serenade (Gevril)

**CENTER RIGHT**

Instrumento No Uno (de Grisogono)

**BOTTOM RIGHT**

World Time (Patek Philippe)

GMT and multiple time-zone watches have become essential instruments for world travelers and people conducting business around the globe. These complex timepieces offer the local time, time in second and third zones—even all 24 zones—around the world. All operate on similar principles, which enable the wearer to locate time here, there and everywhere. Typically, these watches offer a subdial or aperture displaying a second time zone, and a rotating bezel indicating a third time zone or the times in all 24 zones.

# Man is of the essence.

More than 70 years after its initial launch in tribute to the great seafaring nation of Portugal, the legendary Portuguese watch is now available in an elegant new edition: the appeal of the Portuguese Automatic lies in its mechanical movement, automatic Pellaton winding system, seven-day power reserve and case diameter of 42.3 mm. Water-resistant to 30 metres. Ref. 5001 in 18 ct. rose gold. Also available in stainless steel. And in platinum, in a limited edition of 500 watches.

IWC

**Since 1868.**
**And for as long as there are men.**

**IWC Schaffhausen, Switzerland, www.iwc.ch**
For an authorized retailer nearest you, please call (800) 432-9330, or visit our website.

**Gemstone** watches are particularly popular, as trends give way to color, shape, size, and carat weight. Watchmakers have long incorporated sapphires, rubies, emeralds and black diamonds into their gold and platinum creations. Thanks to recent technologies, these jewels now can be placed into steel watches, making it more affordable for gem lovers to own them.

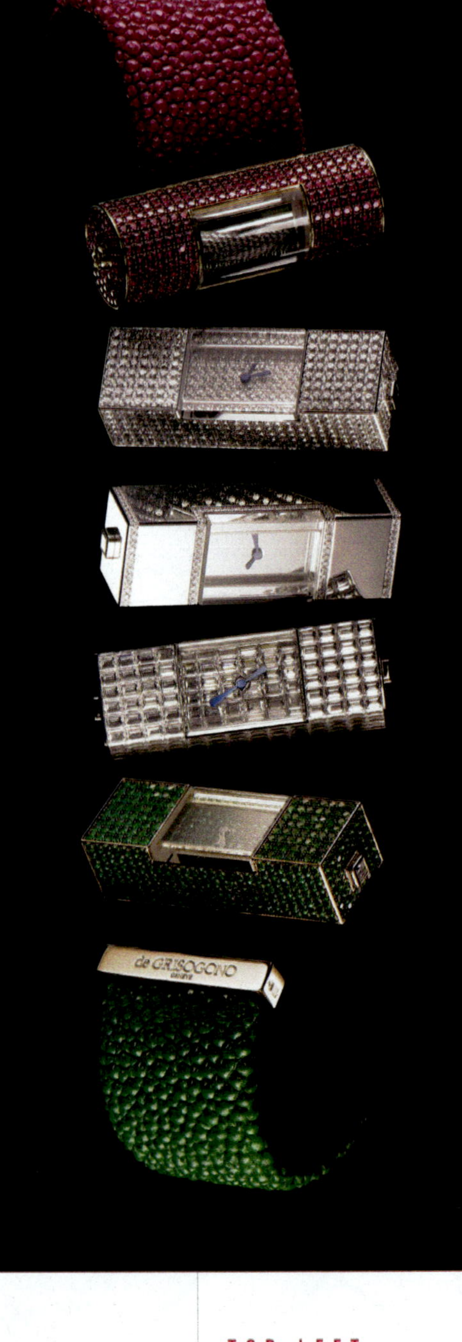

TOP LEFT
J 12 (Chanel)

TOP RIGHT
Lipstick watches (de GRISOGONO)

BOTTOM LEFT
FollowMe (Roger Dubuis)

BOTTOM RIGHT
La Twenty Exclusive (Meyers)

CONCORD
Delirium
SWISS MADE

**TOP LEFT**
Haute Joaillerie watches (Chopard)

**TOP CENTER**
Time Square 2311 MV1 (Guy Ellia)

**CENTER**
Lady Premier Chronograph (Harry Winston)

**TOP RIGHT**
Dentelle de Givre watch (Chaumet)

**FAR LEFT**
Moon Chic (Ebel)

**BOTTOM RIGHT**
XL Miss Protocole (Piaget)

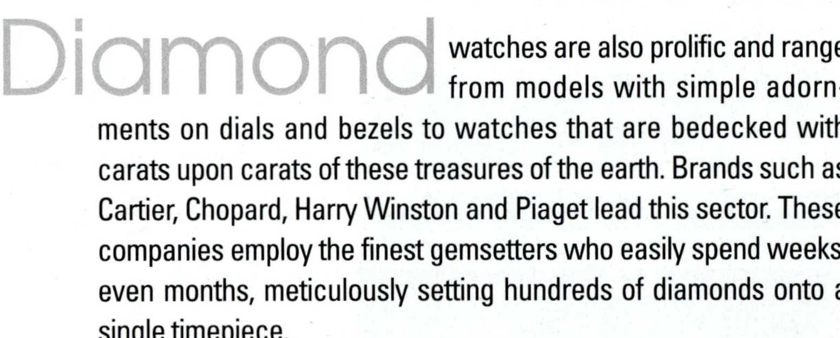

Diamond watches are also prolific and range from models with simple adornments on dials and bezels to watches that are bedecked with carats upon carats of these treasures of the earth. Brands such as Cartier, Chopard, Harry Winston and Piaget lead this sector. These companies employ the finest gemsetters who easily spend weeks, even months, meticulously setting hundreds of diamonds onto a single timepiece.

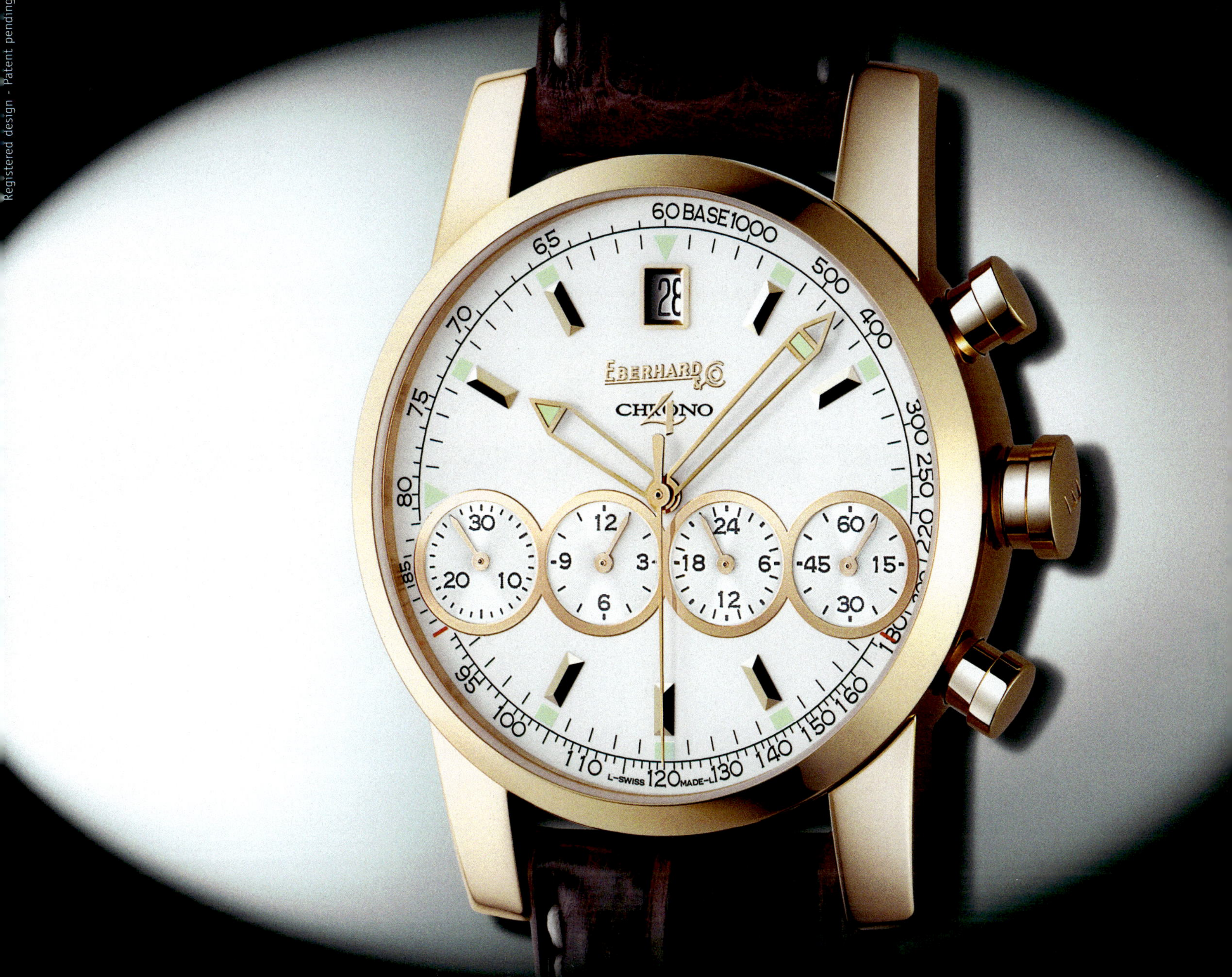

BUTI
GIOTTO GOLD 18K
N°17/50
BUTI
N°17/50
iotto
8k Gold
ited edition
rldwide
50 pieces
me is
endless
ccession of
oments in
hich events and
e changing of
ings take place.

**Fashion** takes over with color, bold styling and unusual case shapes. Many manufacturers offer exquisite straps of fabric, stingray and exotic leathers. Often, these straps are interchangeable so they work well with any wardrobe as the perfect fashion accessory.

TOP LEFT
Five Time Zone Watch (Jacob & Co.)

TOP RIGHT
CSX33 (Michele Watches)

CENTER LEFT
Marrakech 2 (Officina del Tempo)

CENTER RIGHT
Star Open (Zenith)

BOTTOM LEFT
Esperanza™ (Movado)

BOTTOM RIGHT
Lady Charm (Invicta)

Io, comandante del tempo.
RADIOMIR PANERAI
BLACK SEAL
Radiomir Black Seal 45 mm
Polished Steel
PANERAI

**FAR LEFT**
My Dior Malice (Dior)

**ABOVE**
Barénia (Hermès)

**BOTTOM**
Mademoiselle Perles (Chanel)

Designer watches have been popular with luxury enthusiasts for decades.

The timepieces from haute couture fashion icons such as Chanel, Dior and Hermès are updated regularly to reflect the current styles of the house, inspired by seasonal design trends, colors and materials.

MANY
HAPPY RETURNS.
The S. Coifman Flyback.
S. Coifman
Available at selected
watch specialists.
www.scoifman.ch

**Sports** collections make great strides in today's world with chronometers, chronographs, and all types of watches with added functions that enable pilots to fly higher, divers to dive deeper and rugged sports to be enjoyed in any climate. To ensure optimal performance of these professional instruments, sport watches frequently borrow new, cutting-edge materials from other high-tech industries such as medicine, auto racing, and aeronautics. Such materials include titanium, aluminum, and carbon fiber.

TOP CENTER
1970 Titanio (Locman)

TOP RIGHT
Frecce Tricolori Chronomat Evolution (Breitling)

ABOVE
Militare (Anonimo)

FAR LEFT
Aquadyn (Dubey & Schaldenbrand)

CENTER
Admiral's Cup Trophy 41 (Corum)

BOTTOM LEFT
Professional golf Watch (TAG Heuer)

# Chronographs

are hallmarks of many brands. Some offer simple chronographs or more elaborate models with flyback function or the complex chronograph rattrapante. Created in the mid 1800s—perfected and put to use in wristwatches by the early 1900s—chronographs allow for the timing of one or more events simultaneously, depending on the watch's mechanism. Today, chronographs have become must-haves in many connoisseurs' watch wardrobes. They offer hour, minute or second totalizers via one or several pushers.

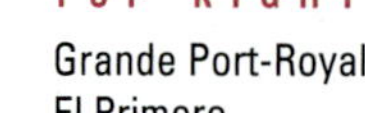

TOP RIGHT
Grande Port-Royal El Primero (Zenith)

CENTER
PanoMaticChrono (Glashütte Original)

FAR LEFT
Giotto GMT Crono Flyback (TB Buti)

BOTTOM LEFT
Lange Double Split (A. Lange & Söhne)

BOTTOM CENTER
Chrono SuperB (Hublot)

CENTER RIGHT
Royal Oak Offshore Juan Pablo Montoya Chronograph (Audemars Piguet)

LOCMAN
ITALY
LOCMAN
ITALY
18
Panorama
18 k Rose Gold

# Chronometers

are important to many watch collectors and sports enthusiasts because of their rugged durability and consistent precision. Usually, a chronometer has undergone rigorous testing over a period of time in several positions and under different conditions. If it is found to meet certain criteria either in-house or by an independent testing observatory, it is deemed a chronometer.

Most countries do not require certification for a watch to be called a chronometer, however Switzerland does. Its stringent testing is executed by the Controle Official Suisse des Chronometres (COSC). There, the watch movement is exposed to tests that confirm water resistance, shock resistance, and accuracy under temperature and pressure extremes. Typically, the watch movement is tested for at least 15 days and is judged by unyielding standards that are set with absolute limits.

**TOP LEFT**
Speedmaster Michael Schumacher The Legend (Omega)

**TOP RIGHT**
The Bentley GT *(left)* and Bentley 6.75 *(right)* (Breitling)

**CENTER**
Cosmograph Daytona (Rolex)

**BOTTOM LEFT**
Chronofighter gold (Graham)

**BOTTOM RIGHT**
Longitude II Blue Ice (Arnold & Son)

Retro is another popular watch category for both men and women. Retro watches' designs are influenced, as the name suggests, by the past. Most popular time periods include the art deco era of the 1920s, from which stunning marcasites and other gemstones and elaborate geometric patterns have inspired many modern timepieces. Also revisited are the 1930s, '40s and '50s, when square and tonneau-shaped watches were trendy. Most recently, a revival of the 1960s and '70s has brought forth more unusual shapes and renditions of cuff watches and bangles.

TOP LEFT
The Santos 100 (Cartier)

TOP RIGHT
Paramount JR 1000 (JeanRichard)

CENTER
The Longines Master Collection (Longines)

ABOVE
Espléndidos Clasico (Cuervo y Sobrinos)

BOTTOM
La Scala™ Tonneau Horizontal (Concord)

MOD. 1 RTM *DIAMONDS*
TO WIND UP ONE
AUTOMATIC WRISTWATCH
R.W. SYSTEM
SCATOLA del TEMPO
the first, the only, the original one.
S.C.S. & Co. Via dei Mille 17 - 23891 Barzanò (LC) Tel. 039 95 52 60 Fax 039 95 89 70

# Visionaries,

watchmakers often are inspired to create extraordinary timepieces with unusual aesthetic ingenuity. Mystery watches belong to this category, as their workings are hidden entirely within a base or bezel. Other intriguing applications are multiple levels or a series of transparent discs in lieu of a typical dial and case.

**TOP**
Tribute to the Great Explorers (Vacheron Constantin)

**CENTER**
Occhio Ripetizione Minuti (de Grisogono)

**BOTTOM LEFT**
RM 008 (Richard Mille)

**BOTTOM CENTER**
Bugatti type 370 (Parmigiani Fleurier)

**BELOW**
UR-103 (Urwerk)

# THE HOUSE OF EIGHT

**The House of Eight SA** is a Swiss luxury goods company that has combined high-precision mechanics, Geneva craftsmanship and fashion to create limited-edition jewelry and belt collections.

The Mecanique de Grand Luxe™ limited-edition collections are objects of art, fashion and time blended together in haute couture. Unveiled by The House of Eight, the collection of mechanical belt buckles for men is an exciting new concept. With U.S. prices ranging from approximately $28,000 to well over $90,000, these belts can arguably be billed among the most expensive buckles in the world.

According to Carol Galiano, board director for The House of Eight, "These are the first-ever belt buckles with Geneva watchmaking tradition and craftsmanship built in."

Made in collaboration with Magnin SA, a high-precision mechanics producer in Geneva, The House of Eight's premiere collection of belt buckles

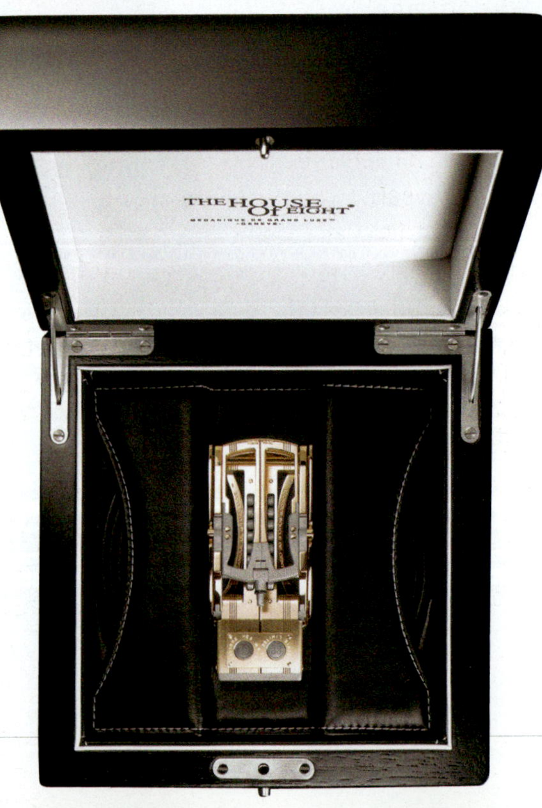


THIS PAGE

The design of these unique Collection C8EVAL belt buckles is protected by a patent and features a two-position mechanism.

**TOP LEFT**

Dedicated to the sport world, this Collection P8LO buckle is created in a limited edition of just 88 pieces.

**RIGHT**

Manufactured and assembled by hand, this Collection R8YAL buckle is entirely gemset.

is called the Calibre 8 Mark 1 and each piece is comprised of more than 108 individually crafted mechanical pieces cut from solid precious metals.

In fact, the company uses only 18-karat rose, white or yellow gold with supporting titanium structures and, in some cases, exotic woods cut more than 100 years ago. Additionally, every piece is assembled, finished and engraved by hand, and set with anywhere from 8 to 2,888 diamonds.

Invented and designed by award-winning Swiss designer Roland Iten, the superior functionality of the belt buckle is delivered through an internationally patented dual-position performance mechanism. The collection offers up to eight styles of buckles with limited and numbered series of only 88 pieces of each style. Two models—the 8CEAN and P8LO—are dedicated to their respective sports worlds.

Manufactured and assembled by hand, these buckles are incredibly exclusive. The leather straps are made from the finest crocodile and other exotic leathers. The House of Eight is currently developing the Calibre 18 collection of belt buckles and an equally intricate collection of mechanical cufflinks. Both are planned for an early 2005 launch.

THE HOUSE Of EIGHT®

www.houseofeight.com

# STARTING ANEW

This past year has been one of incredible pain in the wake of one of the largest natural disasters in history. The tsunami that struck Asia on December 26, 2004 destroyed families around the world by stealing hundreds of thousands of precious lives and wiping out businesses, hospitals, animals and resources. These suffering nations are strong supporters of the world's jewelry and watch industries and it's our turn to lend our support—not just with money for disaster aid, but with our time and services. We at Watches International 2005 would like to dedicate this book to the countries devastated by the tsunami and to their recoveries. We acknowledge the resolve it will take for these countries to rebuild, and we hope that each and every one of us may do our part to refurbish lands and hopes.

Caroline Childers   Roberta Naas   Elizabeth Kindt   Mutsumi Hyuga   Franca Vitali   Igino Schrafl

DP
Doris Panos
Doris Panos
proudly presents
"The Princess"
DP
11
1
7
5
18
SWISS MADE
Beautiful, Sophisticated and Unique describe the long anticipated, exclusive limited edition of
elegant timepieces by Doris Panos.
Swiss made only in 18K white or yellow gold and set with 3.55cts. in diamonds.
Simply put...... Timeless Elegance
Available through select authorized retailers.
For more information call 888.30. PANOS or visit www.dorispanos.com

# A. Lange & Söhne

With roots in the famed Saxony region of Germany, A. Lange & Söhne has re-established itself as a premier German watchmaker—creating incredible mechanical movements within classic timepieces of true distinction.

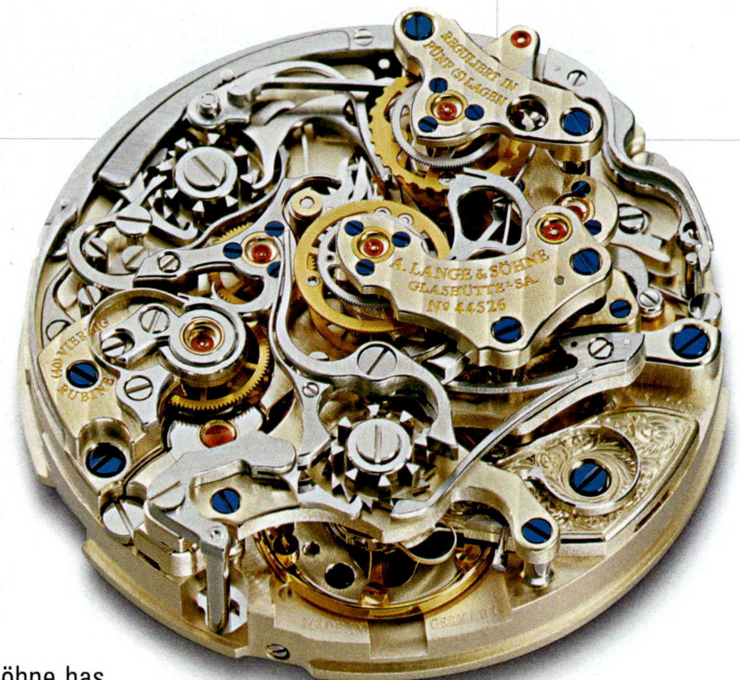

An evolution in the history of watchmaking, A. Lange & Söhne has liberated the rattrapante chronograph from its traditional 60-second lap time and has created the first genuine double rattrapante for the wrist. Aptly named the Lange Double Split, the beautiful timepiece features two rattrapante hands: one for the seconds and one for the minutes to be stopped. Additionally, both the chronograph and rattrapante hands are fly-back hands. With this watch, comparative lap measurements of up to 30 minutes are possible for the first time.

The movement is the result of several years of research and development, and A. Lange & Söhne has filed for a patent for the disengagement mechanism that allows the chronograph sweep-seconds hand to continue revolving while the rattrapante sweep-seconds hand is stopped. A true technological achievement, the watch is also equipped with an in-house-developed balance wheel equipped with poising weights instead of inertia screws. The balance spring is not attached to a hairspring stud, but instead is secured by a balance-spring clamp for which a separate patent registration has been filed. The manually wound Caliber L001.1 movement of the Lange Double Split consists of 465 parts and 40 jewels. It is housed in a platinum case measuring 43mm in diameter.

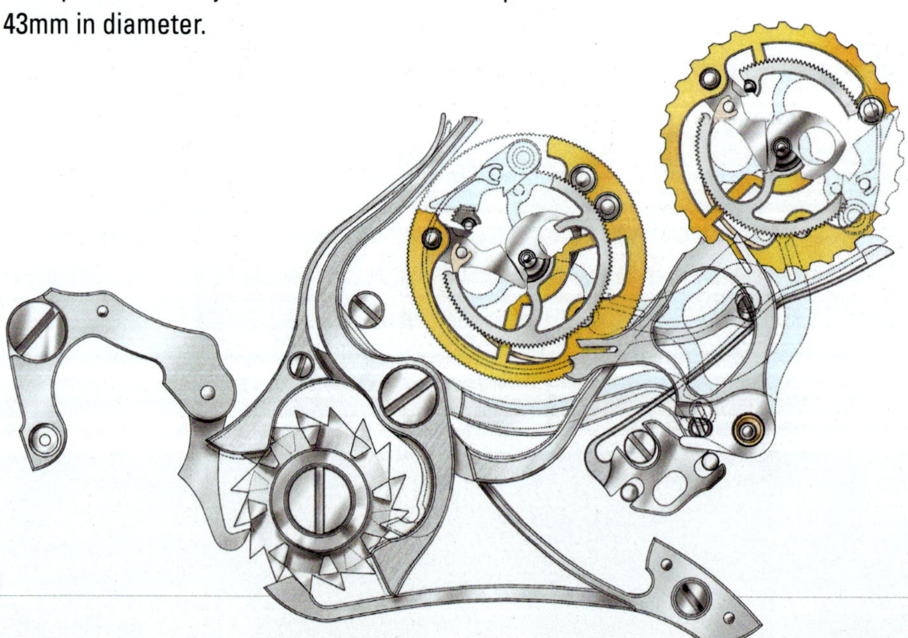

THIS PAGE

ABOVE

The Caliber L001.1 Lange Double Split movement.

BOTTOM

The two possible switching modes of the rattrapante mechanism for the Lange Double Split.

FACING PAGE

The Lange Double Split is the world's first flyback chronograph with double Rattrapante. Controlled by classic column wheels, it now makes possible comparative lap measurements of up to 30 minutes. It is offered in an elegant platinum 43mm case. Its 465-part movement was several years in the making.

A. LANGE & SÖHNE
AB
AUF
BASE 1000 METER
GLASHÜTTE
GERMANY

Further embellishing its successful 1815 series created in tribute to founder Ferdinand Adolph Lange (his birth year), A. Lange & Söhne unveils the 1815 Automatik and the 1815 Chronograph. The 1815 Automatik houses the extraordinary Sax-O-Mat movement with automatic function and patented zero-reset mechanism, which instantly sets the seconds hand to zero when the crown is pulled for accurate synchronization with a time signal. This watch is available in either a three-part gold or platinum case and offers 46 hours of power reserve.

The 1815 Chronograph is created in either 18-karat white or pink gold and houses the Caliber L951.0 movement with pulsimeter scale. The watch measures individual laps and cumulative times from one-fifth of a second to 30 minutes. It is equipped with a precisely jumping minute counter with flyback function, hours, minutes and small seconds with stop seconds.

On the heels of the previous year's astronomical unveiling of the Grand Lange 1 Luna Mundi two-piece set of watches that depict the moon in its true position in both hemispheres, A. Lange & Söhne has added new moonphase depictions to certain watches. Most impressive is a scenic rendering of the waxing and waning moon that now graces the Cabaret watch. The rectangular timepiece already offers outsized date via a patented twin-disc mechanism hidden beneath the double aperture at 12:00. With the added moonphase display at 6:00, the watch takes on even more harmonious appeal. The Cabaret Moonphase houses the Caliber L931.5 movement and offers 42 hours of power reserve.

THIS PAGE

FAR LEFT

The 1815 Automatik houses the Caliber L921.2 Sax-O-Mat movement with patented zero-reset mechanism.

TOP CENTER

Shown here in 18-karat pink gold, the 1815 Chronograph measures individual laps and cumulative times from one-fifth of a second to 30 minutes.

RIGHT

This 1815 Chronograph is created in 18-karat white gold and houses the Calibor L951.0 movement with pulsimeter scale.

FACING PAGE

TOP

The Caliber L931.5 Cabaret Moonphase movement.

BOTTOM

The Cabaret Moonphase watch offers patented outsized-date display and stunning new moonphase display.

## CHRONOLOGY

**1845** Ferdinand Adolph Lange founds Saxony's fine-watch industry in Glashütte.

**1884** Lange introduces the three-quarter-plate caliber, a distinguishing feature of Glashütte watchmaking.

**1866** Adolph Lange develops an astronomical watch.

**1868** Son Richard becomes joint owner of the family business, now renamed "A. Lange & Söhne" (& Sons).

**1895** The company is connected directly to Berlin's observatory for the true time; produces navigational timepieces for naval forces and merchant fleets; Glashütte erects a memorial to honor Adolph Lange, its mayor for 18 years.

**1898** In Constantinople, Kaiser William presents Sultan Abdul Hamit II with an A. Lange & Söhne pocket watch featuring an enamel miniature of the Kaiser.

**1900** Emil Lange represents A. Lange & Söhne on the international jury at the Paris Universal Exhibition and is made a knight of the French Legion of Honour in 1902.

**1908** A Lange Grande Complication repeating clock-watch in a "Louis XV à goutte" case sells for 4930 gold marks—the price of two houses.

**1945** Bombers destroy Lange's main workshops.

**1948** East Germany's communist regime seizes the Lange company; fourth-generation Walter Lange is forced into West Germany.

**1989** Collapse of the communist regime and the Berlin Wall dividing Germany.

**1990** Germany is reunified; Walter Lange founds "Lange Uhren GmbH" of Glashütte, registering the company in Dresden and the traditional trademark of A. Lange & Söhne worldwide.

**1994** The first modern A. Lange & Söhne collection is unveiled with numerous technological innovations and superb hand-wound movements.

**1995** Readers of *Armbanduhren International* vote Lange 1 as Watch of the Year.

**1997** The Langematik with Sax-O-Mat movement is the first automatic watch of the new Lange era. The Lange Watchmaking School opens in Glashütte.

**1998** Walter Lange is the first chairman of House of the Watch Glashütte; A. Lange & Söhne is voted Best New Brand (Italy).

**1999** A 1,000-year moonphase display is integrated into the 1815 Moonphase; distribution expands through Europe to Asia and the United Arab Emirates.

**2000** The firm reacquires the family's original headquarters constructed in 1873 and seized in 1948; the Richemont Group acquires A. Lange & Söhne.

**2001** The Langematik-Perpetual with patented movement is unveiled.

**2003** The company opens its newly built Technology & Development Center. A. Lange & Söhne unveils the Grand Lange 1 Luna Mundi set of two watches: one depicts the correct positioning of the moon in the northern hemisphere and one depicts its phases in the southern.

**2004** Lange presents its new Lange Double Split, the world's first flyback chronograph with double rattrapante.

## LANGE DOUBLE SPLIT — REF. 404.035

**Movement:** manual winding; Lange manufacture cailber L001.1; crafted, assembled, and decorated almost entirely by hand to the highest Lange quality standards; precision-adjusted in five positions; plates and bridges made of untreated cross-laminated German silver; hand-engraved balance cock.
**Functions:** world's first flyback chronograph with double rattrapante, controlled by classic column wheels; precisely jumping chrono minute counter and rattrapante minute counter; flyback function; disengagement mechanism; hours, minutes, small seconds with stop seconds; power-reserve indicator; cumulative and lap-time measurements between 1/6 of a second and 30 minutes; tachometer scale.
**Case:** Ø 43 mm; platinum.
**Dial:** solid silver; two-tiered; black.
**Strap:** hand-stitched crocodile strap with solid platinum Lange prong buckle.

## LANGE 1 MOONPHASE — REF. 109.021

**Movement:** mechanical, manual winding; A. Lange & Söhne L901.5 caliber; hand-finished and hand-engraved.
**Functions:** hour, minute, small seconds; date; moonphase; power reserve.
**Case:** 18K yellow-gold, three-piece case (Ø 38.5mm, thickness: 10.4mm); polished and brushed finish; flat sapphire crystal with antireflection treatment; rectangular date corrector at 10; moonphase corrector between 7 and 8; yellow-gold crown; back attached by 6 screws, displaying the movement through a sapphire crystal; water resistant to 3atm.
**Dial:** solid silver; champagne-colored silvered.
**Indications:** off-center hour and minute at 9; applied gold lozenge markers and Roman numerals; printed minute track; luminescent gold Alpha hands; patented big date bordered in gold with double window at 1; power reserve at 3; small seconds and moonphase between 4 and 5.
**Strap:** crocodile leather, hand-stitched; yellow-gold clasp.
**Also available:** in pink gold; in platinum; bracelet with fold-over clasp on request.

## LANGEMATIK-PERPETUAL — REF. 310.025

**Movement:** mechanical, automatic winding; A. Lange & Söhne L922.1 Sax-O-Mat caliber (L921.4 base + perpetual calendar module); hand-finished and hand-engraved.
**Functions:** hour, minute, small seconds; 24-hour perpetual calendar (date, day, month, year, moonphase); leap year. **Case:** platinum, three-piece case (Ø 38.5mm, thickness: 10.2mm); polished and brushed finish; flat sapphire crystal; white-gold crown; rectangular pusher at 10 for calendar correction; 3 additional correctors on the middle; back attached by 6 screws, displaying the movement through a sapphire crystal; water resistant to 3atm.
**Dial:** solid silver; black rhodium-plated; applied rhodium-plated gold Roman numerals; luminescent dots on a printed railway minute track; luminescent rhodium-plated gold Alpha hands.
**Indications:** month at 3; 4-year cycle at 4; small seconds (with zero-reset device) and moonphase at 6; day and 24-hour day-night display at 9; patented big date with double window bordered in rhodium-plated gold at 12. **Strap:** crocodile leather, hand-stitched; platinum clasp. **Also available:** with bracelet; in yellow gold, silvered champagne-colored dial with leather strap and bracelet.

## DATOGRAPH — REF. 403.031

**Movement:** mechanical, manual winding; A. Lange & Söhne L951.1 caliber; hand-finished and hand-engraved.
**Functions:** hour, minute, small seconds; outsize date; chronograph with fly-back feature and 2 counters.
**Case:** 18K pink-gold, three-piece case (Ø 39mm, thickness: 12.8mm); polished and brushed finish; antireflective flat sapphire crystal; rectangular date-corrector pusher at 10; pink-gold crown; back attached by 6 screws, displaying the movement through an antireflective sapphire crystal; water-resistant to 3atm.
**Dial:** solid silver; black (coloring obtained by a galvanization process); silvered zones; applied pink-gold bâton markers and Roman numerals; luminescent pink-gold Alpha hands; counter hands in rhodium-plated and burnished steel.
**Indications:** minute counter at 4; small seconds at 8; patented big date at 12 with double window bordered in pink gold; center second counter; minute track with divisions for 1/5 of a second; tachometer scale.
**Strap:** crocodile leather, hand-stitched; pink-gold clasp.
**Also available:** in platinum.

## GRAND LANGE 1 LUMINOUS — REF. 115.029

**Movement:** manual winding; Lange manufacture cailber L901.2; crafted, assembled, and decorated almost entirely by hand to the highest Lange quality standards; precision-adjusted in five positions; twin mainspring barrels; patented outsize date; power-reserve indicator; plates and bridges made of untreated cross-laminated German silver; hand-engraved balance cock.
**Functions:** hours, minutes, small seconds with stop seconds; patented outsize date, power-reserve indicator.
**Case:** Ø 41.9mm; 18K white gold.
**Dial:** solid silver, black, rhodium-plated gold appliques, luminous.
**Strap:** hand-stitched buffalo strap with beige seams and Lange prong buckle in solid white gold.

## GRAND LANGEMATIK — REF. 309.025

**Movement:** mechanical, automatic winding; A. Lange & Söhne Sax-O-Mat L921.4 caliber; hand-decorated and hand-engraved.
**Functions:** hour, minute, small seconds; date.
**Case:** platinum, three-piece case (Ø 40mm, thickness: 9.7mm); polished and brushed finish; flat sapphire crystal; rectangular date-corrector pusher at 10; white-gold crown; back attached by 6 screws, displaying the movement through a sapphire crystal; water-resistant to 3atm.
**Dial:** solid silver; rhodium-plated silvered; applied rhodium-plated gold bâton markers; luminescent dots at quarters on a printed minute track; luminescent rhodium-plated gold Alpha hands.
**Indications:** small seconds at 6 (with zero-reset device); patented big date display with double window with rhodium-plated gold border at 12.
**Strap:** crocodile leather, hand-stitched, platinum clasp.
**Also available:** in yellow gold with champagne-colored dial; or in pink gold with black dial.

## GRAND LANGE 1 — REF. 115.021

**Movement:** mechanical, manual winding; A. Lange & Söhne L901.2 caliber; hand-finished and hand-engraved.
**Functions:** hour, minute, small seconds; date; power reserve.
**Case:** 18K yellow-gold, three-piece case (Ø 41.9mm, thickness: 11mm); polished and brushed finish; flat sapphire crystal with antireflective treatment; rectangular date corrector pusher at 10; yellow-gold crown; back attached by 6 screws, displaying the movement through a sapphire crystal; water-resistant to 3atm.
**Dial:** solid silver; champagne-colored argenté; grained silvered subdials.
**Indications:** off-center hour and minute at 9; applied yellow-gold lozenge markers and Roman numerals; printed minute track; yellow-gold Alpha hands; patented big date bordered in yellow gold with double window at 1; power reserve at 3; small seconds between 4 and 5.
**Strap:** crocodile leather, hand-stitched; yellow-gold clasp.
**Also available:** in pink gold with black and gray dial (dial with two colors); in platinum with rhodium-plated and argenté dial; leather strap.

## LANGE 1 — REF. 101.033

**Movement:** mechanical, manual winding; A. Lange & Söhne L901.0 caliber; hand-finished and hand-engraved.
**Functions:** hour, minute, small seconds; date; power reserve.
**Case:** 18K pink-gold, three-piece case (Ø 38.5mm, thickness: 10mm); polished and brushed finish; flat sapphire crystal; rectangular date-corrector pusher at 10; pink-gold crown; back attached by 6 screws, displaying the movement through a sapphire crystal; water-resistant to 3atm.
**Dial:** solid silver; gray.
**Indications:** off-center hour and minute at 9; applied pink-gold lozenge markers and Roman numerals; printed minute track; pink-gold Alpha hands; patented big date bordered in pink gold with double window at 1; power reserve at 3; small seconds between 4 and 5.
**Strap:** crocodile leather, hand-stitched; pink-gold clasp.
**Also available:** in yellow and white gold and platinum, leather strap or bracelet, dials with different colours and materials, for example with mother-of-pearl dial in different colors.

## LANGEMATIK WITH OUTSIZE DATE — REF. 308.027

**Movement:** mechanical, automatic winding; A. Lange & Söhne Sax-O-Mat L921.4 caliber; hand-decorated and hand-engraved.
**Functions:** hour, minute, small seconds; date.
**Case:** 18K white-gold, three-piece case (Ø 37mm, thickness: 9.7mm); polished and brushed finish; flat sapphire crystal; rectangular date corrector at 10; gold crown; back attached by 6 screws, displaying the movement through a sapphire crystal; water resistant to 3atm.
**Dial:** solid silver; black silvered; applied gold bâton markers; luminescent dots at quarters on a printed minute track; luminescent gold Alpha hands.
**Indications:** small seconds at 6 (with zero-reset device); gold-bordered patented big date display with double window at 12.
**Bracelet:** crocodile leather, solid gold buckle.
**Also available:** in yellow and pink gold and platinum.

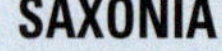

## SAXONIA — REF. 105.022

**Movement:** mechanical, manual winding; A. Lange & Söhne L941.3 caliber; stop seconds; 30 jewels; 42-hour power reserve; Ø 25.6mm, thickness: 4.95mm; shock-resistant screw balance timed to 21,600 alternations per hour; three-quarter plate, plates, bridges made of untreated cross-laminated German silver; screwed gold chatons; hand-engraved balance cock with whiplash precision index adjuster; manually beveled and polished plate edges; plates and bridges damascened and solarized with Glashütte ribbing.
**Functions:** hour, minute, small seconds; patented outsize date.
**Case:** 18K yellow-gold (Ø 33.9mm, thickness: 9.1mm); antireflective sapphire crystal glass and caseback.
**Dial:** solid silver; argenté; blued steel hands.
**Indications:** small seconds at 6; date at 12.
**Strap:** hand-stitched crocodile with solid gold buckle.

## CABARET MOONPHASE — REF. 118.032

**Movement:** manual winding; Lange manufacture cailber L931.5; crafted, assembled, and decorated almost entirely by hand to the highest Lange quality standards; precision-adjusted in five positions; plates and bridges made of untreated, cross-laminated German silver; hand-engraved balance cock.
**Functions:** hours, minutes, small seconds with stop seconds; patented outsize date; moonphase display.
**Case:** 36.3x27.5mm; pink gold.
**Dial:** solid silver in argenté; gold appliques.
**Strap:** hand-stitched crocodile straps and Lange prong buckle in solid gold.
**Also available:** yellow gold.

## CABARET — REF. 107.031

**Movement:** mechanical, manual winding; Lange manufacture cailber L931.3; (size: 25.6x17.6mm, thickness: 4.95mm); 42 hours power reserve; 30 jewels; stop seconds; shock-resistant screw balance timed to 21,600 alternations per hour; three-quarter plate, plates and bridges made of untreated cross-laminated German silver, screwed gold chatons, hand-engraved balance cock with whiplash precision index adjuster, manually bevelled and polished plate edges, plates and bridges damascened and solarised with Glashütte ribbing.
**Functions:** hour, minute; patented outsize date.
**Case:** 18K pink-gold, two-piece case (size: 36.3x25.5mm, thickness: 9.1mm); antireflective sapphire-crystal glass and caseback, pink-gold crown.
**Dial:** solid silver, black; applied pink-gold markers and double window for the outsize date at 12; pink-gold hands.
**Strap:** hand-stitched crocodile strap with solid-gold buckle; pink gold clasp
**Also available:** in white and yellow gold, platinum, jewelled version.

## 1815 CHRONOGRAPH REF. 401.026

**Movement:** manual winding; Lange manufacture cailber L951.0; crafted, assembled, and decorated almost entirely by hand to the highest Lange quality standards; precision-adjusted in five positions; plates and bridges made of untreated, cross-laminated German silver; hand-engraved balance cock.
**Functions:** chronograph with 30-minute counter; flyback and precisely jumping minute counter; hours, minutes, small seconds with stop seconds.
**Case:** Ø 39mm; white gold.
**Dial:** solid silver in argenté.
**Strap:** hand-stitched crocodile straps and Lange prong buckle in solid gold.
**Also available:** pink gold.

## 1815 AUTOMATIK REF. 303.021

**Movement:** self winding; Lange manufacture cailber L921.2 Sax-0-Mat; crafted, assembled, and decorated almost entirely by hand to the highest Lange quality standards; precision-adjusted in five positions; three-quarter plate made of untreated cross-laminated German silver, with integrated three-quarter rotor made of 21K gold and platinum segment, reversing and reduction gear with four ball bearings; hand-engraved balance cock.
**Functions:** hours, minutes, small seconds with stop seconds, zero-reset mechanism.
**Case:** Ø 37mm; yellow gold.
**Dial:** solid silver; argenté; Arabic numerals.
**Strap:** hand-stitched crocodile straps and Lange prong buckle in solid gold.
**Also available:** pink gold or platinum.

## 1815 "UP AND DOWN" REF. 221.032

**Movement:** mechanical, manual winding; A. Lange & Söhne L942.1 caliber; hand-decorated and hand-engraved.
**Functions:** hour, minute, small seconds; power reserve.
**Case:** 18K pink-gold, three-piece case (Ø 35.9mm, thickness: 7.9mm); polished and brushed finish; flat sapphire crystal; back attached by 6 screws, displaying the movement through a sapphire crystal; water resistant to 3atm.
**Dial:** solid silver, argenté; printed Arabic numerals; printed railway minute track; pink-gold Alpha hands.
**Indications:** small seconds at 4; power reserve at 8.
**Strap:** crocodile leather, hand-stitched; pink-gold clasp.
**Also available:** in yellow gold, leather strap; in platinum with leather strap or bracelet (on request).

## ARKADE REF. 801.030

**Movement :** mechanical; manual winding; Lange manufacture cailber L911.4; (size: 25.6x17.6mm, thickness: 4.95mm); 42 hours power reserve; 30 jewels; stop seconds; shock-resistant screw balance timed to 21,600 alternations per hour; three-quarter plate, plates and bridges made of untreated cross-laminated German silver, screwed gold chatons, hand-engraved balance cock with whiplash precision index adjuster, manually beveled and polished plate edges, plates and bridges damascened and solarised with Glashütte ribbing.
**Functions:** hour, minute, small seconds; patented outsize date.
**Case:** 18K white-gold, (size: 31.5x24.9mm, thickness: 8.2mm); set with 38 Top Wesselton (VVS) baguette diamonds; antireflective sapphire crystal glass and caseback.
**Dial:** solid silver, blue; rhodiumed gold hands.
**Strap:** hand-stitched crocodile strap with solid-gold buckle.

## CALIBER L901.0.

Manual-winding movement; with double barrel; 72-hour autonomy.
**Functions:** hours, minutes, small seconds (with stopping device); patented big-sized date (with fast corrector); power reserve.
**Shape:** round. **Diameter:** 30.40mm. **Thickness:** 5.90mm. **Jewels:** 53.
**Balance:** with compensating screws; with two arms; in Glucydur.
**Frequency:** 21,600 vph.

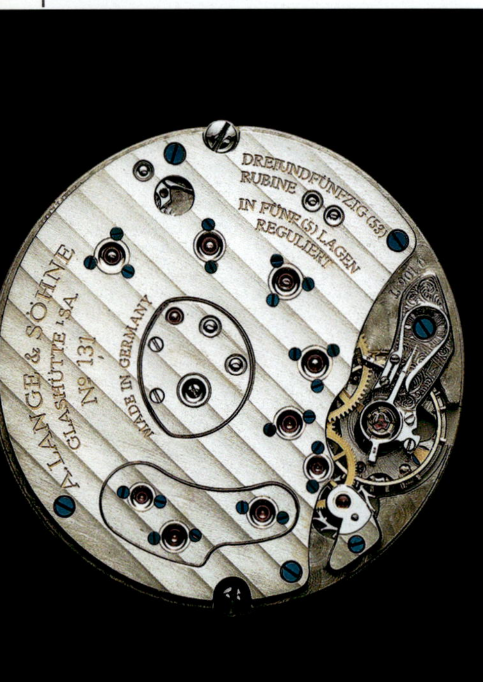


**Balance-spring:** flat; Nivarox 1; with micrometer screw regulating device and swan-neck retaining spring (patented). **Shock-absorber system:** Incabloc.
**Notes:** the alpaca pillar-plate is decorated with a circular graining pattern; the bridges, in alpaca, are decorated by the Glashütte polish and beveled; the upper jewel of the escape wheel is mounted on a gold setting and locked by a polished steel platelet; the balance bridge is hand-engraved. The upper bridge at 3/4 houses 9 gold settings, fastened by blued steel screws, for as many jewels. On the dial side, all the indications are off-center and never superposed (Lange 1).
**Derived calibers:** 901.5 (901.0 with moonphase, 398 components in total, 54 jewels)

## CALIBER L951.1

Manual-winding movement; 36-hour autonomy; consisting of 390 elements.
**Functions:** hours, minutes, small seconds (with stopping device); patented big-sized date (with fast corrector); chronograph with two counters (30 minutes, 60 seconds with fly-back feature).
**Shape:** round. **Diameter:** 30.6mm. **Thickness:** 7.50mm. **Jewels:** 40.
**Balance:** with compensating screws; with two arms; in Glucydur.
**Frequency:** 18,000 vph. **Balance-spring:** Breguet type; Nivarox 1; with micrometer screw regulating device and swan-neck retaining spring.

**Shock-absorber system:** Incabloc.
**Notes:** the bridge of the seconds wheel is additional and separate. The escapement bridge is separate; the balance bridge is hand-engraved. Pillar-plates and bridges are in alpaca and decorated with a circular graining pattern, by the Glashütte polish, beveled and polished; the screws are blued and chamfered; the 4 gold settings are screwed on.
**Chronograph:** the column-wheel is oversized; levers and springs are beveled and polished; the instantaneous jumping minute system with adjustable control lever, mounted on jewels on both sides, is patented; an endless stepped wheel is provided for the exact release of the lever sliding on a jewel.

## CALIBER L911.4

Manual-winding movement; 42-hour autonomy. **Functions:** hours, minutes, small seconds (with stopping device); patented big-sized date (with fast corrector). **Shape:** rectangular with curved short sides. **Size:** 25.60x17.60mm. **Thickness:** 4.60mm. **Jewels:** 30. **Balance:** with compensating screws; with two arms; in Glucydur. **Frequency:** 21,600 vph. **Balance-spring:** flat; Nivarox 1; with micrometer screw regulating device and swan-neck retaining spring. **Shock-absorber system:** Incabloc. **Notes:** Pillar-plate in alpaca; decorated with a circular graining pattern; alpaca bridges decorated by the Glashütte polish and beveled; the upper jewel of the escape wheel is mounted on a gold setting and locked by a polished steel platelet; the balance bridge is hand-engraved. The upper bridge at 3/4 houses 4 gold settings, fastened by blued steel screws, for as many jewels.

## CALIBER L922.1 SAX-O-MAT

By using caliber L921.4 as a time base and adding a calendar module taking automatically into account the different duration of the months, Lange was able to introduce the Langematik Perpetual model (478 components) in its catalog. By such a combination, the complete movement has 43 jewels and is 5.7mm high. These values are strangely lower than those of the movement provided only with the integrated big-sized date. An original feature of this model is represented by the ability of adjusting the calendar display independently through three classic correctors or of letting them advance one day per click by pressing down once the relevant pusher placed at 10.

When realizing its automatic movement, Lange introduced some unique and original technically refined solutions, such as the use of four ball bearings to reduce the friction caused by motion transmission from the rotor to the barrel or the zero-reset device to set the small-second hand to zero and keep it stopped, as long as the crown is pulled out.

## CALIBER L942.1

Manual movement with 45-hour autonomy. **Functions:** hours, minutes, small seconds (with a stopping device); power reserve. **Shape:** round. **Diameter:** 25.60mm. **Thickness:** 3.7mm. **Jewels:** 27. **Balance:** with compensating screws; with two arms; in Glucydur. **Frequency:** 21,600 vph. **Balance-spring:** flat; Nivarox 1; with micrometer screw regulating device and swan-neck retaining spring. **Shock-absorber system:** Incabloc. **Notes:** Pillar-plate in alpaca; decorated with a circular graining pattern; alpaca bridges decorated by the Glashütte polish and beveled; the upper jewel of the escape wheel is mounted on a gold setting and locked by a polished steel platelet; the balance bridge is hand-engraved. The upper bridge at 3/4 houses 7 gold settings, fastened by blued steel screws, for as many jewels. Derived calibers: 943.1 (942.1 with moonphase).

## CALIBER L921.4 — SAX-O-MAT

**Base caliber:** L921.2 (without big date; thickness: 3.80mm). Automatic movement; 46-hour autonomy; off-center rotor in 21K gold with screw-on platinum sector, mounted on a ball bearing. **Functions:** hours, minutes, small seconds (with zero-reset device); patented big-sized date (with fast corrector). **Shape:** round. **Diameter:** 30.40mm. **Thickness:** 5.55mm. **Jewels:** 45. **Balance:** with compensating screws; with two arms; in Glucydur. **Frequency:** 21,600 vph. **Balance-spring:** flat; Nivarox 1; with micrometer screw regulating device and swan-neck retaining spring. **Shock-absorber system:** Incabloc. **Notes:** Pillar-plate in alpaca; decorated with a circular graining pattern; alpaca bridges decorated by the Glashütte polish and beveled; the upper jewel of the escape-wheel with an endstone is mounted on a gold setting and locked by a polished steel platelet; the balance bridge is hand-engraved. Among the features of this movement, the realization of the appreciated automatic-winding and zero-reset features is worthwhile mentioning. The latter allows the continuous second hand to go back to zero, when time is set again.

## THE ZERO-RESET SYSTEM

Thanks to this device, it is possible to synchronize hours, minutes and seconds perfectly with another timepiece. Demonstrated in the photographs shown is the complex play of levers supporting the zero-reset system: when the crown is pulled out, the gray lever is displaced; a bending spring (blue, on the left) locks the balance; the hammer lever (brown) exerts a pressure on the heart-shaped eccentric (green) to set the hand to zero; the stop lever (fuchsia) holds it in place. The dashed lines show the positions reached by the different organs when the winding crown is pushed in again.

The photograph below on the right shows the zero-reset system as it appears on the movement on the dial side. The brass-colored wheel above is the one on whose inner side the hour wheel is fastened, while the minute hand is fixed on the coaxial steel pivot. Visible in a lower vertical position, the pivot standing out from the jewel on which the small seconds hand is mounted.

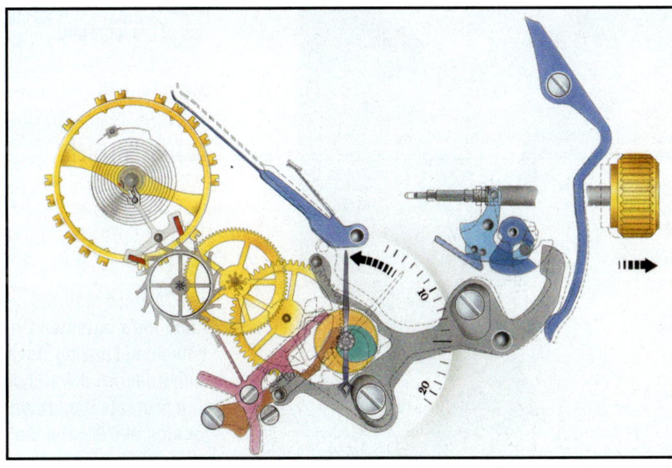

## THE MOONPHASE OF THE L901.5 CALIBER

The Lange 1 Moonphase accurately reproduces our satellite's movement with a minimal gap of 0.002%. On average, the moon rotates around our planet once every 29 days, 12 hours, 44 minutes and 3 seconds. During the year, moonphases have a variable duration. Usually, a wheel with 59 teeth is used to indicate moonphases; therefore, the moon cycle is rounded off to 28.5 days with a gap of 44 minutes and 3 seconds. In two years such a difference results in a gap of an entire day. However, the moonphase wheelwork of the Lange 1 Moonphase is so incredibly complex that it would take the Lange 1 Moonphase 122.6 years to result in this one-day discrepancy. However, by means of the pusher positioned between 7 and 8, it is possible to correct the difference at any time.

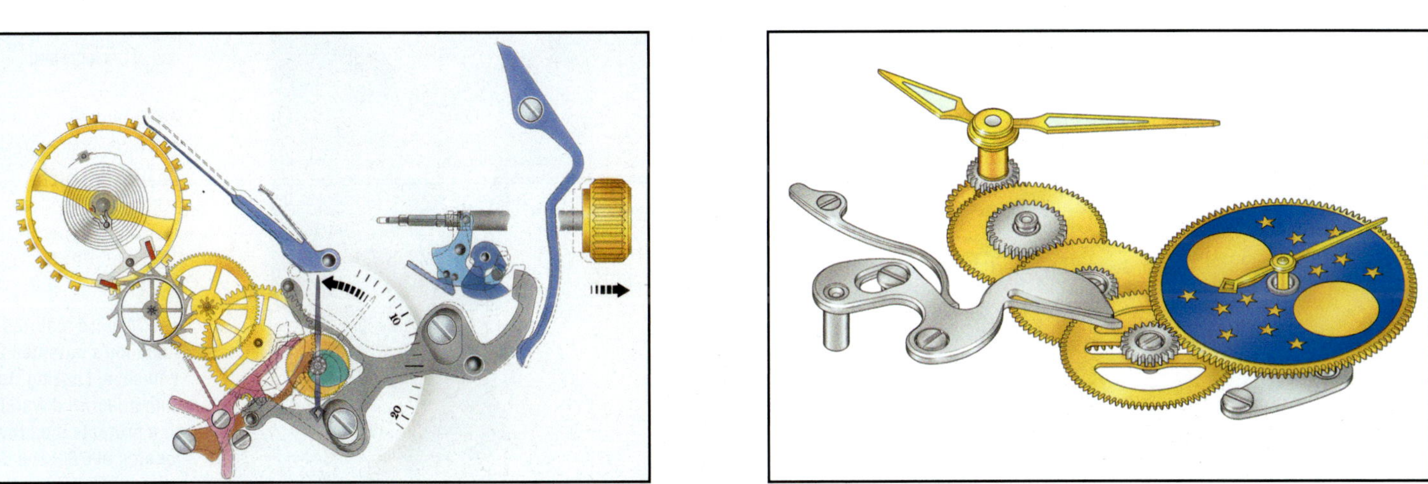

# ANONIMO

Created in the time-honored Florentine tradition, Anonimo watches are strictly mechanical and a definitive testament to bold Italian craftsmanship and technological functioning.

Founded in Florence eight years ago, Anonimo was designed by an entrepreneur with a vision to preserve the art of Florentine watchmaking. Federico Massacesi and his team of veteran watchmakers focused on offering watches with strong personalities that communicate design, innovation and function. Even the name Anonimo, which means anonymous, is designed to enable the wearer to express himself and the watches speak more about the people wearing them than about the brand.

Anonimo is founded on five essential values: Honesty (integrity in relationships); Originality (technological creativity and modern design concepts); Essentials (in the creation of Anonimo watches, anything that is unnecessary is eliminated); Excellence (superior materials and components); Teamwork (both within the company and with retail and consumer partners). This tried and true strategy has infused strength in the brand and its positioning.

THIS PAGE

TOP

The Firenze Dual Time model 2009 houses two automatic movements that function independently and allow for a second time zone or GMT readout. The dial is extra-thick with Super-LumiNova coating for superior day/night readability. It features a time-zone table with the names of the representative cities of the corresponding time zone on the dial for GMT time. There is a plus/minus indication for the adjustment of the table for the use of the local hour.

BOTTOM

The back of the Firenze Dual Time watch.

FACING PAGE

The Militare features Anonimo's patented Crown Vanishing Locking Device with integrated watchstrap that protects the crown located at 6:00. The dial offers military time readout.

MILITARE
AUTOMATICO

# ANONIMO

Anonimo's first mission was to create its own case, and with the combined experience of its team, Anonimo developed the AISI3161 high-quality stainless steel case that serves as the main force for all of its watches. The brand is also one selected by ETA to use a series of master complication movements. In just a short time, due to its earnest investigations and research, Anonimo has already secured two international patents: one for the Kodiak Process it uses to improve the water wearability of its leather straps, and one for its Crown Vanishing Locking Device.

Anonimo developed a process that keeps the leather looking unchanged and unmarred despite long-lasting immersion—even in salt water—enabling the brand to link function and fashion in a manner no other brand can support. The other patent was detained for the brand's Militare 2004 model. It offers innovative water wearability and crown protection security, and provides a unique crown-winding and time-setting system.

The Anonimo collection consists of mechanical timepieces that offer true professional functions. The Millimetri has been successfully tested to a depth of 2,100 meters on a radio-controlled submarine off the coast of Sicily. It houses an automatic-winding Anonimo F1 01.0 movement on an ETA 2824-2 base. It is water wearable to 100atm. The Cronoscopio watch is 45.95mm in diameter and offers chronograph function with 30-minute and 12-hour counters. The movement is an automatic-winding modified Valjoux 7750 caliber with quick-set day and date and 40 hours of power reserve.

The Militare model 2004 is a 43.4mm watch without crown. The watch features the innovative hidden crown protected by a patent. The timepiece houses the oversized manual-winding ETA UT 6497-1 17-jeweled movement. It has an extra-thick dial with luminous coating and Arabic numerals in military format. It also features a concentric military time scale in red and features Super-LumiNova baton-style hour and minute hands. Available with either an orange or yellow dial, this watch is water wearable to 12atm. There is also a Militare Crono model 2007 with automatic-winding Dubois Dépraz 2035 chronograph module that is modified to position the stem at 6:00 and the pushbuttons at 9:00 and 11:00.

**TOP LEFT**

The Militare Crono has been reconfigured to offer pushbuttons at 9:00 and 11:00 and crown at 6:00. The watch features the patented Crown Vanishing Locking Device and offers military time scale.

**TOP CENTER**

The Millimetri model 2000 is water wearable to 100atm and features a helium expulsion valve. It houses an automatic movement and extra-thick domed sapphire crystal.

**TOP RIGHT**

The Cronoscopio features chronograph functions with readouts at 12:00 and 6:00. Day/date windows are offered at 3:00.

## CHRONOLOGY

**1997** Federico Massacesi, Italian designer and entrepreneur, founds Anonimo in Florence Italy. It is his goal to preserve Florentine watchmaking. He assembles an established team of veteran watchmakers and craftsmen to specialize in the production of unique Italian timepieces. Strategically, he opens workshops in the heart of Florence and sets about creating his first collection.

**1998** Anonimo is a hit in Italy and soon begins branching out around the world. It secures a patent for its Kodiak Process of treating leather to make it increasingly water wearable.

**1999** Anonimo secures its second international patent for its Crown Vanishing Locking Device on the Militare 2004 watch.

**2000** The brand first exhibits at the Basel watch and jewelry fair.

**2001** Anonimo sponsors the KTM-Marcuci Team at the Pharaohs Rally in Egypt. The brand also sponsors the Olympic Class Star Massacesi-Montanarini Italian Sail Championship. Also this year, Anonimo is selected to produce the Stradivari 1715 that is presented to leaders of the G8 industrialized nations summit held in Genoa Italy.

**2002** Anonimo collaborates with Cooperative National Sub from Avenza, providing a special-pressure model of its Millimetri watch to be used at major depths in the China Sea by its specialized divers' recovery unit.

**TOP**

The Hi-Dive is water wearable to 120atm and features red, white and green Super-LumiNova on the extra-thick dial.

**ABOVE LEFT AND RIGHT**

The Three Glasses watch houses an oversized manual-winding ETA UT 6497-1 movement and offers a red warning dot on the dial if the crown is left open.

**RIGHT**

The Match Racing Valencia watch offers dial-center countdown of minute and second hands with a synchronized 24-hour counter at 9:00. This race watch features color-coded reaching indicators, flags and signs and is Super-LumiNova treated for superb day/night readability.

Another impressive timepiece is the Firenze Dual Time model 2009. This timepiece houses two automatic movements that are independent in function and enable the dual time, GMT readouts. Equally as stately is the Three Glasses model 5004 watch with ETA UT 6497-1 movement that does not stop running when the crown is extracted. There is, however, a magnified check window on the dial at 4:00 that displays a red dot when the crown is left open.

Other models include the D-Date 2006 that offers full day and date displays, the Wayfarer model 2008 with GMT hour hand and power-reserve readout, and the Hi-Dive automatic-winding watch that is water wearable to 120atm.

All Anonimo watches feature straps finished in the Kodiak Process to allow for extended immersion in water.

# ARMAND NICOLET

Armand Nicolet has created harmonious balance between mechanics and form in its mechanical timepieces for generations.

In line with its founder's work, the Armand Nicolet philosophy revolves around the perfect blend between the technical value of complications and the design of the watch. Even today, the brand uses a movement that it first created in 1948: the UT 176. It represents a true gem in the Maison Nicolet, where everything from movements to cases to dials is made in house.

Located in idyllic Tramelan in the Bernese Jura, the workshops and the team of watchmakers within have a calm, serious demeanor. It is here that the integrated processes of research, development and creation come together. Because Armand Nicolet makes its own components, which are then hand assembled by an individual watchmaker, every Armand Nicolet watch has its own rate control record that is filled in and signed by one person, who follows it through every stage of development from basic idea to official inspection.

Due to the extensive personal attention and man hours required to crate each piece, the Armand Nicolet collection is limited. It includes a chronograph, big date and complete calendar. Also of particular note is the stunning Tramelan Limited Edition watch with mechanical movement and small seconds function. This timepiece houses the UT 176, modified in 2003. This movement has been completely revised so that the spiral balance wheel assembly is protected by the Incabloc system that prevents the axis of the balance wheel from breaking if the watch is dropped. The manual-winding movement with small second hand and 21 rubies, is embellished with blued screws and a swan neck in the regulating mechanism. The guillochéd silvered dial features applied indexes and luminous dots and hands. It is available in 18-karat rose or white gold and is water resistant to 5atm. Only 135 pieces are available in each color of gold.

THIS PAGE

ABOVE

Also delivered in steel, the Complete Calendar M02 watch features an interchangeable Louisiana crocodile strap.

LEFT

The Tramelan Limited Edition watch houses the UT 176 that was first unveiled n 1948 and modified in 2003. The silvered dial features applied indexes and luminous dots and hands.

FACING PAGE

This 18 karat rose gold Complete Calendar M02 houses the AN 9200/2824-2 caliber with day, date, month, year and moonphase readout.

ARMAND NICOLET
TRAMELAN
AUTOMATIC
COMPLETE CALENDAR
SWISS MADE

The Big Date M02 is housed in a stunning 43mm case and houses the AN 14000/2824-2 caliber. The mechanical automatic movement offers big date readout at 12:00 and a small seconds function. It is available in steel and in 18-karat rose gold with a Louisiana crocodile strap. The Chronograph M02 is also offered in steel and in 18-karat rose gold, and houses the AN 2045/2824-2 TND/TNK caliber. This mechanical automatic movement offers chronograph functions with 12-hour and 30-minute totalizers.

The Complete Calendar M02 watch houses the AN 9200/2824-2 caliber that offers complete calendar functions of day, date, month and year. It also features a stunning moonphase display at 12:00. It, too, is delivered in either steel or 18-karat rose gold on a Louisiana crocodile strap.

All of the Armand Nicolet timepieces were inspired by originals created by the founder and therefore offer the classically elegant look of the early 20th century. All of the watches feature sapphire crystal exhibition casebacks and are water resistant from 50 to 200 meters. Straps are interchangeable to offer versatility.

**TOP RIGHT**

The Big Date M02 houses the AN 14000/2824-2 mechanical automatic movement in a 43mm case. It offers big date readout at 12:00 and a small seconds function. This version is created in 18-karat rose gold.

**LEFT**

The Big Date M02 is available in stainless steel.

## CHRONOLOGY

**1884** Armand Nicolet is born, the son of a watchmaker.

**1900** After a brilliant watchmaking apprenticeship and a period of technical experimentation, Nicolet sets up his own workshop in Tramelan, creating mechanical timepieces.

**1902** Nicolet unveils the single-button chronograph with complete calendar and repeating hours, quarter hours and minutes.

**1940s** The brand releases the flyback chronograph. Willy Nicolet inherits his father's company and continues to run it as a symbol of watchmaking luxury.

**1948** Armand Nicolet develops the UT 176 manual-winding mechanical movement with small second hand.

**1950s** The Maison Nicolet acquires the Ajustor patent used to adjust rate without having to open the watch.

**1979** The brand exhibits at the Basel watch fair for the first time.

**2002** Armand Nicolet establishes a small museum of important machinery and period tools in its headquarters.

**2003** Armand Nicolet reconfigures its UT 176 manual movement and releases it in a limited edition timepiece.

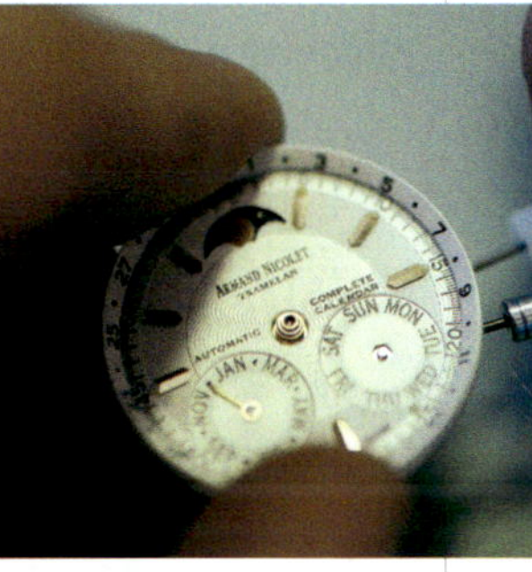

**ABOVE**

The Chronograph M02 is shown here in 18-karat rose gold.

**RIGHT**

This stainless steel Chronograph M02 houses the caliber AN 2045/2824-2 TND/TNK and offers chronograph functions with 12-hour and 30-minute totalizers.

# ARNOLD & SON

It is recorded that Arnold & Son maritime clocks accompanied the most famous of British explorers on their expeditions—Sir John Franklin, Captain Phipps, Sir Ernest Shackleton and the legendary Captain Cook—because of the excellent chronometers that the brand created in response to the Longitude Act.

**TOP**

The 45mm, silver-dialed Arnold & Son True North Perpetual features 7-day power reserve, perpetual calendar, time equation, moonphase and 24-hour indicator. The hand-wound movement offers double time equation, true solar compass and true solar time corrector at 8:00 for entering longitude. The True North Perpetual is water resistant to 100 feet. Shown here in white gold, the watch is also available in a 25-piece platinum limited edition.

Representing the culmination of lengthy, meticulous research, the internationally patented True North Perpetual is a unique achievement in contemporary watchmaking history, strongly influenced by the work of 18th century English master watchmaker John Arnold.

Human lives have always been governed by two universal timekeepers: the regular alternations of day and night (as the earth rotates on its axis) and cold and warm seasons (as the earth orbits the sun).

Devised by Eric A. Loth, reviver of some of England's most distinguished brands and creator of the Arnold & Son Longitude watch, the True North Perpetual complication addresses civil time (average time within a time zone) and the globe as a cosmic clock for the first time in a wristwatch.

Powered by a patented hand-wound movement with 7-day power reserve (produced by Jacquet SA exclusively for Arnold & Son), this features a perpetual calendar accounting for leap years, a moonphase display calculated on a 29.5-day lunar cycle, a 24-hour time-zone indicator also showing mean solar time, and a double equation-of-time display.

The Arnold & Son True North Perpetual is the first timepiece capable of indicating true solar time in a given place and the true geographical North (once a day at true solar noon). Its operating principle is based on the correction of the discrepancies between our mean civil time (valid throughout a time zone), and true solar time (different for each terrestrial longitude and dependent on the date (the earth's position along its ecliptic orbit).

There are currently several watches with equation-of-time indication, but no other has also incorporated summer time or Daylight Saving Time correction and longitude, both of which are quite important factors in determining true solar time.

Via three corrections, the 24-hour solar hand (tipped with a small sun) and the triple dial consisting of a large fixed central dial and two mobile dial rings, enable the wearer to determine true solar time in the place he or she is, without changing the civil time shown on the watch.

The first correction is for summer time: By successively pressing the pushbutton located at 10:00, the 24-hour solar hand can be adjusted to winter time, corresponding in summer to civil time minus one hour. This applies to all regions using Daylight Saving Time (which moves the clock one hour forward during the summer).

The second correction relates to the location: Depending on whether the wearer is to the east, west or in the center of a given time zone, the sun will not always reach its zenith at the same time.

At 8:00, the wearer rotates the outer mobile dial ring by a value equal to the difference between the current longitude and that of the wearer's civil time. The value of this correction is visible at 6:00. For example, the longitude in Geneva is around 6° East. The time zone for Switzerland is "plus 1 hour" from Greenwich (GMT +1), or 15° East, so the correction of the two mobile dials will be 9° to the West.

The third correction is the running equation of time: In order to simplify things, the fluctuating value of the equation of time—according to whether the apparent sun is faster (sun fast) or slower (sun slow) than the mean sun—is indicated directly by the joint movement of the two mobile dial rings. Thus, the value of the equation of time is automatically compensated for in the read-off displayed on the graduated solar hour scale around the outer mobile dial ring.

The True North Perpetual verges on the sublime when the 24-hour solar hand indicates the true solar noon. At this precise moment, you need only to point this 24-hour solar hand in the direction of the sun to make the mobile outer dial ring indicate the true geographical north, independently of any error related to magnetic fields, position (within the Northern hemisphere) or to the date.

The development of the Arnold & Son True North Perpetual watch might not have been possible a few years ago. Using cutting-edge development and production technologies, the English Arnold & Son team and Geneva watchmaker Jean-Marc Wiederrecht, of Agenhor SA, have accomplished several highly original feats in order to achieve the result of true solar time.

BELOW
John Arnold.

## CHRONOLOGY

**1750** John Arnold becomes an apprentice to his father, a clockmaker in Cornwall.

**1764** Arnold establishes his own career in London. His goal is to design a perfect marine timekeeper to determine longitude.

**1774** The bimetallic compensation balance spring is developed by Arnold, though it will not be patented until 1782.

**1775** Arnold patents his chronometer.

**1780** The spring-detent chronometer escapement is developed and is patented in 1782.

**1783** Arnold is admitted into the Clockmakers' Company.

**1787** John Roger joins his father's business, now known officially as Arnold & Son. While other watchmakers can produce about 500 marine chronometers within a lifetime, Arnold & Son will produce more than 5,000—quickly becoming the main supplier to the Royal Navy.

**1799** John Arnold dies at age 63. Abraham-Louis Breguet pays homage to their friendship by incorporating his first operational tourbillon device into a marine chronometer that Arnold had made for Breguet.

**1800s** The brand operates through the end of the century, supplying the Royal Navy and exploration ships with marine timekeepers.

**1990s** The British Masters company is established, honoring the famous English inventor-clockmakers. The firm is headquartered in La Chaux-de-Fonds.

**1998** The British Masters presents the new Arnold & Son collection.

**2002** Arnold & Son unveils a Deck Marine Timekeeper, a Longitude Timekeeper and a stunning GMT Master Tourbillon with mysterious hand-winding system.

**2003** Arnold & Son resumes its close cooperation with the Royal Navy and the Prince Trust. The three partner to launch the Arnold & Son Explorer expedition on a TransAtlantic Arctic route.

**2004** Arnold & Son launches the True North Perpetual. For the first time in the history of watchmaking, a Perpetual Calendar wristwatch displays a time corrected by the time equation. The watch shows the true North and solar time for a given longitude.

ARNOLD & SON
LONDON 1764

## TRUE NORTH PERPETUAL REF. 1QPAW.S01A.C40B

**Movement:** mechanical self-winding caliber A-1794; 41 jewels; 21,600 vph; 7-day power reserve; Côtes de Genève and circular graining patterns; blue steel screws; adjusted 5 positions.
**Functions:** hour, minute, second; date; solar compass; power reserve; equation of time; perpetual calendar; moonphase; 3 correctors for: summer time; location; running equation of time.

**Case:** Ø 45mm; white-gold case; curved sapphire crystal; water resistant to 100 feet.
**Dial:** silver dial with power reserve; perpetual calendar; time equation; moonphase; 24-hour indicator.
**Indications:** quick setting corrector for moonphase at 8 and date at 10; GMT and compass setting at 11; and corrector for longitude rotating inner bezel at 7.
**Strap:** black crocodile leather; polished and engraved white-gold buckle.
**Also available:** platinum (limited edition 25 pieces).

## DESIGN OF CALIBER A-1794

Powered by a manual-wound movement with a 7-day power reserve, this complicated watch is equipped with a perpetual calendar taking into account leap years, a moonphase display based on a 29.5-day lunar cycle, a 24-hour time-zone indication capable of showing also the mean solar time, and with a double equation of time display (equation segment and running equation indication, both giving the difference between true solar time and mean solar time).

**Movement:** mechanical self-winding caliber A-1794; 41 jewels; 21,600 vph; 7-day power reserve; Côtes de Genève and circular graining decoration; blue steel screws; adjusted 5 positions.

## LONGITUDE II BLUE ICE REF. 1L2AS.B04A.K02A

**Movement:** mechanical self-winding caliber A-714; 11" 1/2; 21 jewels; 28,800 vph; 42-hour power reserve; Côtes de Genève and circular graining patterns; blue steel screws; COSC-certified chronometer; adjusted 5 positions.
**Functions:** hour, minute, second; date; solar compass; longitude positioning.
**Case:** Ø 44.5mm; low-carbon, high corrosion-resistant stainless steel three-piece case; transparent sapphire crystal caseback under secret back opened via push-button at 3; water resistant to 160 feet.
**Dial:** blue and black dial with mirror polished indexes; central rotating dial showing North Pole.
**Indications:** longitude calculation with the longitude scale on rotating bezel and equation of time in secret back; central 24-hour solar compass disc; magnified date at 6.
**Strap:** black rubber; polished and engraved oversized steel buckle.

## LONGITUDE II REF. 1L2AS.S02A.K02B

**Movement:** mechanical self-winding caliber A-714; 11" 1/2; 21 jewels; 28,800 vph; 42-hour power reserve; Côtes de Genève and circular graining patterns; blue steel screws; COSC-certified chronometer; adjusted 5 positions.
**Functions:** hour, minute, second; date; solar compass; longitude positioning.
**Case:** Ø 44.5mm; low-carbon, high corrosion-resistant stainless steel three-piece case; transparent sapphire crystal caseback under secret back opened via push-button at 3; water resistant to 160 feet.
**Dial:** silvered with silver rotating bezel and central 24-hour disc; luminescent markers, hour and minute hands; central rotating dial showing North Pole.
**Indications:** longitude calculation with the longitude scale on rotating bezel and equation of time in secret back; central 24-hour solar compass disc; magnified date at 6.
**Strap:** black rubber; polished and engraved oversized steel buckle.

## WHITE ENSIGN SILVER DIAL — REF. 1WEBS.S01A.K02B

**Movement:** mechanical manual-winding caliber A-294E; 11" 1/2; 20 jewels; 21,600 vph / 3 Hz; 7-day power reserve; Côtes de Genève and circular graining patterns; blue steel screws; adjusted 5 positions.
**Functions:** hour, minute, small second at 6; date; 7-day power reserve; bi-directional inner bezel.
**Case:** Ø 44.5mm; low-carbon, high corrosion-resistant stainless steel three-piece case; transparent sapphire crystal caseback held by 7 screws; water resistant to 660 feet.
**Dial:** silver with luminescent markers; British "broad arrow" at 12; central hands; hour hand with extra-long red tip; white hands for power-reserve indicator and small second.
**Indications:** date at 6; English-style power-reserve gauge (fully wound at "0") at 12; small second at 6; rotating inner bezel.
**Strap:** black rubber; polished and engraved oversized steel buckle.
**Also available:** crocodile or calf leather strap.

## WHITE ENSIGN BLACK DIAL — REF. 1WEBS.B01A.K02B

**Movement:** mechanical manual-winding caliber A-294E; 11" 1/2; 20 jewels; 21,600 vph / 3 Hz; 7-day power reserve; Côtes de Genève and circular graining patterns; blue steel screws; adjusted 5 positions.
**Functions:** hour, minute, small second at 6; date; 7-day power reserve; bi-directional inner bezel.
**Case:** Ø 44.5mm; low-carbon, high corrosion-resistant stainless steel three-piece case; transparent sapphire crystal caseback held by 7 screws; water resistant to 660 feet.
**Dial:** black with luminescent markers; British "broad arrow" at 12; central hands; hour hand with extra-long red tip; white hands for power-reserve indicator and small second.
**Indications:** date at 6; English-style power-reserve gauge (fully wound at "0") at 12; small second at 6; rotating inner bezel.
**Strap:** black rubber; polished and engraved oversized steel buckle.
**Also available:** crocodile or calf leather strap.

## GMT II COMPASS ROSE — REF. 1G2AS.B03A.C01B

**Movement:** mechanical self-winding double GMT caliber A-788; 11"; 26 jewels; 28,800 vph; 42-hour power reserve; Côtes de Genève and circular graining decoration; blue steel screws; COSC-certified chronometer; adjusted five 5 positions.
**Functions:** hour, minute, second; date; 2 independent 24-hour time-zone indicators with correctors in addition to the local time (center hands); solar compass.
**Case:** Ø 42mm; low-carbon high corrosion-resistant stainless steel three-piece case; caseback held by 8 screws; royal marine crown engraved on caseback; water resistant to 330 feet.
**Dial:** black with luminescent markers and center hands; bicolor subdials for GMT and third time zones with solar compass; sun hand at 11.
**Indications:** main / local time (center hands); two additional 24-hour time zones adjustable independently; solar compass; magnified date at 6.
**Strap:** black crocodile or alligator leather; polished and engraved steel buckle.

## TIMEKEEPER III — REF. 1M3AP.S01A.C34B

**Movement:** mechanical manual-winding caliber A-294E; 11" 1/2; 20 jewels; 21,600 vph / 3 Hz; 7-day power reserve; Côtes de Genève and circular graining patterns; blue steel screws; adjusted 5 positions.
**Functions:** hours, minutes, small seconds; date; 7-day power reserve.
**Case:** Ø 38mm; 4N18 pink-gold three-piece case; transparent sapphire crystal caseback attached by 8 screws; water resistant to 160 feet.
**Dial:** silvered with pink-gold-plated applied markers and central hands; blued-steel hands for power-reserve indicator and small seconds.
**Indications:** date at 3; small seconds at 6; English-style power-reserve gauge (fully wound to "0") at 12.
**Strap:** black crocodile or alligator leather with polished and engraved pink-gold buckle.

# AUDEMARS PIGUET

One of the most venerable manufactures, Audemars Piguet consistently proves its excellence in all arenas, from grand complications and complicated masterpieces to high-tech sports watches and high-jeweled works of art.

Audemars Piguet unveils beautiful pieces in each of its watch categories. Since the summer of 2002, racecar driver Juan Pablo Montoya has been an ambassador for Audemars Piguet, and now the brand celebrates this alliance in its Royal Oak series—one of the most acclaimed success stories of modern-day watchmaking—with the Royal Oak Offshore Juan Pablo Montoya Chronograph. A mouthful to say, the watch is equally as impressive and massive to look at.

This watch marks a new stage in the history of Audemars Piguet and in the field of haute horlogerie, as it embodies the seamless merging of two avant-garde technologies. The self-winding chronograph encapsulates the most cutting-edge research in Formula 1 motor racing and blends it with incomparable horological expertise. Like the Formula 1 racing cars, which use titanium, steel and carbon because of their sturdiness and lightness, the Royal Oak Offshore Juan Pablo Montoya Chronograph features carbon inserts on its bezel and pushers. And, as one may expect, the watch is offered not only in platinum or pink gold, but also in titanium.

Also in keeping with the theme of Formula 1, Audemars Piguet has bedecked the watch with numerous details to reflect the aesthetics of a racecar. Instead of hexagonal bezel screws, the screws are shaped like cylinder-head screws, the crown is reminiscent of a wheel axle and the pushers resemble cooling flaps. The rotor of the movement, revealed through the sapphire caseback, looks like a clutch disc. Finally, the leather strap features a seam similar to those on driving suits and features a velvet lining of fabric used to cover the steering wheels of the racing machines. The watch is equipped with a tachometric scale to measure speed and is offered in three versions: silver dial on titanium case; black dial on pink-gold case; matte blue dial on platinum case.

THIS PAGE

ABOVE

Only 100 pieces of the platinum Royal Oak Offshore Juan Pablo Montoya Chronograph with matte blue dial will be made.

FACING PAGE

Resulting from a close cooperation between Audemars Piguet and the famous Colombian racecar driver, the Royal Oak Offshore Juan Pablo Montoya is a high-tech self-winding chronograph with tachometer scale. The titanium version with silvered dial is created in a series of 1,000 pieces.

AP
AUDEMARS PIGUET

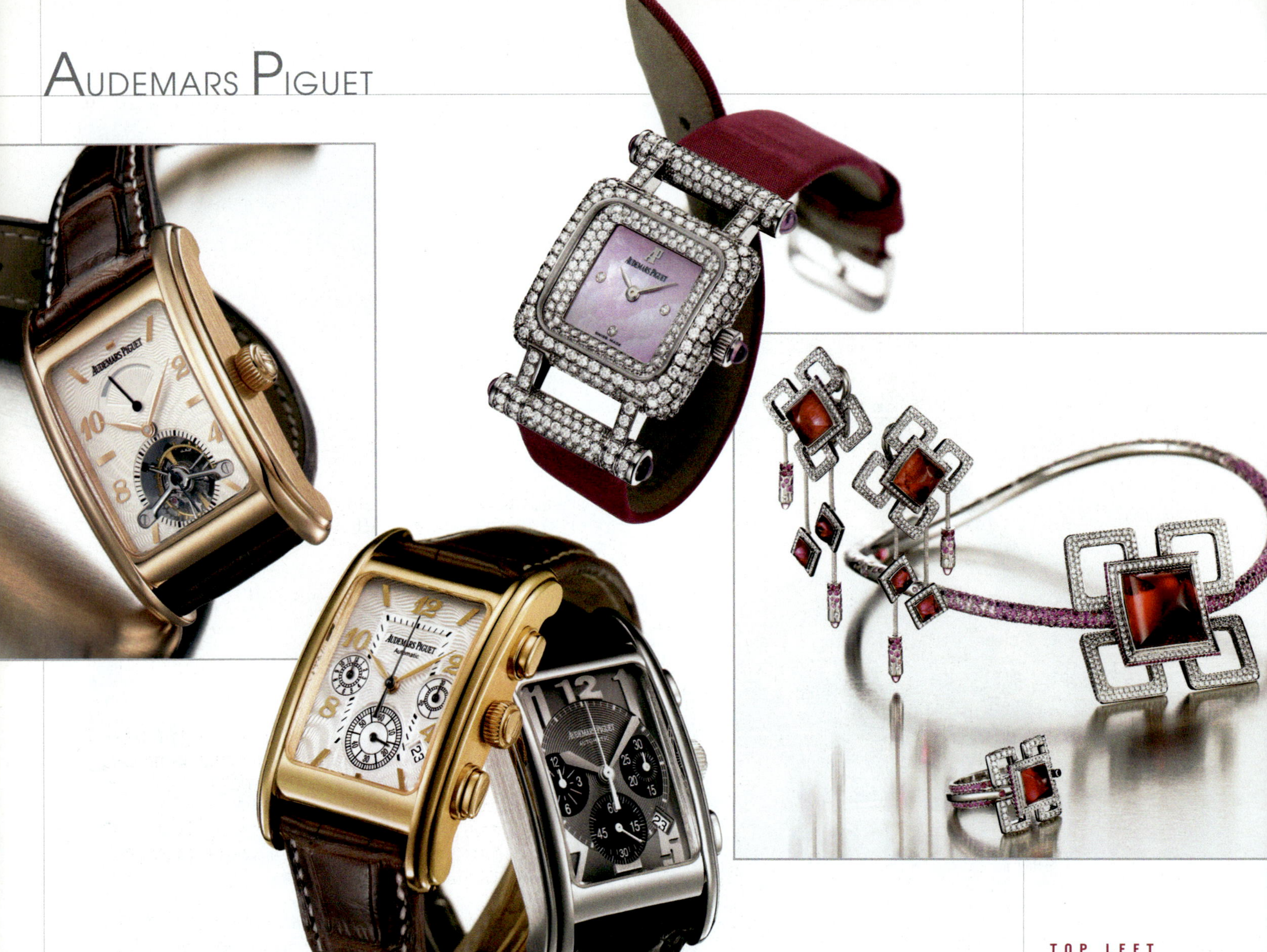

In its Edward Piguet collection—named for one of the company's founders—the brand unveils a stunning rectangular Edward Piguet Tourbillon with 70 hours of power reserve. For several decades, Audemars Piguet has been offering miniaturized tourbillon movements for the wrist. This newest watch is created in platinum, 18-karat white or pink gold, and features a tourbillon aperture at 6:00. It houses the proprietary Caliber 2878 hand-wound movement with 177 parts and 21 jewels.

Also new is the Edward Piguet Selfwinding Chronograph. Classically elegant, the rectangular case is slightly larger than others in the collection. It is crafted in gold and houses the Caliber 2385 self-winding movement with 304 parts and 37 jewels.

Audemars Piguet is also expert at designing women's watches—offering diamond and gemstone pieces that are breathtakingly beautiful. Such is the case with the new Deva watch line with accompanying jewelry. The Deva collection of feminine timepieces is definitively alluring with its cushion-cornered square case shape and open-worked case-to-bracelet attachment that lets some skin show through. Among the new Deva models are 18-karat gold pieces bedecked with varying degrees of diamonds on the case and attachments. One model features 405 brilliants weighing 4.37 carats.

**TOP LEFT**
This 18-karat pink-gold Edward Piguet Tourbillon offers 70 hours of power reserve and houses a 177-part hand-wound movement.

**LOWER CENTER**
The Edward Piguet Self-winding Chronograph is created in 18-karat gold and offered with a choice of classic or contemporary dial.

**TOP CENTER**
The Deva watch features approximately 4.24 carats of diamonds and 1.09 carats of sapphires.

**CENTER RIGHT**
The Deva necklace is set with a 32.25-carat rubellite, 11.68 carats of sapphires, 0.75 carats of rubies and 5.67 carats of diamonds.

**TOP**

This Jules Audemars Chronograph is crafted in 18-karat gold and houses a self-winding movement with 42 hours of power reserve.

**CENTER**

This Millenary ladies' chronograph features a striking black dial with pink numerals to coordinate with the pink strap.

Each watch features a mother-of-pearl dial and a matching color-coordinated strap.

Other jeweled and ladies' watches come in the form of new Millenary chronographs and Jules Audemars Chronographs. The Jules Audemars Chronograph with globe dial is offered in pink and white versions with varying degrees of diamonds. The Millenary chronographs for women are also offered in pastel colors with striking dials and color-coordinated numerals to match the straps.

## CHRONOLOGY

**1875** Jules Audemars and Edward Piguet become business partners in Le Brassus.

**1881** Audemars Piguet & Cie is registered as a firm specializing in extra-flat and complicated watches.

**1889** Audemars Piguet unveils the Grande Complication pocket watch with minute repeater, perpetual calendar, moonphase, split-second chronograph and petite and grande sonnerie.

**1906** The first wristwatch featuring a minute repeater is developed.

**1915** The world's smallest minute repeater (15.8mm diameter) is created by the manufacture.

**1946** Audemars Piguet develops an extra-flat movement for wristwatches—the 9''' ML caliber with a thickness of just 1.64mm.

**1970** The brand's automatic Caliber 2121 with date and center gold rotor is the flattest of its kind at 3.05mm thick.

**1972** With its Royal Oak, Audemars Piguet enters the world of luxury sports watches.

**1992** The Triple Complication wristwatch is unveiled, featuring minute repeater, chronograph function and perpetual calendar indicating the leap years and 52 weeks.

**1994** The Grande Sonnerie, stemming from an illustrious pocket ancestor, is launched as a wristwatch equipped with hour and quarter repeaters.

**1997** The Royal Oak celebrates its 25th anniversary with an automatic movement and a 80-piece limited-edition of the Royal Oak Golf Set in homage to golf champion Nick Faldo.

**1999** The Jules Audemars with tourbillon, minute repeater and split-second chronograph is launched. It is the first of 8 legendary watches and the limited series Tradition d'Excellence.

**2000** For the company's 125th anniversary, the Audemars Piguet Foundation, established in 1992, holds a charity auction at Christie's in New York as its inaugural event. The company unveils the Jules Audemars Equation of Time wristwatch—inspired by a pocket watch of 1925. It is adjusted to the owner's local time at the workshop and indicates the equation of time, sunrise and sunset times, perpetual calendar and moonphase.

**2001** The Metropolis combines a perpetual calendar with the display of 24 time zones.

**2002** Audemars Piguet unveils the Royal Oak Concept watch to celebrate the collection's 30th anniversary. Its hand-wound movement represents a first in the luxury watch industry. It is made of titanium and is equipped with a tourbillon escapement and Dynamograph®.

**2003** Audemars Piguet co-sponsors the Swiss winner of the America's Cup 2003, Team Alinghi, and creates a special Royal Oak version in honor of the event and the team.

## ROYAL OAK CONCEPT WATCH — REF. 25980AI

**Movement:** mechanical manual-winding Audemars Piguet Caliber 2896; tourbillon mounted on shock absorbers; all components manufactured and decorated by hand; chamfering, polishing and sapphire-blasting of the mainplate, bars and bridges.
**Functions:** hour, minute, small second; power-reserve indicator showing the number of barrel turns (1 turn every 6 hours); mainspring torque indicator (Dynamographe); crown function selector.

**Case:** Alacrite 602 (17.51mm thick); sapphire crystal, 4.58mm thick; transparent sapphire caseback, 4.13mm thick; bezel in titanium (grade 1); water resistant to 500 meters.
**Dial:** the bottom plate of the movement serves as dial face.
**Indications:** linear-shaped power-reserve indicator at 3; subdial for the second at 6; tourbillon visible at 9; Dynamographe at 12.
**Strap:** synthetic fiber with AP deployment clasp in titanium and stainless steel.
**Note:** limited series of 150 pieces in Alacrite 602, marking the 30th anniversary of the Royal Oak.

## ROYAL OAK TRADITION D'EXCELLENCE TOURBILLON WITH CHRONOGRAPH — REF. 25969PT

**Movement:** exclusive manual-winding Audemars Piguet Caliber 2893; tourbillon; 10-day power reserve; rhodium-plated movement with Côtes de Genève and circular-graining decorative patterns; all parts decorated by hand.
**Functions:** hour, minute, second; chronograph; double power-reserve indicator (10 days / last 24 hours).

**Case:** platinum; polished and brushed finish; sapphire crystal and caseback; octagonal bezel and 8 recessed hexagonal nuts in white gold, fastening 8 white-gold through-screws of the caseback; water resistant to 20 meters.
**Dial:** partially open-worked dial with Grande Tapisserie pattern.
**Bracelet:** platinum; exclusive Audemars Piguet folding clasp.

## ROYAL OAK PERPETUAL CALENDAR — REF. 25820ST

**Movement:** mechanical automatic-winding, extra-thin Audemars Piguet Caliber 2120/2802; white-gold skeleton rotor; hand-finished and hand-decorated.
**Functions:** hour, minute; perpetual calendar (date, day, month, year, moonphase).
**Case:** stainless steel two-piece case (Ø 38.5mm, thickness: 9.5mm); polished and brushed finish; flat sapphire crystal; octagonal bezel with gasket and 8 recessed hexagon nuts in white gold, fastening 8 white-gold through-screws of the caseback; back displaying the movement through a sapphire crystal; 4 correctors on middle; hexagonal screw-down crown; water resistant to 20 meters.

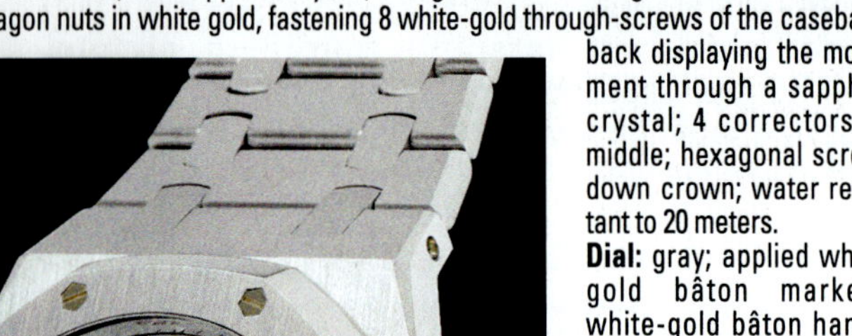

**Dial:** gray; applied white-gold bâton markers; white-gold bâton hands; printed minute track.
**Indications:** date at 3; moonphase at 6; day at 9; month and four-year cycle at 12.
**Bracelet:** brushed stainless steel; fold-over clasp with safety pusher.
**Also available:** with sapphire blue dial; yellow-gold gilded dial; platinum and stainless steel black Grande Tapisserie dial; platinum Tuscany blue dial. Medium size with blue Petite Tapisserie dial Ref. 25800: in stainless steel; in yellow gold. Skeleton Ref. 25829: in steel; yellow gold; in platinum.

## ROYAL OAK CHRONOGRAPH — REF. 26022BA

**Movement:** self-winding Audemars Piguet Caliber 2385; chronograph; 18K gold oscillating weight; 37 jewels; 304 parts and components; power reserve up to 40 hours; rhodium-plated movement with Côtes de Genève and circular-graining decorative patterns.
**Functions:** hour, minute, small second; date display; chronograph.
**Case:** 18K yellow gold; sapphire crystal; water resistant to 50 meters.

**Dial:** exclusive and traditional engine-turned Grande Tapisserie decorative pattern.
**Strap:** alligator leather; 18K yellow-gold Audemars Piguet folding clasp.
**Also available:** 18K white or pink gold.

## ROYAL OAK CHRONOGRAPH — REF. 25860ST

**Movement:** mechanical automatic-winding Audemars Piguet Caliber 2385; manufactured and finished by hand; decorated with Côtes de Genève pattern and beveled.
**Functions:** hour, minute, small second; date; chronograph with 3 counters.
**Case:** stainless steel three-piece case (Ø 39mm, thickness: 11mm); polished and brushed finish; flat sapphire crystal; octagonal bezel with gasket and 8 recessed white-gold hexagon nuts fastening through the caseback; hexagonal screw-down crown; pushers with case protection; water resistant to 50 meters.
**Dial:** silvered, decorated with Grande Tapisserie pattern; counters decorated with circular beads; luminescent applied markers; luminescent bâton hands.
**Indications:** minute counter at 3; date between 4 and 5; small second at 6; hour counter at 9; center second counter; minute track.
**Bracelet:** stainless steel, brushed finish; fold-over clasp with safety pusher.
**Also available:** with black or "cosmos" blue or silvered dial; yellow gold with silvered or blue Petite Tapisserie dial; white gold with silvered dial.

## ROYAL OAK AUTOMATIC — REF. 14790ST

**Movement:** mechanical automatic-winding Audemars Piguet Caliber 2225; manufactured and finished by hand; decorated with Côtes de Genève pattern and beveled.
**Functions:** hour, minute, second; date.
**Case:** stainless steel two-piece case (Ø 37mm, thickness: 8.2mm), polished and brushed finish; flat sapphire crystal; octagonal bezel with gasket and 8 recessed hexagon nuts in white gold fastening through the caseback; hexagonal screw-down crown; water resistant to 50 meters.
**Dial:** black, decorated with Grande Tapisserie pattern; luminescent applied steel bâton markers; luminescent steel bâton hands; printed minute track with 5-minute progression.
**Indications:** date at 3.
**Bracelet:** brushed steel; double fold-over clasp with safety pusher.
**Also available:** with Grande Tapisserie "cosmos" blue, silvered or Petite Tapisserie, dark gray dial; Pilot black dial, leather strap, bracelet; steel/yellow gold, Petite Tapisserie dark gray or silvered Grande Tapisserie dial, bracelet; yellow-gold, silvered Grande Tapisserie dial; with Pilot black dial, luminescent Arabic numerals, leather strap.

## LADY ROYAL OAK — REF. 67601BA

**Movement:** quartz; Audemars Piguet Caliber 2712; rhodium-plated movement, decorated with Côtes de Genève and circular graining. **Functions:** hour, minute; date.
**Case:** satin-brushed 18K yellow-gold case; beveled edges; 18K yellow-gold bezel set with 32 brilliant-cut diamonds; visible through-screws; domed and hollowed sapphire crystal; satin-brushed/polished 18K yellow-gold crown adorned with translucent sapphire cabochon; caseback stamped with the Lady Royal Oak logo; polished letters on a sandblasted base; water resistant to 50 meters.
**Dial:** white natural mother-of-pearl; 11 hour-markers set with brilliant-cut diamonds; applied aperture; elongated oval-shaped luminescent hands.
**Strap:** matte white hand-sewn crocodile leather with stitching in a matching shade; double-folding clasp in polished 18K yellow gold.
**Also available:** in steel or 18K white gold; various diamond setting; silvered or sky-blue dial; wave Tapisserie motif with 11 oval-shaped luminescent hour markers; on white, brown or sky-blue crocodile straps; on steel satin-brushed and polished bracelet or 18K yellow-gold satin-brushed and polished bracelet. Full diamond-set jewelry versions available in 18K white gold.

## ROYAL OAK OFFSHORE JUAN PABLO MONTOYA CHRONOGRAPH — REF. 26030RO

**Movement:** Audemars Piguet Caliber 2226/2840; self-winding chronograph; 21K gold oscillating weight; power reserve up to 42 hours; rhodium-plated movement with Côtes de Genève and circular-graining decorative patterns.
**Functions:** hour, minute, small second; date; chronograph; tachymeter.
**Case:** sturdy construction of 18K pink gold; sapphire crystal and caseback; bezel and pushbuttons decorated with carbon inserts; bezel screws resembling cylinder-head screws on a Formula 1 engine; screw-locked crown echoing the design of a wheel axle; back fitted with sapphire crystal and bearing the name of racecar driver Juan Pablo Montoya; water resistant to 100 meters.
**Dial:** Mega Tapisserie pattern reminiscent of a checkered flag; hollowed gold hands with design dedicated to Juan Pablo Montoya.
**Strap:** leather with reinforced seams and velvet lining; exclusive Audemars Piguet folding clasp.
**Also available:** in titanium or platinum.

## ROYAL OAK OFFSHORE CHRONOGRAPH — REF. 26020ST

**Movement:** Audemars Piguet caliber 2226/2840; self-winding chronograph; 21K gold oscillating weight; power reserve up to 42 hours; rhodium-plated movement with Côtes de Genève and circular-graining decorative patterns.
**Functions:** hour, minute, small second; date display; chronograph; tachymeter.

**Case:** sturdy construction of stainless steel; polished and brushed finish; sapphire crystal; octagonal bezel and 8 recessed hexagonal nuts, fastening the 8 through-screws of the caseback; antimagnetic soft iron movement housing; water resistant to 100 meters.
**Dial:** decorated with Mega Tapisserie pattern; luminescent Arabic numerals.
**Strap:** leather; exclusive Audemars Piguet folding clasp.
**Also available:** in several dial colors and straps.

## ROYAL OAK OFFSHORE CHRONOGRAPH — REF. 25940OK

**Movement:** bi-directional automatic-winding Caliber 2226/2840; 21K gold oscillating weight segment; Ø 11 1/2''', thickness: 6.15mm; 54 jewels; 370 parts; 38-hour power reserve; 28,800 vph; finish: all parts decorated by hand; beveling, circular graining pattern on the mainplate and Côtes de Genève on the bridges.
**Functions:** hour, minute, small second; numerical calendar display; chronometer; 1000-based tachometric scale.

**Case:** 18K pink-gold; rubber bezel; rubber guards for the crown and pushpieces.
**Dial:** slate-gray with "extra" Grande Tapisserie pattern; Arabic numerals and white luminescent hour markers.
**Strap:** black rubber, notched and padded, with steel reinforcements and AP folding clasp in 18K pink gold.
**Also available:** in steel.

## ROYAL OAK OFFSHORE CHRONO LADY — REF. 25986CK

**Movement:** automatic-winding chronograph; Audemars Piguet Caliber 2385; date calendar; rhodium-plated movement with Côtes de Genève decorative pattern and circular graining pattern with 18K gold rotor; Ø 25.60mm, thickness: 5.50mm; 37 jewels; 40-hour power reserve; 21,600 vph.
**Functions:** hour, minute, small second; date; chronograph with 3 counters.
**Case:** 18K white gold; rubber-clad gem-set bezel (32 diamonds: 1.25 carats total) with gemstones certificate; sapphire crystal; water resistant to 50 meters.

**Dial:** exclusive, traditional Grande Tapisserie decorative pattern.
**Strap:** rubber, notched and padded, with steel reinforcements and AP folding clasp in 18K white gold.
**Also available:** in 18K yellow gold with gray rubber strap and in 18K white gold with orange rubber strap and light pink dial.

## JULES AUDEMARS METROPOLIS PERPETUAL CALENDAR — REF. 25919PT

**Movement:** extra-thin automatic Audemars Piguet Caliber 2120/2804; rotor with 21K gold segment; 40 jewels; 19,800 vph; realized and finished by hand; decorated with Côtes de Genève and beveled.
**Functions:** hour, minute; perpetual calendar (date, day, month, year); world time.
**Case:** platinum three-piece case (Ø 39, thickness: 10mm); polished and brushed finish; curved sapphire glass; middle with three correctors; white-gold crown; pusher for the independent hour correction of world time at 4; back attached by 5 screws, displaying the movement through a sapphire crystal; water resistant to 20 meters.

**Dial:** silvered, engraved meridians and parallels; zones decorated with circular beads; with gold rim; applied white-gold Arabic numerals and cabochon markers; printed minute track with 5-minute progression; white-gold leaf-style hands.
**Indications:** date at 3; world time at 6; day at 9; month and four-year cycle at 12.
**Strap:** crocodile leather; platinum fold-over clasp shaped in the firm's logo.
**Also available:** in pink gold.

## JULES AUDEMARS GLOBE REF. 15120BC

**Movement:** automatic-winding Audemars Piguet Caliber 3090; 60-hour power reserve; 40 jewels; 22K gold rotor with engraved sector; realized by hand; finish: all parts decorated by hand; beveled, with Côtes de Genève pattern on the bridges and circular graining on the mainplate.
**Functions:** hour, minute, center second; date.
**Case:** 18K white- or pink-gold three-piece case (Ø 39mm, thickness: 9.9mm); polished and brushed finish; sapphire crystal caseback; water resistant to 20 meters.
**Dials:** the Classic is silvered with Côtes de Genève pattern and applied Roman numerals; the Globe dial features decorative globe pattern in black or silvered with luminescent numerals.
**Strap:** full-grain crocodile leather with optional exclusive 18K AP folding clasp.
**Also available:** in 18K white gold for the Classic version; 18K pink gold for the Globe version.

## JULES AUDEMARS GRANDE COMPLICATION REF. 25866OR

**Movement:** automatic-winding Audemars Piguet Caliber 2885; consisting of more than 600 elements; handmade and hand-finished with Côtes de Genève pattern and beveled.
**Functions:** hour, minute, small second; perpetual calendar (date, day, month, year, week, moonphase); minute repeater; split-second chronograph with 2 counters.
**Case:** 18K pink-gold three-piece case (Ø 42mm, thickness: 13.5mm); flat sapphire crystal; middle with five correctors and slide repeater on case side; pink-gold crown and pushers (with coaxial split-second pusher); snap-on back; moisture protection.
**Dial:** silvered; applied pink-gold bâton markers; burnished-gold leaf-style hands.
**Indications:** minute counter and day of week at 3; month and four-year cycle at 6; date and small second at 9; week and moonphase at 12; center split-second counters; minute track with divisions for 1/5 of a second.
**Strap:** crocodile leather; pink-gold fold-over clasp.
**Also available:** in yellow gold and platinum.

## JULES AUDEMARS EQUATION OF TIME REF. 25934BA

**Movement:** automatic; Audemars Piguet Caliber 2120/2808; realized and finished by hand.
**Functions:** hour, minute; perpetual calendar (date, day, month, year, moonphase); equation of time; sunrise and sunset hours.
**Case:** 18K yellow-gold three-piece case (Ø 39, thickness: 11.7mm); polished and brushed finish; curved sapphire glass; polished bezel with engraved digits for the equation-of-time indication (difference between solar and mean time in minutes); middle with 3 correctors; gold crown; back attached by 5 screws, displaying the movement through a sapphire glass; water resistant to 20 meters.
**Dial:** silvered, center and zones decorated with circular beads; with gold rim; applied faceted gold triangular markers; printed minute track with 5-minute progression; skeletonized burnished-gold Alpha hands.
**Indications:** four-year cycle between 1 and 2; sunset hour at 3; date and day of the week at 6; sunrise hour at 9; month and moonphase at 12; time equation center hand with sun.
**Strap:** crocodile leather; gold fold-over clasp shaped with the firm's logo.
**Also available:** in pink gold, black dial; white gold, dark gray dial.

## EDWARD PIGUET TOURBILLON WITH POWER RESERVE REF. 26006BC

**Movement:** exclusive manual-winding Audemars Piguet Caliber 2878; tourbillon; 21 jewels; 177 parts and components; power reserve up to 70 hours; rhodium-plated movement with Côtes de Genève and circular-graining decorative patterns; all parts decorated by hand.
**Functions:** hour, minute, small second; power-reserve display.
**Case:** new Edward Piguet case with sapphire crystal and caseback.
**Dial:** engine-turned flame pattern; 18K white-gold applied Arabic numerals and hour markers.
**Strap:** large-scale alligator leather; 18K white-gold Audemars Piguet folding clasp.
**Also available:** in pink or white gold; platinum with black dial.

## EDWARD PIGUET SAPPHIRE TOURBILLON — REF. 25924PT

**Movement:** manual-winding Audemars Piguet Caliber 2888; tourbillon regulator; quartz mainplate with rutile inclusions; (size: 28.80x21.80mm, thickness: 6.51mm); 19 jewels; 167 parts; 48-hour power reserve; 21,600 vph; finish: rhodium-plated movement with Côtes de Genève decorative pattern, circular graining and hand engraving.
**Functions:** hour, minute, small second.

**Case:** in 950 platinum; sapphire crystal and caseback.
**Dial:** tourbillon bridge inspired by the shape of Galileo's pendulum.
**Strap:** full-grain crocodile leather with AP folding clasp.

## EDWARD PIGUET CHRONOGRAPH — REF. 25987OR

**Movement:** self-winding Audemars Piguet Caliber 2385; chronograph; 18K gold oscillating weight; 37 jewels; 304 parts and components; power reserve up to 40 hours; rhodium-plated movement with Côtes de Genève and circular-graining decorative patterns.
**Functions:** hour, minute, small second; date display; chronograph.
**Case:** 18K pink gold; sapphire crystal; water resistant to 20 meters.

**Dial:** engine-turned flame pattern; applied and riveted gold numerals and hour markers.
**Strap:** large-scale crocodile leather; 18K pink-gold Audemars Piguet folding clasp.
**Also available:** in white gold.

## MILLENARY CHRONOGRAPH — REF. 26011ST

**Movement:** automatic Audemars Piguet Caliber 2226/2840; 21K gold rotor with sector; realized and finished by hand; decorated with Côtes de Genève and beveled.
**Functions:** hour, minute, small second; date; chronograph with 3 counters.
**Case:** stainless steel three-piece case, in oval shape (size: 37x41, thickness: 11mm); polished-brushed finish; flat sapphire crystal; crown with pink sapphire cabochon; back fastened by 6 screws; water resistant to 20 meters.

**Dial:** black; soleil brushed center; black-polished hour ring; subdials in grené; pink luminescent Arabic numerals with red borders; white printed minute track on the flange with luminescent dots; pink luminescent sword-style hands in steel, white enameled.
**Indications:** date with magnifying glass at 3; hour counter at 6; minute counter at 9; small second at 12; center second counter.
**Strap:** metallic crocodile leather; fold-over clasp in stainless steel in the shape of the house's logo.
**Also available:** with slate-gray dial, light blue luminescent Arabic numerals; bezel with brilliants.

## PROMESSE — REF. 67259ST

**Movement:** quartz; Audemars Piguet Caliber 2508; rhodium-plated movement with Côtes de Genève decorative pattern and circular graining.
**Functions:** hour and minute.
**Case:** ergonomically curved stainless steel case set with two rows of diamonds; curved sapphire crystal; crown is tipped with a sapphire cabochon; Gemstones certificate; 12 diamonds (0.21 carats); Crown: 1 sapphire (0.14 carats); water resistant to 20 meters.

**Dial:** sky-blue; two Arabic numerals (6 and 12) tone-on-tone.
**Bracelet:** stainless steel.
**Also available:** in various sizes and color combinations; in 18K white or yellow gold, mini-size, on leather or 18K white or yellow gold bracelet; mother-of-pearl dials, two Arabic numerals (6 and 12) set with diamonds.

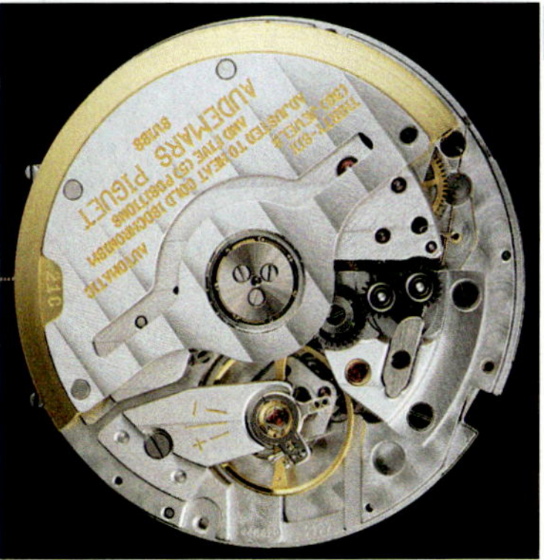

## CALIBER 2124

Automatic-winding movement, 45-hour autonomy, two-piece rotor with a 21K gold sector, on a ball bearing. **Functions:** hours, minutes, date. **Shape:** round. **Diameter:** 26mm. **Thickness:** 3.25mm. **Jewels:** 35. **Balance:** smooth, with two arms, in Glucydur. **Frequency:** 21,600 vph. **Balance-spring:** flat, Nivarox 1, with micrometer screw regulating device. **Shock-absorber system:** Kif. **Notes:** Pillar-plate decorated with a circular-graining pattern, bridges and rotor decorated with a Côtes de Genève pattern and beveled. **Derived calibers:** 2125 (center second); 2124/2825 (day-date; moonphase); 2126/2840 (chronograph; date); 2126/2841 (chronograph); 2127/2827 (hand date, day and month by discs and windows); 2129/2845 (date; p-reserve; two time zones); 2224, 2225, 2226 (28,800 vph); 2224/2814 (annual calendar); 2224/2811 (Star Wheel).

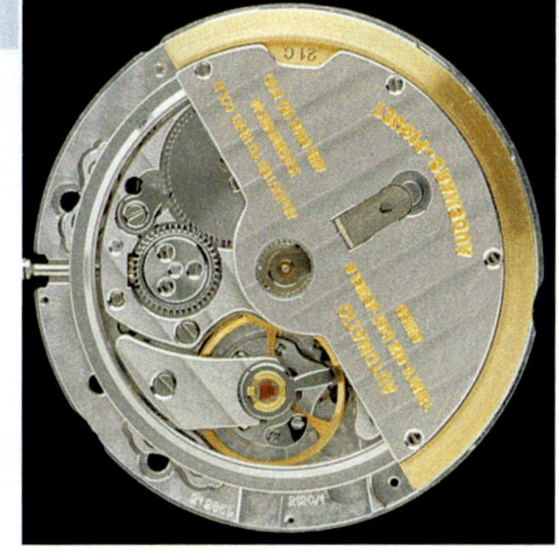

## CALIBER 2120

Automatic-winding movement, 45-hour autonomy; three-piece rotor whose parts are connected by 4 screws: bearing ring rotating on 4 jewel rollers, steel main body, 21K gold sector. **Functions:** hours, minutes. **Shape:** round. **Diameter:** 28mm. **Thickness:** 2.45mm. **Jewels:** 36. **Balance:** smooth, with three arms, in Glucydur. **Frequency:** 19,800 vph. **Balance-spring:** flat, Nivarox 1. **Shock-absorber system:** Kif for both balance and escape wheel. **Notes:** Pillar-plate decorated with a circular-graining pattern, bridges decorated with a Côtes de Genève pattern and beveled. **Derived calibers:** 2120 QP (2120 + modules 2801 or 2802 perpetual calendar; thickness: 4.00mm, 38 jewels); 2120/2804 (perpetual calendar and world time); 2121 (2120 with date; thickness: 3.05mm).

## CALIBER 2120/2808

Automatic-winding movement, 40-hour autonomy; three-piece rotor whose parts are connected by 4 screws; bearing ring rotating on 4 jewel rollers; 21K gold sector. **Functions:** hours, minutes; perpetual calendar (date, day, month, year, moonphase); dawn and sunset time; equation of time. **Shape:** round. **Diameter:** 28mm. **Thickness:** 5.35mm. **Jewels:** 41. **Balance:** smooth, with three arms, in Glucydur, with regulation masses. **Frequency:** 19,800 vph. **Balance-spring:** flat, Nivarox 1. **Shock-absorber system:** Kif for both balance and escape wheel. **Notes:** Pillar-plate decorated with a circular-graining pattern, bridges decorated with a Côtes de Genève pattern and beveled, skeletonized and chased rotor.

## MODULE 2808

Module 2808, view on the dial side. This module, adopted for Jules Audemars Equation of time, displays perpetual calendar indications (date, day, month, four-year cycle and moonphase along a vertical line), dawn and sunset time (respectively at 9 and 3) and equation of time (by center hand with a scale engraved on the bezel). For both dawn/sunset time and equation of time, Audemars Piguet offers models set on the meridians of 16 towns or, at request, on any other place chosen by a client. This is a world premiere for wristwatches, derived from an Audemars Piguet pocket model from 1925.

## MODULE 2840 (CHRONOGRAPH)

**Functions:** chronograph with three counters (center seconds, minutes and hours). **Shape:** round. **Diameter:** 29.90mm. **Thickness:** 2.90mm. **Jewels:** 19.
**Notes:** Module base and bridge are decorated with a circular-graining pattern, levers are beveled. The photograph shows the Module without the upper bridge.

## MODULE 2845

**Functions:** date; power reserve; two time zones. **Shape:** round. **Diameter:** 26.60mm. **Thickness:** 1.60mm. **Jewels:** 2.
**Notes:** the base is decorated with a circular-graining pattern, the bridges with a Côtes de Genève pattern. Screw heads are finished by specular polishing. Combined with the Caliber 2129 in watches with hand subdial for hours and minutes of a second time zone.

## MODULE 2801 (PERPETUAL CALENDAR)

**Functions:** perpetual calendar (day, date, week and leap year by hands; moonphase by disc). **Shape:** round. **Diameter:** 27.50mm. **Thickness:** 1.85mm. **Jewels:** 2.
**Notes:** the base is decorated with a circular-graining pattern, the levers and spring are brushed and beveled. Screw heads are finished by specular polishing. Combined with the Caliber 2120 within the Millenary family. Derived modules: 2802.

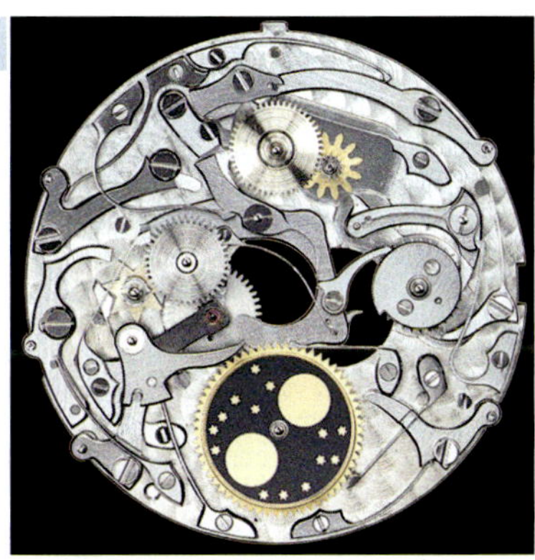

## MODULE 2802

**Functions:** perpetual calendar (day, date, month and leap year by hands; moonphase by disc). **Shape:** round. **Diameter:** 27.50mm. **Thickness:** 1.55mm. **Jewels:** 2.
**Notes:** the base is decorated with a circular-graining pattern, the levers and spring are brushed and beveled. Screw heads are finished by specular polishing. Combined with the Caliber 2120 within the Royal Oak and classic Perpetual Calendar watch families.

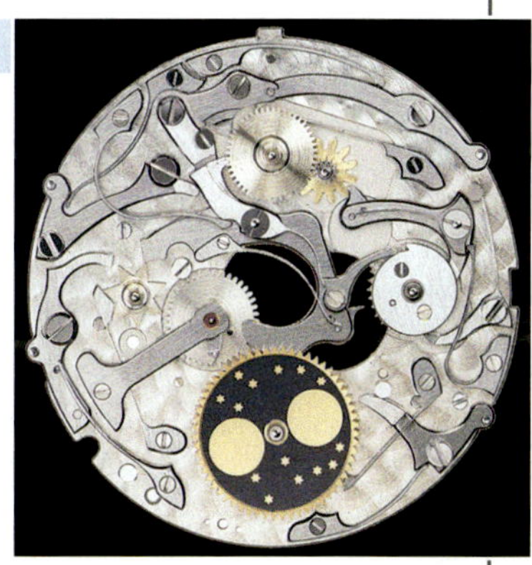

## CALIBER 2140

Automatic-winding movement with more than 40 hours' autonomy, two-piece rotor with a 21K gold sector, mounted on a ball bearing. **Functions:** hours, minutes, seconds; date. **Shape:** round. **Diameter:** 20mm. **Thickness:** 3.95mm. **Jewels:** 31. **Balance:** smooth, two arms, in Glucydur. **Frequency:** 28,800 vph. **Balance-spring:** flat, Nivarox 1, with micrometer screw regulating device. **Shock-absorber system:** Kif.
**Notes:** bridges and rotor are decorated with a Côtes de Genève pattern and beveled.
Derived calibers: 2141 (without center seconds, to be combined with the Module 2806).

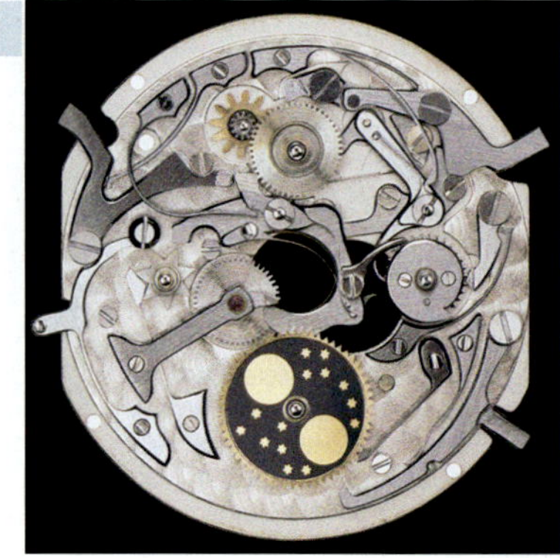

## MODULE 2806 (PERPETUAL CALENDAR)

**Functions:** perpetual calendar (day, date, month and leap year by hands; moonphase by disc). **Shape:** round. **Diameter:** 23mm. **Thickness:** 1.55mm. **Jewels:** 2.
**Notes:** the base is decorated with a circular-graining pattern, the levers and spring are brushed and beveled. Screw heads are finished by specular polishing. Combined with the Caliber 2141 in medium-sized Royal Oak, in Quantième Perpétuel Cambré and combined with the Caliber 2866 in the John Shaeffer Minute Repeater, Perpetual Calendar.

## CALIBER 3120

Bidirectional, automatic-winding movement with 60-hour autonomy; 22K gold rotor.
**Functions:** hours, minutes, center seconds; date. **Shape:** round. **Diameter:** 25.60mm. **Thickness:** 4.26mm **Jewels:** 40. **Balance:** variable inertia balance with 8 inertia-blocks and flat balance-spring. **Frequency:** 21,600 vph.
**Notes:** direct drive center seconds; the performances of the going train are thus enhanced while enabling the hand to move without jumping; cross-through balance-cock; fast date correction.

## CALIBER 2385

Automatic-winding movement with 45-hour autonomy, 18-karat-gold rotor. **Functions:** hours, minutes, small seconds; date; chronograph with three counters (center seconds, minutes and hours). **Shape:** round. **Diameter:** 25.60mm. **Thickness:** 5.40mm. **Jewels:** 37.
**Balance:** smooth, with three arms, in Glucydur. **Frequency:** 21,600 vph. **Balance-spring:** flat, Nivarox 1, with micrometer screw regulating device. **Shock-absorber system:** Kif.
**Notes:** the pillar-plate and bridges are decorated with a circular-graining pattern. The balance-bridge's winding device and the rotor are decorated with a Côtes de Genève pattern and beveled. The components of the regulating system and the screw heads are finished by specular polishing.

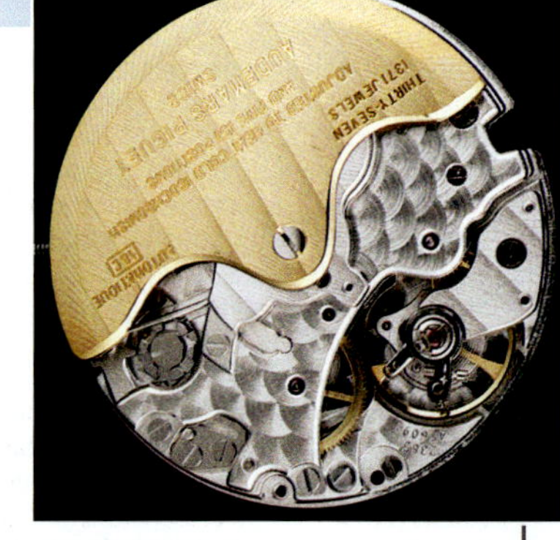

## CALIBER 2875

Automatic-winding movement; 60-hour autonomy; oscillating inertial hammer mass and elastic shock absorbers at trip end. **Functions:** hours, minutes; date; power reserve. **Shape:** round. **Diameter:** 30mm. **Thickness:** 5.70mm. **Jewels:** 41. **Balance:** two arms, with compensating screws, in Glucydur and tourbillon device with titanium carriage. **Balance-spring:** flat. **Notes:** the pillar-plate is decorated with a circular-graining pattern, bridges are decorated with circular graining and Côtes de Genève patterns and beveled. The oscillating mass and the thin titanium carriage of the tourbillon are brushed and beveled. The regulation crown is positioned on the rear side. The photograph shows the dial side. The tourbillon is placed at 6; the hour and minute pivots at 12; the date pivot at 3; the reserve pivot at 9.

## CALIBER 2877

Basic caliber: 2866. Manual-winding movement; 70-hour autonomy. **Functions:** hours, minutes, small seconds; hour, quarter and minute repeater; power reserve of the sonnerie. **Shape:** round. **Diameter:** 22.30mm. **Thickness:** 5mm. **Jewels:** 33. **Balance:** with compensating screws, with two arms, in Glucydur. **Frequency:** 21,600 vph. **Balance-spring:** flat, first quality. **Shock-absorber system:** Kif. **Notes:** the pillar-plate is decorated with a circular-graining pattern, bridges are decorated with a Côtes de Genève pattern. The balance-spring regulation system and the screw heads are finished by specular polishing and beveled. The movement shown in the photograph is the Caliber 2866 (34 jewels and 45-hour autonomy) which originated the 2877, displaying the sonnerie power reserve as well as the sonnerie status.

## CALIBER 2866

Caliber 2866, view on the dial side. The pillar-plate is decorated with a circular-graining pattern; the levers and springs are brushed and beveled. Screw heads are finished by specular polishing. On the John Shaeffer Minute Repeater Skeleton model, today out of production and on which this Caliber was mounted, the dial had been eliminated (time indications were printed directly on the sapphire crystal) to allow following the "life" of this fascinating feature, when the repeater was activated.

## CALIBER 2865

**Basic caliber:** 2866. Manual-winding movement with the same technical features as Caliber 2866 from which it derives, except for the greater thickness due to the modification, on the dial side (shown here), for the jumping hour and minute discs with a window. The basic caliber was used exclusively for the John Shaeffer Minute Repeater series in four versions: basic (Caliber 2866) also with sight movement on the dial side: "Squelette" with a traditional hand display; with jumping hours and minutes: "Saltarello" (Caliber 2865); with a jumping display "Star Wheel" (Caliber 2867) with a big-sized arc window in which hours appear printed on rotating sapphire discs; and finally, a perpetual calendar (Caliber 2866 + Module 2806).

## CALIBER 2868

Manual-winding movement; 48-hour autonomy. **Functions:** hours, minutes, seconds; hour and quarter repeater; grande and petite "au passage" sonneries. **Shape:** round. **Diameter:** 28.20mm. **Thickness:** 5.20mm. **Jewels:** 51 (escape wheel with end-stones). **Balance:** with compensating screws, two arms, in Glucydur. **Frequency:** 18,000 vph. **Balance-spring:** flat, first quality. **Shock-absorber system:** Kif. **Notes:** the pillar-plate is decorated with a circular-graining pattern, bridges are decorated with a Côtes de Genève pattern and beveled. The balance-spring regulation system, the repeater hammers and the screw heads are beveled and finished by specular polishing.

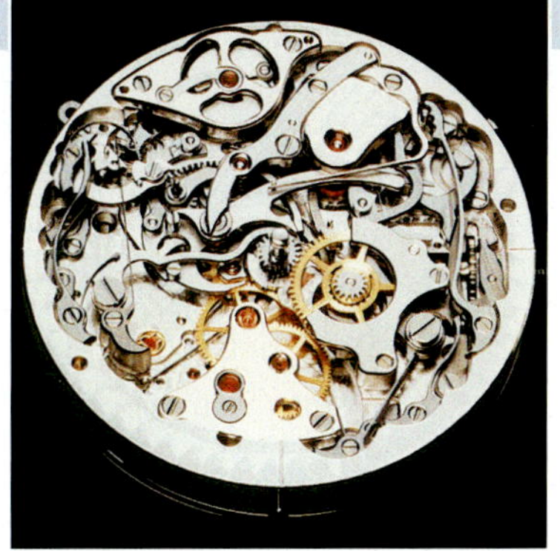

## CALIBER 2868

Caliber 2868 dial-side view. The photograph shows the great complexity of the movement, consisting of 412 pieces. A three-year planning work and over 1,000 construction drawings were needed for its realization. In this case, the hour and quarter repeater—a complication almost as difficult to realize as the hours-quarters-minutes repeater—is combined with the "au passage" sonnerie allowing for three options: "Grande sonnerie" (hours and quarters); "Petite sonnerie" (just hours); or "Mute" that may be selected by means of a cursor positioned on the case middle. The Grande sonnerie has autonomy of 10 hours, the Petite sonnerie of 32 hours and the watch of 48 hours. A special device eliminates the noise of the regulating system, when the sonnerie is working.

## CALIBER 2871

Manual-winding movement; 48-hour autonomy.
**Functions:** hours, minutes, small seconds.
**Shape:** rectangular with arc-shaped pole sides. **Size:** 27x20.30mm. **Thickness:** 6.10mm. **Jewels:** 19.
**Balance:** with compensating screws, two arms, in Glucydur, with tourbillon device.
**Frequency:** 21,600 vph.
**Balance-spring:** Breguet.
**Notes:** the pillar-plate is decorated with a circular-graining pattern and gilded, bridges are decorated with a Côtes de Genève pattern, beveled and gilded. The bridge and tourbillon carriage are brushed and beveled. Derived calibers: 2878 (2871 with power reserve).

## CALIBER 2871

Caliber 2871 dial-side view. The pillar-plate is decorated with a circular graining (concentric circle) pattern. Screw heads are finished by specular polishing. In the complete watch (Tourbillon Cambré) the tourbillon device is visible through a round aperture on the dial and through the sapphire crystal back, which seconds the movement's shape.

## CALIBER 2869

Manual-winding movement; 48-hour autonomy. **Functions:** hours, minutes, small seconds; hour, quarter and minute repeater; perpetual calendar (big-sized date with double disc, day, month, four-year cycle). **Shape:** round. **Diameter:** 29.30mm. **Thickness:** 6.70mm. **Jewels:** 38.
**Balance:** with compensating screws, two arms, in Glucydur, with tourbillon device.
**Frequency:** 21,600 vph.
**Balance-spring:** Breguet.
**Notes:** the pillar-plate is decorated with a circular-graining pattern, bridges are decorated with a Côtes de Genève pattern and beveled. The tourbillon bridge and repeater hammers are beveled and finished by specular polishing. Screw heads are polished and levers are brushed and beveled. Consists of 483 elements.

## CALIBER 2869

Caliber 2869 dial-side view. Outstanding features of this Caliber are the combination of the three most valuable complications (tourbillon, repeater and perpetual calendar), the unusual double-disc big date and the four-year cycle display by a complete circle and three circle arcs (the number of visible marks on the dial indicates the current year). The tens disc of the big-sized date indicates also the digits 10, 20 and 30, which makes the 0 useless on the units disc.

## CALIBER 2891

Manual-winding movement; 48-hour autonomy. **Functions:** hours, minutes, small seconds; hour, quarter and minute repeater; grande and petite chime sonneries with a dynamograph; power reserve of the sonnerie. **Shape:** round. **Diameter:** 29.30mm. **Thickness:** 5.80mm **Jewels:** 57 (escape wheel with end-stones). **Balance:** with compensating screws, two arms, in Glucydur. **Frequency:** 21,600 vph. **Balance-spring:** flat, first quality. **Shock-absorber system:** Kif.
**Notes:** the pillar-plate is decorated with a circular-graining pattern, bridges are decorated with a Côtes de Genève pattern and beveled. The balance-spring regulation system, the repeater hammers and the screw heads are beveled and finished by specular polishing; 491 elements.

## CALIBER 2891

Caliber 2891 dial-side view. The special technical feature—a novelty for the whole horology sector—introduced in this movement is represented by the dynamograph, i.e. the indication of the force transmitted by the barrel to the movement. When the spring is completely wound or almost uncoiled, the movement's functioning may be impaired. By controlling the force transmitted, it is possible to wind the movement manually so that the spring tension always is correct and, hence, the transmission-force optimal. By turning the crown clockwise, the movement's barrel is wound; by turning it counterclockwise, the sonnerie's barrel is wound. The autonomy is
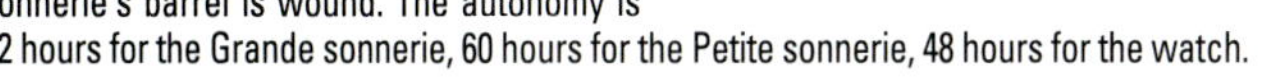
22 hours for the Grande sonnerie, 60 hours for the Petite sonnerie, 48 hours for the watch.

# BAUME & MERCIER

In its Geneva headquarters, Baume & Mercier houses a fully integrated design atelier that focuses on creativity and marked difference in all it produces. As such, the fashions and styles from this house are not only cutting-edge, but always in style.

Perhaps most indicative of the brand's foresight in design and technical prowess is its incredibly successful Hampton collection. The series celebrated its 10th anniversary in 2004, and added a host of new models to its various lines. Among its newest watches are the Hampton Spirit PM line for women. A smaller version of the successful Spirit line that was first introduced in 2002, the new Hampton Spirit PM features similarly gracious curves in its rectangular case, but with a host of different colored straps. Versions include specially designed dials with diamond accents and an incredible mink-covered alligator strap model that features a host of diamonds on the steel case.

Other new Hampton Spirit watches include the Hampton Spirit XL Phase de Lune. The men's watch houses a Dubois Dépraz 5600 automatic movement with moonphase display and a two-touch day and date function. The cambered screen-shaped case is crafted in polished steel and is water resistant to 50 meters. The decorated silvered dial offers day and month counters, applied indexes and a stunning moonphase display at 6:00.

Similarly, the Hampton City line (first unveiled in 2003) gains new models, including the Hampton City Chronograph crafted in steel with an extra-large dial that offers magnitude and beauty at the same time. The watch is also equipped with a tachometer scale. The Hampton City small model for women now adopts a beautiful Milanese bracelet giving it a smoother, contemporary personality.

**ABOVE**

The ladies' Hampton Spirit PM in pale blue has a white mother-of-pearl dial and case set with 28 diamonds. The larger Hampton Spirit XL Phase de Lune features an automatic movement.

**FAR LEFT**

The Hampton City PM is a ladies' watch with steel Milanese buckle and the men's version is the Hampton City Chrono XL with a mechanical self-winding movement offering 42 hours of power reserve.

**BOTTOM LEFT**

The Hampton Milleis PM is set elegantly with 28 diamonds on its rectangular case, while the men's Hampton Milleis houses a self-winding mechanical movement with screw-down caseback.

**BOTTOM RIGHT**

The Hampton Classic PM watch features a three-row polished steel bracelet and sapphire crystal. The men's Hampton Classic Chronograph XL, also housed in steel, has an alligator strap with square scales and is available on a three-row bracelet.

TOP

Taking a walk on the wild side, Baume & Mercier adds genuine mink to the Hampton family.

CENTER

These Hampton watches represent the entire range of ladies' models.

LOWER RIGHT

The Hampton Spirit PM watches feature steel cases, screw-down casebacks and sapphire crystals.

Additionally, a grand-sized Hampton Milleis watch has joined the family. This extra-large masculine piece houses a self-winding mechanical movement and features a date display at 6:00 and a sapphire caseback. Like the glamorous Long Island, New York, community for which the collection was named, the watches in this series all have distinct personalities and alluring charm.

## CHRONOLOGY

**1830** Societé Baume Frères is established in the canton of Berne by Louis Victor Baume and Pierre Joseph Celestin Baume, though the family can trace its watchmaking roots back to the 1500s.

**1851** Baume Bros. is established in London. The watch company regularly creates table- and pocket watches that are exported throughout Europe, Australia and New Zealand.

**1859** Joseph Eugene Baume settles in Geneva and takes over the manufacture of watchcases and watches.

**1876** Baume Bros. becomes Baume & Cie.

**1883-1923** The brand takes part in the Kew Observatory chronometry competitions, winning multiple prizes over the years.

**1893** The company scores 91.9 points out of a possible 100 from the chronometry board for its keyless chronograph with tourbillon escapement. This record will stand for 10 years.

**1912** William Baume becomes close friends with watchmaker Paul (Tchereditchenko) Mercier. The duo will eventually become business partners.

**1918** Leaving Mosimann, William Baume settles in Geneva and registers his name there. This marks the separation of Baume's Swiss and English branches.

**1930** Baume & Mercier SA Geneve becomes a registered trademark.

**1952** Baume & Mercier SA takes over CH Meylan Watch SA in Le Brassus, a manufacturer that specializes in chronographs and extra-thin movements.

**1964** Baume & Mercier forms an alliance with Piaget Watch Company, which later becomes a major shareholder.

**1971** The company unveils the Tronosonic tuning fork watch and enters the electronic era.

**1987** Baume & Mercier unveils the Linea collection.

**1988** The company becomes part of the Vendôme Luxury Group, which will later become the Richemont Group.

**1994** The famed Hampton watch is unveiled.

**1998** Baume & Mercier unveils the Capeland.

**2003** The newest Hampton City line joins the very successful Hampton family.

## HAMPTON SPIRIT XL CHRONO FLYBACK — REF. MOA08452

**Movement:** mechanical automatic-winding BM 11030 caliber.
**Functions:** hour, minute, small second; fly-back chronograph with 2 counters; date.
**Case:** stainless steel; size: 31.9x42.3mm, thickness: 14mm; rectangular galbé; double longitudinal and transversal curve; sapphire crystal with double curve; rectangular pushers; back fastened by 8 screws, with a small bull's eye on the balance; water resistant to 5atm.
**Dial:** argenté; guilloché with Tapisserie decoration; grained subdials; applied polished steel trapezoidal markers and logo at 12; Hampton Milleis polished steel skeleton hands.
**Indications:** small second at 3; date at 6; minute counter at 9; center second; minute track with divisions for 1/5 second.
**Strap:** alligator leather; steel clasp.

## HAMPTON SPIRIT XL CALENDAR MOONPHASE — REF. MOA08487

**Movement:** mechanical automatic-winding Dubois Dépraz 5600 caliber.
**Functions:** hour, minute, second; date, day; moonphase.
**Case:** stainless steel; size: 31.9x42.2mm, thickness: 14mm; polished, rectangular galbé; double longitudinal and transversal curve; sapphire crystal with double curve; 3 correctors on the middle; back fastened by 8 screws, with a small bull's eye on the balance; water resistant to 5atm.

**Dial:** argenté; guilloché with Tapisserie decoration; grained subdials; applied polished steel trapezoidal markers and logo at 12; printed minute track; Hampton Milleis steel skeleton hands.
**Indications:** date at 3; moonphase at 3; day at 9.
**Strap:** alligator leather; steel clasp.

## HAMPTON MILLEIS XL — REF. MOA08483

**Movement:** mechanical automatic-winding ETA 2000-1 caliber; autonomy 42 hours; decorated with Côtes de Genève and circular-graining patterns.
**Functions:** hour, minute, second; date.
**Case:** stainless steel, polished two-piece case; size: 36.9x30mm, thickness: 10.9mm; rectangular galbé at poles; double longitudinal and transversal curve; sapphire crystal with double curve; back fastened by 8 screws, numbered; water resistant to 5atm.

**Dial:** black; hour ring guilloché with soleil decoration; applied trapezoidal markers, Arabic numerals and logo in polished steel; Hampton Milleis steel skeleton hands.
**Indications:** date at 6.
**Strap:** alligator leather; steel fold-over clasp.
**Also available:** silvered dial; bracelet.

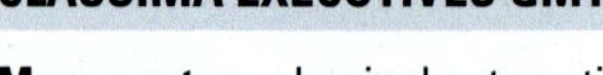

## CLASSIMA EXECUTIVES GMT — REF. MOA08462

**Movement:** mechanical automatic-winding BM 11893-2 caliber.
**Functions:** hour, minute, second; date; second time zone; 24 hour.
**Case:** stainless steel two-piece case; Ø 41.8mm, thickness: 9.25mm; polished finish; flat sapphire crystal; screw-on back; water resistant to 3atm.
**Dial:** white; applied steel bâton markers and Roman numerals; steel leaf-style hands; printed minute track with 5-minute graduation.

**Indications:** date at 3; second 24-hour time zone with center hand with a red arrow tip.
**Strap:** alligator leather; steel clasp.

## CAPELAND POWER RESERVE — REF. M0A08322

**Movement:** mechanical automatic winding.
**Functions:** hour, minute, second; date, day; power reserve.
**Case:** stainless steel three-piece case; Ø 39mm, thickness: 13.3mm; brushed bezel; curved sapphire crystal; screw-down crown; knurled screw-on back; water resistant to 10atm.
**Dial:** slate-gray; soleil brushed; black outer ring and subdials (decorated with circular beads); silver printed embossed Arabic numerals and minute track; steel Capeland skeleton sword-style hands.
**Indications:** date at 3; power reserve at 6; day at 9.
**Strap:** alligator leather; steel fold-over clasp.

## CAPELAND S XXL 1000M AUTOMATIC — REF. M0A8319

**Movement:** mechanical automatic winding.
**Functions:** hour, minute, small second; date.
**Case:** brushed titanium and stainless steel, three-piece case; Ø 44.5mm, thickness: 17.7mm; brushed steel, counterclockwise-turning ring with luminescent pointer and engraved and embossed graduated scale, useful for the calculation of diving times; decompression valve at 9, allowing the release of helium gas during diver's ascent; curved sapphire crystal; screw-down crown with case protection; water resistant to 100atm.
**Dial:** yellow Kevlar fiber; black embossed outer ring; luminescent applied steel bâton markers; luminescent dots at 6 and 12; white printed minute track with 5-minute graduation; luminescent steel sword-style hands.
**Indications:** date at 3.
**Strap:** vulcanized rubber; titanium, double fold-over safety clasp.
**Note:** supplied with 2 interchangeable straps, the first of which is provided with the patented Flexiflit system that allows length adjustments.

## CAPELAND CHRONOGRAPH AUTOMATIC — REF. M0A08491

**Movement:** mechanical automatic-winding BM 13750 caliber (Valjoux 7750 caliber base).
**Functions:** hour, minute, small second; date; chronograph with 3 counters.
**Case:** stainless steel three-piece case; Ø 39mm, thickness: 15.5mm; brushed bezel; curved sapphire crystal; rectangular pushers; knurled screw-on caseback; water resistant to 10atm.
**Dial:** glossy black; hollowed silvered subdials decorated with circular beads; argenté printed Arabic numerals; luminescent, steel sword-style Capeland hands.
**Indications:** date at 3; hour counter at 6; small second at 9; minute counter at 12; center second counter; minute track with divisions for 1/2 second and with luminescent dots.
**Strap:** alligator leather; fold-over steel clasp.
**Also available:** with bracelet; white, tobacco-colored, or black dial; argenté Arabic numerals or argenté dial; black Arabic numerals; black-blue dial, silvered Arabic numerals; rubber strap or bracelet.

## CAPELAND S CHRONOGRAPH AUTOMATIC — REF. M0A08320

**Movement:** mechanical automatic-winding BM 13750 caliber (Valjoux 7750 caliber base). **Functions:** hour, minute, small second; date; chronograph with 3 counters. **Case:** brushed titanium and 18K pink-gold, three-piece case; Ø 41mm, thickness: 16.8mm; polished pink-gold counterclockwise-turning ring with engraved, embossed graduated scale, useful for the calculation of diving times; curved sapphire crystal; pink-gold screw-down crown with case protection; pink-gold trapezoidal pushers; knurled screw-on caseback; water resistant to 20atm.
**Dial:** slate-gray soleil; anthracite subdials decorated with circular beads; luminescent applied pink-gold bâton markers; luminescent, pink-gold sword-style Capeland hands.
**Indications:** date at 3; hour counter at 6; minute counter at 12; center seconds; minute track.
**Strap:** alligator leather; titanium, double fold-over safety clasp.
**Also available:** in steel/yellow fold with white dial on bracelet; in steel, gray dial on bracelet; in steel, black dial on rubber strap or polished/brushed bracelet; with silvered dial and brushed bracelet.

# BLANCPAIN

Blancpain has remained true to its steadfast rule never to create a quartz watch, regularly turning out mechanical watches that are deftly blended works of tradition and technology.

The brand consistently adds exquisite models to its already rich collections. One new masterpiece is a world premiere: the first wristwatch with running equation of time combined with an ultra-thin perpetual calendar and a retrograde moonphase display. The dial of the Le Brassus is fitted with two coaxial minute hands—one that indicates mean solar time and another that indicates real solar time. The watch houses Blancpain's Caliber 3863, which took several years to develop and is comprised of 400 parts. Equipped with 72 hours of power reserve, the watch is masterfully presented in a platinum case.

To its well-known Villeret series—named for the village in which watchmaker Jehan-Jacques Blancpain lived in the 1730s—the brand adds the Chronograph Monopoussoir. This chronograph is operated by a single pushpiece, which fits directly into the stem setting. The watch—which houses a self-winding caliber consisting of 320 components and 37 rubies—offers date, a small-seconds hand and a power-reserve indicator.

Several versions of the Chronograph Monopoussoir are being created, including an 18-karat white-gold watch with brown strap and sunray-patterned Havana-brown dial, a rose-gold model with opaline dial and brown crocodile strap; and a steel version with a matte white dial and black crocodile strap. These Villeret watches feature sapphire casebacks and are water resistant to 50 meters.

On the complicated side, Blancpain unveils the Tourbillon Grand Date in an 18-karat rose- or white-gold Léman case. Sophisticated and elegant, this self-winding watch features a tourbillon aperture at 12:00, and a date indicator at 6:00. Additionally, it offers 169 hours of power reserve, and features a sapphire caseback. The hand-engraved movement, complete with tourbillon escapement, is comprised of more than 300 individual parts and 35 rubies. There is also a Léman Grand Date watch without tourbillon. This watch is water resistant to 100 meters and houses a mechanical movement with 35 rubies and 70 hours of power reserve.

**ABOVE**

The superlative Equation Marchante is the first continually running and visually displayed equation of time with perpetual calendar and retrograde moonphase display.

**LEFT**

The Léman Tourbillon Grand Date features a tourbillon escapement, large date and power-reserve indicator.

ABOVE

The single pusher of the Chronograph Monopoussoir is integrated into the watch crown.

RIGHT

The Villeret Lady 5 Straps houses a self-winding watch with 40 hours of power reserve. It is sold with five different colored, interchangeable straps.

## CHRONOLOGY

**1735** Jehan-Jacques Blancpain sets up shop in Villeret in the heart of the Jura Mountains and begins creating timepieces with his own components.

**1926** Blancpain introduces the first mass-produced self-winding watch to the French market.

**1931** The brand unveils the rectangular Rolls watch.

**1932** With no remaining Blancpain descendants to carry on the watchmaking tradition, the company ceases operations.

**1982** The Blancpain brand enjoys a brilliant revival under the vigilant eye of owners Jean-Claude Biver and Jacques Piguet. Biver insists that the brand remain true to its roots—creating only mechanical timepieces of the highest technical prowess and caliber.

**1988** Blancpain unveils a complex offering of timepieces that are recognized as masterpieces in the watchmaking art: the ultra-slim watch, the perpetual calendar, split-seconds chronograph, minute repeater and tourbillon.

**1991** In tribute to Jehan-Jacques Blancpain, the company unveils the 1735, one of the most complicated watches in the world. Six years in the making, it houses 740 parts and offers numerous functions.

**2000** Blancpain is purchased by The Swatch Group. The brand teams with the Monaco Yacht Show as an official sponsor and begins creation of an annual Monaco watch model.

**2001** Among its newest introductions are the ingenuous Quattro, featuring four important complications in one watch: the tourbillon, chronograph, split-seconds chronograph and perpetual calendar.

**2002** Blancpain unveils the Villeret collection of sophisticated timepieces with automatic movements.

**2003** Blancpain focuses particularly on rounding out its Léman collection, adding an automatic moonphase calendar watch, and a multiple-timezone, flyback-chronograph watch.

## LE BRASSUS EQUATION MARCHING REF. 4238-3442-55B

**Movement:** mechanical automatic-winding 3863 caliber (1150 caliber base + perpetual calendar and moonphase modules) with tourbillon device; 72 hours' autonomy; consisting of approx. 400 elements; hand-chased platinum rotor. **Functions:** hour, minute, small second; perpetual calendar (date, day, month, year, moonphase); equation of time; solar time. **Case:** platinum three-piece case (Ø 42mm, thickness: 12.7mm); polished finish; antireflective curved sapphire crystal; white-gold crown; 5 correctors on the middle; snap-on back, displaying the movement through a sapphire crystal; water resistant to 5atm. **Dial:** silvered with an aperture on the tourbillon; applied rhodium-plated Roman numerals; printed minute track; rhodium-plated leaf-style hands. **Indications:** equation of time between 1 and 2 (difference between solar and civil time in minutes); date at 3; small second integrated with the tourbillon carriage at 6 with center cam for the equation of time; day of the week at 9; moonphase with retrograde hand between 10 and 11; months and 4-year cycle at 12; center true solar time (yellow-gold hand with sun on tip). **Strap:** crocodile leather; fold-over platinum clasp. **Note:** limited edition of 50 pieces.

## LE BRASSUS SPLIT-SECOND CHRONOGRAPH REF. 4246F-3642-55B

**Movement:** mechanical automatic-winding 40F6 caliber; chased skeleton rotor.
**Functions:** hour, minute; date; split-second chronograph with 3 counters; power reserve.
**Case:** 18K pink-gold three-piece case (Ø 42mm, thickness: 15.3mm); polished finish; curved antireflective sapphire crystal; pushers with case protection and crown with coaxial pusher for the split-second chronograph in pink gold; snap-on back, displaying the movement through a sapphire crystal; water resistant to 3atm.
**Dial:** silvered grained; applied pink-gold Roman numerals; pink-gold leaf-style hands.
**Indications:** minute counter at 3; date at 6; hour counter at 9; power reserve at 12; center second and split-second counter; minute track with divisions for 1/5 second and 5-minute graduation.
**Strap:** crocodile leather; fold-over pink-gold clasp.
**Also available:** in platinum with leather strap, 100 pieces.

## LÉMAN TOURBILLON BIG DATE REF. 2825A-1542-53B

**Movement:** mechanical automatic-winding 6825 caliber with tourbillon volant device; 168 hours' autonomy; 35 jewels; decorated with a circular-graining pattern and hand-finished; chased rhodium-plated rotor in 18K yellow-gold.
**Functions:** hour, minute, small second; date; power reserve.
**Case:** 18K white-gold three-piece case (Ø 38mm, thickness: 12.65mm); curved sapphire crystal; 1 corrector on the middle, engraved brand name; screw-down crown with case protection in white gold; screw-on back displaying the movement through an antireflective sapphire crystal; water resistant to 10atm.
**Dial:** argenté opalin with aperture on the tourbillon; applied white-gold bâton markers with a luminescent cabochon on printed minute track; luminescent white-gold skeleton sword-style hands.
**Indications:** big date with double window at 6; power reserve at 9; small second at 12 integral with the tourbillon carriage.
**Strap:** crocodile leather; hand-stitched; white-gold fold-over clasp.
**Note:** limited edition of 50 pieces.
**Also available:** pink gold, 50 pieces.

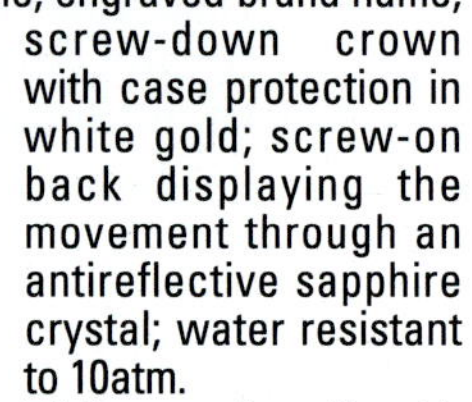

## LÉMAN BIG DATE REF. 2850-1127-53

**Movement:** mechanical automatic-winding, extra-thin 6825 caliber, with 70 hours' autonomy; 35 jewels; rotor decorated with a Côtes de Genève pattern.
**Functions:** hour, minute, second; date.
**Case:** stainless steel three-piece case (Ø 40mm, thickness: 11.45mm); curved antireflective sapphire crystal; engraved brand name on the middle; screw-down crown with case protection; screw-on back displaying the movement through a sapphire crystal; water resistant to 10atm.
**Dial:** white; applied rhodium-plated bâton markers; luminescent dots on printed minute track; luminescent rhodium-plated skeleton sword-style hands.
**Indications:** big date with double window at 6.
**Strap:** crocodile leather; steel clasp.
**Also available:** with opalin black dial; in red gold with black dial; rubber strap 333 pieces; Ø 38mm: stainless steel with black Military dial; leather strap.

## LÉMAN BIG DATE

**Movement:** mechanical automatic-winding, extra-thin 6850 caliber; 70 hours' autonomy; 35 jewels; rotor decorated with a Côtes de Genève pattern.
**Functions:** hour, minute, second; date.
**Case:** 18K red-gold three-piece case (Ø 40mm, thickness: 11.45mm); brushed finish; curved antireflective sapphire crystal; engraved brand name on the middle; screw-down crown with case protection in red gold; screw-on back displaying the movement through a sapphire crystal; water resistant to 10atm.
**Dial:** opalin black; applied red-gold bâton markers and luminescent dots on the printed minute track; luminescent red-gold skeleton sword-style hands.
**Indications:** big date with double window at 6.
**Strap:** rubber; red-gold clasp.
**Note:** limited edition of 333 pieces.
**Also available:** unlimited edition: stainless steel, white or black dial with soleil pattern, crocodile leather. Ø 38mm: stainless steel with black Military dial, leather strap.

## VILLERET CHRONO SINGLE-PUSHER — REF. 6185-3642

**Movement:** mechanical automatic-winding M185 caliber; chased skeleton rotor.
**Functions:** hour, minute; chronograph with 3 counters; date.
**Case:** 18K pink-gold three-piece case (Ø 38mm, thickness: 11.6mm); curved antireflective sapphire crystal; crown with coaxial chronograph pusher in pink gold; snap-on back, displaying the movement through a sapphire crystal; water resistant to 3atm.
**Dial:** silvered opalin; subdials decorated with circular beads; applied pink-gold Roman numerals; pink-gold leaf-style hands.
**Indications:** minute counter at 3; small second and date at 6; hour counter at 9; center second; minute track with 5-minute graduation.
**Strap:** crocodile leather; pink-gold clasp.
**Also available:** fold-over clasp; brown dial, leather strap with fold-over clasp; steel with white dial, leather strap with fold-over clasp.

## VILLERET FULL CALENDAR MOONPHASE — REF. 6763-3642

**Movement:** mechanical automatic-winding, extra-thin 6763 caliber; 100 hours' autonomy; 29 jewels; 18K red-gold rotor with engraved moon.
**Functions:** hour, minute, small second; full calendar (date, day, month, moonphase).
**Case:** 18K pink-gold three-piece case (Ø 37.5mm, thickness: 10.85mm); curved antireflective sapphire crystal; 4 correctors on the middle; pink-gold crown; snap-on back, displaying the movement through a sapphire crystal; water resistant to 5atm.
**Dial:** opalin silvered; applied pink-gold Roman numerals; red-gold leaf-style hands.
**Indications:** moonphase and small seconds at 6; day and month at 12; date with half-moon center hand.
**Strap:** crocodile leather; pink-gold clasp.
**Also available:** fold-over clasp; brown dial; white gold, strap and buckle, fold-over clasp; steel with strap and buckle, fold-over clasp.

## VILLERET LADY 5-STRAPS — REF. 6102-4628-95

**Movement:** mechanical automatic-winding, extra-thin 953 caliber; 40 hours' autonomy; 21 jewels.
**Functions:** hour, minute, second.
**Case:** stainless steel three-piece case (Ø 29.3mm, thickness: 8.85mm); 48 brilliants set on the bezel; curved antireflective sapphire crystal; snap-on back; water resistant to 3atm.
**Dial:** white; set brilliants for markers; white-gold leaf-style hands.
**Indications:** moonphase and small seconds at 6; day and month at 12; date with half-moon center hand.
**Strap:** satin; steel clasp (interchangeable with 4 different crocodile leather or karung straps).
**Also available:** without brilliants, white dial, Roman numerals.

# BOVET

Bovet perpetuates the style and the decorative techniques of its watchmaking heritage, the soul of its origins enshrined in exceptional timekeepers.

In 1822, Edouard Bovet, a native of Fleurier, set up a watch trading post in Canton, China, and met with great success thanks to his pocket watches richly decorated with pearly and miniature enamel paintings. He was the first to reveal the engraved movements through transparent casebacks. Today, the Bovet brand is taking its heritage to fresh peaks of achievement through horological interpretations characterized by a number of inimitable distinguishing characteristics.

Pascal Raffy, President of Bovet, remembers his first encounter with this brand with considerable emotion. He found a company with a human dimension, with a deliberately limited production, working within a context of genuine craftsmanship. He finds his greatest pleasure in cultivating friendly relationships with his partners, in seeing all the watches produced, and in telling clients all about the production process—and especially those times when he is instantly smitten by a unique product.

## WATCHES WITH BOWS

This approach is apparent in the timepieces making up the Bovet range. Bovet's contemporary design is simply incomparable and its difference is profoundly emblematic. The bows typical of the pocket watches of yesterday are now echoed on all current wristwatches by the brand, in the form of attachments placed at 12:00. The Fleurier collection, which is the most classic with its original rounded shapes, is directly inspired by a 19th century model. It houses prestigious mechanical manual-winding or self-winding movements, equipped with simple functions or fascinating complications such as the perpetual calendar, the minute repeater and the tourbillon. Generally crafted in white or rose gold, and sometimes in platinum, these watches come in three sizes with respective diameters of 28, 34 or 39 mm. The Sportster collection—in steel, gold and platinum, measuring 36 or 40mm in diameter—features COSC-certified chronometers with contrasting straight and slanting lines, asserting their sporting nature through self-winding chronograph movements with large date display. Created in accordance with an early 20th century Bovet chronograph and launched in 2001, the Sportster made a particularly striking impression in a version graced with Chinese characters on the dial, a reminder of the origins from which the brand draws its originality.

## SHOWCASING THE DECORATIVE ARTS

Bovet's characteristic pocket watches adapted to the wrist provide the perfect showcase for the traditional forms of decoration inherent to Swiss watchmaking. At the very least, the movements are adorned with Côtes de Genève patterns and blued screws.

**TOP**

Fleurier Tourbillon, Minute Repeater with reversed hand fitting in rose gold with openwork dial and Bovet caliber 12BM06.

**ABOVE**

Bovet pocket watch with enameled Mille Fleurs paint, circa 1840, made for the Chinese market. Equipped with the Chinese duplex escapement.

**BOTTOM LEFT**

This prestige self-winding movement caliber Bovet 12BA03 is fully engraved in Fleurisanne style with half pearls setting. Its 21-karat gold rotor is hand engraved.

FACING PAGE

**BOTTOM CENTER**

Pascal Raffy, President of Bovet Fleurier SA.

**BOTTOM RIGHT**

The 39mm Fleurier in white gold with blue fired enamel flinqué dial and self-winding movement caliber Bovet 11BA04.

THIS PAGE

**ABOVE**

This 39mm rose-gold Fleurier Tourbillon with engraved bridges and openwork dial in black enamel with applied Romand numerals houses the Bovet Caliber 12BM05 in gold.

**BELOW**

Tourbillon Minute Repeater and reversed hand fitting This 39mm Fleurier in platinum with sapphire crystal caseback and openwork dial in black enamel with applied Roman numerals is powered by the Bovet Caliber 12BM06.

The most sophisticated also feature Fleurisanne engraving, a positive engraving typical of Fleurier, which makes the motifs appear in relief.

Some are enriched with pearls, a discreet reminder that in the past they represented a distinguishing sign in the ornamentation of watch covers. The exterior leaves plenty of scope for the talent of gemsetters and, to an extent unmatched in contemporary watchmaking, for that of enamellers. The enameling, which is created through this series of extremely delicate applications and methods of vitrifying, gives the dials in the Fleurier line a wealth of radiance. Almost all possible effects obtained with materials are explored: grand feu enamel, flinqué enamel, cloisonné enamel and, at the pinnacle of the art, the art of miniature painting which so few craftsman still master today. Through the decorative arts, Bovet attracts an atypical clientele with a taste for highly personalized models. One-of-a-kind creations (with motifs created on request) and limited series account for 60% of annual production, which is limited deliberately to an annual average of 1,500.

## FLEURIER QUALITY FOUNDATION CERTIFICATION

Finally, Bovet is a co–founders of a new certification, launched in September 2004. The extremely demanding Fleurier Quality Foundation certification incorporates high-end criteria governing technical, aesthetic aspects and wearer comfort, which all the craftsmen involved in the creation of Bovet watches firmly intend to perpetuate.

## CHRONOLOGY

**1797** Edouard Bovet is born in Fleurier, Switzerland. Son of a local master watchmaker, Jean-Frédéric Bovet. Edouard had four brothers, Frédéric, Alphonse, Gustave, Charles-Henri, and a sister, Caroline.

**1818** Edouard Bovet's employer, the Magniac company, sends him to Canton, the only Chinese port open to Western trade. He leaves England on the East India merchantman, Orwell, on April 20, arriving in Canton via the Cape of Good Hope on August 16.

**1822** Edouard Bovet, now living in Canton, founds a partnership company for the China watch trade with his two brothers in London, Alphonse and Frédéric, and his third brother Gustave, a watchmaker in Fleurier. The company's first charter is drawn up in London on May 1. Business booms, and the company soon transfers production to Fleurier.

**1855** Bovet wins a gold medal in the luxury-watches category at the Paris International Exhibition for a pair of enamelled gold watches commissioned by the Emperor of China.

**1864** The Bovet family sells its watch production to their manufacturing inspectors in Fleurier. The articles of association maintain the Bovet group of companies: Maison Bovet and Bovet Bros. in London; F. and A. Bovet in Canton; and Bovet Frères et Cie in Fleurier.

**1997** The Fleurier model, flagship of the collection, is awarded the Watch of the Year, Prize of the Public by Swiss magazine Montres Passion.

**1998** In Basel, the Fleurier watch is awarded the Best Case Prize by Italian magazine Polso.

**2000** A jury of Swiss watch making experts selects the Fleurier model as one among fifty Montres du siècle (Watches of the century).

**2001** Two new product lines are launched worldwide, Fleurier and Sportster. The first Fleurier Complication is a 39mm minute repeater featuring a mother-of-pearl dial with cloisonné enamel with a miniature painting. The Sportster reflects the company history, yet its look is resolutely modern, unique, and different.

**2003** New Bovet Fleurier Complications are launched: The Tourbillon, Minute Repeater, Perpetual Calendar, Tourbillon and Minute Repeater with reversed hand fitted, all available in gold and platinum. The Sportster is offered in chronograph and a triple-date calendar with moonphase versions, all available in steel, gold and platinum. The Sportster is COSC certified.

**2003** Bovet is member of the Fleurier Quality Foundation along with Chopard and Parmigiani. The Fleurier Certification is given only to watches that pass extremely rigorous tests considered to be the most accurate in the watch industry today.

## SPORTSTER 40MM CHRONOGRAPH REF. SP0002

**Movement:** self-winding haute horlogerie Caliber 13BA01, 13''' 1/2 chronograph movement; 28 jewels; balance frequency of 28,800 vph (4Hz); 42-hour power reserve; entirely finished by hand; bridge decorated with Côtes de Genève pattern; central winding rotor blued; Geneva-quality bridge and dog screws, polished and blued by fire; COSC-certified chronometer. **Functions:** hour, minute; small seconds at 6; large date; chronograph with hour and minute counters. **Case:** Ø 40mm; high-performance stainless steel case; curved, antireflective sapphire crystal; flat, antireflective sapphire caseback; crown at 12 protected by the bow and flanked by shaped chronograph stop/start and reset buttons at 11 and 1, respectively; bow is a creative adaptation of a 19th century pocket watch bow; water resistant to 330 feet.

**Dial:** white dial; painted Chinese zodiac symbols and minute track; Bovet Serpentine chronograph hand; skeleton baton hour and minute hands; hour counter at 3; small second at 6; 30-minute counter at 9; large date at 12.
**Strap:** hand-stitched crocodile leather; steel folding buckle.
**Also available:** yellow-gold or platinum case and different dials; gemstones set on any bezel; stainless steel bracelet.

## SPORTSTER 40MM CHRONOGRAPH REF. SP0184

**Movement:** self-winding haute horlogerie Caliber 13BA01, 13''' 1/2 chronograph movement; 28 jewels; balance frequency of 28,800 vph (4Hz); 42-hour power reserve; movement entirely finished by hand; bridge decorated with Côtes de Genève pattern; central winding rotor blued; Geneva-quality bridge and dog screws, polished and blued by fire; COSC-certified chronometer.
**Functions:** hour, minute; small seconds at 6; large date; chronograph with hour and minute counters.
**Case:** Ø 40mm; 18K rose-gold case; curved, antireflective sapphire crystal; flat, antireflective sapphire caseback; crown at 12 protected by the bow and flanked by shaped chronograph stop/start and reset buttons at 11 and 1, respectively; bow is a creative adaptation of a 19th century pocket watch bow; water resistant to 330 feet.

**Dial:** black polished enamel with Art Deco numbers; skeleton bâton hour and minute hands; Bovet Serpetine chronograph hand.
**Indications:** hour counter at 3; 30-minute counter at 9; large date at 12.
**Strap:** hand-stitched crocodile leather; 18K rose-gold folding buckle.

## SPORTSTER 40MM CHRONOGRAPH REF. SP0210-MA

**Movement:** self-winding haute horlogerie Caliber 13BA01, 13''' 1/4 chronograph movement; 28 jewels; balance frequency of 28,800 vph (4Hz); 42-hour power reserve; movement entirely finished by hand; bridge decorated with Côtes de Genève pattern; central winding rotor blued; Geneva-quality bridge and dog screws, polished and blued by fire; COSC-certified chronometer. **Functions:** hour, minute; small seconds at 6; large date; chronograph with hour and minute counters.
**Case:** Ø 40mm; stainless steel case; curved, antireflective sapphire crystal and caseback; crown at 12 protected by the bow and flanked by shaped chronograph stop/start and reset buttons at 11 and 1, respectively; bow is a creative adaptation of a 19th century pocket watch bow; water resistant to 330 feet.

**Dial:** black polished enamel with white Art Deco numbers; skeleton baton hour and minute hands; Bovet Serpentine chronograph hand.
**Strap:** hand-stitched crocodile leather; steel folding buckle.

## SPORTSTER 40MM TRIPLE CALENDAR REF. QA0003

**Movement:** self-winding Caliber 11BA11, 11''' 1/2; balance frequency of 28,800 vph (4Hz); 72-hour power reserve; COSC-certified chronometer.
**Functions:** hour, minute; date, day and month; moonphase.
**Case:** Ø 40mm; polished stainless steel; domed, antireflective sapphire crystal; flat, antireflective sapphire caseback; water resistant to 330 feet.

**Dial:** white or black polished enamel dial; luminous numerals or applied markers.
**Strap:** hand-stitched crocodile leather; steel ardillon buckle.
**Also available:** white, blue and red dial with triangle indexes and Arabic numerals; Ø 36mm case.

## FLEURIER JUMPING HOURS — REF. CP0156

**Movement:** self-winding Caliber 11BA08, 11''' 1/2; balance frequency of 28,800 vph (4Hz); 32 jewels; 55-hour power reserve; central jumping hours and rotating minutes-ring, winding rotor made in 22K gold engraved with Fleurisanne pattern.
**Functions:** jumping 12 central hours on one disc, hours jump instantaneously as the "Bovet" on the ring reaches 12.
**Case:** Ø 39mm; 18K white-gold case; curved, antireflective sapphire crystal; flat, antireflective sapphire caseback; white-gold crown at 12 with sapphire cabochon, protected by the bow; water resistant to 110 feet.
**Dial:** transparent sapphire dial; mother-of-pearl minute ring.
**Strap:** hand-stitched crocodile leather; central attachment with jointed lugs; sapphire cabochons; white-gold folding clasp.
**Also available:** in 18K white gold and with Wind Compass mother-of-pearl dial.

## FLEURIER PERPETUAL CALENDAR — REF. CP0139

**Movement:** self-winding haute horlogerie Caliber 11BA07, 11''' 1/2; 32 rubies; frequency of 28,800 vph (4 Hz); 55-hour power reserve; double barrel; 22K gold rotor decorated in Fleurisanne pattern; finished by hand; bridges are beveled and decorated with Côtes de Genève pattern; Geneva-quality bridge and dog screws, polished and blued by fire; perpetual calendar module preset for a hundred years; date adjusts automatically every month, including leap years.
**Functions:** perpetual calendar (day, date, month, leap years and moonphase).
**Case:** Ø 39mm; 18K rose-gold case; curved, antireflective sapphire crystal; flat, antireflective sapphire caseback; rose-gold crown at 12 with sapphire cabochon, protected by the bow; water resistant to 110 feet.
**Dial:** mother-of-pearl with jasp moonphase counter.
**Strap:** hand-stitched crocodile leather; central attachment with jointed lugs; sapphire cabochons; rose-gold folding clasp.

## FLEURIER FIRED ENAMEL DIAL — REF. FL0149

**Movement:** self-winding haute horlogerie Caliber 11BA04, 11''' 1/2; 25 rubies; frequency of 28,800 vph (4Hz); double barrel; 22K gold rotor; bridges beveled and decorated with Côtes de Genève pattern; bridges and screws in blued steel with angled and polished edges.
**Functions:** hour, minute.
**Case:** Ø 39mm; 18K white-gold case; curved, antireflective sapphire crystal; flat, antireflective sapphire caseback; white-gold crown at 12 with sapphire cabochon, protected by the bow; water resistant to 110 feet.
**Dial:** hand crafted in "grand feu" black enamel on a domed dial; Grand Roman Numerals and minute track; Bovet Serpentine hands in blued steel.
**Strap:** hand-stitched crocodile leather; hexagonal attachment screws with gold cabochons; white-gold folding buckle.
**Also available:** rose gold; gemstones set on the bezel and bow; customized bezels; variety of sizes, movements and styles.

## FLEURIER JUMPING HOURS — REF. CP0127

**Movement:** self-winding Caliber 11BA08, 11''' 1/2; balance frequency of 28,800 vph (4Hz); 32 jewels; 55-hour power reserve; central jumping hours and rotating minutes-ring, winding rotor made in 22K gold engraved with Fleurisanne style.
**Functions:** 12 jumping central hours on one disc, jumping instantaneously as 60th minute on ring reaches 12.
**Case:** Ø 39mm; 18K white-gold case set with Baguette diamonds; bow and lug set with Baguette diamonds; antireflective sapphire crystal; transparent caseback; white-gold crown at 12 with sapphire cabochon, protected by the bow; water resistant to 110 feet.
**Dial:** "Compass rose" dial; paved with 368 diamonds, 168 black sapphires for a total of 1.40 carats; rotating minute-ring in black mother-of-pearl dial.
**Strap:** hand-stitched crocodile leather; lug set with Baguette diamonds; black sapphire cabochons; white-gold folding clasp.

# BREGUET

Reigning for centuries as one of the finest watchmakers in the world, the House of Breguet continues to offer complications that guarantee its prominent standing within the industry.

Excellence remains the brand's chief priority in its creative horology. Breguet's command of complications keeps it in a leading position amongst watch enthusiasts and collectors. Prime examples are the newest Classique timepieces. For the Tourbillon Regulateur Ref. 5307, Breguet developed a new 31-jeweled self-winding movement with an exquisite engine-turned regulator dial. Similarly, the Perpetual Calendar Ref. 5327 houses an improved self-winding movement with 46 hours of power reserve and stunning moonphase readout at 1:30.

Crafting in the spirit of old-world tradition and elegance, Breguet unveils several new Héritage models in its striking tonneau-shaped case. The Chronograph Héritage Ref. 5469 is crafted in 18-karat white gold and paved with baguette diamonds invisibly set on the curved surface of the case. The crown and chronograph buttons feature briolette diamonds, and the dial is awash with baguettes. This stunning timepiece houses an automatic movement. The Héritage Grand Date Ref. 5480 is housed in a larger-sized Héritage case with a date display using two separate numeral disks and driven by a self-winding movement.

In the sportier realm, Breguet unveils a new Type XXI 3810 Chronograph with extra-large diameter. The black rhodium dial is embraced by a steel case with a bidirectional bezel and fluted design for sporty chic appeal. The automatic movement registers elapsed minutes on a center dial. The day/night indicator's subdial is at 3:00, and the date is displayed at 6:00. Luminous hands and markers ensure easy legibility at any time during any sporting event.

**TOP**

This Classique Grande Complication is crafted in 18-karat gold and houses a tourbillon escapement.

**LEFT**

The engraved automatic movement of this Classique offers perpetual calendar with precise moonphase and power-reserve indicators.

ABOVE

The Héritage Ref. 5480 offers grand date readout at 12:00 and small seconds at 6:00. It is water resistant to 30 meters.

RIGHT

The regulator dial of this Classique watch is crafted of hand-engraved silvered 18-karat gold. The offset chapter ring shows the hours at 12:00.

## CHRONOLOGY

**1775** Abraham-Louis Breguet founds his workshops.

**1777** Breguet is quickly recognized as a jeweler to the French royal family. Simultaneously, he continues to create timepieces and technological inventions.

**1780** Breguet develops the first self-winding watch known as the perpetuelle.

**1783** Breguet invents the gong strip, a metal coil that wraps around the movement to improve sound in a minute repeater. This invention sets the groundwork for slimmer repeaters.

**1795** Breguet develops the famed tourbillon escapement.

**1801** Breguet receives a patent for his tourbillon and houses the tourbillon escapement in a distinguished 18-karat gold pocket watch.

**1823** Abraham-Louis Breguet dies. Watchmaking continues at the hands of his grandson, Louis-Clement Breguet.

**1843** Louis-Clement continues work on chronometers and is nominated to the board of Longitude as his grandfather had been before him.

**1900s** Breguet changes hands several times, from family ownership to private ownership by Georges Brown, to the Chaumet Brothers in 1970 to Investcorp in 1987.

**1994** In addition to its Le Brassus and Le Sentier workshops, Breguet opens a workshop in the village of L'Abbaye.

**1999** The Swatch Group purchases Breguet.

**2000** Breguet celebrates its 225th anniversary.

**2001** Breguet celebrates the 200th anniversary of the tourbillon.

**2002** The brand enhances its Classique collection with additional limited-edition timepieces, including a columnwheel chronograph and an extra-slim mechanical watch with four days of power reserve.

**2004** Breguet unveils the Le Réveil du Tsar alarm watch housing a movement that was co-developed by Breguet and Blancpain. The movement is composed of two patented devices.

## CLASSIQUE TOURBILLON REGULATOR REF. 3358BB/52/986 DD00

**Movement:** mechanical manual-winding Breguet 587caliber; tourbillon device; 120 hours' autonomy; 18K gold rotor; engraved and finished by hand.
**Functions:** hour, minute, small second.
**Case:** 18K yellow-gold three-piece case (Ø 40mm, thickness: 10.8mm); curved sapphire crystal; fluted middle; gold crown; hand-engraved snap-on back displaying the movement through a sapphire crystal; water resistant to 3atm.
**Dial:** solid gold, silvered; guilloché by hand; aperture on the tourbillon; hand-finished blued-steel Breguet hands.
**Indications:** off-center hours and minutes at 12; Roman numerals and minute track on brushed ring with Breguet's signature, all printed; small second at 6 integral with the tourbillon carriage.
**Strap:** crocodile leather; fold-over gold clasp.
**Also available:** in platinum.

## CLASSIQUE PERPETUAL CALENDAR POWER RESERVE REF. 5327BA/1E/9V6

**Movement:** mechanical automatic-winding, extra-thin Breguet 502.3.DRP1 caliber; 46 hours' autonomy; 38 jewels; (12'''); 18K gold rotor; engraved and finished by hand.
**Functions:** hour, minute; perpetual calendar (date, day, month, year, moonphase); power reserve.
**Case:** 18K yellow-gold three-piece case; Ø 39mm; flat sapphire crystal; fluted middle with 4 correctors; gold crown; hand-engraved snap-on back displaying the movement through a sapphire crystal; water resistant to 3atm.
**Dial:** solid gold, silvered, guilloché by hand; Roman numerals and minute track on brushed ring with Breguet's signature, all printed; hand-finished blued-steel Breguet hands.
**Indications:** moonphase between 1 and 2; day of the week at 4; date at 6; 4-year cycle at 8; power reserve between 10 and 11; center month.
**Strap:** crocodile leather; fold-over gold clasp.
**Also available:** in white gold.

## CLASSIQUE REGULATOR REF. 5187BR/15/986

**Movement:** mechanical automatic-winding Breguet 591QSHD caliber; 38 hours' autonomy; 25 jewels; (11 and 1/2'''); mono-metallic annular balance; 18K gold guilloché rotor; finished by hand.
**Functions:** hour, minute; date.
**Case:** 18K pink-gold three-piece case (Ø 36.2mm, thickness: 8.7mm); curved sapphire crystal; fluted middle; pink-gold crown; snap-on back displaying the movement through a sapphire crystal; water resistant to 3atm.
**Dial:** solid gold, silvered, guilloché by hand; minute track printed on the brushed outer ring; hand-finished blued-steel Breguet hands.
**Indications:** off-center hours at 12 with Roman numerals on the brushed ring with Breguet's signature, all printed; date at 6; center minute.
**Strap:** crocodile leather; pink-gold clasp.
**Also available:** in white gold.

## MARINE HOMME REF. 5817ST/12/5V6

**Movement:** mechanical automatic-winding Breguet 517GG caliber; 18K gold rotor; finished and engraved by hand.
**Functions:** hour, minute, second; date.
**Case:** stainless steel three-piece case (Ø 40mm, thickness: 12mm); curved sapphire crystal; fluted middle; crown with case protection; back fastened by 6 screws, displaying the movement through a sapphire crystal; water resistant to 3atm.
**Dial:** solid gold, silvered, stepped, guilloché by hand; printed Roman numerals and minute track with luminescent dots on brushed ring; luminescent hand-finished blued-steel Breguet hands.
**Indications:** oversized date with a double window at 6.
**Strap:** rubber; steel clasp.
**Also available:** blue dial; bracelet.

## TYPE XXI REF. 3810ST/92/SZ9

**Movement:** mechanical automatic-winding Breguet 582Q caliber; numbered and personalized.
**Functions:** hour, minute, small second; date; fly-back chronograph with 3 counters.
**Case:** stainless steel three-piece case (Ø 43.5mm, thickness: 15.4mm); brushed and polished finish; domed sapphire crystal; bi-directional knurled ring with engraved 5-minute graduation; fluted middle; screw-down crown; screw-on back; water resistant to 10atm.
**Dial:** black rhodium-plated, matte center; subdials decorated with circular beads; printed Arabic numerals and applied lozenge hands; luminescent steel bâton hands.
**Indications:** 24 hour at 3; hour counter and date at 6; small second at 9; center minute and fly-back second counter; minute track on the flange.
**Bracelet:** brushed and polished steel; recessed fold-over clasp.
**Also available:** with leather strap.

## REINE DE NAPLES REF. 8918BB/58/864/D00D

**Movement:** mechanical automatic-winding Breguet 537/1 caliber; 18K gold rotor; numbered, personalized and engraved by hand.
**Functions:** hour, minute.
**Case:** 18K white-gold three-piece case in oval shape (size: 37x29mm, thickness: 10.35mm); 117 brilliants set on the bezel (0.99 total carats); domed sapphire crystal; fluted middle; white-gold crown at 4 with a briolette cabochon; back fastened by 6 screws, displaying the movement through a sapphire crystal; water resistant to 3atm.
**Dial:** solid gold covered with white natural mother-of-pearl; Poire-cut diamond at 6; Roman numerals; minute track printed on brushed ring bearing Breguet's signature; blued-steel hand-finished Breguet hands.
**Indications:** off-center hour and minute at 6 on a silvered hand-guilloché dial.
**Strap:** satin; white-gold fold-over clasp with set diamonds.
**Also available:** with bracelet; in yellow gold with strap, bracelet.

## CLASSIQUE TOURBILLON FOR LADIES REF. 3358BB/52/986 DD00

**Movement:** mechanical manual-winding Breguet 558.1T caliber (Lemania 187 caliber base; tourbillon device; 21 jewels; 50 hours' autonomy; engraved and finished by hand.
**Functions:** hour, minute, small second.
**Case:** 18K white-gold three-piece case (Ø 36mm, thickness: 9mm); 73 set brilliants on bezel and lugs (1.31 carats total); flat sapphire crystal; fluted middle; white-gold crown; snap-on back displaying the movement through a sapphire crystal; water resistant to 3atm.
**Dial:** solid gold covered with natural mother of pearl; guilloché by hand with Côtes de Genève pattern; subdial decorated with Clous de Paris; aperture on the tourbillon; hand-finished blued-steel Breguet hands.
**Indications:** off-center hours and minutes at 12; Roman numerals and minute track on smooth ring with Breguet's signature, all printed; small second at 6, hand with 3 tips (each indicating a 20-second sequence) integral with the tourbillon carriage.
**Strap:** crocodile leather; white-gold clasp.

## HÉRITAGE BIG DATE REF. 5480BA/12/996

**Movement:** automatic Breguet caliber; finished by hand.
**Functions:** hour, minute, small second; date.
**Case:** 18K yellow-gold three-piece case; tonneau shaped, ergonomically curved; (size: 41.5x35mm, thickness: 10mm); curved sapphire crystal; fluted middle; yellow-gold crown; back fastened by 8 screws; water resistant to 3atm.
**Dial:** solid silver, guillochéd by hand; Roman numerals and minute track printed on brushed ring with double secret signature; hand-finished blued-steel Breguet hands.
**Indications:** small seconds at 6; big date with double window at 12.
**Strap:** crocodile leather; fold-over yellow-gold clasp.
**Also available:** in white gold.

# Breitling

The Breitling brand is synonymous with true wristwatch instruments for professionals. For more than 120 years, this brand has been creating superb luxury sport timepieces that function above and beyond the call of duty.

In true Breitling style, the brand remains committed to producing exceptional high-function timepieces. Most recently, in celebration of the 20th anniversary of the Chronomat (which heralded the renaissance of the mechanical chronograph) and the brand's 120th anniversary, Breitling introduced the Chronomat Evolution. This newest version of the model that has gained respect as the benchmark in this product category has been restyled in a sophisticated blend of proportions and curves, yet maintains its sturdiness, precision and functionality.

Particular care has been devoted to each and every detail in the restyling of this large, commanding watch. The dial is meticulously crafted and guillochéd. The crown and pushpieces are set firmly in to the protective case sides, and the case horns are ergonomically curved to fit the wrist comfortably. The watch is available in steel, 18-karat yellow or white gold (limited edition), and two-tone. The case is equipped with screw-locked pushpieces enabling the Chronomat Evolution to withstand pressures of 30 bars (300 meters) in depth. This device also provides effective protection against shock. The officially COSC-certified chronometer houses the caliber 13 self-winding chronograph movement. The inaugural series is dedicated to Frecce Tricolori, the famous Italian aerobatic flight team that first approached Breitling in the 1980s to create the Chronomat for them. Today's Breitling Frecce Tricolori Chronomat Evolution is created in a limited edition of 1,000 pieces and features the team emblem and colors on the dial.

**ABOVE**
The Frecce Tricolori Chronomat Evolution is a limited edition piece dedicated to the Italian aerobatic flight team.

**BOTTOM LEFT**
The Chronomat Evolution features screw-locked crown and safety pushpieces set into the case to protect it from shocks.

**BOTTOM RIGHT**
The Chronomat Evolution houses the COSC-certified chronometer chronograph Breitling caliber 13 with 25 jewels.

On the heels of its very successful alliance with world-renowned Bentley Motors, Breitling continues to produce new models in its Breitling for Bentley line. Among the newest pieces are the Bentley 6.75 and the Bentley GT chronographs. This launch heralds the emergence of a full-fledge watch collection distinguished by exclusivity, prestige and performance. The Bentley 6.75—created in homage to the largest Bentley engine—is a chronograph with large date calendar displayed through two windows.

Housing the Breitling caliber 44B, the self-winding chronometer features 38 jewels and chronograph with 30-minute and 12-hour totalizers. The watch naturally incorporates some of the signature Bentley features, such as the knurled finish on the bezel inspired by the Bentley controls. The watch is created in steel and in 18-karat yellow gold. Additionally, 100 pieces are created in rose gold and 50 in white gold.

The Bentley GT (referring to the Grand Touring tradition) is sportier and more compact than the Bentley 6.75. Its dial, with contrasting totalizers, is reminiscent of the Bentley Grand Tourers' dashboards. Breitling uses metallic colors in Bentley shades for this series production dial. The watch houses the COSC-certified chronometer Breitling caliber 13B with day/date calendar. The GT is also endowed with a variable tachometer to measure average speed.

**TOP**

***from left to right***

The Bentley GT house a variable tachometer to measure average speed, no matter the time elapsed, distance covered or speed reached. The variable tachometer is operated by rotating the external bezel.

The Bentley 6.75 chronometer chronograph also has large date displayed via two separate windows.

## CHRONOLOGY

**1884** Léon Breitling opens his first workshop in St. Imier, Switzerland, and manufactures pocket chronographs.

**1892** The Breitling workshop relocates to La Chaux-de-Fonds.

**1915** Léon Breitling's son, Gaston, invents a wristwatch chronograph for pilots.

**1923** Breitling patents the independent chronograph pushpiece.

**1926** The company registers a patent for the 1/10th of a second counter.

**1934** Breitling patents a wrist chronograph with second return-to-zero pushpiece, created by third-generation Willy Breitling.

**1936** Airplanes are equipped with Breitling on-board chronographs and the company begins working with several armed forces.

**1952** Breitling unveils the Navitimer wristwatch. This chronograph is built for aviators and collectors and is capable of measuring both speed and fuel-consumption levels.

**1962** Astronaut Scott Carpenter gives the Navitimer Cosmonaut its first test in orbital flight aboard the Aurora 7.

**1969** Breitling unveils the Chronomat. It houses the Caliber 11 self-winding chronograph movement, developed by Breitling, Heuer and Hamilton-Buren.

**1971** Breitling unveils the Unitime, which offers time in two zones.

**1979** Ernest Schneider and Willy Breitling enter an agreement giving Schneider ownership. The company continues operation under the famed Breitling name.

**1984** The Chronomat becomes the watch of choice for the Italian acrobatic aviation team, the Frecce Tricolori.

**1989** Breitling launches the Chronomat Yachting watch that incorporates a regatta racing counter.

**1995** The Breitling Emergency watch saves the lives of 13 people aboard the Mata-Rangi raft.

**1999** Breitling travels the world with Bertrand Piccard and Brian Jones in the Orbiter 3's successful non-stop around-the-world balloon flight.

**2001** Breitling develops the SuperQuartz™ movement with an annual variation of just 15 seconds.

**2002** Breitling celebrates the 50th anniversary of the Navitimer and unveils an emblematic model. The company also unveils the Avenger Seawolf watch, water resistant to 10,000 feet.

**2003** Breitling forms an alliance with Bentley Motors, wherein Breitling styles the distinctive dashboard instruments for the Bentley Continental GT and supports Team Bentley for the Le Mans race.

## CHRONOMAT EVOLUTION — REF. A1335611

**Movement:** mechanical automatic-winding Breitling Caliber 13 (Valjoux 7750 Caliber base); 25 jewels; COSC-certified chronometer.
**Functions:** hour, minute, small second; date; chronograph with 3 counters.
**Case:** stainless steel three-piece case, antimagnetic (Ø 43.7mm, thickness: 17.05mm, weight: 119.9 gr.); curved double-sided antireflective sapphire crystal; counterclockwise-turning ring with 12 holding screws; luminescent marker; 4 riders at quarters and engraved graduated scale; screw-down crown and pushers with case protection; screw-on back; water resistant to 100atm.
**Dial:** green; gilded subdials decorated with circular beads; applied gold-plated markers and luminescent dots; gold-plated luminescent hands.
**Indications:** date at 3; hour counter at 6; small second at 9; minute counter at 12; center second counter; minute track with divisions for 1/4 second; tachometer scale on the flange.
**Bracelet:** stainless steel.
**Also available:** in stainless steel and 18K yellow-gold details; in 18K yellow gold (10atm); with leather strap or Pilot bracelet of the same metal as the case; various dial colors.

## COCKPIT LADY — REF. B7135612

**Movement:** SuperQuartz™ Breitling Caliber 71; COSC-certified chronometer.
**Case:** stainless steel (Ø 31.8mm, thickness: 12.7mm, weight: 44.6 gr.); diamond-set gold bezel; water resistant to 10atm.
**Dial:** diamond hour markers; calendar.
**Strap:** blue leather.
**Also available:** steel with 18K yellow gold; gold; various gemset versions on strap or bracelet.

## NAVITIMER WORLD GMT — REF. A2432212

**Movement:** mechanical automatic-winding Breitling Caliber 24; COSC-certified chronometer. **Functions:** hour, minute, small second; date; second 24-hour time zone; chronograph with 3 counters. **Case:** stainless steel three-piece case (Ø 46mm, thickness: 15.5mm, weight: 112.8 gr.); curved double-sided antireflective sapphire crystal; bi-directional turning grooved ring integral with the flange; screw-on back with dual time-zone engravings; water resistant to 3atm. **Dial:** soleil; subdials decorated with circular beads; luminescent applied bâton markers in rhodium-plated brass; luminescent bâton hands in rhodium-plated brass. **Indications:** date at 3; hour counter at 6; small second at 9; minute counter at 12; center second counter and second 24-hour time zone with red arrow-tipped hand; minute track with divisions for 1/5 second with luminescent dots; slide-rule. **Bracelet:** Navitimer stainless steel; fold-over safety clasp. **Note:** limited edition of 100 pieces for each dial color. **Also available:** 200 rose-gold pieces; 25 white-gold pieces; various dials, straps, bracelet.

## BENTLEY GT — REF. A1336212

**Movement:** mechanical automatic-winding Breitling Caliber 13B (modified Valjoux 7751 base); COSC-certified chronometer. **Functions:** hour, minute, small second; date/day; chronograph with 3 counters. **Case:** stainless steel three-piece case (Ø 44.8mm, thickness: 15.15mm, weight: 109.4 gr.); curved double-sided antireflective sapphire crystal; ring integrated with the two-way turning flange, knurled with deep grooves, in steel and gold; screw-down crown with case protection; screw-on back, engraved; water resistant to 10atm. **Dial:** metallic bordeaux; gilded subdials decorated with circular beads, flange argenté and brushed; applied bâton markers in gold-plated brass with luminescent dots; luminescent sword-style hands in gold-plated brass. **Indications:** day and date display at 3; hour counter at 6; small second at 9; minute counter at 12; center second counter; minute track with divisions for 1/4 second; fixed and variable tachometer scale on the turning flange (manually, bi-directionally); slide-rule. **Bracelet:** Speed style in steel.
**Also available:** with gold-plated details; steel and gold Speed bracelet; leather strap, Diver Pro strap; stainless steel with leather strap, Diver Pro strap, Speed bracelet; in yellow gold, crocodile strap, Speed bracelet; 50 white-gold pieces; crocodile strap, Speed bracelet.

## BENTLEY 6.75 REF. A4436212

**Movement:** mechanical automatic-winding Breitling Caliber 44B; COSC-certified chronometer. **Functions:** hour, minute, small second; large date; chronograph with 3 counters. **Case:** stainless steel, three-piece case, (Ø 48.7mm, thickness: 17.2mm, weight: 144.7 gr.); curved double-sided antireflective sapphire crystal; ring integrated with the flange; bi-directional; knurled with deep grooves; screw-down crown with case protection; stylized screw-on back, engraved; water resistant to 10atm.

**Dial:** bronze; soleil; subdials decorated with circular beads and flange, all argenté; applied, rhodium-plated bâton markers with luminescent dots; rhodium-plated luminescent bâton hands. **Indications:** small second at 3; hour counter at 6; minute counter at 9; big date display at 12; center second counter; half-minute track with divisions for 1/4 second; fixed and variable tachometer scale on the turning flange (manually, bi-directionally); slide-rule.
**Strap:** leather; steel clasp.
**Also available:** 18K yellow gold; 100 rose-gold pieces; 50 white-gold pieces; various dials, straps, bracelet.

## CHRONO COCKPIT REF. A1335753

**Movement:** mechanical automatic-winding Breitling Caliber 13 (Valjoux 7750 Caliber base); 25 jewels; COSC-certified chronometer. **Functions:** hour, minute, small second; date; chronograph with 3 counters. **Case:** stainless steel, three-piece case, antimagnetic (Ø 39mm, thickness: 16.05mm, weight: 96.2 gr.); curved double-sided antireflective sapphire crystal; counterclockwise-turning mother-of-pearl bezel with a row of set brilliants; 12 holding screws; luminescent marker; 4 gold riders at quarters; screw-down crown and pushers with case protection; screw-on back; water resistant to 10atm.

**Dial:** black mother-of-pearl dial; gilded subdial crowns; applied luminescent gold-plated markers; gold-plated luminescent bâton hands.
**Indications:** date at 3; hour counter at 6; small second at 9; minute counter at 12; center second counter; minute track with divisions for 1/5 second; tachometer scales on the flange.
**Strap:** leather; steel clasp.
**Also available:** without brilliants; stainless steel with gold-plated details; leather or crocodile strap or bracelet; in yellow gold with crocodile leather strap or Pilot bracelet; in stainless steel with leather or crocodile strap or Pilot bracelet.

## AEROMARINE COLT SUPEROCEAN STEELFISH REF. A1736010

**Movement:** mechanical automatic-winding Breitling Caliber 17; COSC-certified chronometer. **Functions:** hour, minute, second; date. **Case:** stainless steel three-piece case (Ø 42mm, thickness: 14.95mm, weight: 100.6 gr.); brushed and polished finish; curved antireflective sapphire crystal; glass-bearing bezel with engravings at markers; counterclockwise-turning ring with 8 holding screws; luminescent marker; 4 riders at quarters and brushed ring with engraved graduated scale; decompression valve at 12 for helium-gas relief during the diver's ascent; screw-down crown with case protection, with double safety device; screw-on back with engraving; water resistant to 150atm.

**Dial:** argenté; decorated with circular beads; luminescent applied round markers and Arabic numerals in rhodium-plated brass; center printed 24-hour scale; railway minute track with 5-minute graduation printed on the flange (with a luminescent dot at 12; luminescent sword-style hands in rhodium-plated brass).
**Indications:** date at 3; large round hour markers.
**Strap:** blue Diver Pro rubber strap.
**Also available:** blue, black or white dial; various Diver Pro rubber strap and Professional steel bracelet.

## COLT GMT REF. A3235011

**Movement:** Breitling Caliber 32; COSC-certified chronometer.
**Function:** second 24-hour time zone.
**Case:** stainless steel (Ø 40.5mm, thickness: 13.6mm, weight: 85.1 gr.); water resistant to 50atm.
**Dial:** blue; stainless steel Arabic numerals.
**Indications:** date at 3; center second counter and second 24-hour time zone with red arrow-tipped hand.
**Bracelet:** stainless steel.
**Also available:** black or silver dial; various straps, bracelet.

# BVLGARI

The extraordinary creativity and emotional impact of Italian design, unusual materials and harmonious sizes make Bvlgari's rich collections instantly recognizable, giving Bvlgari watches their appeal as objects created for our times.

Bvlgari watches are made to the very highest levels of precision and to the most stringent quality standards adopted in Swiss watchmaking, with constant and meticulous attention to detail.

Recently launched in 2004, Ergon takes its inspiration directly from the main attributes of Bvlgari's style: the bold and contemporary design and dynamic volumes. The Ergon watch is a truly unique timepiece, its forceful character and self-assured confidence derives from a perfect blend of sport and elegance. Its energetic personality reflects the ideal balance among luxurious materials, daring sizes and purity of form. The ergonomically arched, encircling shape of the case forms a single unit with the integrated bracelet.

In another of its latest creations, Bvlgari realizes its first in-house grand complication timepiece. The icon of the Bvlgari collection—the Bvlgari-Bvlgari line—is today enriched by a new exclusive Tourbillon watch, which combines its elegant design with a highly complicated movement born from the renowned watchmaking expertise of Bvlgari and Daniel Roth. This prestigious timepiece is created in a limited edition of 25 yellow-gold pieces and 25 white-gold pieces.

THIS PAGE

**TOP**

These Diagono Aluminum timepieces indicate hour and minute via luminescent hands, hour indexes and numerals on black or carbon fiber dials. Their bezels and straps are rubber.

**BOTTOM LEFT**

This Rettangolo Chrono is crafted in 18-karat yellow gold.

**BOTTOM RIGHT**

The 40mm, 18-karat white-gold Ergon Chrono is powered by an automatic movement. Its anthracite, opalin-plated dial features vertical treatment, anthracite counters and date display.

FACING PAGE

**TOP AND CENTER**

The Bvlgari-Bvlgari Tourbillon features a tourbillon aperture at 6:00.

**BOTTOM**

Shown here on a hand-sewn leather strap and a stainless steel bracelet, these Bvlgari-Bvlgari for gents and ladies, respectively, are also available in 18-karat yellow gold.

## CHRONOLOGY

**1884** Jeweler Sotirio Bvlgari, the heir of an ancient dynasty of Greek silversmiths, establishes his first shop on Rome's Via Sistina.

**1905** With sons Costantino and Giorgio, Bvlgari opens the shop in Via Condotti which will become an institution in the Italian capital's old town and a highlight for curious tourists and clients from all over the world.

**1977** Bvlgari presents its first luxury watch collection with the famed signature "Bvlgari-Bvlgari."

**1980s** The Roman house founds the Bvlgari Time company in Neuchâtel, Switzerland. In addition to the Rome, Paris, Geneva and Montecarlo boutiques, others are established in New York, London, Milan, Monaco, St. Moritz, Hong Kong, Osaka, and Tokyo, with the number of points of sale increasing steadily.

**1989** An agreement is signed with GP Manufacture SA for the production of Bvlgari watches to be equipped, from 1994 on, with the new automatic GPM 3000 and 3100 calibers.

**1990** The new quartz Chronograph is born.

**1993** Bvlgari watches are carried by the most exclusive jewelers in the world.

**1994** The brand's first complicated watches have a modern architectural design, such as the Tourbillon and Minute Repeater. At the same time, the new Sport line is presented, comprising sport and diver watches with modern and original designs and automatic movements.

**1995** The Trika is the first "soft" bracelet, a masterpiece by master jewelers. On July 17th, Bvlgari S.p.A., the group's parent company, is quoted at the Italian telematic stock exchange system and at the international London SEAQ.

**1996** The Sport line expands with the addition of a split-second chronograph. Three models enrich the Bvlgari-Bvlgari collection: the Squelette, the Perpétuel with the date programmed until the year 2099, and the GMT.

**1998** Bvlgari sells its shares in the GP Manufacture SA. The Aluminum model is presented and immediately becomes an international success.

**2000** An agreement with The Hour Glass leads to the acquisition of Gérald Genta and Daniel Roth.

**2001** The Bvlgari-Bvlgari collection presents three new automatic watches with its 38mm cases: a chronometer chronograph, an annual calendar and a perpetual calendar.

**2002** Inspired by its bestseller line, Bvlgari launches a new luxury accessory watch for ladies: the B.zero1. The Diagono Professional collection is enriched by the new GMT Tachimetric timepiece.

**2003** Following the incredible success of its jewelry collection, Bvlgari launches a new jewelry watch: Lucea. The Diagono Professional Scuba 2000m is presented as a maximum performance instrument in scuba diving watches. Bvlgari launches the Bvlgari-Bvlgari Annual Calendar and the Bvlgari-Bvlgari Moon Phases timepieces.

**2004** The Ergon is presented at Basel. The Bvlgari-Bvlgari Tourbillon is the first in-house grand complication timepiece. Regatta and GMT Flyback are added to the Diagono Professional collection.

## BVLGARI-BVLGARI TOURBILLON — REF. BBW38GLTB

**Movement:** mechanical manual-winding; made by Bvlgari (Daniel Roth); Caliber 052 with tourbillon device; 64-hour power reserve; Côtes de Genève and satinè soleil treatment.
**Functions:** hour, minute, small second; power reserve.
**Case:** Ø 38mm; 18K white-gold two-piece case; numbered; polished; flat antireflective scratch-resistant sapphire crystal; nylon gasket; bezel with engraved logo; snap-on back, displaying the movement through a sapphire crystal; engraving of the individual limited edition number, water resistant to 30 meters.
**Dial:** anthracite with tourbillon visible at 6; guilloché and Côtes de Genève decoration; applied silver-plated bâton markers.
**Indications:** small second hand at 6 integral with the tourbillon cage; power-reserve indicator on back.
**Strap:** hand-sewn matte crocodile strap; 18K gold deployment buckle.
**Also available:** 18K yellow gold; silver dial.

## BVLGARI-BVLGARI CHRONO — REF. BB38GLDCH

**Movement:** mechanical automatic-winding ETA customized by Bvlgari.
**Functions:** hour, minute, small second; date; chronograph with hour, minute, second.
**Case:** Ø 38mm; 18K yellow-gold two-piece case; numbered; polished; flat antireflective scratch-resistant sapphire crystal; nylon gasket; bezel with engraved logo; snap-on back; water resistant to 30 meters.
**Dial:** white; gold-plated subdials decorated with circular beads; applied gold-plated bâton markers; luminescent dots; luminescent gold-plated bâton hands; painted minute track.
**Indications:** permanent small second at 3; date between 4 and 5; hour counter at 6; minute counter at 9; center chronograph second.
**Strap/Bracelet:** hand-sewn matte crocodile strap; 18K gold buckle.
**Also available:** stainless steel with black dial and silvered counters; bracelet.

## RETTANGOLO AUTOMATIC — REF. RT45C6LSLD

**Movement:** mechanical automatic-winding ETA customized by Bvlgari.
**Functions:** hour, minute; date.
**Case:** stainless steel two-piece rectangular case; size: 35.8x25.8mm; numbered; polished; curved scratch-resistant sapphire crystal; nylon gasket; logo engraved; back fastened by 6 screws; water resistant to 30 meters.
**Dial:** silvered with vertical treatment, applied rhodium-plated bâton markers, painted minute track.
**Indications:** date at 6.
**Strap:** hand-sewn matte leather strap; stainless steel buckle
**Also available:** steel or yellow gold; leather strap or bracelet; white gold with diamonds.

## RETTANGOLO STEEL RUBBER — REF. RT45SVD

**Movement:** mechanical automatic-winding ETA customized by Bvlgari.
**Functions:** hour, minute; date.
**Case:** stainless steel two-piece rectangular case; size: 35.8x25.8mm, thickness 9.8mm; numbered; polished; curved scratch-resistant sapphire crystal; nylon gasket; back fastened by 6 screws; water resistant to 30 meters.
**Dial:** black; applied rhodium-plated bâton markers and Arabic numerals.
**Strap/Bracelet:** black rubber with brushed stainless steel links; recessed double fold-over buckle.
**Also available:** 18K yellow gold.

## DIAGONO ALUMINIUM — REF. AL38BTAVD/SLN

**Movement:** mechanical automatic-winding ETA customized by Bvlgari.
**Functions:** hour, minute, second; date.
**Case:** Ø 38mm; aluminum and titanium brushed three-piece case; rubber fixed bezel; scratch-resistant sapphire crystal; nylon gasket; black PVD-coated satin-finished titanium caseback; numbered; water resistant to 30 meters.
**Dial:** black carbon fiber; white printed luminescent hour indexes and numerals; luminescent rhodium-plated hands.
**Indications:** date at 3.
**Strap/Bracelet:** black rubber with brushed aluminum links; aluminum buckle.
**Also available:** white dial; in 18K yellow gold with rubber bracelet; ladies' size.

## DIAGONO ALUMINIUM CHRONO — REF. AC38TAVD/SLN

**Movement:** mechanical automatic-winding ETA customized by Bvlgari.
**Functions:** hour, minute, small second; date; chronograph with hour, minute, second.
**Case:** Ø 38mm; aluminum and titanium brushed three-piece case; rubber fixed bezel, scratch-resistant sapphire crystal; nylon gasket; black PVD-coated satin-finished titanium caseback; numbered; black PVD-coated titanium pushbuttons (2) and crown; water resistant to 30 meters.
**Dial:** rhodium coated, satin finished; black printed luminescent hour indexes and numeral 12; 3 black printed counters with white printed numbers; black painted luminescent hands.
**Indications:** small second at 3; date between 4 and 5; hour counter at 6; minute counter at 9; center second.
**Strap/Bracelet:** black rubber with brushed aluminum links; aluminum buckle.
**Also available:** carbon fiber dial; 18K yellow gold with rubber bracelet.

## DIAGONO — REF. LCV38WSLD

**Movement:** mechanical automatic-winding ETA customized by Bvlgari.
**Functions:** hour, minute, second; date.
**Case:** Ø 38mm; stainless steel brushed three-piece case; fixed bezel; antireflective scratch-resistant sapphire crystal; nylon gasket; bezel with engraved logo; stainless steel screw-down crown with case protection; satin-finished stainless steel caseback; numbered; water resistant to 30 meters.
**Dial:** white; hand applied hour indexes and numerals 6 and 12.
**Indications:** date at 3.
**Strap:** hand-sewn matte leather strap; stainless steel buckle.
**Also available:** black dial; steel bracelet; stainless steel and 18K yellow gold; 18K yellow gold with crocodile strap or bracelet; ladies' size.

## DIAGONO CHRONO — REF. CH35BSSDAUTO

**Movement:** mechanical automatic-winding ETA customized by Bvlgari.
**Functions:** hour, minute, small second; date; chronograph with hour, minute, second.
**Case:** Ø 35mm; stainless steel brushed three-piece case; antireflective scratch-resistant sapphire crystal; nylon gasket; bezel with engraved logo; stainless steel screw-down crown with case protection; satin-finished stainless steel caseback; numbered; water resistant to 30 meters.
**Dial:** black with rhodium-plated subdials decorated with circular beads; applied rhodium-plated bâton markers; rhodium-plated bâton hands.
**Indications:** small second at 3; date between 4 and 5; hour counter at 6; minute counter at 9; center second.
**Bracelet:** brushed stainless steel with fold-over buckle.
**Also available:** white dial; leather bracelet; stainless steel and 18K yellow gold; 18K yellow gold with crocodile strap or bracelet.

## DIAGONO PROFESSIONAL CHRONO RATTRAPANTE REF. CH40GLTARA

**Movement:** mechanical automatic-winding Jacquet customized for Bvlgari; COSC-certified chronometer.
**Functions:** hour, minute, small second; split-second chronograph with hour, minute, second.
**Case:** Ø 40mm; 18K yellow-gold brushed three-piece case; antireflective scratch-resistant sapphire crystal; nylon gasket; bezel with engraved tachymetric scale; gold screw-down crown with case protection; gold pushers; screw-on back, displaying the movement through a sapphire crystal; numbered; water resistant to 100 meters.
**Dial:** white; applied gold-plated bâton markers; luminescent dots; luminescent gold-plated bâton hands.
**Indications:** minute counter at 3; hour counter at 6; small second at 9; center second and split-second counter; painted minute track with division of 1/5 second.
**Strap:** hand-sewn alligator strap; completely polished 18K yellow-gold recessed double fold-over buckle.
**Also available:** white gold.

## DIAGONO PROFESSIONAL REGATTA REF. SD40SV/RE

**Movement:** mechanical automatic-winding Dubois Dépraz customized for Bvlgari.
**Functions:** hour, minute; flyback chronograph; minute amplification display; tactical functions for Regatta.
**Case:** Ø 40mm; stainless steel brushed three-piece case; antireflective scratch-resistant sapphire crystal; nylon gasket; bi-directional rotating bezel with compass scale; stainless steel screw-down crown with case protection; satin-finished stainless steel caseback; numbered; 2 screwed pushbuttons for chronograph and flyback functions; water resistant to 30 meters.
**Dial:** white painted; hand-applied luminescent round hour indexes and special minute amplification display at 12 (5 holes) for the chronograph; luminescent rhodium-plated hands.
**Indications:** special Regatta indicators for tactical decisions; minute amplification display; compass scale.
**Strap/Bracelet:** black rubber with brushed stainless steel links; recessed double fold-over buckle.

## DIAGONO PROFESSIONAL GMT 40 FLYBACK REF. GMT40SVD/FB

**Movement:** mechanical automatic-winding Dubois Dépraz exclusively developed for Bvlgari, COSC-certified chronometer.
**Functions:** hour, minute, small second; date; flyback chronograph with hour, minute, second.
**Case:** Ø 40mm; stainless steel, brushed three-piece case; antireflective scratch-resistant sapphire crystal; nylon gasket; bi-directional rotating bezel with 24-hour scale; stainless steel screw-down crown with case protection; satin-finished stainless steel caseback; numbered; 3 screwed pushbuttons for chronograph and flyback functions and GMT correction; water resistant to 100 meters.
**Dial:** white dial; hand-applied luminescent hour indexes and numeral 12; luminescent rhodium-plated hands; rhodium-plated GMT hand with red arrow.
**Indications:** GMT 3 time zones with chrono-flyback function; date between 4 and 5.
**Strap/Bracelet:** black rubber with brushed stainless steel links; recessed double fold-over buckle.

## ERGON REF. EG35BSSD

**Movement:** mechanical automatic-winding ETA customized by Bvlgari.
**Functions:** hour, minute, second; date.
**Case:** Ø 35mm; satin-finished stainless steel case with polished edges; antireflective scratch-resistant sapphire crystal; nylon gasket; satin-finished stainless steel caseback; numbered; completely polished stainless steel crown; water resistant to 30 meters. **Dial:** satinè soleil with black galvanic treatment; hand-applied rhodium-plated diamond-treated hour indexes; numerals 6 and 12; luminescent rhodium-plated hands.
**Indications:** date at 3.
**Bracelet:** stainless steel; satin-finished bracelet and fold-over buckle.
**Also available:** hand-sewn matte alligator strap; three different sizes for men and ladies.

## ERGON CHRONO — REF. EGW40C5GLDCH

**Movement:** mechanical automatic-winding ETA customized by Bvlgari.
**Functions:** hour, minute, small second; date; chronograph with hour, minute, second.
**Case:** Ø 40mm; completely polished 18K white gold; antireflective scratch-resistant sapphire crystal; nylon gasket; satin-finished 18K white-gold caseback; numbered; completely polished 18K white-gold pushbuttons and crown; water resistant to 30 meters.
**Dial:** anthracite opalin-plated with central area with vertical treatment and 3 anthracite counters; hand-applied rhodium-plated diamond-treated hour indexes and numeral 12; and luminescent rhodium-plated hands.
**Indications:** date between 4 and 5.
**Strap:** hand-sewn alligator strap; completely polished 18K white-gold deployment buckle.

## ERGON LADIES DIAMONDS — REF. EGW30C5GDLD/12

**Movement:** quartz, ETA customized by Bvlgari.
**Functions:** hour, minute, second; date.
**Case:** Ø 30mm; completely polished 18K white-gold case; antireflective scratch-resistant sapphire crystal; nylon gasket; satin-finished 18K white-gold caseback numbered; completely polished 18K white-gold crown; water resistant to 30 meters.
**Dial:** opalin-plated anthracite; central area with vertical treatment; hand-applied hour indexes with 24 diamonds; luminescent rhodium-plated hands.
**Indications:** 64 diamonds (approx. 1.15 carats); date at 3.
**Strap:** hand-sewn alligator strap; completely polished 18K white-gold deployment buckle.
**Also available:** without diamonds.

## BVLGARI-BVLGARI DIAMONDS — REF. BBW33BGDLAUTO

**Movement:** mechanical automatic-winding ETA customized by Bvlgari.
**Functions:** hour, minute; date.
**Case:** Ø 33mm; 18K white-gold two-piece case; numbered; polished; flat antireflective scratch-resistant sapphire crystal; nylon gasket; bezel set with 40 diamonds (approx. 1.72 carats); snap-on back; water resistant to 30 meters.
**Dial:** black galvanic with a sun satin effect; applied rhodium-plated bâton markers.
**Indications:** date at 3.
**Strap:** hand-sewn matte crocodile strap; 18K gold buckle.
**Also available:** 18K gold bracelet.

## LUCEA — REF. LUW16OGDGDO/12

**Movement:** quartz; ETA customized by Bvlgari.
**Functions:** hour, minute.
**Case:** Ø 16mm; 18K white gold; bezel with diamonds; scratch-resistant sapphire crystal; numbered.
**Dial:** onyx with 12 diamond indexes.
**Indications:** 250 diamonds (3.4 carats); 30 onyx.
**Bracelet:** 18K white gold with diamonds and onyx.
**Also available:** mother-of-pearl dial; 18K white-gold bracelet; white gold and blue topaz; demi-pavè, full-pavè dial with full-pavè bracelet.

# CARTIER

For more than a century and a half, this legendary Parisian house has been a world leader in the creation of high-jeweled masterpieces—both jewelry and watches. Today, its watches are Swiss-made with French high style and adeptly run the gamut from haute joaillerie to haute horlogerie.

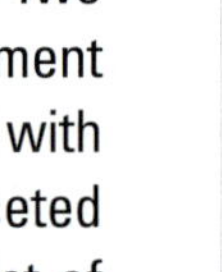

THIS PAGE

ABOVE

The Tank Louis Cartier Skeleton watch is crafted in platinum and houses the 9710MC mechanical manual-wind mechanism.

LEFT

The movement within the Tank Louis Cartier Skeleton.

FACING PAGE

The Tortue Perpetual Calendar with Two Time Zones is created in platinum and houses the 9421MC mechanical movement. With an 18-karat gold dial, each watch features matching numbered case and movement.

Among the newest complex watches from Cartier is the stunning extra-large Tortue Perpetual Calendar. Crafted in pure platinum or in 18-karat rose gold, the Tortue Perpetual Calendar with Two Time Zones houses the 9421MC mechanical movement. The intricate double-complication movement is comprised of 276 parts and 27 jewels. Complete with 18-karat gold rotor, the watch is equipped with 49 hours of power reserve. The watch features an 18-karat gold dial with Roman numerals, a faceted sapphire crown and a sapphire caseback. The movement and case of each timepiece consist of matching numbers. Also this year, Cartier releases a limited edition of 25 Tortue Minute Repeaters crafted in 18-karat rose gold and housing the 24-jeweled 9401MC movement.

Another important addition of beguiling beauty is the Tank Louis Cartier Skeleton. Part of the Collection Privée Paris, the watch is encased in 950 platinum and intricately decorated by hand. Featuring a slightly larger Tank case, the skeletonized watch houses the 9710MC mechanical movement with manual-wind mechanism and C de Cartier index assembly. The movement is comprised of 153 individual parts, 19 jewels, and offers 40 hours of power reserve. Only 50 pieces are being created, each featuring matching numbered case and movement.

In celebration of the Santos watch's 100th anniversary, Cartier unveils the Santos 100—a bold timepiece with a powerful case that is a contemporary interpretation of its legendary predecessor. Created from a block of gold or steel, the watch features an oversized screw-on bezel and luminous hands.

CARTIER
PARIS
SWISS MADE
NOV JAN MAR MAI JUIL SEP
DIM SAM VEN JEU MER

THIS PAGE

FAR LEFT

The Santos 100 is an updated version of the original, created by Louis Cartier in 1904 for his friend Alberto Santos-Dumont.

CENTER TOP

Called the Hypnose, this unusual watch is set with brilliant-cut diamonds and features an offset oval case of 18-karat gold.

FAR RIGHT

The Casque watch features a silver sun motif on the dial and brilliant-cut diamonds.

CENTER BOTTOM

The Sofa watch is created in 18-karat white gold and set with princess-cut diamonds.

FACING PAGE

TOP

Cartier's sporty chic Tortue single-pushbutton chronograph is offered in 18-karat rose gold with diamonds.

CENTER

The Tank Chinoise large model is crafted in platinum and houses the 430MC manual-wind mechanism.

BOTTOM

Cartier unveils the Déclaration watch (first launched in 2003) in different materials, including a rose-gold version with steel rings, and a steel version with ceramic rings (not shown).

Several Santos 100 models exist—all housing the caliber 049 mechanical movement with an automatic-wind mechanism.

In true Cartier tradition, the brand also offers delightfully extravagant high-jeweled watches. Ingenuity reigns supreme with the new asymmetrical oval Hypnose watch that is set slightly askew for an elegant twist. The watch is set meticulously with 357 diamonds in nine sizes, weighing 4.5 carats. Other new jeweled watches include a host of elongated and unusually shaped watches. The Sofa features a D-shaped, horizontal rectangle case created in a limited edition of 25 pieces and set with four carats of diamonds. The Sabot is set with nearly five carats of diamonds on its elongated case. In its much-coveted Animal Kingdom series of enamel- and cloisonné-dialed watches, Cartier releases a stunning dragon that rears its head and flicks its tongue. Available with either blue or red/orange enameling, each watch undergoes approximately 20 paintings and firings.

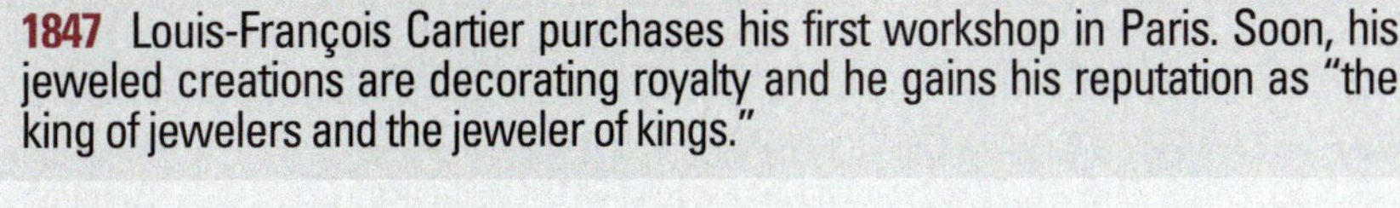

## CHRONOLOGY

**1847** Louis-François Cartier purchases his first workshop in Paris. Soon, his jeweled creations are decorating royalty and he gains his reputation as "the king of jewelers and the jeweler of kings."

**1873** An Egyptian-styled pocket watch signed by Cartier is crafted in gold, diamonds and rubies.

**1874** Alfred Cartier takes over his father's business.

**1899** The fourth (and last) change of address for Cartier. Alfred's son, Louis Cartier, moves the House to Rue de la Paix, 13.

**1907** Louis Cartier and Edmond Jaeger sign a long-lasting agreement in which Jaeger gives Cartier the exclusive commercial rights to Jaeger's watch production and Cartier guarantees orders totaling at least 250,000 francs per year.

**1911** Originally designed as Cartier's first-ever men's wristwatch with leather strap for Louis Cartier's Brazilian friend Alberto Santos-Dumont, the Santos joins Cartier's retail line.

**1913** The launching of the Tortue and a small pendulum clock, Mystérieuse.

**1930s** Cartier creates a water-resistant watch with a special locking system for the Pasha of Marrakech.

**1933** Cartier patents the Vendôme with center-attached mobile lugs.

**1972** A group of investors, led by Joseph Kanouï, buys Cartier Paris and, two years later, Cartier London.

**1976** First appearance of the Vérmeil watches for Les Must de Cartier.

**1979** Cartier Monde is established to unify all of the House's interests.

**1983** Presentation of the Panthère.

**1985** Pasha is presented, inspired by a model from 1943.

**1989** Introduction of the Tank Américaine.

**1993** Launching of the Chrono Reflex-movement versions of the Pasha, Cougar and Diabolo de Cartier watches.

**1996** Launching of the Tank Française watch.

**1997** Cartier celebrates its 150th anniversary with three limited editions, each distinguished by a cabochon ruby: a 1930s Tank; a swinging levered Tank from 1923; and the Driver, featuring a curved case that rests on the top side of the wrist while driving. Some other innovations are a Tank in platinum; a Tank Carrée Obus; a limited-edition Pasha; and an automatic Santos.

**1998** Cartier creates the exceptional Collection Privée Cartier Paris (CPCP), which is launched at the eighth SIHH. New introductions include: the Pasha Tourbillon; the refined Tortue collection with a Tourbillon whose bridges and pillar plates are cut from a single piece of rock crystal; the Three Diamond Trinity (the watch version of the famous Three Golds ring); The Parrot, a sumptuous example of a wristwatch with 187 grams of platinum, 1,013 diamonds and 2 emeralds; and The Pendulette Mystérieuse.

**2002** Cartier creates the Roadster watch, inspired by the world of automobile designs.

**2003** Cartier unveils the Animal Kingdom series of enamel and cloisonné watches set with gemstones.

## TORTUE XL PERPETUAL CALENDAR DUAL TIME COLL. PRIVÉE — REF. W1542851

**Movement:** mechanical automatic-winding Cartier caliber 9421 MC; autonomy approx. 49 hours; 11'''1/2; 27 jewels; 28,800 vph; bridges and rotor (in 18K gold) decorated with Cartier's double interlaced "C" and beveled. **Functions:** hour, minute; perpetual calendar (date, day, month, year); second 24 hour time zone. **Case:** 18K pink-gold two-piece case, Tortue shape (size: 37x38.2mm, thickness: 11.8mm); spherical mineral glass; 4 correctors on the middle; polygonal pink-gold crown with a faceted set sapphire; back fastened by 8 screws, displaying the movement through a sapphire crystal; water resistant to 3atm.
**Dial:** solid gold; argenté guilloché soleil subdials decorated with circular beads; printed Roman numerals and railway minute track; Breguet hands in blued steel.
**Indications:** date at 3; second 24-hour time zone at 6; day at 9; month and year at 12.
**Strap:** hand-stitched alligator leather; pink-gold fold-over clasp.
**Also available:** platinum.
**Note:** each watch comes with a mahogany box containing a watchmaker's lens framed in heathwood, a piece of deerskin and a black leather travel case.

## SANTOS 100 — REF. W20071Y1

**Movement:** mechanical automatic-winding Cartier caliber 049 MC.
**Functions:** hour, minute, second.
**Case:** 18K yellow-gold two-piece case, curved square shape (size: 43x51mm, thickness: 10.35mm); brushed and polished finish; curved sapphire crystal; bezel fastened by 8 screws; polygonal gold crown with a faceted set sapphire with case protection; back fastened by 8 screws; water resistant to 10atm.
**Dial:** argenté flinqué; printed Roman numerals and minute track; luminescent sword-style hands in blued steel.
**Strap:** alligator leather; yellow-gold triple fold-over clasp.
**Also available:** stainless steel; stainless steel and yellow gold.

## SANTOS DUMONT — REF. W2008751

**Movement:** mechanical manual-winding Cartier caliber 430 MC.
**Functions:** hour, minute.
**Case:** 18K yellow-gold two-piece case (size: 36x45mm, thickness: 5.6mm); brushed finish; curved sapphire crystal; recessed polygonal gold crown with a faceted set sapphire; back fastened by 8 screws; water resistant to 3atm.
**Dial:** argenté, brushed; printed Roman numerals and minute track; sword-style hands in black oxidized steel.
**Strap:** alligator leather; yellow-gold fold-over clasp.
**Also available:** in pink or white gold.

## SANTOS DEMOISELLE LM — REF. W25065Z5

**Movement:** quartz Cartier caliber 690.
**Functions:** hour, minute.
**Case:** stainless steel three-piece case, curved square shape (size: 26x36mm, thickness: 7mm); brushed and polished finish; curved sapphire crystal; polygonal crown with a faceted set spinel with case protection; back fastened by 8 screws; water resistant to 3atm.
**Dial:** argenté, guilloché soleil; printed Roman numerals and minute track; sword-style hands in blued steel.
**Bracelet:** stainless steel; fold-over clasp.
**Also available:** stainless steel and yellow gold with bracelet; yellow- and white gold with brilliants.

## SANTOS DEMOISELLE SM — REF. W25063X9

**Movement:** quartz Cartier caliber 690.
**Functions:** hour, minute.
**Case:** 18K yellow-gold three-piece case in curved square shape (size: 22x30mm, thickness: 5.9mm); brushed and polished finish; curved sapphire crystal; polygonal crown with a faceted set spinel with case protection; back fastened by 8 screws; water resistant to 3atm.
**Dial:** argenté, guilloché soleil; printed Roman numerals and minute track; sword-style hands in blued steel.
**Bracelet:** yellow gold; fold-over clasp.
**Also available:** stainless steel and yellow gold with bracelet; yellow- and white gold with diamonds.

## TANK CHINOISE LARGE MODEL — REF. WE300351

**Movement:** mechanical manual-winding Cartier caliber 430 MC.
**Functions:** hour and minute.
**Case:** platinum four-piece case, square (size: 28x28.5mm, thickness: 8mm); a row of brilliants set on lateral bars (fastened by screws) and lugs; curved mineral glass; platinum crown with faceted set diamond and adorned by small spheres; back fastened by 8 screws; water resistant to 3atm.
**Dial:** argenté grené; printed Roman numerals and minute track; sword-style hands in blued steel.
**Strap:** alligator skin; white-gold fold-over clasp.
**Also available:** pink gold without brilliants; small size in pink gold with brilliants; fabric strap; platinum without brilliants.

## TONNEAU — REF. WE400251

**Movement:** mechanical manual-winding Cartier caliber 430 MC.
**Functions:** hour, minute.
**Case:** platinum two-piece case, ergonomically curved tonneau shape (size: 40x26.4mm); brushed finish; a row of brilliants set on the bezel; curved mineral crystal; white-gold octagonal crown with faceted set diamond; back fastened by 4 screws; water resistant to 3atm.
**Dial:** argenté, guilloché soleil, flinqué, curved; printed Roman numerals and minute track; sword-style hands in blued steel.
**Strap:** alligator leather; white-gold fold-over clasp.
**Also available:** small size in white gold; fabric strap; rose gold without brilliants.

## TANK CINTRÉE — REF. W1544451

**Movement:** mechanical manual-winding Cartier caliber 9780 MC.
**Functions:** hour, minute.
**Case:** 18K yellow-gold two-piece case, rectangular and ergonomically curved (size: 46x23mm, thickness: 6.65mm); brushed and polished finish; curved mineral crystal; yellow-gold crown with a set sapphire cabochon; back fastened on the middle by 4 screws; water resistant to 3atm.
**Dial:** solid gold, curved; printed Arabic numerals and railway minute track; Breguet hands in blued steel.
**Strap:** hand-stitched alligator leather; yellow-gold fold-over clasp.
**Note:** limited edition of 150 pieces.

# CHANEL

Inspired by Coco Chanel's creations, the brand's watches bring a new dimension to feminine watchmaking. Today, eight watch collections combine Chanel's creativity with the finest quality of watchmaking.

From the very beginning, Artistic Director Jacques Helleu anticipated watchmaking trends while ensuring that each new model matched house standards of perfection, absolute beauty, purity of line: all creative characteristics that contribute to the avant-garde yet timeless house style.

Chanel's workshops are housed at La Chaux-de-Fonds, the birthplace of Swiss watchmaking. All stages of manufacturing take place there, from computer-assisted design to the final hand adjustments required for the mechanical watches. Its workshops have gained an excellent reputation in the manufacturing of bracelets. For the development of the J12, mastery of the newest technologies has enabled the use of innovative, highly resistant materials, such as high-tech ceramic and tungsten carbide.

All Chanel watches undergo numerous quality and water-resistance controls and are fitted with both a scratchproof sapphire crystal and a safety clasp. Each watch is numbered, equipped with a high-precision Swiss quartz movement and accompanied by a two-year international guarantee.

## WATCHES WITH A UNIQUE STYLE

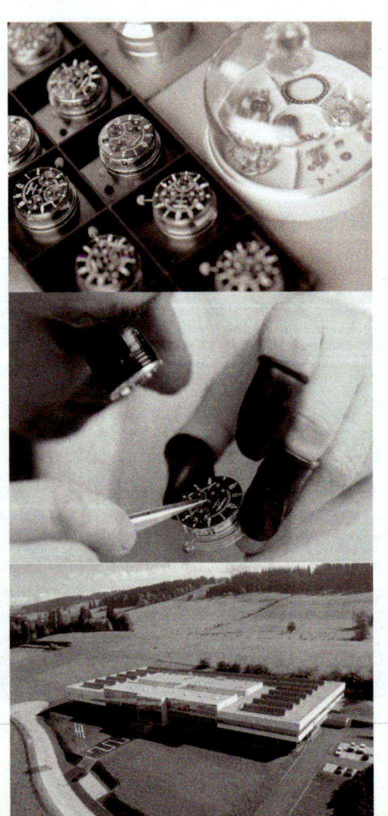

The Première model—or workshop number one—plays a key role in the world of Haute Couture. The octagon shape of the case is inspired by the design of the place Vendôme and the Chanel N°5 bottle and stopper. The chain bracelet, interwoven with leather strips, is a reminder of the famous metal and leather chains of the Chanel bags.

With its large square case, slender Roman numerals and its plain and uncluttered shape, the Mademoiselle line conveys a strong character in the spirit of the 1930s. With the change of a strap or bracelet, this watch becomes sophisticated with cultured pearls (designed as a tribute to Coco Chanel), classic with leather straps, or urban chic with metal bracelets.

The design of the Matelassée is inspired by one of Chanel's timeless designs—quilting—which still today adorns the most celebrated bags in the world.

The bracelet, comprised of links assembled entirely by hand and articulated on invisible axes, is a technical and aesthetic achievement: extremely comfortable to wear for a pure, sensual and feminine watch.

**ABOVE**
Jacques Helleu, Artistic Director of Chanel.

**LEFT**
Chanel workshops In La Chaux-de-Fonds.

## MADEMOISELLE CHANEL, AN AVANT-GARDE WOMAN

**1910** Gabrielle "Coco" Chanel first introduces herself as an avant-garde woman.

**1921** The fashion icon establishes her design house at 31, rue Cambon and launches her first perfume, N°5. From the sailor top to the famous quilted shoulder bag, in trousers, tweeds, and the little black dress, Coco Chanel has invented a new allure.

**1932** Coco Chanel designs a sumptuous exhibition of diamond jewelry that creates a sensation with their simplicity and originality. Most of them can be seen in the Chanel Fine Jewelry Boutiques, like the necklaces Comète and Fontaine.

**1955** Coco Chanel is awarded the Fashion Oscar in Dallas, honoring the "most influential designer of the 20th century."

The J12 sport watch for both men and women combines technological design and innovations. Its name is inspired by the world of yacht racing and its curves by a famous course car. The ceramic case is paired with a ceramic or rubber bracelet of 48 links for aeration and absolute comfort. It is equipped with a curved, ergonomic case and a patented automatic folding buckle. Produced in both black and white ceramic, the J12 is available in several versions encompassing classic to jeweled.

Firmly rooted in the Chanel universe, the Chocolat watch merges luxury with seduction and brings a breath of fresh air to the world of traditional watchmaking with the combination of watchmaking and fine jewelry. With avant-garde allure and a digital display specially designed for Chanel, it is available in steel, steel and diamonds, or white gold and diamonds.

Two new collections of jewelry watches, Camelia and 1932, are inspired by Coco Chanel herself. The Camelia collection, which symbolizes purity, is adorned with diamonds and blue sapphires. It was Coco Chanel's favorite flower. The 1932 collection is inspired by the Art Deco spirit, an alliance of structure and femininity. 1932 is available in different models, all paved with white and black diamonds.

**ABOVE**
Coco Chanel.

**RIGHT**
New release of the Comete brooch in platinum and diamonds, originally created by Coco Chanel in 1932.

## J12 — REF. H0685

**Movement:** Swiss automatic.
**Functions:** hours, minutes, seconds; date.
**Case:** Ø 38mm; black scratchproof high-tech ceramic; water resistant to 20atm.
**Dial:** lacquered black; raised numbered indexes.
**Bracelet:** black high-tech ceramic; triple-folding buckle; adjustable standard size.
**Also available:** leather or rubber strap.

## J12 DIAMONDS — REF. H0950

**Movement:** Swiss automatic.
**Functions:** hours, minutes, seconds; date.
**Case:** Ø 38mm; black high-tech ceramic; bezel set with white diamonds F/G VVS (1.5 carats); water resistant to 20atm.
**Dial:** lacquered black; raised numbered indexes.
**Bracelet:** black high-tech ceramic; triple-folding buckle; adjustable standard size.
**Also available:** bezel set with black diamonds.

## J12 CHRONOGRAPH — REF. H0939

**Movement:** Swiss automatic; COSC certified.
**Functions:** hours, minutes, seconds; date; chronograph.
**Case:** Ø 41mm; black scratchproof high-tech ceramic; water resistant to 20atm.
**Dial:** lacquered black; raised numbered indexes.
**Strap:** black rubber; triple-folding buckle; adjustable standard size.
**Also available:** leather strap or high-tech ceramic bracelet.

## J12 LIMITED EDITION — REF. H1461

**Movement:** Swiss automatic; COSC certified
**Functions:** hours, minutes, seconds; date; chronograph.
**Case:** Ø 41mm; black scratchproof high-tech ceramic and white gold set with baguette-cut rubies (5.40 carats); water resistant to 20atm.
**Dial:** lacquered black; set with white diamonds F/G VVS (0.07 carat).
**Bracelet:** black high-tech ceramic; triple white-gold folding buckle; adjustable standard size.
**Also available:** bezel set with baguette-cut blue sapphires, baguette-cut emeralds, or baguette-cut white diamonds.
**Note:** limited edition of 12 pieces (only upon request).

## J12 REF. H0970

**Movement:** Swiss automatic.
**Functions:** hours, minutes, seconds; date.
**Case:** Ø 38mm; white scratchproof high-tech ceramic; water resistant to 20atm.
**Dial:** lacquered white; raised numbered indexes.
**Bracelet:** white high-tech ceramic; triple-folding buckle; adjustable standard size.
**Also available:** Ø 33mm (high-precision Swiss quartz movement).

## J12 CHRONOGRAPH REF. H1007

**Movement:** Swiss automatic; COSC certified.
**Functions:** hours, minutes, seconds; date; chronograph.
**Case:** Ø 41mm; white scratchproof high-tech ceramic; water resistant to 20atm.
**Dial:** lacquered white; raised numbered indexes.
**Bracelet:** white high-tech ceramic; triple-folding buckle; adjustable standard size.
**Also available:** bezel set with white diamonds.

## J12 DIAMONDS REF. H1422

**Movement:** Swiss automatic.
**Functions:** hours, minutes, seconds; date.
**Case:** Ø 38mm; white scratchproof high-tech ceramic; bezel set with white diamonds F/G VVS (1.5 carats); water resistant to 20atm.
**Dial:** lacquered white, raised numbered indexes.
**Bracelet:** white high-tech ceramic set with white diamonds F/G VVS (4.22 carats); triple-folding buckle; adjustable standard size.
**Also available:** Ø 33mm (high-precision Swiss quartz movement).

## J12 PINK SAPPHIRES REF. H1182

**Movement:** Swiss automatic.
**Functions:** hours, minutes, seconds; date.
**Case:** Ø 38mm; white scratchproof high-tech ceramic; bezel set with pink sapphires (3 carats); water resistant to 20atm.
**Dial:** lacquered white; raised numbered indexes.
**Bracelet:** white high-tech ceramic; triple-folding buckle; adjustable standard size.
**Also available:** Ø 33mm (high-precision Swiss quartz movement); Ø 33mm and Ø 38mm bezel set with blue sapphires.

## PREMIÈRE REF. H0451

**Movement:** high-precision Swiss quartz.
**Functions:** hours, minutes.
**Case:** Ø 20mm; steel; water resistant to 3atm.
**Dial:** lacquered black.
**Bracelet:** steel chain interwoven with black leather; steel clasp; several sizes.

**Also available:** 18K 20-micron gold-plated; steel link bracelet.

## PREMIÈRE REF. H1639

**Movement:** high-precision Swiss quartz.
**Functions:** hours, minutes.
**Case:** Ø 20mm; steel; water resistant to 3atm.
**Dial:** mother of pearl.
**Bracelet:** steel chain interwoven with white rubber; steel clasp; several sizes.

**Also available:** steel link bracelet.

## MADEMOISELLE REF. H1168

**Movement:** high-precision Swiss quartz.
**Functions:** hours; minutes.
**Case:** Ø 22mm; steel; water resistant to 3atm.
**Dial:** lacquered white.
**Strap:** black alligator strap; standard buckle in steel; adjustable standard size.

**Also available:** beige alligator strap; steel bracelet.

## MATELASSÉE REF. H0009

**Movement:** high-precision Swiss quartz .
**Functions:** hours, minutes.
**Case:** Ø 19mm; steel; water resistant to 3atm.
**Dial:** lacquered black.
**Bracelet:** polished quilted steel; double-folding buckle in steel; adjustable standard size.

**Also available:** 18K gold on 18K polished-gold bracelet; steel on leather strap.

## CHOCOLAT REF. H0935

**Movement:** high-precision Swiss quartz.
**Functions:** hours, minutes.
**Case:** 18K white-gold case, pavé-set with white diamonds F/G VVS (0.75 carat); water resistant to 3atm.
**Dial:** digital display.
**Bracelet:** 18K white-gold bracelet, pavé-set with diamonds F/G VVS (2.97 carats), fully articulated; triple-folding buckle in white gold; adjustable standard size.
**Also available:** steel; steel with 4 pavé-set squares with diamonds; yellow gold.

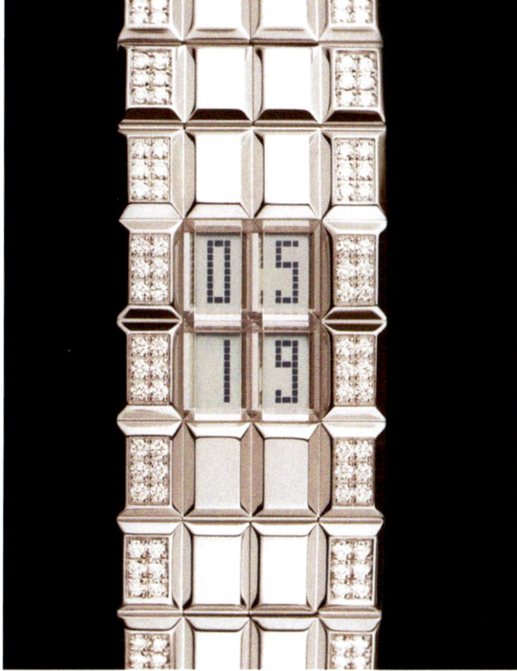


## MADEMOISELLE PERLES REF. H1434

**Movement:** high-precision Swiss quartz.
**Functions:** hours, minutes.
**Case:** Ø 22mm; white gold; water resistant to 3atm.
**Dial:** pavé-set with white diamonds F/G VVS (0.75 carat).
**Bracelet:** white gold; several sizes.
**Also available:** yellow gold with Roman numerals.

## CAMÉLIA REF. H1186

**Movement:** high-precision Swiss quartz.
**Functions:** hours, minutes.
**Case:** white gold; petals set with blue sapphires (2.6 carats) and white diamonds F/G VVS (0.9 carat); water resistant to 3atm.
**Dial:** mother of pearl with 4 diamonds F/G VVS indicators.
**Strap:** lavender-blue satin strap; white-gold buckle; adjustable standard size.
**Also available:** pavé-set petals with blue sapphires and pavé-set dial with diamonds; petals with diamonds and mother-of-pearl dial; or petals with diamonds and pavé-set dial with diamonds.

## 1932 REF. H1183

**Movement:** high-precision Swiss quartz.
**Functions:** hours, minutes.
**Case:** white gold; 3 sections set with white diamonds F/G VVS (0.7 carat); water resistant to 3atm.
**Dial:** lacquered black; 4 white diamond indicators.
**Strap:** black satin strap; white-gold buckle; adjustable standard size.
**Also available:** pavé-set dial with white diamonds and 3 sections set with black diamonds; bezel set with white diamonds and mother-of-pearl dial.

# CHARLES OUDIN PARIS

Once chronometer-maker to the French navy and watch-maker by appointment to the leading dynasties of 19th century Europe, Charles Oudin rediscovers a glorious past in a very Parisian collection of jewelry watches.

THIS PAGE

The Amazone is an 18-karat white-gold Curvex, framed by set diamonds, rubies, sapphires and emeralds. The watch houses a Swiss mechanical, manual-winding or quartz movement and is also available in pink or yellow gold, with other gems and different straps.

FACING PAGE

*from left to right*

Retro 506

Retro 504

Retro 509

In the early years of the 19th century, elegant ladies visited Charles Oudin's workshop in the garden of Palais Royal, where they were sure to see the latest styles of perpetually changing fashions.

As a watchmaker and jeweler, Oudin drew his inspiration from the gardens of the Palais Royal, and the brand retains a deep-rooted attachment to this historical place and its culture, as evidenced in the its collections. Today, in the place Vendôme, the Charles Oudin brand adorns its watches with innovative and original designs, characterized by floral designs that develop and change with the seasons.

The collection subtly weaves an aesthetic link between the past and the present, their typic ally Parisian nature giving Charles Oudin timepieces an instantly recognizable style. Although inspired by the classic creations of the past, the bold originality of their manufacture makes them resolutely contemporary.

Charles Oudin
PARIS
Charles Oudin
PARIS
Charles Oudin
PARIS
CHARLES OUDIN
PARIS

The pure and structured lines of the Falcon model recall the celebrated Buren pillars of the Palais-Royal forecourt, while the Floral collection evokes the magnificent gardens, and the hand-engraved collection the architectural features of the building.

Nature has inspired the settings of the most precious gemstones—sapphires, rubies, emeralds and diamonds—that adorn time with outstanding elegance.

The distinctive style of Charles Oudin is the floral settings of the Amazone model, which has become a glamorous classic.

**TOP**

White-gold Brancard set entirely with diamonds.

**BOTTOM LEFT**

This white-gold Baguette is trimmed with diamonds.

**BOTTOM RIGHT**

The Falcons are 18-karat gold, framed by set diamonds and house Swiss quartz movements. Baguette Falcons are available in two different sizes.

THIS PAGE

TOP LEFT

Princess watch.

RIGHT

*from top to bottom*

Renaissance Noire

Star

Renaissance Grise.

BOTTOM

Tropical watch.

FOLLOWING PAGE

The Full Diamond Curvex Couple is available in two sizes. The 18-karat gold watches are framed by set diamonds and powered by Swiss quartz movements.

BOTTOM

Zellige is an 18-karat white-gold Curvex, engraved by hand and set with diamonds and rubies.

OPPOSITE TO FOLLOWING PAGE

TOP

JET rubis is an 18-karat white-gold Curvex, set with diamonds and rubies.

BOTTOM

This 18-karat pink-gold Oudin Street is framed with set pink rubies. The words Oudin and Paris are displayed in emeralds and diamonds, respectively, and the strap is made of pink satin. The Oudin Street is also available in yellow or white gold, with other gems and different straps. Charles Oudin is able to set a personalized name upon request.

Charles Oudin's men's and ladies' models are made exclusively in gold and platinum, and often set with precious stones. The extensive choice of floral decors and the infinite possibilities of gem combinations allow the creation of one-of-a-kind pieces as well as confidential series. The most recent creations, hand-engraved and delicately set with precious stones, exemplify the superb workmanship and creative design that characterize this watchmaker and jeweler.

# Charles Oudin PARIS

These timepieces are designed and created entirely in Paris by artists and craftsmen of considerable talent. Charles Oudin watches express the fashion-transcending quality that contributes to their enduring value.

In Paris, it is only at 8 Place Vendôme that the lady of fashion can, by appointment, realize her dream of time made to order.

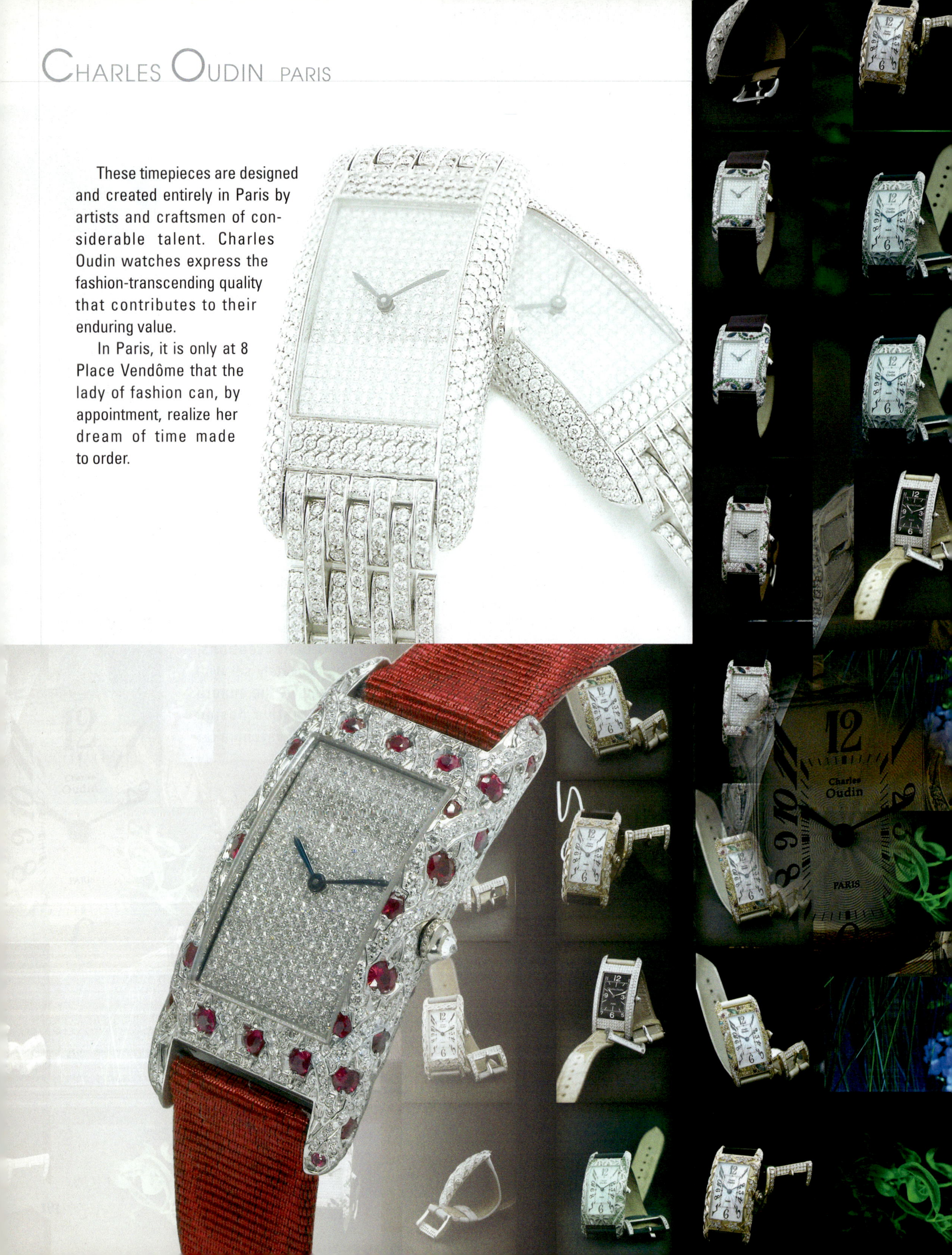

## CHRONOLOGY

**1790** At age 18, Charles Oudin becomes a pupil of legendary watchmaker Abraham-Louis Breguet.

**1804** Oudin establishes his own workshops at 52 Palais Royal.

**1805** Already popular with Europe's royal families, Oudin creates a repeater watch for Empress Josephine.

**1806** Oudin is awarded an honorable mention at the Paris Exhibition for a self-winding watch with moonphase.

**1819** At the Paris Exhibition, Oudin receives a citation for an equation-of-time watch.

**1840** A miniature Six Pence watch is presented to Queen Victoria by the company.

**1859** The brand unveils its first Crucifix watches.

**1860** The company becomes watchmaker to the Pope and introduces its first world-time watches.

**1862** At the Universal Exhibition in London, Charles Oudin presents a gold-and-crystal timepiece with quarter repeater. A Crucifix watch is crafted for the Pope.

**1863** A mourning watch is made for the Empress of Russia, and ivory watches with lever escapements are made for Italian and Greek royalty.

**1867** A mantle regulator is designed and created for Napoleon III.

**1920s** Charles Oudin presents its first collection of wristwatches in gold and platinum.

**1998** Launching of a new Charles Oudin collection.

# CHAUMET

Chaumet draws its creative force from a fertile imagination and pays tribute to beauty.

Inspired by nature, Frisson—the new high-jewelry collection from Chaumet—reflects the firm's heritage and is expressed through the fine details and refined lines for which Chaumet is famous.

Frisson evokes that instant, fragile moment when time and all things turn to the dawn of a new day just as nature drops its winter dew, its sparkling frost.

From the traditional brilliant, pear, baguette and princess cuts to the oldest rose, briolette and cushion cuts, Chaumet has audaciously espoused the mirror cut of a rough diamond for its mysterious reflections.

ABOVE

This Dentelle de Givre watch in white gold features a white mother-of-pearl dial, brilliant-, princess- and baguette-cut diamonds and a gray satin strap.

BOTTOM

The Dentelle de Givre watch is crafted in 18-karat white gold and set with diamonds. It features a gray mother-of-pearl dial and gray satin bracelet with pavé buckle.

PREVIOUS PAGE

From the Frisson collection, the Dentelle de Givre earrings sparkle with 9 carats of diamonds and the three "dew-drop" bracelet shimmers with 24 carats. These white-gold pieces feature different cuts of diamonds: brilliant, baguette, princess, rose and briolette.

Dandy, a watch and jewelry collection for men, evokes the contemporary and eternal dandy style. This collection is composed of rings, cufflinks, shirt studs and wristwatches in steel, yellow gold or pink gold. There is also a steel pocket watch.

Dandy reveals the essence of dapper style: a striped pattern, black taffeta and satin strap, shirt-stud clasp, extra-flat case with taut lines, a manually wound mechanical movement. The design displays attention to every detail, including luminescent gilded hands and extremities of the indicators, and a grooved crown with an onyx cabochon. For daytime, the Dandy watch can be worn with an alligator strap with extra-flat buckle.

For 2005, Chaumet proposes new jeweled Dandy models in white gold with brilliant- or baguette-cut diamonds, black dial with diamond striped patterns and index diamonds, or with an aventurine glass dial from Murano, Italy. Cufflinks are available in white gold, with diamonds and onyx.

THIS PAGE

LEFT

Pink-gold Dandy watch, black bayadere striped dial, silk taffeta and satin strap, pink-gold and onyx button clasp, manual-winding mechanical movement.

## CHRONOLOGY

**1780** The future house of Chaumet is founded by Marie-Etienne Nitot, who sets up shop in Paris and quickly becomes the official jeweler to Emperor Napoleon I. From tiaras to swords, this magnificent jeweler deftly combines the world's finest gems with creative designs.

**1875** Joseph Chaumet marries the daughter of the head this prestigious jewelry house. With foresight, he officially registers the brand's name as Chaumet and takes the house to new heights with his distinct style.

**Late 1800s-Early 1900s** Chaumet leads the world with its Art Nouveau designs of flora and fauna. With the transition into the Art Deco period, Chaumet makes even greater strides and leads with its geometric wonders. Indeed, Chaumet is destined to remain a leader in designs of every epoch and era henceforth.

**1995** The brand launches into the world of timepieces, unveiling Khésis—a deliciously feminine cuff watch.

**1998** Chaumet offers innovative style with its Class One diving watch, featuring a bold combination of sport and glamour. The collection blends diamonds, steel and rubber.

**2003** Chaumet launches a new watch and jewelry collection for men. Complete with wristwatches, a pocket watch, cuff links and ring, the Dandy collection reveals a universe of charisma, sophistication and contemporary spirit for men.

**2004** Chaumet enriches the Dandy collection with jewelry models and launches a collection of jewelry watches called the Liens—already an icon in the jewelry line.

ABOVE

The Liens de Chaumet watch in yellow gold and pavé diamonds with a simple crosstie, black satin bracelet with white dial.

RIGHT

The Liens de Chaumet watch in white gold: one link, one carat. Very contemporary with a hint of vintage; a nighttime beauty that underscores the elegance of each feature.

FAR RIGHT

The Liens de Chaumet watch in white gold: two links, 1.2 carats. Very high fashion with a nod to the corset, but dedicated to the blue-jean cult.

Lovers' links, family links, a hyphen between past and present: interpretations succeed and superimpose each other as they intertwine and cross on rings, bracelets and pendants.

The Liens de Chaumet now presents its first collection of jewelry watches.

An evening watch in white or yellow gold with pavé diamonds that borrows the codes of the single link and the crossed link. Dressed for the occasion with a black satin strap that extends and blends into the graphic dial and is illuminated by the case and link set with diamonds.

A perfect curve, strong shapes, asymmetrical lines, buckle completely pavé set with diamonds—all the details that escape from the ephemeral. The dial has just one numeral (12) as a reference to the brand's headquarters at 12 place Vendôme.

# CHOPARD

Throughout the past 100 years, the Scheufele family has brought its talents, ambition, creativity and passion to the world of watches and jewelry—culminating in a wealth of the most beautiful, technically advanced pieces.

Year after year, this brand delights collectors and watch lovers around the world with its scintillating creations. A family-owned business, Chopard's roots date back to 1904 when Karl Scheufele I founded his jewelry business in Pforzheim. Karl Scheufele II reintroduced the Eszeha brand in 1948, and 15 years later, his son—Karl Scheufele III—purchased the Chopard brand. The family members all turned their sights to creating an internationally famous watch and jewelry company—something they have achieved with grand consequence.

Today Chopard is arguably one of the foremost innovative designers of luxury jewelry and watches. In the brand's manufacture, all jewelry and watchmaking is executed by a team of artisans. From melting the gold, to making the mold, setting the stones and creating the complicated watch movements, everything is done inhouse.

Among the new timepieces in the impressive men's collections is the Anniversary watch created to celebrate the Chopard/Eszeha jubilee. Inspired by an Eszeha gent's watch from the 1940s and equipped with a L.U.C proprietary movement, this watch carries the name Eszeha on the dial as a reminder of the Karl Scheufele Company's origins, and is created in a limited edition of 400 pieces.

In keeping with the vintage feeling, Chopard also unveils the Mille Miglia Vintage watch. A thoroughbred chronograph, the design is inspired by the styles of the 1950s and 1960s but contemporary in execution due to its 41mm diameter. The chronograph is equipped with the Lemania 1874 mechanical hand-wound movement and features a 30-minute counter, a 12-hour counter and an independent small second hand. The dial, available in silver or black, features a tachometer scale on the outer circle to read speeds, and a pulsimeter scale on the inner circle. The watch is available only in 18-karat rose gold in a series of 250 pieces.

In its alluring L.U.C collection, Chopard releases the stunning 4R Quattro Regulateur watch. Crafted in 18-karat rose gold or white gold, the watch houses the L.U.C mechanical hand-wound movement with 224 parts and 39 jewels. Offering nine days of power reserve, the COSC-certified chronometer offers time-zone indicator and semi-instantaneous date display.

The L.U.C Quattro Regulateur was declared Watch of the Year 2004 by the Swiss magazines *Montres Passion* and *Uhrenwelt* for its visual elegance and sophisticated movement.

THIS PAGE

ABOVE

The new Mille Miglia Vintage chronograph.

BOTTOM

Named for the Scheufele family's first jewelry business, the Eszeha features a L.U.C movement.

FACING PAGE

The multi-complication L.U.C 4R Quattro Regulateur is a COSC-certified chronometer and available in yellow or white gold.

CHRONOMETRE

# CHOPARD

Chopard does exquisite gem and diamond setting in its high-jeweled watch and jewelry collections and is internationally known for its innovative designs. Among the newest high-jeweled watches are a stunning pair of exceptional all-diamond-baguette Haute Joaillerie watches crafted in 18-karat white gold and set with 41 or 51 carats of diamonds depending on the size of the watch.

Similarly, in homage to women, Chopard offers deliciously feminine Haute Joaillerie jewelry. Designed by Caroline Gruosi-Scheufele, the newest jewelry pieces illuminate the shimmer of the earth and the beauty of the woman. The Haute Joaillerie necklace of more than 200 diamonds and multicolored sapphire briolettes is at once alluring and breathtaking, as is a series of hoop earrings totally ensconced in more than a thousand brilliant of either diamonds, rubies or sapphires.

ABOVE

Eva Herzigova wears Chopard.

LEFT

The Haute Joaillerie watches are set with 51 carats of baguette diamonds for the larger watch and 41 carats of baguette diamonds for the slightly smaller version.

BOTTOM RIGHT

Eva Herzigova with Happy Spirit Collection.

## CHRONOLOGY

**1860** Louis-Ulysse Chopard founds a high-precision watchmaking manufactory (specializing in pocket watches and chronometers) in Sonvilier, in the Swiss Jura.

**1920** Chopard relocates to Geneva and launches into the production of luxury watches.

**1963** Karl Scheufele takes over Chopard. Representing the third generation of a family of jewelers, he owns the German firm Eszeha, founded in 1904 and specializing in watches and jewelry.

**1976** Creation of the first Happy Diamonds watch with mobile diamonds spinning freely between two sapphire discs on the dial.

**1983** The first Chopard boutique in Asia opens in Hong Kong.

**1986** The first Chopard boutique in Europe opens in Geneva, followed a few years later by another in Vienna.

**1988** Start of the partnership between Chopard and the famous Mille Miglia vintage car race held each year in Italy. Chopard creates the Mille Miglia watch.

**1996** The company returns to its origins by founding a watch manufacture in the Swiss Jura, dedicated to crafting the L.U.C movements.

**1997** The first L.U.C 1860 watch fitted with Caliber 1.96 is voted Watch of the Year by the Swiss magazine Montre Passion/Uhrenwelt.

**1998** Chopard becomes official partner to the International Film Festival held each year in Cannes.

**2000** Premiere of the L.U.C Quattro watch equipped with Caliber 1.98 at the Basel watch and jewelry show. This new movement, fitted with 4 barrels (2 x 2 stacked barrels) can achieve a power reserve of more than 9 days.

**2001** Presentation of the L.U.C Tonneau 3.97 model at the Basel show. Representing a major technological feat, its shaped self-winding movement with off-centered microrotor is perfectly adjusted to the shape of the case.

**2002** Chopard unveils the Golden Diamonds concept of faceted gold as the center stone of jewelry and watches.

**2003** Presentation of the Tourbillon watch at the Basel show. This new L.U.C manufacture-crafted watch represents a new technological accomplishment.

**2004** Chopard's L.U.C Quattro Regulateur is voted Watch of the Year 2004 by judges appointed by *Montres Passion* and *Uhrenwelt* magazines.

TOP LEFT

This stunning Butterfly Collection features diamonds and multicolored sapphires.

CENTER

This Haute Joaillerie Pampille necklace is crafted in 18-karat white gold and set with more than 2,000 sapphire briolettes and diamonds.

## L.U.C QUATTRO — REF. 16/1863

**Movement:** mechanical manual-winding L.U.C 1.98 caliber produced in Chopard's workshops at Fleurier; mounted, decorated and finished by hand with the Côtes de Genève pattern and beveled; COSC-certified chronometer; Poinçon de Genève quality hallmark.
**Functions:** hour, minute, small seconds; date; power reserve.
**Case:** 18K pink-gold three-piece case (Ø 38mm, thickness: 9.6mm); curved sapphire crystal; pink-gold crown; transparent sapphire crystal caseback attached by 8 screws, displaying movement; water resistant to 3atm.

**Dial:** silvered; center guillochéd with sun pattern; brushed hour ring; zone decorated with circular beads; applied faceted pink-gold pointed markers; printed minute track; pink-gold Dauphine-style hands.
**Indications:** date and small seconds at 6; power-reserve indicator at 12.
**Strap:** crocodile leather; pink-gold clasp.
**Also available:** white gold (same price); yellow gold; platinum. All versions available with black, blue or silvered dial.

## L.U.C TONNEAU 6.96 — REF. 16/2267

**Movement:** automatic tonneau-shaped L.U.C 6.96 caliber produced in Chopard's workshops at Fleurier; mounted and finished entirely by hand; bridges decorated with Côtes de Genève pattern; COSC-certified chronometer.
**Functions:** hour, minute, small seconds; date.
**Case:** 18K white-gold three-piece case, ergonomically curved (size: 38.5x40mm, thickness: 10mm); curved sapphire crystal; white-gold crown; transparent sapphire crystal caseback attached by 8 screws, displaying the movement; water resistant to 3atm.

**Dial:** black; center guillochéd with sun pattern; brushed hour ring; applied faceted white-gold pointed markers; printed railway minute track; white-gold Dauphine-style hands.
**Indications:** date and small seconds at 6.
**Strap:** crocodile leather; white-gold clasp.
**Note:** limited edition of 1860 pieces, dedicated to Louis-Ulysse Chopard who founded the firm in that year.
**Also available:** silvered dial; pink or yellow gold.

## L.U.C 1.96 — REF. 16/1860/2

**Movement:** mechanical automatic-winding L.U.C 1.96 caliber produced in Chopard's workshops at Fleurier; mounted and finished entirely by hand with the Côtes de Genève pattern; Poinçon de Genève quality hallmark.
**Functions:** hour, minute, small seconds; date.
**Case:** 18K pink-gold three-piece case (Ø 36mm, thickness: 8mm); curved sapphire crystal; pink-gold crown; transparent sapphire crystal caseback attached by 8 screws, displaying movement; water resistant to 3atm.

**Dial:** silvered gold; center guillochéd; brushed hour ring; applied pink-gold pointed markers; printed minute track; pink-gold Dauphine-style hands.
**Indications:** date and small seconds at 6.
**Strap:** crocodile leather; pink-gold clasp.
**Note:** numbered edition of 1860 pieces, dedicated to Louis-Ulysse Chopard who founded the firm in that year.
**Also available:** with black dial; in white gold with silvered, black, gilded, or coppered dial (same price); in yellow gold with black or silvered dial; in platinum with silvered, black, gilded, or coppered dial. With L.U.C 3.96 movement (without Geneva Seal): white or coppered dial and silvered zone 1860 pieces; in white or pink gold; in yellow gold.

## L.U.C 4R QUATTRO REGULATEUR — REF. 16/1874

**Movement:** mechanical manual-winding L.U.C 4R caliber produced in Chopard's workshops at Fleurier; equipped with 4 barrels (2 sets of 2 stacked); L.U.C Quattro technology; bridges decorated with straight line Côtes de Genève pattern; COSC-certified chronometer; Poinçon de Genève quality hallmark.
**Functions:** hour, minute, small seconds; date; power reserve; 24 hour.
**Case:** 18K white-gold three-piece case (Ø 39.5mm, thickness: 10mm); antireflective curved sapphire crystal; white-gold crown; transparent sapphire crystal caseback; water resistant to 3atm.

**Dial:** guilloché gold dial; applied hour markers; gold hour, minute and small seconds hands.
**Indications:** off-center hour at 3 with printed Arabic numerals; center minutes; small seconds and semi-instantaneous date at 6; second time zone; 24-hour at 9; power reserve at 12.
**Strap:** hand-stitched crocodile leather; white-gold clasp.
**Note:** limited edition of 250 numbered pieces.
**Also available:** 18K yellow gold.

## L.U.C 4T QUATTRO TOURBILLON REF. 16/1869

**Movement:** mechanical manual-winding L.U.C 1.02 caliber with Tourbillon, produced in Chopard's Fleurier workshops; mounted, decorated, and finished by hand; COSC certified; Poinçon de Genève quality hallmark.
**Functions:** hour, minute; power reserve.
**Case:** 18K pink-gold case and crown; caseback fitted with sapphire crystal displaying the movement.
**Dial:** silvered 18K gold; gold hour and minute hands.
**Indications:** "One-minute" tourbillon at 6 with blued-steel seconds hand; gold power-reserve indicator at 12.
**Strap:** hand-stitched crocodile leather, brown or black; fitted with a gold or platinum folding-clasp.
**Also available:** with black dial; two limited series: 100 pieces in 18K pink gold, 100 pieces in platinum.

## L.U.C 4T QUATTRO TOURBILLON (BACK) REF. 16/1869

The L.U.C 4T Quattro Tourbillon is equipped with the 1.02 caliber tourbillon. The mechanical hand-wound movement with 4 barrels (L.U.C Quattro technology) ensures 9 days of power reserve. The adjustment of daily rating is ensured by the rotation of small inertia blocks on a Variner-type balance, for which a patent is pending.

## L.U.C PRO ONE REF. 16/8912

**Movement:** mechanical automatic-winding L.U.C 4.96 caliber produced by Chopard's Fleurier workshops; mounted and finished entirely by hand; COSC certified.
**Functions:** hour, minute, second; date.
**Case:** stainless steel three-piece case, polished and brushed (Ø 42mm, thickness: 13.3mm); counterclockwise-turning brushed and knurled ring with graduated scale, luminescent pointers and polished raised chapters; screw-on crown with case protection; screw-on back with raised rose; water resistant to 30atm.
**Dial:** silvered, brushed; center decorated with a raised wave pattern; hour ring decorated with circular beads; luminescent applied rhodium-plated brass lonzenge markers; printed minute track with 5-minute divisions on the flange; luminescent rhodium-plated brass sport-style hands.
**Indications:** date at 4:30.
**Strap:** rubber with raised wave pattern; steel clasp.
**Also available:** with blue or black dial.

## L.U.C PRO ONE REF. 16/8912/1

**Movement:** mechanical automatic-winding L.U.C 4.96 caliber produced by Chopard's Fleurier workshops; mounted and finished by hand; COSC certified.
**Functions:** hour, minute, second; date.
**Case:** stainless steel; counterclockwise-turning brushed graduated scale and luminescent pointers; screw-on crown with case protection; water resistant to 30atm.
**Dial:** black, brushed; center decorated with a raised wave pattern; orange luminescent markers; orange luminescent sport-style hands.
**Indications:** date at 4:30.
**Strap:** black leather.

## DUAL TEC REF. 16/2274

**Movement:** mechanical automatic-winding for main time; quartz movement for second time zone.
**Functions:** hour, minute; second time zone.
**Case:** solid pink-gold two-piece case in rectangular shape with ergonomic curve.
**Dial:** silvered dial highlighted by a sunburst guilloché pattern and transferred hour circle with printed Roman numerals; sword-style hands in pink gold, luminescent for the main time.
**Indications:** main time at 12; second time zone at 6.
**Strap:** hand-stitched crocodile leather; pink-gold clasp.
**Also available:** 18K white gold.

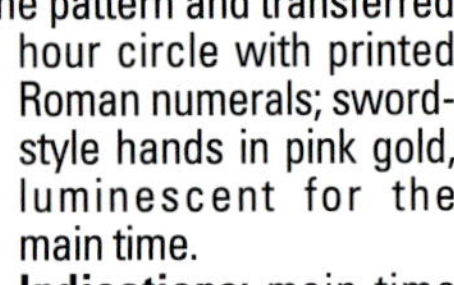

## MILLE MIGLIA RACING COLORS REF. 16/8915/101

**Movement:** ETA 2892A2, self-winding in both directions; 40-hour power reserve; COSC certified.
**Functions:** hour, minute, small second; date; chronograph with 3 counters.
**Case:** titanium.
**Dial:** colors of nations competing in classic and vintage car races: Red/Italy; Green/England; Gray/Germany; Yellow/Belgium. Luminescent Arabic numerals in Super-LumiNova.
**Indications:** date; tachometric scale.
**Strap:** leather.
**Note:** limited series of 1,000 per dial color.

## CHRONOGRAPH "ELTON JOHN" REF. 17/8331/13-20

**Movement:** mechanical automatic-winding ETA 2892A2 caliber + Dubois Dépraz chronograph module; 42 hours' power reserve; COSC-certified chronometer.
**Functions:** hour, minute, small second; date; chronograph with 3 counters.
**Case:** stainless steel three-piece case (Ø 39.85mm, thickness: 12mm); white-gold bezel with a row of set brilliants; curved sapphire crystal, antireflective on both sides; back with Elton John's engraved signature; water resistant to 5atm.
**Dial:** blue mother-of-pearl; silvered hour ring; silvered subdials decorated with circular beads; blue outer ring; black engraved Arabic numerals; luminescent bâton hands in rhodium-plated brass.
**Indications:** small seconds at 3; date at 4:30; hours at 6; minutes at 9; center second counter; minute track with divisions for 1/4 second.
**Strap:** hand-stitched crocodile leather; steel clasp.
**Note:** limited edition of 2,000 pieces; available only in Chopard boutiques.
**Also available:** without brilliants.

## CHRONOGRAPH MILLE MIGLIA GMT 2004 REF. 16/8954

**Movement:** manual-winding mechanism; 46 hours' power reserve; COSC-certified chronometer. **Functions:** hour, minute, small second; date; chronograph with 3 counters, second time zone; 24 hour. **Case:** stainless steel three-piece case (Ø 42.5mm, thickness: 14.9mm); curved sapphire crystal, antireflective on both sides, with a magnifying lens on the date; bezel with engraved 24-hour scale; back fastened by 8 screws, embossed with the race's symbol; water resistant to 5atm. **Dial:** matte black; subdials decorated with circular beads; luminescent bâton markers; luminescent bâton hands in rhodium-plated brass.
**Indications:** date at 3 (with a red arrow, a symbol for the race); 12-hour counter at 6; small seconds at 9; 30-minute counter at 12; center second counter and second time zone; 24-hour hand with luminescent arrow-tip; minute track with divisions for 1/4 second with a luminescent 5-minute graduation; tachometer scale on the flange.
**Strap:** black barennia leather with large holes; fold-over through steel safety clasp; furnished with a rubber strap (replicating a Dunlop Racing tire tread of the 1960s).
**Note:** limited edition of 2,004 numbered pieces.
**Also available:** in pink gold with leather strap, 250 pieces.

## IMPERIAL CHRONOGRAPH REF. 37/3168-23

**Movement:** mechanical with electric drive controlled by a quartz crystal; Frédéric Piguet 1270 caliber.
**Functions:** hour, minute, small second; date; chronograph with 3 counters.
**Case:** 18K white-gold four-piece case (Ø 37mm, thickness: 9mm); flat sapphire crystal; bezel and central attachment with brilliant-cut set diamonds (3.36 carats); brand and progressive number engraced on the left middle side; white-gold octagonal crown, pushers and lugs with sapphire cabochons; back attached by 8 screws; water resistant to 3atm.
**Dial:** white, silvered counters; applied round faceted markers, white-gold lozenge-style hands.
**Indications:** hour counter at 3; date at 4:30; small seconds at 6; minute counter at 9; center second chronograph counter; railway minute track with divisions for 1/5 of a second.
**Strap:** crocodile leather; central attachment with brilliants; white-gold clasp.
**Also available:** with sapphire cabochons in yellow, pink or white gold; with sapphire cabochons on bezel and central attachment Ref. 37/3168-23 in yellow or white gold; with ruby cabochons in yellow, pink or white gold.

## HAPPY SPORT CHRONOGRAPH REF. 28/8267-23

**Movement:** electromachanical; Frédéric Piguet 1270 caliber.
**Functions:** hour, minute, small second; date; chronograph with 3 counters.
**Case:** stainless steel three-piece case (Ø 38.5mm, thickness: 10.5mm); 7 Top Wesselton quality brilliants (totaling 0.39 carats) individually set and moving freely between 2 flat sapphire crystals; sapphire cabochons on crown, pushers and lugs; caseback attached by 8 screws; water resistant to 3atm.
**Dial:** white; silvered counters decorated with circular beads; printed Roman numerals; blued steel bâton-style hands.
**Indications:** hour counter at 3; date at 4:30; small seconds at 6; minute counter at 9; center second counter railway minute track.
**Bracelet:** steel; double fold-over clasp.
**Also available:** iolite cabochon; strap, bracelet; sapphire cab., strap; ruby cab., strap; ruby cab., mother-of-pearl dial, brac. Mother-of-pearl dial: yellow gold, sapphire cab., strap, brac.; yellow gold, ruby cab., strap, brac.; white gold, sapphire cab., strap; brac.; white gold, ruby cab., strap, brac. Bezel with brilliants: yellow gold, mother-of-pearl dial, sapphire cab., strap, brac.; white gold, sapphire cab., strap, brac. In other jeweled versions.

## ICE CUBE REF. 13/6858/42

**Movement:** mechanical automatic-winding ETA 2000 caliber.
**Functions:** hour, minute.
**Case:** 18K burnished white-gold two-piece case, ergonomically curved (size: 31.5x31.5mm, thickness: 8.54mm); studded entirely with square-cut pink sapphires; curved sapphire crystal; recessed burnished gold crown; curved caseback attached by 4 screws; water resistant to 3atm.
**Dial:** white gold; studded with brilliants; blued steel bâton-style hands.
**Strap:** pink satin; white-gold clasp.
**Also available:** with blue sapphires; entirely brilliant pavé; dial with black brilliants.

## LA STRADA REF. 41/6866/8

Presented in 1997, the La Strada collection consists of necklaces, bracelets, rings and earrings characterized by large elements in half-moon shapes and this theme has been carried over into the watch line from the same family. The La Strada timepieces, proposed in numerous combinations according to the subtle psychology of the feminine universe, have 2 case sizes while the movement can be manual—the Omega 730 old-time—or quartz.
The photograph shows the larger version (size: 39.5x32mm, thickness: 9.8mm) in 18K white gold with 3 rows of diamonds on bezel sides and a mother-of-pearl dial with a small seconds zone driven by a quartz movement.

# CLERC

With an immediately identifiable style, Clerc creates authentic Swiss watches with passion and precision.

**ABOVE**

This C-ONE stainless steel watch features a brown Teju lizard strap with steel folding clasp. Individually numbered. C1-L6.

**LEFT**

The CXX Diamond Scuba Chronograph (CXXD113Q) is a stunning version enhanced with diamonds.

**BELOW**

These ladies' C125 watches feature stainless steel bracelets set with at least 100 diamonds and house Swiss precision quartz movements. Individually numbered. C125/S1.

Heir to a longstanding family tradition passed down from one generation to the next, the Clerc brand has been cultivating exceptional watchmaking since 1874. For 130 years, the watches bearing this recognized signature have consistently been known for their unique designs and uncompromising Swiss craftsmanship.

The famed Geneva-based watchmaker-jeweler has always been skilled in capturing the spirit of the times, and has signed prestigious creations for important personalities and royalty. The powerful and distinctive new collections designed by Gérald Clerc reflect this legacy.

15
30
45
CLERC
GENÈVE
CXX
SCUBA
PROFESSIONAL 200 METERS
14
200 METERS
STAINLESS STEEL
N°0000
SWISS MADE

The C-ONE Collection's authentic, radiant and modern style is combined with a level of excellence and quality synonymous with Swiss prestige watchmaking. A perfect blend of style and craftsmanship, C-ONE watches are definitely in tune with their times. Fashioned and sculpted from solid steel and beautifully set with diamonds, C-ONE models are also stunning gem-set jewelry pieces. Crafted in Switzerland, each C-ONE is individually numbered and comes with a three-year international warranty.

PREVIOUS PAGE

The CXX Scuba Chronograph in stainless steel on rubber strap is water resistant to 200 meters and houses a Swiss precision quartz movement. Individually numbered. CXX110Q. (Also available with automatic movement.)

THIS PAGE

These ladies' C-ONE steel watches are set elegantly with diamonds. Individually numbered. C1D-SS2 (Pink), C1D-SS3 (Blue).

FACING PAGE

TOP LEFT

The officially certified C-Collection chronograph. 811.

TOP RIGHT

The 850 is a dual-time-zone watch with power-reserve indicator.

BOTTOM

The CXX Scuba Chronograph is crafted in steel with steel bracelet and houses a mechanical movement.

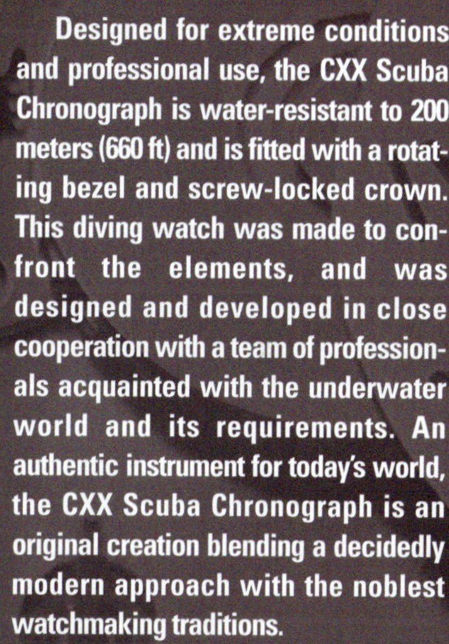

Designed for extreme conditions and professional use, the CXX Scuba Chronograph is water-resistant to 200 meters (660 ft) and is fitted with a rotating bezel and screw-locked crown. This diving watch was made to confront the elements, and was designed and developed in close cooperation with a team of professionals acquainted with the underwater world and its requirements. An authentic instrument for today's world, the CXX Scuba Chronograph is an original creation blending a decidedly modern approach with the noblest watchmaking traditions.

The CXX Scuba 250 Limited Edition Automatic Chronograph houses a mechanical self-winding movement with 25 jewels. The watch features a polished screwed-in steel case, graduated turning fine-brushed and beveled bezel, protective PVD guards around the winding-crown, screw-locked pushpieces and a glare-proof sapphire crystal.

Available on rubber strap or stainless steel bracelet, the CXX Scuba 250 Limited Edition Automatic Chronographs are individually numbered from 1 to 250 and come with three-year international warranties.

1

2

3

4
CLERC
GENÈVE
AUTOMATIC
SWISS MADE

5

6

7

8

FACING PAGE

*celebrities*

**1.** Houston Texans quarterback David Carr sports a CXX Scuba Chornograph on rblack rubber strap.

**2.** Gérald Clerc with an NFL player sporting a Clerc timepiece.

**3.** Swimsuit model Petra Novikova sports a CXX Diamond Chronograph with black dial and strap.

**4.** Gérald Clerc with Leeann Tweeden, host of *Best Damn Sports Show Period*, who is wearing the CXX Diamond Chronograph.

**5.** Kelly Rowland of Destiny's Child is wearing a CXX Diamond Chronograph white dial and strap.

**6.** A member of the NFL dons the Clerc CXX Scuba with PVD black bezel on rubber strap.

**7.** Supermodel Niki Taylor with a CXX Scuba Chronograph with black PVD bezel and rubber strap.

**8.** Actress Holly Robinson Peete poses with a C-One Diamond watch, pink dial and strap.

BOTTOM LEFT

This ladies' 18-karat gold jewelry watch with diamonds and sapphires features an automatic movement, and the Cie de Genève quality hallmark.

THISPAGE

CENTER

Gérald Clerc oversees every aspect of design and development.

RIGHT

This black-dialed CXX Diamond Chronograph is on a black rubber strap. It houses a Swiss precision quartz movement and is individually numbered. CXXD110Q.

## CHRONOLOGY

**1874** The Clerc family establishes itself as a watchmaker and jeweler.

**Early 1900s** Clerc creates watches of the utmost elegance and performance. The company is known for its avant-garde designs.

**1920s** As wristwatches gain in popularity, Clerc rises to the challenge of creating distinctive precious-stone wristwatches.

**1940s-1980s** Clerc develops a host of classic and stylistic watches of each era. Indeed, throughout its history Clerc has been associated with celebrities and crowned heads such as Princess Grace of Monaco, General Charles de Gaulle, Nikita Khrushchev, Maurice Chevalier and a host of others.

**1998** Fourth-generation designer Gerald Clerc signs his first collection of timepieces called the C-Collection. The brand also garners the much-coveted Cie de Genève quality hallmark. Clerc watches are quickly sported by such celebrities as Jack Scalia, Michael Douglas and Ewan McGregor.

**1999** As a world premiere, Clerc launches the Red, White and Blue series of steel watches set with rubies, sapphires and diamonds.

**2003** Clerc pre-launches the CXX Scuba Chronograph collection of bold diving watches.

# CONCORD

For nearly a century, Concord has been creating timepieces of exceptional design, sophistication, elegance and acclaimed technology.

This is a brand that historically creates timeless designs that epitomize contemporary luxury. In 1979, Concord released the ingenious Delirium®, renowned as the thinnest watch in the world. Today, in celebration of this remarkable breakthrough in watch design, Concord introduces the new Delirium® series.

One of Concord's most innovative designs, the new Delirium® collection includes elegantly thin, ergonomically curved, rectangular cased models crafted in solid 18-karat gold. While paying homage to its predecessors, the new collection is distinguished by a bolder bracelet design and new variations on the signature Delirium® dish dial. The case, which angles to a beautifully thin edge in tribute to the groundbreaking thinness of the original Delirium, is exquisitely sculpted and offered in an array of diamond settings. For men, there is the limited edition Delirium® Reserve de Marche—created in just 50 pieces: 25 in rose and 25 in white gold. The watch houses a mechanical hand-winding movement with calendar function and 42 hours of power reserve. Several other important versions exist, including a breathtaking high-jeweled style for men and women.

THIS PAGE

ABOVE

The Delirium® is stunning. The larger watch features 230 diamond brilliants and baguettes. The smaller watch is set wth 232 brilliants and baguettes.

BOTTOM

The Delirium®.

FACING PAGE

This Delirium® Reserve de Marche features a calendar subdial and power-reserve readout.

CONCORD
Delirium
RESERVE DE MARCHE
SWISS MADE

The vintage-inspired Soirée collection captures the spirit of the Concord brand with style, elegance and sophistication. Delicate oval, rectangular, and tonneau-shaped cases are set with sparkling diamonds. A single cubed diamond strand bracelet or an 18K white gold rope lariat bracelet completes the delicate look. One style is offered as a set with a special Judith Leiber bag to complement ladies' evening attire.

Adding to its stunning La Scala™ collection, Concord offers new Art Deco styles. Blending timeless aesthetics and superb craftsmanship, the Concord La Scala™ Tonneau Horizontal is a sophisticated, 18-karat rose-gold horizontal timepiece of retro inspiration. It is offered with a diamond-accented case featuring either 24 or 54 diamonds. There is also a striking version with 126 diamonds on the dial.

The more traditional La Scala™ Tonneau is a vertical tonneau offered with a multifunction chronograph movement for men and in two diamond settings for women: one with 12 diamonds on the bracelet attachments and one that is fully set with 42 diamonds. New versions of the classic La Scala™ round watch are added as well.

In its masterfully engineered Saratoga® line, the brand offers a 36mm chronograph with a bracelet of polished and matte steel links and Concord's patented latched crown protector. In one version, the hallmark of this particular Saratoga® model—its mother-of-pearl dial—is set with a sparkling 15-diamond ribbon center zone. The 36mm chronograph is also unveiled with a rubber strap as the Saratoga® SR. This casual, versatile style is available in choices of either a black PVD-finish case with black rubber strap or a stainless steel case with white rubber strap. Both straps have intertwined stainless steel links. Diamond-set versions are also available.

For a sporty chic look, the Saratoga® XL makes an impact with either a black or silver scallop-engraved dial set inside a 46mm case. This version also features the patented latched crown protector and is water resistant to 50 meters.

Concord's collections are selectively distributed in the finest jewelry and department stores around the world.

TOP LEFT

The La Scala™ Tonneau is offered now in the men's chronograph version and ladies' petite bracelet version.

TOP CENTER

The vintage-inspired 18-karat gold Soirée.

ABOVE RIGHT

The La Scala™ Tonneau Horizontal features a striking, art deco-inspired case. Crafted in 18-karat rose gold, it features graceful contours and rich, contrasting textures. It is water resistant to 30 meters.

## CHRONOLOGY

**1908** Concord Watch Co. SA is founded in Bienne, Switzerland as a manufacturer of high-quality watches.

**1909** An American subsidiary is opened in New York City.

**1918** Following World War I, Concord secures its reputation as jeweler extraordinaire by producing private-label platinum watches bedecked in rubies, emeralds, sapphires and diamonds.

**1945** U.S. President Harry Truman presents the Concord Ring Clock to heads of state, including Winston Churchill and Josef Stalin, at the Potsdam Conference. The Ring Clock is the first portable eight-day winding travel alarm clock.

**1969** Gedalio "Gerry" Grinberg purchases the Concord brand and incorporates it into North American Watch Corporation (which will later become Movado Group Inc.).

**1979** Concord makes headlines around the world with the introduction of the revolutionary Delirium—the world's thinnest, ultra-flat Swiss quartz watch measuring a scant 1.98mm.

**1980** The company breaks its own world record with the Delirium IV, which measures 0.98mm.

**1986** Concord launches the now-famed Saratoga collection. With a distinctive eight-sided bezel and intricate link bracelet, the watch is destined to become an icon of the brand.

**1995** The brand unveils the jeweled Saratoga Exor—one of the most expensive watches ever made.

**1997** Concord unveils a superb collection of geometrically inspired timepieces for women—the stunning La Scala series.

**2002** Concord demonstrates its complex watchmaking expertise with the Saratoga® tourbillon.

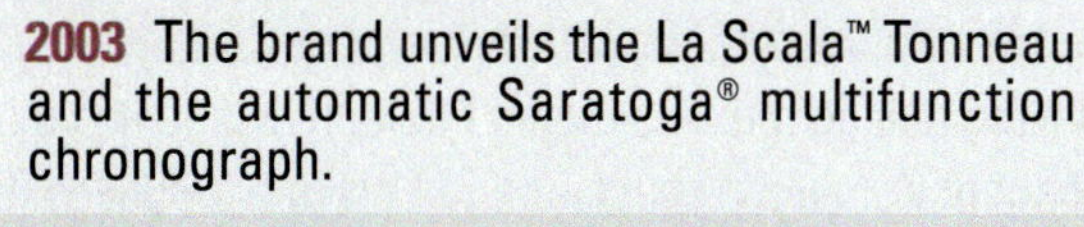

**2003** The brand unveils the La Scala™ Tonneau and the automatic Saratoga® multifunction chronograph.

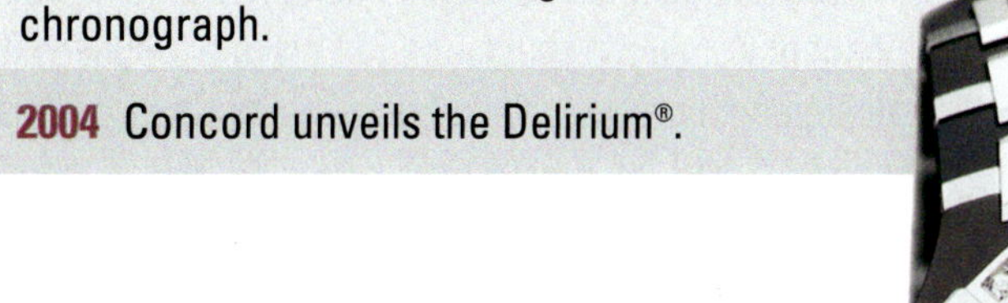

**2004** Concord unveils the Delirium®.

**TOP LEFT**

The sleek, modern Saratoga® is crafted in steel with a diamond-set bezel.

**BOTTOM LEFT**

The Saratoga® XL has a bold 46mm case of steel that is immediately recognized. It is offered with a custom-decorated automatic movement visible through the sapphire caseback.

**BOTTOM RIGHT**

The Saratoga® SR features a rubber strap in either black or white.

# CORUM

The year 2005 marks the 50th anniversary of Corum—a Swiss brand with a fine history that was made even grander five years ago when watch visionary Severin Wunderman purchased it and propelled it to incredible heights.

In its infancy, Corum fast made a reputation for its creative spirit as it unveiled extraordinary watches of distinction—including the now-famed Golden Bridge, the Coin and the Admiral's Cup. All of these timepieces garnered the brand a unique space in watchmaking history. Then, in 2000 Severin Wunderman acquired the controlling interest in the brand—keeping it an independently run firm and infusing it with monumental ingenuity. Under the vigilant and creative mind of Wunderman, collections such as the Bubble watch, the Trapeze and a host of art-inspired enameled watches have become legends of our time.

As Severin Wunderman maintained the position of president and CEO for the brand, he brought his son, Michael, on board and prepared him for the presidency. Michael's keen entrepreneurial spirit and fine business acumen quickly propelled him to that chair in 2004. Today, this father/son duo dynamically runs the Corum brand, reinforcing its Swiss heritage while at the same time dramatically redefining style through inventive designs.

In celebration of its 50th anniversary, Corum is reintroducing the Golden Bridge in a limited edition run. The original Golden Bridge has its roots in 1977, when watchmaker Vincent Calabrese presented to Corum executives his prototype for an extraordinary movement in which all the components were perfectly aligned in a single line. Corum purchased the patent from Calabrese and began further development and reworking of the concept until the first Golden Bridge was unveiled nearly 10 years later. To recreate this watch today, Corum had to completely rework and retool the basics,

**ABOVE**

The Admiral's Cup Trophy 41 is crafted in steel and engraved on the caseback with the Admiral's Cup trophy logo.

**FAR LEFT**

The original Golden Bridge.

**BOTTOM LEFT**

The Classical Chrono Flyback is a triple-complication watch with flyback chronograph and is crafted in a Limited Edition of 500 pieces each according to dial execution.

**BOTTOM CENTER**

The Bubble Dive Bomber watches salute the Flying Tigers missions. They house automatic and chronograph movements and feature lacquered dials.

**BOTTOM RIGHT**

The striking Bubble Skeleton watch houses an automatic movement and is a massive 45mm in diameter. The movement is coated with black PVD.

TOP LEFT

The Potpourri is a stunning watch with pink dial and faceted crystal. Its bracelet is set with diamonds and gemstones.

TOP CENTER

Called Kai Chon, this watch features enameled roosters set with diamonds.

TOP RIGHT

Called the Chevaliers de Monfort, this watch is a tribute to the knights of the Middle Ages.

BOTTOM LEFT

Birds of Paradise with hand-painted mother-of-pearl dial.

BOTTOM RIGHT

The intricate Limited Edition Classical Pearl Dragon features a mother-of-pearl dial carved six layers deep and painted.

as well as dedicate a single watchmaker to the hand assembling of the fine movement. Once again, the movement will be in line and completely visible, but in a modern day work of art. The new Golden Bridge houses the mechanical V7000 movement and is created in 18-karat pink, yellow or white gold, with or without diamonds.

Corum also introduces an entirely new Artisan collection of hand-painted dials. In fact, it has a patent pending for a process developed for carving mother-of-pearl dials and has introduced grand-style enameling. For its limited-edition enamel watches, at least 40 hours of hand painting on a tiny surface is involved to make a single dial. The dials on the new Corum masterpieces reflect a wide range of subject matter, including birds of all types, the macabre, zodiac-inspired pieces and a host of others. These limited-edition enamel watches are the subjects of a year-long international tour Corum is conducting with its master artisans.

For women, Corum is deliciously inventive with styles like the Debutante (with interchangeable bracelet system), and the provocative Potpourri with a stunning bracelet of geometrically shaped, magnificently set gemstones.

## CHRONOLOGY

**1955** Gaston Ries, a watchmaker since 1924, begins the company with daughter Simone and nephew René Bannwart. (The trio names the brand Quorum, but chooses the phonetic spelling "Corum" to eliminate confusion when seen in print.)

**1956** Corum's debut timepieces are very successful at the Basel Fair.

**1966** Corum files a patent for the Romulus model. Jean-René Bannwart, René's son, joins the management.

**1968** Corum watches are distributed in the United States. The Gold Coin watch is presented through an extraordinary campaign launch and strengthens the brand's worldwide reputation.

**1987** On the basis of a patent held by the watchmaker Vincent Calabrese, Corum produces the Golden Bridge. The first model entirely realized by Corum, it is equipped with a mechanical movement built up "in line" and enclosed in a Baccarat crystal parallelepiped. (The piece numbered 001 is offered to the Museum of La Chaux-de-Fonds.)

**2000** Corum's man for the new millennium is Severin Wunderman, an American businessman known for his long lasting success with Gucci Timepieces. Corum is one among the rare independent houses. The first sign of the important change are mainly the Bubble timekeepers, characterized by rounded shapes, domed glasses and striking dials. The new Trapèze enters the catalog.

**2001** New models enlarge the Bubble family, among them a GMT and a diving watch. Unique forms also characterize the new ladies' models such as the Sugar Cube and Padlock.

**2004** Michael Wunderman takes over as president of Corum and Severin Wunderman remains on as CEO.

## BUBBLE DIVE BOMBER SHARK — REF. 082.181.20

**Movement:** automatic ETA 2892.A2.
**Functions:** hour, minute, second; date.
**Case:** Ø 45mm; brushed stainless steel; unidirectional rotating bezel; screw-down crown; 11mm full-cut antireflective sapphire crystal; water resistant to 20atm.
**Dial:** polychrome enamels of a shark's mouth; second hand in shape of a propeller.
**Strap:** leather; military style; stainless steel pushbutton folding clasp.
**Note:** special edition of 2004, dedicated to the World War II Flying Tigers team.

## BUBBLE DIVE BOMBER CHRONO TIGER — REF. 285.181.20

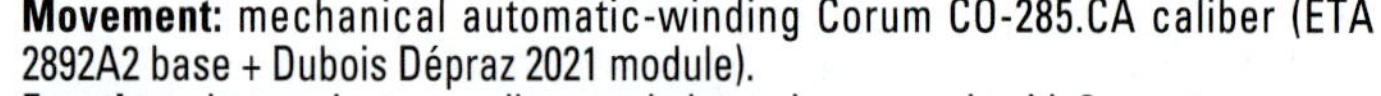

**Movement:** mechanical automatic-winding Corum CO-285.CA caliber (ETA 2892A2 base + Dubois Dépraz 2021 module).
**Functions:** hour, minute, small second; date; chronograph with 3 counters.
**Case:** stainless steel three-piece case (Ø 45mm, thickness: 21.5mm); brushed and polished finish; very thick domed sapphire crystal (11mm at center), antireflective on both sides; counterclockwise-turning bezel, black ring, graduated scale with luminescent dot for calculation of diving times; screw-down crown with rubber O-ring; pushers burnished inside; screw-on engraved back; water resistant to 20atm.
**Dial:** polychrome enamels representing a tiger head; hollowed subdials; luminescent square markers; luminescent black enameled cigar hands.
**Indications:** small second at 3; hour counter and date at 6; minute counter at 9; center second counter with a propeller-shaped hand; minute track.
**Strap:** military style, leather; double fold-over safety clasp in stainless steel.
**Note:** special edition of 2004, dedicated to the World War II Flying Tigers team.

## NIGHT FLYER BUBBLE – COLLECTOR SERIES — REF. 082.157.97

**Movement:** automatic ETA 2892.A2.
**Functions:** hour, minute, second; date.
**Case:** Ø 45mm; stainless steel with black PVD coating; screw-down crown; bezel with 120 brilliants (0.90 carat); domed, 11mm double-sided antireflective sapphire crystal; engraved caseback; water resistant to 20atm.
**Dial:** black dial with winged and helmeted-skull motif in relief; set with 12 diamonds (0.051carat); skeleton hour and minute hands in steel; sword-shaped second hand.
**Indications:** date at 6.
**Strap:** leather on composite material with red stitching.
**Note:** limited edition of 99 pieces worldwide.

## BUBBLE SKELETON — REF. 082.150.20

**Movement:** mechanical automatic-winding ETA 2892A2 caliber; skeletonized and black-PVD treated.
**Functions:** hour, minute, second.
**Case:** stainless steel three-piece case (Ø 45mm, thickness: 18.7mm); very thick domed sapphire crystal (11mm at center), antireflective on both sides; screw-down crown with rubber O-ring; back fastened by 6 screws, displaying the movement through a sapphire crystal; water resistant to 3atm.
**Dial:** skeleton pillar-plate treated with black PVD; luminescent steel cigar hands.
**Strap:** crocodile leather with a rubber rim; double fold-over safety clasp in stainless steel.

## CLASSICAL GRANDE DATE REF. 922.201.56

**Movement:** automatic CO-922; COSC-certified chronometer.
**Functions:** hour, minute, second; date.
**Case:** Ø 42mm; 18K yellow gold; moving lugs; domed antireflective sapphire crystal; engraved 6-screw caseback; water resistant to 5atm.
**Dial:** black guilloché.
**Indications:** off-centered small seconds at 6; large date at 12.
**Strap:** crocodile leather; 18K gold folding clasp.

## CLASSICAL RESERVE DE MARCHE REF. 973.201.20

**Movement:** automatic CO-973.PR; ETA base with Jacquet J3916 module; 42-hour power reserve; COSC-certified chronometer.
**Functions:** hour, minute; date; power reserve.
**Case:** Ø 42mm; stainless steel; moving lugs; open back cover; sapphire crystal with integrated magnifying glass to read date; 8-screw caseback; water resistant to 3atm.
**Indications:** large date at 12.
**Bracelet:** stainless steel; pushbutton folding security clasp.

## CLASSICAL CHRONO FLYBACK REF. 996.201.20 (STAINLESS STEEL)

**Movement:** automatic CO-996; COSC-certified chronometer.
**Functions:** hour, minute; chronograph with 3 counters and flyback function (instant reset-to-zero).
**Case:** concave, stainless steel; Ø 43mm without the lugs; domed antireflective sapphire crystal; transparent caseback; water resistant to 5atm.
**Dial:** black or silver; guilloché; luminescent main hands.
**Indications:** seconds at 3; minutes at 9; hours at 6; large date at 12.
**Bracelet:** stainless steel; folding clasp.
**Note:** black dial (500 pieces); silver dial (500 pieces).

## CLASSICAL CHRONO FLYBACK REF. 996.201.55

**Movement:** mechanical automatic-winding modified DD 4500 caliber; rotor engraved; COSC-certified chronometer. **Functions:** hour, minute; date; flyback chronograph with 3 counters. **Case:** 18K pink-gold three-piece case (Ø 42.6mm, thickness: 15mm); curved antireflective sapphire crystal; hollowed middle; pushers with case protection; back fastened by 6 screws with a sapphire glass aperture; water resistant to 5atm. **Dial:** blue; decorated with circular beads; applied pink-gold subdial crowns; applied steel Arabic numerals and ellipsoidal markers; luminescent pink-gold leaf-style hands. **Indications:** small second at 3; hour counter at 6 (with double hand whose smaller end indicates the hours on the upper half-circle and the larger one on the lower half-circle); minute counter at 9; big date with a double window at 12; center second; minute track with divisions for 1/2 second. **Strap:** hand-stitched crocodile leather; pink-gold double fold-over safety clasp. **Note:** limited edition of 50 numbered pieces. **Also available:** with slate-gray dial, 50 pieces; bracelet.

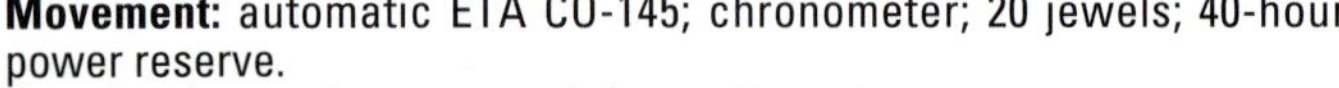

## ADMIRAL'S CUP 29 — REF. 145.440.47

**Movement:** automatic ETA CO-145; chronometer; 20 jewels; 40-hour power reserve.
**Function:** hour, minute, second; date at 6.
**Case:** Ø 29mm; stainless steel; 12-sided; set with 36 full-cut diamonds (0.54 carats); slightly domed antireflective crystal; open back cover engraved; water resistant to 5atm.

**Dial:** white mother-of-pearl; 12 nautical flags as hour markers; Super-LumiNova hands.
**Bracelet:** stainless steel; adjustable folding clasp.
**Also available:** with quartz movement.

## ADMIRAL'S CUP TROPHY 41 — REF. 082.830.20

**Movement:** automatic CO-082.
**Case:** Ø 41mm; stainless steel; antireflective sapphire crystal; caseback engraved with Admiral's Cup trophy logo; crown protected with a latch; water resistant to 10atm.
**Dial:** guilloché; luminescent hour and minute hands; counterweight of second hand in shape of Corum logo key; date at 6 with magnifying loop.

**Bracelet:** vulcanized rubber with stainless steel folding clasp.

## ADMIRAL'S CUP CHRONOGRAPH — REF. 985.630.20

**Movement:** automatic CO-985; COSC-certified chronometer.
**Functions:** hour, minute, second; date at 6; chronograph with 3 counters; sailing indications for Olympic triangle.
**Case:** Ø 45mm; stainless steel; 12-sided; domed antireflective sapphire crystal; partial open back with sapphire crystal; bi-rotational bezel with nautical pennants corresponding to appropriate numeral (1-12); 8-screw caseback; water resistant to 5atm.

**Dial:** luminescent hour and minute hands and hour markers.
**Bracelet:** stainless steel with vulcanized rubber and folding clasp.

## ADMIRAL'S CUP TIDES — REF. 977.630.55

**Movement:** automatic CO-977; Tides COSC-certified chronometer.
**Functions:** hour, minute, second; date at 3; moonphase; high and low tide times; state and height of tide; strength of the currents.
**Case:** Ø 44mm; 18K rose gold; 127.7 grams; antireflective domed sapphire; 12-sided covers, dial and bezel; partial open caseback with sapphire crystal; nautical pennants on bezel corresponding to appropriate numeral (1-12) as used in international maritime code; water resistant to 5atm.

**Bracelet:** 18K rose gold with folding clasp; 114.1 grams.

## $20 DOUBLE EAGLE GOLD COIN — REF. 082.355.56

**Movement:** automatic 12 1/12 Piguet 70.
**Case:** authentic $20 U.S. gold coin; crown set with a diamond; sapphire crystal; water resistant to 3atm.
**Strap:** crocodile with 18K yellow-gold buckle.

## TOURBILLON SAPHIR 2004 — REF. 372.551.55

**Movement:** mechanical manual J3910; 90-hour power reserve.
**Functions:** hour, minute.
**Case:** Ø 40mm; 18K rose gold; sapphire crystal; open caseback with 8-screws; available with diamond.
**Dial:** Sapphire movement; Roman numerals in relief on bezel.
**Strap:** crocodile leather with 18K gold folding clasp.
**Note:** limited edition of 25 rose-gold pieces worldwide.

## CLASSICAL PEARL DRAGON — REF. 154.201.69

**Movement:** automatic CO-982; COSC-certified chronometer.
**Functions:** hour, minute, second.
**Case:** Ø 42mm; 18K yellow, rose or white gold; set with 2.20 carats of diamonds; crown set with 0.20 carat of diamonds; antireflective sapphire crystal; 8-screw caseback; water resistant to 5atm.
**Dial:** engraved and hand-painted mother-of-pearl dial with limited edition number on dial; skeleton hour and minute hands; counter-weight of second hand in shape of Corum key logo.
**Strap:** crocodile leather; 18K gold folding clasp.
**Note:** limited edition of 50 pieces with unique color variations for each dial.

## CLASSICAL KAI CHON

**Movement:** automatic CO-982; COSC-certified chronometer.
**Case:** Ø 42mm; 18K yellow, rose or white gold; case set with 2.20 carats of diamonds; crown set with 0.20 carat of diamonds; antireflective sapphire crystal; 8-screw caseback; water resistant to 5atm.
**Dial:** hand engraved and grand feu enameled dial with limited edition number on dial; set with 0.48 carat of diamonds; skeleton hour and minute hands; counter-weight of second hand in shape of Corum key logo.
**Strap:** crocodile leather; 18K gold folding clasp.
**Note:** limited edition of 50 pieces with unique color variations for each dial.

# Cuervo y Sobrinos

A new line of fine watches based on original designs reminiscent of an era synonymous with refinement, luxury and glamour—this is Cuervo y Sobrinos.

Defined as a brand with a "Swiss Heart – Cuban Soul," the relaunch of Cuervo y Sobrinos marks the comeback of a Cuban legend. This prestigious brand traces its roots back to the elegant old Havana heydays, circa 1882. Originally established as a small family business, the retail watch and jewelry shop became internationally recognized under the direction of the founder's nephew, Armando Rio y Cuervo. This was the store to visit if you were a prominent figure of the day.

So successful was the brand in Havana that the family opened shops in strategic European locations: Paris; Pforzheim, Germany; La Chaux-de-Fonds, Switzerland. They purchased Swiss movements and housed them in cases inspired by Cuban design. This was the grand start of the Cuervo y Sobrinos brand.

Although the Cuervo family fled Cuba during the revolution and there is no longer a Cuervo y Sobrinos jewelry store there, efforts began in the late 1990s to revive the brand to its former great past. When the doors to the old workshops on San Rafael were opened, unfinished pieces were discovered along with drawings and designs. Based on these artifacts, it has been possible to continue in the original brand's cultural spirit.

Today's Cuervo y Sobrinos timepieces are new period watches. They are not replicas of the models that made the brand famous a century ago, but embrace the essence of the brand: Caribbean culture where time bends and forms to a luxurious, warm lifestyle.

Each Cuervo y Sobrinos watch houses a Swiss movement (the heart) in Cuban-inspired designs (the soul). The watches are crafted in steel or in 18-karat gold. The rose-gold versions are subjected to a special fire treatment to emulate the appearance of old gold. Dials are enamel, crystals are sapphire, and movements are automatic. All watches are presented in limited, numbered series

All Cuervo y Sobrinos timepieces are hand crafted and undergo numerous stages of execution. Each gold case is heat tempered, hand numbered and engraved.

THIS PAGE

ABOVE

The Espléndidos Clasico is shown here in three renditions.

BOTTOM

Street of Old Calle San Rafael, Cuba.

FACING PAGE

This Prominente Dual-Time Zone watch houses two automatic movements. It is crafted in 18-karat rose gold with black dial.

Cuervo y Sobrinos
LA HABANA 1882
CUERVO Y SOBRINOS
HABANA
AUTORECARGANTE

**TOP**

*from left to right:*

The single time-zone Prominente crafted in 18-karat rose gold; the steel Torpedo chronograph featuring pulsometer function with an old-world ivory dial; and Espléndidos Clasico crafted in 18-karat rose gold.

**BOTTOM LEFT**

This Prominente features the dual time-zone.

**BOTTOM RIGHT**

The Torpedo with GMT is crafted in steel and houses an automatic movement.

Each phase of manufacture passes through continuous and strict quality controls, and all components are methodically prepared and checked before being used—guaranteeing works of art that are in no way rushed.

There are three main collections that are appropriately named after cigars: Espléndidos, Torpedo, and Prominente. The Espléndidos watches are inspired by the 1940s Art Deco style, in square cases with gracefully, ergonomically curved edges that embody an architectural look and feel.

The Torpedo collection—named for the classic cigar shape—is a series of round watches that are 40mm in diameter and offer a host of different functions. The automatic movements feature Côtes de Genève and perlage decoration. Among the Torpedo timepieces is a classic watch, a GMT watch, and a Chrono/Pulsometer.

The Prominenete is a stunning, ergonomically designed rectangular watch named for one of the largest cigars in production. It is available either as a single or dual time-zone watch and is strikingly elegant. The dual time-zone version is endowed with two mechanical movements that show the two different sets of times.

## CHRONOLOGY

**1882** Ramon Cuervo opens a watch store in Havana. Armando Rio y Cuervos and his brothers later join the watchmaking business started by their uncle. The store quickly becomes highly respected for its watches and jewelry and caters to a demanding international clientele.

**1890s** The family expands the store's locations, adding three European shops. At this time, they begin buying Swiss watch movements and creating their own line: Cuervo y Sobrinos (Cuervo and nephews).

**1950s** Cuervo y Sobrino's success is halted during the Castro era, when the family packs its inventory into suitcases and leaves, never to be seen in Cuba again.

**1997** The quest begins to reestablish the brand's international offices in Lugano, Switzerland.

**2002** The brand is relaunched in Europe by international owners: Marzio Villa and Luca Musumeci.

**2003** On its first anniversary, Cuervo y Sobrinos establishes an annual award: Latino Internacional. The first recipient is Pedro Almodovar, Spanish cinematographer.

**2004** The brand officially launches its North America/Canada subsidiary and exhibits at BaselWorld.

TOP RIGHT

This Espléndidos watch is crafted in gold with diamonds on the case.

CENTER

Water resistant to 3atm, this Espléndidos Clasico watch is assembled in Bordeaux colors with pink sapphires.

BOTTOM

Cased in white gold, this Espléndidos Clasico watch features a pink dial, pink stingray strap and pink sapphires.

The Espléndidos, Prominente and Torpedo are all available with diamond- or gemstone-adorned bezels for added glamour.

Each collection is timeless in nature with classically elegant styles that are meant to measure a different kind of time: "Time that moves slowly... because time in Havana has a different rhythm."

To further underscore the brand's Cuban spirit, all Cuervo y Sobrinos watches are delivered in fully functional humidors made of Spanish cedar.

# DAVID YURMAN

Arguably one of the most prolific designers of our time, David Yurman has built a loyal following with his incredible, distinctive Cable Collection of jewelry and watches.

After establishing his own company in La Chaux-de-Fonds to ensure that his timepieces are 100 percent Swiss manufactured to exacting standards, Yurman continues to intensify his watch collections.

In his newest feminine watch series, the Madison Cable™, Yurman revisits his classic cable design to create a sleek racetrack-shaped case. The contemporary feel of this beautiful series is reinforced by the Madison's handmade link-chain bracelet. The watches are also available with alligator straps. The curved case is crafted in silver and steel or in 18-karat gold. All dials are stunning mother of pearl and subtly reflect David Yurman's latest jewelry collection: South Sea Pearl. The dials are offered in a variety of colors and are available with or without diamond accents. The diamond-adorned watches feature G-VS full-cut diamonds. Limited edition, high-jeweled version of this exquisite timepiece are also available. Designed in America and crafted in La Chaux-de-Fonds, the Madison Cable™ Collection houses ETA movements.

"Like my jewelry, the watches express a casual sense of luxury," says David Yurman. "They work naturally with many of my designs; they are versatile and comfortable to wear."

THIS PAGE

TOP

These Madison Cable™ watches are crafted in silver and steel, or in silver and 18-karat gold, and feature

the specially made Madison link-chain bracelet.

BOTTOM LEFT

From the South Sea Pearl Collection, these stunning necklace and rings are accented with diamonds.

FACING PAGE

The dials of the Madison Cable™ watches are crafted with colored mother-of-pearl dials and color-coordinated straps. These watches are available with or without diamonds.

DAVID YURMAN
SWISS MADE
DAVID YURMAN
SWISS MADE
DAVID YURMAN

# David Yurman

In 2005, David Yurman will launch the Small Madison Cable™ series is the Small Madison Cable watch—a classic cocktail watch. With or without diamond accents, the Small Madison is available in 18-karat yellow, white or pink gold on a variety of alligator or satin straps.

Embellishing 2003's Color Chronograph Watch Collection, David Yurman SA adds splendid new dial and strap colors. The cushion-shaped chronographs feature a variety of mother-of-pearl dials with color-coordinated alligator straps, including a pink, lavender, yellow and orange series.

For men, Yurman reinforces the Mercer Watch Collection™ and the titanium Chronograph Watch Collection with bold new models that feature striking bracelets.

**TOP LEFT**

From the Thoroughbred™ Watch Collection.

**BOTTOM RIGHT**

The Small Madison Cable watch is the perfect cocktail watch, adorned with G-VS full-cut diamonds.

## CHRONOLOGY

**1962** David Yurman begins an apprenticeship with sculptor Jacques Lipchitz.

**1965** Yurman opens his Greenwich Village sculpture studio.

**1970** Yurman is awarded the Court of Honor at ACC Rheinbeck at the Rheinbeck Juried Craft show.

**1979** David and Sybil Yurman found Yurman Designs Inc.

**1983** The Cable Collection of jewelry is introduced and becomes the signature of Yurman Designs Inc.

**1994** The Cable Watch Collection® is launched.

**1999** Launching of the Men's Thoroughbred™ Watch Collection. The David Yurman flagship store opens on Madison Avenue in New York City. Yurman designs a bronze Angel statue to be awarded annually to a humanitarian (the first recipient is Steven Speilberg).

**2000** The Women's Thoroughbred™ Watch Collection is unveiled. Sir Elton John receives the Angel statue.

**2001** The Limited Edition Artist's Series Chronograph Watch Collection and the DualTime™ Watch are launched. The company launches its first lifestyle ad campaign. The David & Sybil Humanitarian and Arts Foundation is established to formalize the company's dedication to supporting charitable efforts.

**2002** The second Yurman retail store opens in Costa Mesa, California.

**2003** Yurman establishes David Yurman SA in La Chaux-de-Fonds. The brand,s corporate headquarters moves into a state-of-the-art facility in New York,s trendy TriBeCa neighborhood. Yurman adds pearls to his collection.

**2004** David Yurman opens new boutiques in Atlanta, Bal Harbour and Houston. The company also launches its Bridal and South Sea Pearl lines.

TOP

This Mercer Watch™ is named for the downtown New York City street and features a sleek black dial with silver subdials.

BOTTOM

The Titanium Chronograph Watch Collection features steel and titanium casse and bracelets.

## THOROUGHBRED CHRONOGRAPH — REF: T3081ACTS-BRACT

**Movement:** automatic; ETA 2894-2.
**Functions:** chronograph with 3 counters; flyback function; date.
**Case:** stainless steel with titanium bezel; water resistant to 3atm.
**Bracelet:** steel and titanium.
**Also available:** stainless steel case; on strap or all-steel bracelet; steel and rubber bracelet.

## THOROUGHBRED COLOR CHRONOGRAPH — REF: T3175QC-ST-BUGAWM

**Movement:** ETA 251.471
**Functions:** chronograph with 3 counters; date.
**Case:** stainless steel with sterling silver; full-diamond bezel.
**Dial:** white mother of pearl; pink subdials.
**Strap:** alligator leather.
**Also available:** blue mother-of-pearl dial with pistachio subdials or rose Arabic dial; stainless steel bracelet or assorted interchangeable alligator straps; without diamond bezel.

## MEN'S LARGE THOROUGHBRED — REF. T3071AL-SS-BRACR

**Movement:** mechanical, automatic winding ETA 2892/A2; 21 jewels; 28,8000 vph.
**Functions:** hour, minute, sweep second; date.
**Case:** oxidized and high-polished sterling silver and high-polished steel six-piece case (Ø 35mm, thickness: 11mm); domed, antireflective sapphire crystal; caseback attached by 4 screws; water resistant to 3atm.
**Dial:** black enamel dial with center guilloché zone; feuille hands; applied bâton markers; applied David Yurman logo.
**Indications:** date at 3.
**Strap:** brushed and polished steel with black rubber bracelet; recessed deployant clasp.
**Also available:** gold case; alligator strap.

## LADIES' THOROUGHBRED — REF. T3144QS-88-BRACD

**Movement:** quartz movement; ETA 956.032; long life; 7 jewels.
**Functions:** hour, minute.
**Case:** high-polished 18K yellow-gold, six-piece case (Ø 25mm, thickness: 7mm); domed, antireflective sapphire crystal; bezel set with diamonds (43 stones); caseback attached by 4 screws; water resistant to 3atm.
**Dial:** natural white mother-of-pearl dial; applied markers set with diamonds; applied Arabic numerals and David Yurman logo; feuille hands.
**Bracelet:** high-polished 18K yellow-gold bracelet with pavé set diamonds (56 stones); recessed deployant clasp.
**Also available:** calf, alligator, or grosgrain strap; gold bracelet.

## LADIES' CABLE REF: T01016M-SS-GG

**Movement:** caliber 792.
**Case:** sterling silver with 14K yellow gold.
**Bracelet:** silver with 14K yellow gold.
**Also available:** pink or blue mother-of-pearl dials.

## MADISON REF. T4194QSSSWHGAM

**Movement:** Swiss.
**Case:** stainless steel; diamond bezel.
**Dial:** blue mother of pearl.
**Strap:** white glossy alligator leather.

## MADISON REF. T4195QSSSPKGA

**Movement:** Swiss.
**Case:** stainless steel; diamond bezel.
**Dial:** pink mother of pearl.
**Strap:** pink glossy alligator leather.

## MADISON REF. T4391QS88BUGA

**Movement:** Swiss.
**Case:** 18K yellow gold; diamond bezel and case.
**Dial:** blue mother of pearl.
**Strap:** burgundy glossy alligator leather.

# De Bethune

Although a relatively young company, De Bethune relies on traditional craftsmanship and watchmaking heritage to create its mechanical masterpieces.

Included in its repertoire of complicated watches are a Mono-Pusher chronograph series, a GMT line, a minute repeater, an equation of time, and a line of split-seconds chronographs.

Most recently, De Bethune unveiled a Perpetual Calendar watch with revolving moonphase readout. First released in only 18-karat yellow gold, the stunning piece is now available in 18-karat white gold. The mechanism of the Perpetual Calendar is the result of a De Bethune in-house project. Called the caliber De Bethune, it is 30mm in diameter and features a double barrel—the thinnest in the world—and has unique balance-spring and regulation properties.

The manual-winding movement houses a new Swiss lever escapement, beats at 28,800 vibrations per hour, and offers four days of power reserve. The winding and time-setting functions are adjusted through the crown in three positions. The caliber De Bethune is hand decorated, and all the steel components are hand polished.

Also new is another Revolving Perpetual Calendar with mechanical complications. It is equipped with the latest perpetual calendar, projected and developed by De Bethune, and is also fitted with a minute repeater that chimes the hours, quarters and minutes. Additionally, the watch houses a tourbillon escapement and the De Bethune balance in titanium and platinum with Breguet balance-spring.

The Revolving Perpetual Calendar's 43mm case is crafted in 18-karat rose gold with ogival lugs, octagonal crown and sapphire caseback. The dial is gold with a hand-guilloché pattern. This watch, which beats at 18,000 vibrations per hour, houses 381 components including 20 jewels, and offers 30 hours of power reserve. The perpetual calendar offers revolving moonphase and leap-year indications and the repeater is fitted with a strike-silent mechanism.

The winding and time-setting functions are adjusted via the crown in two positions; date is adjusted via the button at 4:00; month via the button at 5:00; day via the button at 8:00; and moonphase via the button at 10:00. The mechanism is decorated with Côtes de Genève pattern. All the steel components are polished and hand decorated.

THIS PAGE

ABOVE

This Perpetual Calendar with Revolving Moon Phase watch is also fitted with a minute repeater and a tourbillon. Developed by De Bethune, it is an original system of display and function. The watch houses a 381-part manual-winding mechanism that offers 30 hours of power reserve.

FACING PAGE

TOP CENTER

The De Bethune Perpetual Calendar with Revolving Moon Phase DB15, is crafted in 18-karat white gold and features a unique, original moonphase display: a sphere made of platinum and steel that revolves on its axis. Situated at 12:00, it also offers leap-year indication. The perpetual calendar movement is manufactured entirely in De Bethune's Atelier, and is fitted with an additional function that allows quick setting of the date through the crown in the third position. The leap-year function is depicted by the changing colors of the star under the moon, depending on the year.

## CHRONOLOGY

**2002** De Bethune is established in La Chaux L'Auberson in the Swiss Jura Mountains, co–founded by David Zanetta (consultant to many prestigious watch houses) and Denis Flageollet (watchmaker and watchmaking professor at Le Locle). Utilizing precious materials and watchmaking tradition, combined with contemporary styling for the 21st century, De Bethune gains immediate recognition for its complicated watches.

**2003** Armed with a masterful collection of unique pieces and complicated watches, De Bethune makes its debut at the Basel Fair. Among its watches: an automatic-winding model; a keyless model with 168 hours of power reserve; a chronograph; a marine chronometer with 10 days of power reserve and a strike-silent mechanism; a perpetual calendar with big date and split-seconds chronograph. Demonstrating the brand's complex watchmaking prowess, De Bethune offers a watch with tourbillon-escapement, minute repeater, perpetual calendar and equation of time. De Bethune uses exclusive movements, entirely hand assembled and hand decorated by its own watchmakers. Additionally, the brand specializes in custom-made watches that respect its manufacturing philosophy of meticulous attention to detail and exceptionable finishing. All De Bethune watches submit to many quality controls and are extremely limited in production. In fact, by 2008 production will reach just 1,200 pieces total.

**2004** De Bethune unveils its own caliber, manufactured entirely in house and featuring a revolving moonphase indicator.

DE BETHUNE

## DE BETHUNE MONO PUSHER CHRONOGRAPH REF. DB1

**Movement:** manual-winding caliber De Bethune 2002; decorated with Côtes de Genève pattern; Swiss lever escapement; 21 jewels; 21,600 vph; 36-hour power reserve; 183 components; hand polished.
**Functions:** hour, minute; chronograph with column-wheel, chronographic functions are adjusted through a coaxial pusher included in the crown; winding and time-setting functions are adjusted through the crown in 2 positions.
**Case:** yellow or white gold; Ø 42mm, thickness: 8mm; ogival lugs; octagonal crown; caseback held by palladium screws; water resistant to 3atm.
**Dial:** silver-plated or plain gold; with hand-guilloché pattern; blue Roman numerals; blued steel hands; 30-minute counter at 3; small seconds at 9.
**Strap:** crocodile leather with gold buckle.

## DE BETHUNE GMT 7 DAYS POWER RESERVE REF. DB3

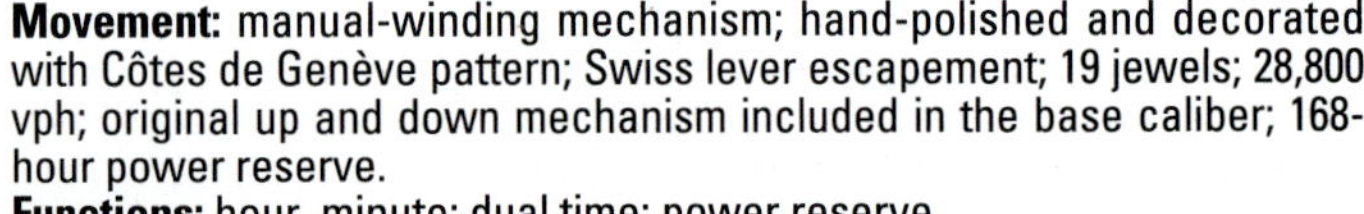
**Movement:** manual-winding mechanism; hand-polished and decorated with Côtes de Genève pattern; Swiss lever escapement; 19 jewels; 28,800 vph; original up and down mechanism included in the base caliber; 168-hour power reserve.
**Functions:** hour, minute; dual time; power reserve.
**Case:** yellow, white, rose gold or in platinum (on request); Ø 42mm; ogival lugs; octagonal crown; caseback held by palladium screws; water resistant to 3atm.

**Dial:** silver-plated or plain gold; hand-guilloché pattern; blue Roman numerals; blued steel hands; power-reserve subdial at 12; 24-hour dual-time subdial at 6.
**Strap:** crocodile leather with gold buckle.

## DE BETHUNE MINUTE REPEATER REF. DB4

**Movement:** manual-winding; decorated with Côtes de Genève pattern and hand polished; Swiss lever escapement; 28,800 vph; 24-hour power reserve.
**Functions:** hour, minute; minute repeater on two gongs; winding and time-setting functions are adjusted through the crown in 2 positions.
**Case:** yellow, white and rose gold, platinum (on request); Ø 42mm; ogival lugs; repeater slide at 9; caseback held by palladium screws; water resistant to 3atm.
**Dial:** silver-plated or plain gold; blue Roman numerals; blued steel hands.
**Strap:** crocodile leather with gold buckle.

## DE BETHUNE AUTOMATIC REF. DB5

**Movement:** self-winding caliber De Bethune 2072; Swiss lever escapement; 20 jewels; 21,600 vph; 36-hour power reserve; decorated with Côtes de Genève pattern; polished and hand decorated; winding mechanism wound by a 18K gold rotor.
**Functions:** hour, minute, center seconds; winding and time-setting functions are adjusted through the crown in two positions
**Case:** yellow, white, rose gold or in platinum (on request); Ø 42mm, thickness: 8mm; original ogival lugs; octagonal crown; caseback held by palladium screws; water resistant to 3atm.
**Dial:** silver-plated or plain gold; hand-guilloché pattern; blue Roman numerals; blued steel hands; center seconds hand.
**Strap:** crocodile leather with gold buckle.

## DE BETHUNE MONO PUSHER CHRONOGRAPH REF. DB8

**Movement:** mechanical manual-winding caliber De Bethune 2003; Swiss lever escapement; 21 jewels; 21,600 vph; single-button chronograph movement with column wheel; 36-hour working power; decorated with Côtes de Genève pattern; polished and hand decorated; 188 components.
**Functions:** 45-minute counter; chronograph with column wheel; start, stop and return to zero are adjusted by a single button included in the crown; winding and time-setting functions through the crown adjusted in 2 positions.
**Case:** yellow, white, pink gold or platinum (on request); Ø 42mm; exclusive ogival lugs; octagonal crown; solid caseback held by palladium screws; water resistant to 3atm.
**Dial:** silver-plated or plain gold; center hand-guilloché pattern; blue Arabic numerals; blued steel hands; 45-minute counter at 6.
**Strap:** crocodile leather with gold buckle.

## DE BETHUNE AUTOMATIC REF. DB10

**Movement:** self-winding caliber De Bethune 2072; Swiss lever escapement; 20 jewels; 21,600 vph; 36-hour working power; winding mechanism wound by 18K gold rotor; decorated with circular Côtes de Genève pattern; polished and hand decorated.
**Functions:** hour, minute, center seconds; winding and time setting functions through the crown adjusted in 2 positions.
**Case:** yellow, white, pink gold or platinum (on request); Ø 42mm; ogival lugs; octagonal crown; water resistant to 3atm.
**Dial:** silver-plated or plain gold; center hand-guilloché pattern; blue Arabic numerals; blued steel hands; center seconds hands.
**Strap:** crocodile leather with gold buckle.

## DE BETHUNE CHRONOGRAPH, MINUTES COUNTER, BIG DATE REF. DB12

**Movement:** manual-winding chronograph; column wheel; Swiss lever escapement; 25 jewels; Breguet balance-spring; "col-de-cygne" regulator; 18,000 vph; 30-hour power reserve; 226 parts; decorated with Côtes de Genève pattern; all hand-polished steel components.
**Functions:** hour, minute, small second at 9; chronograph; large date; month; winding and time-setting adjusted by the crown in 2 positions; start, stop and return to zero adjusted by buttons at 2 and 4; date setting via small button at 10; month setting at 3:30.
**Case:** rose or white gold; Ø 42mm, thickness: 13mm; exclusive ogival lugs; 2 chronograph buttons on each side of the octagonal crown; 1 corrective pusher at 3:30; sapphire crystal; engraved back with 7 paladium screws
**Dial:** silver-plated gold; hand-guilloché pattern; blue Arabic numerals; blued steel hands; 30-minute counter at 3; white-gold subdial for month at 6 and large date at 12.
**Strap:** crocodile leather with gold buckle.

## DE BETHUNE PERPETUAL CALENDAR REVOLVING MOON PHASE REF. DB15

**Movement:** manual-winding caliber De Bethune 30 with double barrel (thinnest in the world); new Swiss lever escapement; 28,800 vph; 4-day power reserve; 24 jewels; hand-polished and -decorated steel components.
**Functions:** hour, minute; perpetual calendar; day/month with moonphase and leap-year indication; winding and time-setting functions adjusted through the crown in 3 positions; quick date correction by the intermediary position of the crown; day, month and moon correction by button on the case.
**Case:** rose or white gold; Ø 43mm, thickness: 13mm; ogival lugs; 2 integrated correctors for moonphase and day of the week; sapphire crystal and caseback.
**Dial:** gold; Roman numerals; blued steel hands; date at 6; moonphase (platinum and steel sphere revolving on its own axis in a circle of stars) at 12.
**Strap:** crocodile leather; gold simple or deployment buckle.

# de GRISOGONO

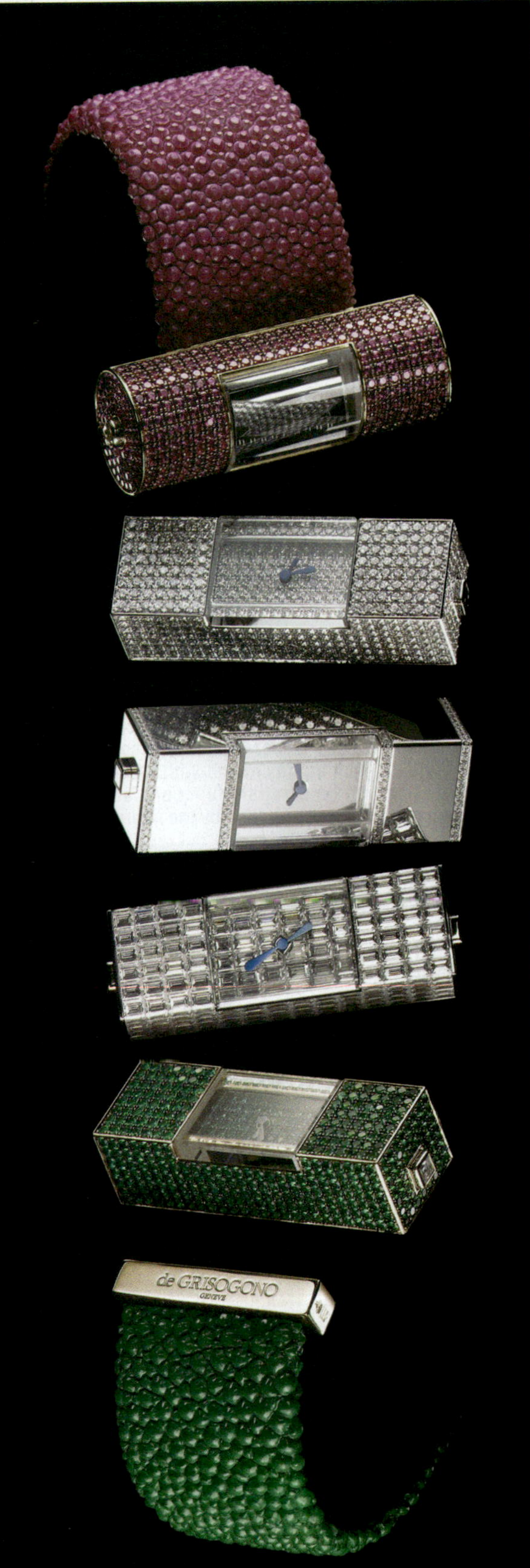


Passion. This might be the only word that truly defines the love Fawaz Gruosi—designer extraordinaire of de GRISOGONO—has for beguiling creations.

Dramatic? Perhaps—but so is de GRISOGONO. Every masterpiece from this esteemed designer is more captivating than the last, and year after year, men and women alike witness the marvels that emanate from Gruosi.

Perhaps the most striking yet, is the new cylindrical Lipstick series of stunning ladies' watches that represent the epitome of feminine must-haves through a blend of bold design and the jeweler's art. The Lipstick is a piece of irresistible feminine jewelry—and extraordinary originality.

To Gruosi, Lipstick is the most beautiful way to embellish the wrist. The aesthetic appeal of Lipstick is its sculpted virtuosity. Crafted in rose or white gold, the construction of this watch is based on a case—either square or an elongated cylinder—that is either lightly set or totally covered with the most precious stones. The case is attached via a secure system to a galuchat bracelet, rounded off with a cylindrical or rectangular decorative cuff-style clasp.

THIS PAGE

LEFT

The array of galuchat-strapped Lipstick watches is spectacular. Shown here from top to bottom:

18-karat pink-gold Cylinder with 588 rubies

18-karat white-gold Square with 608 diamonds

18-karat white-gold Square with 140 diamonds

18-karat white-gold Square with baguette-cut diamonds

18-karat pink-gold Square with 608 emeralds

BOTTOM RIGHT

Fawaz Gruosi.

FACING PAGE

This Lipstick Cylinder watch is crafted in 18-karat white gold with a light pink galuchat bracelet. The case and dial are set entirely with baguette diamonds.

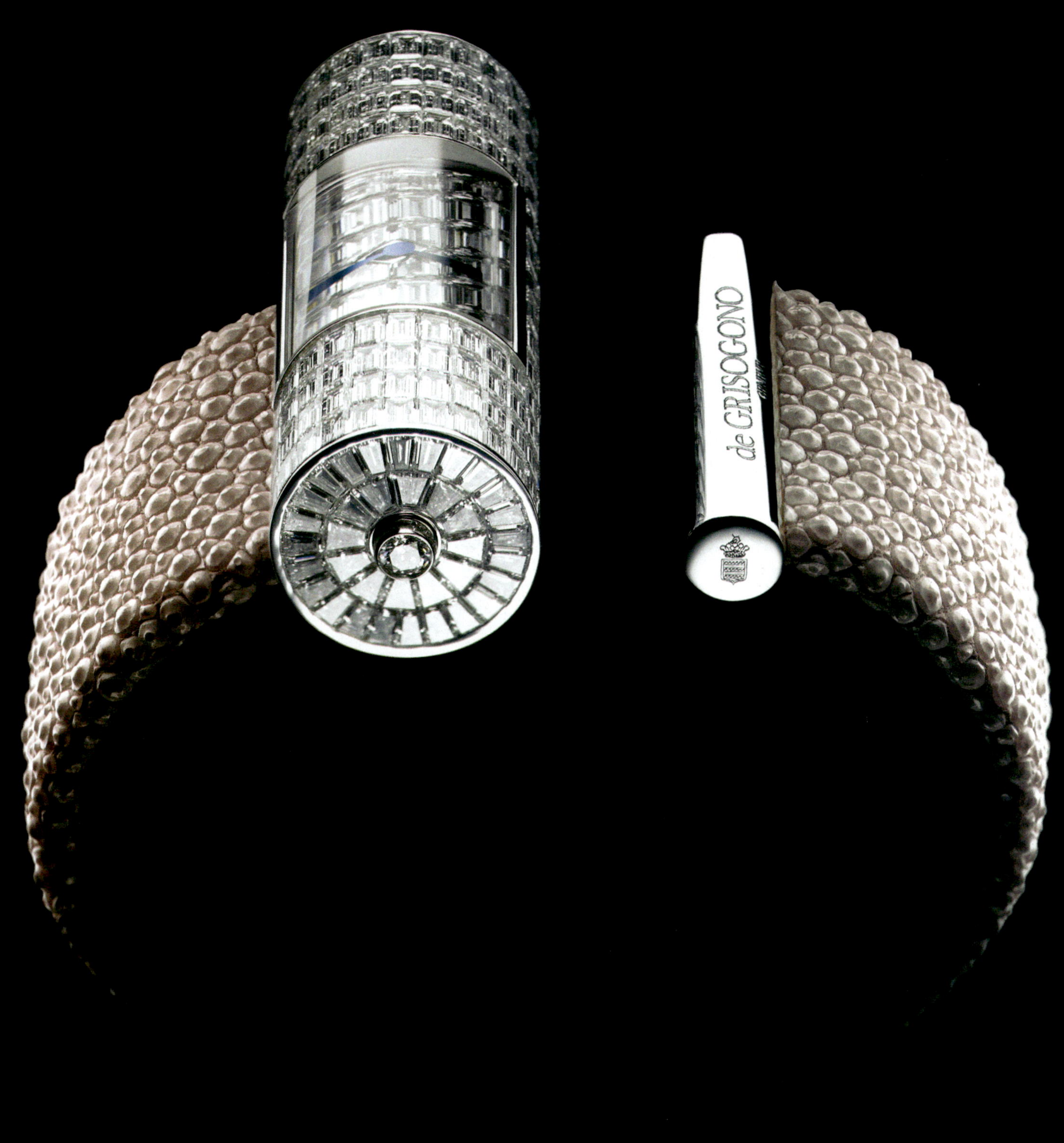
de GRISOGONO

Emeralds, diamonds, rubies or sapphires sparkle with exceptional brilliance in these eye-catching designs. Equally enticing is the fact that the straps are interchangeable thanks to a two-pushbutton system. The Lipstick Cylinder features a convex sapphire case offering superb magnification of the hours. The glass on the Square version is perfectly etched to echo the structure of the case and features two rows of gemstone beneath the glass. There are also two invisibly set diamond baguette versions of both the Cylinder and Square.

The stunning Lipstick collection of watches is matched by a set of holiday jewelry, including a magnificent pair of Cylinder diamond earrings and a spectacular sapphire and diamond Panther brooch.

THIS PAGE

LEFT

Rings abound in topaz, amethyst, peridot, emerald, orange, pink or yellow sapphires, and black diamonds.

BOTTOM

The Instrumento Tondo is crafted in pink gold with a cinnamon galuchat strap. It features a three-level dial with power-resave indicator and 24-hour time zone.

FACING PAGE

TOP

Cannes Film Festival 2004.

***from left to right***

Daryl Hannah wears a de GRISOGONO necklace with turquoise, aqua-marina and black diamonds.

Fawaz Gruosi and Naomi Campbell, who is wearing a necklace set with rubies and 10 carats of white diamonds.

Angie Hill is wearing a necklace with Autumn Icy Diamonds and white diamonds.

CENTER

Crafted in 18-karat white gold, this necklace is set with hundreds of carats of gemstones.

BOTTOM

Fawaz Gruosi and Eva Herzlgova.

# de GRISOGONO

A yummy new series from de GRISOGONO is the Fruit Collection consisting of a host of mouth-watering pieces of fruity jewelry. The freshness of this new series is turning heads with rings, earrings and pendants crafted of huge, magnificently colored gemstones that are carved to resemble eggplants, lemons, melons and more. Two years of development and craftsmanship went into the making of this series and only the finest gemsetters in the world are sought to produce the masterpieces.

Similarly, for the exquisite de GRISOGONO watches, gemsetting takes center stage in the creation of the newest Instrumentinos with varying degrees of diamonds on the dials and cases. The Nº Uno line also offers a range of steel cases without diamonds, set entirely with diamonds, and a sparkling model ensconced in diamonds from dial to case and bracelet attachments.

THIS PAGE

TOP RIGHT

These pink-gold earrings are set with multiple carats of stunning gemstones.

CENTER

This ring is set with 3.05 carats of sapphires and is enhanced by a blue cylinder of 11.13 carats of sapphires.

BOTTOM LEFT

These fanciful earrings are crafted in white gold with just over 25 carats of diamonds and sapphires.

FACING PAGE

TOP LEFT

The Melon earrings are set with 9.10 carats of peridots, 7.40 carats of tsavorites and two yellow sapphires weighing 0.10 carat.

TOP CENTER

The Orange ring in yellow gold is set with 6.10 carats of orange sapphies, 2.30 carats of white diamonds and four cabochon orange sapphires weighing 2.90 carats.

CENTER LEFT

de GRISOGONO's new boutique in New York.

CENTER RIGHT

This Instrumentino is crafted in pink gold with a pink galuchat strap. The watch houses the automatic-winding movement with dual time zone.

BOTTOM LEFT

The Apple ring and earrings are set with rubies, diamonds, emeralds, and one brown diamond.

BOTTOM CENTER

These Watermelon earrings are set with 5.85 carats of dark pink sapphires, 5.80 carats of emeralds 2.30 carats of peridots and 1.05 carats of black sapphires.

The Grape earrings are set with 63.80 carats of green pranites and 3.65 carats of emeralds.

BOTTOM RIGHT

These white-gold Aubergine earrings are set with two cabochon amethysts weighing 90.90 carats.

The Cherry earrings are set with 71.95 carats of pink tourmalines.

de GRISOGONO
de GRISOGONO

de GRISOGONO

SWISS MADE
de GRISOGONO
GENEVE

## CHRONOLOGY

**1995** Fawaz Gruosi founds de GRISOGONO SA and specializes in the creation of his own original designs—luxurious jewelry and objects of art—and makes a name for himself, notably by initiating the revival of black diamonds at a time when all other jewelers are neglecting this gemstone because of its rarity and extreme fragility. Gruosi is fascinated by these noble and mysterious stones, and fashions an entire jewelry collection around them. The enthusiasm of his clientele convinces Gruosi to adopt this stone as the symbol of de GRISOGONO.

**1996** The first de GRISOGONO boutique opens in Geneva.

**1997** A de GRISOGONO boutique is opened in London.

**1998** The brand makes headway with a new shop at the Palace Hotel in Gstaad.

**1999** Gruosi incorporates black diamonds into everyday objects such as sunglasses and mobile telephones, one of which is set with 240 diamonds totaling 18 carats. A fourth de GRISOGONO boutique opens its doors in Rome.

**2000** Gruosi begins his own watch production and unveils the Instrumento Nº Uno.

**2002** The brand unveils the double-sided Instrumento Doppio.

**2003** Two new de GRISOGONO watches are launched (the Instrumento Doppio Tre and the Instrumento Tondo) and new boutiques open in Paris and St. Moritz.

FACING PAGE

Shown here in stainless steel, the Nº Uno is also available with a blackened steel bracelet, in yellow or rose gold, or platinum and white gold set with diamonds. Its two-level, black-lacquered dial is exclusive to de GRISOGONO, the crown features a natural black diamond, and the watch is water resistant up to 30 meters.

THIS PAGE

TOP

The Instrumentino is crafted in pink gold and offered with either bracelet or strap. It houses a mechanical movement with 40 hours of power reserve and offers dual time-zone indicator.

BOTTOM

The Instrumento Tondo is crafted in pink gold with a three-level black dial and 24-hour time-zone readout.

For men, too, de GRISOGONO pulls out all the stops. Elegant men's timepieces run the gamut from the superbly ergonomic round Tondo watch (with 24-hour time-zone indicator and power reserve) to the dual time-zone Instrumentino to the famed Doppio Tre automatic-winding reversible watch. Each of these collections is crafted in the three colors of gold, and each offers striking renditions with masculine dials and sumptuous bracelets or straps.

Indeed, Gruosi spares nothing—imagination, skill nor resources—in the making of his jewelry and watches. For this gentleman with a passionate spirit, jewels (whether they be art, timepieces, or both) are today's method of communication.

# DeWitt

DeWitt was established just five years ago on the premise of creating only the most complex horological works of art—and only in limited editions. By remaining true to this creed, the firm has built a superb collection of masterpieces and a loyal following of collectors.

With perfection and passion at the heart of its new timepieces, DeWitt takes pride in unveiling a marvel: the Pressy Grande Complication 2004. Due to the immense amount of time and hand craftsmanship involved in the building of this watch, only five pieces will ever be made over the course of a year. This stunning platinum watch houses the DW96 movement and offers a wealth of incredible complications. Among them: quarter repeater; tourbillon; bi-retrograde perpetual calendar; retrograde days, months, years; split-seconds chronograph. The mechanical hand-wound movement features 52 jewels and offers 48 hours of power reserve. The elegant dial is a soft silver and blue mother of pearl, hand turned, with Arabic numerals. Naturally, the watch features a sapphire caseback.

To produce the New Emotion Minute Repeater with a sound pure and melodious, master watchmakers, artists and musicians worked together to create miniscule strike hammers of the finest quality. This watch features the DW88 mechanical movement. The complication enables the wearer to request the hours, quarters and minutes to be struck at any time. The strike-function activator is an exclusive DeWitt feature and is located mysteriously below the bezel. The ballet of magnificent hammers can be admired through the exhibition caseback and the movement is decorated with the Côtes de Genève motif.

Also new this year in the New Emotion Joaillerie collection are the Animations and the Caviar, an haute joaillerie piece. The Animations once again demonstrate DeWitt's excellence in

**ABOVE**

World Premiere: The Pressy Grande Complication 2004 houses the DW96 mechanical movement and offers bi-retrograde perpetual calendar, minute repeater, tourbillon and split-second chronograph.

**LEFT**

The New Emotion Minute Repeater features the DW88 mechanical movement and the DeWitt-exclusive strike-function activator, located below the bezel.

## CHRONOLOGY

**1803** Napoléon Bonaparte's brother, King Jérôme of Westphalia, is an avid pocket watch and table clock collector—an interest passed down from generation to generation.

**1999** Jérôme Napoléon DeWitt, fifth-generation descendant of King Jérôme, decides to restore the spirit of the discoverers of watchmaking and develops the DeWitt watch company.

**2002** DeWitt watches are introduced—offering traditional Swiss craftsmanship with innovative techniques and technology. It is the philosophy of the company that only limited editions will be created, thereby putting man in the heart of the creative process. Included in the collection are grand horological works, including a chronograph rattrapante, a tourbillon and a retrograde. Each is crafted of the finest 18-karat red or white gold and is fitted with a stunning lacquer dial.

**2003** DeWitt unveils a stunning array of timepieces and exhibits for the first time at the Basel World Watch and Jewelry Show. Each DeWitt timepiece is completely handmade by a single watchmaker, who signs every watch he completes with his own mark.

**2004** Among the stunning new watches is the Premiere Mondiale, a grand complication watch that offers hours, minutes, perpetual calendar, retrograde date, retrograde hours, months, years, split-second chronograph, minute repeater and tourbillon.

watchmaking but also add diamonds in a creative setting. The 18-karat gold New Emotion watches are now set with round diamonds on the bezel and on the case lugs for a very original look. Additionally, diamonds adorn the dial's uniquely shaped numerals. In all, the mechanical retrograde-seconds watch is set with 282 Top Wesselton VVS diamonds weighing 2.87 carats.

But, to the discerning powers that be at DeWitt, this diamond arrangement was still not enough. As such, it unveils the aptly named Caviar—the New Emotion Tourbillon Haute Joaillerie watch. The magnificent timepiece is set with 11.63 carats of Top Wesselton VVS1, color F baguette diamonds on the bezel and casesides, as well as on the lugs and crown. The watch's non-existent dial allows for viewing of the hand-decorated guilloché bridges and plates, and the tourbillon escapement. Only 11 pieces of this exclusive watch will be produced.

ABOVE

The New Emotion Tourbillon Haute Joaillerie Caviar is set with 89 baguette diamonds weighing 11.63 carats. It houses the DW80 mechanical movement with tourbillon escapement. Instead of a dial, the hands are set mystery-style over the main plate.

RIGHT

The New Emotion Animations are crafted in either 18-karat raised gold or 18-karat white gold and are set with 282 diamonds. The watches offer retrograde seconds and house the DW30 mechanical movement.

## NEW EMOTION MINUTE REPEATER — REF. NE088

**Movement:** DW88 mechanical manual-winding movement; Côtes de Genève finishing.
**Functions:** minute repeater (hours, quarters and minutes); 48 hours of power reserve; hour and minute indications.
**Case:** solid 750 red gold; bezel and middle section engraved with the exclusive DeWitt Imperial Columns; sapphire crystal caseback; water resistant to 30 meters.
**Note:** the radically innovative strike function activator is an exclusive DeWitt feature and is located mysteriously below the bezel.
**Dial:** hand-turned; solid 750 red gold; chocolate lacquered; small seconds hand at 9 and opening from 3 to 9.
**Indications:** minute repeater; small second at 9; hours and minutes.
**Strap:** chocolate brown alligator strap; solid 750 red gold folding clasp.
**Notes:** limited edition of 50 pieces per material.
**Also available:** solid 750 white gold.

## NEW EMOTION TOURBILLON — REF. NE080

**Movement:** DW80 mechanical; mysterious wheels and gear trains in Dents de Loup; manual-winding movement.
**Functions:** 110 hours of power reserve; hour and minute indications.
**Case:** solid 750 white gold; bezel and middle section engraved with the exclusive DeWitt Imperial Columns; sapphire crystal caseback; water resistant to 30 meters.

**Dial:** replaced by a hand-turned azure blue Petit Panier motifs succession on the plate and bridge.
**Strap:** midnight blue alligator strap; solid 750 white-gold folding clasp.
**Notes:** limited edition of 50 pieces per material.
**Also available:** solid 750 red gold.

## NEW EMOTION PERPETUAL CALENDAR BI-RETROGRADE — REF. NE097

**Movement:** DW97 mechanical self-winding movement stamped with the Geneva Seal; solid gold micro-rotor.
**Functions:** 52 hours of power reserve; hours, minutes; date, day, month, year; moonphase.
**Case:** solid 750 white gold; bezel and middle section engraved with the exclusive DeWitt Imperial Columns; sapphire crystal caseback; water resistant to 30 meters.

**Dial:** hand-turned; solid 750 white-gold and chocolate colored sun pattern.
**Indications:** retrograde date at 3; retrograde day at 9; months and year in counter at 12; moonphase display at 6.
**Strap:** brown alligator strap; solid 750 white-gold folding clasp.
**Notes:** limited edition of 50 pieces per material.
**Also available:** solid 750 red gold.

## NEW EMOTION CHRONOGRAPH — REF. NE071

**Movement:** DW71 mechanical; Valjoux base entirely reworked in-house; manual-winding column wheel chronograph movement.
**Functions:** 52 hours of power reserve; chronograph with 2 counters; hour, minute and second indications.
**Case:** solid 750 red gold; bezel and middle section engraved with the exclusive DeWitt Imperial Columns; sapphire crystal caseback; water resistant to 30 meters.

**Dial:** hand-turned; solid 750 red and white gold.
**Indications:** chronograph minute counter at 3; movement seconds in counter at 9; seconds of the chronograph function by a central hand.
**Strap:** black alligator strap; solid 750 red-gold folding clasp.
**Notes:** limited edition of 50 pieces per material.
**Also available:** solid 750 white gold.

## NEW EMOTION GMT DUAL TIME ZONE REF. NE024

**Movement:** DW24 mechanical self-winding movement.
**Functions:** 42 hours of power reserve; dual time; hours, minute and second indications; date.
**Case:** solid 750 red gold; bezel and middle section engraved with the exclusive DeWitt Imperial Columns; water resistant to 30 meters.
**Dial:** hand-turned; solid 750 red-gold and white mother-of-pearl.
**Indications:** small second-time-zone central hand; 24-hours indication in counter at 12; seconds in a central hand; date with magnet at 6
**Strap:** black alligator strap; solid 750 red gold buckle.
**Notes:** limited edition of 99 pieces per material.
**Also available:** solid 750 white gold and four different dials.

## NEW EMOTION RETROGRADE SECOND REF. NE030

**Movement:** DW30 mechanical self-winding movement.
**Functions:** 42 hours of power reserve; hour, minute and retrograde second indications.
**Case:** solid 750 red gold; bezel and middle section engraved with the exclusive DeWitt Imperial Columns; water resistant to 30 meters.
**Dial:** hand-turned; solid 750 red gold and ruthenium sun pattern.
**Indications:** retrograde second in a fan-shaped counter at 6.
**Strap:** black alligator strap; solid 750 red gold buckle.
**Notes:** limited edition of 99 pieces per material.
**Also available:** solid 750 white gold and four different dials

## NEW AGE CHRONOGRAPH REF. NA040

**Movement:** DW40 mechanical self-winding movement.
**Functions:** 48 hours of power reserve; chronograph with 3 counters; hour, minute and seconds indications; date.
**Case:** oval-shaped; polished stainless steel; water resistant to 30 meters.
**Dial:** engine-turned; black and gray.
**Indications:** minute counter for the chronograph function at 3; seconds counter for the movement at 9; chronograph hour counter at 6; seconds of the chronograph function by a central hand; date aperture between 4 and 5.
**Strap:** black alligator strap; polished stainless steel buckle.
**Also available:** one different dial.

## NEW AGE REGULATOR REF. NA050

**Movement:** DW50 mechanical self-winding movement.
**Functions:** 42 hours of power reserve; hours and minutes (by regulator) and seconds indication.
**Case:** oval-shaped; polished stainless steel; water resistant to 30 meters.
**Dial:** engine-turned; black.
**Indications:** hours at 12; seconds at 6; minutes by a single central hand.
**Strap:** black alligator strap; polished stainless steel buckle.

# DIOR

Dior, the French fashion house established in 1947, is a leading trendsetter season after season. Creativity, innovation and provocation are words that best describe the distinctive Dior style.

Dior Watches is the unique result of a harmonious mix between the couture collection, watch creations and fine Swiss watchmaking expertise from Les Ateliers Horlogers in La Chaux-de-Fonds.

Three designers drive Dior's creative and innovative tradition. John Galliano leads the artistic direction of Haute Couture, Ready-to-Wear and Women's Accessories. A master of "mix and match," Galliano has created an audaciously extravagant and consistently fresh timepiece collection for Dior Watches.

Artistic Director of Dior Joaillerie since 1998, Victoire de Castellane now infuses her style—a mix of poetry and eccentricity—into original jewelry watch collections for Dior Watches.

Last year, Hedi Slimane, Artistic Director for Dior Homme since 2000, presented the Chiffre Rouge, Dior's first masculine timepiece.

## DIOR HOMME

Dior's debut watch for men, Chiffre Rouge shares its values of excellence through a partnership with Zenith. The result is a technical watch that mirrors the design excellence of Dior Homme.

Structure: Chiffre Rouge is available in three versions and features the benchmark-quality automatic movement, the Caliber Irreductible. Developed by Zenith for Dior Homme, it contains 278 components and is capable of measuring time to 1/10th of a second with outstanding precision. When fully wound, the Caliber Irreductible offers more than 50 hours' power reserve.

Architecture: The functional asymmetry of Chiffre Rouge's case is unique, with an enlarged right side for the controls and a tooled bezel between 9:00 and 12:00 for better grip. The curved shape, smooth contours, convex surface, extreme flexibility of the bracelet, soft satin finish and use of steel endow this watch with fluid lines.

Appearance: Chiffre Rouge is easy to identify with Dior Homme. The principle of personal, exclusive and mysterious luxury is symbolized by the diamond hidden on the back of the case and the movement visible behind a black sapphire glass. Red, the ritual color for the architectural projects at Dior Homme, highlights the watch's key elements—name, date and pushbutton at 4:00.

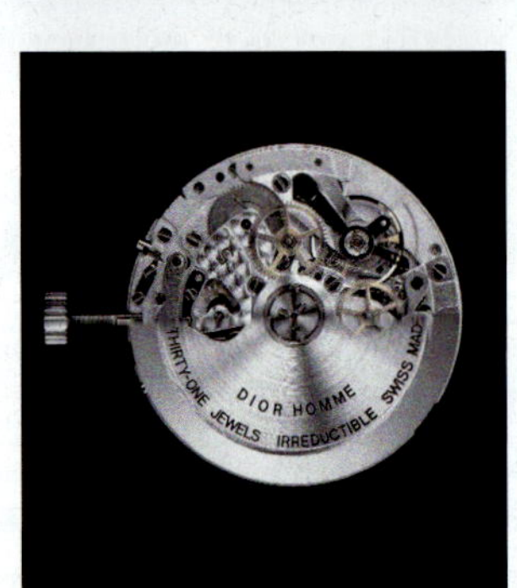


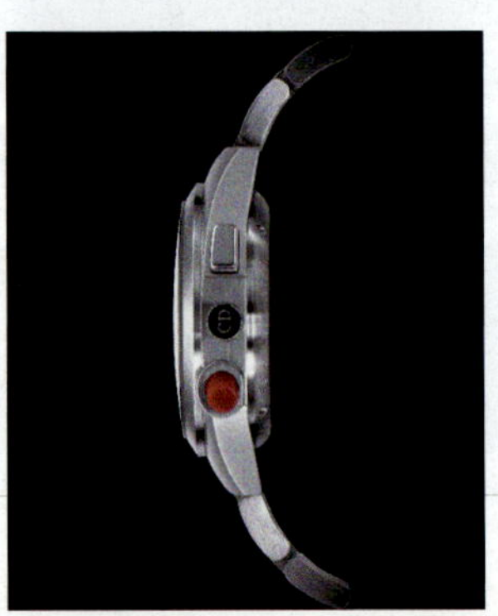

THIS PAGE

ABOVE

Chiffre Rouge A03 with a silver sun-brushed dial houses the automatic movement, Caliber ETA 2824.

LEFT

The sapphire-glass caseback reveals the complex performance of the Caliber Irreductible movement, an automatic COSC-certified chronometer chronograph. All materials used by Dior are of the very finest quality, such as the 316L vertical satin-finish steel for the case and double unfolding-clasp bracelet and the composite material for the red pushbutton.

FACING PAGE

The Caliber Irreductible (by Zenith for Dior) powers the 38mm Chiffre Rouge A01 with black dial by. Numbered limited edition.

55 Dior 5
CHRONOMETRE
IRREDUCTIBLE
SWISS MADE

## MY DIOR COLLECTION

The latest romantic creation by John Galliano for Dior evokes a bygone age and creates a marriage between the steel case and the white of a beautifully worked bracelet.

With its vintage inspiration, My Dior combines refined scallop stitching and British embroidery to set off its subtly finished leatherwork. Available in a selection of accessories and watches, the My Dior style defines femininity for the 2005 spring-summer season.

With Malice and Dior 66 in its wrap version, My Dior will appear contemporary. In its precious and refined jewelry versions, it perfectly associates the purity of white leather with the eternity of diamonds: Malice and Riva Sparkling shine in dazzling finery; Chris 47 reveals a diamond-set bezel; and Dior 66 lights up its style with a galaxy of diamond stars.

**TOP LEFT**
The Chris 47 is fashioned in the My Dior steel-on-white theme.

**TOP CENTER**
Banded version of the Dior 66 (with removable leather band) for the My Dior collection by John Galliano.

**TOP RIGHT**
This My Dior Riva Sparkling Chronograph is sprinkled with 43 diamonds.

**FAR LEFT**
Malice My Dior on a white removable leather bandage.

ABOVE

This 23mm Baby D features a white mother-of-pearl dial with diamond-set indexes and bezel set with 52 diamonds.

TOP RIGHT

This La D de Dior in 38mm case with silver dial features a bezel set with 72 diamonds and a steel bracelet.

BOTTOM RIGHT

The gold 23mm Baby D with a sun-brushed dial and bezel set with 52 diamonds.

## La D de DIOR

The little sister to La D de Dior, Baby D is the latest from Victoire de Castellane. Its new proportions (23mm diameter) give it an unmistakable feminine touch. Items of jewelry, the steel versions of La Baby D de Dior boast 12 indexes. Like its bigger sisters (33 and 38mm), it has all the refinements of Dior Joaillerie—a ribbon presenting the time, flawless finishing, and diamond-set bezels and indexes. It is the newborn addition to an extended family of bracelets in gold, steel, leather and crocodile skin. It is the Baby D.

### CHRONOLOGY

**1947** Presentation of the first Christian Dior collection. Launch of the Miss Dior fragrance.

**1948** Creation of Parfums Christian Dior.

**1955** Opening of the Avenue Montaigne Boutique.

**1957** At 42, Christian Dior suffers a heart attack. Yves Saint Laurent takes over as Artistic Director of the house.

**1967** Presentation of the first Christian Dior Women's Ready-To-Wear collection.

**1969** Launch of the first Christian Dior make-up line.

**1970** Creation of Christian Dior Menswear.

**1975** Introduction of Christian Dior Watches.

**1985** Bernard Arnault is appointed Chairman and Managing Director of Christian Dior.

**1995** Launch of the La Parisienne watch.

**1996** John Galliano is appointed Artistic Director of Dior.

**1997** First Haute Couture Collection by Galliano for Dior is presented.

**1998** Victoire de Castellane is appointed Artistic Director of Dior Jewelry.

**2000** Hedi Slimane is appointed Artistic Director of Christian Dior Homme. Launches of Malice and Riva.

**2001** Launch of Chris 47.

**2003** Launch of La D de Dior.

**2004** Launch of Chiffre Rouge.

# Dubey & Schaldenbrand

In the high-end watch industry, a woman's role is often restricted to sales or marketing. At Dubey & Schaldenbrand, a woman is at the head of the company. Cinette Robert purchased the brand in 1995, and has produced a coveted collector's line of classic watchmaking and superb design.

Cinette Robert may well be the only woman to have risen to ownership of a luxury watch brand. Of Swiss origin and the great-granddaughter of renowned watchmaker Meylan-LeCoultre, Robert honors the traditions of the old horological masters and inventors.

This brand's high-end Swiss timepieces are elegant watches with beautifully curved lines that encompass a feminine sensibility and subtlety. The enchanting 100 percent Swiss-made movements offer a melodious tick-tock and are intricately complex. A look through the transparent caseback reveals a spectacle of 1,001 reflections created by the artistic engravings that decorate the heart of each watch.

The highly skilled craftsmen, carefully selected by Dubey & Schaldenbrand, constantly work their magic using a combination of their gifted hands along with the specialized machines, instruments and tools that they master. The sum of their delicate and time-consuming work—work that is executed today as in the past—defines the identity of each and every one of the unique timepieces that they create. Their work is a perfect symphony of modern, high-tech, micro mechanics and high-end watchmaking. It is these very skills and expertise that perpetuate the reputation of the Neuchâtel mountain region.

Dubey & Schaldenbrand creates exceptional pieces—pieces charged with history and emotion. To truly understand a Dubey & Schaldenbrand watch, one must see it, feel it, listen to it—allow the bracelet to embrace the wrist. Each watch is made by men and women who strive patiently to achieve the perfection and durability of a Dubey & Schaldenbrand timepiece. These highly skilled craftsmen are pleased to entrust you with a part of their passion when they leave you with an exceptional work of art.

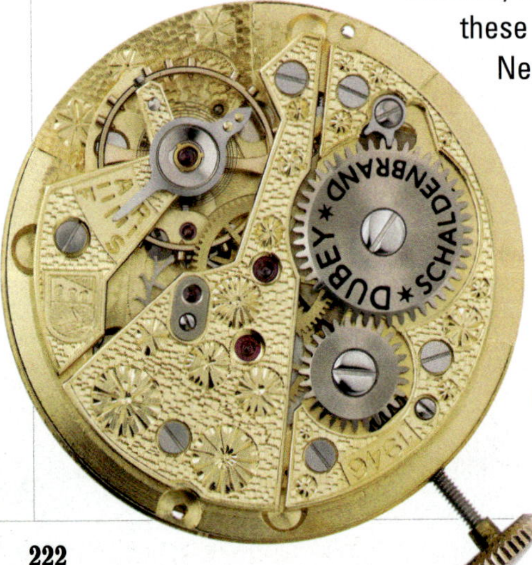


**TOP**

The beautiful Spiral Venus features a spiral recoil spring that rotates around the center axis of the hands on the dial. The movement is delicately hand engraved with flower and bird motifs of the region where the brand's Swiss workshops are located.

**ABOVE**

The Spiral VIP chronograph features triple date and moonphase functions and is available in 18-karat rose gold or stainless steel.

**LEFT**

Engraved vintage movement of the Spiral Venus.

Dubey & Schaldenbrand
SWISS MADE
SUN
JUN

# Dubey & Schaldenbrand

By consistently reviving archival looks in a modernistic mode—then combining them with superlative functions and movements—Dubey & Schaldenbrand offers a rich and exclusive collection of timepieces. Most recent unveilings feature not only complex, finely finished movements, but also themed engravings on the movement parts. Indeed, in its workshops in Les Ponts-de-Martel, Dubey & Schaldenbrand's highly skilled craftsmen work constant magic with their gifted hands to deliver delicate artful engravings that defines the identity of each watch and deems it unique.

The newest hand-engraved models include the Spiral Venus and Spiral VIP. Each of these models carries the engraved motif of a flower or animal. Exceptionally elegant, the Spiral watches feature the original Isoval spiral recoil spring that pivots around the center axis of the hands on the dial. First patented in 1946 as the Index Mobile chronograph, this recoil spring is offered in tribute to Georges Dubey, founder of the brand and originator of the device.

The case of the Spiral Venus borrows its design inspiration from styles of the 1940s and 1950s and adds mobile lugs for flexibility and comfort. The dials are either white, pink or blue mother of pearl and the casebacks are sapphire. The movement of the Spiral Venus is original—produced from 1950 to 1960. Perhaps more impressive than the age and prowess of the movement is its engraving. Tiny birds and flowers from the Les Ponts-de-Martel region grace the tiny parts.

Because of the time-consuming work involved in the creation of the Spiral Venus, just two limited series are being created. The Spiral Venus 220 is created in 80 pieces with white mother-of-pearl dials, and 40 pieces each with blue and pink mother-of-pearl dials. The Spiral Venus 227 is created in just 39 pieces with white mother-of-pearl dial and date window at 3:00. Both models are steel and water resistant to 30 meters.

The Spiral Cap line is designed for the young at heart, with a striking boldness to the design. The Spiral Cap features a big date at 6:00 and a power-reserve indicator at 12:00. Three models are offered including a black-, white-, or blue-dial version. Interestingly, the Spiral Cap's crown is located on the left side of the case and finished with a blue ogival stone. Only 300 pieces of the Spiral Cap will be produced and each will be individually numbered.

Another key watch in the line is the Spiral VIP chronograph. The exceptional character of this watch is evidenced by the moonphase indicator, weekday and month indicators, date, 24-hour counter, and hour, minute and second chronograph counters. The bridge of this model is adorned with two herons, symbolic of the brand's home region. Additionally, the magnificent automatic movement features a skeletonized winding rotor that pirouettes around its axis. The Spiral VIP is offered in steel or in 18-karat rose gold.

PREVIOUS PAGE

The Gran'Chrono Astro features a full triple date (day, date, month) combined with moonphase. These added complications are fitted in the same ergonomic case, on which even the pushers were specially designed to ensure maximum ease and aesthetics. To make the 18-karat gold case, 90 operations are required. It is set with 432 diamonds weighing 8.92 carats. The watch houses the Valjoux 7751 self-winding automatic movement with 25 jewels.

THIS PAGE

ABOVE

The all new Aquadyn sport watch is water resistant to 100 meters and houses a top-quality self-winding automatic movement.

LEFT

Engraved movement.

**TOP**

The very successful Aerochrono is now available in stunning 18-karat rose gold.

**CENTER**

The Spiral Cap features the same spiral recoil spring as the Spiral Venus, but has a more contemporary design thanks to its left-sided crown and bold dial designs.

Also new to Dubey & Schaldenbrand is a collection of sport watches aptly named Aquadyn. The bold Aquadyn features a screw-down crown, an extra-thick domed sapphire crystal with antireflective coating on both sides, and water-resistance to 100 meters. Housing a self-winding automatic 26-jeweled movement specially modified for Dubey & Schaldenbrand, the watch includes a big-date indicator and a small subdial for the seconds. The tonneau case is crafted in steel and the bracelet is a rugged steel-and-rubber combination.

Adding to its incredibly successful Aerochrono line that was first introduced in 2003, Dubey & Schaldenbrand unveils Aerochrono in 18-karat rose gold. The self-winding automatic watch offers three subdials on a Clous de Paris guilloché dial. As with all Dubey & Schaldenbrand timepieces, this series is limited in production.

## CHRONOLOGY

**1946** Georges Dubey, a teacher at the school of horology in La Chaux-de-Fonds, develops the Index Mobile—a new chronographic second-division system based on the principles of 19th century Austrian horologist Josef Winnerl. Dubey pools his talents with skilled watchmaker René Schaldenbrand and Dubey & Schaldenbrand is formed.

**1947** The Index Mobile is registered in Switzerland, France and the United States.

**1950** The brand's production of automatic watches for gentlemen reaches a record of 2,000 pieces. The high-performance chronograph movement is much smaller and less expensive than the equivalent mechanisms produced by Breitling, Butex and Patek Philippe. It is adopted by many sporting events and for military purposes.

**1960** A new 6 3/4" automatic ladies' watch is produced as well as an 11 1/2" caliber with power reserve.

**1980** The brand is not deterred by the quartz boom. In fact, Dubey & Schaldenbrand ignores the new propulsion system and focuses on the restoration of old mechanical masterpieces for a limited elite of collectors.

**1990** Georges Dubey assembles a record 17 pocket tourbillons.

**1995** The Dubey & Schaldenbrand company is sold to Cinette Robert, long-time friend of Georges Dubey. While Dubey was restoring timepieces, Robert was collecting retired mechanical movements. Her first step as owner of the company is to introduce a series of limited editions by using the 6,000 movements she had collected and adapting them into retro-styled cases.

**2000** The brand launches the automatic Gran'Chrono Astro, which combines a triple calendar and moonphase with a chronograph.

**2001** Dubey & Schaldenbrand exports 5,000 watches to 30 countries.

**2004** Aerodyn Lady Star is released housing a self-winding movement with moonphase and pointer calendar.

# Dubey & Schaldenbrand

## GRAN'CHRONO ASTRO — REF. AGCA/RG/BKS/

**Movement:** chronograph 2 counters; self-winding mechanical movement; chronometer-quality escapement; stop seconds; hand-engraved.
**Functions:** hours, minutes; chronograph; day, date, month; moonphase.
**Case:** 18K rose gold (4N); (size: 37.7x50mm, thickness: 15.1mm); Cintrée curvex shape; antireflective sapphire crystal domed on top flat on bottom; water resistant to 3atm.
**Dial:** guilloché; "Losanges diamantés" hands with Super-LumiNova.
**Strap:** Louisiana alligator.
**Also available:** with silver dial.

## GRAN'CHRONO ASTRO — REF. AGCA432/RG/SIB/

**Movement:** chronograph 2 counters; self-winding mechanical movement; chronometer-quality escapement; stop seconds; hand-engraved.
**Functions:** hours, minutes; chronograph; day, date, month; moonphase.
**Case:** 18K rose gold (4N); (size: 37.7x50mm, thickness: 15.1mm); Cintrée curvex shape; set with 432 diamonds TW/VS (8.92ct); antireflective sapphire crystal domed on top, flat on bottom; water resistant to 3atm.
**Dial:** guilloché; "Losanges diamantés" hands with Super-LumiNova.
**Strap:** Louisiana alligator.
**Also available:** with black dial.

## GRAN'CHRONO ASTRO — REF. AGCA/ST/SIB/

**Movement:** chronograph 2 counters; self-winding mechanical movement; chronometer-quality escapement; stop seconds; hand-engraved.
**Functions:** hours, minutes; chronograph; day, date, month; moonphase.
**Case:** polished 316L surgical stainless steel; (size: 37.7x50mm, thickness: 15.1mm); Cintrée curvex shape; antireflective sapphire crystal domed on top, flat on bottom; water resistant to 3atm.
**Dial:** guilloché; "Losanges diamantés" hands with Super-LumiNova.
**Strap:** Louisiana alligator.
**Also available:** with black or blue dial.

## GRAN'CHRONO ASTRO — REF. AGCA54/ST/SIB/

**Movement:** chronograph 2 counters; self-winding mechanical movement; chronometer-quality escapement; stop seconds; hand-engraved.
**Functions:** hours, minutes; chronograph; day, date, month; moonphase.
**Case:** polished 316L surgical stainless steel; (size: 37.7x50mm, thickness: 15.1mm); Cintrée curvex shape; set with 54 diamonds TW/VS (2.16 carats); antireflective sapphire crystal domed on top, flat on bottom;

water resistant to 3atm.
**Dial:** guilloché; "Losanges diamantés" hands with Super-LumiNova
**Strap:** Louisiana alligator.
**Also available:** with black or blue dial.

## AQUADYN — REF. AQUA/ST/WHG/

**Movement:** self-winding mechanical movement; chronometer-quality escapement; stop seconds.
**Functions:** hours, minutes, small seconds; large date.
**Case:** polished 316L surgical stainless steel; (size: 38x47.5mm, thickness: 14.1mm); Cintrée curvex shape; domed antireflective sapphire crystal; screw-down crown; water resistant to 10atm.
**Dial:** white enamel; Poire hands with Super-LumiNova.
**Strap:** rubber with steel elements.
**Also available:** with black, blue or red dial.

## AQUADYN — REF. AQUA/RG/BKW/

**Movement:** self-winding mechanical movement; chronometer-quality escapement; stop seconds.
**Functions:** hours, minutes, small seconds; large date.
**Case:** 18K rose gold (4N); (size: 38x47.5mm, thickness: 14.1mm); Cintrée curvex shape; domed antireflective sapphire crystal; screw-down crown; water resistant to 5atm.
**Dial:** black enamel; Poire hands with Super-LumiNova.
**Strap:** rubber with gold elements.

## SONNERIE GMT — REF. GMTA/ST/WHG/

**Movement:** alarm self-winding mechanical movement with two barrels; chronometer-quality escapement; stop seconds.
**Functions:** hours, minutes, sweep seconds; date; alarm; GMT.
**Case:** polished 316L surgical stainless steel; (size: 37.7x50mm, thickness: 15.1mm); Cintrée curvex shape; antireflective sapphire crystal domed on top, flat on bottom; water resistant to 3atm.
**Dial:** white enamel; "Losanges diamantés" hands with Super-LumiNova.
**Strap:** Louisiana alligator.
**Also available:** with black or blue dial.

## AERODYN DUO — REF. ADUO173/RG/BKW/

**Movement:** self-winding mechanical movement; chronometer-quality escapement; stop seconds.
**Functions:** hours, minutes, sweep seconds; date; second time zone; 24-hours display.
**Case:** 18K rose gold (4N); (size: 33x44mm, thickness: 11.7mm); Cintrée curvex shape; set with 173 diamonds TW/VS (3.5 carats); domed antireflective sapphire crystal; water resistant to 3atm.
**Dial:** black enamel; Poire hands with Super-LumiNova.
**Strap:** Louisiana alligator.
**Also available:** in stainless steel with 173 diamonds.

## SPIRAL ONE — REF. SPI1/RG/BKG/

**Movement:** chronograph 3 counters; self-winding mechanical movement; chronometer-quality escapement; stop seconds; hand-engraved.
**Functions:** hours, minutes, small seconds; chronograph; date.
**Case:** 18K rose gold (4N); (size: 40x46.5mm, thickness: 14.3mm); mobile lugs; blue set crown; antireflective sapphire crystal domed on top, flat on bottom; water resistant to 3atm.
**Dial:** guilloché; "Losanges diamantés" hands with Super-LumiNova.
**Strap:** Louisiana alligator.
**Also available:** in stainless steel.

## SPIRAL VIP — REF. SVIP/RG/SIG/

**Movement:** chronograph 3 counters with triple date and moon; self-winding mechanical movement; chronometer-quality escapement; stop seconds; hand-engraved.
**Functions:** hours, minutes, small seconds; 24-hours hand; chronograph; day, date, month; moonphase.
**Case:** 18K rose gold (4N); (size: 40x46.5mm, thickness: 14.3mm); mobile lugs; blue set crown; antireflective sapphire crystal domed on top, flat on bottom; water resistant to 3atm.
**Dial:** brossé with applied hour markers; "Losanges diamantés" hands with Super-LumiNova.
**Strap:** Louisiana alligator.
**Also available:** in stainless steel.

## SPIRAL VIP — REF. SVIP/ST/SIS/

**Movement:** chronograph 3 counters with triple date and moon; self-winding mechanical movement; chronometer-quality escapement; stop seconds; hand-engraved.
**Functions:** hours, minutes, small seconds; 24-hour hand; chronograph; day, date, month; moonphase.
**Case:** polished 316L surgical stainless steel; (size: 40x46.5mm, thickness: 14.3mm); mobile lugs; blue set crown; antireflective sapphire crystal domed on top, flat on bottom; water resistant to 3atm.
**Dial:** brossé with applied hour markers; "Losanges diamantés" hands with Super-LumiNova.
**Strap:** Louisiana alligator.
**Also available:** with bracelet.

## SPIRAL RATTRAPANTE — REF. SPIR/ST/SIB/

**Movement:** chronograph 4 counters with split-second chronograph; self-winding mechanical movement; chronometer-quality escapement; stop seconds; hand-engraved.
**Functions:** hours, minutes, small seconds; split-second chronograph; date.
**Case:** polished 316L surgical stainless steel; (size: 40x46.5mm, thickness: 14.7mm); mobile lugs; blue set crown; antireflective sapphire crystal domed on top, flat on bottom; water resistant to 3atm.
**Dial:** guilloché; "Losanges diamantés" hands with Super-LumiNova.
**Strap:** Louisiana alligator.
**Also available:** with bracelet.

## CARRE CAMBRE DIPLOMATIC — REF. CCDI/ST/WHB/

**Movement:** self-winding mechanical movement; chronometer-quality escapement; stop seconds.
**Functions:** hours, minutes, sweep seconds; date; second time zone; 24-hour display.
**Case:** polished 316L surgical stainless steel; (size: 34x34mm, thickness: 9.9mm); carré cambré cushion shape; domed antireflective sapphire crystal; water resistant to 3atm.
**Dial:** white enamel; Feuilles hands.
**Strap:** caïman or alligator.
**Also available:** with black dial.

## CARRE CAMBRE CALENDAR — REF. CCCA/ST/SIB/

**Movement:** self-winding mechanical movement; chronometer-quality escapement; stop seconds.
**Functions:** hours, minutes, small seconds; large date.
**Case:** polished 316L surgical stainless steel; (size: 34x34mm, thickness: 9.9mm); carré cambré cushion shape; domed antireflective sapphire crystal; water resistant to 3atm.
**Dial:** guilloché; Alpha hands.
**Strap:** Louisiana alligator.
**Also available:** with black dial.

## SPIRAL CAP — REF. SCAP/ST/WHB/

**Movement:** self-winding mechanical movement; chronometer-quality escapement; stop seconds.
**Functions:** hours, minutes, sweep seconds; large date; power-reserve indicator.
**Case:** polished 316L surgical stainless steel; (size: 35.5x41.5mm, thickness: 10.7mm); mobile lugs; blue set crown; antireflective sapphire crystal domed on top, flat on bottom; water resistant to 3atm.
**Dial:** white enamel; Alpha hands.
**Strap:** ostrich or alligator.
**Also available:** with black dial.
**Note:** limited edition of 300 pieces.

## SPIRAL VENUS — REF. SVEN/ST/PIS/

**Movement:** mechanical manual-winding vintage movement; hand-engraved.
**Functions:** hours, minutes, sweep seconds.
**Case:** polished 316L surgical stainless steel; (size: 35.5x41.5mm, thickness: 10.3mm); mobile lugs; blue set crown; antireflective sapphire crystal domed on top, flat on bottom; water resistant to 3atm.
**Dial:** mother of pearl; Alpha hands.
**Strap:** Louisiana alligator.
**Also available:** with white or blue mother-of-pearl dial.
**Note:** limited edition of 160 pieces.

# Dubey & Schaldenbrand

## AERODYN DATE — REF. ADAT/RG/SIG/

**Movement:** self-winding mechanical movement; chronometer-quality escapement; stop seconds.
**Functions:** hours, minutes, small seconds; large date.
**Case:** 18K rose gold (4N); (size: 33x44mm, thickness: 11.8mm); Cintrée curvex shape; domed antireflective sapphire crystal; water resistant to 3atm.

**Dial:** guilloché; Feuilles hands.
**Strap:** Louisiana alligator.
**Also available:** with black dial.

## AEROCHRONO — REF. AERO/RG/SIB/

**Movement:** chronograph 3 counters; self-winding mechanical movement; chronometer-quality escapement; stop seconds.
**Functions:** hours, minutes, small seconds; chronograph; date.
**Case:** 18K rose rold (4N); (size: 33x44mm, thickness: 12.2mm; Cintrée curvex shape); antireflective sapphire crystal domed on top, flat on bottom; water resistant to 3atm.

**Dial:** guilloché; Stuart hands.
**Strap:** Louisiana alligator.
**Also available:** in stainless steel.

## AERODYN ELEGANCE — REF. AELE/ST/SIB/

**Movement:** self-winding mechanical movement; stop seconds.
**Functions:** hours, minutes, small seconds; date.
**Case:** polished 316L surgical stainless steel; (size: 33x44mm, thickness: 11.5mm); cintrée curvex shape; domed antireflective sapphire crystal; water resistant to 3atm.
**Dial:** white; Dauphine hands.

**Strap:** Louisiana alligator.
**Also available:** with black dial.

## AERODYN DATE — REF. ADAT/ST/SIB/

**Movement:** self-winding mechanical movement; chronometer-quality escapement; stop seconds.
**Functions:** hours, minutes, small seconds; large date.
**Case:** polished 316L surgical stainless steel; (size: 33x44mm, thickness: 11.8mm); cintrée curvex shape; domed antireflective sapphire crystal; water resistant to 3atm.

**Dial:** guilloché; Feuilles hands.
**Strap:** Louisiana alligator.
**Also available:** with black dial.

## ANTICA REF. AANT173/RG/SIG/

**Movement:** mechanical hand-winding vintage movement; hand-engraved.
**Functions:** hours, minutes, sub-seconds.
**Case:** 18K rose gold (size: 27x37mm, thickness: 8.9mm); Cintrée curvex shape in (5N) set with 173 diamonds TW/VS (2.6ct); antireflective sapphire crystal domed on top, flat on bottom; water resistant to 3atm.
**Dial:** guilloché; blued-steel Croix de Malte hands.
**Strap:** Louisiana alligator.
**Also available:** in 18K white gold.
**Note:** limited edition of 100 pieces.

## LADY REF. AL30/ST/SIG/

**Movement:** self-winding mechanical movement; stop seconds.
**Functions:** hours, minutes, sweep seconds.
**Case:** polished 316L surgical stainless steel (size: 27x37mm, thickness: 10.1mm); Cintrée curvex shape; set with 30 diamonds TW/VS (0.4ct); domed antireflective sapphire crystal; water resistant to 3atm.
**Dial:** guilloché; Dauphine hands.
**Strap:** Louisiana alligator.
**Also available:** without diamonds.

## ANTICA REF. AANT/ST/SIB/

**Movement:** mechanical hand-winding vintage movement; hand-engraved.
**Functions:** hours, minutes, sub-seconds.
**Case:** polished 316L surgical stainless steel; (size: 27x37mm, thickness: 8.9mm); Cintrée curvex shape; antireflective sapphire crystal domed on top, flat on bottom; water resistant to 3atm.
**Dial:** guilloché; blued-steel Croix de Malte hands.
**Strap:** Louisiana alligator.
**Also available:** in 18K rose gold.
**Note:** limited edition of 225 pieces.

## LADY REF. ALND/RG/BKW/

**Movement:** self-winding mechanical movement; stop seconds.
**Functions:** hours, minutes, sweep seconds.
**Case:** 18K rose gold (5N); (size: 27x37mm, thickness: 10.1mm); Cintrée curvex shape; domed antireflective sapphire crystal; water resistant to 3atm.
**Dial:** black enamel.
**Strap:** Louisiana alligator.
**Also available:** in stainless steel.

# EBEL

Since 1911, Ebel has dedicated its talents, passion and creativity to designing and crafting distinctive watches.

A brand that celebrates style in all it creates, Ebel has been internationally recognized for its cutting-edge designs and technical mastery since its inception. Today, Ebel is poised on the edge of grand growth under the auspices of the Movado Group—owners of the brand since March 2004. This group is committed to providing product and marketing support that is designed to lead the brand into a new era of luxury.

In addition to the stunning new products unveiled by Ebel, the brand also launches a beautiful new global advertising campaign that features internationally renowned German supermodel Claudia Schiffer as Ebel's new face. In no uncertain terms, Schiffer—with her glamorous beauty and sophistication—possesses and exudes the spirit of Ebel. The black-and-white advertisements, shot by photographer Patrick Demarchelier, feature a dreamy ambience that suggests timelessness. There are five renditions, each with Schiffer wearing a different Ebel timepiece.

The watches include the shining stars of the brand: its Haute Joaillerie Collection, the Beluga, and the Sportwave. The high jeweled watch series is perhaps the fastest growing timepiece series at Ebel, as the brand pushes all envelopes to unveil shimmering beauties. Among the most stunning new models from the Gems of the Night collection is the all-diamond Moon Chic. Sensually curved and deliciously bedecked with 1,175 diamonds, this watch is crafted in 18-karat gold and features diamond brilliants everywhere. In fact, the total weight is nearly 7 carats. True to its name, the brilliance of Moon Chic captures the brightness of the moon in beauty and harmony. Several other versions of the Moon Chic that feature a diamond case and sateen strap are available.

**TOP**

Subtly elegant, this Moon Chic is crafted in 18-karat gold with a case of 218 diamonds. The black dial is set with 12 diamond markers and the strap is black sateen.

**ABOVE**

On an elegant burgundy sateen strap with a mother-of-pearl dial, this Moon Chic watch is set with 218 diamonds on the case weighing 1.72 carats.

**LEFT**

Claudia Schiffer wears the Moon Chic in Ebel's newest advertising campaign.

EBEL

Attuned to the multi-faceted woman and her timely needs, Ebel offers a stunning new variation of the much-loved Beluga Tonneau. Once again, Ebel embraces femininity and sensuality with the Beluga Tonneau's curved lines.

In contrast to highly jeweled Beluga Tonneaus, the newest versions feature a lighter approach to diamonds. In fact, one model features only diamonds as markers on the dial and is offered in steel with an elegant supple link bracelet. Its sister model is an 18-karat gold version with a center-guilloché, mother-of-pearl dial and sleek link bracelet. This watch offers diamonds on the dial and in two rows on the case. Delightfully demure and irresistible, these newest Belugas offer charm and elegance.

PREVIOUS PAGE

This Moon Chic is totally ensconced in more than 1,000 diamond brilliants—all F-G color and IF-VVS clarity. The case is set with 218 diamonds, the bracelet with 764, and the dial with 193. The total diamond weight is 6.98 carats.

THIS PAGE

ABOVE

Claudia Schiffer wears the Beluga Tonneau.

LEFT

The Beluga Tonneau is shown here in steel with 13 diamond markers on the dial, and in 18-karat gold with gold bracelet and 116 diamonds on the case totaling 0.72 carat.

**TOP LEFT AND RIGHT**

The Sportwave Chronograph has an ergonomic design with sleek pushers.

**ABOVE LEFT**

The ladies' Sportwave features diamond markers on the dial and a diamond bezel.

**ABOVE RIGHT**

The gents' size Sportwave offers a seconds hand and a date feature at 6:00.

All new this year is the re-launched Sportwave collection that proudly carries the unmistakable signature of Ebel: The Architects of Time. Primed for action, the Sportwave embodies the brand's values of sophistication and dynamism.

The legendary Ebel sport wave motif has been revamped for this watch to create a very modern look—characterized by the undulating steel bracelet links that offer flexibility and comfort. The dial features hand-applied markers and intermittent Arabic numerals for easy readability. The watch is offered in: a two-hand version with diamond bezel and markers for women; a three-hand version with date for men; a chronograph version with sweep seconds hand and touches of orange on the counters. All versions are offered with either a silver, black, or orange dial. The gents' three-hand model is also offered with a blue dial and the ladies' model is offered with a mother-of-pearl dial. The Sportwave collection is water resistant to 100 meters and feature antireflective sapphire crystals.

## CHRONOLOGY

**1911** Eugène Blum and his wife Alice Lévy found Ebel (Eugène Blum et Lévy) in La Chaux-de-Fonds, Switzerland.

**1912** Ebel releases its first wristwatch.

**1930** Ebello, an exceptional, water-proof watch with patented opening system, is introduced.

**1939-45** The brand is a key supplier of watches to the British army.

**1964** Ebel is awarded First Prize at the Swiss National Exhibition for a jewelry watch, the Lune Etoilée.

**1970** Pierre Alain Blum, grandson of the founders, arrives at the company.

**1977** Ebel introduces the Sport Classic model.

**1983** The Perpetual Calendar Chronograph is unveiled.

**1984** The diver's model Discovery is launched.

**1985** Ebel unveils the iconic Beluga.

**1986** For its 75th anniversary, Ebel creates the popular 1911. It also acquires the Villa Turque in La Chaux-de-Fonds, the mansion built by Le Corbusier in 1916-17.

**1994** The majority interest in the Ebel Group is acquired by Investcorp.

**1998** The Beluga Manchette is introduced.

**1999** Ebel is acquired by the LVMH Group.

**2001** The new versions of the 1911 are introduced and included a chronograph and an automatic with date display. The ladies' Beluga Manchette line is enhanced with precious gemstone versions and the Classic Wave is launched.

**2002** Launchings of the Gems of the Ocean (Haute Joailerie Collection) and the Beluga Tonneau.

**2003** Ebel introduces a host of new products: Midnight (Haute Joaillerie); 1911 La Carrée; Beluga Tonneau Hypnotic; 1911 XXL Chronograph; and Tarawa. Movado Group Inc. announces plans to acquire Ebel. Final closing is expected in early 2004.

**2004** In March, Ebel is purchased by the Movado Group, which vows a long-term commitment to building the brand in a manner consistent with its past. The brand unveils a bold new advertising campaign with Claudia Schiffer co–starring with Ebel watches.

## TARAWA CHRONOGRAPH REF. 9137J40/5435H34–1214260

**Movement:** mechanical automatic-winding Ebel caliber 137; COSC-certified chronometer.
**Functions:** hour, minute, sweep second; date.
**Case:** polished stainless steel triple-curved case; stainless steel crown; triple-curved antireflective sapphire crystal; sapphire crystal caseback; water resistant to 3atm.

**Dial:** black, applied Roman numerals at 12, 3, 6 and 9; minute-track.
**Indications:** 30-minute counter at 3; hour counter at 6; small seconds hand at 9; center-mounted sweep seconds counter; date display at 6; minute track with divisions for 1/5 of a second.
**Strap:** brown "selvaggio" alligator strap; polished stainless steel folding clasp.
**Also available:** in yellow and rose gold (limited editions).

## 1911 LA CARREE REF. 9120I43/15535136–1214002

**Movement:** mechanical automatic-winding.
**Functions:** hour, minute, sweep second; date.
**Case:** brushed or polished stainless steel case; polished stainless steel bezel; stainless steel crown; flat antireflective sapphire crystal; sapphire crystal caseback; water resistant to 3atm.
**Dial:** black; applied Arabic numerals at 12, 2, 4, 8 and 10; 6 applied cabochon markers.

**Indications:** date display at 6; minute track.
**Strap:** black semi-matte alligator strap; polished stainless steel folding clasp.
**Also available:** in yellow gold.

## TARAWA GENT REF. 9127J48/983035217–1214106

**Movement:** mechanical automatic-winding.
**Functions:** hour, minute, small second; date.
**Case:** polished stainless steel triple-curved case set with 22 diamonds (0.39 total carat weight); stainless steel crown; triple-curved antireflective sapphire crystal; sapphire crystal caseback; water resistant to 3atm.

**Dial:** white mother-of-pearl, engine-turned sunburst-engraved center zone; applied Roman numerals at 12, 3, 6, and 9; 8 diamond markers.
**Indications:** date display 3; small seconds counter at 6.
**Strap:** red alligator strap; polished stainless steel folding clasp.

## TARAWA MINI REF. 9656J18/991087–1214823

**Movement:** quartz.
**Functions:** hour, minute.
**Case:** polished stainless steel triple-curved case set with 40 diamonds (0.44 total carat weight); stainless steel crown; triple-curved antireflective sapphire crystal; water resistant to 3atm.
**Dial:** white mother-of-pearl, engine-turned sunburst-engraved center zone, applied Roman numerals at 6 and 12; 10 diamond markers; applied Ebel logo.

**Bracelet:** polished stainless steel bracelet; triple-blade folding clasp.
**Also available:** in steel and gold and in yellow gold.

## BELUGA TONNEAU MINI — REF. 8656G28/9993070–1215103

**Movement:** quartz.
**Functions:** hour, minute.
**Case:** polished yellow-gold case set with 116 diamonds (0.72 total carat weight); yellow-gold crown; antireflective sapphire crystal; water resistant to 3atm.
**Dial:** white mother-of-pearl, engine-tuned sunburst-engraved center zone; 13 diamond markers; applied Ebel logo.
**Bracelet:** polished yellow gold; polished yellow-gold folding clasp.
**Also available:** in stainless steel.

## 1911 CHRONOGRAPH XXL — REF. 9137260/35535606–1214251

**Movement:** mechanical chronograph, automatic-winding Ebel caliber 137; COSC-certified chronometer.
**Functions:** hour, minute, sweep second; date.
**Case:** brushed stainless steel case; polished stainless steel bezel; stainless steel crown; stainless steel pushers with black joints; flat antireflective sapphire crystal; sapphire crystal caseback; water resistant to 10atm.
**Dial:** black with silver subdials; applied Arabic numerals at 12, 4, and 8; applied indexes; minute track flange.
**Indications:** 30-minute counter at 3; hour counter at 6; small second hand at 9; date display at 4:30; center-mounted sweep seconds counter.
**Strap:** black rubber strap; polished stainless steel folding clasp.

## SPORTWAVE CHRONOGRAPH — REF. 9251K51/5711–1215049

**Movement:** quartz.
**Functions:** hour, minute, sweep second; date.
**Case:** brushed stainless steel case; polished stainless steel bezel; 6 stainless steel screws on the bezel; polished stainless steel crown; flat antireflective sapphire crystal; water resistant to 10atm.
**Dial:** black galvanized dial; applied Arabic numeral at 12; 12 applied indexes; minute track flange; tachometer.
**Indications:** tenths-of-a-second counter at 2; date display at 4:30; small second counter at 6; hour counter at 10; red center-mounted sweep seconds hand.
**Bracelet:** brushed stainless steel bracelet; polished stainless steel triple-blade folding clasp.
**Also available:** in steel and gold.

## SPORTWAVE LADY — REF. 9956K24/9811–1215045

**Movement:** quartz.
**Functions:** hour, minute.
**Case:** brushed stainless steel case; polished stainless steel bezel set with 36 diamonds (0.40 total carat weight); 6 stainless steel screws on the bezel; polished stainless steel crown; flat antireflective sapphire crystal; water resistant to 10atm.
**Dial:** white mother-of-pearl, applied Arabic numeral at 12; 11 diamond markers.
**Bracelet:** brushed stainless steel bracelet with polished stainless steel triple-blade folding clasp.
**Also available:** in steel and gold.

# EBERHARD & CO.

Classic elegance and traditional watchmaking are at the heart of the nearly 120-year-old Eberhard & Co., where even sport watches are chic.

Crafting with only the finest materials and using top-quality mechanical movements, Eberhard & Co. regularly produces striking chronographs, calendars and complex timepieces.

In 1887, Georges-Emile Eberhard founded the Manufacture d'Horlogerie Eberhard & Co. in La Chaux-de-Fonds. Thanks to the extraordinary abilities of its founder and to the intuition of his sons and successors, the company was able to grow and stand its ground—an enterprise that has always invested ingenuity, resources and capital into research and quality, constantly evolving pocket and wristwatches according to the highest technical standards.

In the course of its more than one hundred years of company history, Eberhard & Co. has established itself as a synonym of tradition, passion and innovation. In the new millennium, Eberhard & Co. revolutionized chronograph read-off with the Chrono 4 model (patent pending), the first chronograph in the world's history of watchmaking whose counters are arranged in a single row (registered design) across the dial.

Today, Eberhard & Co. is a prestigious symbol of Swiss watchmaking. Through the antiquity of its pocket watches, the uniqueness of its sporty models and the precious elegance of its dress watches, Eberhard & Co. regularly reiterates the company's creed: The value of the human being and its ability to choose.

Most recently, Eberhard & Co. presented the Extra-fort Roue à Colonnes Grande Date, a chronograph that perfectly combines aesthetics with mechanical refinement to create a masterly balance between tradition and innovation. The great novelty lies in the precious technique of the mechanical automatic-winding movement whose chronograph start and stop functions are operated by the column-wheel, a sophisticated mechanism that prevents the accidental setting to zero when the chronograph is working.

**ABOVE**

The Extra-fort Roue à Colonnes Grande Date houses a mechanical chronograph with automatic-winding caliber. It offers column-wheel chronograph functions and big date readout at 12:00. It is crafted in 18-karat pink gold and is 41mm in diameter. Water resistant to 3atm, the watch features a screwed caseback and crown. It is available with either a silvery or black dial with Roman numerals and applied gilded index quarters.

**LEFT**

These Extra-fort Roue à Colonnes Grande Date are crafted in stainless steel. Water resistant to 5atm, the model is available with a black or silvery dial with rhodium-plated index quarters and hands. The strap version is crocodile; the bracelet version is a Chalin bracelet in steel with Déclic deployment clasp.

## CHRONOLOGY

**1865** Georges-Emile Eberhard is born in Saint-Imier, Switzerland. He learns the trade of watchmaking from his father, who passes on a wealth of trade secrets.

**1887** Georges-Emile is only 22 when he founds the Manufacture d'Horlogerie Eberhard & Co. in La Chaux-de-Fonds and presents its first pocket watch chronograph. The company is soon included in the venerable circles noted for making precision timepieces of the highest grade. It is the beginning of a long succession of successful products to be devised over the next century under the company's motto: Innovation with tradition.

**1907** The company celebrates the inauguration of its headquarters on the Rue Léopold Robert in La Chaux-de-Fonds. It is during these years that Eberhard & Co. establishes its place in the world market for chronometers and chronographs. The name Eberhard & Co. becomes synonymous with meticulous workmanship and progressiveness, and attracts the special esteem of people to whom life is a matter of adventure and challenge.

**1919** The founder's sons Georges and Maurice Eberhard join the company. This year also marks the launching of an 18-karat gold wrist chronograph featuring a strap with mobile attachments and a hinged caseback.

**1926** Georges-Emile's heirs take full charge of the brand.

**1930** The innovative potential of Eberhard & Co. is convincingly expressed in the creation of a new chronograph with self-winding movement—a veritable innovation at this time. During the 1930s, chronographs by Eberhard & Co. are supplied to the commissioned officers in the Royal Italian Navy.

**1935** Eberhard & Co's quest for more novelties gives birth to a new chronograph that features two pushbuttons for stopping and starting again without setting to zero—an innovation that opens up a new possibility for the measuring of time.

**1938** For the first time, a wristwatch chronograph with counter device is presented.

**1939** Eberhard & Co. presents its first chronograph wristwatch with a flyback hand that enables double timekeeping.

**1947** After World War II, the company resumes its watchmaking activities. Eberhard & Co. now ventures into the ladies' watch market, offering quality and reliability in the form of luxurious timekeeping pieces of jewelry.

**1950s** Near the end of this decade, Eberhard & Co. presents its Extra-fort model with a pushbutton for stopping and starting the seconds count. This splendid instrument of mechanical watchmaking will retain its status as a much-coveted collectors' piece into the 21st century.

**1960** The 1960s are marked primarily by the introduction of a simultaneous date-setting device.

**1968** Chronometers by Eberhard & Co. enter a new era as movements performing 36,000 vibrations per hour are developed by the brand and now warrant an improved measure of precision.

**1970** The Sirio collection is Eberhard & Co.'s response to the electronic movement. It features elegantly refined contours and a newly conceived quartz-controlled calendar movement.

**1980** In the early 1980s, Eberhard & Co. takes pride in being one of the Swiss companies that relaunches a mechanical chronograph in the market.

**1984** Based on studies and research conducted in cooperation with P.A.N. Frecce Tricolori, the company creates the Chronomaster Frecce Tricolori, a chronograph dedicated to the world's most famous aerobatic squadron.

**1987** Eberhard & Co. celebrates its centennial and introduces its Navymaster chronographs collection with an inscription on the dial commemorating the occasion.

**1992** Eberhard & Co. marks the 100th birthday of the greatest racetrack champion of all times, Tazio Nuvolari—to whom the brand pays homage with a unique chronograph named in his honor.

**1996** The company now focuses on king-size wristwatches: the Traversetolo (43mm), the Tazio Nuvolari Grande Taille (43mm), and the Tazio Nuvolari Rattrapante Géant (51mm).

**1997** Eberhard & Co. achieves another watchmaking feat in the form of a unique 8 Days watch. It is a mechanical manual-winding watch that needs to be rewound only every eight days. The company's innovation here is a special winding device consisting of two overlapping springs (totaling more than 1.5 meters long), as compared to the standard wristwatch with only one spring and measuring about 30cm long.

**1999** The brand relaunches the Extra-fort chronograph.

**2001** Eberhard & Co. revolutionizes chronograph read-off with the Chrono 4, the first chronograph in the history of watchmaking whose counters are arranged in one row.

**2003** Eberhard & Co. unveils the Tazio Nuvolari Vanderbilt Cup chronograph. In this model, the company combines a dedication to technical progress and an exquisite nostalgia for historical details—as shown on the crown with its coaxial pushbutton.

The aesthetics of the Extra-fort Roue à Colonnes Grande Date renews the elegant and harmonious shape of its predecessors in large format. The 41mm case is available in steel or in pink gold, with black or silvery dial. The Extra-fort Roue à Colonnes Grande Date is water resistant to 3atm or 5atm, and features a sapphire caseback to reveal the personalized mechanism.

The steel versions are offered with crocodile strap or steel bracelet with deployment clasp Déclic (patent pending); the pink-gold versions are available exclusively on a crocodile strap with pink-gold buckle.

Extra-fort Roue à Colonnes Grande Date renews the charm and tradition of the great Eberhard & Co. watches.

## TRAVERSETOLO — REF. 21016

**Movement:** mechanical manual-winding caliber 16_", UNITAS/ETA 6498 base.
**Functions:** continuous small second at 6.
**Case:** steel; Ø 43mm, thickness: 10.7mm; caseback minted, with the marks in relief; water-resistant crown, personalized with an E; curved sapphire crystal; polished bezel; water resistant to 5atm.
**Dial:** black with Arabic numerals and 12 luminescent dots or glossy white with 12 black dots and luminescent Arabic numerals; luminescent leaf-style hands.
**Strap:** 21mm strap attachment; ostrich or brown or black leather; steel buckle personalized with E&C logo.
**Also available:** with transparent sapphire caseback, in steel or in 18K pink gold.
Bracelet: steel Chaland.

## 8 DAYS — REF. 21017

**Movement:** mechanical manual-winding caliber E/Co. 896 10_", base Peseux 7001 with the 8 DAYS modulus, exclusive to E&Co; patented power-reserve device in days; 2 main springs (0.3 + 1.25m) total length 1.55m.
**Functions:** small second.
**Case:** polished steel with engravings; Ø 39.4mm, thickness: 11.55mm; curved sapphire crystal; caseback secured by 6 screws; water-resistant crown, personalized with an E; polished bezel; water resistant to 3atm.
**Dial:** silver-color with Roman numerals or white with Arabic numerals; black leaf-style hands and numerals; scale, graduated in days, indicating the power reserve.
**Strap:** 16.5mm strap attachment; black or dark blue crocodile; steel buckle personalized with E&C logo.
**Bracelet:** Charade (steel version only).
**Also available:** blue with Roman or Arabic numerals; nickel leaf-style hands and numerals; 18K gold (Ref. 20017) same dials as for Ref. 21017; gold-plated hands and numerals.

## CHRONO 4 BELLISSIMO — REF. 30059

**Movement:** mechanical automatic-winding caliber EB. 200 12_", base ETA 2894 chronograph with exclusive modulus E&Co. to bring the 4 counters horizontally in a row. **Functions:** 4 counters: 30 minutes, 12 hours, 24 hours, small second; date at 12.
**Case:** 18K pink gold; Ø 40mm, thickness: 13.5mm; oval-shaped pushbuttons; domed, double-sided antireflective sapphire crystal; polished bezel; screw-in water-resistant crown, personalized with an E; flat, polished, engraved caseback locked by 4 screws; water resistant to 3atm.
**Dial:** white with Roman numerals, skeleton hands; white or blue dial with luminescent indexes, skeleton hands with luminescent points; black or blue with Roman numerals, skeleton hands.
**Strap:** 20mm strap attachment; matte brown, blue or black crocodile; 18K pink-gold buckle personalized with E&C logo.
**Also available:** in steel; in steel with "Apricot" dial, Roman numerals, skeleton hands; bracelet with steel version only.
**Note:** registered design with patent pending.

## TAZIO NUVOLARI GOLD CAR COLLECTION — REF. 31037

**Movement:** mechanical automatic-winding caliber 13_", base ETA 7750 chronograph; superbly executed Côtes de Genève embellishments; 25 rubies; 16 blue screws; rotor with 18K gold details: Tazio Nuvolari driving his Alfa Romeo, Côtes de Genève embellishments and gilded engravings (Tazio Nuvolari 1892-1992, Gold Car Collection, Alfa Romeo tipo C).
**Functions:** 2 counters: 30 minutes, 12 hours. **Case:** stainless steel; Ø 39.5mm, thickness: 14mm; steel pushbuttons, rectangular and water tight; antireflective sapphire crystal; steel screw-in crown, water tight and personalized with an E; caseback locked by 8 screws in 18K gold, with rosebud finish, sapphire crystal; water resistant to 3atm.
**Bezel:** rosebud finish, high-gloss flank, scale engravings in black denoting miles, opening of bezel 28.5mm.
**Dial:** black; luminescent Arabic numerals; signature and stylized depiction of Tazio Nuvolari's tortoise mascot next to 9; glossy white, luminescent baton-shaped hands.
**Strap:** 20mm strap attachment; genuine crocodile leather; steel buckle personalized with E&C logo.
**Alternate version:** Grande Taille, Ref. 31038: Ø43mm on strap or stainless steel Charme bracelet. (The bracelet features invisible clasp with special detail: the 18K gold stylized tortoise mascot)

## CHRONO — REF. 31041

**Movement:** mechanical automatic-winding caliber EB. 200 12_", base ETA 2894 chronograph, device by Eberhard & Co.; 53 rubies. **Functions:** 4 counters arranged in a row: minute, hour, 24 hours and small second; date at 12. **Case:** stainless steel; Ø 40mm, thickness: 13.8mm; stainless steel pushbuttons; polished bezel; curved sapphire crystal; steel, water-resistant screw-in crown; polished, beveled and engraved caseback, fixed by 8 screws; water resistant to 5atm. **Dial:** white with white or black counters; black with black or white counters; blue; 12 luminescent dots; 7 applied indexes; applied date counter, counter contour and brand name; tachometer scale outside.
**Strap:** 20mm strap attachment; crocodile leather; buckle personalized with E&C logo.
**Also available:** on stainless steel Chalin bracelet; in 18K pink gold (Ref. 30058, same dials as for Ref. 31041); dial on 2 levels; white with white or black counters; black with black or white counters; blue with white counters; polished outer surface; concave and decorated inner surface; 7 luminescent applied indexes; applied date; counters' contour and brand name raised; tachometer scale outside; sword-shaped skeleton hands with luminescent points.
**Note:** registered design, patent pending.

## TAZIO NUVOLARI VANDERBILT CUP — REF. 31045

**Movement:** mechanical automatic-winding caliber 13_" 8102, base ETA 7750 chronograph; 28,800 vph; antimagnetic; shock-resistant; Glucydur balance wheel; movement with blue screws, rubies and gold-plated circular engraving; rotor with personalized details and Côtes de Genève-style embellishments; chrono bridge with Côtes de Genève-style embellishments; other lower bridges, circular grained. **Functions:** 3 counters: 30 minutes, 12 hours, small second. **Case:** steel; Ø 42mm, thickness: 16.3mm; double-sided antireflective sapphire crystal; polished bezel; steel, water-resistant crown with coaxial pushbutton for setting to zero, personalized with an E; unique start-stop pushbutton (round, steel, personalized with TN); hinged steel cover, snap closing—a vertical sliding pushbutton at 4 assists opening. The internal part of the cover is reserved for special engravings: the lucky stylized tortoise's carapace, Tazio Nuvolari's initials and a scroll for personal engravings and dedications; flat sapphire caseback locked by 6 screws with Nuvolari's signature; water resistant to 3atm.
**Dials:** white dial; blue Arabic numerals painted in relief; large blue leaf-shaped hands; 3 large counters; tachometer scale; baton-shaped luminescent hands.
**Strap:** 20mm strap attachment; yellow-stitched leather; personalized boucle with E&C logo or deployment clasp Déclic (patent pending).
**Also available:** steel Charmant bracelet, deployment clasp Déclic (patent pending); in 18K pink gold; white dial with luminescent Arabic numerals, oxide contour.

## EXTRA-FORT GRANDE DATE RESERVE DE MARCHE — REF. 40036

**Movement:** mechanical automatic-winding caliber 11_", base ETA 2892A2.
**Functions:** hour, minute, small second; big date at 12; power reserve at 6.
**Case:** 18K pink-gold; Ø 37.5mm, thickness: 10.8mm; curved sapphire crystal; screw-in crown; bassiné back fastened by 6 pink-gold screws, displaying the movement through a sapphire crystal; polished bezel; screw-in water-resistant crown, personalized with an E; water resistant to 5atm.
**Dial:** argenté soleil or black; raised index and gilded date contour; 42-hour power-reserve indicator with radial milled embellishment; gilded Dauphine-style hands.
**Strap:** 19mm strap attachment; black, "honey" or brown crocodile; buckle personalized with E&C logo.
**Also available:** steel; 18K white gold.

## LES GRANDES COURBÉES — REF. 41022

**Movement:** mechanical automatic-winding caliber 11_", base ETA 2824-2.
**Functions:** hour, minute, second; date at 6.
**Case:** stainless steel; 30.6x45.1mm, thickness: 10.3mm; domed sapphire crystal; flat polished caseback, slightly curved profile, locked by 4 screws; polished bezel; steel screw-in water-resistant crown, personalized with an E; water resistant to 3atm.
**Dial:** white; applied nickel-plated index and 12 and 6 in Arabic numerals; nickel-plated baton-shaped hands.
**Strap:** 22mm strap attachment; black or "honey" crocodile; buckle personalized with E&C logo.
**Also available:** black or gray-green mother-of-pearl dial.

# F.P. JOURNE- INVENIT et FECIT-

With the Latin philosophy "Invenit et Fecit" (invented and made) guiding his way, François-Paul Journe is a watchmaker extraordinaire who—in just six short years—has brought a superb collection of handcrafted complex mechanical watches to successful international heights.

## A SUCCESS STORY IN MECHANICAL WATCHMAKING

This multi-faceted inventor has created not only a stellar series of high-caliber chronometers—made in his workshops in Geneva—but he also has opened a unique store in the Omotesando district of Tokyo. Spread over 300 square meters, F.P. Journe's new boutique encompasses a welcome area, library, bar and showroom, as well as an after-sales service center.

"I felt strongly that Japan was the right market for me, but I needed a place where my watches would be promoted correctly. I was not satisfied with the existing stores and circumstances pushed me to open a store in Omotesando, in a famous building conceived by Tadao Ando, architect of spirituality. I could not dream of a better place!" says Journe.

In addition to this bold move, Journe also implemented a truly unique plan in the industry: the creation of 18-karat gold movements. To create the finest of the finest in timepieces, Journe has set a new standard for his own timepieces. With just under 2,000 F.P. Journe watches with brass movements in the market, Journe has now vowed to utilize only 18-karat gold movements (thereby deeming the brass movements collectors' items and the gold movements the coveted newcomers).

**ABOVE**

First generation of the Chronomètre à Résonance with brass mechanism. These models are becoming collectors and are now replaced by models with gold mechanisms.

**TOP LEFT**

The Chronomètre à Résonance is the unique wristwatch working with résonance phenomenon and giving the best accuracy in a mechanical watch. The new model has a 18K red-gold movement with Ø 40mm platinum case.

**CENTER**

The Tourbillon Souveraine offers a remontoir and dead second mechanism, offering a better visibility of time. First model with 18K red-gold movement.

## WATCHMAKING ALCHEMY: TRANSFORMING BRASS TO GOLD

Additionally, Journe has increased his annual production plan to approximately 700 watches per year so that the 18-karat gold movements will become the brand standard over the next two years. Naturally, all the watch movements are numbered and entirely crafted in house.

Again F.P. Journe is offering a unique status with his watches: innovation, authenticity and performance. All models of the Souveraine or Octa collections are world premieres and exclusive in terms of chronometry.

### CHRONOLOGY

**1977** François-Paul Journe graduates from the School of Watchmaking in Paris as a master watchmaker. At the age of 20, he presents his first Tourbillon pocket watch and starts to work for private collectors, creating one or two one-of-a-kind pieces per year.

**1987** Journe builds a new Sympathique pendulum clock for the British house of John Asprey. During this year, he receives the Award from the Fondation de la Vocation Bleustein-Blanchet.

**1989** Approched by numerous luxury brands to develop specific products, Journe decides to open his first movement-manufacturing firm in Switzerland to create on request exclusive mechanisms for the most famous houses in the watchmaking industry.

**1999** Journe launches a collection of mechanical wristwatches (Souveraine and Octa lines) signed F.P. Journe-Invenit et Fecit-, offering innovative and exclusive mechanisms. The brand is distributed by Montres Journe SA and is represented all over the world by the best retailers. All models are world firsts: the Tourbillon Souverain with its original constant energy release remontoir system offering the best possible precision for a wristwatch tourbillon; the incredible Chronomètre à Résonance, the second model of the Souveraine collection and the only wristwatch driven by two movements reaching the state of "sympathy" through the effect of resonance and offering a level of precision unrivaled by any mechanical watches.

**2000** A new workshop with exhibition rooms is opened in the heart of old Geneva. Launching of the Octa line designed to incorporate a variety of complications (chronograph, power reserve, annual calendar, etc.). This collection is built around a totally innovative mechanical caliber offering an automatic-rewind system with more than five days of power reserve.

**2001** Montres Journe SA begins its horological collection with the acquisition of the Janvier Pendulum working with resonance phenomenon and made in 1781. A direct link with the model in the Souveraine line: the Chronomètre à Résonance. This acquisition was followed by a 17th century planetarium.

**2002** Journe unveils the Octa Annual Calendar, which is awarded the honor of Grand Prix d'Horlogerie de Genève. Montres Journe SA purchases a building for its new company headquarters in Geneva.

**2003** Journe creates his first watch for women, the Octa Divine. F.P. Journe-Invenit et Fecit- establishes the brand's presence in the Japanese market with the opening of a new boutique. Journe receives the Grand Prix d'Horlogerie de Genève award in the men's watch category for his new Octa Lune model.

**2004** Journe receives the highest honor (the Gold Hand Award) for his Tourbillon Souverain at the Grand Prix d'Horlogerie de Genève.

## NEW TOURBILLON SOUVERAIN—SOUVERAINE COLLECTION

**Movement:** world-exclusive mechanical manual-winding F. P. Journe caliber 1403; 42-hour power reserve; original concept and production by F.P. Journe.
**Functions:** hour, minute; dead seconds.
**Case:** platinum (Ø 40mm, thickness: 10mm); numbered; curved sapphire crystal; knurled crown; back attached by 6 screws displaying the movement through sapphire crystal.
**Dial:** 18K white gold; blued steel hands; tourbillon cage visible at 9.
**Indications:** hour and minute at 3; "dead beat" seconds at 6; power-reserve display at 12.
**Bracelet:** platinum.
**Also available:** pink-gold case with bracelet; with crocodile strap; dial in white or pink gold.

## NEW CHRONOMÉTRE À RÉSONANCE—SOUVERAINE COLLECTION

**Movement:** world-exclusive mechanical manual-winding F. P. Journe caliber 1499-2; 40-hours power reserve; original concept and production by F. P. Journe; working with resonance phenomenon.
**Functions:** hour and minute (dual time zones); small second; power reserve.
**Case:** platinum two-piece case (Ø 40mm, thickness: 9mm); numbered; curved sapphire crystal; knurled crowns (at 12 for winding and time adjustment on both dials, at 4 for the automatic synchronization of the second hands); back attached by 6 crews displaying the movement through a sapphire crystal; water resistant to 3atm.
**Dial:** 18K white gold; hour dial with symmetric solid silver engine-turned (guilloché) zones; printed Arabic numerals and railway minute track with five-minute progression; blued steel hands in an exclusive shape.
**Indications:** symmetric off-center dual time display (hour; minute; small second); power reserve at 12.
**Strap:** crocodile leather; platinum clasp.
**Also available:** pink-gold case; with bracelet in platinum or gold; dial in white or pink gold.

## OCTA RÉSERVE DE MARCHE—OCTA COLLECTION

**Movement:** world-exclusive mechanical automatic-winding F. P. Journe caliber 1300-2; 120-hour power reserve; designed and produced entirely by F. P. Journe; 22K gold rotor; personalized and engine-turned (guilloché).
**Functions:** hour, minute, small second; date; power reserve.
**Case:** platinum two-piece case (Ø 38mm, thickness: 10.50mm); numbered; curved sapphire crystal; knurled crown; back attached by 6 screws displaying the movement through sapphire crystal; water resistant to 3atm.
**Dial:** 18K white gold; hour dial with solid silver engine-turned (guilloché) zones; blued steed hands in an exclusive shape.
**Indications:** off-center hour and minute at 3 with printed Arabic numerals and railway minute track with five-minute progression; small second between 4 and 5; power reserve at 9; patented big-sized date with double-disc below 11.
**Strap:** crocodile leather; platinum clasp.
**Also available:** pink-gold case; with bracelet in platinum or gold; dial in white or pink gold.

## OCTA LUNE—OCTA COLLECTION

**Movement:** world-exclusive mechanical automatic-winding F. P. Journe caliber 1300-2; 120-hour power reserve; designed and produced entirely by F. P. Journe; 22K gold rotor; personalized and engine-turned (guilloché).
**Functions:** hour, minute; second; date; moonphase; power reserve.
**Case:** platinum two-piece case (Ø 38.3mm, thickness: 10.05mm); numbered; curved sapphire crystal; knurled crown; back attached by 6 screws displaying the movement through sapphire crystal; water resistant to 3atm.
**Dial:** 18K white gold; hour dial with solid silver engine-turned (guilloché) zones; blued steed hands in an exclusive shape.
**Indications:** off-center hour and minute at 3 with printed Arabic numerals and railway minute track with five-minute progression; small second between 4 and 5; power reserve at 9; moonphase at 7; large date at 11.
**Strap:** crocodile leather; platinum clasp.
**Also available:** pink-gold case; with bracelet in platinum or gold; dial in white or pink gold.

## OCTA CHRONOGRAPHE—OCTA COLLECTION

**Movement:** world-exclusive mechanical automatic-winding F. P. Journe caliber 1300-2; designed and produced entirely by F. P. Journe; 22K gold rotor; 120-hour power reserve; personalized and engine-turned (guilloché); 3-level chronograph mechanism flattened to just 1mm combined zero-stop and zero-restart features.
**Functions:** hour; minute; small second; large date; chronograph with 2 counters.
**Case:** platinum two-piece case (Ø 38mm, thickness 10.05mm); numbered; curved sapphire crystal; knurled crown and pushers; back attached by 6 screws displaying the movement through a sapphire crystal; water resistant to 3atm.
**Dial:** 18K white gold; solid silver engine turned (guilloche) zones; blued steel hands in an exclusive shape.
**Indications:** off-center hour and minute at 3 with printed Arabic numerals and railway minute track with five-minute progression; small second between 4 and 5; minute counter at 9; large date at 11; center second counter.
**Strap:** crocodile leather; platinum clasp.
**Also available:** pink-gold case; with bracelet in platinum or gold; dial in white or pink gold.

## OCTA CALENDRIER—OCTA COLLECTION

**Movement:** world-exclusive mechanical automatic-winding F. P. Journe caliber 1300-2; 120-hour power reserve; designed and produced entirely by F. P. Journe; 22K gold rotor; personalized and engine-turned (guilloché). The calendar that displays the day and month through 2 separate windows advances instantaneously and self-adjusts for the months of 29, 30 and 31 days. **Functions:** hour; minute; small second; retrograde date; day and month in 2 separate windows; power reserve. **Case:** platinum two-piece case (Ø 38mm, thickness: 10.50mm); numbered; curved sapphire crystal; knurled crown; back attached by 6 screws displaying the movement through a sapphire crystal; water resistant to 3atm. **Dial:** 18K white gold; hour dial with solid silver engine-turned (guilloché) zones; blued steel hand in an exclusive shape.
**Indications:** off-center hour and minute at 3 with printed Arabic numerals and railway minute track with five-minute progression; small second between 4 and 5; power reserve at 9; patented big-sized date with double-disc below 11. **Strap:** crocodile leather; platinum clasp.
**Also available:** pink-gold case; with bracelet in platinum or gold; dial in white or pink gold.
**Note:** Special award of the Jury "Grand Prix d'Horlogerie de Genève 2002."

## OCTA DIVINE SERTIE—OCTA COLLECTION

The Octa Divine (36mm) is the first model by F. P. Journe-Invenit et Fecit-to be set with diamonds and feature center hour and minute hands. Nevertheless, the recognizable F. P. Journe aesthetic elegance has been retained, with the seconds circle in the lower right-hand section and the hour and minute circles screwed to the dial, a brand-specific patented feature. This watch indicates the power-reserve and moonphase displays thanks to a metallic sapphire disc, which moves one notch forward when the date changes. The bezel is set with loupe-clean DE Top River diamonds, as is the folding clasp or pin buckle.

**Movement:** automatic-winding movement; 120-hour power reserve.
**Case:** Ø 36mm platinum case; set with a total of 2.61 carats.
**Dial:** white or red gold.

## OCTA DIVINE HOMME—OCTA COLLECTION

A worthy heir to the Octa Collection, The Octa Divine (38mm) features center hour and minute hands. The recognizable F. P. Journe aesthetic elegance has been retained, with the seconds circle in the lower right-hand section and the hour and minute circles screwed to the dial, a brand-specific patented feature. This watch indicates the power-reserve and moonphase displays thanks to a metallic sapphire disc, which moves one notch forward when the date changes. The bezel is set with loupe-clean DE Top River diamonds, as is the folding clasp or pin buckle.

**Movement:** automatic-winding movement; 120-hour power reserve.
**Case:** Ø 38mm platinum case.
**Dial:** white or red gold.

# FRANCK MULLER

The Franck Muller brand creates complicated timepieces on the cutting-edge of both design and technology. From crazy numbers to rising tourbillons, this company offers unusual timepieces to a faithful following.

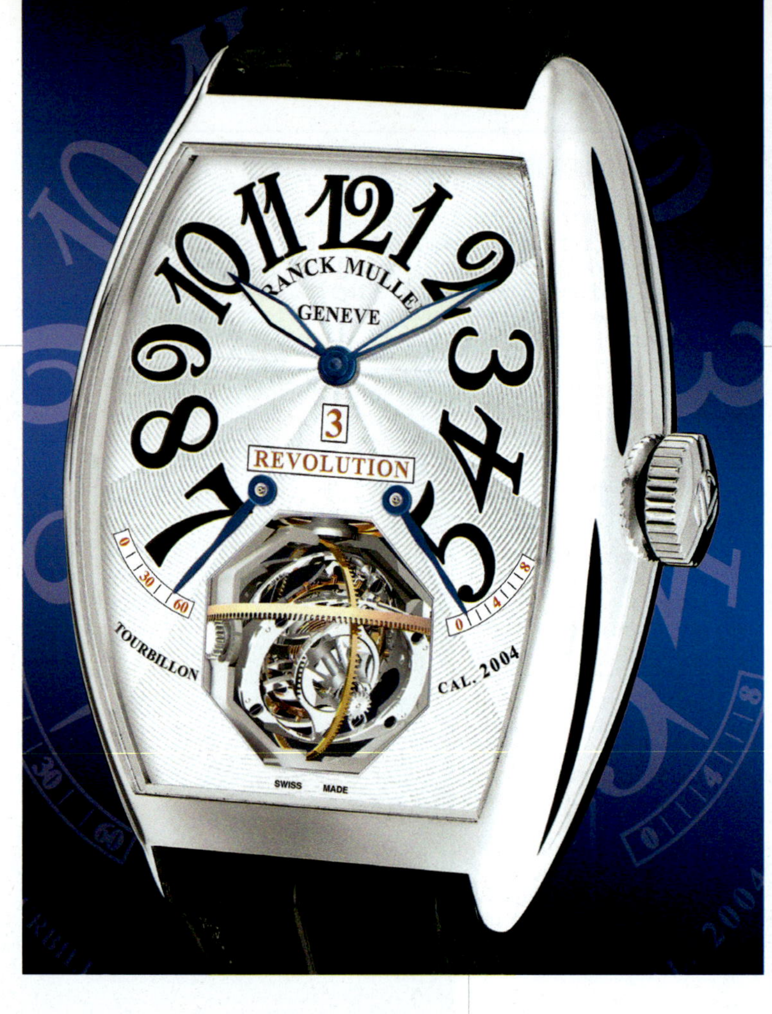


Among the brand's new complications are the Tourbillon Revolution 3, the Crazy Hours Tourbillon and the Tourbillon Minute Repeater with three patents.

The Tourbillon Revolution 3 is significant in that it reduces the variations in the operation of the tourbillon to an incredible minimum via a tri-axial tourbillon wherein the balance wheel and escapement rotating around its axis are contained in Cage A. Cage A is then mounted inside Cage B so it can turn on another axis, and Cage B is mounted inside Cage C, that turns on an axis fixed in relation to the timepiece. With all three axes perpendicular to one another, the system renders the watch impervious to earth's gravity.

The Crazy Hours Tourbillon is a contemporary tourbillon housed in the famed rectangular Long Island Case or in the Cintrée Curvex case—each with a Crazy Hours dial upon which the numbers are placed in a seemingly random manner. The Tourbillon Minute Repeater is a stunning new piece with a patent for the hammer-adjustment system, the new rack design, and a new click system. The watch produces a stunning striking sound.

**ABOVE**
The Tourbillon Revolution 3 is cased in platinum and houses 289 components and 20 jewels.

**BOTTOM LEFT**
The Cintrée Curvex Crazy Hours Tourbillon with power reserve of 60 hours features randomly placed numerals on the dial and a tourbillon aperture at 6:00.

**BOTTOM RIGHT**
The Cintrée Curvex Minute Repeater Tourbillon is comprised of 371 components in a platinum or 18-karat gold case.

**TOP LEFT**

The Long Island Crazy Hours Tourbillon features a lacquered dial and a movement comprised of 244 parts and 21 jewels.

**TOP RIGHT**

This Conquistador Cortez King Chronograph is crafted in stainless steel with an automatic movement.

**ABOVE LEFT**

This Crazy Color Dreams watch features a full-diamond case.

**ABOVE RIGHT**

This Casablanca watch celebrates the 10th annivesary of the Casablanca line.

Also new is Franck Muller's bold square-shaped Conquistador Cortez line, which includes a center-seconds version for men and women and a chronograph for men (available in a 10000 King size).

Franck Muller also unveils the Crazy Color Dreams collection with dials of mixed-up numerals in brilliant colors. The series is offered in both the Cintrée Curvex case and the Long Island case, with black, white, or blue dial backgrounds.

All Franck Muller timepieces are created by an impressive team of the finest master watchmakers in the brand's Genthod workshops, outside of Geneva.

## CHRONOLOGY

**1981** At 23 years old, Franck Muller completes his watchmaking studies at Ecole d'Horlogerie in Geneva. He immediately secures work performing master restorations and building his own creations on the side.

**1983** Muller begins creating watches bearing his name and incorporating multiple complications.

**1987** Muller presents for the very first time his tonneau-shaped Cintrée Curvex at the International Show in Vicenza, Italy.

**1992** Master watchmaker Muller enters a partnership and establishes a workshop in Genthod, outside of Geneva.

**1993** The Franck Muller brand unveils a multi-complex timepiece with split-seconds chronograph, minute repeater, perpetual calendar and internal temperature indicator billed as a world premiere.

**1994** The company launches the Caliber 94 with minute repeater with a striking-mechanism indicator, perpetual calendar, monthly retrograde equation of time, patented tourbillon, retrograde second hand, and an internal temperature indicator.

**1995** The company opens Watchland—a watchmaking château on an estate overlooking Lake Geneva in Genthod. This is the future site of additional watchmaking buildings.

**1996** The Master Banker with three time zones on a single automatic movement is launched.

**1997** The double-faced Conquistador is unveiled with multiple complications.

**1998** The Master City with jumping hour and second time zone with a choice of 14 cities is released.

**1999** The Caliber 99 with Double Mystery dial and the Vegas are introduced.

**2000** The Stunning Long Island double retro-seconds watch is released.

**2001** Franck Muller unveils the Caliber 2001, A Whirlwind of Light, housing the Master Imperial Tourbillon developed by Franck Muller's watchmakers. The company launches into jewelry with a variety of stunning diamond collections. Watchland is opened to the public.

**2002** Franck Muller launches the Revolution, a watch with a tourbillon cage that rotates and lifts closer to the surface of the watch crystal for better viewing. This watch holds several patents and required three years in the research and development stages.

**2003** The company unveils the one-of-a-kind Tourbillon Revolution 2 with dual-flyback readout with the tourbillon on two axes.

## RONDE CHRONOGRAPH QP EQUATION OF TIME — REF. 7008 CC QPE I

**Movement:** mechanical automatic-winding Franck Muller 7000 caliber + exclusive QP Dubois Dépraz module; autonomy 42 hours; 26 jewels; balance with 28,800 vph; first-quality balance-spring; rotor in platinum; beveled and decorated with Côtes de Genève pattern and circular graining.
**Functions:** hour, minute; 24 hour; perpetual calendar (date, day, month, year, moonphase); equation of time.

**Case:** 18K white-gold three-piece case; Ø 44mm, thickness 1.2mm; curved sapphire crystal; 4 correctors on the middle; white-gold crown; snap-on back; water resistant to 2.5atm.
**Dial:** black; subdials and hour ring decorated with circular beads; curved; printed Roman numerals; white enameled leaf-style hands.
**Indications:** four-year cycle at 2; date at 3; moonphase at 6; day and 24 hour at 9; month with equation-of-time indication via retrograde hand at 12; center second; minute track with divisions for 1/5 second.
**Strap:** hand-stitched crocodile leather; white-gold clasp.
**Note:** 50-piece limited edition.
**Also available:** with white dial; in yellow or pink gold; in platinum.

## RONDE TOURBILLON IMPERIAL VOLANT — REF. 7002 T

**Movement:** mechanical manual-winding Franck Muller 2000-2R caliber with tourbillon volant device; bridges and pillar-plate engraved and finished by hand; beveled and decorated with Côtes de Genève pattern.
**Functions:** hour, minute.
**Case:** 18K white-gold three-piece case; Ø 4.2mm, thickness 12.85mm; curved sapphire crystal; white-gold crown; snap-on back displaying the movement through a sapphire crystal; water resistant to 2.5atm.

**Dial:** matte white; aperture on tourbillon; applied blued steel Arabic numerals; 3 blued steel markers and cabochon minute track; blued steel Pomme hands.
**Strap:** hand-stitched crocodile leather; white-gold clasp.
**Also available:** in yellow, red or pink gold; in platinum.

## RONDE CHRONOGRAPH PERPETUAL BI-RETRO — REF. 7000 QP BI RET

**Movement:** mechanical automatic-winding Franck Muller 5888 BR caliber (base with chronograph + calendar module); autonomy 45 hours; 45 jewels; (Ø 26.20mm); 21,600 vph; flat balance-spring; Incabloc shock-absorber system; rotor in platinum; hand-finished; blued screws.
**Functions:** hour, minute; perpetual calendar (date, day, month, year, moonphase); chronograph with three counters.

**Case:** 18K white-gold three-piece brushed case (size: 40x35mm, thickness: 12.7mm); curved sapphire crystal; white-gold pushers and crown; 4 correctors on the fluted middle; snap-on back; water resistant to 3atm.
**Dial:** black; flinqué; silvered subdials (decorated with circular beads) and hour ring; luminescent lozenge hands in blued steel.
**Indications:** date and day of the week with off-center retrograde hand; minute counter at 3; moonphase at 6; month and four-year cycle at 12; center seconds; minute track with divisions for 1/5 second.
**Strap:** crocodile leather, hand-stitched; screwed attachment; white-gold clasp.
**Also available:** with silvered dial; bracelet in yellow, red, pink or gold platinum with leather strap or bracelet.

## RONDE CHRONOGRAPH PERPETUAL CALENDAR — REF. 7000 QP E DF

**Movement:** automatic Franck Muller 7000 caliber base + exclusive QP Dubois Dépraz calendar module; autonomy 42 hours; 26 jewels; 28,800 vph; top-quality flat balance-spring; rotor in platinum; beveled, decorated with Côtes de Genève and circular graining patterns.
**Functions:** hour, minute; 24-hour; perpetual calendar (date, day, month, year, moonphase); chronograph with two counters.
**Case:** 18K pink-gold three-piece double-face case (Ø 39mm, thickness: 14.5mm); curved sapphire crystal; pink-gold crown; 4 correctors on the middle; snap-on back displaying the movement through a sapphire crystal.

**Dial:** black; applied square markers and Pomme hands in pink-gold-plated steel.
**Indications:** date and 24-hour at 3; month with retrograde hand at 6 (with equation of time); four-year cycle at 8; date at 9; minute counter and moonphase at 12; center seconds; minute track with divisions for 1/5 second; telemeter; pulsometer and tachometer scales on the rear side.
**Strap:** crocodile leather, hand-stitched; screwed attachment; pink-gold clasp.
**Also available:** in yellow, red or white gold, platinum with leather strap or bracelet; silvered dial, non-double face, in yellow, red or pink-gold with leather strap or bracelet; in platinum with bracelet, closed caseback (on request). Ø 36mm (on request).

## RONDE DIAMOND CHRONOGRAPH AUTOMATIC REF. 7000 CC D

**Movement:** automatic Franck Muller 7000 caliber (Valjoux 7750 base); autonomy 42 hours; 25 jewels; (Ø 30mm, thickness: 7.90mm); special patented escapement; 28,800 vph; Incabloc shock-absorber system; 28,800 vph; top-quality flat balance-spring with micrometer screw regulation system; rotor in platinum; beveled, decorated with Côtes de Genève and circular graining patterns; blued-steel screws.
**Functions:** hour, minute; small seconds; chronograph with three counters.
**Case:** stainless steel three-piece case (Ø 39mm, thickness: 13.4mm); brilliant pavé; curved sapphire crystal; snap-on back; water resistant to 3atm.
**Dial:** silvered; decorated with circular beads; black enameled subdials; applied star-shaped markers (12 as Arabic numeral) and leaf-style hands in nickel-plated steel.
**Indications:** minute counter at 3; hour counter at 6; small seconds at 9; center seconds; minute track with divisions for 1/5 second.
**Strap:** crocodile leather, hand-stitched; screwed attachment; steel clasp.
**Also available:** in yellow, pink or red gold, or platinum with leather strap or bracelet. Other jewel versions (on request); Ø 36mm (on request). With black, silvered, green, blue or bordeaux dial.

## RONDE MASTER BANKER HAVANA REF. 3800 MB HV

**Movement:** automatic Franck Muller 2800 caliber; autonomy 47 hours; 21 jewels; modified for three time zones; 28,800 vph; rotor with sector in platinum; beveled, decorated with Côtes de Genève and circular graining patterns; blued screws. **Functions:** hour, minute, seconds; date; three time zones. **Case:** 18K white-gold three-piece case (Ø 36mm, thickness: 10.5mm); curved sapphire crystal; white-gold crown for the independent adjustment of three time zones and date; fluted middle; snap-on back displaying the movement through a sapphire crystal; water resistant to 2.5atm.
**Dial:** silvered; grained, subdials decorated with circular beads; luminescent applied pointed markers and Arabic numerals in white-gold-plated steel; printed railway minute track; luminescent Alpha hands in white-gold-plated steel.
**Indications:** date at 3; second and third time zones with two hands at 12 and 6; center second; minute track with divisions for 1/5 second.
**Strap:** crocodile leather, hand-stitched; screwed attachment; white-gold clasp.
**Also available:** in yellow, pink, or red gold, platinum or stainless steel, with leather strap or bracelet; with white or black dial (same versions); Ø 39mm size with white or black Havana dial (on request).

## RONDE MASTER MYSTERY 42MM

**Movement:** mechanical automatic-winding Franck Muller FM98 caliber; rotor with sector in platinum; beveled, decorated with Côtes de Genève and circular graining patterns; blued screws.
**Functions:** hour, approximate minute.
**Case:** 18K white-gold three-piece case (Ø 42mm, thickness: 10.2mm); curved sapphire crystal; bezel with baguette-cut Top Wesselton-quality diamonds in invisible settings; white-gold crown with sapphire cabochon; fluted middle; snap-on back displaying the movement through a sapphire crystal.
**Dial:** "mysterious" pavé of Top Wesselton-quality brilliants; baguette-cut sapphire markers; central disc with a triangular sapphire marker for the hour and approximate minute display.
**Strap:** crocodile leather; white-gold clasp.
**Also available:** in yellow, pink, red gold or platinum. With ruby or emerald markers; in 39mm, 36mm, 33mm or 30mm sizes; Master Double Mystery with hour and minute indication.

## CHRONOGRAPH ENDURANCE GT REF. 7008 CC RC

**Movement:** mechanical automatic-winding Franck Muller 7000 caliber; autonomy 42 hours, 25 jewels (Ø 30mm, thickness 7.9mm); smooth balance with 28,800 vph; flat balance-spring, stable at temperature variations; rotor in platinum; Incabloc shock-absorber system; beveled and decorated with a Côtes de Genève pattern and circular graining. **Functions:** hour, minute, small second; split-second chronograph with 3 counters. **Case:** stainless steel three-piece case (Ø 42mm, thickness 14.5mm); curved sapphire crystal; crown with case protection with split-second pusher; snap-on back displaying the movement through a sapphire crystal; water resistant to 2.5atm.
**Dial:** silvered; subdials and hour ring silvered and decorated with circular beads; applied star-shaped markers; blued steel 12 as Arabic numeral; blued steel Pomme hands.
**Indications:** minute at 3; hour at 6; small second at 9; center second and split-second counters; minute track with divisions for 1/5 second; tachometer scale.
**Strap:** hand-stitched crocodile leather; steel clasp.
**Note:** realized in 2004 for the Endurance World Championship.
**Also available:** with black dial; Ø 44mm.

## CINTRÉE CURVEX DOUBLE MYSTERY REF. 5850 DBLE MYSTERY D CD

**Movement:** mechanical automatic-winding Franck Muller 2800 V caliber; rotor with sector in platinum; hand-finished, beveled and decorated with Côtes de Genève; blued screws. **Functions:** hour, minute. **Case:** 18K white-gold two-piece case in tonneau shape; anatomically curved (size: 38x32mm, thickness: 11.8mm); Top Wesselton brilliant pavé; curved sapphire crystal; white-gold crown with faceted sapphire; back fastened by 4 screws; water resistant to 3atm. **Dial:** "mysterious" pavé of Top Wesselton quality brilliants; baguette-cut sapphire markers; turning disc and circular sector with triangular sapphire markers for hours and minutes.
**Strap:** crocodile leather; hand-stitched; white-gold clasp. **Also available:** in yellow, pink, red gold or platinum with leather strap or bracelet. Mystery FM98 caliber, hour indication only.

## CINTRÉE CURVEX VEGAS REF. 5850 VEGAS D

**Movement:** automatic Franck Muller 2800 caliber; autonomy 44 hours; 21 jewels (Ø 25.60mm, thickness: 3.6mm); 28,800 vph; balance-spring with micrometer screw regulation; rotor with sector in platinum; Incabloc shock-absorber system; beveled, decorated with Côtes de Genève and circular graining patterns. **Functions:** hour, minute; roulette. **Case:** 18K white-gold two-piece case in tonneau shape; anatomically curved (size: 38x32mm, thickness: 11.5mm); brilliant pavé; curved sapphire crystal; white-gold crown with coaxial pusher to activate and stop the roulette disc; back fastened by 4 screws; water resistant to 3atm. **Dial:** black; flinqué; center disc with brilliant pavé, curved; luminescent Arabic numerals; luminescent lozenge hands in blued steel.
**Indications:** central turning "mysterious" roulette disc with a ruby indicator; start-stop control by the pusher coaxial with crown.
**Strap:** crocodile leather; hand-stitched; white-gold clasp.
**Also available:** with sapphire or emerald indicator; in yellow, red or pink gold; platinum (on request) without brilliants; stainless steel with strap; platinum, yellow, white, pink or red gold with leather strap or bracelet; with black, blue, green or silvered dial.

## CINTRÉE CURVEX DIAMOND CHRONOMÈTRE REF. 7500 S6 CHR D

**Movement:** mechanical manual-winding Franck Muller 7500 caliber; autonomy 44 hours; 37 jewels; (Ø 23.30, thickness: 2.50mm); smooth balance; 21,600 vph; balance-spring with micrometer screw regulation; Incabloc shock-absorber system; beveled, decorated with Côtes de Genève and circular graining patterns; blued screws; officially COSC-certified chronometer. **Functions:** hour, minute, small seconds. **Case:** 18K white-gold two-piece case, in tonneau shape; anatomically curved (size: 34x28mm, thickness: 7.85mm); brilliant pavé; curved sapphire crystal; white-gold crown; back fastened by 4 screws; water resistant to 3atm. **Dial:** gold; flinqué; blue; curved, silvered hour ring; printed Arabic numerals and railway minute track, Stuart hands in white-gold-plated steel. **Indications:** small seconds at 6.
**Strap:** crocodile leather, hand-stitched; white-gold clasp.
**Also available:** in yellow, pink or red gold or platinum with strap or bracelet (on request); without brilliants. Ref. 1750 with or without brilliants (on request).

## CINTRÉE CURVEX TOURBILLON REVOLUTION 3 REF. 9880 T 3

**Movement:** mechanical manual-winding caliber realized and produced entirely by Franck Muller; with a tourbillon device turning around three orthogonal axes; autonomy 60 hours; 20 jewels (size 44.66x38mm, thickness 9.5mm); 18,000 vph; 289 parts; bridges and pillar-plate engraved and finished by hand. **Functions:** hour, minute.
**Case:** platinum two-piece case; 49.5x42.5mm, thickness 20mm; tonneau shape, anatomically curved; curved sapphire crystal; white-gold crown; back fastened by 4 screws, displaying the movement through a sapphire crystal and provided with a magnifying lens; water resistant to 2.5atm.
**Dial:** white flinqué; curved; with an aperture on the tourbillon.
**Indications:** off-center hour and minute at 12 with printed blued steel Arabic numerals and Stuart hands; indicators of the rotational state on the axes: at 5 for the minutes of rotation of the carriage on the vertical axis; at 7 for the seconds of the normal carriage rotation (the third carriage makes a full rotation every hour).
**Strap:** hand-stitched crocodile leather; platinum clasp.
**Note:** 2-piece limited edition.
**Also available:** with black, blue, bordeaux, green, gray, bronze, sand-color, light blue, light green or pink dial.

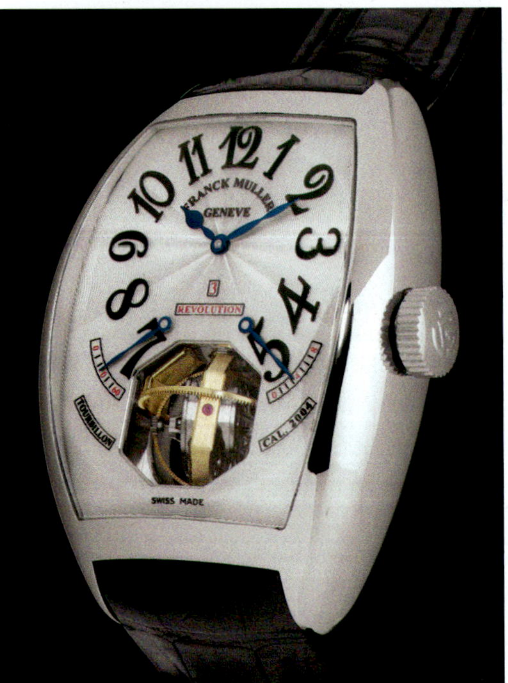

## CINTRÉE CURVEX REPEATER TOURBILLON — REF. 7880 RM T

**Movement:** mechanical manual-winding Franck Muller 3300 caliber in tonneau shape; realized and produced entirely by Franck Muller; with a tourbillon device; autonomy 60 hours; 32 jewels (size 34.80x28.8mm, thickness 6.45mm); 18,000 vph; 371 parts; beveled and decorated with Côtes de Genève pattern. **Functions:** hour, minute, small second; minute repeater. **Case:** platinum two-piece case; 42x35.5mm, thickness 14.35mm; tonneau shape, anatomically curved; curved sapphire crystal; repeater slide on middle; white-gold crown; back fastened by 4 screws, displaying the movement through a sapphire crystal; water resistant to 2.5atm.
**Dial:** silvered flinqué; curved; aperture on the tourbillon; printed Arabic numerals; blued steel Stuart hands.
**Indications:** small second at 6 integral with tourbillon carriage; patented sonnerie-end indicator at 10 (the signal means that the sonnerie device can be activated again without damaging the mechanism).
**Strap:** hand-stitched crocodile leather; platinum clasp.
**Note:** 2-piece limited edition.
**Also available:** with black, blue, bordeaux, green, gray, bronze, sand-color, light blue, light green or pink dial; in yellow, pink or red gold; in jeweled version.

## C. CURVEX CHRONO CASABLANCA 10TH ANNIVERSARY — REF. 8880 C CC

**Movement:** mechanical automatic-winding; platinum rotor.
Functions: hour, minute, small second; chronograph with 2 counters.
**Case:** stainless steel two-piece case; 46.5x39mm, thickness 15.5mm; tonneau shape, anatomically curved; brushed finish; curved sapphire crystal; pushers with case protectors; back fastened by 4 screws; water resistant to 2.5atm.
**Dial:** matte black; curved; luminescent Arabic numerals; luminescent lozenge hands in blued steel.
**Indications:** minute at 3; small second at 9; center second; minute track with divisions for 1/5 second; tachometer scale.
**Bracelet:** brushed steel; double fold-over clasp.
**Note:** realized in 2004 for the Endurance World Championship.
**Also available:** with white or salmon dial and luminescent markers; with leather strap.

## CINTRÉE CURVEX CASABLANCA — REF. 8880 C

**Movement:** mechanical automatic-winding Franck Muller 2800 caliber; autonomy 47 hours; 21 jewels (Ø 26.2mm, thickness 3.6mm); smooth balance with 28,800 vph; balance-spring with micrometer-screw regulation; rotor in platinum; Incabloc shock-absorber system; beveled and decorated with a Côtes de Genève pattern and circular graining; blued screws.
**Functions:** hour, minute, second.
**Case:** stainless steel two-piece case; 46.2x39mm, thickness 15.6mm; tonneau shape, anatomically curved; brushed finish; curved sapphire crystal; pushers with case protectors; back fastened by 4 screws; water resistant to 2.5atm.
**Dial:** matte salmon; curved; luminescent Arabic numerals; luminescent lozenge hands in blued steel.
**Strap:** hand-stitched leather; steel clasp.
**Also available:** with white or black dial and luminescent markers; with bracelet.

## CINTRÉE CURVEX CRAZY HOURS COLOR DREAMS — REF. 5850 CH

**Movement:** mechanical automatic-winding; autonomy 40 hours.
**Functions:** jumping hour, minute.
**Case:** 18K pink-gold two-piece case; 38x32mm, thickness 11.6mm; tonneau shape, anatomically curved; curved sapphire crystal; pink-gold crown; back fastened by 4 screws; water resistant to 2.5atm.
**Dial:** blue flinqué; curved; printed Arabic numerals in different colors; luminescent leaf-style hands in pink gold-plated steel.
**Strap:** hand-stitched crocodile leather; pink-gold clasp.
**Also available:** in yellow, pink or red gold, in stainless steel, all with leather strap or bracelet; in jeweled version.
**Ref. 7851:** 41.5x35mm; in yellow, pink or red gold, in stainless steel; leather strap or bracelet.

## LONG ISLAND CRAZY HOURS COLOR DREAMS — REF. 1200 CH COL DREAMS

**Movement:** mechanical automatic-winding; autonomy 40 hours.
**Functions:** jumping hour, minute.
**Case:** 18K pink-gold two-piece case; 45x32.3mm, thickness 11.7mm; rectangular shape, anatomically curved; 2 rows of set brilliants on bezel and lugs; curved sapphire crystal; pink-gold crown; back fastened by 4 screws; water resistant to 3atm.

**Dial:** silvered flinqué; curved; luminescent Arabic numerals in different colors; luminescent leaf-style hands in blued steel.
**Strap:** hand-stitched crocodile leather; pink-gold clasp.
**Also available:** in other jeweled versions; without brilliants in yellow, pink, white or red gold or in stainless steel with leather strap or bracelet.

## LONG ISLAND COLOR DREAMS — REF. 1000 SC COL DREAMS

**Movement:** mechanical automatic-winding.
**Functions:** hour, minute.
**Case:** 18K white-gold two-piece case; 45x32.5mm, thickness 11.3mm; rectangular shape, anatomically curved; curved sapphire crystal; white-gold crown; back fastened by 4 screws; water resistant to 3atm.
**Dial:** black flinqué; curved; printed Arabic numerals in different colors; railway minute track; Stuart hands in white gold-plated steel.

**Strap:** hand-stitched crocodile leather; screwed attachment; white-gold clasp.
**Also available:** with bracelet; in yellow, pink or red gold or in stainless steel with leather strap or bracelet; in jeweled version.

## LONG ISLAND — REF. 1000 D CD

**Movement:** mechanical automatic-winding.
**Functions:** hour, minute.
**Case:** 18K white-gold two-piece case; 43x30.6mm, thickness 8.4mm; rectangular shape, anatomically curved; 2 rows of set brilliants on bezel and lugs; curved sapphire crystal; white-gold crown; back fastened by 4 screws; water resistant to 3atm.

**Dial:** brilliant pave; curved; luminescent applied Arabic numerals in white gold-plated steel; luminescent Stuart hands in blued steel.
**Strap:** hand-stitched crocodile leather; screwed attachment; white-gold clasp.

## CONQUISTADOR CORTEZ — REF. 10000 SC

**Movement:** mechanical automatic-winding Franck Muller 2800 caliber; autonomy 44 hours; 21 jewels (Ø 26.2mm, thickness 3.6mm); smooth balance with 28,800 vph; balance-spring with micrometer-screw regulation; rotor in platinum; Incabloc shock-absorber system; beveled and decorated with Côtes de Genève pattern and circular graining; blued screws. **Functions:** hour, minute, second; date.
**Case:** 18K pink-gold two-piece case; 41x41mm, thickness 14.15mm; square shape, anatomically curved; curved sapphire crystal; pink-gold crown; back fastened by 4 screws; water resistant to 3atm.

**Dial:** silvered flinqué; curved; luminescent Arabic numerals; printed minute track with five-minute graduation; luminescent leaf-style hands in blued steel.
**Indications:** date at 6 with magnifying lens.
**Strap:** hand-stitched crocodile leather; pink-gold clasp.
**Also available:** with bracelet; in yellow, pink or red gold, in platinum with leather strap or bracelet; in jeweled version.
**Ref. 9000 SC:** in yellow, white, pink or red gold or platinum, all with leather strap; with brilliants; with white, black, blue, bordeaux, green, gray, bronze, sand-color, light blue, light green or pink dial.

## CONQUISTADOR CORTEZ CHRONO — REF. 10000 CC

**Movement:** mechanical automatic-winding Franck Muller 7000 caliber; autonomy 42 hours; 25 jewels (Ø 30mm, thickness 7.9mm); patented escapement; balance with 28,800 vph; first-quality balance-spring with micrometer-screw regulation; Incabloc shock-absorber system; rotor in platinum; beveled and decorated with Côtes de Genève pattern and circular graining; blued screws. **Functions:** hour, minute, small second; date, chronograph with 2 counters. **Case:** 18K white-gold, two-piece case; 41x41mm, thickness 14mm; square shape, anatomically curved; curved sapphire crystal; white-gold screw-down crown and drop-shaped pushers with case protection; back fastened by 4 screws; water resistant to 3atm. **Dial:** gray, flinqué, subdials silvered and decorated with circular beads, curved; luminescent Arabic numerals; luminescent leaf-style hands in white-gold-plated steel. **Indications:** minute at 3; date at 6 with a magnifying lens, small second at 9; center second counter, minute track. **Strap:** hand-stitched crocodile leather; white-gold clasp. **Also available:** with bracelet; in yellow, pink or red gold or platinum, all with leather strap or bracelet. **Ref. 9000 CC:** in yellow, white, pink or red gold or platinum, all with leather strap; with brilliants; white, black, blue, bordeaux, green, gray, bronze, sand-color, light blue, light green or pink dial.

## CONQUISTADOR CORTEZ CHRONO KING — REF. 10000 CC KING D.1P

**Movement:** mechanical automatic-winding Franck Muller 7000 caliber; autonomy 42 hours; 25 jewels (Ø 30mm, thickness 7.9mm); patented escapement; balance with 28,800 vph; first-quality balance-spring with micrometer-screw regulation; Incabloc shock-absorber system; rotor in platinum; beveled and decorated with Côtes de Genève pattern and circular graining; blued screws. **Functions:** hour, minute, small second; date; chronograph with 2 counters. **Case:** 18K white-gold two-piece case; 44x44mm, thickness 15.6mm; square shape, anatomically curved; entirely brilliant pavé; curved sapphire crystal; white-gold screw-down crown and drop-shaped pushers with case protection; back fastened by 4 screws; water resistant to 3atm. **Dial:** blue; curved; silvered subdials decorated with circular beads; center with brilliant pavé; luminescent Arabic numerals; luminescent leaf-style hands in white gold-plated steel. **Indications:** minute at 3; date at 6 with a magnifying lens; small second at 9; center second; minute track. **Strap:** hand-stitched crocodile leather; white-gold clasp. **Also available:** in other jeweled versions; without brilliants: in yellow, white, pink or red gold, in platinum, all with leather strap or bracelet. **Ref. 9000 CC King:** in yellow, white, pink or red gold, platinum, all with leather strap or bracelet; with white, black, blue, bordeaux, green, gray, bronze, sand-color, light blue, light green or pink dial.

## CONQUISTADOR CORTEZ LADY — REF. 10000 LADY

**Movement:** mechanical automatic-winding Franck Muller 2800 caliber; autonomy 44 hours; 21 jewels (Ø 26.2mm, thickness 3.6mm); smooth balance with 28,800 vph; balance-spring with micrometer-screw regulation; rotor in platinum; Incabloc shock-absorber system; beveled and decorated with Côtes de Genève pattern and circular graining; blued screws. **Functions:** hour, minute, second; date. **Case:** 18K pink-gold two-piece case; 32x32mm, thickness 10.25mm; square shape, anatomically curved; curved sapphire crystal; pink-gold screw-down crown; back fastened by 4 screws; water resistant to 3atm. **Dial:** blue; guilloché soleil; curved; luminescent Arabic numerals; printed minute track with five-minute graduation; luminescent leaf-style hands in pink gold-plated steel. **Indications:** date at 6 with magnifying lens. **Strap:** hand-stitched crocodile leather; pink-gold clasp. **Also available:** with bracelet; in yellow, white, pink or red gold, in platinum or stainless steel with leather strap or bracelet. **Ref. 9000 Lady:** in yellow, white, pink or red gold or platinum, all with leather strap; with brilliants; with white, black, blue, bordeaux, green, gray, bronze, sand-color, light blue, light green or pink dial.

## CONQUISTADOR CORTEZ LADY — REF. 10000 LADY

**Movement:** mechanical automatic-winding Franck Muller 2800 caliber; autonomy 44 hours; 21 jewels (Ø 26.2mm, thickness 3.6mm); smooth balance with 28,800 vph; balance-spring with micrometer-screw regulation; rotor in platinum; Incabloc shock-absorber system; beveled and decorated with Côtes de Genève pattern and circular graining; blued screws. **Functions:** hour, minute, second; date. **Case:** 18K white-gold two-piece case; 32x32mm, thickness 10.25mm; square shape, anatomically curved; 1 row of brilliants on bezel and lugs; curved sapphire crystal; white-gold crown; back fastened by 4 screws; water resistant to 3atm. **Dial:** light blue; guilloché soleil; curved; luminescent Arabic numerals; printed minute track with five-minute graduation; luminescent leaf-style hands in blued steel. **Indications:** date at 6 with magnifying lens. **Strap:** hand-stitched crocodile leather; white-gold clasp. **Also available:** in other jeweled versions; without brilliants: in yellow, white, pink or red gold, in platinum or stainless steel, all with leather strap or bracelet. **Ref. 9000 Lady:** in yellow, white, pink or red gold or platinum, all with leather strap; with white, black, blue, bordeaux, green, gray, bronze, sand-color, light blue, light green or pink dial.

# GEVRIL

**A** maverick brand intriguing collectors around the world, Gevril's roots date back hundreds of years.

Perhaps the most exciting news from Gevril comes in the form of the incredibly beautiful and complex Serenade. Part of the Avenue of Americas collection, the Serenade is a stunning new rendition of light and time. It offers two time zones with day and night indicators monitoring the flow of time from dawn to day, dusk to night.

The Serenade houses a patented Gevril movement with a 23-karat gold rotor. Sapphire crystals protect the beautifully guillochéd, curved dial on the front and reveal the GV A0ASE movement on the back. The Serenade is produced in a limited edition of just 50 pieces each in 18-karat white gold, rose gold, and platinum.

Forever linking time, speed and the Serenade, Gevril recently partnered with Champ Car and the Herdez racing team to host the Serenade of Time and Speed event in New York City. Mario Andretti, Paul Newman and Herdez Champion driver Mario Dominguez suited up in full racing gear for the event. Andretti and Newman drove from the Plaza Hotel to the Tourneau Time Machine where the Herdez team performed a real pit stop.

At the event, Gevril auctioned off artwork donated by distinguished racing circuit artists. The auction raised tens of thousands of dollars for Paul Newman's charity, Hole in the Wall Camps. Other celebrities attending the Gevril Serenade of Time and Speed event included Joan Collins and Anne Hathaway, who also sported Gevril watches on their wrists.

THIS PAGE

ABOVE

The Serenade is produced in 50-piece limited editions of 18-karat white gold, 18-karat rose gold, and platinum.

BOTTOM LEFT

The Gevril/Herdez champion car.

BOTTOM RIGHT

Mario Andretti and Paul Newman attend the launching of the Serenade of Time and Speed event in New York City.

FACING PAGE

Part of the Avenue of Americas collection, the Serenade offers two time zones with two day and night indicators to monitor the flow of time. The watch houses a patented Gevril GV A0ASE movement with a 23-karat gold rotor.

GEVRIL
Established in 1758
TIME ZONE ONE
TIME ZONE TWO
Automatic

Recently, Gevril added the Avenue of Americas Mini Collection to the line of the existing rectangular beauties. Created in colorful designs that cater to women, the Mini Collection is available with several dial variations including four exquisite colors of mother of pearl. The Mini is studded with Top Wesselton diamonds and complemented by a choice of 29 strap colors or a classic steel bracelet.

Also new to the Avenue of Americas Collection are several new Glamour watches. Like the Mini, the Glamour is offered with a variety of mother-of-pearl dials including pink, white, green and blue. The watch is powered by a Gevril automatic movement and features a bezel set with up to 2.25 carats of Top Wesselton diamonds.

The men's Avenue of Americas timepieces include the Date Automatic, GMT Power Reserve, Chronograph and Day Date Moonphase—all beautifully rendered in numbered limited editions of 18-karat gold or steel. Gevril also adds to its round Lafayette series and its Sea Clouds series.

Gevril watches have attracted many celebrities, including Sting, Martin Sheen, Brad Garrett, Joe Mantegna, Joan Rivers, and Heidi Klum.

**LEFT**

The Avenue of Americas GMT Power Reserve watch features a mechanical movement.

**BOTTOM LEFT**

This striking Avenue of Americas Day Date Moonphase is crafted in 18-karat gold.

**BOTTOM RIGHT**

*from top to bottom:*

Actors Joe Mantegna, Brad Garrett, and Martin Sheen.

ABOVE

This Gevril pocket watch from the year 1800 is on display at the the Muse de l'Horlorgerie of Geneva, Inventory No. 169-49.

RIGHT

This antique pocket watch by Gevril is a part of the Rolex Wilsdorf Collection.

BOTTOM LEFT

The automatic Avenue of Americas Glamour features a bezel set with up to 2.25 carats of Top Wesselton diamonds.

BOTTOM RIGHT

*from top to bottom*

Actresses Anne Heche and Anne Hathaway.

## CHRONOLOGY

**1722** Jacques Gevril is born in Le Locle, Switzerland.

**1743** Gevril creates his first chrono-meter.

**1758** Gevril is one of the first exporters of Swiss timepieces when he partners with Pierre Jaquet-Droz and journeys to Madrid to present his pieces to the King of Spain.

**1784** Gevril's son Moyse achieves the status of master clockmaker.

**1800** The Gevril family extends its business to include enameling of dials.

**1867** At an exhibition in Paris, a timepiece associated with Gevril is displayed as one of the world's most exclusive chronometers.

**1959** Author Alfred Chapuse writes *Grands Artisans De La Chronometrie* and includes Jacques Gevril as an important contributor to the history of fine Swiss watchmaking in Le Locle.

**1990s** UTC relaunches the Gevril brand.

**1994** Gevril patents the unlocked crown indicator and publishes a book about its new timepieces and the history of Jacques Gevril.

**1999** The company introduces the TriBeCa automatic chronograph, named for the New York City neighborhood.

**2001** Gevril is acquired by First SBF Holding, Inc., spearheaded by Samuel Friedmann.

**2002** Gevril introduces three new collections: the high-tech sporty Sea Clouds line, the Lafayette for women, and the Avenue of Americas collections.

**2003** Gevril gains popularity and introduces the diamond-studded Avenue of Americas Glamour Collection. Hollywood takes note and celebrities appear wearing Gevril timepieces.

**2004** Gevril introduces the complicated, patented Seranade.

## AVENUE OF AMERICAS DATE AUTOMATIC — REF. 5100

**Movement:** automatic; GV-AOM3J1; 25 jewels; 40-hour autonomy; Incabloc, Adouci and engraved.
**Function:** date.
**Case:** 18K rose-gold; size: 44x34mm; 18K rose-gold bezel; exclusive sapphire crystal; sapphire crystal caseback; water resistant to 5atm.
**Dial:** silver with raised rose-gold numerals.
**Strap:** Louisiana crocodile with 18K rose-gold buckle.
**Note:** limited edition of 99 pieces.

## AVENUE OF AMERICAS CHRONOGRAPH — REF. 5111

**Movement:** automatic; GV-AOAWZ1; 51 jewels; 40-hour autonomy; Incabloc, Adouci and engraved.
**Functions:** chronograph; power reserve; date.
**Case:** 18K rose-gold; size: 44x34mm; 18K rose-gold bezel; exclusive sapphire crystal; water resistant to 5atm.
**Back:** sapphire crystal.
**Dial:** black with raised rose-gold numerals.
**Strap:** Louisiana crocodile with 18K rose-gold buckle.
**Note:** limited edition, 00-99.

## AVENUE OF AMERICAS GMT POWER RESERVE — REF. 5022B

**Movement:** automatic; GV-AOAX32; 25 jewels; 40-hour autonomy; Incabloc, Adouci and engraved.
**Functions:** GMT; power reserve; date.
**Case:** stainless steel 316L; size: 44x34mm; sapphire crystal caseback; polished steel bezel; exclusive sapphire crystal; water resistant to 5atm.
**Dial:** black with luminous numerals.
**Bracelet:** stainless steel.
**Note:** limited edition of 500 pieces.

## AVENUE OF AMERICAS DAY-DATE-MOONPHASE — REF. 5131

**Movement:** automatic GV-AOA71L; 25 jewels; 40-hour autonomy; Incabloc, Adouci and engraved.
**Functions:** day/date/month; moonphase.
**Case:** 18K rose-gold; size: 44x34mm; 18K rose-gold bezel; exclusive sapphire crystal; water resistant to 5atm.
**Back:** sapphire crystal.
**Dial:** black with raised rose-gold numerals.
**Strap:** Louisiana crocodile with 18K rose-gold buckle.
**Note:** limited edition of 00-99.

## AVENUE OF AMERICAS GLAMOUR DATE AUTOMATIC REF. 6206NT

**Movement:** automatic; GV-AOM3J1; 25 jewels; 40-hour autonomy; Incabloc, Adouci and engraved.
**Functions:** date.
**Case:** stainless steel 316L; size: 44x34mm; Top Wesselton diamonds on polished steel bezel; exclusive sapphire crystal caseback; water resistant to 5atm.
**Dial:** silver with pink mother-of-pearl; raised stainless steel numerals and hands.
**Strap:** Louisiana crocodile with diamond-set buckle.
**Note:** limited edition of 100 pieces.

## AVENUE OF AMERICAS GLAMOUR DATE AUTOMATIC REF. 6207NE

**Movement:** automatic; GV-AOM3J1; 25 jewels; 40-hour autonomy; Incabloc, Adouci and engraved.
**Functions:** date.
**Case:** stainless steel 316L; size: 44x34mm; Top Wesselton diamonds on polished steel bezel; exclusive sapphire crystal caseback; water resistant to 5atm.
**Dial:** silver with blue mother-of-pearl; raised stainless steel numerals and hands.
**Strap:** Louisiana crocodile with diamond-set buckle.
**Note:** limited edition of 100 pieces.

## AVENUE OF AMERICAS GLAMOUR DATE AUTOMATIC REF. 6208RL

**Movement:** automatic; GV-AOM3J1; 25 jewels; 40-hour autonomy; Incabloc, Adouci and engraved.
**Functions:** date.
**Case:** stainless steel 316L; size: 44x34mm; Top Wesselton diamonds on polished steel bezel; exclusive sapphire crystal caseback; water resistant to 5atm.
**Dial:** silver with green mother-of-pearl; raised stainless steel numerals and hands.
**Strap:** Louisiana crocodile with diamond-set buckle.
**Note:** limited edition of 100 pieces.

## AVENUE OF AMERICAS GLAMOUR DATE AUTOMATIC REF. 6209RV

**Movement:** automatic; GV-AOM3J1; 25 jewels; 40-hour autonomy; Incabloc, Adouci and engraved.
**Functions:** date.
**Case:** stainless steel 316L; size: 44x34mm; sapphire crystal caseback; polished steel bezel; Top Wesselton diamonds on bezel and sides; exclusive sapphire crystal; water resistant to 5atm.
**Dial:** silver with pink mother-of-pearl; raised rose-gold numerals and hands.
**Strap:** Louisiana crocodile with diamond-set buckle.
**Note:** limited edition of 100 pieces.

## AVENUE OF AMERICAS MINI COLLECTION — REF. 7042 RB

**Movement:** GV quartz.
**Functions:** date.
**Case:** stainless steel; size: 32x25mm; bezel with Top Wesselton diamonds; exclusive sapphire crystal; water resistant to 5atm.
**Dial:** black with rose-gold numerals.
**Bracelet:** stainless steel.
**Note:** limited edition of 500 pieces.

## AVENUE OF AMERICAS MINI COLLECTION — REF. 7247NE

**Movement:** GV quartz.
**Functions:** date.
**Case:** stainless steel; size: 32x25mm; bezel with Top Wesselton diamonds; exclusive sapphire crystal; water resistant to 5atm.
**Dial:** blue mother-of-pearl.
**Strap:** Louisiana crocodile.
**Note:** limited edition of 500 pieces.

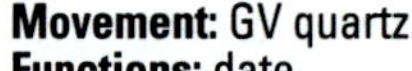

## AVENUE OF AMERICAS MINI COLLECTION — REF. 7248 RL

**Movement:** GV quartz.
**Function:** date.
**Case:** stainless steel; size: 32x25mm; bezel with Top Wesselton diamonds; exclusive sapphire crystal; water resistant to 5atm.
**Dial:** pink mother-of-pearl.
**Strap:** Louisiana crocodile.
**Note:** limited edition of 500 pieces.

## AVENUE OF AMERICAS MINI COLLECTION — REF. 7249 NV

**Movement:** GV quartz.
**Functions:** date.
**Case:** stainless steel; size: 32x25mm; bezel and sides with Top Wesselton diamonds; exclusive sapphire crystal; water resistant to 5atm.
**Dial:** white mother-of-pearl.
**Strap:** Louisiana crocodile.
**Note:** limited edition of 500 pieces.

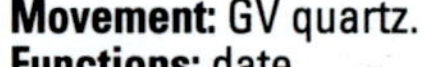

## GRAMERCY REF. 2401

**Movement:** automatic; GV-182; 31 jewels; 40-hour autonomy.
**Functions:** regulator automatic.
**Case:** stainless steel 316L; Ø 39mm; stainless steel bezel; sapphire crystal; water resistant to 5atm.
**Back:** exhibition.
**Dial:** guilloché silvered.
**Bracelet:** stainless steel.
**Note:** limited edition of 500 pieces.

## MADISON REF. 2502

**Movement:** automatic; GV-834; 30 jewels; 40-hour autonomy.
**Functions:** small seconds; date.
**Case:** stainless steel 316L; Ø 39mm; sapphire crystal; water resistant to 5atm.
**Back:** exhibition.
**Dial:** guilloché silvered.
**Strap:** Louisiana crocodile.
**Note:** limited edition of 500 pieces.
**Also available:** 18K gold.

## SOHO DELUXE REF. 2605

**Movement:** automatic; GV-613; 25 jewels; 40-hour autonomy.
**Functions:** complete calendar, day/date/month; moonphase.
**Case:** 18K yellow-gold; Ø 39mm; 18K yellow-gold bezel; sapphire crystal; water resistant to 5atm.
**Back:** exhibition.
**Dial:** guilloché silvered.
**Strap:** Louisiana crocodile.
**Note:** limited edition of 100 pieces.

## LAFAYETTE CHRONOGRAPH REF. 2912

**Movement:** automatic; GV-993; 51 jewels; 40-hour autonomy.
**Functions:** chronograph.
**Case:** stainless steel 316L; Ø 37mm; bezel set with 56 Top Wesselton diamonds; hesalite crystal; decorated stainless steel 316L caseback; water resistant to 10atm.
**Dial:** blue natural mother-of-pearl; raised metallic numerals.
**Strap:** Louisiana crocodile.
**Note:** limited edition of 500 pieces.

# Girard-Perregaux

For more than 200 years, Girard-Perregaux has been heralded for producing unrivaled masterpieces of high watchmaking and has laid claim to numerous awards and patents over the centuries.

A master at the production of complications, Girard-Perregaux's significant claim to fame is the renowned Tourbillon with three gold Bridges. Its newest line up includes several complicated introductions, including the Richeville Tourbillon with gold Bridge and the Vintage XXL three Bridge Quantiéme Perpetual.

The Richeville Tourbillon with gold Bridge is a classically elegant timepiece. Crafted in 18-karat gold, the tonneau-shaped watch features an aperture at 6:00 through which the rose-gold bridge can be seen. The tourbillon and cage consist of 72 components and have a combined weight of just 0.3 grams. The automatic mechanical movement is the GP 9610 T, with 30 rubies and 48 hours of power reserve.

The Vintage XXL three Bridge Quantiéme Perpetual watch is an interesting departure for the brand in that it is the first time a Girard-Perregaux tourbillon escapement is not visible through the watch dial, but rather through the caseback. This approach allows for more space on the dial for the perpetual calendar readouts.

Another important Vintage introduction for the brand is the Vintage 1945 Chronograph GMT, King Size. Available in all three colors of gold, the Chronograph GMT houses the automatic mechanical GP 033 CO movement with 61 rubies. The bold square watch features four counters: a small seconds at 3:00, hours at 6:00, minutes at 9:00, and a GMT 24-hour indicator at 12:00.

THIS PAGE

The Richeville Tourbillon with gold Bridge is bold and sophisticated with its 18-karat gold tonneau-shaped case and single-bridge aperture. The watch houses the GP 9610 T automatic mechanical movement.

FACING PAGE

The Sport Classique R&D 01 Chronograph is a new piece that features pushpieces for the chronograph on the left side of the case making it easier to use. The automatic watch is sculpted in steel and features a carbon fiber dial.

GIRARD-PERREGAUX
GP
SWISS MADE

**TOP LEFT**
The Laureato Evo-3 Chronograph features a silvered dial with black-ringed counters and red accents for the eight hands.

**TOP RIGHT**
This vertical oval Cat's Eye houses an automatic movement with 32 rubies and features a stunning mother-of-pearl dial with moonphase indicator.

Girard-Perregaux unveils a sporty new look for the Laureato Evo-3 Chronograph. Launched in 2003, the automatic Laureato Evo-3 gains a bolder more voluminous look thanks to the new silvered dial and black-ringed counters. Among other functions, the watch's eight hands majestically track seconds at 3:00, hour at 6:00, 24-hours at 9:00, and date at 12:00.

Girard-Perregaux also puts strong emphasis on its women's collections this year and has unveiled an entire Cat's Eye line dedicated to women. The sensual watches are housed in striking oval cases—set vertically in some instances and horizontally in others. The Cat's Eye watches are powered by either the automatic mechanical GP 033 LO, or the GP 033 RO movement, which beats at 28,800 vibrations per hour and has 32 rubies. With 46 hours of power reserve, these watches are beautiful blends of aesthetics and technology.

Among the new Cat's Eye models are a diamond-adorned moonphase version with a stunning mother-of-pearl dial, and a date version with power-reserve readout and a small seconds subdial. This version is crafted with a stunning black mother-of-pearl dial, a silver flinqué dial, or a translucent blue flinqué dial. All of the Cat's Eye watches feature diamonds on the dial, a superb diamond bezel, and are adorned with matching colored silk straps.

In its pour Ferrari collection, Girard-Perregaux unveils the Enzo Tourbillon with three gold Bridges. Created in honor of the new Enzo Ferrari, the Enzo Tourbillon is enhanced with a variety of functions, including a chronograph and perpetual calendar. The watch houses the GP 9982 manual-winding movement and offers 70 hours of power reserve. The barrel is decorated with a motif replicating the Enzo's engine. The watch is available in either 18-karat gold or platinum, both with a carbon-fiber dial and calendar readout using the same color scheme as the Enzo Ferrari instrument panel.

**TOP**

Placed horizontally on its silk strap, this Cat's Eye houses the GP 033 RO movement and offers a small subseconds dial and date readout.

**BOTTOM**

This Baguette Diamonds watch houses a hand-wound mechanical movement with 17 jewels. Its 18-karat gold case is set meticulously with Top Wesselton diamonds. Only 500 individually numbered pieces are being created.

## CHRONOLOGY

**1791** Jean François Bautte opens a manufactory in Geneva.

**1854** Husband-and-wife team Constant Girard and Marie Perregaux acquire the company and change its name two years later.

**1867** The Tourbillon with three gold Bridges pocket watch is introduced by Constant Girard, and is a spectacular masterpiece.

**1901** The Tourbillon with three gold Bridges is so ahead of its time, it is deemed ineligible to compete for awards at the Universal Exhibitions in Paris.

**1969** The entire watch industry is disrupted by the invasion of quartz and many houses view it with distrust—not so Girard-Perregaux. The brand is the first to produce Swiss-made quartz models on an industrial scale. Its oscillator's frequency (32,768 hz) is later adopted as the industry standard.

**1987** Girard-Perregaux unveils the 7000 chronograph—its first true sports watch.

**1991** Girard-Perregaux presents the Tourbillon with three gold Bridges in wristwatch format. This model represents the brand's commitment to its past and to horological perfection, as it is the first time the company has been able to fit the tourbillon escapement, complete with three bridges, into a wristwatch.

**1993** Girard-Perregaux presents the Tribute to Ferrari watch—the first in a series that defines the company's co-branding agreement with Ferrari. The Tribute to Ferrari watch is an automatic split-second chronograph with an engraving of the famed Ferrari symbol on the red dial. This is the first watch in the famous "pour Ferrari" collection.

**1994** Girard-Perregaux develops additional movements, including the GP 3000 and GP 3100.

**1996** The brand unveils the F50 chronograph to celebrate the 50th anniversary of Ferrari.

**1998** Girard-Perregaux unveils the Petit Tourbillon, a miniaturized version of the famed Tourbillon with three gold Bridges. The watch measures 31mm in diameter and compromises none of its sibling's technical features.

**1999** Girard-Perregaux joins the SIHH of Geneva. Opera One is developed, a complicated watch combining the Tourbillon with three gold Bridges with a Westminster chime and a minute repeater.

**2000** Release of the ww.tc with world time indication.

**2002** For the first time, the company unveils the Tourbillon with three gold Bridges in its distinctive, tonneau-shaped Vintage 1945 case.

**2003** Girard-Perregaux introduces the Opera Three, Tourbillon Magistral, and the automatic, skeletonized Tourbillon with three gold Bridges.

**2004** The Tourbillon Magistral is unveiled, housing a tourbillon, sonnerie and offering power-reserve indicator of the sonnerie.

## VINTAGE 1945 TOURBILLON WITH THREE GOLD BRIDGES — REF. 99870

**Movement:** mechanical automatic-winding GP 9600 caliber, with tourbillon device mounted on three 18K rose-gold bridges; over 40-hour autonomy; 21,600 vph; platinum micro-rotor mounted under the winding barrel (patented system); rhodium-plated and chased pillar-plate and barrel cover; realized, finished and decorated entirely by hand by GP's watchmakers. **Functions:** hour, minute, small second.

**Case:** 18K rose-gold three-piece square, anatomically curved case (size: 32x32mm, thickness: 12.5mm); antireflective curved sapphire crystal; rose-gold crown; snap-on back; water resistant to 3atm.
**Dial:** made up of the silvered rhodium-plated brass pillar-plate with vertical engravings, the three arrow-shaped tourbillon bridges in solid rose gold, cut out on the chased barrel and the tourbillon, rose-gold Dauphine hands.
**Indications:** small seconds at 6 integrated with the tourbillon carriage.
**Strap:** crocodile leather, hand-stitched; rose-gold fold-over clasp.
**Also available:** in yellow and gray gold; in platinum.

## VINTAGE 1945 XXL TOURBILLON CHRONOGRAPH PERPETUAL CALENDAR — REF. 99860

**Movement:** mechanical manual-winding GP 9800 caliber with tourbillon device; mounted on three 18K pink-gold bridges; 21,600 vph; 20 jewels; 12'''3/4; decorated with a Côtes de Genève pattern and beveled; modified, finished and decorated by hand by GP's watchmakers. **Functions:** hour, minute, small second; perpetual calendar (date, day, month, four-year cycle, moonphase). **Case:** 18K white-gold two-piece case; rectangular, ergonomically curved; size: 37x36mm, thickness: 15.5mm; curved antireflective sapphire crystal; 4 correctors on the middle; rectangular pushers and crown, both in white gold; back fastened by 4 screws, displaying the movement through a sapphire crystal; water resistant to 3atm.

**Dial:** matte black; subdials decorated with circular beads; applied white gold-plated brass Arabic numerals; printed railway minute track; luminescent white gold-plated brass Dauphine hands.
**Indications:** date at 3; moonphase and small seconds at 6; day of the week at 9; months divided over the four-year cycle at 12.
**Strap:** hand-stitched crocodile leather; white-gold fold-over clasp.
**Also available:** ivory dial; in pink or yellow gold; in platinum.

## VINTAGE 1945 XXL TOURBILLON MAGISTRAL — REF. 99710

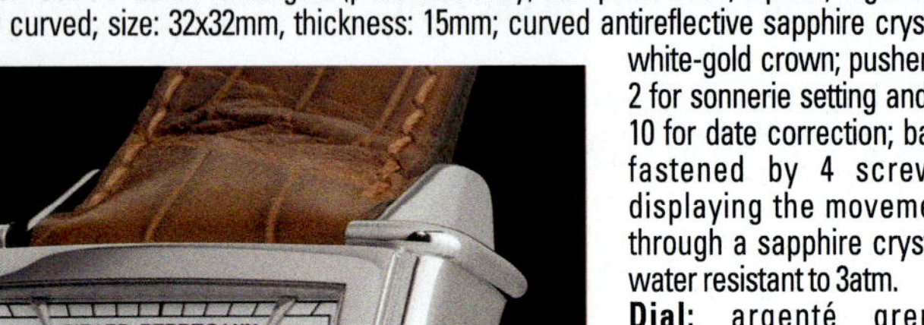

**Movement:** mechanical automatic-winding GP 09700.3950 caliber with tourbillon device; mounted on an 18K pink-gold bridge; approx. 110 hours' autonomy; 21,600 vph; size: 31x33mm; realized, finished and decorated by hand by GP's watchmakers.
**Functions:** hour, minute, small second; sonnerie au passage (hours); date; sonnerie power reserve. **Case:** white-gold (palladium alloy) two-piece case; square, ergonomically curved; size: 32x32mm, thickness: 15mm; curved antireflective sapphire crystal; white-gold crown; pusher at 2 for sonnerie setting and at 10 for date correction; back fastened by 4 screws, displaying the movement through a sapphire crystal; water resistant to 3atm.

**Dial:** argenté grené; curved; aperture on the tourbillon; sectors guilloché with ray-pattern; applied white gold-plated brass pointed markers; printed railway minute track; white gold-plated brass Dauphine hands.
**Indications:** sonnerie power reserve at 2; small seconds at 6 integral with the tourbillon carriage; date with retrograde hand at 10.
**Strap:** hand-stitched crocodile leather; white-gold fold-over clasp.
**Also available:** in pink, white or yellow gold; in platinum.

## VINTAGE 1945 XXL CHRONOGRAPH — REF. 25840

**Movement:** mechanical automatic-winding GP 033C0 caliber; autonomy 46 hours; 63 jewels; 11'''1/2; balance with 28,800 vph; decorated with a Côtes de Genève pattern and beveled; modified, finished and decorated by hand by GP's watchmakers. **Functions:** hour, minute, small second; date; chronograph with 3 counters. **Case:** 18K pink-gold two-piece case; square, ergonomically curved; size: 36.65x36.8mm, thickness: 13.1mm; curved antireflective sapphire crystal; rectangular pushers and crown, both in pink gold; back fastened by 4 screws, displaying the movement through a sapphire crystal; water resistant to 3atm.

**Dial:** argenté; brushed; subdials decorated with circular beads; applied pink gold-plated brass Arabic numerals; pink gold-plated brass Dauphine hands.
**Indications:** small seconds at 3; date between 4 and 5; hour counter at 6; minute counter at 9; center second; railway minute track.
**Strap:** hand-stitched crocodile leather; pink-gold fold-over clasp.
**Also available:** black dial; in white gold.

## VINTAGE 1945 "KING SIZE" PERPETUAL CALENDAR REF. 90285

**Movement:** mechanical automatic-winding GP 33Q0.D caliber; autonomy 50 hours; 27 jewels; 11'''1/2; balance with 28,800 vph; decorated with a Côtes de Genève pattern and beveled; modified, finished and decorated by hand by GP's watchmakers. **Functions:** hour, minute, second; perpetual calendar (date, day, month, four-year cycle, moonphase). **Case:** 18K pink-gold two-piece case; rectangular, ergonomically curved; size: 31.6x31.75mm, thickness: 11.35mm; curved antireflective sapphire crystal; 4 correctors on the middle; rectangular pushers and crown, both in pink gold; back fastened by 4 screws, displaying the movement through a sapphire crystal; water resistant to 3atm.
**Dial:** matte black; subdials decorated with circular beads; applied pink gold-plated brass Arabic numerals; printed railway minute track; pink gold-plated brass Dauphine hands.
**Indications:** small date at 3; moonphase at 6; day of the week et 9, months divided over the four-year cycle at 12.
**Strap:** hand-stitched crocodile leather; pink-gold fold-over clasp.
**Also available:** cream-colored dial.

## VINTAGE 1945 "KING SIZE" CHRONOGRAPH GMT REF. 25975

**Movement:** mechanical automatic-winding GP 033C0 caliber; autonomy 46 hours; 61 jewels; 11'''1/2; balance with 28,800 vph; decorated with a Côtes de Genève pattern and beveled; modified, finished and decorated by hand by GP's watchmakers. **Functions:** hour, minute, small second; 24 hour; date; chronograph with 3 counters. **Case:** 18K pink-gold two-piece case; rectangular, ergonomically curved; size: 31.9x31.5mm, thickness: 13.3mm; curved antireflective sapphire crystal; rectangular pushers (at 10 for the second time zone) and crown, both in pink gold; back fastened by 4 screws, displaying the movement through a sapphire crystal; water resistant to 3atm.
**Dial:** matte black; subdials decorated with circular beads; applied pink gold-plated brass Arabic numerals; pink gold-plated brass Dauphine hands.
**Indications:** small seconds at 3; date between 4 and 5; hour counter at 6; minute counter at 9; second time zone 24 hour at 12; center second; railway minute track.
**Strap:** hand-stitched crocodile leather; white-gold fold-over clasp.
**Also available:** silvered dial; in white gold.

## VINTAGE 1945 "KING SIZE" SMALL SECOND, DATE REF. 25830

**Movement:** mechanical automatic-winding GP 03390 caliber; autonomy 46 hours; 28 jewels; 11'''1/2; balance with 28,800 vph; decorated with a Côtes de Genève pattern and beveled; modified, finished and decorated by hand by GP's watchmakers. **Functions:** hour, minute, small second; date.
**Case:** stainless steel two-piece case; square, ergonomically curved; size: 32x32mm, thickness: 11.4mm; curved antireflective sapphire crystal; back fastened by 4 screws, displaying the movement through a sapphire crystal; water resistant to 3atm.
**Dial:** silvered; center grained; subdial decorated with circular beads; applied pink gold-plated brass Arabic numerals; printed railway minute track; luminescent pink gold-plated brass Sports hands.
**Indications:** date between 1 and 2; small seconds at 9.
**Strap:** hand-stitched crocodile leather; steel fold-over clasp.
**Also available:** leather strap and buckle; with black or blue dial; with black dial, luminescent Arabic numerals and markers; with silvered or gray dial, applied Arabic numerals and markers.

## VINTAGE 1945 SMALL SECOND AND DATE REF. 25932

**Movement:** mechanical automatic-winding GP 03290 caliber; autonomy 40 hours; 28 jewels; 10'''1/2; balance with 28,800 vph; decorated with a Côtes de Genève pattern and beveled; modified, finished and decorated by hand by GP's watchmakers. **Functions:** hour, minute, small second; date. **Case:** stainless steel two-piece case; square, ergonomically curved; size: 28x28mm, thickness: 11.15mm; curved antireflective sapphire crystal; back fastened by 4 screws, displaying the movement through a sapphire crystal; water resistant to 3atm. **Dial:** blue; center disc and small second guilloché; silvered circular railway minute track; applied rhodium-plated brass pointed markers (6 and 12 as Arabic numerals); printed; rhodium-plated brass Dauphine hands.
**Indications:** date between 1 and 2; small seconds at 9.
**Strap:** hand-stitched crocodile leather; steel fold-over clasp.
**Also available:** leather strap and fold-over clasp; with bracelet; with silvered or ruthenium dial; silvered dial; 11 applied Arabic numerals; with blue dial; 8 brilliant markers and mother-of-pearl subdial.

## OPERA THREE — REF. 99790

**Movement:** manual-winding GP 00950.9100 caliber 13''' 1/2; 45 jewels; 28,800 vph; power reserve; 2 melodies.
**Case:** Ø 43mm.
**Dial:** silver.
**Indications:** small second at 6; power-reserve display; selected melody indicator.

**Strap:** crocodile leather (basic colors: black, brown, honey brown).
**Also available:** 18K yellow gold, pink gold or white gold; platinum.
**Note:** Opera Three is an extremely refined musical watch, which marks the passing time with a melody at each hour. The heart of this model is a miniature carillon with a keyboard of 20 keys and one drum set with 150 hand-assembled parts. It is possible to choose 2 different melodies by reversing the drum rotation with a small lever. Another lever with 3 positions allows the wearer to deactivate the melody, play it on command, or program it to play each hour.

## RICHEVILLE TONNEAU TOURBILLON SOUS UN PONT D'OR — REF. 99310

**Movement:** mechanical automatic-winding GP 9610T caliber with a tourbillon device; mounted on an 18K pink-gold bridge; autonomy 48 hours; 21,600 vph; 30 jewels; realized, mounted, adjusted, finished and decorated by hand by GP's watchmakers.
**Functions:** hour, minute.
**Case:** 18K pink-gold two-piece case; tonneau shape; size: 37x37mm, thickness: 12.75mm; curved antireflective sapphire crystal; pink-gold crown; back fastened by 4 screws, displaying the movement through a sapphire crystal; water resistant to 3atm.
**Dial:** cream colored; aperture on the tourbillon; applied pink gold-plated brass Arabic numerals; printed minute track; pink gold-plated brass Dauphine hands.
**Indications:** minute counter at 3; small seconds at 9; center second counter.
**Strap:** hand-stitched crocodile leather; pink-gold fold-over clasp.
**Also available:** in yellow or white gold; in platinum.

## TOURBILLON WITH THREE GOLD BRIDGES AUTOMATIC — REF. 99250

**Movement:** mechanical automatic-winding GP Manufacture 9600 caliber, with tourbillon device mounted on three 18K rose-gold bridges; over 40-hour autonomy; 21,600 vph. Platinum micro-rotor mounted under the winding barrel (patented system); rhodium-plated and chased pillar-plate and barrel cover; realized, finished and decorated entirely by hand by GP's watchmakers. **Functions:** hour, minute, small second.

**Case:** 18K rose-gold, three-piece case (Ø 38mm, thickness: 10mm), polished and brushed finish; antireflective flat sapphire crystal; rose-gold crown; back attached by 6 screws; water resistant to 3atm.
**Dial:** 3 solid gold tourbillon bridges, arabesqued pillar-plate, barrel and tourbillon are all visible; rose-gold Dauphine hands.
**Indications:** small second at 6 integrated in the tourbillon carriage.
**Strap:** crocodile leather, hand-stitched; rose-gold clasp.
**Also available:** in yellow or white gold; in platinum.

## TOURBILLON WITH THREE GOLD BRIDGES AUTOMATIC — REF. 99060

**Movement:** automatic GP 9600S caliber 12'''3/4; 30 jewels; 21,600 vph; minimum power reserve of 48 hours.
**Case:** Ø 39mm, thickness: 9.9mm; sapphire crystal cambered above, flat below; transparent caseback fastened with 6 screws; water resistant to 3atm.
**Dial:** skeleton.
**Strap:** crocodile leather (basic colors: black, brown, honey brown).
**Also available:** 18K yellow gold, pink gold or white gold; platinum.

## RICHEVILLE TONNEAU CHRONOGRAPH — REF. 27650

**Movement:** mechanical automatic-winding GP 033C0 caliber; autonomy 45 hours; 28,800 vph; 63 jewels; 11'''1/2'; decorated with a Côtes de Genève pattern and beveled; modified, finished and decorated by hand by GP's watchmakers. **Functions:** hour, minute, small second; date; chronograph with 3 counters. **Case:** stainless steel two-piece case; tonneau shape; size: 37x37mm, thickness: 12.7mm; curved antireflective sapphire crystal; oval pushers; back fastened by 4 screws, displaying the movement through a sapphire crystal; water resistant to 3atm. **Dial:** silvered; 2 levels, brushed center; subdials decorated with circular beads, grained hour ring; printed Roman numerals; blued steel leaf-style hands. **Indications:** small seconds at 3; date between 4 and 5; hour counter at 6; minute counter at 9; center second counter; railway minute track. **Strap:** crocodile leather; steel fold-over clasp. **Also available:** silvered or blue dial, applied Arabic numerals; with black dial, silvered subdials and 12 as printed Arabic numeral; in yellow or white gold.

## LADY BAGUETTE — REF. 25610

**Movement:** mechanical manual-winding GP 0900 caliber; autonomy 35 hours; 17 jewels; balance with 21,600 vph; realized, finished and decorated by hand by GP's watchmakers. **Functions:** hour, minute, small second; date. **Case:** 18K white-gold two-piece case; tonneau shape, ergonomically curved; size: 30x20mm, thickness: 9.2mm; pavé of set brilliants; curved antireflective sapphire crystal; white-gold crown; pusher at 2 for sonnerie setting and at 10 for date correction; back fastened by 4 screws, displaying the movement through a sapphire crystal; water resistant to 3atm. **Dial:** white mother of pearl; center with brilliant pavé; printed bâton markers; applied white-gold 6 and 12 as Arabic numerals; blued steel sword-style hands. **Indications:** sonnerie power reserve at 2; small seconds at 6 integral with the tourbillon carriage; date with retrograde hand at 10. **Strap:** techno-satin; white-gold clasp. **Note:** limited edition of 500 numbered pieces. **Also available:** in other jeweled versions; in pink or white gold without brilliants; silvered dial or gray or white mother-of-pearl dial; crocodile leather strap.

## TOURBILLON SOUS TROIS PONTS D'OR ENZO FERRARI — REF. 99190

**Movement:** mechanical manual-winding GP 9982 caliber with tourbillon device; mounted on three 18K gold bridges; autonomy 70 hours; 46 jewels; 21,600 vph; 20 jewels; 12'''3/4; realized, finished and decorated by hand by GP's watchmakers. **Functions:** hour, minute, small second; 24 hour; perpetual calendar (date, day, month, moonphase); chronograph with 3 counters. **Case:** 18K white-gold three-piece case; Ø 43mm, thickness: 17mm; polished and brushed finish; curved antireflective sapphire crystal; 4 correctors on the middle; pushers and crown in white gold; back fastened by 6 screws, displaying the movement through a sapphire crystal; water resistant to 3atm. **Dial:** matte black; subdials decorated with circular beads; luminescent applied Arabic numerals with red borders: luminescent, rhodium-plated brass sword-style hands. **Indications:** moonphase and 24 hour at 3; day of the week and hour counter at 6; months divided over the four-year cycle and minute counter at 9; date and small seconds at 12; center second; tachometer scale. **Strap:** hand-stitched crocodile leather; white-gold fold-over clasp. **Also available:** in pink or yellow gold; in platinum.

## GP POUR FERRARI CHRONO WW.TC "F1 053" — REF. 49800

**Movement:** mechanical automatic-winding GP 033C0 caliber; autonomy 46 hours; 63 jewels; 28,800 vph; 11'''1/2; decorated with a Côtes de Genève pattern and beveled; modified, finished and decorated by hand by GP's watchmakers. **Functions:** hour, minute, small second; date; world time; 24 hour; chronograph with 3 counters. **Case:** aluminum three-piece case; Ø 43mm, thickness: 13.75mm; polished and brushed finish; curved antireflective sapphire crystal; screw-down crowns (at 9 for the reference-town disc) and rectangular pushers in titanium; back fastened by 6 screws, displaying the movement through a sapphire crystal; water resistant to 3atm. **Dial:** carbon fiber; black subdials decorated with circular beads; luminescent applied Arabic numerals with red borders: luminescent in white-enameled brass Sports hands. **Indications:** date between 1 and 2; small seconds at 3; hour counter at 6; minute counter at 9; center second; minute track; 24-hour day-night (red-white) ring turning together with the main time; turning ring with reference towns for the 24 time zones. **Strap:** rubber; titanium fold-over clasp. **Also available:** in pink or yellow gold; in platinum.

## GP POUR FERRARI CHRONO SPORT "F1 052" REF. 49540

**Movement:** mechanical automatic-winding GP 019C0 caliber; autonomy 48 hours; 28,800 vph; 11'''1/2; decorated with a Côtes de Genève pattern and beveled; modified, finished and decorated by hand by GP's watchmakers.
**Functions:** hour, minute, small second; date; chronograph with 3 counters.
**Case:** titanium two-piece case; Ø 40mm, thickness: 13.6mm; polished and brushed finish; curved antireflective sapphire crystal; screw-down crown; back fastened by 7 screws, displaying the movement through a sapphire crystal; water resistant to 3atm.

**Dial:** carbon fiber; red enameled subdials decorated with circular beads; Ferrari logo beneath 12; luminescent Arabic numerals; luminescent, rhodium-plated brass sword-style hands.
**Indications:** small seconds at 3; date between 4 and 5; hour counter at 6; minute counter at 9; center second; minute track with divisions for 1/5 second and tachometer scale.
**Strap:** rubber; titanium clasp.
**Note:** limited edition of 200 numbered pieces.
**Also available:** in pink or yellow gold; in platinum.

## SPORT CLASSIQUE R&D1 CHRONO REF. 49930

**Movement:** mechanical automatic-winding GP 033C0 caliber (GP 3300 base + DD 2070 modulo); autonomy 46 hours; 28,800 vph; 52 jewels; modified, finished and decorated by hand by GP's watchmakers. **Functions:** hour, minute, small second; date; chronograph with 3 counters. **Case:** stainless steel three-piece case; Ø 38mm, thickness: 14.2mm; polished and brushed finish; flat sapphire crystal; brushed bezel; drop-shaped pushers; screw-down crown at 9 for winding and hour setting, at 4 for flange rotation, with case protection; date corrector at 3; back fastened by 6 screws, displaying the movement through a sapphire crystal; water resistant to 3atm.

**Dial:** carbon fiber; green-bordered subdials, flange with graduation; luminescent red-bordered Arabic numerals; luminescent, white-enameled brass Sports hands.
**Indications:** 24 hour with day-night indication at 3; date at 6; small seconds at 9; hour counter at 12; center minute counter (with red arrow-shaped tip) and second counter; minute track with divisions for 1/5 second.
**Strap:** rubber; double steel fold-over clasp.
**Also available:** leather strap and clasp; bracelet.

## SPORT CLASSIQUE SEA HAWK II PRO REF. 49940

**Movement:** mechanical automatic-winding GP 033R0 caliber (GP 3300 base); autonomy 46 hours; 28,800 vph; 26 jewels; modified, finished and decorated by hand by GP's watchmakers.
**Functions:** hour, minute, small second; date; power reserve.
**Case:** titanium three-piece case; Ø 45mm, thickness: 20.3mm; brushed finish; flat antireflective sapphire crystal; counterclockwise-turning titanium ring with knurled rim and grained upper face with embossed scale and luminescent dot at 12; recessed screw-down titanium crown at 4; with case protection; back fastened by 6 screws; water resistant to 30atm.

**Dial:** black; luminescent bâton markers (12 triangular); printed minute track; luminescent, white-enameled brass Sports hands.
**Indications:** date between 1 and 2; power reserve at 6.
**Bracelet:** titanium, brushed; double fold-over clasp.
**Also available:** rubber strap.

## LAUREATO EVO III AUTOMATIC REF. 80180

**Movement:** mechanical automatic-winding GP 33C0 caliber (GP 3300 base + DD 2070 module); autonomy 46 hours; 52 jewels; 28,800 vph. **Functions:** hour, minute, small second; date; second time zone; 24 hour; chronograph with 3 counters. **Case:** stainless steel two-piece case; Ø 44mm, thickness: 15.1mm; polished and brushed finish; octagonal bezel with black rubber gasket; curved antireflective sapphire crystal; 1 corrector on the middle; screw-down crown with case protection and anti-skid pushers; back fastened by 6 screws, displaying the movement through a sapphire crystal; water resistant to 5atm.

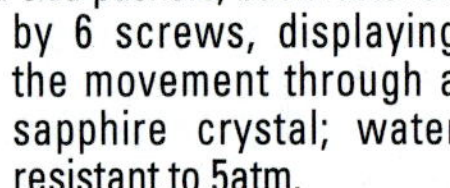

**Dial:** silvered; decorated with Clous de Paris, grained hour ring; subdials with circular beads and black crowns; applied luminescent round markers in rhodium-plated brass; luminescent sword-style rhodium-plated brass hands.
**Indications:** small seconds at 3; hour counter at 6; 24-hour second time zone at 9; date at 12; center minute counter (with red arrow-shaped tip) and second counter; minute track and tachometer scale.
**Bracelet:** polished and brushed stainless steel; recessed double fold-over safety clasp.
**Also available:** black dial; silvered subdial rings.

## CAT'S EYE MOONPHASE — REF. 80490/08049

**Movement:** mechanical automatic-winding GP 033L0 caliber; autonomy 46 hours; 32 jewels; 11'''1/2; 28,800 vph; realized and finished by hand by GP's watchmakers.
**Functions:** hour, minute, small second; moonphase.
**Case:** 18K yellow-gold three-piece case; oval shape; size: 30x35mm, thickness: 10.45mm; curved sapphire crystal; bezel with one row of set brilliants; yellow-gold crown with an onyx cabochon; back fastened by 4 screws, displaying the movement through a sapphire crystal; water resistant to 3atm.
**Dial:** white mother of pearl; silvered subdials; applied yellow-gold markers as set brilliants and 4 Arabic numerals; luminescent yellow-gold leaf-style hands.
**Indications:** small second and moonphase at 6.
**Strap:** techno-satin; yellow-gold clasp (fold-over clasp on request).
**Also available:** gray mother-of-pearl dial or silvered or blue enameled dial; in other jeweled versions; in yellow, pink or white gold; without brilliants, crocodile or satin strap with buckle or fold-over clasp.

## CAT'S EYE SMALL SECOND POWER RESERVE — REF. 8048/08048

**Movement:** mechanical automatic-winding GP 033R0 caliber; autonomy 46 hours; 27 jewels; 11'''1/2; 28,800 vph; realized and finished by hand by GP's watchmakers. **Functions:** hour, minute, small second; date; power reserve. **Case:** 18K white-gold three-piece case; oval shape; size: 35x30mm, thickness: 10.6mm; with one row of set brilliants; curved sapphire crystal; white-gold crown with an onyx cabochon; back fastened by 4 screws, displaying the movement through a sapphire crystal; water resistant to 3atm. **Dial:** white mother of pearl; subdial with blue crown; applied white-gold markers with set brilliants and 4 Arabic numerals; luminescent white-gold leaf-style hands.
**Indications:** date between 1 and 2; power reserve between 4 and 5; small seconds at 9.
**Strap:** techno-satin; white-gold clasp (fold-over clasp on request).
**Also available:** gray mother-of-pearl dial or silvered or blue enameled dial; in other jeweled versions; in yellow, pink or white gold; without brilliants, crocodile or satin strap with buckle or fold-over clasp.

## CLASSIQUE ELEGANCE "375" — REF. 80520

**Movement:** mechanical automatic-winding GP 3290 caliber; autonomy 40 hours; 28 jewels; 10'''1/2; 28,800 vph; 20 jewels; 12'''3/4; decorated with a Côtes de Genève pattern and beveled; modified, finished and decorated by hand by GP's watchmakers.
**Functions:** hour, minute, small second; date.
**Case:** 18K white-gold two-piece case; rectangular, ergonomically curved; size: 36x31mm, thickness: 9.6mm; polished and brushed finish; curved antireflective sapphire crystal; white-gold crown; back fastened by 4 screws; water resistant to 3atm.
**Dial:** gray; brushed with a soleil pattern, black subdial; applied bâton markers and Arabic numerals in white gold-plated brass; printed railway minute track; luminescent, white gold-plated brass Sports hands.
**Indications:** date between 1 and 2; small seconds at 9.
**Strap:** hand-stitched crocodile leather; white-gold fold-over clasp.
**Also available:** pink gold.

## CLASSIQUE ELEGANCE

**Movement:** mechanical automatic winding; decorated with a Côtes de Genève pattern and beveled; modified, finished and decorated by hand by GP's watchmakers.
**Functions:** hour, minute, second; date.
**Case:** stainless steel three-piece case; Ø 38mm, thickness: 8.8mm; polished and brushed finish; curved antireflective sapphire crystal; back fastened by 6 screws, displaying the movement through a sapphire crystal; water resistant to 3atm.
**Dial:** black; applied rhodium-plated brass Arabic numerals; printed minute track; luminescent, rhodium-plated brass Alpha hands.
**Indications:** date at 3.
**Strap:** hand-stitched crocodile leather; steel fold-over clasp.
**Also available:** silvered or blue dial, applied Arabic numerals; with black dial, silvered subdials and 12 as printed Arabic numeral; in yellow or white gold.

# Glashütte Original

Fine German watchmaking is a tradition at Glashütte Original, whose roots date back more than 150 years. Since its reemergence on the watchmaking scene just about 15 years ago, this Saxony brand has been developing and constructing its own movements and timepieces in house.

Complex works of art, Glashütte Original's watches rival the finest in the world. Now, the brand celebrates the opening of a new watchmaking factory, bringing all facets of the development and building processes under one roof.

Within its new state-of-the-art workshops, Glashütte Original recently developed its newest automatic-winding Caliber 95, panorama date, classic column-wheel chronograph, and flyback function. The movement features a rotor with bilateral winding via step gear. It beats at 28,800 vibrations per hour, offers 42 hours of power reserve and features a twin spring barrel, hand-engraved balance cock and skeletonized gold rotor.

The exquisite Caliber 95 is housed in a stunning new PanoMaticChrono with an inventive presentation of chronograph readouts and time. The dial offers the time readout in a large subdial at 6:00, and the chronograph seconds readout in a large subdial at 12:00, superimposed over the other subdials. The PanoMaticChrono is produced in platinum with two different dial choices, each in a limited edition of 200 pieces. An 18-karat rose-gold version is available with two dial choices.

Also new from Glashütte Original is the Senator Panorama Date with Moonphase watch that houses the automatic-winding Caliber 39-41. The 18-karat rose-gold watch displays the movement through a screw-on sapphire crystal caseback. The dial is clean with date readout at 4:00 and moonphase indication at 10:00.

**ABOVE**

This PanoMaticChrono is crafted in platinum and houses the new Caliber 95. It offers panorama date and column-wheel chronograph with flyback function.

**LEFT**

Crafted in 18-karat rose gold, this PanoMaticChrono features a silvered dial with a unique counter layout.

## CHRONOLOGY

**Mid 1800s** In the Saxony region of Germany, watchmaking as a trade takes root.

**1845** Timepieces are being produced in Saxony by a variety of master watchmakers—establishing what is today Glashütte Original.

**1904** The Ernst Kassiske watch factory gives rise to Glashutter Prazisions-Uhrenfabrik AG.

**1927** Uhren-Rohwerke-Fabrik Glashütte AG (Urofa) is founded to produce fine watches that are distributed throughout Europe.

**1940s** The watchmaking trade here is disrupted by World War II bombings and political unrest.

**1946** Glashütte produces its first complicated movements.

**1951** The East German government merges the various watch brands of the region into one company, VEB Glashutter Uhrenbetriebe. The economic isolation of the land leads watchmakers to develop independent technologies and designs, while expanding international distribution.

**1990** Following the German reunification, the dream of the return of German branded watchmaking becomes a reality. Watchmakers set about reestablishing their brands.

**1994** The Glashütte Original brand is established, and embarks on a quest to create fine complex mechanical timepieces.

**1996** The signature elements of the brand—excellent craftsmanship, elegant design, interesting history, and dedication to survival—come together and the Glashütte Original watches are released. One of the first pieces is the Alfred Helwig Tourbillon watch based on a model created by its namesake around 1920.

**2000** The brand, popular with connoisseurs and collectors, is purchased by The Swatch Group, which is determined to maintain Glashütte's purity of tradition.

**2001** Glashütte unveils the Alfred Helwig Tourbillon 2 watch. It houses a Glashütte Original movement, Caliber 41-02, with manual winding and a frontally placed one-minute flying tourbillon. The watch also offers 48 hours of power reserve, a subdial to indicate the hour and minute displays, and a retrograde date display.

**2002** The company unveils a column-wheel chronograph movement and a caliber fitted with a tourbillon escapement. By now, the company has created 10 proprietary movements and offers a watch line comprised of five different collections complete with master complications.

**2004** The brand opens its new manufacturing facility.

TOP LEFT AND RIGHT

The new Glashütte Original manufactory brings all aspects of watchmaking under one roof.

ABOVE

One of Glashütte Original's newest movements, the Caliber 95 offers panorama date, a column-wheel chronograph with flyback function.

RIGHT

The Senator Panorama Date with Moonphase is crafted in 18-karat rose gold and houses the automatic-winding Caliber 39-41.

## PANOMATICTOURBILLON — REF. 93.01.03.03.04

**Movement:** mechanical automatic-winding Glashütte Original 93 caliber with tourbillon volant device.
**Functions:** hour, minute, small seconds; date.
**Case:** platinum three-piece case; Ø 39.3mm, thickness: 12.4mm; polished-brushed finish; curved sapphire crystal; crown and ellipsoidal pusher at 10 for date correction in platinum; back fastened by 5 screws, displaying the movement through a sapphire crystal; water resistant to 10atm.
**Dial:** white gold; argenté; cannelé; with an aperture on the tourbillon, guilloché soleil subdial; brushed hour ring; applied bâton markers in nickel-plated brass; blued steel Alpha hands; with diamonds.
**Indications:** off-center hours and minutes at 9; big date 3; small seconds integrated with the tourbillon carriage at 8.
**Strap:** hand-stitched alligator leather; platinum clasp with applied logo.
**Note:** limited edition of 50 numbered pieces.

## PANOMATICLUNAR — REF. 90.02.03.03.04

**Movement:** mechanical automatic-winding Glashütte Original 90-02 caliber.
**Functions:** hour, minute, small seconds; date; moonphase.
**Case:** platinum three-piece case; Ø 39.3mm, thickness: 11.7mm; polished-brushed finish; curved sapphire crystal; platinum crown; 1 corrector in the middle; back fastened by 5 screws, displaying the movement through a sapphire crystal; water resistant to 10atm.

**Dial:** matte black; hour ring and brushed silvered subdial crowns; with applied bâton markers and Alpha hands in nickel-plated brass; with diamonds.
**Indications:** hour, minute at 9; moonphase at 2; big date at 4; small seconds at 8.
**Strap:** alligator leather; steel fold-over clasp with applied logo.
**Note:** limited edition of 200 numbered pieces.
**Also available:** pink gold, silvered dial; stainless steel, silvered dial.

## PANORETROGRAPH — REF. 61.01.04.03.06

**Movement:** mechanical manual-winding Glashütte Original 60 caliber.
**Functions:** hour, minute, small second; date; fly-back chronograph with 2 counters, countdown with acoustic elapsed-time signal.
**Case:** 18K pink-gold three-piece case; Ø 39mm, thickness: 13.2mm; polished and brushed finish; curved sapphire crystal; smoothed rectangular pushers and crown, all in pink gold; back fastened by 5 screws, displaying the movement through a sapphire crystal; water resistant to 3atm.

**Dial:** white gold; matte black; silvered zones.
**Indications:** off-center hour; minute and second at 9; applied bâton markers in gilded brass with diamonds; Alpha hands in gilded brass; minute counter at 2 with a three-arm scalar hand (each arm indicates a 20-second sequence on 3 concentric sectors); big date with 2 co-axial and complanar discs at 4; small seconds at 8; minute track.
**Strap:** alligator leather; pink-gold fold-over clasp with applied logo.
**Also available:** silvered dial; 150 pieces in white gold, silvered dial; 50 pieces in platinum, silvered dial.

## PANOMATICCHRONO — REF. 95.01.03.03.04

**Movement:** mechanical automatic-winding Glashütte Original 95 caliber.
**Functions:** hour, minute, small second; date; fly-back chronograph with 2 counters. **Case:** platinum three-piece case; Ø 39mm, thickness: 12.8mm; polished and brushed finish; curved sapphire crystal; crown with a sapphire cabochon and smoothed rectangular pushers at 10 for date correction, all in platinum; back fastened by 5 screws, displaying the movement through a sapphire crystal; water resistant to 3atm.

**Dial:** white gold; matte black; silvered guilloché jonquille; guilloché soleil hour dial; brushed hour ring.
**Indications:** off-center hour and minute at 6 with applied bâton markers in nickel-plated brass with diamonds and luminescent Alpha hands in blued steel; minute counter at 2 (with an inclined initial "0"); big date with 2 co-axial and complanar discs between 3 and 4, small seconds at 10 (with an inclined initial "0"); second counter at 12 with raised subdial.
**Strap:** hand-stitched alligator leather; platinum fold-over clasp with applied logo.
**Note:** limited edition of 50 numbered pieces.
**Also available:** pink gold with leather strap and fold-over clasp or bracelet.

## PanoReserve — Ref. 65.01.02.02.04

**Movement:** mechanical manual-winding Glashütte Original 65-01 caliber.
**Functions:** hour, minute, small seconds; date; power reserve.
**Case:** stainless steel three-piece case; Ø 39mm, thickness: 10.8mm; polished-brushed finish; curved sapphire crystal; back fastened by 5 screws, displaying the movement through a sapphire crystal; water resistant to 3atm.
**Dial:** silvered, grained.
**Indications:** off-center hour, minute and second at 9 with applied bâton markers and Alpha hands; minute counter at 2; big date with two coaxial and complanar discs at 4; small seconds at 8; minute track.
**Strap:** crocodile leather; fold-over clasp with applied logo.
**Also available:** in 18K pink-gold with silvered Ref. 65.01.01.01.04; in platinum with black dial Ref. 65.01.03.03.04, 100 piecesl.

## Senator Klassik Perpetual Calendar — Ref. 39.50.15.21.04

**Movement:** mechanical automatic-winding Glashütte Original 39-50 caliber.
**Functions:** hour, minute, second; date; perpetual calendar (date, day, month, year, moonphase).
**Case:** 18K pink-gold three-piece case; Ø 39mm, thickness: 11mm; polished finish; stepped bezel with polished zones; antireflective curved sapphire crystal; crown in pink gold; 4 correctors on the middle; back fastened by 5 screws, displaying the movement through a sapphire crystal; water resistant to 5atm.
**Dial:** gray, galvanized; applied bâton markers in gilded brass with diamonds on the printed minute track; Régate hands in gilded brass.
**Indications:** month between 2 and 3; big date with 2 co-axial and complanar discs at 4; moonphase between 7 and 8; day of the week between 9 and 10; four-year cycle between the center and 12.
**Strap:** hand-stitched alligator leather; pink-gold fold-over clasp with applied logo.
**Also available:** stainless steel; in pink gold with silvered dial; in stainless steel with silvered dial; 100 pieces in platinum with blue dial; 50 pieces in platinum with silvered dial.

## Senator Karree Perpetual Calendar — Ref. 39.51.01.01.04

**Movement:** mechanical automatic-winding Glashütte Original 39-51 caliber.
**Functions:** hour, minute; perpetual calendar (date, day, month, year, moonphase).
**Case:** 18K pink-gold four-piece square case; 37.5x34.8mm, thickness: 13mm; polished and brushed finish; curved sapphire crystal; pink-gold crown; 4 correctors in the middle; back fastened by 5 screws, displaying the movement through a sapphire crystal; water resistant to 3atm.
**Dial:** solid silver; applied faceted pointed markers in gilded brass; printed minute track; gilded brass Régate hands.
**Indications:** month at 2; big date with two coaxial and complanar discs at 4; moonphase between 7 and 8; day of the week at 10; four-year cycle between center and 12.
**Strap:** crocodile leather; pink-gold clasp with applied logo.
**Also available:** in stainless steel Ref. 39.51.02.02.04.

## Senator Karree Chronograph — Ref. 39.31.06.04.04

**Movement:** mechanical automatic-winding Glashütte Original 39-31 caliber.
**Functions:** hour, minute, small seconds; chronograph with 3 counters.
**Case:** stainless steel four-piece square case; 37.5x34.8mm, thickness: 12.5mm; polished and brushed finish; curved sapphire crystal; beveled rectangular pushers; back fastened by 8 screws, displaying the movement through a sapphire crystal; water resistant to 3atm.
**Dial:** solid silver; subdials decorated with circular beads; applied faceted pointed markers in nickel-plated brass; printed minute track; nickel-plated brass Régate hands.
**Indications:** small seconds at 3; 6-hour counter at 6; 30-minute counter at 9; center second; minute track with divisions for 1/5 second.
**Strap:** crocodile leather; steel clasp with applied logo.
**Also available:** in pink gold, silvered dial Ref. 39.31.09.05.04; 50 pieces in platinum, silvered dial Ref. 39.31.06.10.04.

# GRAHAM

Since 1695, Graham has stood in tribute to a golden age of timepiece engineering and design, a time when watchmakers were under tremendous pressure from The Royal Society to improve precision timekeeping.

Before all else, a word of warning: This vigorously sensual in-your-face chronograph is not for the shy at heart. The Swordfish, as it is named, is resolutely designed for high-profile individuals with a fresh, youthful attitude and a strong penchant for arousing curiosity-and satisfying their own. Swordfish catches and holds the gaze in a hypnotic grip, drawing the fascinated observer into the infinite depths of time.

Swordfish is the stunning result of a competition among top-flight young designers, organized within the framework of the Europe-wide Erasmus program. The demanding brief was mind-blowing for some, irresistibly stimulating for others: the outcome is all those emotions wrapped into one. In keeping with the revived and perpetuated Graham spirit of invention, this new and entirely uncompromising expression of luxurious technical sophistication is packed with novelties.

The essence of the Graham genius lies in unique technical features that make a Graham watch stand out from the crowd. The Swordfish is no exception: witness the tip of the crown that has been cleverly recessed and ridged to ensure a perfect grip and serves as a subtle reminder of brand identity. Then there are the distinctive chronograph pushbuttons with their Clous de Paris motif, creating a texture that offers optimal grip and easy handling, in addition to a pleasing aesthetic effect. Additionally, the original mirror-polished section on either side of the raised bezel makes a striking contrast with the rest of the fine-brushed surface.

For those already won over by the Drive Left concept introduced by Graham for optimal timekeeping efficiency using the thumb, an "L" just above 6:00 on the black dial draws attention to the fact that the controls are indeed placed on the left. Meanwhile, an "R" (for right) signals what is probably the only conventional thing about this chronograph! The sturdy stainless steel 46mm case, with its back secured by 8 screws, ensures water resistance to a depth of 160 feet (50 meters). It is attached to the wristband with architectonic dipping lugs that ensure optimal penetration and a perfect fit on all wrist sizes. The hypoallergenic

**ABOVE**

Graham's automatic Swordfish is powered by a chronograph movement with two counters (minute and hour), with the small seconds included in the hour counter. Swordfish also features a special case with bi-convex sapphire magnifying lenses for the counters. Pushers and crown are available in left or right position. Its 46.2mm case features a curved sapphire crystal and is water resistant to 160 feet (50 meters). The watch is offered on either a special rubber strap or sport calf strap with plain steel buckle.

**LEFT**

Profile of Swordfish.

silicon rubber strap is equipped with an extra-large stainless steel buckle.

The key to the powerful, sensual charm of this model undoubtedly lies in the sapphire crystals protecting the 12-hour sweep seconds and 30-minute chronograph counters. They reinforce the intriguing optical effect of depth created by the upward sloping case and confer a whole new dimension on time itself. By widening the gap between the protuberant eyes of the Swordfish, Graham has simultaneously freed up space for an additional circle in the middle to facilitate reading of information. This priority given to legibility is confirmed by the hour-markers and numerals that are luminescent for improved nighttime visibility, as are the hour and minute hands—also skeletonized for extra clarity. In a fascinating design trick, the center seconds hand with its elongated red tip is very much reminiscent of the extended upper jaw of the aquatic creature after which this model is named.

TOP

George Graham.

GRAHAM
LONDON

## CHRONOLOGY

**1700s** In 18th century London, George Graham is becoming famous for his timepieces. Most of his inventions—the cylinder escapement, the mercurial pendulum, the chronograph and the minute repeater with damper—remain used in horology.

The Royal Society ensures that Graham's inventions enjoy international acclaim as he publishes over 21 scientific papers on horology in the official publication of the Royal Society's journal. He is the first-ever clock-maker to be honored with membership.

In the very first years of the 18th century, what had escaped so many for so long is achieved by Graham: the precise measurement of time. Graham builds the very first clock with one-second-per-day accuracy, and time can, at last, be measured and read with precision and confidence. Perhaps the greatest accolade for the master watchmaker is the commission by the Greenwich Royal Observatory to build its Master Clock. For over 75 years, the timepiece that Graham designed and built enables astronomers, scientists, navigators and military planners to accurately conduct their work. It is displayed at the Greenwich Royal Observatory's museum, one of London's most famous landmarks.

In the later years of his life, Graham concentrates on perfecting astronomical instruments. Edmund Halley, the British astronomer with whom Graham became close friends, is able to draw his famous sidereal maps thanks to an extremely precise instrument invented by Graham for the Royal Observatory.

It is, however, Graham's invention of the chronograph for which he will be best remembered and known as the "Father of the Chronograph." As the movement from which all modern watch companies evolved their own mechanisms, the chronograph is a monument to Graham's work and incredible ingenuity.

**1997** Infused with a heritage unlike any other, George Graham's legacy of invention and innovation is renewed and fulfilled by The British Masters SA, in the Swiss Jura Mountains. In tribute to Graham, each watch in the collection is an authentic wrist instrument, driven by a complex movement unparalleled in its craftsmanship and originality.

**1998** Graham completes the development of and launches its trademark, the world-first Foudroyante Split (1/8th of a second) chronograph.

**2000** The self-winding COSC-certified chronometer, called the Chronofighter is unveiled. This thumb-operated chronograph features the patented left-hand side "fast action start/stop lever" mechanism.

**2004** Graham launches the Swordfish, a strong contemporary design. The two bi-convex magnifying lenses and the concept make the product sophisticated and powerful.

## SWORDFISH — REF. 2SWAS.B02A.K06B

**Movement:** mechanical automatic-winding G-1710 caliber; 33mm; 28,800 vph; 34 jewels; Côtes de Genève and circular graining decoration; blued steel screws; adjusted 5 positions.
**Functions:** hour, minute, small second; bicompax chronograph with 2 counters.
**Case:** Ø 46.2mm; stainless steel case with special biconvex sapphire magnifying lenses for counters; pushers and crown available in left or right position (dials are marked with L or R); water resistant to 160 feet.
**Dial:** black; luminescent hour markers; luminescent Arabic numerals 6 and 12; printed minute track; luminescent center second with red marker, white hands and red marker for counters.
**Indications:** left model: 12-hour counter at 3 and 30-minute counter at 9; right model: 30-minute counter at 3 and 12-hour counter at 9.
**Strap:** special rubber strap; plain steel buckle.

## SWORDFISH — REF. 2SWAS.B02A.L31B

**Movement:** mechanical automatic-winding G-1710 caliber; 33mm; 28,800 vph; 34 jewels; Côtes de Genève and circular graining decoration; blued steel screws; adjusted 5 positions.
**Functions:** hour, minute, small second; bicompax chronograph with 2 counters.
**Case:** Ø 46.2mm; stainless steel case with special biconvex sapphire magnifying lenses for counters; pushers and crown available in left or right position (dials are marked with L or R); water resistant to 160 feet.
**Dial:** black; luminescent hour markers; luminescent Arabic numerals 6 and 12; printed minute track; luminescent center second with red marker, white hands and red marker for counters.
**Indications:** left model: 12-hour counter at 3 and 30-minute counter at 9; right model: 30-minute counter at 3 and 12-hour counter at 9.
**Strap:** brown calf leather strap; plain steel buckle.

## CHRONOFIGHTER STEEL MIRROR — REF. 2CFPS.B08A.L31B

**Movement:** mechanical automatic-winding G-1722 caliber; 13''' 1/4; 28,800 vph; 30 jewels; Côtes de Genève and circular graining decoration; blued steel screws; adjusted 5 positions; COSC-certified chronometer.
**Functions:** hour, minute, small second; bicompax chronograph; coaxial command fast-action start/stop lever.
**Case:** stainless steel; Ø 43mm, thickness: 16mm; crown: Ø 8.5mm; domed sapphire crystal; mirror-polished finish on stainless steel bezel; back attached by 8 screws; embedded Royal Marine crown on caseback; stainless steel lever mechanism; water resistant to 160 feet.
**Dial:** black; luminescent hour markers; printed minute track; luminescent center second with red marker; white hands for counters.
**Indications:** small seconds at 3; 30-minute counter at 9.
**Strap:** leather strap "aviator" in brown or black calf with a classic buckle in plain stainless steel with mechanical engraving Graham or a new "Deployante" folding buckle with double-lever system.

## CHRONOFIGHTER GOLD — REF. 2CFAR.S02A.C54B

**Movement:** mechanical automatic-winding G-1722 caliber; 13''' 1/4; 28,800 vph; 30 jewels; Côtes de Genève and circular graining decoration; blued steel screws; adjusted 5 positions; COSC-certified chronometer.
**Functions:** hour, minute, small second; bicompax chronograph; coaxial command fast-action start/stop lever.
**Case:** red gold; Ø 43mm, thickness: 16mm; crown: Ø 8.5mm; domed sapphire crystal; mirror-polished finish on red-gold bezel; back attached by 8 screws; embedded Royal Marine crown on caseback; stainless steel lever mechanism; water resistant to 160 feet.
**Dial:** silver with black subdials; applied red-gold hour markers and numerals 6 and 12; printed minute track.
**Indications:** small seconds at 3; 30-minute counter at 9.
**Strap:** crocodile strap in brown or black with a classic buckle in solid red gold with mechanical engraving Graham.

## MASTERSPLIT REF. 2MSBR.B01A.C40B

**Movement:** mechanical manual-winding G-4445 caliber; column-wheel chronograph with direct effect-rattrapante function; Ø 31mm; 18,000 vph; 24 jewels; 42-hour power reserve; nickel-plated; circular graining decoration; blued steel screws; adjusted 5 positions.
**Functions:** hour, minute, small second at 9; central rattrapante second hand; integrated rattrapante and reset functions (single pushbutton); tachymeter (km/h base 1,000 meters); telemeter (base 15°C).
**Case:** Ø 44mm; red-gold 5N18, three-piece case; transparent sapphire crystal; caseback held by 8 screws; water resistant 100 feet.
**Dial:** guilloché sunray black dial; red gold-plated hands and applied Arabic numerals; openwork spear minute and hour hands; printed minute track; tachymeter scale and telemeter scale.
**Indications:** rattrapante hand for intermediary timing; minute counter at 3; small seconds at 9.
**Strap:** black crocodile leather; polished and engraved red-gold buckle.

## MASTERSPLIT REF. 2MSBR.S01A.C40B

**Movement:** mechanical manual-winding G-4445 caliber; column-wheel chronograph with direct effect-rattrapante function; Ø 31mm; 18,000 vph; 24 jewels; 42-hour power reserve; nickel-plated; circular graining decoration; blued steel screws; adjusted 5 positions.
**Functions:** hour, minute, small second; central rattrapante second hand; integrated rattrapante and reset functions (single pushbutton); tachymeter (km/h, base 1,000 meters); telemeter (base 15° C).
**Case:** Ø 44mm; red-gold 5N18, three-piece case; transparent sapphire crystal; caseback held by 8 screws; water resistant to 100 feet.
**Dial:** guilloché sunray silver dial; red gold-plated hands and applied Arabic numerals; openwork spear minute and hour hands; printed minute track; tachymeter scale and telemeter scale.
**Indications:** rattrapante hand for intermediary timing; minute counter at 3; small second at 9.
**Strap:** black crocodile leather; polished and engraved red-gold buckle.

## SILVERSTONE GOLD REF. 2SIAR.S01A.C01B

**Movement:** mechanical automatic-winding G-1721 caliber; 13 1/4'''; 28,800 vph; 28 jewels; Côtes de Genève and circular graining decoration; blued steel screws; adjusted in 5 positions.
**Functions:** hour, minute, small second; chronograph with 2 counters; second time-zone indicator; big date with double disc; center flyback seconds.
**Case:** Ø 41.6mm; red-gold 5N18, three-piece case; curved sapphire crystal; caseback attached by 8 screws; engraved Royal Marine crown on caseback; water resistant to 160 feet.
**Dial:** silvered dial; luminescent red gold-plated Roman numerals and center hands; red gold-plated second time-zone hand; printed minute track.
**Indications:** minute counter at 3; date at 6; small second at 9; center second time zone.
**Strap:** crocodile strap in black; polished and engraved red-gold buckle.
**Also available:** brown leather strap.

## SILVERSTONE BLACK REF. 2SIAS.B01.C01B

**Movement:** mechanical automatic-winding G-1721 caliber; 13 1/4'''; 28,800 vph; 28 jewels; Côtes de Genève and circular graining decoration; blued steel screws; adjusted in 5 positions.
**Functions:** hour, minute, small second; chronograph with 2 counters; second time-zone indicator; big date with double disc; center flyback seconds.
**Case:** Ø 41.6mm; low carbon, high corrosion-resistant, stainless steel three-piece case; curved sapphire crystal; caseback attached by 8 screws; engraved Royal Marine crown on caseback; water resistant to 160 feet.
**Dial:** black dial; luminescent Arabic numerals and center hands; yellow second time-zone hand; printed minute track.
**Indications:** minute counter at 3; date at 6; small second at 9; center second time zone.
**Strap:** crocodile strap in black; polished and engraved stainless steel buckle.
**Also available:** silver or blue dial with brown leather strap.

# GREUBEL FORSEY

With a creed to invent, validate and progress, two watchmakers join forces and vow to take haute horology to new heights. The Greubel Forsey brand is borne with one model—a watch the inventors bill as the tourbillon of the new millennium.

When watchmaker-inventors Robert Greubel and Stephen Forsey teamed up, their intention was to create a company dedicated to the development of complicated movements for prestige watchmaking. Their goal continues to be to create new complications in very small numbers that are marvels for collectors and connoisseurs.

In their atelier in La Chaux-de-Fonds, Greubel and Forsey worked tirelessly for nearly four years to perfect a movement that would surpass the accomplishments of existing tourbillons and offer ever more precise functioning. The fruit of their efforts: a tourbillon within a tourbillion that permanently compensates for rate errors in all wristwatch positions.

Named the Double Tourbillon 30° because of the angle that links the two mobile carriages, the double-tourbillon system is patented. Essentially, the invention of significance is the 30-degree inclination of the small carriage in relation to the rotational speed of the two tourbillon carriages.

Inside a large carriage (which is 15mm in diameter and turns once in a four-minute period), is a second smaller carriage inclined at a 30-degree angle, revolving once in 60 seconds. Thisinclination and speed creates the optimal conditions for the balance wheel to oscillate permanently in all positions. Hence, the compensation of the difference in rate due to gravity is no longer limited to the vertical position as in other tourbillons. An added mark of sophistication in the watchmaking of Greubel Forsey is the fact that the two carriages together contain 128 elements yet weigh a mere 1.17 grams.

THIS PAGE

ABOVE

A close-up look at the detailing of the stunning 18-karat gold case of the Double Tourbillon 30°.

FACING PAGE

The Double Tourbillon 30° named for the angle that links the two mobile carriages—features a patented double-tourbillon system. The 30° inclination of the small carriage in relation to the rotational speed of the two tourbillon carriages improves timekeeping performance.

GREUBEL FORSEY
DOUBLE
TOURBILLON
30°
SWISS

The Double Tourbillon 30° is driven by twin barrels, one of which is equipped with a slipping spring to avoid any defect caused by excess tension placed on the mechanism during winding. The watch is comprised in total of 301 components, including 39 domed jewels, and has a power reserve of at least 72 hours.

The exquisite movement is housed in a 43.5mm case in the three colors of gold. The case is closed with white-gold security screws ensuring that only the watchmakers trained by Greubel Forsey—and equipped with a special tool—can access the movement. The first wristwatch carrying the Greubel Forsey name, the Double Tourbillon 30° lays evidence to history in the making.

THIS PAGE

The Double Tourbillon 30° features a large carriage within which is a second smaller carriage inclined at a 30-degree angle, revolving once in 60 seconds. This inclination and speed enables the balance wheel to oscillate permanently in all positions.

FACING PAGE

The two carriages of the Double Tourbillon 30° together contain 128 elements, yet weigh a mere 1.17 grams.

## CHRONOLOGY

**1960** Robert Greubel is born in Alsace, France. He grows up repairing watches in his father's shop and later graduates from the Ecole d'Horlogerie in Dreux, France.

**1967** Stephen Forsey is born in St. Albans, England.

**1980s** Greubel works as a prototypist for IWC and participates in the Grand Complication project. He later joins Renaud & Papi, where he works on a variety of projects and then becomes co–general director.

**1987** Forsey joins Asprey London and later becomes responsible for its watch restoration and after-sales service department.

**1992** Forsey meets Greubel at Renaud & Papi and begins working on grand sonneries, repeaters and tourbillons.

**2001** Greubel and Forsey create CompliTime SA, a company dedicated to the development of complicated movements for prestige watchmaking.

**2004** Greubel Forsey creates a watchmaker-oriented Experimental Watch Technology (EWT) testing platform allowing them to implement engineering concepts and to validate the precision of their movement innovations. At BaselWorld, the brand unveils its first timepiece, the Double Tourbillon 30°, in extremely limited numbers.

# GUY ELLIA

Guy Ellia is a brand defined by its originality. Indeed, in all Ellia creates, this perfectionist lives by a simple motto: To conceive, to create, to innovate and to reject restrictions.

Guy Ellia timepieces deftly demonstrate the careful balance of subtlety and audacity, of traditionalism and bold invention. They are an evolution of a designer's insight and innovation. Guy Ellia started in the jewelry and watch world more than 20 years ago as a diamond dealer. From there, he branched into colored stones and later created a stunning collection of high jewelry. This effervescent designer with a warm and inviting nature enjoyed creating these pieces but wanted something more challenging and with stronger brand identity, so he decided to build a watch brand and launched his first timepiece, the Time Square, about six years ago. While his jewelry company was headquartered in Paris, he based his watch production in Geneva.

THIS PAGE

ABOVE

This stunning Time Square Convex represents the spirit of jeweled time by Guy Ellia. It features a mother-of-pearl dial, diamond bezel and superb gold mesh-link bracelet.

BOTTOM LEFT

This elegantly curved jewerly watch features a navy dial with color-coordinated strap and diamond accents. Oversized stylized numerals are hand applied.

FACING PAGE

This Times Square watch is bold and beautiful. It features a midnight blue mother-of-pearl dial and is crafted in rose gold with diamonds.

As a creator rather than a technical watchmaker, Ellia looked at watch design differently, and developed a line that was as pure in spirit as his jewelry. In fact, his first watch was set with 1,559 brilliants, infinitely small to give it particular shine. Still, Ellia wanted to push the technical envelope in his timepieces as well, and set his sights on designing complex men's watches. He approached the finest movement manufacturers and ordered not just simple calibers, but calibers that are further embellished and are more unusual than the norm.

High complications, men's watches, ladies' watches...today as yesterday, Guy Ellia preserves the art of being unique and combines its standards of perfectionism and savoir faire. How to recap GUY ELLIA : Creativity, subtlety and design.

# Guy Ellia

The Guy Ellia line consists of several main series, including the Time Square collection of watches. The Time Square Convex, with its square case crafted in each of the three colors of gold and set with diamonds. The dial is mother of pearl and bears four Arabic numerals—either painted or applied in gold. The Time Square Convex houses a Frederic Piguet caliber 820 movement. Another watch, the 2311 Squelette, also features white, black, pink or yellow main plate and bridges in the caliber 117 movement created by Parmigiani.

There is a stunning high-jewelry Time Square model called the Dream, which is bedecked with 148 emerald-cut diamonds weighing 35 carats. Ensuring the unique spirit of invention and performance that characterize Guy Ellia, this watch is created in a limited edition of just five pieces.

Most recently, Guy Ellia turns his sights to the complicated watches and offers a line of complexities called the Time Square Z 1 series that includes grand dates, moonphases, jumping seconds and perpetual calendars. In addition to this collection, Guy Ellia's crowning glory is the all-new Tourbillon Magistère biconvex timepiece.

The Time Square Z 1 watches are immediately recognizable in their full, curved square cases that are quite flat. The watches feature specially stylized Roman numerals and dials that offer sobriety.

**ABOVE**

The Time Square Z 1 Tourbillon Magistère is a stunning masterpiece. It houses a one-minute rotating tourbillon that was created for Guy Ellia by Swiss watchmaker Christophe Claret. The movement is skeletonized to offer maximum beauty.

## CHRONOLOGY

**1983** Parisian designer Guy Ellia enters the jewelry world as a diamond dealer in Antwerp. His first sale is a single-carat diamond.

**1986** Ellia extends his business to include precious stones. He begins traveling to Burma for rubies, Colombia for emeralds, and to other lands where he buys, negotiates and sells gemstones.

**1990** Ellia yearns for something more creative than buying and selling stones and begins to pave the way for his own jewelry collection, returning to Paris and starting on his own designs.
Ellia introduces his own high-jewelry collection.

**1999** With the jewelry series under his belt, Guy Ellia decides to launch his own watch brand.

**2002** At the Basel Watch Fair, Guy Ellia unveils the Time Square Squelette, with the caliber 117 with 8 days of power reserve from Parmigiani Fleurier.

**2003** The Guy Ellia brand begins its international expansion and development.

**2004** The brand unveils its first high complication timepieces.

The retrograde watch features a jumping seconds readout in a semi-circular counter at 6:00 and houses the Frédéric Piguet movement. The Big Date is an automatic watch with Frédéric Piguet movement and large-date aperture at 12:00. The Date Hand watch offers day of the week and month readouts in an aperture, along with the phases of the moon. The date is shown by a hand whose circular scale runs around the face. This watch houses a Frédéric Piguet movement, as does the perpetual calendar watch that is adjustment free to 2100. There is also a Perpetual Calendar watch that features the Frédéric Piguet movement and offers elegant redouts.

The Time Square Tourbillon Magistère is a biconvex tourbillon that is created for Guy Ellia by Swiss watchmaker Christophe Claret. It features a one-minute rotating tourbillon whose cage weighs less than one gram. The movement of this elegant watch is skeletonized to offer maximum, essential beauty. Christophe Claret built a highly technical movement with 110 hours' power reserve, which rewinds using the Mysterieus transmission of physical energy.

With the Time Square Tourbillon, Guy Ellia positions himself at the top of the complications references in luxury Swiss watchmaking.

**ABOVE**

This Time Square Z 1 Quantième à Aiguille Moonphase watch. It is crafted in18-karat gold and automatic Frédéric Piguet movement.

**CENTER**

This Time Square Z 1 Grande Date watch is an automatic with Frédéric Piguet movement.

**BOTTOM RIGHT**

This Time Square Z 1 Perpetual Calendar is an automatic with Frédéric Piguet movement.

## TIME SQUARE 2315 LV6 CONVEX N°1

**Movement:** Frédéric Piguet caliber PGE 820; cage: Ø 18.8mm, movement thickness: 1.95mm.
**Functions:** hour, minute.
**Case:** 18K solid gold case set with 100 diamonds (diamonds: Ø 1.5mm); 41x41mm, case thickness: 7.1mm; sapphire glass; crown set with one Ø 2.3mm diamond; bottom cover with deep mechanical engraving water resistant at 3atm (30m).

**Dial:** mother-of-pearl dial; 4 gold Arabic figures; Dauphine-shaped 18K gold hands.
**Indications:** hour setting by a 2-position stem.
**Strap:** alligator; 18K solid gold ardillon buckle set with 40 diamonds (diamonds: Ø 1.5mm); ardillon set with one Ø 0.9mm diamond.
**Also available:** white and pink gold, 8 different colors of mother-of-pearl dial (white, ivory, yellow, pink, lilas, burgundy, jeans, navy); 4 outlined Arabic figures.

## TIME SQUARE 2315 LV6 CONVEX N°2

**Movement:** Frédéric Piguet caliber PGE 820; cage: Ø 18.8mm, movement thickness: 1.95mm.
**Functions:** hour, minute.
**Case:** 18K solid gold case set with 100 diamonds (diamonds: Ø 1.5mm); 41x41mm, thickness: 7.1mm; sapphire glass; crown set with one Ø 2.3mm diamond; bottom cover with deep mechanical engraving; water resistant at 3atm (30m).

**Dial:** mother-of-pearl dial; 4 outlined Arabic figures; Dauphine-shaped 18K gold hands.
**Indications:** hour setting by a 2-position stem.
**Strap:** 18K solid gold bracelet: 32x32 in white, pink and yellow gold.
**Also available:** white and pink gold; 8 different colors of mother-of-pearl dial (white, ivory, yellow, pink, lilas, burgundy, jeans, navy); 4 gold Arabic figures.

## TIME SQUARE 2311 MV1 N°3

**Movement:** Frédéric Piguet caliber PGE 820; cage: Ø 18.8mm, movement thickness: 1.95mm.
**Functions:** hour, minute.
**Case:** 18K solid gold case set with 1,249 diamonds (diamonds: Ø 0.9mm); 37.8x33mm, thickness: 5.4mm; sapphire glass; crown set with the diamond (diamonds: Ø 2.3mm); bottom cover with deep mechanical engraving; water resistant at 3atm (30m).

**Dial:** mother-of-pearl dial; 4 diamonds (diamonds: 1.2mm); Dauphine-shaped 18K gold hands.
**Indications:** hour setting by a 2-position stem.
**Strap:** alligator or satin; 18K solid gold ardillon buckle set with 88 diamonds (diamonds: Ø 0.9mm); ardillon set with 4 diamonds.
**Also available:** white and pink gold, 6 different colors of mother-of-pearl dial (white, ivory, pink, lilas, jeans, black); dial set with 310 diamonds (diamonds: Ø 0.9mm).

## TIME SQUARE 2311 SKELETON N°4

**Movement:** mechanical Parmigiani GE 117 caliber; cage: Ø 32.86x28.06mm, thickness: 7.9mm.
**Functions:** hour, minute, second at 6; power reserve at 12.
**Case:** 18K solid gold case; 37.8x33mm, thickness: 9.2mm; sapphire glass; crown set with Ø 3mm sapphire; water resistant at 3atm (30m).
**Dial:** mother-of-pearl dial; Dauphine-shape 750 gold hands.

**Indications:** 8-day power reserve by spherical differential; winding and hour setting via a 2-position stem.
**Strap:** alligator; 18K solid gold ardillon buckle.
**Also available:** 18K solid gold case set with 775 diamonds (diamonds: Ø 0.9mm).

## ROUND SQUARE 2320 LV6 CONVEX N°5

**Movement:** Frédéric Piguet caliber PGE 820; cage: Ø 18.8mm, movement thickness: 1.95mm.
**Functions:** hour, minute.
**Case:** 18K solid gold case set with 81 diamonds (diamonds: Ø 1.5mm); 55x35mm, thickness: 5.6mm; sapphire glass; crown set with one Ø 2.5mm diamond; bottom cover with deep mechanical engraving; water resistant to 3atm (30m).
**Dial:** mother-of-pearl dial; gold Roman figures (CRO); Dauphine-shaped 18K gold hands.
**Indications:** hour setting by a 2-position stem.
**Strap:** alligator; 18K solid gold ardillon buckle set with 9 diamonds (diamonds: Ø 1.5mm); ardillon set with one Ø 0.9mm diamond.
**Also available:** 9 different colors of mother-of-pearl dial (white, ivory, yellow, light green, pink, lilas, burgundy, jeans, navy); dial with painted Roman figures (white, orange, gold, khaki, brown, red, bordeaux, dark blue, black).

## TIME SQUARE 2311 MV6 4 CAS LS N°6

**Movement:** Frédéric Piguet caliber PGE 820; cage: Ø 18.8mm, movement thickness: 1.95mm.
**Functions:** hour, minute.
**Case:** 18K solid gold case set with 132 diamonds (diamonds: Ø 0.9mm); 37.8x33mm, thickness: 5.4mm; sapphire glass; crown set with one Ø 2.3mm diamond; bottom cover with deep mechanical engraving; water resistant at 3atm (30m).
**Dial:** mother-of-pearl dial; 4 gold Arabic figures in 18K solid gold set with 97 diamonds (diamonds: Ø 0.8mm); Dauphine-shaped 18K gold hands.
**Indications:** hour setting by a 2-position stem.
**Strap:** alligator or satin; 18K solid gold ardillon buckle set with 163 diamonds (diamonds: Ø 0.9mm); ardillon set with 4 diamonds.
**Also available:** white and yellow gold; 6 different colors of mother-of-pearl dial (white, ivory, yellow, pink, lilas, jeans, black).
**Additional option:** 18K solid gold deployment buckle set with 163 diamonds (diamonds: Ø 0.9mm).

## TIME SQUARE 2315 Z1 CONVEX GRANDE DATE N°7

**Movement:** automatic Frédéric Piguet caliber PGE 6860; cage: Ø 25.6mm, movement thickness: 4.35mm; 3-day power reserve; semi-instantaneous Grande Date.
**Functions:** hour, minute, second at 6; Grande Date at 12.
**Case:** 18K solid gold case; 45x45mm, thickness: 11mm; sapphire glass; crown set with one Ø 1.2mm diamond; bottom cover with deep mechanical engraving; water resistant at 3atm (30m).
**Dial:** 18K solid gold; painted Roman figures; Dauphine-shaped 18K gold hands.
**Indications:** hour setting by a 3-position stem.
**Strap:** alligator; 18K solid gold deployment buckle.
**Also available:** yellow gold and pink gold.

## TIME SQUARE 2315 Z1 CONVEX QUANTIEME A AIGUILLE PHASES DE LUNE N°8

**Movement:** automatic Frédéric Piguet caliber PGE 6763; cage: Ø 26.2mm, movement thickness: 5.02mm; 3-day power reserve.
**Functions:** hour, minute; moonphase and co-axial second at 6; date, days and months via discs.
**Case:** 18K solid gold case; 45x45mm, thickness: 11mm; sapphire glass; crown set with one Ø 1.2mm diamond; bottom cover with deep mechanical engraving; water resistant at 3atm (30m).
**Dial:** 18K solid gold; painted Roman figures; Dauphine-shaped 18K gold hands.
**Indications:** hour setting by a 2-position stem; correctors via push rods; days at 10; months at 2; day of the month at 4; moonphase at 8.
**Strap:** alligator; 18K solid gold deployment buckle.
**Also available:** yellow gold and pink gold.

# HARRY WINSTON

Ever the prolific jewelry and watchmaker, Harry Winston never ceases to amaze with its gemstone watches and technical fury.

Among the incredible achievements of Harry Winston is the Opus series of watches that the brand makes in cooperation with individual watchmakers to ensure the future of the art. In 2004, Harry Winston unveiled the Opus Four, created with Christophe Claret—master of the chiming watch. Opus Four is a completely reversible minute repeater that strikes on cathedral gongs. Through one side of the watch, the tourbillon is revealed; the reverse side features a large moonphase indicator and date. The platinum watch consists of 423 parts, including 40 jewels, and has a power reserve of 53 hours. Opus Four is created in a limited edition of 18 platinum pieces and two high-jeweled versions.

Ronald Winston, who takes a very active role in the company's watchmaking business, also unveils a new collection in which he took particular interest: the Project Z1. It features a high-tech sports watch designed with three world firsts: an automatic chronograph with three off-center retrograde indications; a radically different design; and a totally new material in watchmaking. Backed by Ronald Winston himself, the material for the Project Z1 watches is a rare alloy named Zalium—for its major component, zirconium. Used in jet engines, Zalium has never been used in watchmaking because it is very hard and extremely difficult to manipulate. In fact, it must be very carefully machined from the ingot because the dust can catch fire. A personal endeavor of Ronald Winston, the Project Z1 is made in a limited edition of 100 pieces.

In its classically elegant collections, Harry Winston unveils several new models. For men, the new Avenue C Jumping Hours watch embodies the constant zest for invention indicative of the house of Harry Winston. The stunning watch houses a manually wound movement, a tonneau-shaped caliber corresponding to the case. A sapphire crystal caseback reveals the classic Côtes de Genève decoration.

THIS PAGE

The Opus Four is created by Harry Winston in cooperation with Christophe Claret, and is a reversible tourbillon with minute repeater that strikes on cathedral gongs, and moonphase indicator with date.

FACING PAGE

The Avenue C Jumping Hours watch houses a tonneau-shaped manually wound movement and features the jumping hour in a trapeze-shaped aperture at 12:00.

HARRY WINSTON
HARRY WINSTON

Only 25 watches are being created with a blue/silver dial and 25 with a ruthenium/silver dial. The jumping hour appears alone in a trapeze-shaped aperture at 12:00. Off-center dials for the minutes and seconds overlap in a daring display of asymmetry.

For women, Harry Winston releases the gorgeous Avenue C chronograph. The curved rectangular watch houses an automatic chronograph movement and is offered in 18-karat white gold. The case is set spectacularly with 172 diamonds on the bezel, crown and case sides totaling 5.17 carats. The watch features a white mother of pearl dial and a white hand-stitched crocodile strap. Also stunning in white and diamonds is the Lady Premier Chronograph, a round watch with a white rubber and gold, diamond-studded strap. In fact, the water resistant watch is set with 211 diamonds, totaling 5.18 carats.

THIS PAGE

Ronald Winston's personal project, the Project Z1, is a high-tech automatic chronograph with three off-center retrograde indications. The Project Z1 is made from an alloy named Zalium that has never been used before in watchmaking. Only 100 pieces of the Project Z1 are being created.

FACING PAGE

TOP

The Avenue C chronograph houses an automatic movement and is offered in 18-karat white gold. The case is set with 172 diamonds totaling 5.17 carats.

BOTTOM

The Lady Premier Chronograph is created in 18-karat white gold with a gold and rubber strap that is bedecked with diamonds. The watch is set with 211 diamonds, weighing 5.18 carats.

## CHRONOLOGY

**1920** At 28, Harry Winston founds his first jewelry business: The Premier Diamond Company, at 535 Fifth Avenue in New York City.

**1932** Winston incorporates the Premier Diamond Co. into Harry Winston, Inc.

**1947** For the first time, Harry Winston lends jewelry to be worn on Oscar night in Hollywood.

**1949** Harry Winston purchases the collection of jewels from the estate of Evalyn Walsh McLean, which includes the Hope Diamond and the Star of the East diamond.

**1955** A Harry Winston Salon opens in Geneva, followed two years later by one in Paris.

**1958** Harry Winston donates the Hope Diamond to the Smithsonian Institution as a gift to the American people.

**1966** Winston acquires a 241-carat uncut diamond, from which he produces a 61.42-carat pear-shaped jewel that will come to be known as the Taylor-Burton Diamond.

**1978** Winston dies in New York, and his son Ronald takes control of the firm.

**1986** Harry Winston opens a Salon in Beverly Hills, followed two years later by one in Tokyo.

**1989** Ronald Winston establishes Harry Winston's first series of watches, The Ultimate Timepieces.

**1990** The Ultimate Timepiece collection presents the Biretrograde Perpetual Calendar.

**1997** The Harry Winston Gallery opens at the Smithsonian Institution in Washington DC.

**1998** Harry Winston unveils the world's first platinum diving watch, the Ocean Chronograph.

**2001** Harry Winston embarks on a creative mission, Opus One, working with master watchmaker François-Paul Journe to develop 18 unique complicated timepieces.

**2002** Harry Winston and Antoine Preziuso collaborate on the Opus Two tourbillon.

**2003** Harry Winston presents the Opus Three, developed in collaboration with Vianney Halter.

**2004** Harry Winston and Christophe Claret collaborate on Opus Four. Harry Winston also launches a new collection with the Project Z1.

## OPUS 4

**Movement:** mechanical manual-winding; realized by Christophe Claret, with tourbillon device; repeater with Westminster chime; 18,000 vph; autonomy 53 hours; consists of 423 elements.
**Functions:** hour, minute, minute repeater; date; moonphase.
**Case:** platinum three-piece case (Ø 44mm); brushed and polished finish; reversible, double face; jointed lugs and fastened to a rotational system inside the 3 arcs of the case; bezel fastened by 8 screws; flat sapphire crystal, antireflective on both sides; white-gold crown; 2 rectangular pusher correctors; repeater slide on the left side; water resistant to 3atm.
**Dial 1:** made of a white-gold ring with engraved Arabic numerals and minute track; blued-steel bâton hands.
**Dial 2:** blue enameled with white-gold hour ring; engraved Arabic numerals; minute track; white-gold hands; moonphase with hand-engraved white-gold disc at 12; center date with sickle-shaped hand.
**Strap:** hand-stitched crocodile leather; platinum clasp.
**Note:** limited edition of 18 pieces.
**Also available:** in platinum and diamonds (unique piece).

## OPUS 4

The 44mm case of the Opus 4 is unusually impressive (compared to Harry Winston's other models) in order to allow for optimal resonance of the Cathedral's chime, and it boasts considerable water-resistance (guaranteed up to 3atm) for a minute-repeater watch. A rotational system allows turning the case 180° by means of the mobile lugs fastened inside 3 arcs as a symbol of Harry Winston: by pulling them outwards, the lugs are released and the case displays the rear side with a new face. On both dials the function of the watch is displayed thanks to a manual-winding mechanism (developed by Christophe Claret), which reverses the hands' direction. The hour, quarter and minute repeater is obtained by means of a Westminster bell rotating twice around the movement so as to obtain a deep resonance. Gongs are realized in hardened Swedish steel of the "Sandwik type," a flexible and resistant material assuring an ideal sound transmission.

## PROJECT Z1 — REF. 400/MCRA 44ZC.A

**Movement:** mechanical automatic-winding FP1185 caliber base + HW2831A module; toothed compensating wheel.
**Functions:** hour, minute; chronograph with 3 counters.
**Case:** zalium (an alloy derived from zirconium) three-piece case (Ø 44mm, thickness: 12.45mm); brushed finish; jointed lugs; flat sapphire crystal, antireflective on both sides; screw-down crown with case protection; integral pusher; back fastened by screws, displaying the movement through an antireflective sapphire crystal; water resistant to 10atm.

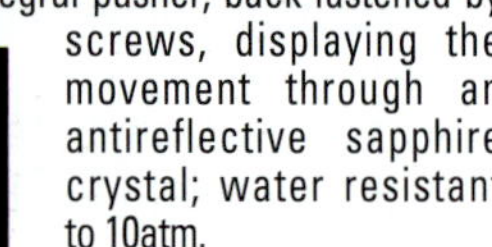

**Dial:** anthracite, brushed; subdial decorated with circular beads, grained sectors; luminescent rhodium-plated sword-type hands with Super-LumiNova.
**Indications:** off-center hour and minute at 12 with luminescent Arabic numerals with Super-LumiNova; minute counter with retrograde hand at 4; run indicator and second counter with retrograde hand; minute track with divisions for 1/6 second and 5-minute graduation at 6; hour counter with retrograde hand at 8.
**Strap:** rubber; brushed zalium clasp.
**Note:** limited edition of 100 numbered pieces.

## EXCENTER CHRONO — REF. 200/MCRA39RL

**Movement:** Frédéric Piguet 1185 self-winding column wheel chronograph with module HW2831 with compensating wheel.
**Functions:** off-centered hour and minute at 12; chronograph with triple retrograde indications; chronograph seconds at 6; 30-minute counter at 4; 12-hour counter at 8.
**Case:** Ø 39mm; rose or white gold (or diamond-set white gold); double-sided antireflective sapphire crystal; water resistant to 3atm.
**Dial:** anthracite; silvered opaline; or white mother-of-pearl with diamonds.
**Strap:** hand-stitched alligator with 18K gold folding clasp; or 18K gold and rubber.

## EXCENTER — REF. 200/MASR37WL.W

**Movement:** GP3106 automatic movement with HW2811 module.
**Functions:** hour, minute, bidirectional seconds.
**Case:** 18K white-gold round case (Ø 37mm); water resistant to 3atm.
**Dial:** silvered white dial with anthracite scales and off-center second.
**Strap:** crocodile strap with 18K white-gold folding clasp.
**Also available:** versions available with various types of settings and bracelets.
**Note:** a world's first.

## EXCENTER TIMEZONE — REF. 200/MMTZ39WL.A

**Movement:** mechanical Jaquet 7060 movement with HW2821 module.
**Functions:** hour, minute; retrograde time zone indicator; day and night indicator; power-reserve indicator; date.
**Case:** 18K white-gold case (Ø 39mm); water resistant to 3atm
**Strap:** crocodile strap with 18K white-gold folding clasp.
**Dial:** anthracite dial.
**Also available:** versions available with various types of settings and bracelets.

## BIRETROGRADE — REF. 200/MABI37RL.W

**Movement:** GP3106 automatic movement with HW300 module.
**Functions:** hour, minute, retrograde second; retrograde day of the week.
**Case:** 18K pink-gold case (Ø 37mm); water resistant to 3atm.
**Dial:** silvered white dial.
**Strap:** crocodile strap with 18K pink-gold folding clasp.
**Also available:** versions available in 18K white gold with various types of settings and bracelets.

## SEMIRAMIS

**Movement:** quartz.
**Functions:** hour, minute.
**Case:** square, platinum 950PT; double-sided antireflective sapphire crystal; bezel set with 24 baguette-cut diamonds; case sides set with 16 round-cut diamonds; crown set with 1 round-cut diamond; water resistant to 3atm.
**Dial:** pavé set.
**Strap:** satin with folding buckle; set with 4 baguette-cut diamonds. Total carat weight: 7.35 carats.

## LADY PREMIER CHRONOGRAPH REF. 200/UCQ32WW1.MD/D3.1/D2.1

**Movement:** electromechanical FP1270 caliber.
**Functions:** hour, minute, small second; chronograph with 3 counters.
**Case:** 18K white-gold three-piece case (Ø 32mm, thickness: 10mm); 35 set brilliants on bezel and lugs (2.17 carats); flat sapphire crystal, antireflective on both sides; white-gold crown and pusher; back fastened by 8 screws, displaying the movement through a sapphire crystal; water resistant to 3atm.
**Dial:** white mother of pearl; subdials with 86 set brilliants (0.19 carats); applied white-gold crowns; printed Arabic numerals; white-gold bâton hands.
**Indications:** hour at 3; small seconds at 6; minute counter at 9; center second counter; minute track.
**Strap:** rubber and white gold with 90 set brilliants (2.82 carats); recessed double fold-over white-gold clasp.

## PREMIER CHRONOGRAPH REF. 200/UCQ32WL.MD/04

**Movement:** meca-quartz chronograph.
**Functions:** chronograph functions; hour, minute and seconds.
**Case:** 18K white-gold case (Ø 32mm); set with white diamonds and pink baguette sapphires; water resistant to 3atm.
**Dial:** mother-of-pearl dial set with white diamonds on chronograph counters.
**Carats:** 1.66 carats of white diamonds and 1.55 carats of pink baguette sapphires.
**Strap:** crocodile strap with 18K white-gold folding clasp.
**Also available:** versions available with blue and yellow baguette sapphires.

## AVENUE C JUMPING HOURS REF. 330/UMJP

**Movement:** mechanical manual-winding HW315 caliber, in tonneau shape; with blued screws; decorated with a Côtes de Genève pattern.
**Functions:** hour, minute, small second.
**Case:** platinum two-piece case, rectangular, ergonomically curved (size: 35.7x26mm, thickness: 11mm); domed, antireflective sapphire crystal; white-gold crown; back fastened by 4 screws, displaying the movement through an antireflective sapphire crystal; water resistant to 3atm.
**Dial:** blue; subdials decorated with circular beads with silvered crowns; brushed outer ring; printed minute track with 5-minute graduation; black enameled bâton hands.
**Indications:** off-center jumping hour and minute at 12; small seconds at 6.
**Strap:** hand-stitched crocodile leather; white-gold clasp.
**Note:** limited edition of 25 pieces.
**Also available:** with ruthenium/silvered dial; 25 pieces.

## AVENUE BLACK RHODIUM

**Movement:** quartz.
**Functions:** center hour and minute.
**Case:** rectangular, 18K white-gold case; double-sided antireflective sapphire crystal; black rhodium plated; set with 25 white diamonds (0.33 carats; Quality: IF to VVS; Color: D, E, F) and 49 pink, purple or blue sapphires (04.73 carats); water resistant to 3atm.
**Dial:** galvanic black; 2 applied, rhodium-plated and polished hour markers.
**Strap:** black satin; 18K white-gold folding clasp.

## AVENUE C MIDSIZE REF. 330/UMWL.MD/D31

**Movement:** mechanical manual-winding HW315 caliber, in tonneau shape; blued screws; decorated with a Côtes de Genève pattern.
**Functions:** hour, minute, small second.
**Case:** white-gold two-piece case, rectangular, ergonomically curved (size: 35.7x26mm, thickness: 11mm); entirely brilliant pavé; domed antireflective sapphire crystal; white-gold crown; back fastened by 4 screws, displaying the movement through an antireflective sapphire crystal; water resistant to 3atm.
**Dial:** white mother of pearl; subdial decorated with circular beads, crowns with set brilliants; applied white-gold bâton markers; printed minute track; white-gold bâton hands.
**Indications:** off-center hour and minute at 12; small seconds at 6.
**Strap:** hand-stitched crocodile leather; white-gold clasp with set brilliants.

## AVENUE C CHRONOGRAPH REF.330/MCAWL.M/D3.1

**Movement:** quartz chronograph.
**Functions:** chronograph functions; hour, minute and seconds.
**Case:** 18K white-gold rectangular case set with white diamonds on bezel and sides of case; water resistant to 3atm.
**Strap:** crocodile strap with 18K white-gold folding clasp.
**Dial:** mother of pearl.
**Carats:** 5.65 carats of white diamonds.
**Also available:** versions available in 18K pink gold with various types of settings.

## LADY AVENUE REF. 310/LQRL.M/A04

**Movement:** quartz.
**Functions:** hour, minute and small second.
**Case:** 18K pink-gold rectangular case set with white diamonds and pink diamonds; water resistant to 3atm.
**Dial:** mother of pearl.
**Strap:** satin strap with 18K pink-gold folding clasp.
**Carats:** 1.55 carats of white diamonds and 0.30 carats of pink diamonds.
**Also available:** versions available in 18K white or yellow gold with various types of settings and bracelets.

## AVENUE C REF. 330/LQWW31.M/D3.1/D2.1

**Movement:** quartz.
**Functions:** hour and minute.
**Case:** 18K white-gold rectangular case set with white diamonds; water resistant to 3atm.
**Bracelet:** 18K white-gold captive bracelet set with white diamonds.
**Dial:** mother of pearl.
**Carats:** 4.45 carats of white diamonds.
**Also available:** versions available in 18K yellow gold with various types of settings and bracelets.

# HERMÈS

For approximately 85 years, Hermès has been creating leather of the finest quality—first for saddlebags, and eventually for watchstraps to accessorize its own fine timepieces. Indeed, this legendary company offers watches that perfectly express the spirit of Hermès.

Located in the traditional Swiss watchmaking center, Hermès is led by a unique Parisian creativity that gives rise to many exciting models each year. On the fashion-forward side, the brand unveils the Barénia collection, which fully represents the spirit of its saddler roots. Its name is derived from the strap—which is crafted of barénia calfskin. A very strong yet supple leather, the strap is nourished with oil and is soft to the touch. The Barénia watch is a seamless length of this rich leather that wraps around the rectangular steel case, folds back over itself and closes with a snap onto the saddle tack bearing the Hermès Paris seal.

On the sporty side, the company expands its very successful Nomade line, which was first introduced in 2001. Like other Nomades, the newest was designed by Philippe Mouquet and is distinctive for its numerals and H-shaped lugs. However, this Nomade houses a self-winding mechanical movement and is water resistant to 50 meters. It is further accentuated with shadowed Arabic numerals for an avant-garde design. The Nomade automatic features a date window at 3:00 and is housed in a brushed steel case.

Demonstrating its classically elegant profile, Hermès also unveils the new Arceau watch. First designed by

THIS PAGE

ABOVE
The Barénia is crafted in steel and accessorized with either a black or natural-colored barénia-calfskin strap.

LEFT
The Barénia watchstrap folds back over itself and closes with a saddle tack. The watch was designed by Frederick Vidal.

FACING PAGE

ABOVE
Water resistant to 50 meters, the Nomade automatic offers hours, minutes, seconds and date readout.

CENTER
The Arceau offers timeless style in a 41mm steel case.

Henri d'Origny in 1978, Arceau timepieces are recognized by their horse-shoe-shaped upper lugs and sloped numerals. The newest version includes these signature features, but now houses an automatic movement with date at 6:00. It is also built in a larger, 41mm steel case. Water resistant to 50 meters, the mechanical Arceau is offered with a choice of superior leathers: natural or black barénia calfskin, an Hermès-red Epsom calfskin, or a Havana alligator strap.

## CHRONOLOGY

**1837** Thierry Hermès opens his saddle and harness workshop in Paris.

**1867** Hermès wins the First Class Medal at the World's Fair.

**1878** Charles-Emile Hermès succeeds his late father at the helm of the family business.

**1892** An ancestor to the famed Kelly bag is introduced. The Haut à Courroies is a deep strap-bag.

**1920s** Emile-Maurice Hermès expands the product line to include leather accessories: belts, gloves; jewelry; sports and automobile accessories; and timepieces.

**1928** Hermès offers its first wristwatch.

**1937** The first Hermès silk scarf is fashioned from the silk of a horse jockey's blouse.

**1940s** The brand's signature orange box, "bolduc" ribbon and legendary Horse and Carriage logo are adopted.

**1975** The Kelly watch is launched.

**1978** Under the reorganization of Jean-Louis Dumas-Hermès, the brand instates its own watch manufacturing plant, La Montre Hermès S.A.

**1980s** The Clipper, Croisière, Rallye and Sellier watch models are introduced.

**1990s** The Cape Cod, Belt, Médor, Harnais, H-Our and Espace lines are launched.

**1999** Hermès inaugurates its own state-of-the-art workshops in Bienne.

**2001** Hermès unveils Nomade, the brand's first autoquartz watch collection.

**2002** Hermès reinvents some of its most famed archival pieces such as the H-Our and the Kelly, giving them updated twists in design.

**2003** Hermès celebrates the 25th anniversary of its La Montre Hermès workshops in Biel, and the 75th anniversary of its watchmaking tradition. In honor of these milestones, the brand unveils its first mechanical watch, the Dressage.

**2004** Hermès continues in its mechanical mode—offering automatic movements in the heart of several of its most successful collections.

## LADIES' H-OUR — REF. HH1.230.271/CRV

**Movement:** quartz ETA 5 1/2 901.001.
**Functions:** hour, minute.
**Case:** Ø 21mm, 6.2mm thick; steel with diamonds; sapphire crystal; water resistant to 3atm
*Also available: steel without diamonds; 750 yellow or white gold with or without diamonds.*

**Dial:** silver.
*Also available: blue jeans, black, orange, copper, white, gilt, mother of pearl with or without diamonds, mauve, pale blue, pale orange, pale green.*
**Strap:** bright red crocodile leather.
*Also available: on Hermès-leather strap (standard: gulliver, nepal calf, epsom calf, doblis suede calf, crocodile; double tour: gulliver, barenia calf, epsom calf and liege calf); steel with or without diamonds; 750 yellow or white gold with or without diamonds.*
**Also available:** mini, maxi, medium and men's sizes.

## LADIES' CAPE COD — REF. CC1.210.220/VBA1

**Movement:** quartz ETA 5 1/2 976.001.
**Functions:** hour, minute.
**Case:** Ø 23mm, 6.45mm thick; steel; sapphire crystal; water resistant to 3atm.
*Also available: 750 yellow gold (ladies' model: 750 yellow gold with diamonds or white gold with or without diamonds or white gold set with diamonds and rubies, blue sapphires or emeralds).*

**Dial:** silver, painted Arabic numerals.
*Also available: black, white mother of pearl for gold version only.*
**Strap:** double tour natural barenia calf.
*Also available: on Hermès-leather strap (standard: epsom calf, ostrich, crocodile; double tour: gulliver, barenia calf, bridle leather, epsom calf, chamonix); steel; 750 yellow gold (for ladies: 750 yellow gold with diamonds, white gold with or without diamonds).*
**Also available:** mini and men's sizes; with a second time zone.

## LADIES' TANDEM — REF. TA1.231.280/3800

**Movement:** quartz ETA 5 1/2 976.001.
**Functions:** hour, minute.
**Case:** 24.5x18.8mm, 6.3mm thick; steel set with diamonds; beveled sapphire crystal; water resistant to 5atm.
*Also available: in steel, steel and gold, 750 yellow or white gold with or without diamonds; for ladies only: white gold with diamonds baguette and white gold set with diamonds and rubies, blue sapphires or emeralds.*

**Dial:** silver.
*Also available: blue or white mother of pearl, black, copper, thalassa blue*
**Bracelet:** steel.
*Also available: on Hermès-leather strap (standard: fjord, barenia calf, epsom calf, crocodile; double tour: gulliver, barenia calf, liege calf); for ladies: 750 yellow gold or white gold.*
**Also available:** men's and maxi sizes.

## LADIES' KELLY — REF. KE1.201.170/UGO

**Movement:** quartz ETA 5 1/2 901.001.
**Functions:** hour, minute.
**Case:** Ø 20mm, 8.48mm thick; gold plated; mineral crystal; non-water resistant. *Also available: steel.*
**Dial:** white.
*Also available: silver, red, black, red H, orange, blue jeans, gilt, green, blue.*

**Strap:** gold epsom calf.
*Also available: on Hermès-leather strap (standard: ostrich, fjord, gulliver, epsom calf, lizard; double tour: gulliver, epsom calf, barenia calf).*
**Also available:** Kelly Clochette.

## MEN'S MECHANICAL DRESSAGE REF. DR1.770.213/MHA

**Movement:** automatic, mechanical Hermès 11 1/2 lignes movement; Vaucher P 1928; rhodium plated; 32 jewels; 28,800 vph for (or 4Hz frequency); 55-hour power reserve; hand-chamfered bars, special Hermès décor; 22K-gold oscillating weight, decorated with Hermès symbol; made by craftsmen in the Vaucher manufacturer in Fleurier, Switzerland.
**Functions:** hour, minute, center seconds; date at 3.
**Case:** Ø 40mm, 9.72mm thick; 750 rose gold; antireflective sapphire crystal; screw-on antireflective sapphire-crystal caseback; water resistant to 3atm.
*Also available: 750 yellow or white gold.*
**Dial:** white mother of pearl.
*Also available: blue mother of pearl, silver.*
**Strap:** Havana alligator leather.
*Also available: on Hermès-leather strap (black alligator, etruscan crocodile and natural barenia calf).*
**Also available:** Dressage complication with moonphase module and simple retrograde calendar.

## MEN'S CHRONOGRAPH DIVERS CLIPPER REF. CL2.915.331/3770

**Movement:** quartz men's chronograph ETA 13 1/4 251.262.
**Functions:** hour, minute, small seconds; date; chronograph with 3 counters.
**Case:** Ø 38.5mm, 11.95mm thick; steel; unidirectional rotating bezel in steel and rubber; antireflective sapphire crystal; screw-on caseback; water resistant to 20atm and 10atm for ladies' model.
*Also available: steel, steel and gold, steel and colored rubber bezel (orange, blue, red H).*
**Dial:** black with green Super-LumiNova.
*Also available: black, orange, blue and red H with white Super-LumiNova.*
**Strap:** rubber with steel core.
*Also available: on Hermès shark-leather strap, steel, steel and gold, or colored rubber (orange, blue, red H) with steel core.*
**Also available:** ladies' size.

## MEN'S CHRONOGRAPH CAPE COD REF. CC1.910.130/VBA

**Movement:** quartz ETA 10 1/2 251.471.
**Functions:** hour, minute, second; date; chronograph with 3 counters.
**Case:** 31.5x31mm, 10mm thick; steel; sapphire crystal; water resistant to 3atm.
**Dial:** white.
*Also available: black.*
**Strap:** natural barenia calf leather.
*Also available: on Hermès-leather strap (bridle leather, chamonix, epsom calf, alligator).*

## MEN'S TANDEM REF. TA1.710.280/VBA

**Movement:** quartz ETA 7 3/4 956.032.
**Functions:** hour, minute.
**Case:** 31.6x25.6mm, 7.38mm thick; steel; beveled sapphire crystal; water resistant to 5atm.
*Also available: steel with diamonds; 750 yellow or white gold with or without diamonds.*
**Dial:** silver.
*Also available: black, copper, blue thalassa, mother of pearl for 750 yellow and white gold only.*
**Strap:** natural barenia calf leather.
*Also available: on Hermès-leather strap (fjord, barenia calf, crocodile, epsom calf); steel; for ladies: 750 yellow or white gold.*
**Also available:** ladies' and maxi sizes.

# HUBLOT

Exactly 25 year ago, Hublot stunned the industry when it entered the watch world with its 18-karat gold luxury watch—complete with rubber strap. The first to transform rubber into luxury, Hublot's trend has taken root and the brand regularly incorporates new and precious materials with rubber for its timepieces.

## Hublot: A Philosophy Of Life

Hublot watches have been a striking presence on elite wrists since the company's foundation in 1980. With its trademark black rubber strap and innovative double-hinged clasp, the Hublot brand makes a distinct visual statement while producing timepieces powered by the finest Swiss movements and accessible sporting complications. In such pieces, high regard has been achieved and maintained with novel designs, within the unique Hublot mono-product concept. When Carlo Crocco presented the Hublot watch at the Basel Fair in 1980, the watch industry was quickly won over and it quickly became the sensation of the year.

ABOVE

Hublot's latest creation, the Regulateur presents an additional technical mechanism fitted with a regulator and is adorned with a black guilloché dial, hour subdial at 12, small second subdial at 6 and center minutes. The Regulateur is water resistant to 50 meters and available in steel or 18-karat pink, white or yellow gold.

LEFT

***The FUSION of Hublot***

In 2004, Carlo Crocco *(above)*, busy with his position as founder and president of MDM Foundation (a charity benefiting underprivileged children), was looking for the right man to take the helm of Hublot. In May 2004, Jean-Claude Biver took up his post as CEO with his head full of amazing plans for the company.

FACING PAGE

The new steel Hublot 1910 has masculine attitude with an innovative, handmade circular grained Perlé dial. The exclusive piece features a tailored look reminiscent of vintage sports cars' dashboards.

HUBLOT
MDM
GENEVE

THIS PAGE

The Chrono SuperB in 18-karat gold divulges an outstanding personality as a revelation of new elegance. Totally contemporary with its enlarged case, it combines noble materials and Italian design with Swiss watch-making technology. The heart of this timekeeper reveals a mechanical movement with automatic winding.

The exclusive rubber rings with UPTS© security device launched by Hublot guarantees an optimum water-resistance security.

**TOP**

This splendid 18-karat gold chronograph is set with an elegant combination of Top Wesselton white and cognac diamonds on the bezel. The heart of this timekeeper reveals precious watchmaking technology with a mechanical movement with automatic winding further enhanced with a flyback and a water resistance to 100 meters.

**BOTTOM**

This Elegant Duo divulges a bezel set with diamonds, as well as diamonds running on the elegant rounded sides of the Hublot case. The dials are burgundy or black with solar reflections and diamond indexes. Both are water resistant to 50 meters.

The prestigious Hublot High Jewellery collection demonstrates the innovative talent of the brand and its elegant distinction in the close circle of Swiss haute horology. It divulges a new challenge between the pure design of the traditional porthole and the renowned Hublot black strap in natural rubber combined with diamonds and precious stones that embellish the elegant tradition of Hublot watches.

**ABOVE**

An exquisite Chrono Lady with blue mother-of-pearl dial and diamonds.

**TOP LEFT AND BOTTOM RIGHT**

The Floreales creations are decorated with three flowers on the side of the case and are set with colored stones in lavender amethyst, mint tsavorite and narcissus yellow diamonds. Ultimately refined, the dials are realized with dial plates made of similar colored stones.

## Hublot: Color

Within the fusion, Hublot is introducing a great new aspect to its 2005 collections: color joins the Hublot black rubber straps. Metallic gray and bronze will be available on the ladies' Classic models. Also, the diamonds on the bezel are intertwined with 12 titanium screws to emphasize the new Hublot label. This new Hublot Color collection is adorned with color-coordinated mother-of-pearl dials enhanced with diamond indexes.

O V E

Among the numerous celebrity afficionados of Hublot watches: Céline Dion, Alicia Keys and Michael Douglas have been seen wearing their favorite Hublot pieces during the World Music Award 2004 in Las Vegas, USA.

## Hublot: A Success Story

Since 1980, the brand's vanilla-scented rubber strap and elegant porthole shape watches have captured the attention of Royal families, celebrities and watch connoisseurs world wide, making Hublot a classic of Swiss Prestige Watchmaking.

### CHRONOLOGY

**1980** Italian designer Carlo Crocco brings the Hublot rubber-strapped luxury sports watch line to the Basel Watch and Jewelry Fair.

**1981** The Hublot wristwatches are a hit when released to the public, and the watches are soon sported by the kings of Spain and Sweden, among others.

**1985** Hublot unveils its Plongeur Professional watch, water resistant to 300 meters.

**1987** Crocco unveils the first Hublot automatic watch with a Frédéric Piguet movement.

**1988** The Hublot Chronograph is unveiled.

**1990** The GMT, featuring Hublot's new water-resistance system, is introduced.

**1991** A platinum automatic chronograph with a 350-piece caliber 1185 Piguet movement is unveiled.

**1993** Hublot implements the Hublot Service program and begins offering customers substitution watches while theirs are undergoing maintenance.

**1995** The Hublot Classic watch houses an automatic movement.

**1996** The Colonial bracelet is presented, the first to accompany an Hublot watch. Production of custom-made cloisonné and champléve dials begins.

**1997** The Elegant Chronograph is unveiled with rounded lines and an 18-karat gold-and-steel case.

**1998** The first Hublot steel watch is set with diamonds.

**2000** Hublot celebrates its 20th anniversary and unveils the Grand Quantième watch.

**2001** A 200-pieced limited edition of the Grand Quantième is released in 18-karat pink gold. A fly-back Elegant Chronograph also makes its debut.

**2002** Inspired by the Elegant Chronograph, Hublot designs a smaller case for women and unveils the new Chrono Lady with colored mother-of-pearl dials and eight diamond markers.

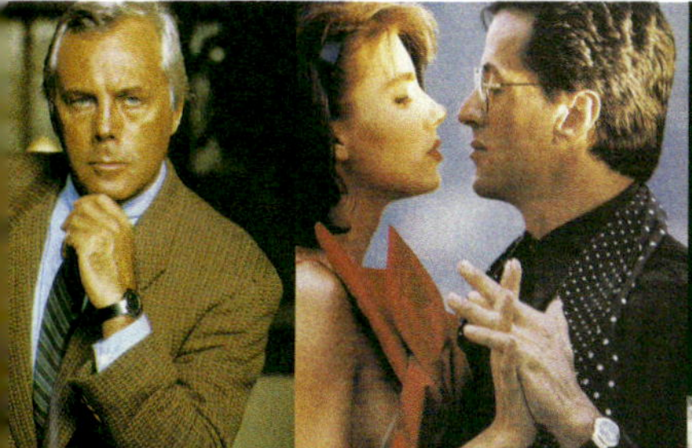

# INVICTA

Big, brash, brassy and bold, the Invicta Watch Group has become a major player in the crowded watch industry, and it's standing in the middle of it all throwing elbows.

Few companies have had the kind of impact on the watch industry that the Invicta Watch Group has. By being true to its Swiss flagship's original 1837 mission, Invicta helped turn the balance of power in the watch industry by changing the dynamic between who could and couldn't possess a true luxury timepiece. With each new offering, the brand forced buyers and makers alike to change the way they think about, market, and appreciate watches. In the process, the once little-known brand emerged as one of the most innovative and influential watch groups in the world.

At the beginning of 2004, the never-satisfied company was still altering itself as much as it was the watch world. It officially announced it was changing its name to Invicta Watch Group, and had added luxury brand S. Coifman and its line of ultra-complicated Swiss-made timepieces to the roster along with the Invicta and Activa brands. From there, the changes kept coming and were as measured and metamorphic as they were meteoric, much like the brand's ascent into public consciousness had been. Most notably was the increase of completely Swiss-made products for the Invicta nameplate. The group owns workshops around the world, but moved a larger percentage of its Invicta production to its facility in Switzerland. Several of the new pieces in the 2005 Collection, such as the incredible Sapphire Ghost and new Ocean Ghost and Speedway chronographs, proudly carry the Swiss Made designation.

Invicta also became the first watchmaker to use the Ronda Startech 5040.B and 5050.C caliber movements. The 5050.C is the world's first day, big date chronograph movement with three eyes and features automatic big date correction. One such model using a Startech is the Diamond Meteorite ACERO 3500. Available in both men's and ladies' versions, the ACERO employs the 13-jeweled 5040.B with automatic big date correction. Bestowed with 136 genuine white diamonds and a genuine stingray strap, the ACERO is another dazzler in the brand's flourishing Diamond Collection. But it's the genuine meteorite stone dial that is the focus of this masterpiece.

THIS PAGE

ABOVE

Created by popular demand, the Lady Lupah Diver is a fitting counterpart to the original, and much larger Lupah Diver. It features a genuine mother-of-pearl dial, and a genuine copperhead snakeskin strap.

LEFT

With its icy cool colors and fine hand-crafted construction, the Diamond Meteorite ACERO 3500 is another masterful offering from the Diamond Meteorite collection. A wintry green genuine stingray strap is the perfect complement to the wonderland shine of the genuine meteorite dial and diamonds.

FACING PAGE

The remarkable Sapphire Ghost owes its name to the genuine sapphire encasement and exhibition windows that surround the skeletonized Invicta 11283 caliber movement.

The stone is obtained from pieces of the Gibeon Meteorite, which was located in Great Namaqualand, Nambia, Africa. Its existence was first reported in 1838. It is estimated that the meteorite fell to earth during prehistoric times, and radiometric dating places the age of the Gibeon at four billion years. Invicta began using the stone for its dials in 2003, mainly on limited-edition pieces. True to Invicta form, the offerings were unveiled with lower-than-expected prices. While this consumer-first philosophy might be a boon for collectors, it can put suppliers of such luxury materials as the Gibeon ill at ease. But that is a risk the mavericks at Invicta have been willing to take. There are more than five Invicta models using the Gibeon stone, with more planned.

Sure to be included in that list are more meteorite versions of the Lupah. Since its inception, the patented Lupah has been Invicta's most successful and most recognized timepiece worldwide. So it was not surprising that it was also selected to be the watch group's first-ever COSC-certified chronometer. Produced in a limited edition, the Dragon Series Lupah is driven by a Valjoux 7750 caliber automatic movement and is layered with 23K Swiss rose-gold plating. At 48mm wide, it also features one of the largest genuine mother-of-pearl dials and genuine sapphire crystals ever produced. In true rebel fashion, the brand did something no other watchmaker had: It included the fully detailed COSC-testing sheet with the purchase of the piece, and engraved the COSC serial number on the movement and caseback to confirm its authenticity and the timepiece's hand assembly. It also included one of the most affordable prices ever offered for a Swiss-made chronometer.

But it's the Sapphire Ghost that will be the highlight of the 2005 collection. Part engineering marvel, part art exhibit, the Sapphire Ghost was in development for over two years at the Invicta workshop in Le Chaux de Fonds where it is completely built by hand. The unique multi-piece sapphire and steel case was developed to display the highly elaborate Invicta 11283 caliber movement. The surgical-grade stainless steel case is constructed from eight individual pieces to form a cage assembly for the genuine sapphire viewing windows.

**ABOVE LEFT**

The Lady Strap with Diamond Elements features one of the smallest Swiss movements ever made. Handset diamonds adorn the sunray satin dial, as well as the genuine leather strap and stainless steel buckle.

**ABOVE RIGHT**

The Lady Charm features a Swiss quartz movement in an hourglass case of solid surgical-grade stainless steel finished with a genuine stingray strap. But it's the unique Invicta charm that makes it a trendsetter.

ABOVE

A hip blend of function and style, the black ionic-plated Lupah Dragon Big Date features an exclusive Swiss-made Startech caliber 5040.B big date movement modified to include an auto correction function.

Each sapphire is cut specific to its respective window, and is curved and free of imperfections to assure a clear viewing experience. The genuine farm-raised large grain alligator custom cut strap was designed specifically for this piece and features a new yellow strap backing designed exclusively for Invicta. The backing will soon become a standard hallmark feature on all Invicta watches.

With its fine timepieces being sold on every continent and in over forty countries, and three well-positioned brands on the roster, the still independent and still rebellious Robin Hood of the watch world is determined as ever to turn the balance of power. The timepieces it creates will push the limits of Swiss perfection, and will always be guided by that same radical notion from 1837: Give customers more than they pay for.

## CHRONOLOGY

**1837** Latin for "invincible," Invicta is founded in La Chaux-de-Fonds, Switzerland, by Raphael Picard. Invicta handcrafts its first watches with the belief that fine Swiss timepieces could be offered at modest prices.

**1837-1970s** For more than a century, the assiduous company creates manual- and automatic-winding pieces of exceptional design and construction. Like many Swiss brands of its day, the brand nearly disappears during the quartz revolution of the early 1970s.

**1991** Descendants of the Invicta family reestablish the brand and hold firm to the company's founding principles. With rebellious zeal, they quickly determine that Invicta will be positioned to give a large segment of the watch-buying public unprecedented access to fine Swiss quality at prices well within their reach.

**1990s** Invicta unveils the successful Angel and Elite lines, which utilize high-quality materials like antireflective sapphire crystals, Swiss-made manual- and automatic-winding movements, and beautifully crafted packaging. Its Pro Diver series, with its jeweled automatic movements, high water resistance and rugged construction achieves a cult-like status among collectors. Indeed, with its collections, Invicta proves that it has successfully gambled with the concept of creating watches of comparable standards to more expensive watches, and the company generates tremendous intrigue, winning over enthusiasts and retailers and confounding higher-priced competitors.

**2000** The brand delves into the making of its own calibers, which have today evolved into Technica Swiss ébauche. New complications include skeletonized movements, and new processes include a unique Swiss gold-layering technique. This addition transforms Invicta into one of the watch world's most technically capable watchmakers. Invicta's non-conformist attitude also works its way into the design of the unisex Lupah Swiss Chronograph. With oversized case, rounded crystal, distinctive dials and colorful straps, this line creates a major sensation. Each watch is equipped with a Swiss ETA quartz movement housed in a polished and brushed, solid stainless steel case patented by the company.

**2002** Invicta is a member of an elite group of watch brands officially certified by ETA to continue using its movements. The Invicta Watch Group has evolved into one of the fastest growing watch companies and has helped spark a movement for bold Swiss timepieces at competitive prices. In accordance with its growth, it moves key production from Chiasso to a new facility in L'Abbeye, Switzerland.

**2004** Invicta officially becomes Invicta Watch Group and adds the S. Coifman brand to its stable. The company also unveils the Invicta brand's first COSC-certified chronometer.

## SAPPHIRE GHOST

**Movement:** mechanical automatic-winding Swiss ETA Valjoux base, modified to Invicta 11283 caliber; 25 jewels; skeletonized and finished with a rare PVD coating in furnace blue or metallic charcoal.
**Functions:** hour, minute, seconds.
**Case:** Ø 46mm; eight-piece case assembly; polished and brushed surgical-grade 316L solid stainless steel; 7 individual genuine sapphire crystals displaying movement from all sides; water resistant to 30 meters.
**Dial:** through genuine sapphire to exhibit the architecture of the finely skeletonized movement; steel sword-style hour and minute hands with Tritnite® luminescence on the tips; bâton sweep-seconds hand.
**Strap:** genuine farm-raised large-grain alligator leather, custom-cut strap with new yellow strap backing made exclusively for Invicta.

## SAPPHIRE GHOST

Part engineering marvel, part art exhibit, the Sapphire Ghost was in development for over two years at the Invicta workshop in La Chaux-de-Fonds, Switzerland where it is completely built by hand. The unique multi-piece sapphire and steel case was developed to display the highly elaborate Invicta caliber 11283, one of the most complicated movements in Invicta history. The surgical-grade steel case is constructed from eight individual pieces to form a cage assembly for the genuine sapphire viewing windows. Each sapphire is cut specific to the window it is destined for, and is curved and free of imperfections to assure clear viewing. The genuine farm-raised large-grain alligator leather, custom-cut strap was designed specifically for this piece and features a new yellow strap backing designed exclusively for Invicta. The backing will soon become a standard hallmark feature of all Invicta timepieces.

## LIMITED-EDITION SPEEDWAY COSC-CERTIFIED CHRONOMETER

**Movement:** mechanical automatic-winding Swiss ETA 2894-2 caliber; ball bearing; stop second device; date corrector; chronograph; 37 jewels; 28,800 vph; decorated; metallic blue finish; COSC-certified chronometer.
**Functions:** hour, minute, seconds; date; chronograph with 3 counters.
**Case:** Ø 42mm; polished and brushed surgical-grade 316L solid stainless steel; engraved tachymeter on the bezel; screw-down crown and pushers; engraved logo; custom screw-down exhibition back; genuine sapphire crystals front and back; water resistant to 200 meters, tested.
**Dial:** silver; checkered flag pattern; printed minute track on the flange; applied Tritnite® luminescent filled markers; bâton hour, minute and counter hands with Tritnite® luminescence.
**Indications:** small seconds at 3; date between 4 and 5; hours at 6; minutes at 9; sweep-seconds hand.
**Bracelet:** polished and brushed surgical-grade 316L solid stainless steel; emblazoned Invicta Speedway logo.

## LIMITED-EDITION SPEEDWAY COSC-CERTIFIED CHRONOMETER

Invicta collectors have been waiting years for an automatic version of the popular Speedway series. It is now available in the second COSC-certified chronometer from the Invicta workshop in La Chaux-de-Fonds, Switzerland. Handsomely rugged, the fit and finish of the new Speedway heralds the company's intense attention to detail. Through the custom exhibition back is a view of the beautifully decorated Swiss ETA 2894-2 movement that is finished with blue screws and a custom rotor treated with a metallic blue titanium-based alloy.

## LIMITED-EDITION DRAGON LUPAH CHRONOMETER

**Movement:** mechanical automatic-winding Valjoux 7750 caliber base modified to support the chronograph and off-center hours and minutes functions; ball-bearing rotor; stopping of seconds; 42-hour autonomy; 25 jewels; 28,800 vph; ETACHRON with regulator adjuster; date corrector; decorated; COSC-certified chronometer. **Functions:** hour, minute, seconds; date; chronograph with 3 counters. **Case:** Ø 48mm; surgical-grade 316L solid stainless steel patented Invicta case design; 23K Swiss rose-gold layered plating front and back; 316L solid stainless steel crown and pushers with rubber O-rings; rounded genuine sapphire crystal; screw-on exhibition caseback with sapphire crystal; water resistant to 100 meters.
**Dial:** genuine mother-of-pearl dial; guilloché pattern; applied Swiss rose gold-plated Arabic markers; Swiss rose gold-plated lozenge hour and minute hands with Tritnite® luminescence; Swiss rose-gold bâton sweep-seconds hand and Javeline counter hands.
**Indications:** 30-minute counter at 12; date at 4; 1/10th of a second at 6; subseconds at 9; sweep-seconds hand with stop feature.
**Strap:** genuine farm-raised large-grain alligator leather strap with quickset pin; push-button deployment clasp plated in Swiss rose gold.
**Also available:** limited edition.

## LIMITED-EDITION DRAGON LUPAH CHRONOMETER

This is the first chronometer ever produced by Invicta. True to form, the brand is doing something no other watchmaker has: it is including the fully detailed COSC-testing sheet with the purchase of the piece, as well as engraving the COSC's serial number on the movement and caseback to confirm its authenticity and the timepiece's hand assembly. This piece also features one of the largest genuine sapphire crystals and genuine mother-of-pearl dials ever produced.

## SPEEDWAY CHRONOGRAPH DAY AND DATE

**Movement:** Swiss-made Ronda Startech caliber 5050.C; world's first day and big date movement with 3 counters; automatic big date correction; 13 jewels. **Functions:** hour, minute, seconds; date and day; chronograph with 3 counters; automatic date correction. **Case:** Ø 44mm; polished and brushed surgical-grade 316L solid stainless steel; engraved tachymeter; 316L solid stainless steel triple screw-down security crown and pushers; antireflective mineral crystal; screw-on caseback; water resistant to 200 meters.
**Dial:** slate; enamel finish; guilloché pattern; printed Tachymeter on the flange; applied Swiss rose gold-plated Roman markers; Swiss rose gold-plated Javeline hour and minute hands with Tritnite® luminescence; Swiss rose-gold Javeline sweep-seconds hand and Dauphine counter hands. **Indications:** day at 12; subseconds at 3; big date and 1/10th of a second at 6; 30 minutes and 12 hours at 9; sweep-seconds hand with stop feature.
**Bracelet:** polished and brushed surgical-grade 316L solid stainless steel; deployment buckle.
**Also available:** in all stainless steel or stainless steel with Swiss rose-gold accents.

## LUPAH BIJOUX CHRONOGRAPH DAY AND DATE

**Movement:** Swiss-made Ronda Startech caliber 5050.C; world's first day and big date movement with 3 counters; automatic big date correction; 13 jewels. **Functions:** hour, minute, seconds; date and day; chronograph with 3 counters; automatic date correction. **Case:** Ø 44mm; polished and brushed surgical-grade 316L solid stainless steel patented Invicta design; Swiss yellow gold-plated bezel; 316L solid stainless steel crown and pushers with rubber O-rings; rounded mineral crystal; screw-on caseback; water resistant to 100 meters. **Dial:** genuine mother-of-pearl dial; applied Swiss yellow gold-plated Arabic markers; Swiss yellow gold-plated Dauphine hour and minute hands with Tritnite® lumine-scence; Swiss yellow-gold bâton sweep-seconds and counter hands.
**Indications:** day at 12; subseconds at 3; big date and 1/10th of a second at 6; 30 minutes and 12 hours at 9; sweep-seconds hand with stop feature.
**Bracelet:** polished and brushed surgical-grade 316L solid stainless steel; some with Swiss yellow-gold plating; individual hand-woven links; deployment buckle.
**Also available:** ladies' version.

## LIMITED-EDITION METEORITE & DIAMOND DRAGON LUPAH

**Movement:** Swiss-made Ronda Startech caliber 5040.B; automatic big date correction; 13 jewels. **Functions:** hour, minute, seconds; date; chronograph with 3 counters; automatic date correction. **Case:** Ø 48mm; polished and brushed surgical-grade 316L solid stainless steel patented Invicta case design; genuine white diamonds handset in 4-prong jeweler's settings in bezel; 316L solid stainless steel crown and pushers with rubber O-rings; rounded genuine sapphire crystal; screw-on caseback with Dragon design; water resistant to 100 meters. **Dial:** genuine Gibeon meteorite stone dial, approx. 4 billion years old; applied stainless steel markers; stainless steel Dauphine hour and minute hands with Tritnite® luminescence; stainless steel Javeline sweep-seconds hand in red with luminescent tip; stainless steel lozenge counter hands.

**Indications:** date at 12; subseconds at 3; 1/10th of a second and 12 hour at 6; 30 minute at 9; sweep-seconds hand with stop feature.

**Strap:** genuine farm-raised large-grain alligator leather with quickset pin; hand stained in Italy; no two are the same.

**Also available:** ladies' version.

## DIAMOND METEORITE ACERO 3500

**Movement:** Swiss-made Ronda Startech caliber 5040.B; automatic big date correction; 13 jewels.

**Functions:** hour, minute, seconds; date; chronograph with 3 counters; automatic date correction.

**Case:** Ø 45mm; polished and brushed surgical-grade 316L solid stainless steel; 136 genuine white diamonds handset in 4-prong jeweler's settings in bezel; 316L solid stainless steel crown and pushers; mineral crystal; screw-on caseback; water resistant to 100 meters.

**Dial:** genuine Gibeon meteorite stone dial, approx. 4 billion years old; applied stainless steel Arabic markers; stainless steel Dauphine hour and minute hands with Tritnite® luminescence; stainless steel bâton sweep-seconds hand; stainless steel Dauphine counter hands.

**Indications:** date at 12; subseconds at 3; 1/10th of a second and 12 hour at 6; 30 minute at 9; sweep-seconds hand with stop feature.

**Strap:** genuine stingray.

**Also available:** ladies' version.

## LIMITED-EDITION METEORITE DRAGON LUPAH MOP

**Movement:** Swiss-made Ronda Startech caliber 5040.B; automatic big date correction; 13 jewels. **Functions:** hour, minute, seconds; date; chronograph with 3 counters; automatic date correction. **Case:** Ø 48mm; polished and brushed surgical-grade 316L solid stainless steel patented Invicta case design; 316L solid stainless steel crown and pushers with rubber O-rings; rounded mineral crystal; screw-on caseback with Dragon design; water resistant to 100 meters.

**Dial:** genuine Gibeon meteorite stone center dial, approx. 4 billion years old; genuine mother-of-pearl dial border; applied stainless steel markers; stainless steel Dauphine hour and minute hands with Tritnite® luminescence; stainless steel Javeline sweep-seconds hand in red with luminescent tip; stainless steel lozenge counter hands.

**Indications:** date at 12; subseconds at 3; 1/10th of a second and 12 hour at 6; 30 minute at 9; sweep-seconds hand with stop feature.

**Strap:** genuine farm-raised large-grain alligator leather with quickset pin.

**Also available:** in Swiss rose gold.

## LIMITED-EDITION METEORITE AUTOMATIC PRO DIVER

**Movement:** Swiss ETA; 25 jewels; shock resistant.

**Functions:** hour, minute, seconds; date.

**Case:** Ø 43mm; surgical-grade 316L solid stainless steel; 23K Swiss rose gold-layered plating front and back; unidirectional rotating bezel with engraved diver's scale; triple screw-down crown; genuine sapphire crystal with magnifier; screw-on exhibition caseback with genuine sapphire crystal; water resistant to 200 meters.

**Dial:** genuine Gibeon meteorite stone center dial, approx. 4 billion years old; printed minute track; Swiss rose gold-plated applied markers, sports hands and sweep-seconds hand with Tritnite® luminescence.

**Indications:** date window at 3; sweep-seconds hand.

**Bracelet:** surgical-grade 316L solid stainless steel; 23K Swiss rose gold-layered plating front and back; diver buckle with safety clasp.

**Also available:** limited edition.

## DUAL ZONE TRANSATLANTIC

**Movement:** dual Swiss-made movements.
**Functions:** hour, minute.
**Case:** Ø 29mm inner case; Ø 39mm outer case; surgical-grade 316L solid stainless steel; patented Invicta easy touch dual-face case system; hand-detailed case cradle and caseback; dual crowns; mineral crystal; screw-down construction; water resistant to 30 meters.
**Dial:** genuine mother-of-pearl on one side, enamel-finished guilloché on the other; applied Arabic markers and inner minute ring; Dauphine hour and minute hands with Tritnite® luminescence.
**Indications:** 5-minute progressions.
**Strap:** genuine leather tapered strap with buckle lug.
**Also available:** in a variety of finishes and color combinations.

## DUAL ZONE TRANSATLANTIC

The TransAtlantic is a highlight of the 2005 Invicta Collection. The twin Swiss-made movements are housed in a patented easy touch dual-face case system that effortlessly flips to reveal the genuine mother-of-pearl and intricately detailed guilloché dials. The hand detailing on the solid surgical-grade stainless steel inner case cradle is also something to admire the watch switches from zone to zone. It's fast becoming a must-have piece for discerning business travelers.

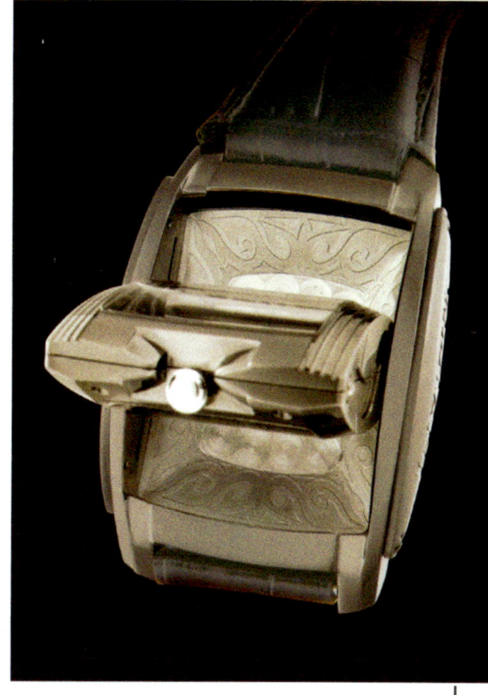

## 1959 RUSSIAN DIVER

**Movement:** mechanical automatic Swiss UNITAS caliber 6498; 55-hour autonomy; 17 jewels; 21,600 vph; INCABLOC shock resistance; skeletonized, decorated and finished with blue alloys.
**Functions:** hour, minute.
**Case:** Ø 53mm (58mm with crown); surgical-grade 316L solid stainless steel; reed pattern; triple screw-down crown with screw on diver's cap with chain; mineral crystal nearly 6mm thick; screw-on exhibition caseback with mineral crystal; water resistant to 100 meters.
**Dial:** military black; markers, Arabic numerals and bâton hands filled with Tritnite® luminescence; Invicta name written in Russian.
**Indications:** hour, minute.
**Strap:** thick genuine leather; tapers; single-tang stainless steel buckle.

## 1959 RUSSIAN DIVER

In 1959, the USSR's Council of Labor and Defense contracted Invicta Switzerland to develop a unique Swiss-made watch exclusively for the elite divers of the naval fleet. Only 100 pieces were made, and never marketed to the public. Invicta was one of the last Swiss makers to be commissioned by the USSR. Now, 45 years later, Invicta proudly introduces a replica piece based on the original Russian Diver. Everything about this piece is large, from the 53mm diameter and oversized numerals to the 6mm-thick mineral crystal.

## OCEAN GHOST CHRONOGRAPH

**Movement:** Swiss-made Ronda Startech caliber 5050.C; world's first day and big date movement with 3 counters; automatic big date correction; 13 jewels.
**Functions:** hour, minute, seconds; day, date; chronograph with 3 counters; automatic date correction. **Case:** Ø 47mm; polished and brushed surgical-grade 316L solid stainless steel; 23K Swiss yellow gold-plated accents; unidirectional rotating bezel with engraved diver's scale; triple screw-down security crown and pushers; antireflective mineral crystal; screw-on caseback; water resistant to 200 meters.
**Dial:** white; enamel finish with sunray pattern; genuine mother-of-pearl subdials; printed Tachymeter on the flange; applied Swiss yellow gold-plated markers; Swiss yellow gold-plated Dauphine hour and minute hands with Tritnite® luminescence; Swiss yellow-gold bâton sweep-seconds hand; Swiss yellow-gold Dauphine counter hands.
**Indications:** day at 12; subseconds at 3; big date and 1/10th of a second at 6; 30 minutes and 12 hours at 9; sweep-seconds hand with stop feature.
**Bracelet:** polished and brushed surgical-grade 316L solid stainless steel; 23K Swiss yellow gold-plated center links; diver buckle with safety clasp.

## AUTOMATIC PRO DIVER DAY AND DATE MOP

**Movement:** mechanical automatic-winding Japanese movement; 21 jewels; shock resistant.
**Functions:** hour, minute, seconds; day, date.
**Case:** Ø 43mm; polished and brushed surgical-grade 316L solid stainless steel; unidirectional rotating bezel with diver's scale; triple screw-down crown; mineral crystal with magnifier; screw-on exhibition caseback with mineral crystal; water resistant to 200 meters.

**Dial:** genuine mother-of-pearl dial; stainless steel outer ring; applied markers and carbon fiber Javeline hands with Tritnite® luminescence.
**Indications:** day and date windows at 3; sweep-seconds hand.
**Bracelet:** polished and brushed surgical-grade 316L solid stainless steel; diver buckle with safety clasp.
**Also available:** in a variety of color combinations.

## TIMES SQUARE CHRONOGRAPH

**Movement:** chronograph; modified for unique counter, crown and pusher positions.
**Functions:** hour, minute, seconds; chronograph with 3 counters.
**Case:** Ø 36mm; surgical-grade 316L solid stainless steel; 23K Swiss rose gold-layered plating front and back; off-set crown and pushers; mineral crystal curved at 6; screw-on caseback; water resistant to 100 meters.

**Dial:** enamel finished; guilloché and sunray patterns; applied Swiss rose gold-plated markers; Swiss rose gold-plated Dauphine hour and minute hands with Tritnite® luminescence; Swiss rose-gold bâton sweep-seconds hand and counter hands.
**Indications:** subseconds at 4; 12 hour at 8; 1/60th of a second at 10; sweep seconds hand with stop feature.
**Strap:** genuine leather with dimple pattern; Italian made; embossed Times Square name on reverse side.
**Also available:** with platinum finish and in a variety of color combinations.

## CORDUVA CHRONOGRAPH

**Movement:** sports chronograph.
**Functions:** hour, minute, seconds; date; chronograph with three counters.
**Case:** Ø 61mm; surgical-grade 316L solid stainless steel; screw-down crown with diver's crown cap; mineral crystal; screw-on caseback; water resistant to 200 meters.
**Dial:** military black; markers, Arabic numerals, bâton hands, sweep-seconds hand and counter hands filled with Tritnite® luminescence; stainless steel counter rings; printed minute track on flange; printed military track on inner circle.

**Indications:** 24 hour at 3; date between 4 and 5, subseconds at 6; minutes at 9; sweep seconds hand with stop feature.
**Strap:** Italian-made Corduva diver strap; durable marine canvas; Velcro fastens.
**Also available:** as an automatic and in a variety of colors.

## LUPAH VÓRTICE

**Movement:** Swiss-made Ronda Startech caliber 5050.C; world's first day and big date movement with three counters; automatic big date correction; 13 jewels. **Functions:** hour, minute, seconds; date and day; chronograph with 3 counters; automatic date correction.
**Case:** Ø 43mm; polished and brushed surgical-grade 316L solid stainless steel patented Invicta design; 316L solid stainless steel crown and pushers with rubber O-rings; rounded mineral crystal; screw-on caseback; water resistant to 100 meters.
**Dial:** enamel finish; guilloché pattern; applied Swiss rose gold-plated Arabic markers; Swiss rose gold-plated Dauphine hour and minute hands with Tritnite® luminescence; Swiss rose-gold bâton sweep-seconds and counter hands.
**Indications:** day at 12; subseconds at 3; big date and 1/10th of a second at 6; 30 minutes and 12 hours at 9; sweep-seconds hand with stop feature.
**Strap:** genuine ostrich; special grain.
**Also available:** in a variety of color combinations.

## LADY WAVE

**Movement:** Swiss; modified to position crown at 12.
**Functions:** hour, minute, seconds; date.
**Case:** Ø 34.5mm at widest point; polished and brushed surgical-grade 316L solid stainless steel; unique wave design; crown at 12; specially made wave-cut mineral crystal; screw-down back; water resistant to 50 meters.
**Dial:** enamel finished; combination guilloché sunray and wave patterns; applied stainless steel Roman markers; stainless steel vintage-style hands; stainless steel bâton sweeps-second hand.
**Indications:** date at 6.
**Strap:** genuine leather; crocodile pattern.
**Also available:** in a variety of matching dial and strap colors.

## TIMES SQUARE AUTOMATIC

**Movement:** mechanical automatic-winding Swiss.
**Functions:** hour, minute, seconds; date.
**Case:** Ø 36mm; surgical-grade 316L solid stainless steel; patented Invicta dual-pusher flip-release case opens to reveal exhibition back with mineral crystal and high-polished mirror; mineral crystal curved at 6; screw-on caseback; water resistant to 100 meters.
**Dial:** genuine mother-of-pearl dial; guilloché and sunray patterns; applied stainless steel Arabic markers; stainless steel Javeline hour and minute hands with Tritnite® luminescence; stainless steel bâton sweep-seconds hand.
**Indications:** date at 6; sweep seconds hand with stop feature.
**Strap:** genuine leather; Italian made; embossed Times Square name on reverse side.
**Also available:** as a chronograph and in a variety of color combinations.

## TIMES SQUARE AUTOMATIC

Big and exciting like the entertainment center for which it is named, the new Times Square Automatic is a powerful symbol of Invicta's increasing watch making prowess. It is highlighted by the patented dual-pusher flip-case that opens to reveal the fine automatic Swiss movement and a high-polished mirror that adds to the viewing experience. The thick mineral crystal with curvature at 6 is another noteworthy design feature.

# IWC

Long respected for its technical mastery of the most complicated watchmaking feats, IWC continues to surpass expectations of even the most critical collectors with its technological advancements and innovative thinking.

IWC embarked on an incredible adventure that took watchmakers outside of their typical realm and into the deep. In 2004, the brand teamed up with the Cousteau Society in a grand Red Sea Expedition, supplying an important timepiece to be worn by the divers throughout the expedition.

Originally founded by Jacques Cousteau and now headed by his widow, the Cousteau Society carries on its namesake's underwater work. Fifty years after Cousteau's first expedition with the Calypso to the coral reefs in the Red Sea, IWC facilitated the start of a second expedition to the original diving sites. The 80-day scientific dive was held to conduct a comparative survey of the coral reefs of then and now. Accompanying the divers was the newest IWC Aquatimer timepiece: the Aquatimer Minute Memory.

In order to enable divers to track time to the very minute while underwater, IWC created an horological and technical marvel for this watch: it is the first divers' watch to be equipped with a separately operated minute-memory mechanism. Divers working with IWC indicated that the ability to measure a second intermediate time independently (for instance, the duration of the ascent) would be an extremely sensible and practical improvement. Essentially, in addition to the chronograph function, this watch offers an additional flyback minute hand that can be activated under water at any point in the operating depth range, and which can serve also as an emergency system in the event of the decompression computer's failure. The Aquatimer Minute Memory watch is offered exclusively in titanium and is pressure- and water-resistant to 2,000 meters. IWC has filed for several patents for this professional instrument.

Also in honor of the expedition, IWC has created a special limited-edition Cousteau Divers watch as part of the Aquatimer family. A symbol of the partnership between the Cousteau Society and IWC, the Cousteau Divers watch is limited to 1953 pieces—marking the year of Cousteau's first Red Sea Expedition.

**ABOVE**

The Minute Repeater Squelette houses 250 individual parts, including the repeater mechanism, all elegantly etched and refined to a minimum framework.

**BOTTOM LEFT**

The new Portuguese Automatic timepieces utilize the IWC Caliber 50010 with Pellaton automatic-winding mechanism and seven days of power reserve.

**BOTTOM CENTER AND RIGHT**

The new Da Vinci perpetual-calendar watches house its 500-year synchronized-calendar mechanism in a massive 41.5mm case.

**TOP LEFT**

The IWC Aquatimer Minute Memory offers a 10-minute countdown flyback hand for additional underwater timing.

**CENTER**

The Cousteau Divers watch commemorates the great undersea activities of Jacques Cousteau and the Cousteau Society.

IWC also continues to excel in the production of complicated timepieces. Top among its new models are the Portuguese Tourbillon Mystère and the Portuguese Minute Repeater Squelette. In the Tourbillon Mystère, IWC master watchmakers combine 81 micro-components with a total weight of only 0.433 grams and condense it to occupy the visual focal point of the dial—forming the tourbillon escapement. The Caliber 50900 automatic movement offers seven days of power reserve. The watch is created in a limited edition of 50 pieces in platinum and 250 in rose gold.

Similarly, because of the sheer amount of hand craftsmanship involved in its making, the Minute Repeater Squelette is strictly limited to only 50 pieces each in rose or white gold. The Squelette takes the 250 individual parts of the minute-repeater movement (already an exquisite complication) and further refines and reduces it to a minimum framework—offering supreme precision and aesthetics.

Three new Portuguese Automatic watches also join the famed family. These new timepieces incorporate the largest automatic movement available on the world market-the IWC Caliber 50010 with Pellaton automatic-winding mechanism and seven days of power reserve. The watch offers date indicator and small-seconds indicator. It is available in rose gold and stainless steel, and in a limited edition of 500 platinum pieces.

IWC's new lineup would not be complete without a new Da Vinci rendition. This year the brand unveils the Da Vinci with perpetual calendar in a larger 41.5mm case. The bold watch marks time for 500 years mechanically with synchronized calendars and a century slide for the years 2200-2499.

## CHRONOLOGY

**1868** American Florentine Ariosto Jones partners with Johann Heinrich Moser to establish IWC, International Watch Company, in Schaffhausen, Switzerland where they can harness the power of the Rhein falls for energy.

**1869** IWC produces the Caliber Jones movement—one of the first to be wound with a crown.

**1890** IWC creates its first Grand Complication pocket watch comprised of more than 1,300 parts.

**1900** IWC becomes a supplier to the British Royal Navy and the Imperial German Navy.

**1940** IWC works tirelessly to create a fully antimagnetic watch for aviators. It houses an inner iron case. The company launches its Portuguesier collection of oversized watches.

**1954** IWC develops an automatic-rewinding mechanism and positions it in its Ingenieur collection.

**1978** The company forms a bond with Ferdinand Porsche that will last 20 years, wherein IWC creates Porsche Design watches by IWC.

**1985** IWC creates the Da Vinci, the first watch to house a revolutionary perpetual-calendar mechanism that is accurate for 500 years.

**1990** The Grand Complication wristwatch is born. With 659 parts, it is the most complex watch of its era.

**1997** The GST collection of sport watches is launched.

**1998** The Aquatimer makes its debut. This is the first watch to be water resistant to 2,000 meters.

**2000** The Caliber 5000 is a seven-day automatic movement with IWC's patented Pellaton winding system.

**2003** The Big Pilot's Watch with the Caliber 5000 movement is launched. It offers 8.5 days of autonomy and features a device that stops the movement after seven days to assure precision.

**2004** The brand unveils the incredible Portuguese Perpetual Calendar with the Caliber 5000 and Pellaton winding system. The patented watch offers representation of the moon's phases in the northern and southern hemispheres.

## DOPPELCHRONOGRAPH SPITFIRE — REF. 3713

**Movement:** mechanical automatic-winding IWC 79230 caliber (chronograph integrated with the module for the split-second feature).
**Functions:** hour, minute, small seconds; date, day; split-second chronograph with three counters.
**Case:** stainless steel three-piece case (Ø 42mm, thickness: 16.6mm); brushed; additional ductile iron inside case for the deviation of magnetic fields; curved, very thick sapphire crystal; depressurization-resistant to 6atm; screw-down crown; pushers with case protection, the one for the split-second chronograph at 10; screw-on back; water resistant to 6atm.
**Dial:** opalin; soleil brushed; grained hour ring; luminescent applied Arabic numerals and bâton markers in rhodium-plated brass; luminescent lozenge hands in rhodium-plated brass.
**Indications:** day of the week and date at 3; hour counter at 6; small seconds at 9; minute counter at 12; center second and split-second counter; minute track with divisions for 1/4 second.
**Strap:** crocodile leather; steel clasp.
**Also available:** with Spitfire or Classic black dial; with bracelet.

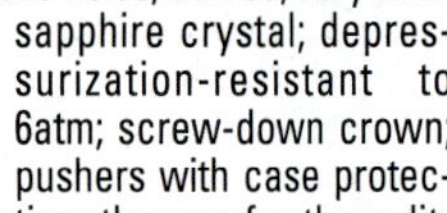

## FLIEGERCHRONOGRAPH AUTOMATIC SPITFIRE — REF. 3706

**Movement:** mechanical automatic-winding IWC 7922 caliber (integrated chronograph); 44-hour autonomy; 25 jewels; shock-resistant and antimagnetic according to NICHS 91-10 standards.
**Functions:** hour, minute, small seconds; day, date; chronograph with three counters.
**Case:** stainless steel three-piece case (Ø 39mm, thickness: 14.6mm); brushed; additional ductile iron inside case for magnetic field deviation; curved, very thick sapphire crystal; depressurization-resistant to 6atm; screw-down crown; pushers with case protection; screw-on back with engraved logo; water resistant to 6atm.
**Dial:** opalin; soleil brushed; grained hour ring; luminescent Arabic numerals and bâton markers in rhodium-plated brass; luminescent lozenge hands in rhodium-plated brass.
**Indications:** day and date at 3; hour counter at 6; small seconds at 9; minute counter at 12; center second counter; minute track with divisions for 1/4 second.
**Bracelet:** brushed steel; fold-over clasp with safety pusher.
**Also available:** with black Spitfire or Classic dial; with strap.

## FLIEGERUHR UTC WORLD TIME SPITFIRE — REF. 3251

**Movement:** mechanical automatic-winding IWC 37526 caliber; 44-hour autonomy; 28,800 vph; shock-resistant and antimagnetic according to NICHS 91-10 standards.
**Functions:** hour, minute, second; date; second time-zone time; 24 hour.
**Case:** stainless steel three-piece case (Ø 39mm, thickness: 13.5mm); brushed; additional ductile iron inside case for magnetic field deviation; curved, very thick sapphire crystal; depressurization-resistant; screw-down crown; screw-on back; water resistant to 6atm.
**Dial:** black grené; luminescent applied Arabic numerals and bâton markers in rhodium-plated brass; luminescent lozenge hands in rhodium-plated brass (hour hand independently adjustable with crown pulled out at an intermediate notch).
**Indications:** date at 3; second time-zone time under 12.
**Strap:** crocodile leather; fold-over clasp with safety pusher.
**Also available:** silvered Spitfire or black Classic dial; with bracelet; in platinum with leather strap and blue dial.

## FLIEGERUHR MARK XV SPITFIRE — REF. 3253

**Movement:** mechanical automatic-winding IWC 37524 caliber; shock-resistant and antimagnetic according to NICHS 91-10 standards.
**Functions:** hour, minute, second; date.
**Case:** stainless steel three-piece case (Ø 38mm, thickness: 9mm); brushed; additional ductile iron inside case for magnetic field deviation; curved, very thick sapphire crystal; depressurization-resistant; screw-down crown; screw-on back; water resistant to 6atm.
**Dial:** opalin; soleil brushed; grained hour ring; luminescent applied Arabic numerals and bâton markers in rhodium-plated brass; black printed minute track with five-minute graduation; luminescent lozenge hands in rhodium-plated brass.
**Indications:** date at 3.
**Strap:** leather; steel fold-over clasp.

## GRANDE COMPLICATION REF. 3770

**Movement:** mechanical automatic-winding IWC 79091 caliber (integrated chronograph + calendar and repeater modules); finished by hand.
**Functions:** hour, minute, small seconds; perpetual calendar (date, day, month, year, moonphase); chronograph with three counters; minute repeater.
**Case:** platinum (Ø 42.2mm, thickness: 16.3mm); polished and brushed finish; curved sapphire crystal; repeater slide on the middle; screw-down crown for the correction of the whole calendar and rectangular pushers, all in platinum; back fastened by 6 screws; waterproof and antimagnetic.
**Dial:** black; subdials; applied bâton markers in white gold; bâton hands in white gold.
**Indications:** date at 3; hour counter and month at 6; 4-digit year between 7 and 8; small seconds and day at 9; moonphase and minute counter at 12; center second counter; minute track with divisions for 1/4 second.
**Strap:** crocodile leather; platinum clasp.
**Note:** produced as a limited edition of 50 pieces per year.
**Also available:** with silvered or white dial; with bracelet; in yellow gold with silvered or white dial; with strap.

## PORTOFINO AUTOMATIC REF. 3533

**Movement:** mechanical automatic-winding IWC 30110 caliber; 42-hour autonomy; 21 jewels; 28,800 vph.
**Functions:** hour, minute, second; date.
**Case:** stainless steel two-piece case (Ø 38mm, thickness: 8.65mm); flat sapphire crystal; semi-recessed crown; back fastened by 6 screws; water resistant to 3atm.
**Dial:** white; bâton markers in steel; printed minute track; steel bâton hands.
**Indications:** date at 3.
**Strap:** crocodile leather; steel clasp.
**Also available:** with black dial; with bracelet; in yellow gold with white dial and strap.
Ref. 3513, Ø 34mm, 37521 caliber: in stainless steel with white dial; applied markers;crocodile leather strap or bracelet; applied Arabic numerals; black caribou leather strap or bracelet; in yellow gold with applied markers or printed Roman numerals; with quartz movement.

## DA VINCI SPLIT-SECOND REF. 3754

**Movement:** mechanical automatic-winding IWC 79252 caliber (integrated chronograph modified by the addition of the split-second device + calendar module).
**Functions:** hour, minute, small seconds; perpetual calendar (date, day, month, year, moonphase); split-second chronograph with three counters.
**Case:** platinum three-piece case (Ø 41.5mm, thickness: 16mm); jointed lugs with central attachment; domed Plexiglas glass; screw-down crown for the correction of the whole calendar; pusher for the split-second chronograph at 10; back fastened by 6 screws; water resistant to 3atm.
**Dial:** opalin; subdials decorated with circular beads; printed Arabic numerals and luminescent applied steel square markers; luminescent steel Alpha hands.
**Indications:** date at 3; month and hour counter at 6; 4-digit year between 7 and 8; day and small seconds at 9; moonphase and minute counter at 12; center second and split-second counter; minute track with divisions for 1/4 second.
**Strap:** crocodile leather; platinum clasp.
**Note:** produced as a limited edition of 500 pieces.
**Also available:** with blue dial; in pink gold with silvered dial.

## PICCOLO DA VINCI REF. 3736

**Movement:** with electric drive controlled by a quartz crystal and mechanical timing; IWC 630 caliber.
**Functions:** hour, minute, small seconds; date; moonphase; chronograph with three counters.
**Case:** 18K yellow-gold three-piece case (Ø 29mm, thickness: 8.3mm); jointed lugs with central attachment; curved sapphire crystal; screw-down yellow-gold crown; snap-on back; water resistant to 3atm.
**Dial:** white; applied yellow-gold bâton markers and luminescent dots; luminescent yellow-gold bâton hands.
**Indications:** hour counter at 3; date between 4 and 5; small seconds at 6; minute counter at 9; moonphase at 12; center second counter; minute track with divisions for 1/4 second.
**Strap:** crocodile leather; yellow-gold clasp.
**Also available:** with dial in blue mother-of-pearl; with bracelet; in stainless steel with white or black dial, strap or bracelet; jeweled version (upon request).

## PORTUGUESE TOURBILLON MYSTÈRE REF. 5042

**Movement:** mechanical automatic-winding IWC 50900 caliber with tourbillon volant device; autonomy 7 days; 44 jewels; 19,900 vph; yellow-gold rotor with the Probus Scafusia seal; finished by hand.
**Functions:** hour, minute, small second; power reserve.
**Case:** 18K pink-gold three-piece case (Ø 44.2mm, thickness: 15.45mm); polished and brushed finish; domed sapphire crystal; pink-gold crown; numbered middle; back fastened by 6 screws, displaying the movement through a sapphire crystal; water resistant to 3atm.
**Dial:** argenté, subdial decorated with circular beads; aperture on the tourbillon inside a sector decorated with a Côtes de Genève pattern; applied gilded Arabic numerals and hollowed minute track; gilded leaf-style hands.
**Indications:** power reserve between 4 and 5; small second at 9.
**Strap:** hand-stitched crocodile leather; pink-gold fold-over clasp.
**Note:** limited edition of 50 numbered pieces.
**Also available:** in platinum, 250 pieces.

## PORTUGUESE PERPETUAL CALENDAR REF. 5021

**Movement:** mechanical automatic-winding IWC 50611 caliber; 7-day autonomy; 66 jewels; 18,800 vph; rotor in yellow gold with the "Probus Scafusia" seal; finished by hand. **Functions:** hour, minute, small seconds; perpetual calendar (date, day, month, year, moonphase); power reserve. **Case:** 18K pink-gold three-piece case (Ø 44.2mm, thickness: 15.75mm); curved sapphire crystal; pink-gold-plated crown; back fastened by 6 screws, displaying the movement through a sapphire crystal; water resistant to 3atm.
**Dial:** black; power reserve sector argenté; subdials decorated with circular beads; embossed doré Arabic numerals and hollowed minute track, all rhodium-plated; pink-gold leaf-style hands.
**Indications:** date and power reserve at 3; month at 6; 4-digit year between 7 and 8; small seconds and day at 9; moonphase (of the Northern and Southern hemispheres) at 12.
**Strap:** crocodile leather, hand-stitched; double fold-over clasp in pink gold.
**Note:** produced as a limited edition of 250 pieces.
**Also available:** in yellow gold with silvered dial; in platinum with silvered dial, 250 pieces.

## PORTUGUESE CHRONOGRAPH AUTOMATIC REF. 3714

**Movement:** mechanical automatic-winding IWC 79240 caliber (integrated chronograph); 44-hour autonomy; 31 jewels; 28,800 vph.
**Functions:** hour, minute, small seconds; chronograph with two counters.
**Case:** stainless steel three-piece case (Ø 41mm, thickness: 12.7mm); polished and brushed finish; curved sapphire crystal; back fastened by 4 screws; water resistant to 3atm.
**Dial:** opalin with black subdials; embossed doré Arabic numerals and hollowed minute track, all rhodium-plated; rhodium-plated leaf-style hands.
**Indications:** small seconds at 6; minute counter at 12; center second counter; minute track with divisions for 1/4 second on the flange and five-minute graduation.
**Strap:** crocodile leather, hand-stitched; steel clasp.
**Also available:** with all-silvered or black dial; in yellow gold with silvered dial; in white gold with black dial and silvered zones; in pink gold with black or silvered dial.

## PORTUGUESE SPLIT-SECOND CHRONOGRAPH REF. 3712

**Movement:** mechanical manual-winding IWC 76240 caliber (integrated chronograph).
**Functions:** hour, minute, small seconds; split-second chronograph with two counters.
**Case:** 18K yellow-gold three-piece case (Ø 41mm, thickness: 12.7mm); curved sapphire crystal; yellow-gold crown and pushers, pusher for the split-second function at 10; back fastened by 4 screws; water resistant to 3atm.
**Dial:** opalin; subdials decorated with circular beads; embossed doré Arabic numerals and hollowed minute track, all gold-plated; leaf-style gold-plated hands.
**Indications:** small seconds at 6; minute counter at 12; center second and split-second counter; minute track with divisions for 1/4 second on the flange and five-minute graduation.
**Strap:** crocodile leather, hand-stitched; yellow-gold clasp.
**Also available:** in pink gold with black or silvered dial; in stainless steel with silvered dial.

## GST PERPETUAL CALENDAR — REF. 3756

**Movement:** mechanical automatic-winding IWC 79261 caliber (integrated chronograph + calendar module); shock-resistant and antimagnetic according to the NICHS 91-10 standards.
**Functions:** hour, minute, small seconds; perpetual calendar (date, day, month, year, moonphase); chronograph with three counters.
**Case:** stainless steel three-piece case (Ø 43mm, thickness: 16.7mm); polished and brushed finish; perforated bezel; curved sapphire crystal, antireflective; screw-down crown; screw-on back; water resistant to 12atm.
**Dial:** white grené, on three levels; bâton markers in blued steel; rhodium-plated luminescent bâton hands.
**Indications:** date at 3; hour counter and month at 6; 4-digit year between 7 and 8; small seconds and day at 9; minute counter and moonphase at 12; center second counter; minute track with divisions for 1/4 second and five-minute graduation.
**Bracelet:** stainless steel, polished and brushed; recessed fold-over clasp with safety pusher.
**Also available:** with silvered, black, salmon or gray rhodium-plated dial; in titanium with black dial.

## GST SPLIT-SECOND — REF. 3715

**Movement:** mechanical automatic-winding IWC 79230 caliber (integrated chronograph modified by the addition of the split-second device); shock-resistant and antimagnetic according to the NICHS 91-10 standards.
**Functions:** hour, minute, small seconds; day, date; split-second chronograph with three counters.
**Case:** stainless steel three-piece case (Ø 43mm, thickness: 17mm); polished and brushed finish; perforated bezel; curved sapphire crystal, antireflective; screw-down crown; pusher at 10 for the split-second chronograph; screwed-on back; water resistant to 12atm.
**Dial:** black, on three levels; subdials decorated with circular beads; applied faceted rhodium-plated bâton markers; rhodium-plated luminescent bâton hands.
**Indications:** day of the week and date at 3; hour counter at 6; small seconds at 9; minute counter at 12; center second and split-second counters; minute track with divisions for 1/4 second and five-minute graduation.
**Bracelet:** in stainless steel, polished and brushed; recessed fold-over clasp with safety pusher.
**Also available:** with blue, gray rhodium-plated or salmon dial; in titanium with black dial.

## THE PELLATON WINDING SYSTEM

For the transmission of motion from the rotor to the barrel, this particular winding system uses the rotation of an eccentric cam (gold colored, on the right), integral with the rotor (removed here), and causes the big rocking bar meshing with it (center, in a fork shape with two big evolving jewel bearings at its ends) perform limited oscillations. The rocking bar, by its oscillations, controls two pawls (dial center, above, gold colored); these drive alternately-and always clockwise-the nearby wheel provided with wolf-teeth (left). Thus, motion is transmitted, after a series of reductions, in such a way as to wind up the long and strong barrel spring, which is planned so as to assure a working autonomy of 8.5 days. A mechanical device, linked with the power-reserve visualizing system, stops the movement 36 hours before the normal stop, thus avoiding the movement's functioning with a motive force of lower intensity with respect to the optimal value. In fact, this could cause balance oscillations of more reduced amplitude and, hence, losses in accuracy.

## CALIBER 5000

Automatic-winding movement; 204-hour autonomy, i.e. 8.5 days (a special device stops the movement after 168 hours, 7 days, to assure the highest precision at any time).
**Functions:** hour, minute, small seconds; power reserve. **Shape:** round.
**Diameter:** 38.20mm. **Thickness:** 7.20mm. **Jewels:** 46. **Balance:** with two arms, with compensating screws and fine regulation system by 2 eccentric screws positioned at both arms' ends.
**Frequency:** 18,000 vph.
**Balance-spring:** Breguet, in Nivarox 1, with eccentric screw regulating device and mobile balance-spring stud holder provided with an eccentric screw regulating device.
**Shock-absorber system:** Incabloc.
**Notes:** the pillar-plate is decorated with a circular-graining pattern, bridges with a concentric-circle pattern. The rotor is skeletonized, coin stamped and provided with a gold medallion showing the House's motto "Schaffhausen's good produce."
**Derived calibers:** 5011 (5000 with center second and date).

# JACOB & CO.

In a world where bling has become commonplace, Jacob & Co. is a major player—producing high-end diamond watches of mega size and style.

Jacob Arabo founded his own company in New York City nearly 25 years ago. A young immigrant from Russia, Arabo had come to America when he was 15 years old. At the age of 16, he enrolled in a jewelry design school and rose to the top of his class. He soon opened a small booth in New York's famed diamond district and began designing jewelry for a number of brands and for private clients. His business grew as word of his designing talents spread. By the mid 1990s, Arabo had established great relationships with well-known rap artists and celebrities and quickly became a big jewelry name in the music world. Jacob & Co became the place to go for custom jewelry and Arabo was nicknamed Jacob the Jeweler. After designing jewelry for many years, Arabo made the natural progression and unveiled his first timepiece—the Five Time Zone Watch.

The most popular Jacob & Co. timepiece today—and the one that put this brand on the bling map—is the Five Time Zone Watch. The design of the Five Time Zone Watch is bold and beautiful. It features a main dial set to local time and four subsidiary dials showing the time in New York, Los Angeles, Tokyo and Paris. Available in a host of styles ranging from mid-sized (40mm) to full-size (47mm), and from unadorned to totally diamond adorned, the Five Time Zone Watch is created in steel, and in 18-karat yellow, white or rose gold. It houses ETA movements—the ETA 956.112 for the main dial with date and the ETA 280.002 for the subdials.

THIS PAGE

ABOVE

The 40mm automatic chronograph offers small seconds, 30-minute and 12-hour counters and features an exhibition caseback. It is available with an interchangeable diamond bezel and comes with enamel or mother-of-pearl dials.

BOTTOM

*from left to right*

Jimmy Fallon, Giselle Bundchen, P. Diddy, Jorge Pasada.

FACING PAGE

The World is Yours watch is part of the Five Time Zone collection and features a world map on the dial created with 4 carats of pavé multicolored diamonds. It offers date and five time-zone readouts.

&Co
JACOB & Co.
789

Prices for the Five Time Zone Watch range from $6,000 to $150,000 depending on carat weight, which varies from a 2-carat bezel to a full-pavé 27-carat model. In total, more than 50 different styles exist in the versatile Five Time Zone collection. Each watch is sold with four straps in different colors matching the watch dial; they can be changed by the wearer without any tools.

**TOP CENTER**

Fondly referred to as the mid-size Five Time Zone Watch, this 40mm version is available with a range of diamond options.

**FAR LEFT**

*from top to bottom*

Justin Timberlake, David Beckham and Elton John, 50 Cent.

**BOTTOM RIGHT**

This full-size 47mm Five Time Zone Watch features a main dial time, and offers time in New York, Los Angeles, Tokyo and Paris. It also offers date readout and is sold with four different colored interchangeable deployment straps. It is available with a plain bezel or diamond bezel of 3.25 carats or 5 carats. A full-pavé case and bracelet are also available, bringing the total weight up to 27 carats.

**TOP LEFT**

The mid-size Five Time Zone Watch.

**BOTTOM RIGHT**

From the Angel Collection, this rectangular watch is offered in steel or in 18-karat gold. It is created with 10.50 carats of diamonds and offers a dual time-zone dial. The dial is made of Blackstone with a mother-of-pearl or diamond inlay main dial. A host of other exotic stone dials is available, as are enamel dials.

## CHRONOLOGY

**1981** Jacob Arabo—a recent immigrant to America from Russia—opens a small booth in New York City's diamond district at the age of 16. He begins designing for a number of jewelry companies and for private clients. He later opens Diamond Quasar and designs under the brand name Jacob & Co.

**1990s** Arabo meets up-and-coming singer Faith Evans, who enters his shop while looking for jewelry to wear for her CD cover. Taken by his creations, she returns with her husband, the late Notorious B.I.G.—a well-established rap artist. The couple becomes loyal customers and recommends Jacob & Co to their high-profile friends in the music industry.

**2002** A natural progression from his pendants and rings, Arabo designs the Five Time Zone Watch for his jet-set clients.

**2004** Jacob & Co unveils the Angel collection of dual time-zone watches.

In addition to this series, Jacob & Co offers the Angel line of rectangular dual time-zone watches. Also created in steel or 18-karat gold, these rectangular beauties feature dials of either enamel or semi-precious stones with mother-of-pearl or diamond inlays.

There is also a new Automatic Chronograph collection that features 30-minute and 12-hour counters, and is available with an interchangeable diamond bezel.

As with all Jacob & Co. timepieces, the newest watches are sold with accompanying certificates of authenticity.

# JAEGER-LECOULTRE

Among the most revered watch brands in the world, Jaeger-LeCoultre boasts a history rich in invention and advancement in both technology and design. This complete manufacture regularly defies the constraints of watchmaking and breaks boundaries in the creation of complications.

Adding to its very successful Master series, Jaeger-LeCoultre unveils the Master Compressor Dualmatic, a sporty yet chic timepiece. Elegantly housed in a 41mm case, the watch's asymmetrical dial bears the hallmark of the famed Master Compressor line. The watch indicates the hours and date in local (travel) time through window apertures on the dial, and includes the 24-hour indicator. The minutes and hours of home time are displayed traditionally, and there is a subseconds dial. The watch is surprisingly easy to use. To change time on this watch, the wearer unscrews the compression key on the lower crown (as opposed to a main crown on most other dual time-zone watches), pulls the key out, moves the hour hand forward the appropriate number of hour leaps and closes the compression key. The function works equally as well in the opposite direction.

The Master Compressor Dualmatic houses the automatic Jaeger-LeCoultre caliber 972 handcrafted movement, comprised of 230 parts and 29 jewels. Tested for 1,000 hours and water resistant to 10atm, the watch is crafted in steel with the 1,000-hours Control Seal engraved in 18-karat gold on the caseback.

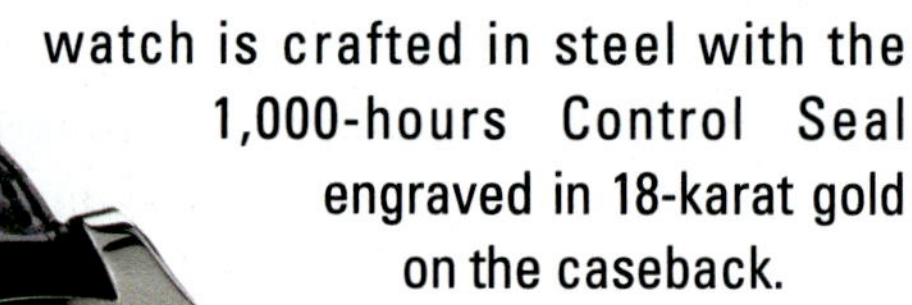

THIS PAGE

The Master Eight Days is available in 18-karat gold and platinum.

FACING PAGE

The Master Compressor Dualmatic offers dual time-zone readouts with an incredibly easy-to-use compressor setting.

JAEGER-LECOULTRE
DUALMATIC
SWISS MADE

In its famed Reverso line, Jaeger-LeCoultre unveils a host of models, including: Reverso Grand GMT; Reverso Duetto Classique with different dials on its front and back; Reverso Gran'Sport Automatic; Reverso Gran'Sport Lady with manually wound movement; Reverso Volga with diamonds set on the case in elegant circles resembling bubbles; and Reverso Florale with 178 full-cut diamonds cloud-set in a floral motif.

In typical Jaeger-LeCoultre style, the brand also unveiled a rare gem in high-watchmaking: the Gyrotourbillon I. A grand complication of the highest magnitude, the Gyrotourbillon I is a spectacular feat. Nearly four years in the development stages, it features a patented spherical tourbillon that beats much like a heart. It also houses one of the most difficult watchmaking complications—a running equation of time. Essentially, the equation of time

FACING PAGE

TOP LEFT

By adding diamonds to the case of this Reverso Gran'Sport Lady watch, it becomes a sporty chic beauty.

TOP RIGHT

Crafted in 18-karat gold, the Reverso Florale watch features Jaeger-LeCoultre's own diamond setting technique.

LEFT

The Reverso Grand GMT offers GMT time and day/night indicator on one side.

BOTTOM

Crafted in steel,the Reverso Gran'Sport features a large date readout.

THIS PAGE

TOP

The Gyrotourbillon I houses a spherical tourbillon that is tilted in its axis and rotates in all directions to offer maximum precision.

indicates the difference between the average sun day and the true sun day.

In reality, time is not consistent from one day to the next in relation to the meridian. In order to have consistency, all of the days in a year were calculated and an average sun day of 24 hours was fixed. However, the true sun day can vary from just over 14 minutes to 16 minutes on certain days of the year. The equation of time displays the difference on a daily basis. The Gyrotourbillon also offers hours, minutes, seconds, power reserve, perpetual date via two retrograde indicators and a retrograde perpetual indication of the month and leap year on the back of the watch. Incredibly complicated, it takes about four days just to assemble the tourbillon escapements and four weeks to assemble the entire platinum timepiece. Only 25 pieces will be made per year, totaling no more than 75.

## CHRONOLOGY

**1833** Antoine LeCoultre opens a workshop at Le Sentier. As a man of great innovation, he designs machines to make components. The first machine-cut pinions are of his invention.

**1847** LeCoultre & Co. invents a lever-based winding system that replaces the traditional key.

**1903** Antoine LeCoultre's grandson Jacques-David pairs with Parisian chronometer-maker Edmond Jaeger, forming Jaeger-LeCoultre. The company develops the world's slimmest pocket watch caliber.

**1928** The Atmos clock is invented by engineer Jean Léon Reutter. It draws its energy from temperature variations and is billed as "the clock that lives on air."

**1929** The Caliber 101 is created. The smallest mechanical movement in the world, it consists of 98 elements and weighs just under 0.9 grams.

**1931** Created for polo-playing British officials, the Reverso features a swivel case and offers an excellent solution to the frequent breakage of watch crystals.

**1956** Memovox is the first automatic wristwatch equipped with an alarm device.

**1958** Jaeger-LeCoultre's Geophysic features a chronometer antimagnetic at 600 amp/meter. This proves valuable to the exploration crew aboard The Nautilus.

**1992** The Master Control 1000 Hours by Jaeger-LeCoultre establishes a new benchmark for quality within the watchmaking world.

**1994** The Reverso Duo watch features two time zones.

**1998** Jaeger-LeCoultre makes its foray into the world of luxury sport with the Reverso Gran'Sport—the fruit of seven years of intense research and development.

**2002** This year marks the 70th anniversary of the Reverso. The house unveils the first platinum Reverso with a skeleton movement and also expands its high-jeweled Reverso collection.

**2003** Launching of the Grande Reverso line—the most generously sized Reverso with an 8-day power-reserve movement—and the Master Antoine LeCoultre, honored by the Grande Prix of Genève with its Special Jury Prize.

## GYROTOURBILLON I — REF. 600 64 20

**Movement:** mechanical manual-winding Jaeger-LeCoultre 177; Ø 36.3mm, 10.85mm high; 77 jewels; 512 elements; two barrels with sapphire-crystal lid and base; 8-day power reserve; tested 1,000 hours; crafted, assembled and decorated by hand.
**Spherical tourbillon:** monometallic balance in 14K gold with outlying 14K-gold setting inertia blocks; freely oscillating, quality 1 Breguet balance spring; 21,600 vph; Ø 13.86mm; weight: 0.336 grams; 100 elements; rotation: exterior carriage in aluminum 1/minute, interior carriage in titanium and aluminum 2.5/minute; 6 anti-shock devices.
**Functions:** hours, minutes, seconds; power reserve; time equation; perpetual date; perpetual retrograde month; retrograde leap year.
**Case:** 950 platinum; Ø 43mm; height: 14.9mm including sapphire crystal; sapphire crystal caseback, revealing retrograde leap year.
**Indications:** dual retrograde hands indicating perpetual date (left hand indicates the 1st to the 16th, the right hand the16th to the 28th, 29th, 30th or 31st); retrograde leap year on back, **Dial:** upper part in glass and brushed rhodium-plated gold; lower part in gold, charcoal gray; black transferred Arabic numerals.
**Strap:** hand-stitched alligator leather; 950 platinum folding clasp. **Note:** limited production of 20 pieces per year.
**Approx. retail price:** 390,000 CHF.

## MASTER EIGHT DAYS PERPETUAL — REF. 161 24 2A/F/D

**Movement:** mechanical manual-winding Jaeger-LeCoultre Caliber 876; 6.6mm high; 37 jewels; 262 elements; two barrels with sapphire-crystal lid and base; 8-day power reserve; 28,800 vph; tested 1,000 hours; crafted, assembled and decorated by hand. **Crown:** 1 crown to rewind the movement and adjust the hour, minute, day/night; 1 corrector to adjust the entire set of functions of the perpetual calendar: 1 push = 1 day. **Functions:** hours, minutes; date; day, month, 4-digit year display; moonphase; power reserve; day/night indicator with red safety zone for the changing of the perpetual calendar. **Case:** 18K pink-gold; Ø 41.5mm; cambered sapphire crystal, hardness no. 9; sapphire base through which the movement can be viewed; water resistant to 5atm; platinum model has Antoine LeCoultre's signature engraved on the case's middle.
**Dial:** sunray-finished silvered, gold- or rhodium-plated applied hour-markers and numerals; 12 applied luminescent dots.
**Hands:** hour and minute hands are alpha, rhodium-plated or gilded brass; date, day and month hands are rhodium-plated or gilded brass, varnished, blued; moonphase hand is rhodium-plated or gilded brass; power-reserve hand is rhodium-plated or gilded brass, baton shaped, varnished, blued.
**Indications:** day/night indicator at 1; day at 3; month at 6; year at 8; moonphase at 9; power reserve at 11. **Strap:** matte chocolate-colored alligator leather; 18K pink-gold folding clasp.
**Also available:** 950 platinum (Ref. 161 64 2A/F/D).

## REVERSO GRANDE GMT — REF. 302 84 20

**Movement:** mechanical manual-winding Jaeger-LeCoultre Caliber 878; 5.6mm high; 35 jewels; 276 parts; 8-day power reserve; 28,800 vph; tested 1,000 hours; crafted, assembled and decorated by hand. **Crown:** 1 crown to rewind the mechanism and to reset the time on the front and back dials as well as the date; 2 pushbuttons adjust the second time zone: 1 button at 10 to move an hour forward, 1 button at 8 to move an hour back; 1 pushbutton corrector for the synchronization of the GMT indication. **Functions:** Front Dial: hours, minutes, small seconds; large date; day/night indicator.
Back Dial: hours, minutes for second time zone; 24-hour display; 8-day power reserve; indication of time difference in relation to the GMT reference (or another reference of time). **Case:** stainless steel, pivoting Reverso Grande case; sapphire crystal, hardness no. 9; made of more than 50 parts; water resistant to 3atm. **Dial:** Front: silvered guilloché wave pattern and black transferred numerals. Back: brilliant black with silvered zones and white, luminescent transferred numerals.
**Strap:** matte brown alligator leather 20/18 with 18mm stainless steel folding clasp.
**Also available:** 18K pink-gold version with pink-gold folding clasp (Ref. 302 24 20); both versions available with 5-linked bracelet (stainless steel: Ref. 302 81 20 or 18K pink gold: Ref. 302 21 20) with exclusive clasp and length adjustable over 2x4mm.

## MASTER HOMETIME — REF. 162 84 20

**Movement:** mechanical manual-winding Jaeger-LeCoultre Caliber 975; 5.7mm high; 29 jewels; 230 parts; 50-hour power reserve; 28,800 vph; tested 1,000 hours; 22K-gold oscillating weight segment; crafted, assembled and decorated by hand. **Crown:** 1crown for starting the watch and setting of both local and home/reference times, minute, date and day/night indicator.
**Functions:** local ("travel time") hour hand that can be moved both forward- and backwards; date function synchronized with the local hour hand, setting in both directions; "home time" or reference-time hour hand; day/night indicator, linked to the reference-time hand; minutes and small seconds. **Case:** stainless steel; Ø 40mm; cambered sapphire crystal, hardness no. 9; sapphire caseback, displaying movement; water resistant to 5atm. **Dial:** silvered sunray finish; applied numerals and hour markers, either rhodium or gold plated; 12 luminescent dots.
**Hands:** alpha, rhodium-plated or gilded-brass minutes and local hour hands; alpha, openworked blued home time and seconds hands; rhodium-plated or gilded-brass, varnished and blued seconds hand.
**Strap:** matte brown alligator leather 20/16, with 18mm stainless steel folding clasp.
**Also available:** 18K pink gold with matte brown alligator strap (Ref. 162 24 20); stainless steel with stainless steel bracelet, patented with length change enabling fine adjustment over 2x4mm (Ref. 162 81 20).

## MASTER COMPRESSOR DUALMATIC REF. 173 84 70

**Movement:** mechanical automatic Jaeger-LeCoultre Caliber 972; 6.14mm high; 29 jewels; 230 parts; 50-hour power reserve; 28,800 vph; tested 1,000 hours; 22K-gold oscillating weight segment; crafted, assembled and decorated by hand.
**Crowns:** 1 crown with compression key at 2 to adjust the rotating bezel; 1 crown with compression key at 4 for initial setting/starting and moving the principal hour marker forwards and backwards in 1-hour intervals. **Functions:** hour, minutes, small seconds; date of the travel time; hours of reference time; 24-hour indicator synchronized with reference time; rotating flange protected against accidental rotation. **Case:** stainless steel; Ø 41.5mm; cambered sapphire crystal, hardness no. 9; stainless steel caseback with 1000 Hours Control seal in 18K gold; water resistant to 10atm. **Dial:** brilliant black with luminescent numerals and dial markers. **Hands:** trapeze-shaped, openworked, luminescent hour and minute hands in rhodium-plated brass; trapeze-shaped, openworked, white lacquered reference-time hand; white lacquered brass small seconds hand.
**Strap:** caramel-colored calfskin strap, double-stitched with stainless steel folding clasp. **Also available:** 18K pink-gold model with charcoal-gray dial and luminescent numerals and markers on matte chocolate-colored alligator strap with 18K pink-gold folding clasp (Ref. 173 24 40); 18K white-gold model with slate-gray dial and luminescent numerals and markers on matte honey-colored alligator strap with 18K white-gold folding clasp (Ref. 173 34 40); stainless steel model on bracelet with patented, 5 dual-axis links (3 brushed central and 2 brushed lateral links) and patented clasp, made of 52 parts, with length change enabling fine adjustment over 2x4mm (Ref. 173 81 70); 18K pink-gold model on bracelet with patented, 5 dual-axis links (polished) and patented clasp, made of 52 parts, with length change enabling fine adjustment over 2x4mm (Ref. 173 21 40).

## MASTER COMPRESSOR GEOGRAPHIC REF. 171 24 40

**Movement:** mechanical automatic Jaeger-LeCoultre Caliber 923; crafted, assembled and decorated by hand; 28,800 vph; approx. 45-hour power reserve; 31 jewels; thickness: 4.90mm (heavy metal oscillating weight segment). **Functions:** hour, minute, center seconds; date; 24 time zones; day-night indicaton (AM/PM). **Adjusting functions:** 1crown fitted with a compressor key to wind the watch, set the hours and minutes and synchronize the time zones; 1 crown fitted with a compressor key to adjust the second time zone; 1 corrector at 3 to adjust the date. **Case:** 18K pink-gold (Ø 41.5mm); cambered sapphire crystal, hardness no. 9; 18K gold Master Compressor seal on the caseback; water resistant to 100 meters.
**Dial:** brilliant black, charcoal gray or slate gray; luminescent numerals; 7 luminescent hour markers; luminescent trapeze-shaped hour and minute hands in rhodium-plated brass; white lacquered-brass small-seconds hand with red tip.
**Strap:** matte chocolate-colored strap, 18K pink-gold deployment buckle.
**Also available:** 18K pink-gold bracelet; 18K white-gold with matte honey-colored strap; in stainless steel bracelet or with caramel-colored calfskin strap.
**Note:** bracelet: patented, 5 dual-axis links, polished for gold models; clasp: on metal bracelet, exclusive to Jaeger-LeCoultre, 52 parts, with fast summer/winter or morning/evening length-change enabling fine adjustment over 2x4mm.

## MASTER COMPRESSOR AUTOMATIC REF. 172 24 40

**Movement:** mechanical automatic Jaeger-LeCoultre Caliber 960M; crafted, assembled and decorated by hand; 28,800 vph; approx. 44-hour power reserve; 31 jewels; approx. 226 parts; thickness: 4.2mm (heavy metal oscillating weight segment).
**Functions:** hour, minute, center seconds; date at 3; secure graduated rotating bezel.
**Adjusting functions:** 1 crown at 4 to wind the watch and set the hours, minutes and date; 1 crown at 2 to adjust the rotating bezel; crowns fitted with a compressor key.
**Case:** 18K pink-gold (Ø 36.8mm); cambered sapphire crystal, hardness no. 9; 18K gold Master Compressor seal on the caseback; water resistant to 200 meters.
**Dial:** charcoal gray; luminescent numerals; 8 luminescent hour markers; open-worked, luminescent trapeze-shaped hour and minute hands in rhodium-plated brass; white lacquered-brass small-seconds hand with red tip.
**Strap:** matte chocolate-colored crocodile strap.
**Also available:** in stainless steel with calf strap or patented 5 dual-axis link bracelet; clasp exclusive to Jaeger-LeCoultre with 52 parts with fast summer/winter or morning/evening length-change enabling fine adjustment over 2x4mm.

## MASTER COMPRESSOR AUTO WITH DIAMONDS REF. 172 84 01

**Movement:** mechanical automatic Jaeger-LeCoultre Caliber 960M; crafted, assembled and decorated by hand; 28,800 vph; approx. 44-hour power reserve; 31 jewels; approx. 226 parts; thickness: 4.2mm (heavy metal oscillating weight segment).
**Functions:** hour, minute, center seconds; date at 3; secure graduated rotating bezel.
**Adjusting functions:** 1 crown at 4 to wind the watch and set the hours, minutes and date; 1 crown at 2 to adjust the rotating bezel; crowns fitted with a compressor key.
**Case:** stainless steel (Ø 36.8mm); cambered sapphire crystal, hardness no. 9; 18K gold Master Compressor seal on the caseback; 68 F-G Top Wesselton VVS1 full-cut diamonds (Ø 1.3mm, +/- 0.64 carats); water resistant to 200 meters.
**Dial:** brilliant black or charcoal gray; 62 diamonds; luminescent numerals; 8 luminescent hour markers; version with gem-set numerals and hour markers; open-worked, luminescent trapeze-shaped hour and minute hands in rhodium-plated brass; white lacquered-brass small-seconds hand with red tip.
**Strap:** raspberry-colored calfskin strap.
**Also available:** 18K pink-gold with chocolate dial and matte chocolate-colored strap.

## REVERSO GRAN'SPORT LADY — REF. 296 84 01

**Movement:** mechanical manual-winding Jaeger-LeCoultre Caliber 864; 3.45mm high; 19 jewels; 164 parts; 50-hour power reserve; 21,600 vph; crafted, assembled and decorated by hand.
**Crown:** 1 double-jointed crown to rewind watch and to set the hours and minutes; 1 corrector at 10 to set the hour hand of the second time zone in 1-hour intervals.

**Functions:** Front Dial: hours, minutes, seconds at 6. Back Dial: hours and minutes for second time zone, day/night disk.
**Case:** reversible in stainless steel, more than 50 pieces; cambered sapphire crystal, hardness no. 9; water resistant to 5atm.
**Dial:** Front: matte white with silvered soleillées zones, Gran'Sport numerals and silver powdered markers. Back: black, silvered powdered Gran'Sport numerals, transferred rhodium-plated markers.
**Hands:** luminescent, articulated fan-shaped hour and minute hands; black brass-nickel seconds hand with red tip.
**Strap:** orange alligator leather with stainless steel folding clasp.

## REVERSO GRAN'SPORT LADY — REF. 296 81 20

**Movement:** manual Jaeger-LeCoultre Caliber 864; 19 jewels; 21,600 vph; consisting of 164 parts; beveled and Côtes de Genève hand-decorated. **Functions:** hour, minute, small seconds; date; day-night indicator; second time zone; day-night. **Case:** stainless steel, barrel-shaped, reversible double-face case (only case size 27.5x24.5mm, thickness: 9.5mm); engraved with sand-blasted transverse grooves; 32 diamonds set on the second face; curved sapphire crystal on both sides; corrector for the adjustment of the second time zone on the middle; carrier with brushed finish and circular graining decoration; water resistant to 5atm. **Dial:** silvered, guilloché; Linton Arabic numerals; printed minute track with 3 luminescent dots; nickel-plated brass hands.

**Indications:** small seconds at 6; night-day at 12. Rear dial: silvered, engine-turned (guilloché) panels; applied rhodium-plated drop-shaped markers and printed blue "flower" Arabic numerals; luminescent steel bâton hands; second time zone, night-day at 6.
**Strap:** polished/brushed steel; double fold-over clasp and safety pushers.
**Also available:** in yellow gold with bracelet or rubber strap.

## REVERSO DUETTO — REF. 266 11 20

**Movement:** mechanical manual-winding Jaeger-LeCoultre Caliber 844; crafted, assembled and decorated by hand; 21,600 vph; approx. 42-hour power reserve; 18 jewels; 100 parts; thickness: 3.45mm.
**Functions:** hour and minute, identical on both sides.
**Adjusting functions:** 1 crown for winding the watch and setting the hours and minutes simultaneously on both faces. **Case:** 18K yellow-gold; reversible; more than 50 parts; ladies' size; sapphire crystal, hardness no. 9; caseback set with 32 F-G Top Wesselton VVS1 full-cut diamonds (Ø 1.2mm, +/- 0.22 carats).
**Front dial:** silvered; brushed; engine-turned (guilloché) perimeter; printed Eastern-style Arabic numerals and minute track; fan-shaped, blued steel bâton-style hands.
**Rear dial:** mother-of-pearl; dagger-shaped Dauphine hands, 4N gold plated.
**Bracelet:** 18K yellow-gold.
**Also available:** stainless steel; 18K yellow-gold and stainless steel.

## REVERSO DUO — REF. 271 24 70

**Movement:** mechanical manual-winding Jaeger-LeCoultre Caliber 854; patented.
**Functions:** main time zone: minute and small seconds; second time zone: minute and 24-hour.
**Case:** 18K pink-gold, rectangular, reversible, double-face case (with carrier size: 42x26mm, thickness: 9.8mm; case size: 30.5x26mm, thickness: 8.5mm); engraved sand-blasted transverse grooves; curved sapphire crystal on both sides; second time-zone corrector on the middle; pink-gold crown. **Front dial:** in solid silver, Art Déco design, with engine-turned (guilloché) center, printed Arabic numerals and minute track; blued steel bâton hands; small seconds at 6. **Rear dial:** black, engine-turned (guilloché), with luminescent applied pink-gold pointed markers and Arabic numerals, luminescent gold hands and 24-hour display at 6.

**Strap:** black alligator strap.
**Also available:** in white gold, black/silver dials, day/night indicator on brown strap or bracelet; in yellow gold, silver dials on brown strap or bracelet; in steel, black/silver dials on brown ostrich strap or bracelet.

## CALIBER 844 (1997)

**Basic caliber:** 846/1 (1992). Manual-winding movement, 42-hour autonomy.
**Functions:** hours, minutes. **Shape:** tonneau.
**Size:** 13.00x15.20mm. **Thickness:** 3.45mm.
**Jewels:** 18 (escape wheel with end-stones).
**Balance:** smooth, with three arms, in Glucydur.
**Frequency:** 21,600 vph. **Balance-spring:** flat, Nivarox 1, with Spirofin micrometer screw regulating device. **Shock-absorber system:** Kif.
**Notes:** the pillar-plate is decorated with a circular-graining pattern, the bridges are decorated with a Côtes de Genève pattern and beveled. Screw heads are finished by specular polishing. This caliber is realized for the purpose of being mounted on the "Reverso Duetto." Its peculiarity is that it indicates the same time on both sides: in the middle of the main dial and slightly off-center towards 12 on the rear dial. **Derived calibers:** 865; 864.

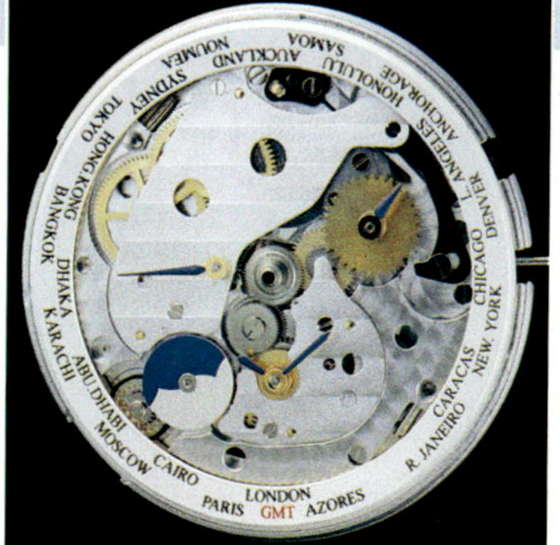

## CALIBER 929/3 (1990/1996)

**Basic caliber:** 889/2. Same characteristics, decorations and finishing as the 889 family with the following variants: date (with fast corrector); world time, second time-zone, 24 hours; power reserve; ring adapter for the disc with the indications of the reference cities for the 24 time zones.
**Thickness:** 4.85mm; **Jewels:** 38.
**Notes:** the photograph shows Caliber 929/3 on the dial side in the version adopted for the "Master Geographic" with all the components for the indications (except for hours and minutes) put in place. Outside the city disc, at 7 the two-color disc for day/night window display; respectively at 2 and 6; at 9 the hands of the date, second time-zone time and power-reserve displays.

## CALIBER 889-440/2 (1987/1996)

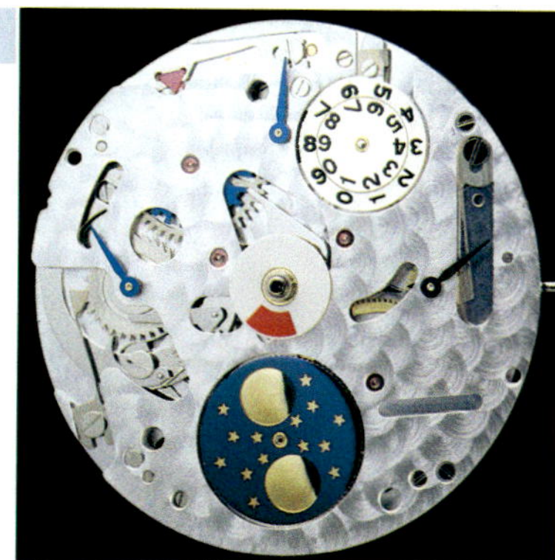

**Basic caliber:** 889/2. Same characteristics, decorations and finishing as Caliber 889/2 with some variants. **Functions:** hours, minutes, seconds (with stopping device); perpetual calendar (date, day, month, year, moonphase with fast corrections). **Total diameter (base +.module):** 28.00mm (12'''1/2). **Thickness:** 4.55mm. **Jewels:** 50. **Notes:** the photograph shows a dial-side view with all the components for the indications (except for hours, minutes, seconds) put in place. Day, date and month applied by hand respectively at 3, 9, 12; 2-digit year, moonphase and consent indicator (for calendar corrections) by discs and windows respectively at 1, 6 and at the center. The perpetual-calendar correction is possible by advancing only a single corrector.

## CALIBER 891/2-448 (1997)

**Basic caliber:** 889/2.
Same characteristics, decorations and finishing as Caliber 889/2 with some variants.
**Functions:** hours, minutes, center seconds (with stopping device); full calendar (day, date, month and moonphase with fast corrections).
**Thickness:** 3.25mm.
**Jewels:** 36 (escape wheel with end-stones).
**Notes:** the caliber derives from 891/2-447 (of 1993, without moonphase). The photograph shows a dial-side view with all the components for the indications (except for hours, minutes, seconds) put in place: center and date; day, month and moonphase by disc, respectively at 9, 3 and 6.

## CALIBER 101/4 (1994)

**Basic caliber:** 101 (1929). Manual-winding movement, 33-hour autonomy.
**Functions:** hours, minutes.
**Shape:** rectangular. **Size:** 4.80x14.00mm.
**Thickness:** 3.40mm.
**Jewels:** 19.
**Balance:** smooth, with two arms, in 14K gold.
**Frequency:** 21,600 vph.
**Balance-spring:** flat, Nivarox 1.
**Shock-absorber system:** Kif.
**Notes:** the pillar-plate is decorated with a circular-graining pattern, the bridges are decorated with Côtes de Genève and circular-graining patterns and beveled. Screw heads are finished by specular polishing. The winding crown is positioned on the rear of the dial side.

## CALIBER 854

Caliber 854, dial-side view. This movement, realized for the purpose of being used in the "Reverso Duoface" model, has the peculiarity that it indicates the time of two different time zones on one of the two opposite dials: in the middle of the main dial and slightly off-center towards 12 on the rear dial. The complex mechanism (patented and consisting of 180 components) also allows quick adjustment of the local time on the main dial by actuating a small pusher positioned on the case middle. On the rear side (the one indicating the "home" time zone when travelling) there is the indispensable 24-hour display at 6.

## CALIBER 854 (1994)

**Basic caliber:** 822 (1992). Manual-winding movement, 45-hour autonomy.
**Functions:** hours, minutes, small seconds; second time-zone (with fast corrector), 24 hours.
**Shape:** tonneau. **Size:** 17.20x22.60mm.
**Thickness:** 3.80mm. **Jewels:** 21 (escape wheel with end-stones).
**Balance:** with compensating screws, with two arms, diameter: 8.50mm, in Glucydur.
**Frequency:** 21,600 vph.
**Balance-spring:** flat, Nivarox 1, with Spirofin micrometer screw regulating device.
**Shock-absorber system:** Kif for balance and escape wheel.
**Notes:** the pillar-plate and bridges are decorated with a circular-graining pattern and beveled. Screw heads are finished by specular polishing.

## CALIBER 849 (1994)

**Basic caliber:** 838 (1975). Manual-winding movement, 35-hour autonomy.
**Functions:** hours, minutes.
**Shape:** round. **Diameter:** 21.10mm (9'''1/4).
**Embedding diameter:** 20.80mm.
**Thickness:** extra-thin, 1.85mm.
**Jewels:** 18 (escape wheel with end-stones).
**Balance:** smooth, with two arms, diameter: 8.40mm, in Glucydur.
**Frequency:** 21,600 vph.
**Balance-spring:** flat, Nivarox 1.
**Shock-absorber system:** Kif for balance and escape wheel.
**Notes:** the pillar-plate is decorated with a circular-graining pattern, the bridges are decorated with a Côtes de Genève pattern and beveled. Screw heads are finished by specular polishing.

# Jaquet Droz

This Swiss manufacture of haute horlogerie upholds the principles of its founder Pierre Jaquet Droz and responds, just as he did, to the demands of a prestigious clientele.

THIS PAGE
This Grande Seconde pocket watch dates back to 1785.

FACING PAGE
The Grande Seconde Émail is a jumping hour watch that is extraordinarily elegant in its presentation both inside and out.

Today, the Jaquet Droz brand is proud to be perpetuating the spirit of this exceptional watchmaker, with exclusive state-of-the-art products, combining non-conformist avant-garde designs with traditional Swiss craftsmanship. As in the days of Pierre Jaquet Droz, the brand's luxury timekeepers are distinguished by their aesthetic refinement and embodiment of meticulous attention to detail and exquisite craftsmanship.

Jaquet Droz timepieces are a tribute to timeless design, while faithfully illustrating the spirit and techniques of the company founder. Some, like the legendary Grande Seconde, have been inspired directly by pocket watches manufactured in the Jaquet Droz workshops of those days. With their large and gently rounded curves, the Grande Seconde watches embody a majestic expression of the beauty of the 18th century pocket watches: generously proportioned, classically styled dials. Through its mastery and refinement, Jaquet Droz confers a resolutely poetic touch on time itself.

Thus far, Jaquet Droz has consistently presented timepieces of rare beauty that are unique in terms of their configuration and their complexity, garnering the company an excellent international reputation. To enhance the sense of privilege enjoyed by its clientele, it has issued extremely limited editions of some of its grand complication watches.

JAQUET DROZ

# Jaquet Droz

TOP RIGHT

The Petite Hour Minute Émail watch houses the self-winding Jaquet Droz caliber 2653-4 movement with double barrel and 22-karat gold rotor. It features off-centered hours and minutes and is water resistant to 30 meters.

FAR LEFT

The Chrono Monopoussoir émail watch is a single-pusher chronograph that houses the self-winding Jaquet Droz 2688M movement with 37 jewels and 40 hours of power reserve.

RIGHT CENTER

This Les Douze Villes émail houses a mechanical movement with jumping hour display and jumping second time-zone indicator. It is created in a limited-edition of 88 pieces and houses the Jaquet Droz caliber 3663-4 self-winding mechanical movement with double barrels.

BOTTOM RIGHT

The Grande Seconde Marine is a bolder-cased watch with off-centered hours and minutes.
It houses the self-winding COSC-certified Jaquet Droz 2663-4 mechanical movement.

Today, as the ultimate luxury, the brand caters to the desires of its demanding clients by providing the opportunity to develop and embellish their own model in keeping with their own preferences. Lapis lazuli, rhodonite, Venus hair, meteorite, onyx, ruby heart, spectrolite, rutilium quartz, black obsidian, snowflake obsidian or Kandertal slate may each be used to adorn the dial of a unique and personal Jaquet Droz watch. Whether one chooses a Grande Seconde, Petite Heure Minute, Les Douze Villes, Les Lunes or a striking Chrono Monopoussoir, the brand offers the possibility of replacing the slate-gray dial with a dial composed of a rare mineral carefully selected by the company or the customer, and skilfully crafted by the dextrous hands of one of its master dial makers. Given the difficulty and extraordinary level of mastery needed to make such a dial, Jaquet Droz produces only one for each natural mineral.

Not only will such a timepiece reveal its true splendor while indicating the time with flawless precision, but also it will accompany its wearer through the beneficial virtues attributed to the chosen mineral, samples of which are harmoniously presented at the most prestigious retailers.

TOP

The 43mm 18K white-gold Tourbillon Répétition Minutes epitomizes the Jaquet Droz style with its slate-gray dial and opaline silvered subdials in an applied 18K white-gold beveled ring (which is drawn out with a file). The Tourbillon Répétition Minutes features a center hour and minute dial, while the subseconds is placed at 9:00, an unique arrangement for Jaquet Droz. This piece is powered by a mechanical, manually wound movement with its tourbillon visible via the caseback.

CENTER

The Les Douze Villes Réhaut is powered by the Jaquet Droz caliber 3663-4, self-winding mechanical movement with jumping hours, 12 time zones and 72-hour power reserve.

BOTTOM

The Grande Seconde Réhaut houses the Jaquet Droz caliber 2663-4 with 72-hour power reserve. The self-winding mechanical movement beats at 28,800 vibrations per hour.

## CHRONOLOGY

**1721** Pierre Jaquet Droz is born in La Chaux-de-Fonds, in the principality of Neuchâtel, Switzerland.

**1738** After his studies of theology at the University of Neuchâtel and physics and mathematics at the Academy of Basel, Jaquet Droz chooses a career in horology and returns to La Chaux-de-Fonds, where he opens his first workshop.

**1758** Following a request from the governor of Neuchâtel, the young watchmaker embarks on a 49-day trip to Spain to demonstrate before King Ferdinand VI the extent of his talents. This venture succeeds beyond his wildest hopes—the young man's timepieces are universally admired in court circles and the king ultimately purchases Jaquet Droz's entire stock for his Madrid and Villaviciosa palaces.

**1774** The money earned in Spain enables Jaquet Droz to concentrate on building the watches, clocks and automata he prefers. With his son Henry-Louis and his adopted son Jean-Frédéric Leschot, he establishes the Jaquet Droz & Leschot Company, opening a second set of workshops in London. Its production is designed essentially for the far-away Chinese market with the Chinese Emperor as his biggest client. At about the same time, Jaquet Droz develops and builds even more elaborated automata, in particular human-like figures known as The Writer, The Musician and The Draughtsman, that will definitely establish the venture's reputation.

**1784** After presenting his automata to Louis XVI and Marie-Antoinette at the French court, business flourishes and the workshops remain busier than ever. Having succumbed to extreme fatigue, Henry-Louis leaves La Chaux-de-Fonds for Geneva, where he opens the city's very first watchmaking workshops.

**1790** Pierre Jaquet Droz passes away in Bienne, Switzerland and his watchmaking is carried on by his two sons.

## GRANDE SECONDE EMAIL — REF. J003034201

**Movement:** Jaquet Droz 2663-4, self-winding mechanical movement; 28,800 vph; 30 jewels; 72-hour power reserve; double barrel; 22K white-gold oscillating weight.
**Case:** Ø 43mm; 18K white gold; individual series number engraved on the caseback; water resistant to 3atm.
**Dial:** ivory colored "grand feu" enameled dial, hand finishing.
**Indications:** off-center hour, minute; extra large subsecond.
**Strap:** rolled-edge handmade black alligator leather; 18K white-gold ardillon buckle.

## GRANDE SECONDE ONYX — REF. J003034222

**Movement:** Jaquet Droz 2663-4, self-winding mechanical movement; 28,800 vph; 30 jewels; 72-hour power reserve; double barrel; 22K white-gold oscillating weight.
**Case:** Ø 43mm; 18K white gold; individual limited series number engraved on caseback; water resistant to 3atm.
**Dial:** onyx; applied 18K white-gold ring beveled and drawn out with a file; secured by blued steel screws.
**Indications:** off-center hour, minute; extra large subsecond.
**Strap:** rolled-edge handmade black alligator leather; 18K white-gold ardillon buckle.
**Note:** limited edition of 8 pieces.

## PETITE HEURE MINUTE ÉMAIL — REF. J005034202

**Movement:** Jaquet Droz 2653-4, self-winding mechanical movement; 28,800 vph; 30 jewels; 72-hour power reserve; double barrel; 22K white-gold oscillating weight.
**Case:** Ø 43mm; 18K white gold; individual series number engraved on the caseback; water resistant to 3atm.
**Dial:** ivory colored "grand feu" enameled dial; ivory colored applied "grand feu" subdial, hand finishing; individual limited series number painted on the dial.
**Indications:** off-center hour and minute.
**Strap:** rolled-edge handmade black alligator leather; 18K white-gold ardillon buckle.
**Note:** limited edition of 88 pieces.

## PETITE HEURE MINUTE RÉHAUT — REF. J005034201

**Movement:** Jaquet Droz 2653-4, self-winding mechanical movement; 28,800 vph; 30 jewels; 72-hour power reserve; double barrel; 22K white-gold oscillating weight.
**Case:** Ø 43mm; 18K white gold; individual series number engraved on the caseback; water resistant to 3atm.
**Dial:** slate gray and opaline silver; applied 18K white-gold ring, beveled and drawn out with a file; secured by blued steel screws.
**Indications:** off-center hour and minute.
**Strap:** rolled-edge handmade black alligator leather; 18K white-gold ardillon buckle.
**Note:** limited edition of 88 pieces.

## GRANDE SECONDE MARINE — REF. J020034201

**Movement:** Jaquet Droz 2663-4; self-winding mechanical movement; 28,800 vph; 30 jewels; 72-hour power reserve; double barrel; 22K white-gold oscillating weight
**Case:** Ø 43mm; 18K white gold; individual limited series number engraved on caseback; screwed bezel, backplate and crown; off-centered bezel, fixed by three screws; water resistant to 10atm.
**Dial:** ivory colored "grand feu" enameled, hand finished; blued hands.
**Indications:** off-center hour, minute; extra large subseconds.
**Note:** limited edition of 88 pieces.

## GRANDE SECONDE CERCLÉE SERTIE DIAMANTS — REF. J003034212

**Movement:** Jaquet Droz 2663-4; self-winding mechanical movement; 28,800 vph; 30 jewels; 72-hour power reserve; double barrel; 22K white-gold oscillating weight.
**Case:** Ø 43mm; 18K white gold; individual limited series number engraved on the caseback; water resistant to 3atm.
**Dial:** opaline slate-gray or black dial; silvered subdials; blued hands, screws; 18K white-gold ring set with 62 diamonds.
**Indications:** off-center hour, minute; extra large subseconds.

## GRANDE SECONDE GRAVÉE — REF. J003034207

**Movement:** Jaquet Droz 2663-4; self-winding mechanical movement; 28,800 vph; 30 jewels; 72-hour power reserve; double barrel; 22K white-gold oscillating weight.
**Case:** Ø 43mm; 18K white gold; individual limited series number engraved on the caseback; water resistant to 3atm.
**Dial:** engraved champagne-colored dial, silvered subdials; applied 18K white-gold ring, beveled and drawn out with a file; secured by blued steel screws.
**Indications:** off-center hour, minute; extra large subseconds.
**Note:** limited edition of 88 pieces.

## GRANDE SECONDE GRAVÉE — REF. J003033201

**Movement:** Jaquet Droz 2663-4; self-winding mechanical movement; 28,800 vph; 30 jewels; 72-hour power reserve; double barrel; 22K white-gold oscillating weight.
**Case:** Ø 43mm; 18K red gold; individual limited series number engraved on the caseback; water resistant to 3atm.
**Dial:** engraved silver dial, silvered subdials; applied 18K red-gold ring, beveled and drawn out with a file; secured by blued steel screws.
**Indications:** off-center hour, minute; extra large subseconds.
**Note:** limited edition of 88 pieces.

## LES DOUZES VILLES ÉMAIL — REF. J010124202

**Movement:** Jaquet Droz 3663-4; self-winding mechanical movement; 28,800 vph; 28 jewels; 72 hour power reserve; double barrel; 22K gold oscillating weight.
**Case:** Ø 40.5mm; 18K white gold; individual limited series number engraved on caseback; water resistant to 3atm.
**Dial:** ivory colored "grand feu" enameled dial; ivory colored applied "grand feu" subdial, hand finishing; individual limited series number painted on the dial.
**Indications:** jumping hour and 12 time zones (12 cities) through an aperture; pointer-type minute display.
**Strap:** rolled-edge handmade black alligator leather; 18K white-gold ardillon buckle.
**Note:** limited edition of 88 pieces.

## LES DOUZE VILLES RÉHAUT — REF. J010124201

**Movement:** Jaquet Droz 3663-4; self-winding mechanical movement; 28,800 vph; 28 jewels; 72 hour power reserve; double barrel; 22K gold oscillating weight.
**Case:** Ø 40.5mm; 18K white gold; individual series number engraved on caseback; water resistant to 3atm.
**Dial:** slate gray and opaline silver; applied 18K white-gold ring, beveled and drawn out with a file; secured by blued steel screws.
**Indications:** jumping hour and 12 time zones (12 cities) through an aperture; pointer-type minute display.
**Strap:** rolled-edge handmade black alligator leather; 18K white-gold ardillon buckle.

## LES LUNES EMAIL — REF. J012624201

**Movement:** Jaquet Droz 6553-4, self-winding mechanical movement, complete calendar; 28,800 vph; 28 jewels; 72-hour power reserve; double barrel; 22K gold oscillating weight.
**Functions:** hour, minute; complete calendar with days and months through aperture; pointer-type date; retrograding moonphase hand.
**Case:** Ø 40.5mm; 18K white gold; individual limited series number engraved on caseback; water resistant to 3atm.
**Dial:** ivory colored "grand feu" enameled dial; hand finishing; individual limited series number painted on the dial.
**Strap:** rolled-edge handmade black alligator leather; 18K white-gold ardillon buckle.
**Note:** limited edition of 88 pieces.

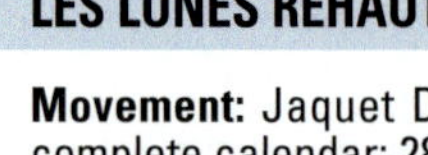

## LES LUNES RÉHAUT — REF. J012624205

**Movement:** Jaquet Droz 6553-4, self-winding mechanical movement, complete calendar; 28,800 vph; 28 jewels; 72-hour power reserve; double barrel; 22K gold oscillating weight.
**Functions:** hour, minute; complete calendar with days and months through aperture; pointer-type date; retrograding moonphase hand.
**Case:** Ø 40.5mm; 18K white gold; individual limited series number engraved on caseback; water resistant to 3atm.
**Dial:** slate gray and opaline silver; applied 18K white-gold ring, beveled and drawn out with a file; secured by blued steel screws.
**Strap:** rolled-edge handmade black alligator leather; 18K white-gold ardillon buckle.

## CHRONO MONOPOUSSOIR EMAIL — REF. J007634201

**Movement:** Jaquet Droz 2688M, single pushbutton self-winding chronograph movement; 21,600 vph; 37 jewels; 40-hour power reserve double barrel; 22K gold oscillating weight.
**Case:** Ø 43mm; 18K white gold; individual series number engraved on caseback; water resistant to 3atm.
**Dial:** ivory colored "grand feu" enameled dial; ivory colored applied enameled "grand feu" subdial; hand finishing; individual series number painted on the dial.
**Indications:** hour, minute (subdial at 12), subsecond at 6; central chronograph sweep seconds hand; chronograph counter at 9; chronograph minute counter at 3.
**Strap:** rolled-edge handmade black alligator leather; 18K white-gold ardillon buckle.
**Note:** limited edition of 88 pieces.

## CHRONO MONOPOUSSOIR RÉHAUT — REF. J007634202

**Movement:** Jaquet Droz 2688M, single pushbutton self-winding chronograph movement; 21,600 vph; 37 jewels; 40-hour power reserve; double barrel; 22K gold oscillating weight.
**Case:** Ø 43mm; 18K white gold; individual series number engraved on caseback; water resistant to 3atm.
**Dial:** slate gray and opaline silver; applied 18K white-gold ring beveled and drawn out with a file; secured by blued steel screws.
**Indications:** hour, minute (subdial at 12); subsecond at 6; central chronograph sweep seconds hand; chronograph counter at 9; chronograph minute counter at 3.
**Strap:** rolled-edge handmade black alligator leather; 18K white-gold ardillon buckle.

## TOURBILLON RÉPÉTITION MINUTES — REF. J011834202

**Movement:** Jaquet Droz 2629.T, mechanical movement with tourbillon visible on the movement side; 18,800 vph; 36 jewels; 48-hour power reserve; monometallic thermally compensated balance wheel with screws and Breguet hairspring; minute repeater, striker to order on two gongs with two hammers.
**Case:** Ø 43mm; 18K white gold; individual limited series number engraved on caseback.
**Dial:** slate gray and opaline silver; applied 18K white-gold ring bevelled and drawn out with a file; secured by blued steel screws.
**Indications:** central hour, minute; subsecond at 9.
**Strap:** rolled-edge handmade black alligator leather; 18K white-gold ardillon buckle.
**Note:** limited edition of 8 pieces.

## BACK OF TOURBILLON RÉPÉTITION MINUTES — REF. J011834205

**Movement:** Jaquet Droz 2629.T, mechanical movement with tourbillon visible on the movement side; 18,800 vph; 36 jewels; 48-hour power reserve; monometallic thermally compensated balance wheel with screws and Breguet hairspring; minute repeater, striker to order on two gongs with two hammers.

# JEAN-MAIRET & GILLMAN

A young brand based on an old history—one wrapped in adventure and intrigue—Jean-Mairet & Gillman creates mechanical timepieces for today's international traveler.

THIS PAGE

TOP

This stainless steel Hora Mundi is set with a row of diamonds. The watch offers an alarm and world timer.

FACING PAGE

The brand new Caesar Augusto with one-minute tourbillon and 110 hours of power reserve.

With a very rich family history in the worlds of watchmaking and exploration, César A. Jean-Mairet founded his firm intent on personifying his family's traditions in his timepieces. Among the exciting timepieces from this brand are the Grand Voyageur (its first watch ever unveiled), the Seven Days, and the Hora Mundi. Each of these 18-karat-gold timepieces is handcrafted in the company's Geneva workshops in very limited numbers.

Another piece characteristic of Jean-Mairet & Gillman is the Chronographe Alexandre No. 2. First unveiled in 2003, this chronograph is crafted in 18-karat gold or platinum and is now available with a stunning white dial that is strikingly clean and sophisticated. A new Lady Fiona Diamonds was recently unveiled as the brand's first foray into steel. This watch features a shimmering five-row steel bracelet and a bezel with diamond accents. The automatic Lady Fiona Diamonds has a slate blue-gray mother-of-pearl dial.

Typical of this brand, all timepieces house mechanical movements that have been hand-embellished in house and individually finished to exacting standards.

At BaselWorld 2005, Jean-Mairet & Gillman will reveal to watch aficionados a tri-retrograde timepiece and its first tourbillon, the Caesar Augusto.

## CHRONOLOGY

**1766** Jean-Henry Mairet invents industry tooling for watchmaking.

**1800s** Horologist Sylvain Jean-Mairet begins building precision timepieces. Over the years he creates a double-stem-wind watch and perfects several lever devices.

**1884** Sylvain Jean-Mairet develops a carriage watch movement.

**1900s** André Jean-Mairet is appointed chief of workshops at one of Switzerland's key watchmaking schools. He wins more than 115 first prizes for creative watchmaking and technical advancements from the Neuchâtel Observatory.

**1999** César A. Jean-Mairet initiates development of his own collection of exclusive timepieces.

**2000** A combination of César's paternal and maternal heritages (the famous Bovets of Fleurier), Jean-Mairet & Gillman is registered, and he creates the brand's first prototype, the Grand Voyageur. The collection includes the Grand Voyageur automatic timepiece with second time zone and mechanical alarm. The Seven Days watch offers seven days of power reserve in its manual-wind movement.

**2001** The brand unveils the Grand Voyageur and Seven Days collections as the signature series of Jean-Mairet & Gillman.

**2002** The company makes its world debut at the Basel Watch and Jewelry Fair. It unveils the Hora Mundi (Hours of the World) watch with GMT timing and mechanical alarm function.

**2003** Jean-Mairet & Gillman unveils the Chronographe Alexandre 2 with automatic caliber.

**2004** Lady Fiona, the brand's first women's automatic watch in stainless steel with diamonds, is introduced. The Chronographe Alexandre 2 is available in stainless steel.

## GRAND VOYAGEUR "HALF MOON" AUTOMATIC DUAL TIME / LIMITED EDITION

**Movement:** automatic Dual Time and Alarm; caliber JMG 1999/AS 5900; engraved oscillating mass; 31 jewels; 4Hz / 28,800 vph; 42-44 hours' power reserve.
**Functions:** hours, minutes, center seconds; date; self-winding alarm system; second time zone. All functions operated by two crowns.
**Case:** polished stainless steel; round; Ø 41mm, 14mm thick; bezel set with 44 Top Wesselton diamonds (0.86 carats); sapphire crystal caseback, individually numbered and engraved on the back; water resistant to 3atm.
**Dial:** lacquered black; 12 applied rhodium markers; round date-window; printed minute track with luminescent dots; luminescent arrow-shaped hands.
**Strap:** hand-stitched alligator with folding clasp in stainless steel.
**Also available:** 39mm; 18K rose or white gold.
**Note:** 200-piece limited edition in steel; 50-piece limited edition in 18K gold.

## GRAND VOYAGEUR AUTOMATIC DUAL TIME / LIMITED EDITION

**Movement:** automatic Dual Time and Alarm; caliber JMG 1999/AS 5900; decorated 18K rose-gold oscillating mass; 31 jewels; 4Hz / 28,800 vph; 42-44 hours' power reserve.
**Functions:** hours, minutes, center seconds; date; self-winding alarm; second time zone. All functions operated by two crowns.
**Case:** polished 18K rose gold; round; Ø 41mm, 14mm thick; sapphire crystal bezel caseback, individually numbered and engraved on the back; water resistant to 3atm.
**Dial:** lacquered white; 12 blue applied markers; printed minute track; round date-windows at 4:30; large second time-zone window at 12; arrow-shaped hands.
**Strap:** hand-stitched alligator with folding clasp in 18K rose gold.
**Also available:** in steel or 18K white gold.
**Note:** 200-piece limited edition in steel; 50-piece limited edition in 18K gold.

## GRAND VOYAGEUR LADY AUTOMATIC DUAL TIME / LIMITED EDITION

**Movement:** automatic Dual Time and Alarm; caliber JMG 1999/AS 5900; decorated 18K gold oscillating mass; 31 jewels; 4Hz / 28,800 vph; 42-44 hours' power reserve.
**Functions:** hours, minutes, center seconds; date; self-winding alarm; second-time zone. All functions operated by two crowns.
**Case:** polished 18K rose gold; round; Ø 41mm, 14mm thick; bezel set with 144 pink sapphires (1.9 carats); sapphire crystal caseback, individually numbered and engraved on the back; water resistant to 3atm.
**Dial:** pink mother-of-pearl; 12 applied blue markers; printed minute track; round date-window; large second time-zone window at 12; arrow-shaped hands.
**Strap:** hand-stitched alligator with folding clasp in 18K rose gold.
**Also available:** 39mm; 18K white gold.

## LADY FIONA AUTOMATIC / LIMITED EDITION

**Movement:** automatic; caliber JMG 2003-2 / ETA 2000; 20 jewels; 28,800 vph; 42-44 hours' power reserve.
**Functions:** hours and minutes.
**Case:** polished stainless steel; round; Ø 37mm, 10mm thick; individually numbered and engraved on the back; water resistant to 3atm; rotating bezel set with 72 Top Wesselton diamonds (0.75 carats).
**Dial:** black mother-of-pearl with 6 applied rhodium Arabic markers and 6 applied diamonds dots; 18K white-gold arrow-shaped hands.
**Bracelet:** stainless steel with folding clasp.
**Also available:** on leather strap with folding clasp; can be set with colored stones or diamonds.
**Note:** 100-piece limited edition.

## HORA MUNDI AUTOMATIC WORLDTIME + ALARM / LIMITED EDITION

**Movement:** automatic Worldtime and Alarm; caliber JMG 1999 / AS 5900; decorated 18K rose-gold oscillating mass; 31 jewels; 4Hz / 28,800 vph; 42-44 hours' power reserve.
**Functions:** hours, minutes, center seconds; date; self-winding alarm; 24-hour worldtime. All functions operated by two crowns.
**Case:** polished 18K rose gold; round; Ø 41mm, 14mm thick; sapphire crystal caseback, individually numbered and engraved on the back; water resistant to 3atm.
**Dial:** matte black/silver zone with printed cities; open center with 24-hour disc; 12 pink-gold applied dots; printed minute track; arrow-shaped hands.
**Strap:** hand-stitched alligator with 18K rose-gold folding clasp.
**Also available:** in steel or 18K white gold.
**Note:** 200-piece limited edition in steel; 50-piece limited edition in 18K gold.

## CAESAR AUGUSTO TOURBILLON

**Movement:** one-minute tourbillon; flat balance spring; 21,000 vph; aligned barrel; center wheel and hand-chamfered carriage; approx. 110 hours' power reserve; pink-gold guilloché bridges; mystery winding; wheel with curved, hand-chamfered arms; wheels, ratchet-wheel and barrel with wolf teeth.
**Functions:** day/night; days, weeks; retrograde hours for 12-hour second time zone.
**Case:** pink gold case; Ø 44mm, thickness: 16mm; sapphire crystal; back attached with screws, displaying the movement through a sapphire crystal.
**Dial:** fired-enameled dial; blued steel hands.

## CHRONOGRAPHE ALEXANDRE 2 AUTOMATIC / LIMITED EDITION

**Movement:** automatic Chronograph; caliber JMG 2003 / DD2046; decorated 18K rose-gold oscillating mass; 39 jewels; 4Hz / 28,800 vph; 42-44 hours' power reserve.
**Functions:** chronograph with central counter on 45 minutes; small seconds at 12.
**Case:** polished 18K rose gold; round; Ø 41mm, 14mm thick; sapphire crystal caseback, individually numbered and engraved on the back; water resistant to 3atm.
**Dial:** dark gray; 12 applied 4N markets and luminescent dots; printed minute track on 45 minutes in white at center; 18K rose-gold and luminescent arrow-shaped hands.
**Strap:** hand-stitched alligator with 18K rose-gold folding clasp.
**Also available:** in steel or 18K white gold.
**Note:** 100-piece limited edition in steel; 50-piece limited edition in 18K gold.

## CHRONOGRAPHE ALEXANDRE 2 "DISC" AUTOMATIC / LIMITED EDITION

**Movement:** automatic Chronograph; caliber JMG 2003 / DD2046; decorated 18K rose-gold oscillating mass; 39 jewels; 4Hz / 28,800 vph; 42-44 hours' power reserve.
**Functions:** chronograph with central counter on 45 minutes; small seconds shown on a disc in large window.
**Case:** polished 18K rose gold; round; Ø 41m, 14mm thick; sapphire crystal caseback, individually numbered and engraved on the back; water resistant to 3atm.
**Dial:** sand-blasted in silver; 12 applied 4N markers and luminescent dots; printed minute track on 45 minutes at center; 18K rose-gold and luminescent arrow-shaped hands.
**Strap:** hand-stitched alligator with 18K rose-gold folding clasp.
**Also available:** in steel or 18K white gold.
**Note:** 100-piece limited edition in steel; 50-piece limited edition in 18K gold.

# JEANRICHARD

Young but incredibly innovative in design, JeanRichard is a brand dedicated to originality blended with watchmaking tradition.

In just a few short years, JeanRichard has built a stellar reputation with its retro-styled TV Screen and Chronoscope watches. Owned and operated by the Sowind Group (which owns Girard-Perregaux), the brand thrives on a free-spirited independence inspired by the legendary Gino Macaluso.

Now, JeanRichard unveils its first proprietary movement, an example of the purest values of traditional watchmaking. The JR 1000, designed by and for JeanRichard, is made entirely within the Sowind Manufacture. It is an automatic mechanical movement with a unidirectional rotor featuring the circular Côtes de Genève decoration. The movement houses 142 components and 32 rubies. Beating at 28,800 vibrations per hour, the movement offers 48 hours of power reserve, center hour and minute, small second at 9:00 with stop second, and date window with instant date change.

The JR 1000 has two interesting technical features. One is a double third wheel and pinion that makes it possible to have a direct-drive center seconds hand, comprising of a single pinion and created in a space suitable for a larger barrel, which allows for more power reserve. There is also a small seconds at 9:00 that is driven by micro-modular gears (or micro-toothing) that allows for instantaneous time setting and starting of the minute hand.

To house this all-new movement, JeanRichard created an all-new case, and thus, an all-new watch: the Paramount JR 1000. This stunning square timepiece features bold contours that are unequivocally contemporary. The spear-head of an entire new line, the Paramount JR 1000 watch features a transparent caseback displaying the precision mechanism. Presented with either a black or silvered dial with gilded Arabic numerals and faceted skeleton sword-style hands, the watch is created in a limited edition of 1,000 pieces in steel and 25 pieces in pink gold.

THIS PAGE

ABOVE

The JR 1000 is the brand's first proprietary movement. The automatic caliber offers 48 hours of power reserve.

FACING PAGE

The Paramount JR 1000 combines a completely new JeanRichard case with the new JR 1000 movement. The retro-styled watch is superb with subseconds at 9:00 and date at 4:30.

JEANRICHARD
JR1000
SWISS MADE

Offering a vast array of beauties in its Lady Collection, JeanRichard presents the stunning TV Screen Milady Joaillerie in a variety of subtle colors that belie femininity. This model is created for contemporary women who appreciate bold creativity. It is adorned with precious stones for chic glamour. The watch is then color-coordinated with a pastel mother-of-pearl dial and a matching galuchat strap. Even the hands on the watch are color-coordinated.

The watch is available in striking green, blue or purple. Gemstones include sapphires, emeralds, rubies, amethysts, spessartites and diamonds in varying degrees. Styles range from models with 50 full-cut stones on the bezel, to those with 70 full-cut gems on the bezel and lugs, to the totally bedecked 150 full-cut stone version with gems on the bezel, lugs and case. The watch houses the mechanical automatic-winding JR 25 caliber with 25 rubies and 38 hours of power reserve.

THIS PAGE

LEFT

The TV Screen Milady Joaillerie features color-coordinated gemstones with pastel mother-of-pearl dials with a matching galuchat strap.

ABOVE

JeanRichard Villa North.

FACING PAGE

TOP

JeanRichard Villa South.

CENTER

A statue of Daniel JeanRichard stands proudly in front of the watchmaking school in Le Locle.

BOTTOM

This pocket watch is signed "Daniel JeanRichard, Le Locle, beginning 17th C."

## CHRONOLOGY

**1665** Daniel JeanRichard, considered one of the founders of the watchmaking industry in the Swiss Jura Mountains, is born.

**Late 1980s** The brand Daniel JeanRichard is acquired by Dr. Luigi "Gino" Macaluso, President of the Sowind Group. He sets out to restore the brand to its former eminence.

**Early 1990s** Production begins again and the brand focuses on the Italian market.

**1996** Through its successful integration into the world's most prominent watch markets, Daniel JeanRichard confirms a powerful international presence that it will carry into the third millennium.

**1999** In its first showing at the Salon International de la Haute Horlogerie in Geneva, the brand presents a special, gold, limited series of the TV Screen Chronograph and TV Screen Split-seconds along with the Bressel Chronograph and Chronoscope. These models are extremely well received by Daniel JeanRichard's agents and international distributors.

**2000** The brand makes some prudent additions to its collection, notably the Grand TV Screen Flyback chronograph with large date, and a Bressel GMT chronograph; Daniel JeanRichard pursues the development of its image and increases its presence in markets such as Italy, the United States and Japan through the Sowind Group's Tradema subsidiaries.

**2001** Daniel JeanRichard continues its steady development and increases its international points of sale—each carefully selected to match the specific nature of the company's models; At the Salon International de la Haute Horlogerie, the brand presents its first line for ladies: the TV Screen Lady features a steel case adorned with a diamond bezel.

**2003** Daniel JeanRichard is officially referred to as JeanRichard.

# LOCMAN ITALY

Today, the Locman Group represents the most important Italian watchmaking enterprise in the industry.

The heart of Locman's watches strikes on Elba, in the premises overlooking on the bay of Campo, where a team of professionals works together like a well-oiled machine. Living on an island of Tuscany is their choice of life, friendship and style. Here, close to the seaside, ideas are borne and strategies devised, both technical and commercial. But this is not all. Marina di Campo houses Locman's administrative offices, technical laboratories, the quality management, as well as the assembly department of the most sophisticated lines, warehouses and logistics.

Further production stages are carried out in Milan, inside the Genesi industrial compound, where a staff of 25 master watchmakers works in compliance with the highest quality standards. It is considered the most efficient and modern Italian watchmaking factory. Cases and high-tech components are produced inside the laboratories of Materie Future, the Group's industrial company based on the Island of Elba with its factory in Vicenza. At Materie Future, in a highly sophisticated and protected environment, a team of skilled engineers is devoted to the research and mechanics of technologically advanced materials, such as carbon fiber, titanium, aluminum and alternative alloys. Communication strategies and relations with the mass-media sector are managed by Marchio Giallo, the internal advertising agency of the Locman Group in Milan.

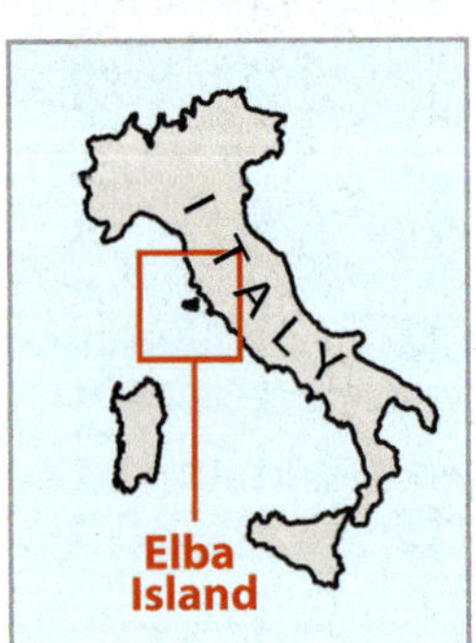

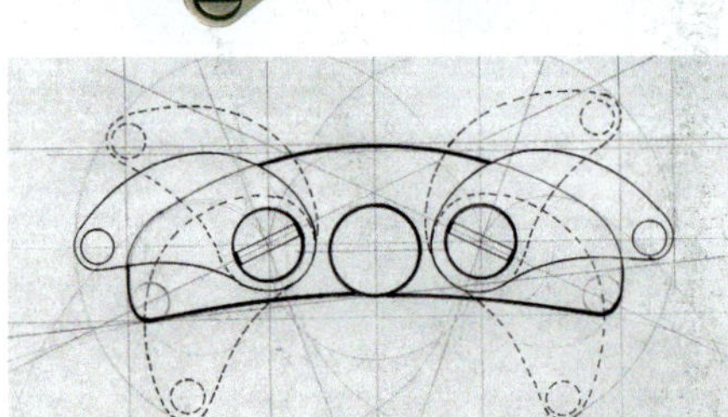

THIS PAGE

FAR LEFT

***top:*** Marco Mantovani (left) with Ben Feigenbaum, presidents of Locman Italy and Locman USA.

***center:*** Detail of Locman's Elba headquarters.

TOP RIGHT

The Latin Lover features an extreme bend in its dial.

ABOVE

The Latin Lover is available with and without diamonds.

FACING PAGE

Modern and casual, the new pink-gold Panorama is powerd by a mechanical automatic-winding ETA movement. The ladies' version is available with brilliants.

LOCMAN
ITALY
AUTOMATIC
18
LOCMAN
ITALY

## DIAMOND COLLECTIONS

Locman lit a firecracker when it created the Diamond Aluminum Collection five years ago, completely altering the face of time.

Since, it has launched a host of scintillating diamond-adorned models with many faces and cases in all shapes and materials. The newest lines include the bold Latin Lover and the Panorama Diamond, which together expand the Locman Diamond collection to offer thousands of combinations.

The steel Latin Lover Diamond is a romantic rendition with moveable lugs that hug the wrist and offers date indication. The ladies' automatic Panorama Diamond is available in pink gold and also features date indication.

**TOP RIGHT**

Locman's signature Diamond Aluminum Tonneau collection appeals to collectors with a wide selection of models in three sizes, varying degrees of diamonds, and chronograph versions.

**FAR LEFT**

The Nuovo Oval is an elegant timepiece with a curvaceous design, a steel case and mother of pearl dial framed by a line of glittering diamonds weighing 0.5 carat. The face and coconut-fiber strap come in many soft pastel colors such as pink, baby blue, ivory, and white.

**TOP**

Cavallo Pazzo collection. The lugs—covered with handset natural brilliants in the diamond version—flow over the rounded case and shaped pushers. The strap is available in colored iguana or rubber. The Cavello Pazzo offers chronograph functions and is water resistant to 5atm.

**BOTTOM**

Locman's Classic Diamond.

The Cavallo Pazzo (Crazy Horse) is an alluringly bold collection of watches that bears the colors of New York City graffiti, the warmth of Hispanic dancing places, and the shine of exclusive Parisian partiers. This is a trendy watch, extremely innovative and impressive with excessive luxury.

## HIGH-TECH MATERIAL

Locman is marrying high-tech and tradition, combining materials such as aluminum, carbon and titanium with classic elements such as diamonds and mother-of-pearl, to the effect of unmistakable Italian style. Locman's production distinguishes itself by embracing the newest, most advanced technologies. In 2002, the company founded a new enterprise, Materie Future Srl, for the study and production of high-tech materials, such as titanium and carbon fiber.

The latter is a product offering shock-resistance, compressive strength and anticorrosive features unknown in nature and particularly suitable for technological applications requiring extreme resistance and lightness. It is a modern material with a future, as sharp as diamond: in fact, diamond is pure carbon. Carbon fiber was a challenge for Locman's engineers, but finally the result achieved was surprising: a texture, a kind of fabric with extraordinary features, extremely light, hard and above all highly resistant.

Thus, the first watches with carbon-fiber cases were produced, waterproof and provided with scratchproof sapphire crystals and titanium components.

FACING PAGE

TOP LEFT

Profile of the 1970 Titanio.

TOP CENTER

Available in a mechanical automatic version with an ETA 2824.2 movement and in a quartz chronograph version, the 1970 Titanio is water resistant to 5atm and comes with a matching Lorica sport strap.

RIGHT

Watchmakers at work in Locman's factory.

BOTTOM

Locman's sporty Nuovo Carbonio.

Titanium is also an extremely light material, resistant and incredibly compatible with our bodies—which makes it very useful to surgeons as a perfect material for prostheses and other biomedical products. Locman adopted it for the brand's ergonomic cases and gave it the brilliance and reflection of more precious materials. Thus, the famous Titanio Lucidato Locman metal was born, a white and brilliant material used for the bezel of the Mare Carbonio model and the case of the Tonneau Titanio. Finding new design solutions through new technology presents constant challenges for Locman's research units—challenges they embrace in order to propose futuristic watches with soul, capable of imposing fashions and trends. Years of research and investment in high-tech materials has led to very prestigious achievements for Locman: the House of Elba is the first horology business in the world to realize watches equipped with cases in carbon fiber and titanium.

THIS PAGE

BOTTOM

The Mare Carbonio.

## CHRONOLOGY

**1986** Locman Italy is established on the idyllic Isle of Elba, with additional offices in Milan. The brand's debut collection, the Radica, features briarwood bezels crafted from Mediterranean trees dating back 300 years.

**1987-1998** The Radica collection grows to include more than 36 styles. It evolves into a steel-cased line with wood bezels.

**1999** The Locman Aluminum Sport watch collection is introduced in Italy. Its lightweight case and extreme design makes it an immediate hit.

**2000** The Locman Diamond Aluminum represents the first time a watch company has paired diamonds with aluminum—demonstrating Locman's confidence and adventurous spirit. There is one tonneau-shaped time-only model and one chronograph model launched within the original line. Several months later, Locman unveils the Full Pavé with more than 2 carats of diamonds on the regular watch and nearly 4 carats on the chronograph.

**2001** The Mother-of-pearl Full Pavé collection is launched and features vibrant or pastel-colored dials and coordinated straps.

**2002** Locman wins the prestigious Premio Argo award in Italy for innovation in men's fashions. Also this year, the brand unveils its first full-titanium line, called the Titanio; the Luna, an oversized domed-crystal aluminum watch; and the striking square Quadrato collection of aluminum watches with and without diamonds are launced. Locman becomes involved with international yacht racing as a sponsor of the first annual Toscana Elba Cup Trophy Locman Regatta. Locman also opens a store in the high-end Ginza district of Tokyo, Japan and moves its American headquarters to Madison Avenue in New York City. The brand founds a sibling company, Materie Future.

**2003** On the famed Via Tornabuoni in Florence, Italy, the brand opens an exclusive Locman-only store in one of the most historic palaces in the city, Palazzo Tornabuoni. In addition to Locman timepieces, the store sells its new collection of fine leather goods and writing tools. Locman introduces an expanded collection of titanium watches and the powerful Latin Lover.

**2004** Introduction of the rose-gold Panorama and the Cavallo Pazzo collections.

## BOUTIQUES

Locman watches are found in the best jeweler's shops around the world and, of course, the exclusive Locman boutiques, whose design philosophies reflect that of the watches—perfect blends of technology and tradition. Locman shops are marked with the distinct style of Tuscany, from those in Tokyo to Porto Cervo to the streets of the Island of Elba. Typically, Lombard elegance and simplicity are the inspiration behind the Brescia and Salò boutiques. In Florence, Locman renovated an exquisite location in the 15th century Loggia del Cigoli, in the lower floors of one of the city's most ancient buildings, Palazzo Tornabuoni near Palazzo Strozzi. The newest Locman boutique is on the Namichi Dori, Tokyo—Japan's capital's most exclusive street, where the international fashion sector's leading ateliers are located.

THIS PAGE

FAR LEFT

Interiors of Locman boutiques *(from top to bottom)*: in Florence, Brescia, Marina di Campo and Salo.

ABOVE

Front façade of Locman boutique in Port Ferraio, Island of Elba.

BOTTOM

A brand new Locman boutique in Namichi Dori, the most exclusive street in Tokyo, Japan.

FACINNG PAGE

The stunning Locman store in Florence, Italy is located in the famed Palazzo Tornabuoni.

LOCMAN
ITALY

# LONGINES

With its roots in the early 19th century, Longines has grown from a three-man partnership in a tiny workshop surrounded by meadow land situated in the Jura mountain range of western Switzerland into a center of all-round traditional horological excellence whose products are highly regarded the world over. Early in its history, the company set its sights on the design and production of superlative watch movements.

THIS PAGE

ABOVE

**First Longines watch (1867)**

With the inauguration of a new factory in 1867, the production of the first Longines movement, the L20A, began. Breaking with traditional construction, the watch featured a lever movement, wound and set by the crown. The design won a bronze medal at the Paris Universal Exhibition that year.

LEFT

**First Longines stopwatch (1878)**

Collaborating with caliber designer H.-A. Lugrin, Longines developed its first pocket chronograph with a subdial for the seconds: caliber L20H. It was the first in a long series of chronographs and timers with which the company built an enviable reputation over the years.

FACING PAGE

**L2.631.4.78.2**

This patented self-winding mechanical movement encased in this GMT wristwatch from The Longines Master Collection not only indicates time and date but also allows the time to be read in any of the world's 23 other time zones, thanks to its rotating 24-hour inner disc and time-zone ring. It is housed in a stainless steel case on a brown, genuine leather strap.

In 1867, its very first proprietary caliber L20A, wound by a crown instead of a key, earned the company the first of the many distinctions it was to win at international shows, fairs and exhibitions. That initial success was followed in 1878 by the L20H single-pushpiece chronograph caliber, the first single-pushpiece chronograph L13.13 for the wrist in 1913, the L13ZN flyback design of 1936 and the 24-line L262 chronograph caliber in 1939. In 1945 Longines also produced the first self-winding movement with a bi-directional oscillating weight, the L22A, along with two truly exceptional movement designs: its celebrated caliber L360 in 1959, the "observatory caliber" (the most distinguished wristwatch movement for its precision at the time), and caliber L990 in 1977, the world's slimmest of its day with twin barrels, center seconds and date aperture.

L'ELEGANCE DU TEMPS DEPUIS 1832

THE LONGINES
MASTER
COLLECTION

ABOVE

**Olympic Timer (1939)**

1939 saw the introduction of Longines's famed "Olympic timer" to a $1/10^{th}$ of a second, available with or without a flyback split-seconds hand and fitted with a very rare type of movement for the period, beating at 36,000 vibrations per hour.

Swiftly upgraded for the 1940 Olympic Games in Helsinki, for which Longines had been appointed official timekeeper, the "Olympic timer" featured a totalizer that completed a dial rotation in three minutes. Alas, World War II caused the cancellation of the Games and consigned Longines's exceptional instruments to its Saint-Imier workshops.

When Charles A. Lindbergh designed his famed "hour-angle watch," the company to which he entrusted its production was naturally none other than Longines.

In short order, the company reorganized and expanded its production, decided to call itself Longines, adopted its winged hourglass symbol and focused its attention and energy on the two areas of watchmaking that have ensured its sterling reputation ever since: impeccable design totally in tune with market expectations and high-quality watch and chronograph movements. Longines chronographs, timers and photo-finish installations starred decade after decade at Olympic Games and international competitions.

That heritage has been evidently infused into Longines product lines ever since.

LEFT

**L990 movement (1977)**

Introduced in early 1977, the pride and joy of Longines's seasoned team of watchmakers was the self-winding L990 caliber (the last it was to design and build) and it proved highly successful. The company kept it in production for an entire decade. The L990 was later purchased by Nouvelle Lémania, a complex-movement specialist who upgraded the design and continues to produce it today.

# The Longines MasterCollection

## Styled for today

With so distinguished a track record, Longines's latest entry displays the full measure of the company's experience and expertise. Elegantly masculine in character and dimensions, The Longines Master Collection comprises ten designs, all housed in stainless steel cases ranging in diameter from 38.5 to 47.5mm to suit all wrist sizes. Every model is equipped with a mechanical movement, either hand-wound or self-winding, with, in every case but one, a standard power reserve of 42 hours. Nearly all include one or more additional features.

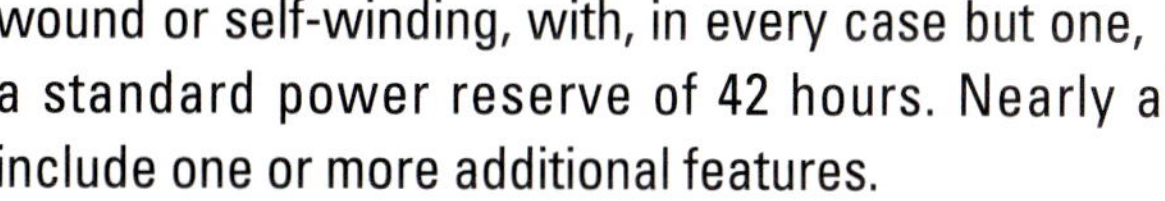

**TOP LEFT**

**L2.629.4.78.6**

Featuring a sleek stainless steel case and bracelet, this wrist chronograph from The Longines Master Collection records and displays time spans from $1/5^{th}$ second to 30 minutes, read off its center chronograph hand and 30-minute totalizer. Blued-steel hands also indicate the time of day to the second and the watch features a date aperture.

**FAR RIGHT**

**L2.666.4.78.6**

Along with the precise time of day and date, the dial of this stainless steel wristwatch from The Longines Master Collection indicates the remaining energy stored in the mainspring of its self-winding mechanical movement. The broad, uncluttered flinqué enamel dial is decorated with a classical barleycorn pattern.

**BOTTOM LEFT**

**L2.628.4.78.2**

This stainless steel watch from The Longines Master Collection is powered by a self-winding mechanical movement with a power reserve of 42 hours. Hours, minutes, center seconds and date aperture at 6:00 are arranged on a silver-finished flinqué enamel dial with a brown, genuine leather strap.

**BOTTOM RIGHT**

**L2.640.4.78.2**

From The Longines Master Collection, the dial's width reveals the subtle refinement of its flinqué enamel face. Stamped on a silvery background, a classic barleycorn pattern coated in transparent enamel provides a stylish backdrop for its blued-steel hands. A stainless steel case houses a hand-wound mechanical movement and is complemented with a brown, genuine leather strap.

# THE LONGINES MASTER COLLECTION

Along with a display of the hours, minutes and seconds, The Longines Master Collection offers a choice of single or double date aperture, a power-reserve indicator, a chronograph with center seconds and a 30-minute totalizer, a GMT display with a rotating interior setting disc and a 24-hour timezone display (on a Longines-patented movement) or a moonphase display and a chronograph with center seconds, 30-minute and 12-hour totalizers plus a 24-hour hand and a circular calendar.

In short, a variety of practical, easy-to-operate additional features makes The Longines Master Collection an attractive choice for any man whose interests extend to sport and leisure activities, and of course travel, along with his professional tasks. All the more reason that Longines watch dials display a rare styling refinement under its scratch-resistant sapphire crystal: a flinqué finish featuring a silver-toned dial neatly stamped with a traditional barleycorn pattern and coated with a fine layer of transparent enamel, over which two or more handsome blued-steel hands move.

**TOP LEFT**

**L2.676.4.78.6**

With its perfect balance of traditional and contemporary features, this wristwatch from The Longines Master Collection is sure to appeal worldwide to a broad range of tastes. The subdial for the seconds, historic hour figures and blued-steel hands recall the early years of the 20th century while the generous dimensions of its flawlessly integrated stainless steel bracelet and case, double date aperture and tried and tested low-maintenance self-winding mechanical movement reflect the best of watchmaking today.

**RIGHT**

**L2.665.4.78.6**

Its stainless steel case and bracelet give this model from The Longines Master Collection its eminently asser-tive character. Under the broad expanse of its barleycorn patterned flinqué enamel dial beats steadily the self-winding mechanical movement that brings to life its three blued-steel hands. Equally suited to business and leisure environments, it testifies to the professional acumen of Longines watchmakers and designers.

**BOTTOM**

**L2.673.4.78.2**

Both practical and crisply handsome, these wristwatches from The Longines Master Collection are an examples of the full measure of the professional care and expertise with which its watchmakers approach design: a flinqué enamel dial makes an elegantly contrasting background to a moonphase display, a chronograph to 30 minutes and a circular date aperture along with the hours, minutes, seconds, day and month display.

**1832: Longines's Early Years Auguste Agassiz**

The Longines story began in 1832 when Auguste Agassiz settled in Saint-Imier and became an associate of the Comptoir horloger Raiguel Jeune trading company.

**1867: Longines's Early Years Ernest Francillon**

One of Agassiz's sisters married Charles-Marc Francillon, a shopkeeper from Lausanne. In 1834 they had a son, Ernest, who later joined the company, succeeding his uncle in 1862. A new company, known as Ancienne Maison Auguste Agassiz, Ernest Francillon, Successeur, was established. At that time, watchmaking was essentially a cottage industry, with people doing piecework in their own homes.

## CHRONOLOGY

**1832** With two associates, Auguste Agassiz opens a modest workshop to assemble and finish watches. His associates' retirement in 1847 leaves him alone at the helm of the still-modest venture.

**1852** Ernest Francillon, the founder's nephew, joins the company.

**1862** Succeeding his uncle, Francillon adds his name to the company.

**1867** The new owner-manager reorganizes production under one roof and begins turning out "Longines" brand watches. With the inauguration of the new factory, Longines launches its first movement, the L20A, with a lever escapement and a winding crown. It wins a bronze medal at the 1867 Paris Universal Exhibition.

**1878** In collaboration with the caliber designer H.-A. Lugrin, Longines develops its first pocket chronograph with a subdial for the seconds: the caliber L20H.

**1889** The Longines trademark and its winged hourglass logo are first registered under patent number 2684 on May 27, 1889 and under patent number 14 on March 27, 1893 at the International Office of Intellectual Property (today the World Intellectual Property Organization). In 2005, Longines will be the oldest international trademark registered at the WIPO that hasn't been altered, always renewed and still being used in its original form.

**1885** Longines receives its first Grand Prize at an international exhibition in Antwerp, which will be followed by nine more in the ensuing decades. Its record of ten Grand Prizes and 28 Gold Medals at such events will not be surpassed as of 2005.

**1905** Longines turns out its first wristwatches, completely reorganizing its manufacturing facilities and methods.

**1911** Longines's first tonneau-shaped wristwatch reaches market as part of an 18-karat gold collection, marking the start of the square and rectangular watch styles that define the Longines style for much of the 20th century.

**1912** Longines enters the world of gymnastics at the Swiss Federal Gymnastics Meeting in Basel, Switzerland. Longines's recourse to an electromechanical system featuring start and finish tapes marks the introduction of automatic timing methods, a world first.

**1926** When Longines participates in its first International Horse Show in Geneva, the brand begins its legacy of constant involvement in equestrian sport, a perfect example of the precision and elegance so valued by Longines.

**1927** Longines officially times the non-stop solo flight of Charles A. Lindbergh across the North Atlantic. The pilot then entrusts the production of his famed "hour-angle watch" to Longines.

**1945** The creation of the caliber L22A marks the birth of the self-winding movement by Longines.

**1960s** Longines is one of the first brands to introduce miniaturized electronic movements. Its gem-set designs also wins four Diamond Academy Prizes while another model wins the Prize of Honor at the 1964 Swiss National Exhibition.

**1970s** Longines leads the field again, this time as one of the first watch manufacturers to introduce quartz-piloted wristwatches.

**1980s** The diminutive L960 ladies' caliber gives Longines designers unsurpassed creative freedom, marked by, among other things, a silver medal at the Paris' Bijorhca Show. Its Clip design also wins at the Montres et Bijoux de Genève Show.

**1984** Longines launches its Conquest model with VHP (very high precision) movement, a Longines development. Because of its built-in thermocompensation system, such watches are five to ten times more precise than a normal quartz watch.

**1990** Based on the sleek 18-karat gold Agassiz collection, La Grande Classique de Longines designs in stainless steel make an elegant name for themselves.

**1997** Based on its models from the 1920s and 1930s, the company launches its Longines DolceVita collection. Two years later, the Longines DolceVita chronograph design will win France's prestigious Cadran d'Or prize in the Luxury Watches for Men category.

**2001** Longines produces its thirty millionth watch and launches a commemorative collection to celebrate.

**2002** Introduction of Les Élégantes, a commemorative collection of three vintage jewelry watches, at a reception celebrating 170 years of elegance staged at the Pavillon Ledoyen, on Paris's celebrated Champs Élysées.

**2003** Based on a tonneau-shaped design from 1925, the Longines's "evidenza" collection demonstrates the brand's unique approach to contemporary styling.

**2005** The Longines Master Collection sums up Longines's expertise and experience spanning three centuries.

# MAURICE LACROIX

Independent watch manufacturer Maurice Lacroix crafts timekeeping classics with passion and tireless attention to detail-always offering a synergy of excellent design, perfect craftsmanship, precious materials and masterful finishings.

Maurice Lacroix stands for decades of experience in the production of high-quality watches. Around 150,000 top-quality timepieces leave the state-of-the-art assembly facility in Saignelégier each year. Today, Maurice Lacroix, which has a total of 220 employees worldwide, is one of the most successful Swiss watch brands, both nationally and internationally, and is represented in more than 4,000 select specialist shops in 45 countries all over the world. Maurice Lacroix also manufactures its own cases in Saignelégier—one of the few Swiss brands to do so.

THIS PAGE

The case of the Masterpiece Vénus houses the fine Vénus 175 caliber. The heart of this complex historical chronograph movement is the column-wheel, an ingenious mechanism that activates the three specific functions: start, stop, and zero.

FACING PAGE

Roger Federer, ranked Number 1 in men's tennis (October 2004), has been the official international ambassador for Maurice Lacroix since June 2004. Here, the Swiss tennis player sports a Masterpiece Réveil Globe.

## The Maurice Lacroix Philosophy—Tomorrow's Classics

In spite of the rapid change and growth, one thing has always remained the same—the company's love of design, perfection, and fine materials. Maurice Lacroix is particularly proud of its crown jewels: the mechanical watches of its Masterpiece Collection. For these traditional masterpieces of the watchmaker's art, the brand uses historic watch calibers or contemporary mechanical movements (painstakingly finished by hand and provided with sophisticated additional mechanisms) developed especially for this collection. The experience Maurice Lacroix has gained from this precise art of watchmaking is also incorporated into its classic collections such as Miros and Pontos, which were revised and enhanced in 2004.

Also in 2004, Maurice Lacroix expanded the Masterpiece Collection with three attractive new models: The Masterpiece Vénus, the Masterpiece Jours Rétrogrades Tonneau, and the Masterpiece Grand Guichet Dame.

The Masterpiece Vénus is a superlative chronograph. Its artistically guillochéd case houses the fine Vénus 175 caliber and Maurice Lacroix offers this Masterpiece in two limited editions: 150 pieces in pink gold and 100 pieces in white gold.

MAURICE LACROIX
Réveil

# Maurice Lacroix

THIS PAGE

The exclusive Masterpiece Collection by Maurice Lacroix includes three watch models with retrograde displays: The Masterpiece Calendrier Rétrograde (far left) with retrograde date display; the Masterpiece Double Rétrograde (top center) with a retrograde date display and a 24-hour display for a second time zone; and the Masterpiece Jours Rétrogrades Tonneau (bottom right) with a retrograde weekday display. A separate mechanism, perfectly matched to the specific watch and display, is used for each of these three watches.

The Masterpiece Jours Rétrogrades Tonneau features a retrograde weekday display. The special mechanism of this display was developed especially for the Jours Rétrogrades Tonneau and the date display of this Masterpiece is oversized. Yet the caliber ML 102 is a rarity in itself: While the base movement is round, the plate carrying the complications has been designed in a tonneau shape.

The date display area was more than doubled for the Masterpiece Grand Guichet Dame and the small seconds near 6:00 provide the perfect optical counterpoint to the large date display at 12:00. With its five cabochons of genuine sapphire or 750 18-karat yellow gold, optional 50 Top Wesselton diamonds (0.835 carats), a dial of solid silver 925 with or without a genuine mother-of-pearl hour ring and 6 diamonds, and watchbands of genuine leather in various colors, the Grand Guichet Dame is the ideal companion for women who strive for perfection.

## CHRONOLOGY

**1961** Zurich-based Desco von Schulthess AG acquires an assembly facility in Saignelégier, a town in the Jura Mountains. Here the company produces private label watches.

**1975** The company introduces its first watch under the name of Maurice Lacroix in Austria.

**1976** The brand is launched in Spain.

**1979** Maurice Lacroix expands, establishing its own sales organization in Germany.

**1989** The company acquires its own case manufacturer.

**1990** Maurice Lacroix launches its Masterpiece Collection of complicated mechanical timepieces.

**1995** The brand opens Maurice Lacroix USA and begins distribution in the United States market.

**2001** Maurice Lacroix SA, previously a division of Desco von Schulthess AG, becomes an independent legal entity.

**2002** The brand founds its Great Britain subsidiary and targets overall international growth.

**2004** Maurice Lacroix is represented in over 4,000 select specialist shops in 45 countries around the world.

**TOP**

The Masterpiece Grand Guichet Dame—the second model in the Masterpiece Collection designed exclusively for women—epitomizes the efforts by Maurice Lacroix to continuously expand the line of attractively shaped, feminine ladies' wrist watches with sophisticated, helpful complications.

**CENTER**

With its timeless, purist design and high quality, hand-wound mechanical movement, this enhanced Pontos model appeals to demanding buyers. The generously sized small-seconds display expresses the design consciousness of its wearer.

**BOTTOM**

The new chronograph of the Miros collection appeals to watch aficionados with a flair for sporting elegance. This model pleases not only with its precise time measurements recorded with 30-minute and 10-hour counters, but also with small seconds at 3:00 and a convenient large date display at the 12:00.

# MEYERS

**Meyers is a young brand taking the world by storm with its imaginative dangling jeweled timepiece.**

Just two, years ago Jean Christophe Niarquin and Cyril Waskoll formed their auspicious partnership that brought to life a unique and creative timepiece to the world at the Basel Watch and Jewelry Fair. The patented watches featured stunning gemstones hanging freely from the bezel in an array of geometrical cuts and briolette in a variety of choices.

The Meyers collection has successfully united fine watchmaking and jewelry into a Swiss watch that is a fine piece of jewelry in the true sense of the word. Each unique bezel is hand finished by master jewelers who normally would never see the inside of the watch factory. This unique approach is vastly different from the way many other Swiss watches are made in that the jewelry aspect is pure.

Truly a visual feast, dazzling bezels shimmer with diamond streamers, geometrical rectangles and triangles of diamonds. "Pompons" of colorful briolette sapphires or pearls and bezel-set mixtures of colored gems that hang and shake freely. Each version is more captivating than the next. Even in mere words the timepieces are exciting, but the collection can be truly appreciated only when gloriously dancing and shimmering on one's wrist.

The response this collection invokes is truly amazing. Consumers find Meyers's watches as subtle as lighting bolts and the sophisticated luxury consumer's typical reaction is an open jaw and awestruck eyes.

Celebrities have flocked to Meyers's alluring charm and have been in hot pursuit to wear the pieces. Eve, Ashley Simpson, Mary J. Blige, Victoria Gotti, Christina Milian and countless others are finding the collection thanks to the word of mouth of their peers. Editors of top publications also find the collection to be the perfect fit with the world of high fashion in today's trendy market. Most recently, Meyers watches were strutted on the New York Fashion runways in the couture shows of Italian designer Rosita & Disarno. Victoria Gotti fell in love with the brand and featured it on her television show, A&E's *Growing Up Gotti*. Shortly after, other top shows like *Extra* and *Deco Drive* featured the collection in "mini" spots.

THIS PAGE

ABOVE

This stunning Star features 288 diamonds, 12 sapphires and 12 pearls, mother-of-pearl dial with diamond index and 45 diamonds around chronograph dials.

BOTTOM LEFT

This youthful LadyBeach I Love You Diamond Pavé collection features the brand's signature hanging elements but with sweet messages and a sporty look with its colored rubber straps embossed with the Meyers logo.

FACING PAGE

Mother-of-pearl dial with diamond pave counters, on black stingray strap and flowing with 18-karat gold strands.

MEYERS
60
45
SWISS
MADE

Members of the international market have been quick to recognize the hot brand and have moved to stake their claim in the success this collection is bringing. Japan, Italy, China, Hong Kong, Korea, Spain, Greece and Ukraine are some of the newest markets to carry Meyers's watches and the product has stayed true to its character, attracting the top echelon of consumers in these countries. Of course, primary markets like the USA, Europe and the Middle East continue to be strong and are growing rapidly.

Meyers has created a world of creativity and exploration that opened the doors to new levels of designs and textures. The extent of the collection and its personality have not just pushed the envelope but blown it wide open.

The excitement that the collection is generating has spurred Meyers to create matching jewelry to complement the watches and Meyers eagerly anticipates Fall 2005 for the launch of the Meyers Jewelry Collection.

Meyers will be unveiling its first men's collection, also in Fall 2005. This collection will feature automatics and complications with a jeweled twist only Meyers could achieve.

**TOP LEFT**

From the new Pearls collection, this breathtaking Pearls in Black and White is set with 18-karat gold "pineapples" with pave diamonds.

**TOP RIGHT**

The After Eight Lady is shown with full pave diamonds and on a black stingray (galuchat) strap. Temperatures rise with this hot timepiece in cool ice.

## CHRONOLOGY

**2000** Born into the watch business, Jean Christophe Niarquin learns the industry inside and out from his father, a successful distributor of luxury watches. However, it is Niarquin's dream to create his own brand of timepieces and, at the age of 30, he leaves his father's company to start his own.

**2001** Niarquin creates and unveils the Meyers watch brand, a line of patented timepieces featuring jeweled bezels.

**2002** Born into the jewelry business, famous designer Cyril Waskoll joins Meyers as the head of creation. The joint venture between the two ambitious entrepreneurs gives rise to the Samba watch, a magnificent spectacle of diamond, ruby or sapphire pompons set in either 18-karat white or yellow gold. Other models feature gemstone or diamond pineapples dangling deliciously from the watches' bezels.

**2003** Meyers exhibits for the first time at key jewelry and watch fairs around the world. When first launched, the Meyers brand was distributed in France, the Middle East, Japan and the Antilles Islands. Today, Meyers watches are sold in many major markets including England, Germany, Austria, Russia, South Africa, Morocco and the USA.

**2004** The USA market is taken over by Doron Basha, previously Vice President of Charriol USA. His joining results in renewed energy and immediate growth for the brand, especially among exclusive top retailers such as Saks Fifth Avenue, Mayors Jewelers, London Jewelers, Geary's, and Westime Watches.

TOP

Aptly named, the La Twenty Exclusive is a striking watch featuring 20 multicolored sapphires on the bezel, dripping with deep colors.

BOTTOM

Pave accents float in a sea of French enamel in deep colors.

## CHRONO MOUNA SUMMER EXCLUSIVE

**Movement:** Swiss ETA 251.272.
**Functions:** hour, minute, small seconds at 6; chronograph 1/10 second; chronograph in the center; 1/10 second at 2; minute at 10.
**Case:** stainless steel 316L; 39mm; sapphire crystal; bezel with 45 full-cut white diamonds and 15 white-gold brillolette sapphires (23 carats of sapphires); water resistant to 330 ft/100 meters. **Strap:** stingray strap with stainless steel buckle.
**Dial:** white mother of pearl with 45 diamonds set around counters and 8 diamonds indexes. *Also available with white mother of pearl with pavé counters in white diamonds or full pavé in white diamonds.*
**Packaging:** brown wooden box with beige ultra suede.
**Warranty:** 1 year.
**Also available:** in ladies' size.

## CHRONO MOUNA SPRING

**Movement:** Swiss ETA 251.272.
**Functions:** hour, minute, small seconds at 6; chronograph 1/10 second; chronograph in the center; 1/10 second at 2; minute at 10.
**Case:** stainless steel 316L; 39mm; sapphire crystal; bezel with 120 full-cut white diamonds and 16 white-gold brillolette sapphires (24 carats of sapphires); water resistant to 330 ft/100 meters.

**Strap:** stingray strap with stainless steel buckle.
**Dial:** white mother of pearl with pavé counters in white diamonds. *Also available in mother of pearl with 45 diamonds set around counters and 8 diamonds indexes, or full pavé in white diamonds.*
**Packaging:** brown wooden box with beige ultra suede.
**Warranty:** 1 year.
**Also available:** in ladies' size.

## CHRONO MOUNA AUTUMN

**Movement:** Swiss ETA 251.272.
**Functions:** hour, minute, small seconds at 6; chronograph 1/10 second; chronograph in the center; 1/10 second at 2; minute at 10.
**Case:** stainless steel 316L; 39mm; sapphire crystal; bezel with 120 full-cut white diamonds and 16 white-gold brillolette sapphires (24 carats of sapphires); water resistant to 330 ft/100 meters.

**Strap:** stingray strap with stainless steel buckle.
**Dial:** white mother of pearl with pavé counters in white diamonds. *Also available in mother of pearl with 45 diamonds set around counters and 8 diamonds indexes, or full pavé in white diamonds.*
**Packaging:** brown wooden box with beige ultra suede.
**Warranty:** 1 year.
**Also available:** in ladies' size.

## CHRONO MOUNA WINTER

**Movement:** Swiss ETA 251.272.
**Functions:** hour, minute, small seconds at 6; chronograph 1/10 second; chronograph in the center; 1/10 second at 2; minute at 10.
**Case:** stainless steel 316L; 39mm; sapphire crystal; bezel with 120 full-cut white diamonds and 15 white-gold brillolette sapphires (20 carats of sapphires); water resistant to 330 ft/100 meters.

**Strap:** stingray strap with stainless steel buckle.
**Dial:** white mother of pearl with 45 diamonds set around counters and 8 diamonds indexes. *Also available with white mother of pearl with pavé counters in white diamonds or full pavé in white diamonds.*
**Packaging:** brown wooden box with beige ultra suede.
**Warranty:** 1 year.
**Also available:** in ladies' size.

## CHRONO MOUNA DIAMOND EXCLUSIVE

**Movement:** Swiss ETA 251.272.
**Functions:** hour, minute, small seconds at 6; chronograph 1/10 second; chronograph in the center; 1/10 second at 2; minute at 10.
**Case:** Ø 39mm; stainless steel 316L; sapphire crystal; bezel with 45 full-cut white diamonds, 15 white-gold "briollette" diamonds; water resistant to 330 ft/100 meters.
**Dial:** full pavé white diamonds.
*Also available in mother of pearl with 45 diamonds set around counters and 8 diamonds indexes or with white mother of pearl with pavé counters in white diamonds.*
**Strap:** crocodile strap; stainless steel buckle.
**Also available:** white mother-of-pearl dial; white mother-of-pearl dial with pavé counters (white diamonds).
**Packaging:** brown wooden box with beige ultra-suede.
**Warranty:** 1 year.

## CHRONO MOUNA COGNAC DIAMOND

**Movement:** Swiss ETA 251.272.
**Functions:** hour, minute, small seconds at 6; chronograph 1/10 second; chronograph in the center; 1/10 second at 2; minute at 10.
**Case:** stainless steel 316L; Ø 39mm; sapphire crystal; bezel with 120 full-cut white diamonds, 16 white-gold briollette brown diamond; water resistant to 330 ft/100 meters.
**Dial:** white mother of pearl with pavé counters in white diamonds.
*Also available in mother of pearl with 45 diamonds set around counters and 8 diamonds indexes, or full pavé in white diamonds.*
**Also available:** with white mother-of-pearl dial, full pavé (white diamonds).
**Packaging:** brown wooden box with beige ultra-suede.
**Warranty:** 1 year.

## LADY MOUNA DIAMOND

**Movement:** Swiss ETA 956.412.
**Functions:** hour, minute, small seconds.
**Case:** stainless steel 316L; Ø 32mm; sapphire crystal; bezel with 96 full-cut white diamonds, 10 white-gold briollette diamond; water resistant to 330 ft/100 meters.
**Dial:** full pavé (white diamonds).
**Strap:** crocodile strap; stainless steel buckle.
**Also available:** white mother-of-pearl dial
**Packaging:** brown wooden box with beige ultra-suede.
**Warranty:** 1 year.

## SQUARE MOUNA DIAMOND

**Movement:** Swiss ETA 956.402.
**Functions:** hour, minute.
**Case:** stainless steel 316L; Ø 32mm; sapphire crystal; bezel with 104 full-cut white diamonds, 12 white-gold briollette diamond; water resistant to 165 ft/50 meters.
**Dial:** white mother of pearl.
**Strap:** crocodile strap; stainless steel buckle.
**Also available:** full pavé dial with (white diamonds).
**Packaging:** brown wooden box with beige ultra-suede.
**Warranty:** 1 year.

## TWENTY MULTI

**Movement:** Swiss ETA 251.272.
**Functions:** hour, minute, small seconds at 6; chronograph 1/10 second; chronograph in the center; 1/10 second at 2; minute at 10.
**Case:** stainless steel 316L; Ø 39mm; sapphire crystal; bezel with 120 full-cut white diamonds, 20 white-gold briollette multicolored sapphires; water resistant to 330 ft/100 meters.

**Dial:** full pavé white diamonds.
*Also available in mother of pearl with 45 diamonds set around counters and 8 diamonds indexes or with white mother of pearl with pavé counters in white diamonds.*
**Strap:** crocodile strap; stainless steel buckle.
**Also available:** white mother-of-pearl dial; pavé white mother-of-pearl dial with white diamond counters.
**Packaging:** brown wooden box with beige ultra-suede.
**Warranty:** 1 year.

## TWENTY PINK EXCLUSIVE

**Movement:** Swiss ETA 251.272.
**Functions:** hour, minute, small seconds at 6; chronograph 1/10 second; chronograph in the center; 1/10 second at 2; minute at 10.
**Case:** stainless steel 316L;39mm; sapphire crystal; bezel with 40 full-cut white diamonds, 20 white-gold "briollette" pink sapphires; water resistant to 330 ft/100 meters.

**Dial:** white mother of pearl with 45 diamonds set around counters and 8 diamonds indexes.
*Also available with white mother of pearl with pavé counters in white diamondsor full pavé in white diamonds.*
**Strap:** crocodile strap; stainless steel buckle.
**Also available:** white mother-of-pearl dial with white-diamond pavé counters or full pavé (white diamonds).
**Packaging:** brown wooden box with beige ultra-suede.
**Warranty:** 1 year.

## LADY SUPER TWELVE PINK

**Movement:** Swiss ETA 956.412.
**Functions:** hour, minute, small seconds.
**Case:** stainless steel 316L; Ø 32mm; sapphire crystal; bezel with 96 full-cut white diamonds, 12 white-gold briollette pink sapphires; water resistant to 330 ft/100 meters.
**Dial:** full pavé (white diamonds).

**Strap:** crocodile strap; stainless steel buckle.
**Also available:** white mother-of-pearl dial.
**Packaging:** brown wooden box with beige ultra-suede.
**Warranty:** 1 year.

## SQUARE SUPER TWELVE MULTI

**Movement:** Swiss ETA 956.402.
**Functions:** hour, minute.
**Case:** stainless steel 316L; 26mm; sapphire crystal; bezel with 104 full-cut white diamonds, 12 white-gold "briollette" multicolored sapphires; water resistant to 165 ft/50 meters.
**Dial:** white mother of pearl.

**Strap:** crocodile strap; stainless steel buckle.
**Also available:** full white-diamond pavé dial.
**Packaging:** brown wooden box with beige ultra-suede.
**Warranty:** 1 year.

## LA PERLE WHITE PAVÉ

**Movement:** Swiss ETA 251.272.
**Functions:** hour, minute, small seconds at 6; chronograph 1/10 second; chronograph in the center; 1/10 second at 2; minute at 10.
**Case:** full pavé white diamonds.
*Also available in mother of pearl with 45 diamonds set around counters and 8 diamonds indexes or with white mother of pearl with pavé counters in white diamonds.*
**Dial:** full pavé (white diamonds).
**Strap:** crocodile strap; stainless steel buckle.
**Also available:** white mother-of-pearl dial; white mother-of-pearl dial with white-diamond pavé counters.
**Packaging:** brown wooden box with beige ultra-suede.
**Warranty:** 1 year.

## LA PERLE GREY EXCLUSIVE

**Movement:** Swiss ETA 251.272.
**Functions:** hour, minute, small seconds at 6; chronograph 1/10 second; chronograph in the center; 1/10 second at 2; minute at 10.
**Case:** stainless steel 316L;39mm; sapphire crystal; bezel with 45 full-cut white diamonds, 15 white gold gray pearls; water resistant to 330 ft/100 meters.
**Dial:** white mother of pearl with pavé counters in white diamonds.
*Also available in mother of pearl with 45 diamonds set around counters and 8 diamonds indexes, or full pavé in white diamonds.*
**Strap:** steel bracelet.
**Packaging:** brown wooden box with beige ultra-suede.
**Warranty:** 1 year.

## LA PERLE BLACK

**Movement:** Swiss ETA 251.272.
**Functions:** hour, minute, small seconds at 6; chronograph 1/10 second; chronograph in the center; 1/10 second at 2; minute at 10.
**Case:** Ø 39mm; stainless steel 316L; sapphire crystal; bezel with 120 full-cut white diamonds, 15 white-gold black pearls; water resistant to 330 ft/100 meters.
**Dial:** white mother of pearl with pavé counters in white diamonds.
*Also available in mother of pearl with 45 diamonds set around counters and 8 diamonds indexes, or full pavé in white diamonds.*
**Strap:** crocodile strap; stainless steel buckle.
**Also available:** white mother-of-pearl dial, full pavé (white diamonds).
**Packaging:** brown wooden box with beige ultra-suede.
**Warranty:** 1 year.

## LA PERLE PINK

**Movement:** Swiss ETA 251.272.
**Functions:** hour, minute, small seconds at 6; chronograph 1/10 second; chronograph in the center; 1/10 second at 2; minute at 10.
**Case:** stainless steel 316L; Ø 39mm; sapphire crystal; bezel with 120 full-cut white diamonds, 15 white-gold pink pearls; water resistant to 330 ft/100 meters.
**Dial:** mother of pearl with 45 diamonds set around counters and 8 diamonds indexes.
*Also available with white mother of pearl with pavé counters in white diamonds or full pavé in white diamonds.*
**Strap:** crocodile strap; stainless steel buckle.
**Also available:** white mother-of-pearl dial with pavé counters (white diamonds) or full pavé (white diamonds).
**Packaging:** brown wooden box with beige ultra-suede.
**Warranty:** 1 year.

## CHRONO SAMBA RUBY PAVÉ EXCLUSIVE

**Movement:** Swiss ETA 251.272. **Functions:** hour, minute, small seconds at 6; chronograph 1/10 second; chronograph in the center; 1/10 second at 2; minute at 10. **Case:** stainless steel 316L; 39mm; sapphire crystal; bezel with 40 full-cut diamonds, 10 white-gold pompons with diamonds and 10 yellow-gold pompons with rubies (3x4mm) (2.2 carats of rubies); water resistant to 330 ft/100 meters. **Dial:** full pavé white diamonds. *Also available in mother of pearl with 45 diamonds set around counters and 8 diamonds indexes or with white mother of pearl with pavé counters in white diamonds.*
**Strap:** crocodile strap with stainless steel buckle.
**Packaging:** brown wooden box with beige ultra suede.
**Warranty:** 1 year.
**Also available:** with emerald pompons.

## CHRONO SAMBA BLUE PAVÉ

**Movement:** Swiss ETA 251.272. **Functions:** hour, minute, small seconds at 6; chronograph 1/10 second; chronograph in the center; 1/10 second at 2; minute at 10. **Case:** stainless steel 316L; 39mm; sapphire crystal; bezel with 120 full-cut white diamonds, 10 white-gold pompons with diamonds and 10 white-gold pompons with blue sapphires (3x4mm) (2.2 carats of sapphires); water resistant to 330 ft/100 meters. **Dial:** full pavé white diamonds. *Also available in mother of pearl with 45 diamonds set around counters and 8 diamonds indexes or with white mother of pearl with pavé counters in white diamonds.*
**Strap:** crocodile strap with stainless steel buckle.
**Packaging:** brown wooden box with beige ultra suede.
**Warranty:** 1 year.
**Also available:** with black diamond dial.

## CHRONO SAMBA PINK

**Movement:** Swiss ETA 251.272.
**Functions:** hour, minute, small seconds at 6; chronograph 1/10 second; chronograph in the center; 1/10 second at 2; minute at 10.
**Case:** stainless steel 316L; 39mm; sapphire crystal; bezel with 120 full-cut white diamonds; 10 white-gold pompons with diamonds and 10 white-gold pompons with pink sapphires (3x4mm) (2.2 carats of sapphires); water resistant to 330 ft/100 meters.
**Dial:** pink mother of pearl with 45 diamonds set around counters and 8 diamonds indexes.
*Also available with white mother of pearl with pavé counters in white diamondsor full pavé in white diamonds.*
**Strap:** crocodile strap with stainless steel buckle.
**Packaging:** brown wooden box with beige ultra suede.
**Warranty:** 1 year.

## CHRONO SAMBA MULTICOLORS EXCLUSIVE

**Movement:** Swiss ETA 251.272. **Functions:** hour, minute, small seconds at 6; chronograph 1/10 second; chronograph in the center; 1/10 second at 2; minute at 10. **Case:** stainless steel 316L; 39mm; sapphire crystal; bezel with 40 full-cut white diamonds, 10 white-gold pompons with diamonds and 10 white-gold pompons with multicolored sapphires (3x4mm) (2.2 carats of sapphires); water resistant to 330 ft/100 meters. **Dial:** mother of pearl with 45 diamonds set around counters and 8 diamonds indexes.
*Also available with white mother of pearl with pavé counters in white diamonds or full pavé in white diamonds.*
**Strap:** crocodile strap with stainless steel buckle.
**Packaging:** brown wooden box with beige ultra suede.
**Warranty:** 1 year.
**Also available:** with 20 white-gold pompons with diamonds.

## LADY SAMBA RUBIES

**Movement:** Swiss ETA 956.412.
**Functions:** hour, minute, small seconds.
**Case:** stainless steel 316L; 32mm; sapphire crystal; bezel with 96 full-cut white diamonds, 6 white-gold pompons with diamonds and 6 yellow-gold pompons with rubies (3x4mm); water resistant to 330 ft/100 meters.
**Dial:** white mother-of-pearl with 8 diamond indexes. Also available with full-pavé white diamonds.
**Strap:** crocodile strap with stainless steel buckle.
**Packaging:** brown wooden box with beige ultra suede.
**Warranty:** 1 year.

## LADY SAMBA PINK SAPPHIRE

**Movement:** Swiss ETA 956.412.
**Functions:** hour, minute, small seconds.
**Case:** stainless steel 316L; 32mm; sapphire crystal; bezel with 96 full-cut white diamonds, 6 white-gold pompons with diamonds and 6 white-gold pompons with pink sapphires (3x4mm); water resistant to 330 ft/100 meters.
**Dial:** pink mother-of-pearl with 8 diamond indexes. Also available with white mother-of-pearl with 8 diamond indexes and with full-pavé white diamonds.
**Strap:** crocodile strap with stainless steel buckle.
**Packaging:** brown wooden box with beige ultra suede.
**Warranty:** 1 year.

## LADY SAMBA DIAMOND

**Movement:** Swiss ETA 956.412.
**Functions:** hour, minute, small seconds.
**Case:** stainless steel; 316L; 32mm; sapphire crystal; bezel with 96 full-cut white diamonds and 12 white-gold pompons with diamonds; water resistant to 330 ft/100 meters.
**Dial:** full-pavé white diamonds. Also available with white, blue, pink, beige, black, mother-of-pearl with 8 diamond indexes.
**Strap:** black stingray strap with stainless steel buckle.
**Packaging:** brown wooden box with beige ultra suede.
**Warranty:** 1 year.

## LADY SAMBA LADYCOLORS

**Movement:** Swiss ETA 956.412.
**Functions:** hour, minute, small seconds.
**Case:** stainless steel 316L; 32mm; sapphire crystal; bezel with 96 full-cut white diamonds, 6 white-gold pompons with diamonds and 6 white-gold pompons with multicolored sapphires (3x4mm); water resistant to 330 ft/100 meters.
**Dial:** full-pavé white diamonds. Also available with white mother-of-pearl with 8 diamond indexes.
**Strap:** crocodile strap with stainless steel buckle.
**Packaging:** brown wooden box with beige ultra suede.
**Warranty:** 1 year.

## LADYBEACH I LOVE YOU DIAMOND

**Movement:** Swiss ETA G15.
**Functions:** hour, minute, small seconds at 6; chronograph 1/10 second; chronograph in the center; 1/10 second at 2; minute at 10.
**Case:** stainless steel 316L; Ø 36mm; bubble crystal; bezel with 17 full-cut white diamonds, letters and heart setting; water resistant to 330 ft/100 meters.
**Dial:** white mother of pearl; white figures.
**Strap:** white rubber strap; stainless steel buckle.
**Packaging:** pink and raspberry ultra-suede box.
**Warranty:** 1 year.

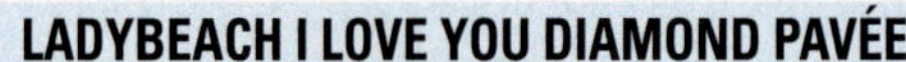

## LADYBEACH I LOVE YOU DIAMOND PAVÉE

**Movement:** Swiss ETA G15.
**Functions:** hour, minute, small seconds at 6; chronograph 1/10 second; chronograph in the center; 1/10 second at 2; minute at 10.
**Case:** stainless steel 316L; Ø 36mm; bubble crystal; bezel with 17 full-cut white diamonds, letters and heart setting; water resistant to 330 ft/100 meters.
**Dial:** full pavé (white |diamonds).
**Strap:** blue rubber strap; stainless steel buckle.
**Packaging:** pink and raspberry ultra-suede box.
**Warranty:** 1 year.

## LADYBEACH I LOVE YOU

**Movement:** Swiss ETA G15.
**Functions:** hour, minute, small seconds at 6; chronograph 1/10 second; chronograph in the center; 1/10 second at 2; minute at 10.
**Case:** stainless steel 316L; Ø 36mm; buble crystal; bezel with 17 full-cut white diamonds, steel letters and setting heart; water resistant to 330 ft/100 meters.
**Dial:** white mother of pearl; black figures.
**Strap:** black crocodile strap; stainless steel buckle.
**Packaging:** pink and raspberry ultra-suede box.
**Warranty:** 1 year.

## LADYBEACH I LOVE YOU

**Movement:** Swiss ETA G15.
**Functions:** hour, minute, small seconds at 6; chronograph 1/10 second; chronograph in the center; 1/10 second at 2; minute at 10.
**Case:** stainless steel 316L; Ø 36mm; bubble crystal; bezel with 17 full-cut white diamonds, steel letters and setting heart; water resistant to 330 ft/100 meters.
**Dial:** white mother of pearl; pink figures.
**Strap:** pink crocodile strap; stainless steel buckle.
**Packaging:** pink and raspberry ultra-suede box.
**Warranty:** 1 year.

## CHRONO CRAZY PAVÉ

**Movement:** Swiss ETA 251.272.
**Functions:** hour, minute, small seconds at 6; chronograph 1/10 second; chronograph in the center; 1/10 second at 2; minute at 10.
**Case:** stainless steel 316L; Ø 39mm; sapphire crystal; bezel with 120 full-cut white diamonds, 60 white-gold chains; water resistant to 330 ft/100 meters.
**Dial:** full pavé white diamonds.
*Also available in mother of pearl with 45 diamonds set around counters and 8 diamonds indexes or with white mother of pearl with pavé counters in white diamonds.*
**Strap:** galuchat strap; stainless steel buckle.
**Also available:** white mother-of-pearl dial; white mother-of-pearl dial with pavé counters (white diamonds).
**Packaging:** brown wooden box with beige ultra-suede.
**Warranty:** 1 year.

## CHRONO CRAZY

**Movement:** Swiss ETA 251.272.
**Functions:** hour, minute, small seconds at 6; chronograph 1/10 second; chronograph in the center; 1/10 second at 2; minute at 10.
**Case:** stainless steel 316L; Ø 39mm; sapphire crystal; bezel with 120 full-cut white diamonds, 60 white-gold chains; water resistant to 330 ft/100 meters.
**Dial:** white mother of pearl with pavé counters in white diamonds.
*Also available in mother of pearl with 45 diamonds set around counters and 8 diamonds indexes, or full pavé in white diamonds.*
**Strap:** galuchat strap; stainless steel buckle.
**Also available:** white mother-of-pearl dial with pavé counters (white diamonds) or full pavé (white diamonds).
**Packaging:** brown wooden box with beige ultra-suede.
**Warranty:** 1 year.

## LADY CRAZY

**Movement:** Swiss ETA 956.412.
**Functions:** hour, minute, small seconds.
**Case:** stainless steel 316L; Ø 32mm; sapphire crystal; bezel with 96 full-cut white diamonds, 48 white-gold chains; water resistant to 330 ft/100 meters.
**Dial:** white mother of pearl.
**Strap:** galuchat strap; stainless steel buckle.
**Also available:** full pavé dial (white diamonds)
**Packaging:** brown wooden box with beige ultra-suede.
**Warranty:** 1 year.

## SQUARE CRAZY PAVÉ

**Movement:** Swiss ETA 956.402.
**Functions:** hour, minute.
**Case:** stainless steel 316L; Ø 32mm; sapphire crystal; bezel with 104 full-cut white diamonds, 28 white-gold chains; water resistant to 165 ft/50 meters.
**Dial:** full pavé (white diamonds). Also available: white mother-of-pearl dial.
**Strap:** crocodile strap; stainless steel buckle.
**Packaging:** brown wooden box with beige ultra-suede.
**Warranty:** 1 year.

## CHRONO FLOWER MULTICOLORS

**Movement:** Swiss ETA 251.272. **Functions:** hour, minute, small seconds at 6; chronograph 1/10 second; chronograph in the center; 1/10 second at 2; minute at 10. **Case:** stainless steel 316L; 39mm; sapphire crystal; white-gold bezel with 250 full-cut white diamonds, 16 multicolored sapphires and pompons with multicolored sapphires; water resistant to 330 ft/100 meters. **Dial:** white mother of pearl with 45 diamonds set around counters and 8 diamonds indexes. *Also available with white mother of pearl with pavé counters in white diamonds or full pavé in white diamonds.* **Strap:** stingray strap with stainless steel buckle. **Packaging:** brown wooden box with beige ultra suede. **Warranty:** 1 year. **Also available:** ladies' size; non-chronometer version.

## CHRONO FLOWER BLUE

**Movement:** Swiss ETA 251.272. **Functions:** hour, minute, small seconds at 6; chronograph 1/10 second; chronograph in the center; 1/10 second at 2; minute at 10. **Case:** stainless steel 316L; 39mm; sapphire crystal; white-gold bezel with 250 full-cut white diamonds, 16 blue sapphires and pompons with blue sapphires; water resistant to 330 ft/100 meters. **Dial:** full pavé white diamonds. *Also available in mother of pearl with 45 diamonds set around counters and 8 diamonds indexes or with white mother of pearl with pavé counters in white diamonds.* **Strap:** stingray strap with stainless steel buckle. **Packaging:** brown wooden box with beige ultra suede. **Warranty:** 1 year. **Also available:** ladies' size; non-chronometer version (inset).

## CHRONO FLOWER PINK

**Movement:** Swiss ETA 251.272. **Functions:** hour, minute, small seconds at 6; chronograph 1/10 second; chronograph in the center; 1/10 second at 2; minute at 10. **Case:** stainless steel 316L; 39mm; sapphire crystal; white-gold bezel with 250 full-cut white diamonds, 16 pink sapphires and pompons with pink sapphires; water resistant to 330 ft/100 meters. **Dial:** full pavé white diamonds. *Also available in mother of pearl with 45 diamonds set around counters and 8 diamonds indexes or with white mother of pearl with pavé counters in white diamonds.* **Strap:** stingray strap with stainless steel buckle. **Packaging:** brown wooden box with beige ultra suede. **Warranty:** 1 year. **Also available:** ladies' size; non-chronometer version (inset).

## CHRONO FLOWER RUBY

**Movement:** Swiss ETA 251.272. **Functions:** hour, minute, small seconds at 6; chronograph 1/10 second; chronograph in the center; 1/10 second at 2; minute at 10. **Case:** stainless steel 316L; 39mm; sapphire crystal; yellow-gold bezel with 250 full-cut white diamonds, 16 rubies and pompons with rubies; water resistant to 330 ft/100 meters. **Dial:** white mother of pearl with 45 diamonds set around counters and 8 diamonds indexes. *Also available with white mother of pearl with pavé counters in white diamonds or full pavé in white diamonds.* **Strap:** stingray strap with stainless steel buckle. **Packaging:** brown wooden box with beige ultra suede. **Warranty:** 1 year. **Also available:** ladies' size and in emerald.

## AFTEREIGHT DIAMOND

**Movement:** Swiss ETA 251.272.
**Functions:** hour, minute, small seconds at 6; chronograph 1/10 second; chronograph in the center; 1/10 second at 2; minute at 10.
**Case:** stainless steel 316L; Ø 39mm; sapphire crystal; white-gold bezel with 612 full-cut white diamonds, 24 white-gold diamond pompon and 24 white-gold springs with diamonds; water resistant to 330 ft/100 meters.
**Dial:** white mother of pearl with pavé counters in white diamonds.
*Also available in mother of pearl with 45 diamonds set around counters and 8 diamonds indexes, or full pavé in white diamonds.*
**Strap:** crocodile strap with stainless steel buckle.
**Also available:** white mother-of-pearl dial with pavé counters (white diamonds) or full pavé (white diamonds).
**Packaging:** brown wooden box with beige ultra-suede.
**Warranty:** 1 year.

## AFTEREIGHT MULTI SAPPHIRES PAVÉ

**Movement:** Swiss ETA 251.272.
**Functions:** hour, minute, small seconds at 6; chronograph 1/10 second; chronograph in the center; 1/10 second at 2; minute at 10.
**Case:** stainless steel 316L; Ø 39mm; sapphire crystal; white-gold bezel with 576 full-cut white diamonds and 36 multi sapphires, 24 white-gold multi sapphires pompon and 24 white-gold springs with diamonds; water resistant to 330 ft/100 meters.
**Dial:** full pavé white diamonds.
*Also available in mother of pearl with 45 diamonds set around counters and 8 diamonds indexes or with white mother of pearl with pavé counters in white diamonds.*
**Also available:** white mother-of-pearl dial and white mother-of-pearl dial with pavé counters (white diamonds).
**Strap:** crocodile strap with stainless steel buckle.
**Packaging:** brown wooden box with beige ultra-suede.
**Warranty:** 1 year.

## AFTEREIGHT PINK SAPPHIRES

**Movement:** Swiss ETA 251.272.
**Functions:** hour, minute, small seconds at 6; chronograph 1/10 second; chronograph in the center; 1/10 second at 2; minute at 10.
**Case:** stainless steel 316L; Ø 39mm; sapphire crystal; white-gold bezel with 576 full-cut white diamonds and 36 pink sapphires, 24 white-gold pink sapphires pompon and 24 white-gold springs with diamonds; water resistant to 330 ft/100 meters.
**Dial:** white mother of pearl with 45 diamonds set around counters and 8 diamonds indexes.
*Also available with white mother of pearl with pavé counters in white diamonds or full pavé in white diamonds.*
**Also available:** white mother-of-pearl dial with pavé counters (white diamonds).
**Strap:** crocodile strap with stainless steel buckle.
**Packaging:** brown wooden box with beige ultra-suede.
**Warranty:** 1 year.

## AFTEREIGHT BLUE SAPPHIRES

**Movement:** Swiss ETA 251.272.
**Functions:** hour, minute, small seconds at 6; chronograph 1/10 second; chronograph in the center; 1/10 second at 2; minute at 10.
**Case:** stainless steel 316L; Ø 39mm; sapphire crystal; white-gold bezel with 576 full-cut white diamonds and 36 blue sapphires, 24 white-gold blue sapphires pompon and 24 white-gold springs with diamonds; water resistant to 330 ft/100 meters.
**Dial:** white mother of pearl with 45 diamonds set around counters and 8 diamonds indexes.
*Also available with white mother of pearl with pavé counters in white diamonds or full pavé in white diamonds.*
**Strap:** crocodile strap with stainless steel buckle.
**Also available:** white mother-of-pearl dial with pavé counters (white diamonds) or full pavé (white diamonds).
**Packaging:** brown wooden box with beige ultra-suede.
**Warranty:** 1 year.

# MICHELE WATCHES

Michele Watches is internationally known for creating fascinating, fashion-forward timepieces that utilize cutting-edge styles and materials.

Family owned and operated with three generations of watch experience, Michele Watches is incredibly adept at interpreting the fashion world and translating it into timepieces using coordinated colors, gemstones, steel, rose gold and goldplate in avant-garde designs. Each year, the brand adds new pieces to its signature lines, and also develops accent collections.

Michele Watches is careful to take all details of fashion and style into consideration in the creation of its timepieces. This includes colors and hues that carry through from strap to dial to gemstone adornments. Additionally, all straps are interchangeable to allow for a keen edge, and include exotic leathers, lacquered leathers, sateen, stingray and grosgrain. Bracelets are also available to match cases and are created in either steel, rose gold or goldplate. Additionally, Michele Watches uses aluminum for the cases of some of its sportier collections.

Key collections that have been added to recently are the CSX series of sporty, elegant chronographs and the Deco line of rectangular timepieces. New CSX watches include the CSX33 Pavé with diamond pavé dial. There are also new diamond-cased models, as well. New Deco watches include the Deco Color—set with gemstones on the case—and the Deco non-diamond in an array of metals including stainless steel, gold and rose gold.

THIS PAGE

ABOVE

These Coquette Retro watches offer tonneau-shaped, retro-inspired cases of distinction.

BOTTOM LEFT

These CSX33 watches feature varying degrees of diamonds. The watch on the left is totally diamond ensconced—dial, bezel, case. The watch on the right features a diamond case and bezel and a mother-of-pearl dial.

FACING PAGE

These CSX33 watches offer bold beauty with color-coordinated straps and dials.

CHRONOGRAPH
CSX33
MW

These elegant square watches are ergonomically curved chronographs. The diamond-cased models feature 108 handset diamonds.

Similarly, new diamond-adorned models join the MW2 family of square watches. The watches herein feature 62 diamonds on the case set in the traditional MW style at both the 12:00 and 6:00 positions. The addition of diamonds brings the sporty rectangular look to a new level of chic. The Coquette series of stunning elongated tonneau-shaped watches also now dons a pavé addition with 163 diamonds set on the pillow-shaped case. These watches are offered in steel, goldplate or rose goldplate and feature guilloché dials.

The Extreme Fleur watches join the chronograph series that was first revealed in 2003 and was an immediate hit. New gem-set models feature cases sprinkled with tsavorites, sapphires, rhodolithes and more.

As with all Michele Watches, these newest pieces feature Swiss movements, the MW signature crown, and sapphire crystals.

TOP LEFT

These Deco watches depict the various metal finishes available in the striking square collection.

TOP RIGHT

These CSX33 watches use gemstone accents for powerful color coordination.

BOTTOM RIGHT

Fresh and alluring, these Extreme Fleur watches feature gems set in the steel case to emulate flowers.

## CHRONOLOGY

**1940s** Jack Barouh, son of a European watchmaker, is raised in a family dedicated to the watch and diamond trades.

**1985** Barouh moves to Miami, Florida, and establishes Michele Watches—named for his daughter. He begins selling his innovative timepiece collection in Latin America.

**1990s** Barouh develops a branding and marketing strategy designed to bring Michele Watches to the U.S. market.

**2000** Michele Watches unveils its diamond watches. The fashion-forward collection is an immediate hit thanks to its unusual designs and its mix of color and diamonds. The first collection presented is the CSX Diamond Collection of sporty chic steel-cased, diamond-bezeled watches with colorful interchangeable straps.

**2002** Michele Watches is one of the top selling brands of diamond watches at leading luxury American retailers such as Neiman Marcus, Bloomingdale's, Nordstrom, Saks Fifth Avenue and Barneys. Attesting to its popularity in America, the brand's watches are selected for the 2002 Presenter's Gift Box for the Golden Globe Awards.

ABOVE

These Seaside watches depict ocean- and beach-inspired designs.

CENTER

Stone Cuff watches are all the rage from Michele Watches, especially in pastel hues.

BOTTOM RIGHT

These MW2 watches are crafted in stainless steel with colorful straps and dials.

# MOVADO

For more than a century, Movado has been recognized for its ability to artistically blend luxury and simple elegance in watches of innovative, modern, immediately recognizable design.

In both its world-famous Museum watch line and its other modern collections, Movado regularly breaks out of the typical watch mold, surprising and fascinating watch lovers with its design and technical prowess. Such is the case with its stunning new Trembrili™ collection. This family embodies an all-new expression of the iconic Movado dot motif, with dots forming a striking new five-row link bracelet. Crafted in stainless steel, this watch is offered with a classic black, silver-mirror finish, or white mother-of-pearl Museum dial. The bezel is available simply polished, or brilliant with one or two rows of diamonds. The watch is water resistant to 30 meters.

The innovative look of the Trembrili™ series is perhaps matched only by the dramatic appeal of the sleek, asymmetrical Timema™ collection. The Timema™ features a unique, deeply elongated asymmetrical case that contours from top to bottom. With its interesting integrated bracelet/strap design, the Timema™ is available on a bangle, a link bracelet or a strap fashioned of exotic pale blue, rose or silver snakeskin. Styled with a petite white mother-of-pearl or black Museum dial, the Timema™ is offered with and without diamonds.

Movado has also expanded its popular and elegant Esperanza™ collection. Crafted in solid or two-tone stainless steel, the Esperanza™ is distinguished by its Art Deco-inspired, open-link bracelet that flows seamlessly into a new, modern double-ring bezel. It is available in two sizes with an elegant white mother-of-pearl or black Museum dial. The diamond-set versions feature either 12 or 20 sparkling brilliants that appear to float between the outer and inner rings of the bezel.

THIS PAGE

TOP

The Timema™ features an elongated, asymmetrical case and an integrated bracelet design.

BOTTOM

The sleek Esperanza™ is now available with diamond-adorned bezels that accent the open-linked bracelet and bezel motif. The diamonds are set between the two rings of the bezel, creating the illusion of floating.

FACING PAGE

This new Trembrili™ watch features an unusual expression of the famed Movado dot motif.

SWISS MOVADO MADE

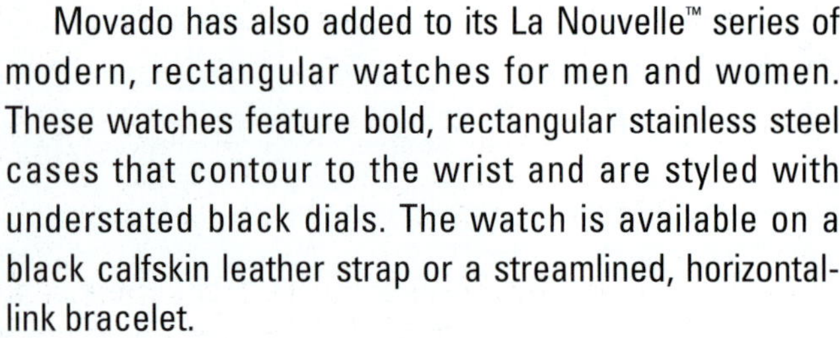

Movado has also added to its La Nouvelle™ series of modern, rectangular watches for men and women. These watches feature bold, rectangular stainless steel cases that contour to the wrist and are styled with understated black dials. The watch is available on a black calfskin leather strap or a streamlined, horizontal-link bracelet.

Other new sporty yet elegant men's models are found in the aerodynamically designed SE® Automatic collection. Crafted in stainless steel, the sleek, contoured bracelet and bezel are punctuated by concave dots. Each distinguished timepiece houses a sophisticated automatic movement visible through its sapphire crystal caseback. The SE® Automatic is water resistant to 30 meters and available in a chronograph version.

As with all Movado watches, these newest models are crafted to the brand's high standards, and supported by an extensive marketing program that highlights Movado's longtime involvement with the cultural arts.

**TOP LEFT**

The La Nouvelle™ is water resistant to 30 meters.

**TOP RIGHT**

The larger sized La Nouvelle™ for men is dramatic and bold.

**BOTTOM**

The chic La Nouvelle™ watch for women has an elegant rectangular case.

THIS PAGE

The SE® Automatic features a sculpted bracelet and is crafted in steel and in gold.

## CHRONOLOGY

**1881** Achille Ditesheim founds A.I. Ditesheim & Frères in La Chaux-de-Fonds, Switzerland.

**1905** The company name is changed to Movado, which means "always in motion" in Esperanto.

**1912** The Polyplan debuts as the first wristwatch contoured to follow the curve of the wrist. Elongated and rectangular in shape, it also boasts a revolutionary movement constructed on three levels, patented shortly after its introduction.

**1925** The first chronometers are produced. In honor of Hollywood heartthrob, Rudolph Valentino, Movado introduces the Valentino Watch as both a wristwatch and pocket watch with snakeskin cover.

**1935** Introduction of the first waterproof watches.

**1947** Nathan George Horwitt, a follower of the Bauhaus Movement, designs a black watch face with no ornamentation except a golden dot at 12:00, representing the sun at high noon.

**1959** Horwitt's dial is accepted into the Design Collection of the New York Museum of Modern Art.

**1960** Movado acquires Horwitt's design and begins production of the world-famous Museum Watch.

**1983** Movado is purchased by North American Watch Corporation, which will become Movado Group in 1996.

**1988** Movado presents the first Movado Artists' Series watch—the Times/5—by pop artist Andy Warhol.

**1991** US Open champion Pete Sampras becomes associated with Movado.

**1994** Movado opens its flagship store at Rockefeller Center in New York City. It features an extensive display of Movado's corporate collection of vintage timepieces.

**1996** On April 15th, it is announced that the North American Watch Corporation is changing its name to Movado Group, Inc.

**1998** Wynton Marsalis, the most acclaimed Jazz musician and composer of his generation, becomes associated with the Movado brand.

**1999** The Movado Time Sculpture clock at Lincoln Center is unveiled. The fifth Movado boutique store opens in the Grand Canal Shoppes at The Venetian Resort in Las Vegas.

**2001** Movado unveils a breakthrough watch design based on the 1912 Polyplan: the Elliptica.

**2003** The brand unveils the Museum automatic watch, uniting the internationally renowned design of the Museum watch dial with a 21-jeweled self-winding movement.

**2004** Movado celebrates the Museum dial with a one-of-a-kind platinum Tourbillon. Celebrated dancer Mikhail Baryshnikov joins the Movado Art of Time international advertising campaign.

# OFFICINA DEL TEMPO

Officina del Tempo is all about bold Italian styling and knock-out colors. The watches from this Italian company use Swiss movements for a winning combination.

Launched in Italy five years ago, Officina del Tempo is a high-fashion brand with trendy, cutting-edge designs presented in a host of outrageous colors. Instantly recognizable thanks to their oversized cases, Officina del Tempo watches are created with and without diamonds. All of its distinctive cases are produced in 316L surgical-grade stainless steel. Straps are made by world-famous Morellato, which creates the finest bands of genuine leather and stingray.

Officina del Tempo watches include both quartz and mechanical movements and consist of several collections. The Marrakech collection features curved, rectangular cases with rounded edges. Dials are bold and striking. There are chronographs, big dates, and watches with small seconds subdials. Models are available with gel/rubber or leather straps and come in several sizes. Some of the Marrakech watches are even set with diamonds, including a ladies' 23-diamond Medio gel watch, a chronograph with 82 diamonds, and a men's chronograph with 188 diamonds.

Also in the Marrakech collection is a limited edition 18-karat rose-gold version. The men's rose-gold Marrakech 6497 is produced in a limited edition of 100 pieces and features a numbered caseback with four screws and a sapphire porthole to reveal the movement. Water resistant to 3atm, the watch has beautiful contour and is created using a Swiss-made Unitas manual-winding movement with a customized rotor.

THIS PAGE

ABOVE

Crafted in 18-karat rose gold, this limited edition watch is released in 100 pieces and features the Swiss Unitas mechanical movement.

BOTTOM

The Marrakech Gel Chrono features a mineral glass with magnifying effect, silicon-gel strap that is completely hypoallergenic, and water resistance to 5atm.

FACING PAGE

The Marrakech 2 is encased in 316L steel set with 46 brilliant-cut natural diamonds in an exclusive shape and a customized steel crown. The high-tech silicon-gel strap with steel deployant buckle, permits pinpoint adjustments and the special composition is used also in the medical sector because it is hypoallergenic; can withstand temperatures ranging from 60° to 180° and it neither fades in sunlight nor hardens from acid solutions; it is softer than the best hides available on the market. The Marrakech 2 is water resistant to 10atm.

MARRAKECH
QUARTZ

The Tonneau series of watches are also bold, set with varying amounts of diamonds. Cases are highly polished or of brushed steel, and the collection includes big dates and chronographs set with anywhere from 44 to 360 diamonds. The 360-diamond version is a simple three-hand watch with an all-diamond case. Strap and dial colors include white, black, cream and blue. There is also a date version with fewer diamonds on the case that comes in pink, turquoise, chocolate, orange, lime green and a host of other colors.

The newest Tonneau Big Date in a brushed steel case features a customized crown and offers a double-window date indicator at 12:00. It is water resistant to 10atm. The Tonneau Chronograph is water resistant to 5atm and is released on a special limited-edition leather strap. A bracelet version of the Tonneau Chrono is also available, with a stunning steel mesh bracelet with deployant buckle.

Another key collection is the Agadir series of rectangular watches with quartz or automatic movements. Both versions are offered in steel with a customized crown and screw-down back. The automatic version features a sapphire porthole revealing the movement. The watches are water resistant to 5atm and models include a chronograph and a three-hand version. All Officina del Tempo watches are sold in a precious inlaid wooden box.

THIS PAGE

LEFT

This elegant Tonneau watch is set with 360 diamonds on the case.

BOTTOM

The Tonneau watch features a custom crown, steel curved back with four screws and is individually numbered. The strap is silicon-gel.

FACING PAGE

TOP

A special limited-edition piece, this Agadir GMT is crafted in 18-karat rose gold with embossed dial. It houses the 2893-2 ETA mechanical movement with custom rotors. It is created in a limited edition of 100 pieces.

BOTTOM LEFT

Powered by a compact FSOO caliber quartz movment, the Agadir is housed in a 316L steel case, handset with 180 brilliant-cut natural diamonds (1.08 carats) and featuring a large customized steel crown. The high-tech silicon-gel strap with steel deployant buckle, permits pinpoint adjustments and the special composition is used also in the medical sector because it is hypoallergenic; can withstand temperatures ranging from 60° to 180° and it neither fades in sunlight nor hardens from acid solutions; it is softer than the best hides available on the market.

BOTTOM RIGHT

Crafted in steel, this Agadir watch features 23 handset brilliants. The dial is elegantly textured and finished and the strap is available in either stingray or leather.

## Chronology

**2000** Officina del Tempo is founded in Ancona, Italy. The Tonneau Limited model is the most sought after, followed by the Marrakech 2 with silicon-gel strap.

**2003** Officina del Tempo makes its debut at the Basel Fair. It also begins to expand distribution to countries such as Spain, Portugal, Brazil.

**2004** The new Tonneau collection is unveiled in February in Milan. By summer, the Agadir makes its debut and in late 2004, the Marrakech Medio Gel watch, with gel strap, is enjoying great popularity. The brand makes its foray into the United States, the Middle East and Taiwan.

# OMEGA

For 157 years, this stellar company has been creating timepieces that run the gamut from technical precision instruments to beautiful jeweled watches while forming strong sport and celebrity alliances.

In its four key collections, Omega regularly unveils new Speedmasters, Seamasters, Constellations and Devilles. The brand most recently enhanced its Speedmaster series with automatic versions for women with stunning diamond bezels. Omega also unveiled the 35th anniversary edition of the Speedmaster Professional Moon Landing and the 6,000-piece limited edition Speedmaster Michael Schumacher The Legend model.

In the Seamaster series, the ladies' automatic Aqua Terra joins the lineup in several versions of 18-karat yellow gold, rose gold or steel. The line also pays homage to the old railroad days with its COSC-certified Railmaster watch. Complications come into play with the Omega Seamaster Professional 300 GMT and the Aqua Terra chronographs.

The Constellation—a favorite for decades—is joined by a Quadrella (tonneau-shaped) series and by the Double Eagle Chronograph men's watch fitted with the Co-Axial Escapement caliber 2500. The COSC-certified chronometer offers 44 hours of power reserve. Specialty watches include the skeletonized Omega Central Tourbillon and new Co-axial Deville watches with big date and small seconds. Indeed, the scope of watches released by Omega continues to earn it a top spot among the most prolific brands on the market.

**TOP**

The steel Speedmaster Michael Schumacher The Legend commemorates the famed Formula 1 champion and Omega ambassador. The 6,000-piece limited edition watch is a COSC-certified chronometer features a tachometer scale and is powered by the Omega caliber 3301 self-winding column-wheel chronograph movement with 55 hours of power reserve.

**BOTTOM LEFT**

The 42.2mm, steel Railmaster Chronograph's black dial features luminous hour markers. The watch houses the Omega caliber 3205 self-winding chronograph chronometer movement.

**BOTTOM CENTER**

This ladies' gold, automatic Seamaster Aqua Terra is set with 42 diamonds and houses the caliber 2520 mechanical movement with 42 hours of power reserve.

**BOTTOM RIGHT**

The Seasmaster Professional 300 GMT houses the caliber 2628 self-winding COSC-certified chronometer movement with Co-Axial escapement and 44 hours of power reserve. Water resistant to 300 meters, it offers a 24-hour scale and second time-zone readout.

**RIGHT**

This stunning skeletonized Central Tourbillion is crafted in platinum and houses the hand-chased self-winding caliber 2633 with COSC certification.

**BELOW**

Called the Constellation Double Eagle, this self-winding model features the Co-Axial Escapement. It is an officially certified chronometer and water resistant to 100 meters.

## CHRONOLOGY

**1848** Louis Brandt founds Omega in La Chaux-de-Fonds with the goal of producing watches that will surpass others in precision timing.

**1879** Brandt dies and his sons, Louis-Paul and Cesar, abandon the assembly workshop system and start an in-house manufacturing system in Bienne.

**1894** The first series-produced calibers (Labrador, Gurzelen, and the Caliber 1894) are unveiled.

**1903** With the deaths of Louis-Paul and Cesar, Omega—with 240,000 watches produced annually and employing 800 people—is left in the hands of 24-year-old Paul-Emile Brandt.

**1930** Paul-Emile merges Omega into the SSIH group, which later acquires a host of other brands.

**1931** Omega times the Olympic Games in Los Angeles, marking the first time a single company becomes the official timekeeper of the Olympics. This year also marks the purchase of the famous Lémania chronograph-movement factory.

**1965** Omega's Speedmaster is declared flight-qualified by NASA for all manned space missions. This year, Edward White wears the watch on the first American astronaut's walk in space.

**1967** Omega pioneers in the field of electronics by contributing—in conjunction with the Electronic Watch Center of Neuchâtel—to the 1967 introduction of the world's first quartz caliber, the famous Beta 21.

**1969** Omega lands on the moon with astronauts Neil Armstrong and Buzz Aldrin.

**1970** The Omega Speedmaster actively contributes to the rescue of Apollo 13. The crew is forced to switch down all power circuits and use their Speedmaster watches to time the rocket firing for re-entry into Earth's atmosphere. The performance earned Omega the Snoopy Award, the astronauts' highest honor given to their suppliers.

**1985** Omega's holding company is overtaken by a group of private investors under the strategy and leadership of Nicolas Hayek. It is renamed SMH.

**1988** Omega's Seamaster 200 Meters sets a new world record when the French scientific submarine Nautilus of the Faré mission descends to a depth of 4,400 meters in the Atlantic Ocean.

**1990s** Personalities in fashion, sports and the performing arts align themselves with Omega, including Cindy Crawford, Pierce Brosnan, tennis aces Martina Hingis and Anna Kournikova, Olympic-champion swimmer Alexander Popov, two-time America's Cup winner and head of "blakexpeditions" Sir Peter Blake, golfer Ernie Els, and Formula 1 champion and speedmaster Michael Schumacher.

**1999** The company launches the revolutionary Co-Axial caliber—designed and built by English watchmaker George Daniels. The caliber functions with practically no lubrication and is a technological advancement in watchmaking.

**2001** Omega is the official sponsor of the blakexpeditions to the Antarctic. The brand unveils its Museum collection.

**2002** Omega unveils the America's Cup Chronograph watch in honor of its involvement with the event.

## SPEEDMASTER DATE, LOS ANGELES 1932 — REF. 3513.20.00

**Movement:** mechanical automatic-winding Omega 1152 caliber (Valjoux 7750 base); rhodium-plated bridges and pillar-plate.
**Functions:** hour, minute, small second; date; chronograph with 3 counters.
**Case:** stainless steel three-piece case; Ø 39mm, thickness: 13.9mm; polished and brushed finish; antireflective domed sapphire crystal; engraved tachometer scale on the bezel; partially recessed screw-down crown and pushers; screw-on back with embossed medallion; water resistant to 3atm.
**Dial:** white; black printed Arabic numerals; red printed logo; luminescent blued-steel bâton hands.
**Indications:** date at 3; hour counter at 6; small second at 9; minute counter at 12; center second; minute track with divisions for 1/5 second.
**Bracelet:** polished and brushed steel; fold-over safety clasp.
**Note:** part of the Olympic Collection, dedicated to the 1932 Olympic Games in Los Angeles.

## SEAMASTER CHRONOGRAPH, LONDON 1948 — REF. 2894.51.91

**Movement:** mechanical automatic-winding Omega 3303 caliber; COSC-certified chronometer. **Functions:** hour, minute, small second; date; chronograph with 3 counters. **Case:** stainless steel three-piece case; Ø 41.5mm, thickness: 15.1mm; polished and brushed finish; antireflective domed sapphire crystal; counterclockwise-turning shaped brushed ring with an embossed graduated scale and a luminescent dot; decompression valve at 10, allowing the freeing of helium gas during ascent; screw-down crown with an O-ring and pushers with case protections; screw-on back with embossed medallion; water resistant to 30atm.
**Dial:** matte black; white printed Arabic numerals; red printed logo; luminescent sword-style hands.
**Indications:** minute counter at 3; date and hour counter at 6; small second at 9; center second; minute track with divisions for 1/5 second.
**Strap:** rubber; clasp in brushed steel.
**Note:** part of the Olympic Collection, dedicated to the 1948 Olympic Games in London.

## SPEEDMASTER BROAD ARROW, MELBOURNE 1956 — REF. 3556.50.00

**Movement:** mechanical automatic-winding Omega 3303 caliber; COSC-certified chronometer.
**Functions:** hour, minute, small second; date; chronograph with 3 counters.
**Case:** stainless steel three-piece case; Ø 42mm, thickness: 14.3mm; polished and brushed finish; antireflective domed sapphire crystal; engraved tachometer scale on the bezel; partially recessed screw-down crown and pushers; screw-on back with embossed medallion; water resistant to 10atm.
**Dial:** matte black, subdials decorated with circular beads; white printed Arabic numerals; red printed logo; luminescent rhodium-plated Broad Arrow, hands. Indications: minute counter at 3; date and hour counter at 6; small second at 9; center second; minute track with divisions for 1/5 second and luminescent dots.
**Bracelet:** polished and brushed steel; fold-over safety clasp.
**Note:** part of the Olympic Collection, dedicated to the 1956 Olympic Games in Melbourne.

## DE VILLE CO-AXIAL CHRONOGRAPH, ROMA 1960 — REF. 4841.20.00

**Movement:** mechanical automatic-winding Omega 3313 caliber, produced by Frédéric Piguet provided with the Co-Axial Escapement, a balance and balance-spring without regulator and column-wheel; COSC-certified chronometer.
**Functions:** hour, minute, small second; date; chronograph with 3 counters.
**Case:** stainless steel three-piece case; Ø 41mm, thickness: 13.1mm; curved sapphire crystal; crown with case protection; screw-on back displaying the movement through a sapphire crystal; water resistant to 10atm.
**Dial:** white; black printed Arabic numerals; red printed logo; luminescent Alpha hands.
**Indications:** minute counter at 3; date and hour counter at 6; small second at 9; center second; minute track with divisions for 1/4 second.
**Strap:** alligator leather; steel fold-over safety clasp.
**Note:** part of the Olympic Collection, dedicated to the 1960 Olympic Games in Rome.

## SPEEDMASTER MICHAEL SCHUMACHER THE LEGEND REF. 3559.32.00

**Movement:** mechanical automatic-winding Omega 3301 caliber; COSC-certified chronometer.
**Functions:** hour, minute, small second; date; chronograph with 3 counters.
**Case:** stainless steel three-piece case; Ø 38.8mm, thickness: 14.25mm; polished and brushed finish; antireflective domed sapphire crystal; engraved tachometer scale on the bezel; partially recessed screw-down crown and pushers; screw-on back with embossed medallion; water resistant to 10atm.
**Dial:** argenté grené; outer ring and black subdials decorated with circular beads; rhodium-plated bâton markers; luminescent rhodium-plated bâton hands.
**Indications:** minute counter at 3; date and hour counter at 6; small second at 9; center second; minute track with divisions for 1/4 second and luminescent dots.
**Bracelet:** polished and brushed steel; fold-over safety clasp.
**Note:** 6,000-piece limited edition celebrating Michael Schumacher's performance during the 2003 F1.

## SPEEDMASTER AUTOMATIC LADY REF. 3515.71.00

**Movement:** mechanical automatic-winding Omega 3220 caliber; rhodium-plated, gold-plated and decorated with a circular-graining pattern.
**Functions:** hour, minute, small second; chronograph with 3 counters.
**Case:** stainless steel three-piece case; Ø 35.5mm, thickness: 14.1mm; polished and brushed finish; curved hexalite glass; bezel with 49 set brilliants (1.28 carats in total); partially recessed crown and pushers; snap-on back; water resistant to 3atm.
**Dial:** white mother-of-pearl; blue printed Arabic numerals; luminescent bâton hands.
**Indications:** small second at 3; hour counter at 6; minute counter at 9; center second; minute track with divisions for 1/4 second.
**Bracelet:** steel with fluted central link; fold-over safety clasp.
**Also available:** with white, red or gray Arabic numerals; with black mother-of-pearl dial and white Arabic numerals; with brilliants at markers; in stainless steel without brilliants, leather strap or bracelet.

## SEAMASTER AQUA TERRA RAILMASTER REF. 2806.52.00

**Movement:** mechanical manual-winding Omega 2201 caliber (Ø 37.2mm); autonomy 60 hours; COSC-certified chronometer; beveled; decorated with Côtes de Genève and circular-graining patterns.
**Functions:** hour, minute, small second.
**Case:** stainless steel three-piece case; Ø 49.2mm, thickness: 12.7mm; polished and brushed finish; curved sapphire crystal, antireflective on both sides; partially recessed crown; screw-on back displaying the movement through a sapphire crystal; water resistant to 15atm.
**Dial:** Railmaster matte black; luminescent Arabic numerals and triangular markers; printed minute track; luminescent Dauphine hands (Broad Arrow steel minute hand). Indications: small second at 6.
**Strap:** alligator leather; steel fold-over safety clasp.

## CONSTELLATION DOUBLE EAGLE CHRONOGRAPH REF. 1514.20.00

**Movement:** mechanical automatic-winding Omega 3313 caliber, produced by Frédéric Piguet provided with the Co-Axial Escapement; balance and balance-spring without regulator and column-wheel; COSC-certified chronometer; rhodium-plated, gold-plated and decorated with a Côtes de Genève pattern.
**Functions:** hour, minute, small second; date; chronograph with 3 counters.
**Case:** stainless steel three-piece case; Ø 41mm, thickness: 13.1mm; brushed finish; curved sapphire crystal, antireflective on both sides; bezel with engraved Roman numerals and riders; 3 and 9 polished; crown with case protection, rectangular pushers; screw-on back displaying the movement through a sapphire crystal; water resistant to 10atm.
**Dial:** white enameled; subdials decorated with circular beads; applied rhodium-plated bâton markers; luminescent rhodium-plated Dauphine hands.
**Indications:** minute counter at 3; date and hour counter at 6; small second at 9; center second; minute track with divisions for 1/4 second and luminescent dots.
**Bracelet:** polished and brushed steel; recessed fold-over safety clasp.
**Also available:** with black dial.

# PANERAI

Intimately involved in the world of underwater exploration and equipment, Panerai has been creating bold, advanced, high-tech instruments for 145 years.

A long-time supplier to various international naval forces and U.S. Navy SEALs programs, Panerai is known globally for its highly specialized production of superior wristwatch instruments. Its timepieces have stood out decade after decade thanks to particular trademarks of its lines: including super luminosity, incredible deep-water resistance, protected crowns and grandly oversized cases.

Today, the Panerai legend continues as the brand rolls out equally superb timepieces such as the recently presented host of new instruments in its Radiomir line. Perhaps most notable is the Panerai Radiomir Black Seal®, which celebrates the Radiomir's 1930s style created for the Royal Italian Navy in a modern format. The newest cushion-cased timepiece is 45mm in diameter and features a streamlined profile for a more classic, distinguished look.

The watch, like its original predecessor, features a screw-down winding crown and screw-on back for a high level of water resistance. The case of this time-only watch consists of three parts (bezel, case band and back) and is water resistant to 100 meters. Crafted of AISI 316L—the highest quality steel alloy—it is completely free of phosphorus. The caseback is transparent sapphire, displaying the mechanically wound Panerai OP XI caliber. The dial of the watch has a three-dimensional effect, achieved by the superimposition of two separate discs: the top one is black with perforated numerals and hour markers, while the lower disc is treated with SuperLumiNova.

Also new in the Radiomir line is the 8 Days watch, which employs an innovative hand-wound 8-day movement. The Panerai OP XIV caliber has a Jaeger-LeCoultre 1877 base with 33 jewels. The 45mm three-part case is fitted with the patented slim wire-loop strap attachments and is water resistant to 100 meters thanks to its screw-in crown and screw-on back. This watch is created in steel and in 18-karat raised gold with a black dial.

THIS PAGE

ABOVE

The Radiomir 8 Days watch houses the hand-wound Panerai OP XIV caliber with Jaeger-LeCoultre 1877 base and 33 jewels.

BOTTOM

The Radiomir Black Seal® pays homage to the men of the Royal Italian Navy. It houses a hand-winding movement with 17 jewels. The COSC-certified chronometer is anti-magnetic, features an Incabloc anti-shock device and offers 56 hours of power reserve.

FACING PAGE

Water resistant to 100 meters, the Radiomir 8 Days watch is also available in 18-karat rose gold.

RADIOMIR
PANERAI
8 DAYS

The elegant Radiomir GMT watch is offered in steel and in gold. This timepiece houses the GMT function in its 42mm case. It features two adjusting crowns: one at 2:00 and one at 4:00. The second time-zone hand makes one complete rotation in 24 hours, indicating the secondary time on the rotating flange surrounding the dial. The flange is subdivided into 24 hours in a clean, uncluttered manner. The flange can be advanced in one-hour clicks by the crown at 2:00; time and date are adjusted via the crown at 4:00. The automatic Radiomir GMT houses the Panerai OP XII caliber on a Jaeger-LeCoultre 897 base with 35 jewels, beating at a rate of 28,800 vibrations per hour. The COSC-certified chronometer is water resistant to 100 meters.

Taking this complex watch one step further, Panerai also unveils the Radiomir GMT/Alarm watch with dual time-zone readout. The movement is a mechanical Girard-Perregaux caliber 59, with an automatic-winding mechanism that winds both the time train and the alarm train. It is personalized with the inscription "Panerai" on the bridges and rotor. Only 500 of these watches will be produced annually. Total functions in addition to hours, minutes and seconds include date, second time zone and alarm.

**TOP**

The Radiomir GMT watch offers GMT time via a rotating flange on the outer dial that is adjusted by the crown at 2:00. The automatic watch is a COSC-certified chronometer and water resistant to 100 meters.

**BOTTOM**

The Radiomir GMT/Alarm offers alarm, date and dual time-zone readout.

ABOVE

Also in celebration of its relationship with the U.S. Navy SEALs, Panerai has created a Black Seal® Compass in a 60mm case for the wrist.

Also in celebration of its relationship with the U.S. Navy SEALs, Panerai has created a Black Seal® Compass in wristwatch format. The case is an impressive 60mm in diameter and is created in titanium and steel with a monobloc dome of Plexiglas to protect the compass dial. Inside this capsule and immersed in a special petroleum-based floating liquid is the rotating device with permanent magnets to which the black dial is fixed. Water resistant to 100 meters, only 100 pieces will be produced.

## CHRONOLOGY

**1938** Creation of the first military diver's watch in history, the Panerai Radiomir: 47mm in diameter, wire-loop strap attachments, Rolex movement.

**1940** The wire-loop strap attachments are replaced by horn lugs integral with the case. Luminosity is ensured by a dial constructed of superimposed layers: metal base; coating layer of luminous material; and the numerals and markings cut out of the metal of the dial. The material seen through these cut-outs provides an exceptionally bright degree of luminosity in complete darkness. The watch's water resistance is ensured by a lever, locking the crown integrated into a half-moon-shaped bridge fixed to the case.

**1943** Development of the Mare Nostrum chronograph. This model designed for deck officers remains in the prototype stage.

**1956** Creation of a Panerai Radiomir watch commissioned by the National Egyptian Navy. It is distinguished from previous versions by the rotating bezel with reference marks at 5-minute intervals.

**1980** Panerai creates a diver's prototype in titanium capable of resisting a depth of 1,000 meters.

**1993** The enterprise creates its first numbered and limited series of models for the public: the Panerai Luminor Marina and the Mare Nostrum.

**1995** At the request of Sylvester Stallone, Panerai creates a special, extremely limited series of the Panerai Luminor Marina named the Slytech. Each piece carries the actor's signature engraved on the back.

**1997** Officine Panerai is bought by Richemont (at the time the Vendôme Luxury Group). The following year the brand is launched on the international market.

**2001** Reopening of the Bottega Panerai at Piazza San Giovanni 16r, Florence. This is the shop originally opened by the Panerai family at the beginning of the 20th century under the name Orologeria Svizzera.

**2002** The Panerai Manufacture at Neuchâtel, Switzerland is opened in September. Opening of a Panerai Boutique in Hong Kong.

**2003** Opening of a new Panerai Boutique in Portofino, Italy.

## RADIOMIR BLACKSEAL — REF. PAM 183

**Movement:** mechanical manual-winding Panerai OP XI caliber; 16 1/2'''; 56-hour autonomy; 17 jewels; balance in Glucydur with 21,600 vph; Nivarox balance-spring, swan-neck detent spring, Incabloc shock-absorber system; finished by hand with the "Panerai" decoration engraved on the bridges; COSC-certified chronometer.
**Functions:** hour, minute, small second. **Case:** stainless steel three-piece case, in carré galbé shape (Ø 45mm, thickness: 13.35mm); polished and brushed finish; curved sapphire crystal, antireflective; conic screw-down crown; screw-on dodecagonal back displaying the movement through a sapphire crystal; water resistant to 10atm.
**Dial:** matte black; luminescent recessed applied Arabic numerals and bâton markers; luminescent black enameled steel bâton hands.
**Indications:** small second at 9.
**Strap:** leather, hand-stitched; removable thread lugs; stainless steel clasp.
**Note:** limited edition of 1500 pieces for 2004.

## RADIOMIR 8 DAYS — REF. PAM 190

**Movement:** mechanical manual-winding Panerai OP XIV caliber (Jaeger-LeCoultre base) with a double barrel; 8-day autonomy; swan-neck detent spring; finished by hand with the "Panerai" decoration engraved on the bridges; COSC-certified chronometer. **Functions:** hour, minute, small second; power reserve. **Case:** pink-gold three-piece case, in carré galbé shape (Ø 45mm, thickness: 15.1mm); curved sapphire crystal (1.90mm thick); antireflective; pink-gold conic screw-down crown; screw-on dodecagonal back displaying the movement through a sapphire crystal; water resistant to 10atm.
**Dial:** black; decorated with a Clous de Paris pattern; luminescent recessed Arabic numerals and bâton markers; luminescent pink-gold bâton hands.
**Indications:** small second at 9; power reserve on back.
**Strap:** hand-stitched crocodile leather; removable thread lugs; pink-gold clasp.
**Also available:** in stainless steel with leather strap.

## RADIOMIR GMT / ALARM — REF. PAM 98

**Movement:** automatic G.P. Manufacture 59 caliber (A. Schild 5008 base); 47-hour autonomy; 31 jewels; Glucydur balance with 28,800 vph; Incabloc shock-absorber system; finished by hand with the Panerai decoration engraved on bridges and rotor. **Functions:** hour, minute, second; date; alarm, second time zone; 24-hour. **Case:** stainless steel, three-piece case, in carré galbé shape (size: Ø 42mm, thickness: 14mm); curved sapphire crystal (thickness: 1.5mm); antireflective, with internal magnifying glass on the date; crown at 2 for hour, second time zone and date setting; crown at 4 for sonnerie setting and actuation; screw-on dodecagonal back displaying the movement through a sapphire crystal; water resistant to 3atm. **Dial:** matte black; bâton markers and Arabic numerals, both luminescent; printed railway minute track with luminescent triangles; luminescent steel bâton hands. **Indications:** date at 3; second time zone at 6; sonnerie with center hand with an arrow-shaped tip.
**Strap:** alligator leather; removable thread lugs; steel clasp.

## LUMINOR BASE — REF. PAM 176

**Case:** Ø 44mm; titanium.
**Dial:** black.
**Note:** from the Historical Collection.

## LUMINOR MARINA 44MM — REF. PAM 111

**Movement:** hand-wound mechanical; Panerai OP XI caliber with swan's neck regulator; 16 1/2 lignes; 17 jewels; Panerai bridges; monometallic Glucydur balance with Nivarox I spring; 21,600 vph; Incabloc anti-shock device; 56-hour power reserve; COSC-certified.
**Functions:** hour, minute, small seconds.
**Case:** AISI 316L polished steel or brushed titanium, (Ø44mm, thickness: 3.5mm); device protecting the crown (protected as a trademark); bezel polished steel or brushed titanium; transparent sapphire crystal caseback; sapphire, formed of corundum; antireflective coating; water resistant to 30atm.
**Dial:** white, black or brown with luminous markers and Arabic numerals.
**Indications:** small seconds at 9.
**Strap:** leather with Panerai personalized buckle; supplied with a steel screwdriver and a second interchangeable strap.

## LUMINOR MOVEMENT — REF. PAM 111

The Panerai Historical Collection—the Luminor Base and the Luminor Marina—is reinforced by the significant developments to its content, the movement. Quality, transformation and excellence mark out the introduction of the new OP XI caliber, a direct transformation of the previous OP I and OP II calibers.
Three hand-wound mechanical movements have been the objects of significant developmental work following the standards of traditional Swiss horology. The bridges have been entirely redesigned and personalized.
The balance wheel assembly, the heart of the movement, has been modifies and is now fitted with a "swan's neck" regulator, conforming to the best Swiss watchmaking tradition. The movement makes 21,600 alternations per hour and is fitted with a Nivarox balance spring and and Incabloc anti-shock device. Its power reserve is 56 hours. The OP XI caliber has hour, minute and second functions.
The Panerai Luminor Historical Collection, the origins of the brand, is evolving so far as its own history is concerned while preserving all its attributes. Cased in steel or fashioned of titanium, it has a transparent back that allows the latest transformation of the Panerai Laboratory of ideas to be admired.

## LUMINOR MARINA AUTOMATIC 44MM — REF. PAM 104

**Movement:** automatic mechanical; exclusive Panerai OP III caliber; 13 1/4 lignes; 21 jewels; bridges and oscillating weight personalized Panerai; monometallic Glucydur balance; 28,800 vph; Incabloc anti-shock device; 42-hour power reserve; COSC-certified.
**Functions:** hour, minute, small seconds; date.
**Case:** polished steel, (Ø44mm, thickness: 3.5mm); device protecting the crown (protected as a trademark) in polished steel; screw-on steel caseback; sapphire, formed of corundum; magnifying lens over the date at 3; antireflective coating; water resistant to 30atm.
**Dial:** black with luminous Arabic numerals and hour markers.
**Indications:** small seconds dial at 9; date at 3.
**Strap:** alligator with Panerai personalized adjustable clasp; supplied with a steel screwdriver and a second interchangeable strap.

## LUMINOR MARINA AUTOMATIC 44MM — REF. PAM 164

**Movement:** automatic mechanical; exclusive Panerai OP III caliber; 13 1/4 lignes; 21 jewels; bridges and oscillating weight personalized Panerai; monometallic Glucydur balance; 28,800 vph; Incabloc anti-shock device; 42-hour power reserve; COSC-certified.
**Functions:** hour, minute, small seconds; date.
**Case:** polished steel, (Ø44mm, thickness: 3.5mm); device protecting the crown (protected as a trademark) in polished steel; screw-on steel caseback; sapphire, formed of corundum; magnifying lens over the date at 3; antireflective coating; water resistant to 30atm.
**Dial:** black with luminous Arabic numerals and hour markers.
**Indications:** small seconds dial at 9; date at 3.
**Strap:** alligator with Panerai personalized adjustable clasp; supplied with a steel screwdriver and a second interchangeable strap.

## LUMINOR MARINA AUTOMATIC 44MM — REF. PAM 140

**Movement:** automatic; Panerai OP III 13 1/4''' caliber (Valjoux 7750-P1 caliber base); 42-hour autonomy; 21 jewels; Glucydur balance with 28,800 vph; Incabloc shock-absorber system; personalized bridges and rotor; COSC-certified chronometer.
**Functions:** hour, minute, small seconds; date. **Case:** 18K yellow-gold, three-piece case, in carré galbé shape (Ø 44mm, thickness: 15.5mm); curved sapphire crystal (thickness: 3.5mm); antireflective, gold crown waterproofed by a patented system consisting of a bridge, fastened on the middle by two screws, with an unique lever pressing the crown against the waterproofing gasket; screw-on back; water resistant to 30atm. **Dial:** carbon fiber; black subdial; luminescent Arabic numerals and bâton markers; luminescent bâton hands.
**Indications:** date at 3; small seconds at 9.
**Strap:** alligator leather; attachment with pivots closed by screws; gold fold-over clasp (supplied with a second strap).

## LUMINOR MARINA AUTOMATIC — REF. PAM 180

**Movement:** mechanical automatic-winding Panerai OP III caliber (Valjoux 7750-P1 caliber base); finished by hand with the "Panerai" decoration engraved on the bridges; COSC-certified chronometer.
**Functions:** hour, minute, small second; date.
**Case:** white-gold three-piece case, in carré galbé shape (Ø 44mm thickness: 15.4mm); curved sapphire crystal with magnifying glass on the date; crown waterproofed by a patented system made up of a bridge, fastened on the middle by two screws, with an eccentric lever pressing the crown against the waterproofing gasket; screw-on back; water resistant to 30atm.
**Dial:** black; decorated with small hollows, subdial decorated with circular beads; luminescent applied steel bâton markers and Arabic numerals; luminescent steel bâton hands.
**Indications:** date at 3; small second at 9.
**Strap:** alligator, attachment with pivots closed by screws; white-gold double fold-over clasp.

## LUMINOR MARINA — REF. PAM 50

**Movement:** automatic.
**Case:** Ø 40mm; steel.
**Dial:** black.
**Bracelet:** steel.
**Note:** from the Contemporary Collection.

## LUMINOR POWER RESERVE — REF. PAM 90

**Movement:** automatic; Panerai OP IX caliber (Valjoux 7750-P1 caliber base); finished by hand with the Panerai decoration engraved on the bridges; COSC-certified chronometer. **Functions:** hour, minute, small seconds; date; power reserve. **Case:** stainless steel; three-piece case, in carré galbé shape (size: Ø 44mm, thickness: 15.8mm); curved sapphire crystal (thickness; 3.5mm); antireflective, with magnifying glass on the date; crown waterproofed by a patented system consisting of a bridge, fastened on the middle by two screws, with an unique lever pressing the crown against the waterproofing gasket; screw-on back; water resistant to 30atm. **Dial:** matte black; subdial; bâton markers and Arabic numerals, both luminescent; printed minute track; luminescent steel bâton hands.
**Indications:** date at 3; power reserve at 5; small seconds at 9.
**Strap:** alligator leather; attachment with pivots closed by screws; steel clasp (supplied with a black rubber strap).

## LUMINOR SUBMERSIBLE — REF. PAM 25

**Movement:** automatic; Panerai OP III 13 1/4''' caliber (Valjoux 7750-P1 caliber base); 42-hour autonomy; 21 jewels; Glucydur balance; 28,800 vph; Incabloc shock absorber system; bridges and rotor personalized; COSC-certified chronometer.
**Functions:** hour, minute, small seconds; date.
**Case:** titanium, three-piece case, in carré galbé shape (Ø 44mm, thickness: 16mm); brushed; curved sapphire crystal (thickness: 3.5mm); antireflective, with magnifying glass on the date; counterclockwise-turning ring with graduated scale represented by small recessed cylinders and engraved minute track; crown waterproofed by a patented system consisting of a bridge, fastened on the middle by two screws, with an unique lever pressing the crown against the waterproofing gasket; screw-on back; water resistant to 30atm.
**Dial:** black Clous de Paris; subdial decorated with circular beads; luminescent embossed round markers and Arabic numerals; skeletonized luminescent steel bâton hands.
**Indications:** date at 3; small seconds at 9.
**Strap:** rubber; attachment with pivots closed by screws; titanium clasp (supplied with a Velcro strap).

## LUMINOR SUBMERSIBLE 1000M — REF. PAM 87

**Movement:** automatic; Panerai OP III 13 1/4'' caliber (Valjoux 7750-P1 base); 42-hour autonomy; 21 jewels; Glucydur balance 28,800 vph; Incabloc shock absorber system; bridges and rotor personalized; COSC-certified chronometer. **Functions:** hour, minute, small seconds; date. **Case:** stainless steel, three-piece case, carré galbé (Ø 44mm, thickness: 18.4mm); brushed; curved sapphire crystal (thickness: 5.1mm); antireflective, with magnifying glass on the date; clockwise turning ring with graduated scale represented by small recessed cylinders (12 luminescent) and engraved minute track; crown waterproofed by a patented system consisting of a bridge, fastened on the middle by two screws, with an unique lever pressing the crown against the waterproofing gasket; helium valve on the middle; screw-on back; water resistant to 100atm.
**Dial:** blue grené, subdial; steel bâton markers and two luminescent Arabic numerals; printed minute track; skeletonized luminescent steel bâton hands.
**Indications:** date at 3; small seconds at 9.
**Strap:** rubber; attachment with pivots closed by screws; steel clasp (supplied with a Velcro strap).

## LUMINOR SUBMERSIBLE 1000M — REF. PAM 187

**Movement:** mechanical automatic-winding Panerai OP XII caliber; 28,800 vph; hand-finished with the "Panerai" decoration engraved on the bridges; COSC-certified chronometer.
**Functions:** hour, minute, small second; date; chronograph with 3 counters.
**Case:** stainless steel three-piece case; carré galbé (Ø 46.4mm, thickness: 19.2mm); brushed finish; curved antireflective sapphire crystal; counterclockwise-turning ring with embossed graduated scale (12 luminescent); screw-down crown waterproofed by a patented system made up of a bridge, fastened on the middle by two screws, with an eccentric lever pressing the crown against a gasket; pushers with case protections; helium valve on the middle; screw-on back; water resistant to 100atm.
**Dial:** black; grené; subdials decorated with circular beads; luminescent steel bâton markers (12 as Arabic numeral); skeletonized luminescent steel bâton hands.
**Indications:** minute counter at 3; date between 4 and 5; hour counter at 6; small second at 9; center second; minute track on the flange.
**Strap:** rubber; attachment with pivots closed by screws; steel clasp.

## LUMINOR CHRONO 44MM DAYLIGHT — REF. PAM 188

**Movement:** mechanical automatic-winding Panerai OP XII caliber; 28,800 vph; hand-finished with the "Panerai" decoration engraved on the bridges; COSC-certified chronometer. **Functions:** hour, minute, small second; date; chronograph with 3 counters. **Case:** stainless steel three-piece case, carré galbé (Ø 44mm, thickness: 16.4mm); brushed finish; polished bezel with engraved tachometer scale; curved sapphire crystal, antireflective; screw-down crown waterproofed by a patented system made up of a bridge, fastened on the middle by two screws, with an eccentric lever pressing the crown against a gasket; pushers integral with the crown-protecting bridge; 1 corrector on middle; screw-on back; water resistant to 10atm. **Dial:** white; printed bâton markers and Arabic numerals; luminescent black enameled steel bâton hands.
**Indications:** minute counter at 3; date between 4 and 5; hour counter at 6; small second at 9; center second; minute track with divisions for 1/2 second and luminescent dots.
**Strap:** alligator; attachment with 2 pivots closed by screws; steel fold-over clasp.
**Note:** limited edition of 850 pieces for 2004.

# Parmigiani Fleurier

Perhaps one of the most traditional watchmakers of our time, Michel Parmigiani is dedicated to preserving the old-world craftsmanship of haute horlogerie encased in incredibly modern masterpieces.

Michel Parmigiani was born just over fifty years ago in the Val-de-Travers, a region historically rich in the culture of fine micromechanics. Since his earliest years Parmigiani has been enthralled with artistic watchmaking, and the field of his research was devoted entirely to the restoration of ancient timepieces. Great collectors quickly put their confidence in him and entrusted him with many famous pieces. Michel Parmigiani has seen more than four hundred years of horological history unfolding through his hands.

With his own creations, his style is unique. The making of a curve on a case or a figure on a dial, the tapering outline of a hand, the double milling of a bezel, the positioning of an indication, the size of a date window—everything is a matter of proportion. Parmigiani's creative instinct is guided by a special golden rule: Harmony guides the intelligence of the hand.

Distributed throughout the world, Parmigiani Fleurier timepieces are coveted by an exclusive circle of connoisseurs and enthusiasts of beautiful mechanisms.

In 2003, some important developments took place at Parmigiani Fleurier. At the heart of the company, a new organizational structure guaranteed the continuance of the brand's unique, exclusive character. This reorganization has been extended to strengthen the manufacture of movements (Vaucher Manufacture Fleurier SA), achieving vertical integration and at the same time meeting the demands of quality and excellence demanded by the brand. In fact, for some time, the manufacture has been equipped with important facilities in the fields of case making, micro-mechanics and precision bar tuning (making parts for movements). This rich diversity of production helps to preserve an unequalled level of horological technical expertise within the company.

THIS PAGE

ABOVE

The Bugatti type 370 inherits every detail of its design from the automobile.

FACING PAGE

The Bugatti type 370 took three years to design and create due to the wealth of non-watchmaking techniques developed totally in house for this project.

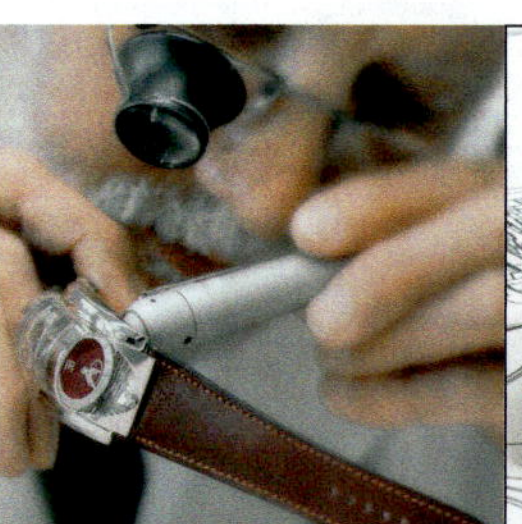

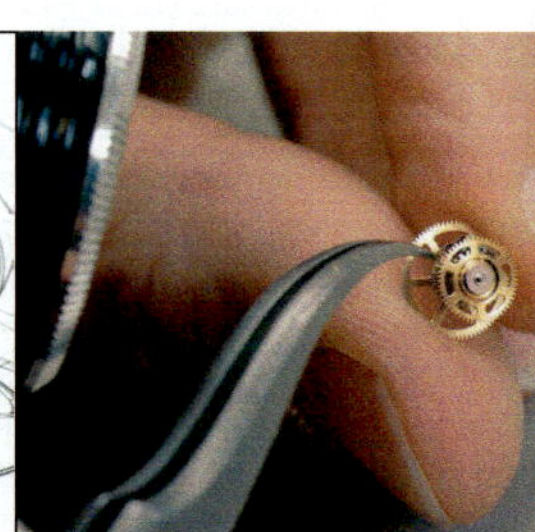

PARMIGIANI
FLEURIER

As part of this initiative, two buildings were opened in November 2003 at Fleurier to accommodate the horological workshops and the making of component parts, as well as the complete production of dials.

The newest Parmigiani Fleurier collection is a demonstration of exceptional creative aesthetic and technical richness. The Forma line holds a place of honor, inaugurating a new approach in Parmigiani Fleurier mechanical timepieces with complications. The Forma XL 30-second Tourbillon houses the Parmigiani Fleurier Calibre 500. The hand-wound movement is developed in the workshops of the manufacture. The Forma XL Minute Repeater is driven by the Parmigiani Fleurier Calibre 350, striking the hours, the quarters and the minutes on request.

Also new and incredibly innovative is the Bugatti type 370 with the Parmigiani Fleurier 370 caliber. This timepiece took Michel Parmigiani and a team of experts three years to perfect. It is the first wristwatch to be built totally on a transverse axis. Every detail of the watch is designed with the automobile in mind. Only 50 pieces of the Bugatti type 370 will be crafted annually for the next three years in three different dial colors—black, silver and red.

Parmigiani Fleurier has devoted meticulous attention to each detail of the 370 caliber. For the first time, movement wheels have been designed in the watch to reflect the aesthetic appearance of the wheel rim invented by Ettore Bugatti in the 1930s. The two dedicated wheels in the movement feature arms cut according to the same design.

Michel Parmigiani's original concept for the Bugatti type 370 was to create "an engine block on the wrist that also happens to tell the time." Crafted in 18-karat white gold, its eight-part case makes observing the movement both accessible and entertaining thanks to the six sapphire crystals, cambered and domed to the extreme. The cre-

**TOP**
The steel Forma XL Automatic is available with a black, silvered or blue lavender dial on an Hermès strap. Its mechanical self-winding movement, Parmigiani Fleurier Calibre 331, is crafted in the Fleurier workshops.

**CENTER**
The Forma XL Automatic is available in 18-karat white or rose gold with a black or a silvered dial. It is equipped with the mechanical self-winding movement, Parmigiani Fleurier Calibre 331.

**BOTTOM**
The Forma XL Minute Repeater, powered by the mechanical hand-wound movement Parmigiani Fleurier Calibre 350, strikes the hours, quarters, and minutes on request via two gongs. It is available in 18-karat rose gold or platinum.

**BOTTOM**

The Forma XL 30-second Tourbillon is equipped with an eight-day power-reserve. Full attention is focused on rotation speed to enhance regularity of rating: two complete revolutions in one minute, the goal being to enhance regularity of rating. Entirely developed and crafted in the Fleurier workshops, the 30-second Tourbillon is created in limited editions of 18-karat rose gold, and 950 platinum.

ation of the case called for a large number of sophisticated sets of tools, and custom-machinery never before seen in watchmaking. In order to protect its transversal movement and to guarantee optimal shock-absorption, the workshops of the Manufacture Parmigiani Fleurier specializing in watch exteriors developed a system comparable to the chassis of an automobile: the movement is therefore placed on "silent blocks" that absorb vibrations and preserve the watch from external stress. These shock absorbers are a first in watchmaking. Indeed, the entire construction of this masterpiece represents a true foray into another world—a world Parmigiani masterfully blends with watchmaking.

## CHRONOLOGY

**1975** Michel Parmigiani establishes an independent restoration business, Parmigiani Mesure et Art du Temps. Although the high-quality mechanical watch is enduring its most difficult moments due to the quartz revolution, Michel Parmigiani launches himself enthusiastically into the adventure and builds the foundation of an horological style with increasing success.

**1978** The Private Label division is developed.

**1994** Parmigiani completes the very long and difficult restoration of the Breguet Pendule Sympatique clock, which was considered by many horologists to be beyond repair. He also officially establishes Parmigiani Fleurier SA to create his own collection.

**1995** The Sandoz Family Foundation acquires a majority shareholding in the company. Michel Parmigiani is awarded the Prix GAIA (a prize presented by the Institute L'homme et le Temps), to honor his activities and research connected with time.

**1996** Launch of the Parmigiani Fleurier collection of ladies' and gentlemen's wristwatches, pocket watches and table clocks, crowned by unique pieces including the Fleur d'Orient (Flower of the Orient) with a grand complication movement.

**1997** Parmigiani Fleurier participates in the SIHH in Geneva for the first time, launching the Toric Chronograph wristwatch.

**1998** The brand introduces the tonneau-shaped eight-day movement in the Ionica model. Parmigiani restores the Breguet Carriage Clock for the Art Decoration Museum in Paris.

**2000** The Sandoz Family Foundation acquires a company in the Jura region (Atokalpa) that makes key mechanical components of high quality, and a second company (Elwin SA) specializing in lathe-work, precision profile-turning and fabrication of micromechanical horological components used in the manufacture of movements—creating a center of watchmaking excellence at the service of the Parmigiani Fleurier brand and other prestigious names.

**2001** International presentation of the first self-winding mechanical movement manufactured entirely in-house, the Parmigiani Fleurier Calibre 331. The Forma is introduced.

**2002** Parmigiani Fleurier establishes an alliance with the house of Bugatti to create a world-premiere mechanical watch in the spirit of the famous cars.

**2003** Parmigiani Mesure et Art du Temps integrates Parmigiani Fleurier SA and Vaucher Manufacture Fleurier SA to set up a true movement manufactory to meet the standards of quality and excellence required by prestige brands.

**2004** International launch of Bugatti type 370 in Milan. In partnership with Chopard and Bovet, the brand creates and develops the "certification Qualité Fleurier," which officially launches in September 2004.

## FORMA GRANDE AUTOMATIC — REF. PF006794

**Movement:** PF331.01; automatic winding; 55-hour power reserve; caliber 11′′′; Ø 25.6mm; 4 Hz–28,800 vph; 32 jewels; double-spring barrel; Côtes de Genève decoration; chamfered bridges; 22K gold oscillating weight.
**Functions:** hours, minutes, seconds; date.
**Case:** polished 18K rose-gold, tonneau-shaped case (size: 46.6x34mm, thickness: 9.25mm); sapphire crystal with antireflective treatment; sapphire crystal caseback; Ø 5.5mm winding crown; individual number engraved on back; water resistant to 30 meters.
**Dial:** silvered; guilloché center; applied Arabic numerals; large date window; Delta-shaped hands.
**Strap:** Hermès alligator with tongue buckle; polished finish.

## FORMA GRANDE AUTOMATIC — REF. PF006797

**Movement:** PF331.01; automatic winding; 55-hour power reserve; caliber 11′′′; Ø 25.6mm; 4 Hz–28,800 vph; 32 jewels; double-spring barrel; Côtes de Genève decoration; chamfered bridges; 22K gold oscillating weight.
**Functions:** hours, minutes, seconds; date.
**Case:** polished 18K white-gold, tonneau-shaped case (size: 46.6x34mm, thickness: 9.25mm); sapphire crystal with antireflective treatment; sapphire crystal caseback; Ø 5.5mm winding crown; individual number engraved on back; water resistant to 30 meters.
**Dial:** black; guilloché center; applied Roman numerals; large date window; Delta-shaped hands.
**Strap:** Hermès alligator with tongue buckle; polished finish.

## FORMA GRANDE AUTOMATIC STEEL — REF. PF006802

**Movement:** PF331.01; automatic winding; 55-hour power reserve; caliber 11′′′; Ø 25.6mm; 4 Hz–28,800 vph; 32 jewels; double-spring barrel; Côtes de Genève decoration; chamfered bridges.
**Functions:** hours, minutes, seconds; date.
**Case:** polished steel, tonneau-shaped case (size: 46.6x34mm, thickness: 9.25mm); sapphire crystal with antireflective treatment; sapphire crystal caseback; Ø 5.5mm winding crown; individual number engraved on back; water resistant to 30 meters.
**Dial:** silvered; guilloché center; lacquer-printed index; large date window; Delta-shaped hands with black lacquer.
**Bracelet:** Forma-type metal bracelet; polished finish; folding clasp.

## FORMA XL AUTOMATIC — REF. PF008625

**Movement:** PF331.01; automatic winding; 55-hour power reserve; caliber 11′′′; Ø 25.6mm; 4 Hz–28,800 vph; 32 jewels; double-spring barrel; Côtes de Genève decoration; chamfered bridges; 22K gold oscillating weight.
**Functions:** hours, minutes, seconds; date.
**Case:** polished 18K rose-gold, tonneau-shaped case (size: 53x37.2mm, thickness: 10.7mm); sapphire crystal with antireflective treatment; sapphire crystal caseback; Ø 7mm winding crown; individual number engraved on back; water resistant to 30 meters.
**Dial:** silvered; guilloché center; applied Roman numerals; large date window; Delta-shaped hands in blued steel.
**Strap:** Hermès alligator with folding clasp; polished finish.

## FORMA XL AUTOMATIC STEEL — REF. PF009236

**Movement:** PF331.01; automatic winding; 55-hour power reserve; caliber 11'''; Ø 25.6mm; 4 Hz–28,800 vph; 32 jewels; double-spring barrel; Côtes de Genève decoration; chamfered bridges.
**Functions:** hours, minutes, seconds; date.
**Case:** polished steel, tonneau-shaped case (size: 53x37.2mm, thickness: 10.7mm); sapphire crystal with antireflective treatment; sapphire crystal caseback; Ø 7mm winding crown; individual number engraved on back; water resistant to 30 meters.
**Dial:** Blu Lavanda with applied snailed center; applied Arabic numerals; large date window; Delta-shaped hands with black lacquer.
**Bracelet:** Forma-type bracelet metal; satin-finished central link; folding clasp.

## TORIC CHRONOGRAPH — REF. PF006780

**Movement:** PF190.01; automatic winding; 50-hour power reserve; caliber 13'''; Ø 29.8mm; 5 Hz–36,000 vph; 31 jewels; column-wheel chronograph; Côtes de Genève decoration; hand-chamfered bridges; steel stoned lengthwise; 18K gold oscillating weight; 22K gold oscillating weight.
**Functions:** hours, minutes, small seconds at 9; date; 1/5 second chronograph (large seconds, 30-minute counter, 12-hour counter).
**Case:** polished 18K white-gold case (Ø 40mm, thickness: 12.3mm); bezel with double milling; sapphire crystal with antireflective treatment; sapphire crystal caseback; Ø 6mm winding crown (cabochon sapphire); individual number engraved on back; water resistant to 30 meters.
**Dial:** black and silvered; guilloché center; black snailed counters; transfer-printed Arabic numerals; Delta-shaped hands with luminous material.
**Strap:** Hermès alligator with tongue buckle; polished finish.

## TORIC CHRONOGRAPH — REF. PF006782

**Movement:** PF190.01; automatic winding; 50-hour power reserve; caliber 13'''; Ø 29.8mm; 5 Hz–36,600 vph; 31 jewels; column-wheel chronograph; Côtes de Genève decoration; hand-chamfered bridges; steel stoned lengthwise; 22K gold oscillating weight.
**Functions:** hours, minutes, small seconds at 9; date; 1/5 second chronograph (large seconds, 30-minute counter, 12-hour counter).
**Case:** polished 18K rose-gold case (Ø 40mm, thickness: 12.3mm); bezel with double milling; sapphire crystal with antireflective treatment; sapphire crystal caseback; Ø 6mm winding crown (cabochon sapphire); individual number engraved on back; water resistant to 30 meters.
**Dial:** black and gilded; guilloché center; snailed counters; applied Arabic numerals; Delta-shaped hands.
**Strap:** Hermès alligator with tongue buckle; polished finish.

## TORIC CHRONOGRAPH — REF. PF006783

**Movement:** PF190.01; automatic winding; 50-hour power reserve; caliber 13'''; Ø 29.8mm; 5 Hz–36,000 vph; 31 jewels; column-wheel chronograph; Côtes de Genève decoration; hand-chamfered bridges; steel stoned lengthwise; 22K gold oscillating weight.
**Functions:** hours, minutes, small seconds at 9; date; 1/5 second chronograph (large seconds, 30-minute counter, 12-hour counter).
**Case:** polished platinum 950 (Ø 40mm, thickness: 12.3mm); bezel with double milling; sapphire crystal with antireflective treatment; sapphire crystal caseback; Ø 6mm winding crown (cabochon sapphire); individual number engraved on back; water resistant to 30 meters.
**Dial:** Blu Lavanda; guilloché center; black snailed counters; applied Arabic numerals; Delta-shaped hands.
**Strap:** Hermès alligator with tongue buckle; polished finish.

# Patek Philippe

Patek Philippe is a brand renowned for its technological expertise, constantly raising the standards of watchmaking and continuing to represent the benchmark of excellence in haute horology.

In both the men's and women's lines, Patek Philippe offers striking new pieces. The Annual Calendar Ref. 5135 represents a new caliber for the brand. Housed in the Gondolo tonneau case, and officially called the Gondolo Calendario, the watch offers a patented annual calendar function and a moonphase display. The proprietary annual calendar caliber was developed in 1996 and was the first wristwatch that automatically advanced the month, day and date with only one manual correction on March 1. The Gondolo Calendario houses this system, but with new display. It shows the date, day and month in three apertures arranged on an arc between 10:00 and 2:00. The subdial at 6:00 has a 24-hour scale and a moonphase display.

At the heart of the watch is the caliber 324 self-winding mechanical movement with the Gyromax balance wheel (for which Patek Philippe garnered patents more than 50 years ago). A closer look at the microcosm of this movement reveals an entirely new toothing system—one that took two years to perfect. The new teeth assure constant force transmission, positively impacting the watch's accuracy rate. The caliber 324 is finished to meet the meticulous specifications of the Geneva Seal, and is revealed through a sapphire caseback.

With its new Calatrava models, Patek Philpe evolves the collection. The new 37mm watches are offered in 18-karat yellow, rose and white gold, as well as in platinum. Its new Twenty-4® pieces feature diamond-set cases in rose or white gold with a chic satin strap in four different hues.

**ABOVE**

The new Twenty-4® 18-karat gold watches feature diamond-set cases and satin straps. Shown from left to right:

White-gold case with Eternal Gray dial

Rose-gold case with Chocolate Dream dial

White-gold case with Timeless White dial

Rose-gold case with Timeless White dial

**BOTTOM LEFT**

The Gondolo Calendarios offer the Annual Calendar Ref. 5135 with three aperture displays and moonphase display with 24-hour dial.

**BOTTOM RIGHT**

The Gondolo Calendario houses this new caliber 324 self-winding movement with numerous innovations, including the four-spoke Gyromax balance and a new toothing system.

## CHRONOLOGY

**1839** Antoine Norbert de Patek and François Czapek form the Genevan pocket-watch manufacturer Patek, Czapek & Co.

**1844** Patek is introduced to the talents of Jean Adrien Philippe.

**1845** The pair launches Patek & Co.

**1851** Patek & Co. becomes Patek Philippe & Co. and wins a gold medal at the first World's Fair (London's Crystal Palace Exhibition).

**1863** The brand's free mainspring leads to the invention of the automatic watch.

**1881** A particular index regulating system by an eccentric cam is patented and the Gondolo pocket watches are equipped with this device. The same name is used later for a series of wristwatches.

**1889** A special perpetual-calendar system is patented and the calendar is self-regulated according to the different duration of months and leap-year cycles.

**1901** The family firm becomes a stock corporation.

**1902** A split-second chronograph is patented.

**1910** The Duca di Regla model is realized; a unique and never matched piece, it features a Westminster sonnerie with five tones.

**1915** Patek's first complicated wristwatch is produced (for women); it is provided with hour-, quarter- and five-minute repeaters.

**1925** A wristwatch with a perpetual calendar is realized.

**1932** Patek Philippe is acquired by Charles and Jean Stern, long-time providers of watch dials to Patek Philippe. The Classic Calatrava is born.

**1933** Henry Graves, Jr. purchases the Graves watch for $11,570. It will re-sell in 1999 for $11 million.

**1942** Through his New York-based company, Charles Stern's son Henri is responsible for sales and distribution of Patek Philippe timepieces in America.

**1948** Creation of Electronics Division and the development of quartz technology.

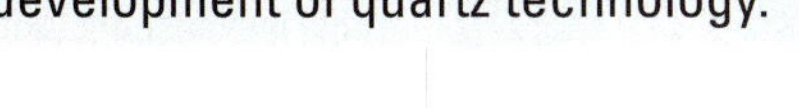

**1959** A watch with dual time-zone indication is realized.

**1962** Patek Philippe sets an unbroken precision record for mechanical watches at the competition of the Geneva Observatory.

**1976** Nautilus is introduced, the house's first sports diver's watch.

**1986** A new patent is registered; it is a secular perpetual calendar with a retrograde indicator. No adjustment will be needed for 400 years.

**1989** Caliber 89, the most complicated existing pocket watch, commemorates the company's 150th Anniversary. Nine years and 1,728 components were required to produce this historical masterpiece featuring 35 horological functions—33 of which are complications. Caliber 89 auctions for $3.2 million.

**1996** A patent is registered for the annual calendar. A 1939 Calatrava (a unique piece in platinum with minute repeater, perpetual calendar and moonphase) fetches a record $1.3 million at auction; the same watch sold for about $115,000 in 1981.

**1999** The Twenty-4® is Patek Philippe's first bracelet watch in steel and diamonds.

**2000** Star Caliber 2000, a high-horology pocket watch, features 21 complications and includes six patented components.

**2001** The Sky Moon Tourbillon is the most complicated wristwatch model and the first to show a complete replica of the night sky above the town chosen by the wearer. On a second dial, it indicates the motion of stars, angular motion and moonphases, as well as sideral time in hours and minutes of the same place. In November, the Patek Philippe Museum is opened, displaying more than 2,000 Patek Philippe inventions.

**2002** Patek Philippe unveils the Celestial watch, Ref. 5102—an astronomical wonder that depicts the exact configuration of the night sky, complete with movement of the stars, the position of the moon and the moonphases within the lunar cycle—all on the watch's front dial. Two years in the making, this watch incorporates achievements and developments previously accomplished by Patek Philippe for its Star Caliber 2000 pocket watch and the Sky Moon Tourbillon.

**2003** Patek Philippe unveils the 10 Day Tourbillon, a COSC-certified tourbillon with no aperture on the dial.

**RIGHT**

Calatrava Ref. 5196, from left to right:

18-karat rose gold with a slightly domed silvery dial

18-karat yellow gold with a slightly domed silvery dial

18-karat white gold with a slightly domed silvery dial

Platinum with a silvery dial, applied white-gold Breguet numerals and a small diamond set between the lugs at 6:00.

## CHRONOGRAPH, PERPETUAL CALENDAR — REF. 5970 R

**Movement:** mechanical manual-winding Patek Philippe CH 27-70 Q caliber; decorated with Côtes de Genève pattern and beveled; hallmarked with the Geneva Seal. **Functions:** hour, minute, small second; 24 hour; chronograph with 2 counters; perpetual calendar (date, day, month, year, moonphase). **Case:** 18K pink-gold three-piece case (Ø 39.7mm, thickness: 13.35mm); curved sapphire crystal; hollowed bezel; 4 correctors on the middle; crown and rectangular pushers in pink gold; two screw-on backs: one closed and one displaying the movement through a sapphire crystal; water resistant to 2.5atm. **Dial:** gold, silvered, subdials decorated with circular beads; applied pink-gold bâton and square markers; pink-gold leaf-style hands.
**Indications:** minute counter and four-year cycle at 3; moonphase and date at 6; small second and 24-hour at 9; day and month at 12; center second counter, tachometer scale, minute track with divisions for 1/5 second.
**Strap:** crocodile leather; pink-gold fold-over clasp.
**Also available:** in white gold.

## GONDOLO CALENDAR — REF. 5135 G

**Movement:** mechanical manual-winding Patek Philippe 324 S QA LU 24H caliber; 21K gold rotor; Gyromax balance with 4 rays and 4 adjustable regulation masses; 28,800 vph; hallmarked with the Geneva Seal. **Functions:** hour, minute, second; 24 hour; annual calendar (date, day, month, moonphase). **Case:** 18K white-gold two-piece case in tonneau shape (39.5x38.5mm, thickness: 11.6mm); bezel in coussin shape; curved sapphire crystal; 2 correctors on the middle; crown in white gold; screw-on back, displaying the movement through a sapphire crystal; water resistant to 2.5atm.
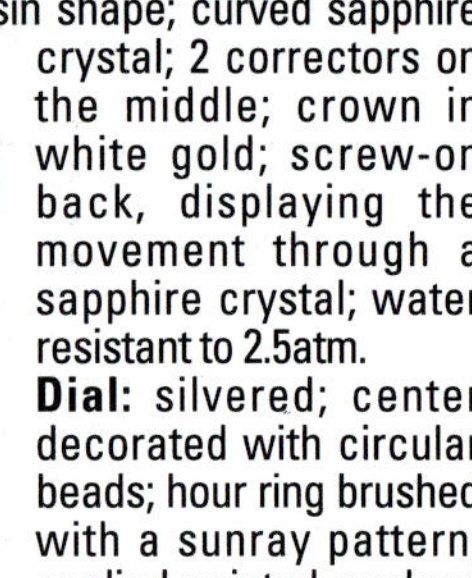
**Dial:** silvered; center decorated with circular beads; hour ring brushed with a sunray pattern; applied pointed markers and 2 white-gold Arabic numerals; white-gold Dauphine hands.
**Indications:** month at 2; moonphase and 24-hour at 6; day at 10; date at 12 with white-gold rim.
**Strap:** crocodile leather; white-gold clasp.
**Also available:** with slate-gray dial; in yellow gold with opalin silvered dial.

## GONDOLO — REF. 5109 P

**Movement:** mechanical manual-winding Patek Philippe 215 PS caliber; hallmarked with the Geneva Seal.
**Functions:** hour, minute, small second.
**Case:** platinum two-piece case in rectangular shape (34x30mm, thickness: 6.4mm); curved sapphire crystal; crown in white gold; back fastened by 4 screws; water resistant to 2.5atm.
**Dial:** solid gold, silvered, brushed, subdial decorated with circular beads; applied bâton markers (Arabic numeral 12) in black-oxidized gold; printed railway minute track; leaf-style hands in black-oxidized gold.
**Indications:** small second at 6.
**Strap:** crocodile leather; platinum clasp.

## NAUTILUS — REF. 3711/1G

**Movement:** mechanical automatic-winding Patek Philippe 315 S C caliber; 21K gold rotor; hallmarked with the Geneva Seal.
**Functions:** hour, minute, second; date.
**Case:** 18K white-gold two-piece case in tonneau shape (38x41.8mm, thickness: 8.7mm); polished and brushed finish; curved sapphire crystal; crown in white gold with two gaskets and case protection; sandwich structure with longitudinal fastening screws, displaying the movement through a sapphire crystal; water resistant to 12atm.
**Dial:** black, tooled with a linear profile; luminescent applied bâton markers in white gold; white printed minute track; luminescent white-gold bâton hands.
**Indications:** date at 3.
**Bracelet:** brushed white gold; polished central links; double fold-over safety clasp.
**Note:** limited edition.
**Also available:** in stainless steel with anthracite dial with a linear profile, bâton markers or smooth black dial and Roman numerals; in yellow gold with silvered dial and bâton markers.

## CALATRAVA REF. 5107 P

**Movement:** mechanical automatic-winding Patek Philippe 315 SC caliber; hallmarked with the Geneva Seal.
**Functions:** hour, minute, second; date.
**Case:** platinum three-piece case (Ø 37mm, thickness: 8.8mm); set brilliant at 6; curved sapphire crystal; screw-down crown in white gold with case protection; screw-on back displaying the movement through a sapphire crystal; water resistant to 2.5atm.
**Dial:** matte black; applied faceted bâton markers in white gold; applied cabochon minute track in white gold; white-gold faceted Dauphine hands.
**Indications:** date at 3.
**Strap:** alligator; platinum clasp.
**Note:** limited edition.
**Also available:** in pink or yellow gold with opalin dial.

## CALATRAVA REF. 5196 R

**Movement:** mechanical manual-winding Patek Philippe 215 PS caliber; hallmarked with the Geneva Seal.
**Functions:** hour, minute, small second.
**Case:** 18K pink-gold three-piece case (Ø 37mm, thickness: 7.65mm); polished and brushed finish; curved sapphire crystal; pink-gold crown; snap-on back; water resistant to 2.5atm.
**Dial:** silvered; applied faceted bâton markers and cabochon minute track in pink gold; pink-gold faceted Dauphine hands.
**Indications:** small second at 6.
**Strap:** crocodile leather; pink-gold clasp.
**Also available:** in white or yellow gold; in platinum.

## CALATRAVA OFFICIER REF. 5196 P

**Movement:** mechanical manual-winding Patek Philippe 215 PS caliber; hallmarked with the Geneva Seal.
**Functions:** hour, minute, small second.
**Case:** platinum three-piece case (Ø 33.5mm, thickness: 6.85mm); set brilliant at 6; curved sapphire crystal; crown in white gold; snap-on back; water resistant to 2.5atm.
**Dial:** silvered, center with diamonds, brushed hour ring, subdial decorated with circular beads; applied Breguet Arabic numerals and cabochon minute track in white gold; white-gold leaf-style hands.
**Indications:** small second at 6.
**Strap:** crocodile leather; platinum clasp.
**Also available:** in white, pink or yellow gold.

## CALATRAVA TRAVEL TIME REF. 5134 P

**Movement:** manual-winding Patek Philippe 215 PS FUS 24H caliber; 44-hours autonomy; 18 jewels; Ø 21.90mm, thickness: 3.35mm; Gyromax balance; 28,800 vph; flat balance-spring; made up of 178 elements; hallmarked with the Geneva Seal.
**Functions:** hour, minute, small second; second time zone; 24 hour.
**Case:** platinum three-piece case (Ø 37, thickness: 10.1mm) with set brilliant at 6; curved sapphire crystal; platinum crown with case protection; 2 pushers on the middle (at 8 to put the GMT hand forward, at 10 to put it back); screwed-on back displaying the movement through a sapphire crystal; water resistant to 2.5atm.
**Dial:** silvered grained center; brushed ring; subdials with circular beads; applied bâton markers, in white gold; printed railway minute track; white-gold Dauphine hands (GMT hand in burnished gold).
**Indications:** small second at 6; 24-hour at 12.
**Strap:** crocodile leather, hand-stitched; fold-over clasp with logo in platinum.
**Also available:** applied Arabic numerals; white or pink gold, white dial; yellow gold.

## TOURBILLON, MINUTE REPEATER REF. 3939 HJ

**Movement:** mechanical manual-winding Patek Philippe RTO 27 PS QR caliber; with tourbillon device; hallmarked with the Geneva Seal.
**Functions:** hour, minute, small second; minute repeater.
**Case:** 18K yellow-gold three-piece case (Ø 33mm); curved sapphire crystal; gold crown; 4 correctors and repeater slide on the middle; two snap-on backs: one closed and the other displaying the movement through a sapphire crystal.
**Dial:** gold; white enameled; applied gold Arabic numerals; printed minute track; gold Pomme hands.
**Indications:** small second at 6.
**Strap:** crocodile leather; gold clasp.
**Also available:** in white or pink gold; in platinum with closed caseback.

## TOURBILLON, MINUTE REPEATER

Minute repeaters were the first watches realized by Patek Philippe 150 years ago. In 1915 it was the first to introduce this complication in a wristwatch—in the small case of ladies' watch, no less. A curious detail is common with all two-hammer minute repeaters: the maximum number of strokes is reached at 12:59 with 32 in total. The finish of the movement equipped with a tourbillon (bottom) is very refined. On the top, there is the symbol of the famous Genevan manufacture—the Calatrava cross—partly hiding the repeater disconnecting-gear, whose purpose is to disconnect the transmission of motive force coming from the sonnerie spring, thus slowing down the frequency of strokes, allowing the user to count them. This model, as well as the "simple" minute repeater, is adorned with an enamel dial, for which many oven-processes are required.

## SPLIT-SECOND CHRONOGRAPH, PERPETUAL CALENDAR REF. 5004 J

**Movement:** mechanical manual-winding Patek Philippe CHR 27-70 Q caliber; decorated with Côtes de Genève and beveled; hallmarked with the Geneva Seal.
**Functions:** hour, minute, small second; 24-hour; split-second chronograph with two counters; perpetual calendar (date, day, month, year, moonphase).
**Case:** 18K yellow-gold three-piece case (Ø 37mm); curved sapphire crystal; gold crown with split-second pusher; 4 correctors on the middle; two screw-on backs: one closed and the other displaying the movement through a sapphire crystal; water resistant to 2.5atm.
**Dial:** gold; opalin silvered; applied gold Arabic numerals and cabochon markers; gold leaf-style hands.
**Indications:** minute counter and four-year cycle at 3; small second and 24-hour at 9; day and month at 12; center second and split-second; minute track with divisions for 1/5 second.
**Strap:** crocodile leather; gold clasp.
**Also available:** in white or pink gold with silvered or black dial; in platinum with silvered or black dial.

## SPLIT-SECOND CHRONOGRAPH, PERPETUAL CALENDAR

This model, realized in 1955 (Ref. 2571) with a Valjoux caliber base and proposed again in 1995 with a new caliber base (Ref. 5004 J), is one among the most important in modern horology. It may be controlled by actuating a third pusher coaxial with the winding crown: this concept is the concrete result of the whole experience and technology that made Patek Philippe famous and appreciated all over the world. The mechanics are based on the sophisticated CH 27-70 chronograph caliber integrated by the traditional Patek calendar module. The movement shows the boomerang-shaped bridge supporting the wheels of the chronograph and the split-second chronograph seconds. Immediately to the left, one notices the working mechanics: the clam locking the additional-hand wheel (acting upon the steel wheel) and the control column-wheel with an ornamental element on top in a sea-star shape with curved arms (also acting as a stop lever).

## ANNUAL CALENDAR PLATINUM — REF. 5056 P

As an intermediate step between the classic calendar watch (typically automatic with date or day display in a window and center seconds) and the complex perpetual calendar, Patek Philippe's annual calendar recognizes the months of 30 or 31 days over a whole year from the 1st of March to the end of February (when the date has to be moved forward by hand). Ref. 5056 P is an edition revisited with new colors and housed in a new platinum case. From the aesthetic point of view, with its white-gold hands and markers, it matches the safari-gray crocodile strap and the slate-gray dial nicely. A new distinctive mark of Patek Philippe's complicated watches in platinum is the Top Wesselton Pur diamond set on the middle at 6.

## ANNUAL CALENDAR — REF. 5035 P

**Movement:** mechanical automatic-winding Patek Philippe 315 SQA 24 H caliber; autonomy 48 hours; rotor in 21K gold; 35 jewels; Ø 30mm; Gyromax balance with 21,600 vph; flat balance-spring; consisting of 316 elements; hallmarked with the Geneva Seal. **Functions:** hour, minute, second; 24-hour; annual calendar (date, day, moonphase, month—with automatic storage of the days of a month for the whole year). **Case:** platinum three-piece case (Ø 36.5mm, thickness: 11mm) with a Top Wesselton brilliant set between the lugs; curved sapphire crystal; hollowed bezel; platinum crown; 3 correctors on the middle; screw-on back displaying the movement through a sapphire crystal; water resistant to 2.5atm.
**Dial:** silvered; luminescent applied white-gold Roman numerals; printed railway minute track; luminescent white-gold leaf-style hands.
**Indications:** month at 3; 24-hour and date at 6; day at 9.
**Strap:** crocodile leather; white-gold clasp.
**Also available:** with slate-gray or black dial; in pink gold with silvered or black dial; in white gold with silvered, copper, slate-gray or black dial; in yellow gold with black dial.

## WORLD TIME — REF. 5110 J

**Movement:** mechanical automatic-winding Patek Philippe 240/188 caliber; autonomy 48 hours; 33 jewels; micro-rotor in 22K gold; Gyromax balance with 21,600 vph; flat balance-spring; consisting of 235 elements; hallmarked with the Geneva Seal. **Functions:** hour, minute; world time; 24-hour. **Case:** 18K yellow-gold three-piece case (Ø 37mm, thickness: 9.65mm); curved sapphire crystal; gold crown with case protection; rectangular gold pusher at 10 for basic setting and time zone adjustment (by hourly steps to move the hours hand forward clockwise and the setting of 24-hour discs and the reference town names of the 24 time zones counter-clockwise); screw-on back displaying the movement through a sapphire crystal; water resistant to 2.5atm. **Dial:** opalin; guilloché center; applied gold bâton markers; gold lozenge hands.
**Indications:** world time and 24-hour day-night.
**Strap:** crocodile leather, hand-stitched; fold-over gold clasp.
**Also available:** in white or pink gold; in platinum with blue soleil dial.

## POWER RESERVE, SMALL SECONDS, DATE AND MOONPHASE — REF. 5055 G

**Movement:** mechanical automatic-winding Patek Philippe 240 PS IRM C LU caliber; micro-rotor in 22K gold; hallmarked with the Geneva Seal.
**Functions:** hour, minute, small second; date; moonphase; power reserve.
**Case:** 18K white-gold two-piece case (Ø 36.5mm, thickness: 9.25mm); curved sapphire crystal; 2 correctors on the middle (at 4 and 8); white-gold crown; screw-on back displaying the movement through a sapphire crystal; water resistant to 2.5atm.
**Dial:** white enameled; applied Arabic numerals in white gold; printed minute track with luminescent dots; luminescent bâton hands in white gold.
**Indications:** small second between 4 and 5; date and moonphase at 7; power reserve between 10 and 11.
**Strap:** crocodile leather; fold-over white-gold clasp with round skeleton stop in the shape of the house's logo (Calatrava cross).
**Also available:** with black dial; in pink gold, rosé dial; in yellow gold with white dial.

## SKY MOON TOURBILLON REF. 5002 J

**Movement:** mechanical manual-winding Patek Philippe 109 (RTO 27 QR SID LU CL) caliber; decorated with Côtes de Genève and beveled; hallmarked with the Geneva Seal; COSC-certified chronometer. **Functions:** hour, minute; perpetual calendar (date, day, month, year, moonphase); minute repeater; sidereal hour; sky map; lunation. **Case:** 18K yellow-gold three-piece case (Ø 43mm, thickness: 16.2mm); double curved sapphire crystal; gold crown: at 2 for the sky map and sidereal hour, at 4 for the movement; 4 correctors and repeater slide on the middle decorated with engraved Calatrava crosses.
**Dial:** gold, silvered; applied gold Roman numerals; printed railway minute track; gold Poire hands.
**Rear dial:** blue sapphire crystal with white enameled Poire skeleton hands.
**Indications:** month at 3; moonphase at 6; day at 9; four-year cycle at 12; date with retrograde center hand.
**Indications:** sidereal hour; lunation; visible sky part.
**Strap:** crocodile leather; gold clasp.

## SKY MOON TOURBILLON REAR DIAL

The Sky Moon Tourbillon is a complicated watch equipped with a tourbillon device, a minute repeater and a perpetual calendar; but the real rarity is represented by the functions linked with the displays of the sidereal hour and the visible sky part (reproduced upon request on the basis of the sky really visible from any town). The white hands indicate the sidereal hour, i.e. the time referred to the passage of the same meridian with respect to a certain star (and not to the sun); as it occurs every 23 hour, 56' and 4.1". The orientation of the sky vault inside the gold oval is the one visible at the moment. The moon disc shows not only the phases but also the lunation period (29 days, 12 hours, 44' and 2.82"). The errors accumulated for these indications because of the imperfect transmission ratio of the gears of the "astronomic" module are minimal ones, i.e. some seconds every century. The orders for this watch must be addressed exclusively to the Patek Philippe's Geneva headquarters in Rue du Rhône.
**Also available:** in platinum.

## SKY MOON REF. 5102

**Movement:** automatic Patek Philippe 240 CL LU caliber (240 base + 165 module for astronomic functions, patented); 301 components; micro-rotor in 18K gold integrated in the movement's volume; decorated with Côtes de Genève and circular graining patterns and beveled; hallmarked with the Geneva Seal. **Functions:** hour, minute; moonphase; sky map. **Case:** 18K white-gold three-piece case (Ø 43.5mm, thickness: 9.78mm); curved sapphire crystal; white-gold crown; pushbuttons at 2 for the hands and at 4 for the movement; middle with engraved Calatrava cross as a symbol of the house; screw-on back displaying the movement through a sapphire crystal; water resistant to 2atm.
**Dial:** blue sapphire crystal; sky part visible from any town (reproduced upon request; in the piece shown here, the town is Geneva); sapphire discs for the astronomic indications; white enameled gold leaf-style hands.
**Indications:** the white-gold oval represents the visible horizon of the sky vault whose orientation varies following the position of the Earth; position and sidereal hour of Sirius and Moon; moonphase display in a window.
**Strap:** crocodile leather; white-gold clasp.
**Note:** unique piece available on request.

## CHRONOGRAPH, PERPETUAL CALENDAR REF. 3970 EG

**Movement:** mechanical manual-winding Patek Philippe CHR 27-70 Q caliber; decorated with Côtes de Genève and beveled; hallmarked with the Geneva Seal. **Functions:** hour, minute, small second; 24-hour; chronograph with 2 counters; perpetual calendar (date, day, month, year, moonphase). **Case:** 18K white-gold three-piece case (Ø 36mm, thickness: 12mm); curved sapphire crystal; hollowed bezel; white-gold crown; 4 correctors on the middle; two screw-on backs: one closed and the other displaying the movement through a sapphire crystal; water resistant to 2.5atm. **Dial:** gold, silvered; subdials decorated with circular beads; applied white-gold bâton and square markers; white-gold bâton hands.
**Indications:** minute counter and four-year cycle at 3; moonphase and date at 6; small second and 24-hour at 9; day and month at 12; center second; minute track with divisions for 1/5 second.
**Strap:** crocodile leather; white-gold clasp.
**Also available:** with black dial; in pink or white gold with silvered dial; in platinum with silvered or black dial or with black dial and brilliant markers.

## TWENTY-4® REF. 4909/50 R

**Movement:** mechanical manual-winding Patek Philippe 16/250 caliber; hallmarked with the Geneva Seal.
**Functions:** hour, minute.
**Case:** 18K pink-gold two-piece case (22.7x21.9mm, thickness: 6.7mm); rectangular, anatomically curved, lateral juts; pavé with set brilliants of Top Wesselton quality; curved sapphire crystal; pink-gold crown with a faceted set brilliant; back fastened by 4 screws displaying the movement through a sapphire crystal; water resistant to 2.5atm.
**Dial:** solid pink-gold; pavé of brilliants; Roman numerals in black oxidized gold; bâton hands in black oxidized gold.
**Strap:** satin with brilliant pavé attachment; recessed double fold-over clasp with logo in pink gold.
**Also available:** in white gold.

## TRAVEL TIME LADY REF. 4864 G

**Movement:** mechanical manual-winding Patek Philippe 215 PS FUS 24H caliber; autonomy 44 hours; 18 jewels (Ø 21.90mm, thickness: 3.35mm). Gyromax balance; 28,800 vph; flat balance-spring; made up of 178 elements; hallmarked with the Geneva Seal.
**Functions:** hour, minute, small second; second time zone; 24-hour.
**Case:** 18K white-gold two-piece case (Ø 29.5mm, thickness: 8.4mm); curved sapphire crystal; milled bezel; white-gold crown in Louis XV style with a sapphire cabochon; 2 pushers on the middle (at 8 to advance the GMT hand, at 10 to move it backward); snap-on back; water resistant to 2.5atm.
**Dial:** white enameled; applied Arabic numerals in white gold; printed railway minute track; black enameled gold leaf-style hands (GMT hand in burnished gold).
**Indications:** small second at 6; 24-hour at 12.
**Strap:** crocodile leather; white-gold clasp.
**Also available:** in pink or yellow gold.

## SMALL SECOND, MOONPHASE REF. 4858 G

**Movement:** mechanical manual winding Patek Philippe 16-250PS/LU caliber; hallmarked with the Geneva Seal.
**Functions:** hour, minute, small second; moonphase.
**Case:** 18K white-gold three-piece case (Ø 29mm, thickness: 7.8mm); curved sapphire crystal; bezel with 60 brilliants (approx. 0.39 carats); one corrector on the middle; white-gold crown with cabochon brilliant (approx. 0.05 carats); snap-on back; water resistant to 2.5atm.
**Dial:** opalin, guilloché soleil center; grained hour ring; applied markers in white gold with set brilliants (approx. 0.02 carats); printed minute track; leaf-style hands in black oxidized gold.
**Indications:** moonphase at 4; small second at 8.
**Strap:** satin; white-gold clasp.
**Also available:** white gold; bronze dial; bezel without brilliants; brilliant markers. Ref. 4857: yellow gold, white dial and blue subdials; white gold with gray dial.

## SMALL SECONDS, MOONPHASE REF. 4858 J

**Movement:** mechanical manual-winding Patek Philippe 16-250PS/LU caliber; hallmarked with the Geneva Seal. **Functions:** hour, minute, small second; moonphase. **Case:** 18K yellow-gold three-piece case (Ø 29mm, thickness: 7.65mm); curved sapphire crystal; bezel with 60 set brilliants (approx. 0.39 carats); one corrector on the middle; gold crown with a cabochon brilliant (approx. 0.05 carats); snap-on back; water resistant to 2.5atm. **Dial:** bronze; guilloché center; grained hour ring; applied gold markers with set brilliants; printed railway minute track; gold leaf-style hands.
**Indications:** moonphase at 4; small second at 8.
**Strap:** crocodile leather; gold clasp.
**Also available:** without brilliants on bezel, but with brilliant markers. Ref. 4857: in yellow gold with white dial and blue subdials; white gold with gray dial.

## CALIBER 16.250

Manual-winding movement; autonomy of 38 hours; Geneva Seal. **Functions:** hours, minutes. **Shape:** round. **Diameter:** 16.00mm (7'''). **Thickness:** 2.50mm. **Jewels:** 18 (escape wheel with end-stones). **Balance:** smooth. **Frequency:** 28,800 vph. **Balance-spring:** flat, with "Triovis" index and micrometer screw regulation device. **Shock-absorber system:** Incabloc. **Notes:** the pillar-plate is decorated with a circular-graining pattern, the bridges are decorated with a Côtes de Genève pattern and beveled. Noticeable on the balance bridge is the special "Triovis" index and the balance spring stud holder allowing the regulation of the oscillations of the balance without disturbing the alignment of both the roller-table and the escapement line. **Derived caliber:** 16.250 PS LU (16.250 with small seconds and moonphase; diameter: 16.30mm, thickness: 2.95mm, 115 components).

## CALIBERS 175 AND 177

Manual-winding movement; autonomy of 43 hours; Geneva Seal. **Functions:** hours and minutes. **Shape:** round. **Diameter:** 20.80mm (9'''1/4). **Thickness:** extra-thin, 1.77mm. **Jewels:** 18 (escape wheel with end-stones). **Balance:** Gyromax, diameter: 7.40mm, in beryllium bronze, with 4 regulation inertia-blocks. **Frequency:** 18,000 vph; Caliber 177: 21,600 vph. **Balance-spring:** flat. **Shock-absorber system:** Kif. **Notes:** the pillar-plate is decorated with a circular-graining pattern, the bridges are decorated with a Côtes de Genève pattern and beveled. At present, only Caliber177/02 is produced; it has the same technical features as the 175, differing only in its vibration per hour datum.

## CALIBER 215

Manual movement; autonomy of 44 hours; Geneva Seal. **Functions:** hours, minutes. **Shape:** round. **Diameter:** 21.50mm (9'''1/2). **Thickness:** 2.55mm. **Jewels:** 18 (escape wheel with end-stones). **Balance:** Gyromax, with 8 regulation inertia-blocks. **Frequency:** 28,800 vph. **Balance-spring:** flat. **Shock-absorber system:** Kif. **Notes:** pillar-plate decorated with a circular-graining pattern, bridges decorated with a Côtes de Genève pattern and beveled. **Derived calibers:** 215 PS (215 with small seconds); 215 PS FUS 24H (215 PS with two time zones with fast correction and 24 hours; diameter: 21.90mm, thickness: 3.35mm, 178 components).

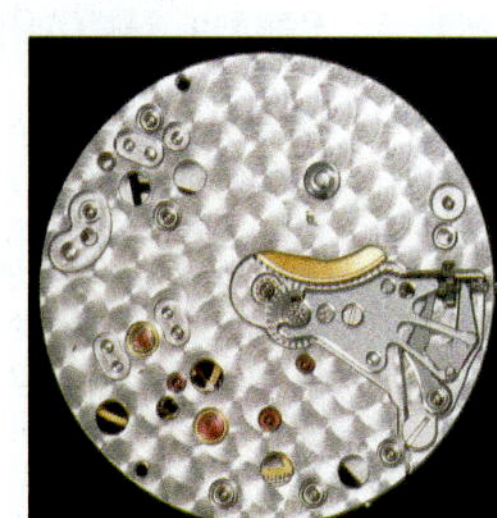

## CALIBER 215 PS FUS 24H

This movement equips the Travel Time and Calatrava Travel Time models. It allows the display of two time zones by two different hour hands. When this function is not needed, the second hour hand may remain completely hidden behind the first one. The mechanisms added on the dial side of the pillar-plate allow controlling of the second hour hand simply by pressing down two pushers to make it move forward or backward in hourly increments. Furthermore, a protection device prevents the mechanism from being damaged by simultaneous pressure exerted on both pushers. The colors of the hands, including the 24-hour hand, help to immediately distinguish local time (burnished hand like the hour hand actuated by the pushers) and home time (gold colored) with the corresponding hand remaining fixed.

## CALIBER 28-20/220

Manual-winding movement; autonomy of 240 hours (10 days); two series-mounted winding barrels; Geneva Seal. **Functions:** hours, minutes, small seconds; power reserve. **Shape:** rectangular. **Size:** 28.00x20.00mm. **Thickness:** 5.05mm. **Jewels:** 29 (9 in gold settings and escape wheel with end-stones). **Balance:** Gyromax, with 8 regulation inertia-blocks. **Frequency:** 21,600 vph. **Balance-spring:** flat. **Shock-absorber system:** Kif. **Notes:** pillar-plate decorated with a circular-graining pattern; bridges are decorated with a Côtes de Genève pattern and beveled. Officially certified "chronometer" (COSC). Above: the dial-side view of the movement provided with the 10-days feature shows the wheelwork of the power-reserve display (it has its pivot at the center of the clear-colored great wheel); below, the particular positioning of the jewels of the regulating organ and escapement on the pillar-plate are visible. The jewels are positioned in a slightly hollowed area in a sinusoid shape, including the balance jewel (recognizable by the shock-absorber spring) on one side and the escape-wheel jewel (with the ninth gold setting which is not visible on the main side of the movement) on the other side. On the right is the hour-setting system with a rocking spring and setting-lever, all brushed and beveled. From here, a gear cascade (under a bridge fastened by two screws) transmits motion from the winding—stem to the center hour—and minute wheels.

## CALIBER 315 SQA IRM LU (ANNUAL CALENDAR)

Thanks to the introduction of this complication, it was possible to near the performances of a perpetual calendar (here the manual date-correction must be initiated once a year, to pass from the 28th or 29th of February to the 1st of March), but with an extremely simplified mechanical construction. The real "brain" of this system is the small wheel provided with five projections, indicated within the circle. These projections "decide"—by engaging a feeler lever (under the same wheel)—the correct date change at the end of the months with 31 days (feeler lever on the circumference of the tooth bases) or 30 days (feeler lever on the projections, as on the drawing), except for the month of February that would be of 30 days without manual correction. The simplification of the annual calendar mechanism allowed realizing a module functioning almost exclusively by toothed wheels and gears, thus excluding rocking bars and levers which would otherwise be necessary for the correct functioning of a perpetual calendar.

The original version is Caliber 315 SQA 24H (patent N° CH685585 G, March 1, 1996—the first day of its first annual cycle), features the basic caliber 315 SC and the annual calendar module 198 with digital date display and digital 24 hours at 6, analogue day and month respectively at 10 and 2; with respect to the base, it has 316 elements, autonomy of 48 hours, 35 jewels, diameter: 30.00mm, thickness: 5.22mm.

## CALIBER R 27 PS (MINUTE REPEATER)

Automatic-winding movement; autonomy of 48 hours; 22K gold off-center micro-rotor mounted on a ball bearing; Geneva Seal.
**Functions:** hours, minutes, small seconds; double-tone minute repeater. **Shape:** round. **Diameter:** 28.00mm (12'''1/2). Embedding diameter: 27.60mm. **Thickness:** 5.05mm. **Jewels:** 39 (escape wheel with end-stones). **Balance:** Gyromax, with 8 regulation inertia-blocks.
**Frequency:** 21,600 vph. **Balance-spring:** flat.
**Shock-absorber system:** Kif.
**Notes:** the pillar-plate is decorated with a circular-graining pattern, the bridges are decorated with a Côtes de Genève pattern and beveled, the micro-rotor, included within the movement's total thickness is guilloché engraved, the Calatrava cross is skeletonized and gilded.
**Derived calibers:** R 27 Q (R 27 PS without small seconds + perpetual calendar module, 24 hours, visible in Caliber 240 Q on the previous pages; thickness: 6.90mm); R 27 PS-QR (R 27 PS + 126 perpetual calendar module with retrograde date, visible below).

## CALIBER R 27 PS (MINUTE REPEATER)

Caliber R 27 PS, dial-side view. The repeater gears are visible in this image. At 11 is the 14-toothed rack for the minute strokes. Below the minutes reel at the center of the movement is the minutes volute (with four bowed arms), almost hiding the smaller sized quarters volute (spiral-shaped, stepped). Also visible nearby is the hours volute, on the left below.
The functioning of a repeater mechanism depends on a series of feeler levers (one respectively for the hours, quarters and minutes) and on their positions on these volutes (representing a very memory of the sonnerie mechanism). When the sonnerie mechanism is actuated by the cursor positioned on the case side, the positions of said levers determine the number of strokes.
It is because of the mechanical complexity of the whole that a repeater represents one among the most expensive complications in horology.
Besides that, the complication of Caliber R 27 PS constitutes a highly refined technical solution, as all of the repeater mechanisms are housed on the same pillar-plate and not on an additional module. For this reason, a manufacturer is obliged to design the movement as a whole.

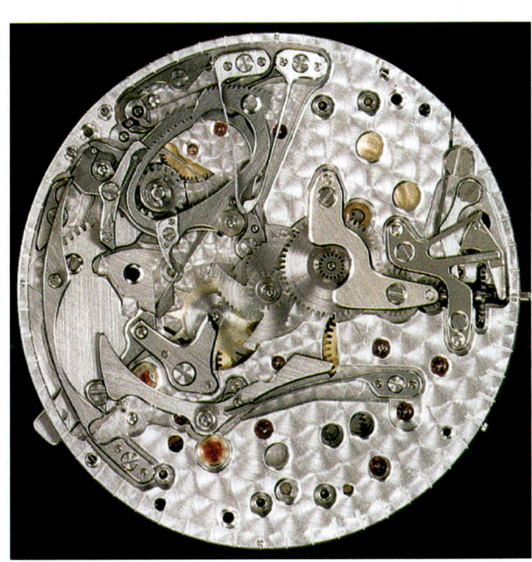

## CALIBER R 27 PS-QR (MINUTE REPEATER, PERPETUAL CALENDAR)

**Basic caliber:** R 27 PS. Automatic movement; autonomy of 48 hours; 22K gold off-center micro-rotor mounted on a ball bearing; Geneva Seal. **Functions:** hours, minutes, small seconds; perpetual calendar (retrograde date, day, month, leap year, moonphase with 4 fast correctors); minute repeater. **Shape:** round.
**Diameter:** 28.00mm (12'''1/2). **Embedding diameter:** 27.60mm. **Thickness:** 6.98mm.
**Jewels:** 39 (escape wheel with end-stones). **Balance:** Gyromax, with 8 regulation inertia-blocks. **Frequency:** 21,600 vph. **Balance-spring:** flat.
**Shock-absorber system:** Kif.
**Notes:** pillar-plate decorated with a circular-graining pattern, bridges decorated with a Côtes de Genève pattern and beveled, micro-rotor included within the movement's total thickness, guilloché engraved, Calatrava cross skeletonized and gilded. The 126 module includes the mechanisms of a perpetual calendar with date display by retrograde hand. Below 12 there is a 4-point star wheel for the digital indication of the four-year cycle (leap year included); at 2 and 9 there are the wheels for the month and day-of-the-week indications through windows. The same perpetual calendar module is also used for the basic calibers RTO 27 PS-QR (repeater, tourbillon, manual-winding perpetual calendar) and 315 SQR (automatic-winding perpetual calendar).

# PAUL PICOT

Jura-based Paul Picot presents elegant, classic timepieces handcrafted under the strict mandate of attention to precision and detail.

Each year this fine brand unveils limited collections adhering to the highest Swiss watchmaking standards. Most recently, Paul Picot SA extended its most successful Firshire collection to include the Firshire Tonneau 3000. Created by master craftsmen, the Firshire Tonneau 3000 timepieces are a rarity in watchmaking: a tonneau-shaped case housing a Paul Picot-exclusive complicated regulator movement bearing official COSC-chronometer certification. The Regulator was developed based on the exclusive PP1100 caliber. The Firshire Tonneau 3000 line is available in three self-winding models: a classic three hands watch with calendar; a retrograde seconds; complicated regulator.

The new three-hand chronometer beats at a rate of 28,800 vibrations per hour and houses 21 jewels in its intricate movement. The Retrograde Seconds features a 30-seconds retrograde and is built on a PP1300 movement with 34 jewels. The Complicated Regulator Firshire Tonneau 3000 with PP1100 caliber, features 30 jewels, and is meticulously finished in harmonious proportions. Crafted in steel, the Firshire Tonneau 3000 Limited Edition offers hours, minutes, seconds, date and power-reserve display on the dial in vivid color. This limited-series regulator is created in just 400 pieces with sapphire crystals with antireflective coating. Expanding its Majestic collection, Paul Picot unveils two richly studded diamond models—each in a limited edition of 10 pieces. One model is the Majestic Sertie—a unique trilogy that features an 18-karat gold case with a bezel set delicately with 62 VVS diamonds.

THIS PAGE

ABOVE

This Firshire Tonneau 3000 Second Retrograde features a return-to-zero-after-30-seconds function. The self-winding caliber PP1300 is a COSC-certified chronometer.

BOTTOM

The Majestic Rattrapante Pavé features a self-winding chronograph movement that is COSC-certified and houses 31 jewels. Crafted in 18-karat gold, the case is set with 447 diamonds.

FACING PAGE

Named for the fir trees in the Jura Mountains that is home to Paul Picot, these Firshire Tonneau 3000s feature self-winding, exclusive Regulator movements and are COSC-certified chronometers. The version on the right is produced in a limited edition.

PaulPicot
Chronometer
Automatic
REGULATOR
SWISS MADE
PaulPicot
No.01/100
Chronometer
Automatic
REGULATOR
SWISS MADE

THIS PAGE

TOP LEFT

The C-Type Le Plongeur 43mm Chronograph is a COSC-certified chronometer with a self-winding Valjoux 7753 movement with 27 jewels. It is water resistant to 300 meters.

CENTER

Crafted in steel, the Gentleman Chrono GMT watch is 42mm in diameter and is water resistant to 50 meters.

TOP RIGHT

The Gentleman Chrono GMT 42mm watch offers classic elegance in a larger size suited for every occasion. The rose-gold watch features a caseback embossed with the GMT medallion and the name "Gentleman." It offers a dual time-zone display and a chronograph, all based on a self-winding Valjoux movement.

FACING PAGE

TOP

The Majestic Gold Chrono Rattrapante houses an automatic COSC-certified chronometer movement.

BOTTOM

The Firshire Tonneau 3000 Classic is elegant and sophisticated with its Roman numerals and blue dial.

Additionally, the dials of the Majestic Sertie watches are set with another 78, 83 or 84 diamonds (depending on the movement), adding dazzling beauty. All movements are COSC-certified chronometers and house self-winding movements. The choices include a complicated calendar, a chronograph with split-second function, or a power-reserve indicator and calendar. The superbly decorated movements with 22-karat gold oscillating weights are visible through a transparent caseback.

Further demonstrating its watchmaking and jewelry prowess, Paul Picot unveils the Majestic Studded watch for true connoisseurs with an 18-karat white-, rose- or yellow-gold case ensconced with 447 diamonds (with the same models that are available in the Majestic Sertie). Because of the incredible success of the Majestic line, Paul Picot also offers several unique pieces with a self-winding chronograph, chronometer movement with rattrapante function on the crown.

Other new models include the striking C-Type Le Plongeur in a 43mm size. A yellow anti-friction ring inserted between the bezel and case, yellow accents on the dial and a yellow rubber strap highlight the incredible divers' chronometer chronograph. Crafted in a limited edition of 999 pieces, the watch is water resistant to 300 meters and is also offered with a steel bracelet. The watch's Protector Case contains a Swiss navy knife, a spare yellow rubber strap and a screwdriver.

## CHRONOLOGY

**1976** Mario Boiocchi launches the brand Paul Picot.

**1982** Paul Picot achieves Best Seller status for the first time with the sport-elegant Mediterranée.

**1986** The company begins to produce chronographs. Two of these models, U-Boot and Le Chronographe, will be very successful.

**1987** Paul Picot introduces the model Minichron, one of the smallest automatic chronographs with calendar.

**1988** Unveiling of Le Plongeur N. 1, a revolutionary professional diver watch that is water resistant to 30atm.

**1990** Paul Picot settles into a watch factory in the Jura Mountains in Le Noirmont, at an altitude of 100atm; The Le Chronographe is voted Watch of the Year at the Basel Fair.

**1991** The elegant model Carré Galbé is chosen as the new face of Paul Picot and the advertising campaign, developed by Helmut Newton, shocks the traditional world of watches.

**1993** Unveiled in Basel and arguably the Masterpiece of Paul Picot, Technicum is the first automatic split-second chronograph with calendar and power reserve; Atelier collection expands with a 310 La Rattrapante with complete calendar—a 1200 automatic chronometer with power reserve.

**1994** Paul Picot introduces the Firshire collection. The power-reserve version is named one of the best watchcases in the world at Basel Exhibition; Atelier Regulator is introduced.

**1995** Atelier Minute Repeater is unveiled at Basel.

**1996** Launch of Atelier Flinqué collection, special pieces are enameled.

**1997** The Perpetual Calendar is introduced into the Firshire collection.

**1998** Firshire 1937 is presented with a special caliber that Paul Picot based on a tonneau-shaped movement from 1930.

**1999** Paul Picot introduces the first models of the Firshire Ronde collection. These watch cases house the finest complications; At Basel, Paul Picot introduces a very exclusive collection in Atelier style—it is crafted in platinum with diamond and full pavé dial.

**2000** New to the Firshire Ronde collection, an automatic chronograph fly-back with big date at 12.

**2001** The Firshire collection adds an automatic chronometer Retrograde 30 seconds; The Gentleman collection is introduced and Paul Picot makes plans to further the development of this line within the upcoming years.

**2003** Paul Picot presents the prestigious Majestic line. With a choice of three movements fitted into steel or 18-karat gold cases. Accompanying the individual watches is a 50-piece three-gold-watch set in a special presentation box. This year, too, the brand unveils its exclusive divers watches, the C-Type Le Plongeur.

**2004** The brand expands its Majestic line, unveiling superbly gem-stone-adorned complicated watches. Launch of the new collection Firshire Tonneau 3000. Models are nominated to the Grand Prix D'Horlogerie de Genève 2004 and for Watch of the Year 2004.

## FIRSHIRE TONNEAU 3000 REGULATOR LIMITED EDITION

**Movement:** self-winding exclusive Regulator movement, caliber PP1100, base 2892-A2; 30 jewels; 28,800 vph; COSC-certified chronometer. A world first.
**Functions:** hour, minute, second; date; power reserve.
**Case:** high-grade stainless steel; 40.5mm wide with crown (37mm wide without); 52mm high with lugs (49mm high without); antireflective sapphire crystal; water resistant to 5atm.
**Dial:** multicolored lacquered dial with painted numerals (black or white base with red or blue hour counter).
**Indications:** center minutes; hours at 12; power reserve at 3; small seconds at 6; date at 9.
**Strap:** leather straps, available in different colors.
**Also available:** metal bracelet.
**Note:** limited edition of 400 pieces (4 versions, 100 numbered pieces of each).

## FIRSHIRE TONNEAU 3000 CLASSICAL

**Movement:** self-winding, base 2892-A2; 21 jewels; 28,800 vph; COSC-certified chronometer.
**Functions:** hour, minute, second; date.
**Case:** high-grade stainless steel; 40.5mm wide with crown (37mm wide without); 52mm high with lugs (49mm high without); antireflective sapphire crystal; water resistant to 5atm.
**Dial:** painted, available in several colors: Roman or Arabic numerals.
**Indications:** date at 6.
**Strap:** leather straps, available in different colors.
**Also available:** metal bracelet.

## FIRSHIRE TONNEAU 3000 REGULATOR

**Movement:** self-winding exclusive Regulator movement, caliber PP1100, base 2892-2; 30 jewels; 28,800 vph; COSC-certified chronometer. A world first.
**Functions:** hour, minute, seconds; date; power reserve.
**Case:** high-grade stainless steel; 40.5mm wide with crown (37mm without); 52mm high with lugs (49mm without); antireflective sapphire crystal; water resistant to 5atm.

**Dial:** lacquered dial with painted luminescent numerals; painted recessed counters.
**Strap:** leather straps, available in different colors.
**Also available:** metal bracelet.

## FIRSHIRE TONNEAU 3000 SECOND RETROGRADE

**Movement:** self-winding movement caliber PP1300, base 2892-2; 34 jewels; 28,800 vph; COSC-certified chronometer.
**Functions:** hour, minute, 30-second retrograde.
**Case:** high-grade stainless steel; 40.5mm wide with crown (37mm without); 52mm high with lugs (49mm without); antireflective sapphire crystal; water resistant to 5atm.

**Dial:** lacquered dial with painted Arabic numerals.
**Strap:** leather straps, available in different colors.
**Also available:** metal bracelet.

## LE PLONGEUR C-TYPE 43MM CHRONOGRAPH

**Movement:** self-winding, base Valjoux 7753; 27 jewels; 28,800 vph; COSC-certified chronometer.
**Functions:** hour, minute, small second; date; 3 counters.
**Case:** high-grade stainless steel; Ø 43mm; antireflective sapphire crystal; unidirectional rotating bezel with anti-friction ring; screw-down crown and pushers; water resistant to 30atm.
**Dial:** luminescent numerals and indexes.
**Indications:** minutes at 3; date at 4:30; hour counter at 6; small second at 9.
**Bracelet:** metal bracelet.
**Also available:** yellow and black rubber strap.
**Note:** limited edition of 999 pieces.

## LE PLONGEUR C-TYPE 43MM CLASSIC

**Movement:** self-winding, base 2824-2; 25 jewels; 28,800 vph; COSC-certified chronometer.
**Functions:** hour, minute, second; date.
**Case:** high-grade stainless steel; Ø 43mm; antireflective sapphire crystal; unidirectional rotating bezel with anti-friction ring; screw-down crown; water resistant to 30atm.
**Dial:** luminescent numerals and indexes.
**Indications:** date at 3; minute track.
**Strap:** yellow and black rubber strap.
**Also available:** metal bracelet.
**Note:** limited edition of 999 pieces.

## MAJESTIC RATTRAPANTE PAVEE

**Movement:** self-winding chronograph movement with split-second-hand function, base 8932; 31 jewels; 28,800 vph; 22K-gold oscillating weight; COSC-certified chronometer.
**Functions:** small seconds at 9.
**Case:** 18K white, rose or yellow gold studded with 447 diamonds; pusher on crown; antireflective, domed sapphire crystal; sapphire crystal tonneau-shaped back; water resistant to 5atm.
**Dial:** 925 solid silver, engine-turned dial set with 332 diamonds.
**Strap:** Louisiana alligator leather.
**Note:** wristlet attachments with 90 diamonds.

## GENTLEMAN'S CHRONO GMT

**Movement:** self-winding chronograph, base Valjoux 7750; 28 jewels; 28,800 vph.
**Functions:** small seconds at 9; date; GMT (second time zone).
**Case:** high-grade stainless steel; Ø 42mm; screw-down crown (steel version only); antireflective, domed sapphire crystal; water resistant to 5atm.
**Dial:** engine-turned dial with painted Arabic numerals or applied indexes.
**Strap:** blue or black Louisiana alligator leather.
**Also available:** 18K rose-gold version with decorated caseback; metal bracelet.

# PIAGET

An alluring name in both jewelry and watches, the esteemed Piaget creates rich masterpieces. From complicated watches to high-jeweled works of art, the brand remains in the top echelon of watchmaking prowess.

Every year Piaget unveils a wealth of incredible watches that lure connoisseurs. Naturally top among them are the highest achievements in watchmaking: Tourbillons. Indeed, Piaget adds two key tourbillons to its highly successful Emperador Skeleton and Piaget Polo collections.

The Emperador Skeleton Tourbillon is an ultra-thin (another category in which Piaget holds top-ranking) watch whose tourbillon movement has been intricately carved and etched to superb clarity. Just 3.5mm thick, the Emperador Skeleton Tourbillon is the slimmest tourbillon movement in the world. Additionally, because more than 75 percent of the metal has been honed away, and because the flying tourbillon carriage consists of just 42 elements and weighs 0.2 grams, this is one of the lightest tourbillons in the world. It is housed in the elegantly curved Emperador case, offering further beauty and expression. Due to the immense amount of hand craftsmanship involved in the making of this timepiece, only 11 watches will be created in 18-karat pink gold, and 11 in 18-karat white gold.

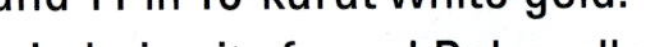

Imbuing its famed Polo collection with complications, Piaget offers the bejeweled Piaget Polo Tourbillon. The entirely gemset timepiece—with 759 diamonds weighing nearly 61 carats—houses an exquisite flying tourbillon movement. In addition to the diamond-bedecked dial, case, caseback and bracelet, the tourbillon aperture and the power-reserve indicator on the dial are outlined with 40 sapphires.

In typical Piaget style, its newest jeweled watches are breathtaking. In its well-loved Miss Protocole collection, several new models emerge, including a horizontal rectangular XL Miss Protocole watch that sports 360 diamonds.

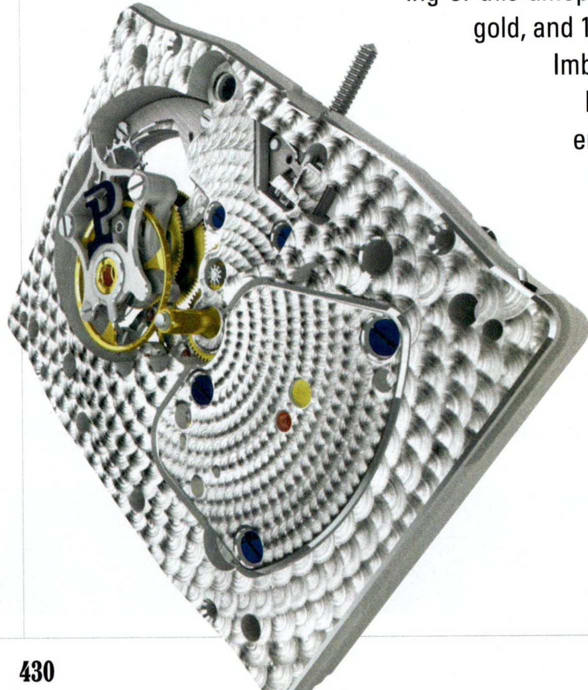

THIS PAGE

ABOVE

Piaget's Emperador Skeleton Tourbillon houses a tourbillon movement with 42 elements. The Manufacture Piaget 600P skeleton movement is a manual-winding piece with 24 rubies and a power-reserve indicator.

LEFT

The Piaget Tourbillon movement beats to a tune of 21,600 vibrations per hour.

FACING PAGE

This exquisite work of technical and artistic beauty is the Piaget Polo Tourbillon. It is set with 759 diamonds weighing 60.9 carats and 40 sapphires weighing 0.9 carat. The tourbillon manual-winding movement is the Piaget 600P.

PIAGET

Also alluring are the sumptuous new Limelight collection renditions: the cuff, oval and ring watches.

The Limelight snowflake watch pays hommage to the brand's roots in the snow-filled Jura Mountains. It is a sparkling Limelight cuff-style watch that uses 27.7 carats of diamonds and 16.2 carats of sapphires to emulate snowflake in an exotic and enticing form. From the tiny center dial, diamond and sapphire snowflake flow into a triangular cuff-watch. The piece features navette-, square-, brilliant- and emerald-cut diamonds for shimmering beauty. The Limelight oval watch is adorned with 130 round diamonds. As has been tradition at Piaget, a stunning ring watch completes the series. The ring is set with 292 brilliant-cut diamonds weighing nearly 3 carats and features a center that spins around to reveal a tiny watch dial. Additionally, there are exceptional cufflink watches for men—totally adorned in diamonds and gemstones.

The Piaget Polo watch, one of the most famous watches in history, returns to its original aesthetics and is available in two jewelry versions for its 25th anniversary. In each version—white gold, either fully or semi-paved—a large self-winding model accompanies a smaller quartz model. They display their taste for certain ostentation in an elegantly casual style.

THIS PAGE

FAR LEFT

From the Miss Protocole collection, the new XL is set with 3.44 carats of diamonds.

TOP CENTER

The 130 brilliant diamond adornments on the case of this Limelight oval watch give it an elongated look at the top and bottom.

RIGHT

Piaget Polo 25th anniversasay watch is available in two jeweled versions.

FACING PAGE

TOP LEFT

The tiny center dial of this Limelight Snowflake cuff-designed watch is ensconced by nearly 40 carats of diamond and sapphire snowflakes.

CENTER

Savvy Piaget cufflinks offer dual time—one zone on each wrist. This pair features the Japanese flag on one and the Swiss flag on the other.

BOTTOM LEFT

As has been tradition at Piaget, a stunning ring watch completes the series. The Ring is set with 443 brilliant-cut diamonds weighing nearly 6.7 carats.

## CHRONOLOGY

**1874** At age 19, Georges-Édouard Piaget establishes the family business in La Côte-aux-Fées in the Swiss Jura.

**1925-1928** Piaget manufactures ultra-thin, high quality movements.

**1943** The Piaget trademark is registered.

**1945** A new workshop in La Côte-aux-Fées manufactures movements for a few prestigious brands and a small number of watches bearing the Piaget trademark.

**1952** Production of the 2P caliber (21,600 vph).

**1956** Creation of the 9P caliber, the world's first manually wound ultra-thin movement.

**1957** Creation of the legendary "A" bracelet.

**1959** Piaget Watch Corporation is founded in New York City.

**1960** Piaget presents the 12P caliber (19,800 vph). At just 2.3mm, it is the slimmest automatic-winding mechanism.

**1969** Piaget participates in the manufacture of the first Swiss quartz movement watch—the bêta 21 caliber—with the Electronic Watch Centre in Neuchâtel; the French Committee of Good Taste awards Piaget its Gold Cup.

**1980** Piaget creates the most expensive men's jeweled wristwatch with 87.87 carats of diamonds mounted on 154 grams of platinum.

**1984** Hans Erni creates the Piaget d'Or, minted by the Swiss Federal Mint.

**1988** Piaget is acquired by Cartier.

**1989** Piaget sponsors the Deauville "Courses d'Or" races.

**1990** The new Tanagra watch and jewelry collection is named for the Greek village renowned for its terracotta figurines of the 4th and 3rd centuries BC.

**1992** Montres et Merveilles, the first exhibition of the Piaget Private Collections, is shown at the Palazzo Reale in Milan. The 500-piece limited-edition Georges Piaget series is unveiled.

**1997** The City of Venice commissions Piaget to fully restore San Marco Tower's famous clock, originally built in 1499 by Rainieri and Son.

**1999** Celebrating its 125th anniversary, Piaget launches the 8-Day Emperador watch housing its 12P caliber.

**2001** A new production center is inaugurated in Geneva.

**2003** After three years of research and development, Piaget unveils the Emperador Tourbillon with a 3.5mm caliber, the slimmest shaped tourbillon movement on the market. The flying tourbillon consists of 42 parts and weighs just 0.2 grams.

**2004** On the heels of the Emperador Tourbillon's great success, Piaget embarks on the creation of an Emperador Skeleton Tourbillon. At the same time, the brand releases a host of scintillating jewelry watches.

## PIAGET EMPERADOR SQUELETON REF. G0A29108

**Movement:** manual-winding skeleton movement Piaget 600P; tourbillon with 3 titanium bridges; 21,600 vph; 24 rubies; thickness: 3.5mm; oscillating organce-balance Ø 7.75mm; approx. 40 hours' power reserve; mainspring torque 310gmm.
**Functions:** hour, minute, second; flying tourbillon (1 revolution per minute); planetary gears system.

**Case:** 18K white-gold three-piece case (size: 32x41mm); polished and brushed finish; antireflective curved sapphire crystal; white-gold crown; back fastened by 4 screws, displaying the movement through a sapphire crystal; water resistant to 3atm.
**Dial:** skeleton pillar-plate, engraved and finished by hand; white-gold faceted Dauphine hands.
**Indications:** power reserve at 6; small second at 12, integral with flying tourbillon with titanium bridges and P.
**Strap:** hand-stitched crocodile leather; white-gold folding clasp.
**Note:** limited edition of 11 pieces.

## RECTANGLE À L'ANCIENNE XL REF. G0A29115

**Movement:** mechanical automatic-winding Piaget 561P (base 500/560P); 40-hour autonomy; 21,600 vph; decorated with Côtes de Genève pattern; blued screws.
**Functions:** hour, minute, retrograde small second; date; power reserve.
**Case:** 18K white-gold two-piece case, rectangular curved (size: 46x31mm); set with 472 brilliant-cut diamonds (approx. 6 carats); curved sapphire crystal; white-gold crown; back fastened by 8 screws.
**Dial:** white gold, black; center set with 88 brilliant-cut diamonds (approx. 0.3 carat); silvered sectors; silvered printed Roman numerals; white-gold faceted Dauphine hands.
**Indications:** power reserve and date at 6; small second with retrograde hand at 12.
**Strap:** hand-stitched crocodile leather; white-gold folding clasp.
**Also available:** in pink gold, non-set versions available in pink and white gold.

## PIAGET POLO CHRONOGRAPH REF. G0A29014

**Movement:** mechanical automatic-winding Piaget 1188P.
**Functions:** hour, minute, small second; chronograph with 3 counters.
**Case:** Ø 38mm; 18K white-gold three-piece case, round; polished and brushed finish; brushed bezel with deep polished lateral grooves; curved sapphire crystal; white-gold crown and square pushers with case protections; back fastened by 6 screws; water resistant to 3atm.

**Dial:** meteorite; slate-gray counters; applied white-gold Arabic numeral 12 and 11 trapezoidal markers; white-gold luminescent Dauphine hands.
**Indications:** minute counter at 3; small second at 6; hour counter at 9; center second; minute track with divisions for 1/2 second.
**Strap:** hand-stitched crocodile leather; white-gold folding clasp.

## LIMELIGHT REF. G0A29060

**Movement:** quartz movement 690P.
**Case:** white-gold case set with 101 brilliant-cut diamonds (approx. 4.4 carats); crown set with 1 brilliant-cut diamond (approx. 0.1 carat).
**Dial:** white mother of pearl; black painted Arabic numerals and indexes.
**Strap:** pink alligator; white-gold buckle set with 18 brilliant-cut diamonds (approx. 0.2 carat).

**Also available:** in white-gold case set with brilliant-cut diamonds with set Arabic numerals on a leather strap and in high-jewelry version.

## ALTIPLANO — REF. G0A29106 – BOUTIQUE EXCLUSIVITY

**Movement:** quartz movement 690P.
**Case:** 18K white-gold squared case (size: 30x30mm, thickness: 5.4mm); bezel with a row of 48 brilliant-cut diamonds (approx. 1.5 carats); flat sapphire crystal; white-gold crown; back fastened by 8 screws; water resistant to 3atm.
**Dial:** gold; set with 256 brilliant-cut diamonds (approx. 1.3 carats); 3 painted Arabic numerals under the glass; sword-style hands.
**Strap:** black satin; white-gold clasp.
**Also available:** in white gold with brilliants on the bezel, fuchsia, set gray or sand-colored dial, satin and crocodile leather strap; in yellow gold with brilliants on the bezel, gilded dial and satin strap; in pink or white gold without brilliants, silvered or slate-gray dial, crocodile leather strap.
Ref. G0A25027 in white gold with quartz movement 690P caliber.

## ALTIPLANO ULTRA-THIN XL — REF. G0A29120

**Movement:** mechanical manual-winding, extra-thin Piaget 430P (derived from the famous Piaget 9P caliber realized in 1956); decorated with Côtes de Genève pattern; rhodium-plated and hand-finished bridges.
**Functions:** hour, minute.
**Case:** Ø 38mm; 18K yellow-gold three-piece case; curved sapphire crystal; gold crown; back fastened by 6 screws; water resistant to 3atm.
**Dial:** white; printed bâton markers; faceted Dauphine hands in yellow gold.
**Strap:** hand-stitched crocodile leather; gold ardillon buckle.
**Also available:** in white gold with anthracite or white dial.

## ALTIPLANO ULTRA-THIN XL — REF. G0A29112

**Movement:** mechanical manual-winding, extra-thin Piaget 430P (derived from the famous Piaget 9P caliber realized in 1956); decorated with Côtes de Genève pattern; rhodium-plated and hand-finished bridges.
**Functions:** hour, minute.
**Case:** Ø 38mm; 18K white-gold three-piece case; curved sapphire crystal; gold crown; back fastened by 6 screws; water resistant to 3atm.
**Dial:** white; printed bâton markers; faceted Dauphine hands in gold.
**Strap:** hand-stitched crocodile leather; gold ardillon buckle.
**Also available:** with anthracite dial; in yellow gold with white dial.

## LIMELIGHT — REF. G0A29066

**Movement:** quartz movement 59P.
**Case:** tonneau-shaped, small; white-gold case set with 86 brilliant-cut diamonds (approx. 1 carat); crown set with 1 brilliant-cut diamond (approx. 0.1 carat).
**Dial:** black flinqué dial with diamond-set Arabic numerals 6 and 12 (22 brilliant-cut diamonds, approx. 0.1 carat).
**Strap:** black satin; clasp set with 14 brilliant-cut diamonds (approx. 0.2 carat).
**Also available:** in polished white or yellow gold on satin strap; in set yellow gold, satin strap; in white-gold or yellow-gold fully paved bracelet

# RAYMOND WEIL

In less than 30 years, this creative, modern family-owned company has established itself as a key Swiss brand. Regularly pursuing perfection in both style and technique, RAYMOND WEIL offers distinguished collections that attract very arts-conscious customers.

By developing mechanical movements and stylish designs, RAYMOND WEIL demonstrates its true strengths. Under the vigilant eye of president and CEO Olivier Bernheim, RAYMOND WEIL constantly strives to reach new heights.

RAYMOND WEIL's most recent stars include the Don Giovanni Così Grande Two Time Zones watch—a superlative modern globetrotter. Quite elegant, this watch continuously displays time in two zones on two dials on the watch face. A mechanical timepiece, the watch functions with one single movement. The first time zone is displayed using the traditional 12-hour timing principle. The second time zone uses a 24-hour timing display to avoid confusion. With this watch, RAYMOND WEIL blends technical prowess with beautiful contemporary design. The watch features a sapphire caseback to reveal the mechanical movement with traditional circular-grained bridges and the decorated rotor with the Côtes de Genève motif. The rectangular curved case is fitted with a leather strap.

Also new to the family is the Don Giovanni Diamonds. Riding high on the wave of success enjoyed by the Don Giovanni mechanical line, the rectangular steel case of this watch is bedecked with 114 diamonds on the bezel. The watch is powered by a mechanical automatic-winding movement that oscillates at 28,800 vibrations per hour and has 38 hours of power reserve. The Swiss caliber features circular-grained bridges, as well as a rotor embellished with the traditional Côtes de Genève motif. The feminine mechanical timepiece is fitted nicely with a black leather strap.

Similarly, the very successful flagship Parsifal collection also emerges with a diamond-adorned version for women. The solid steel Parsifal Diamonds bezel is embellished with 48 diamonds. The dial is black mother of pearl and the hours are depicted with applied Roman numerals.

THIS PAGE

ABOVE

The Don Giovanni Così Grande Two Time Zones watch houses a mechanical movement with automatic wind and 38 hours of power reserve. The caseback is sapphire for viewing of the movement.

FACING PAGE

The Parsifal Automatic Large Date and Power Reserve Indicator watch houses a mechanical movement with automatic wind and 42 hours of power reserve. It is water resistant to 100 meters.

12
RAYMOND WEIL
GENEVE
Parsifal
RESERVE
DE MARCHE
42H
Automatic
SWISS MADE

The screw-down caseback guarantees the watch's water resistance to 100 meters.

In this collection, too, RAYMOND WEIL unveils another premier mechanical watch: the Parsifal Automatic Large Date and Power Reserve Indicator. This timepiece displays its 42 hours of power reserve in an elegant modernistic readout. The large date system operates with two discs displayed in adjacent windows at 12:00. The luxurious dial is embellished with 12 luminescent pearls and 11 Roman numeral appliques. In a beautiful move, the designers have also decorated the crown of the watch with 18 pearls and an anthracite sapphire. The caseback is transparent, revealing the automatic movement. The watch is water resistant to 100 meters, providing a harmonious balance between the technical and aesthetic.

In its more fashion-forward Tango line, RAYMOND WEIL unveils new Spirit watches. These timepieces feature integrated genuine leather straps of a particular color—white, black, orange, red, blue—with white mother-of-pearl dial and nearly a half-carat of diamonds on the dial and bezel.

LEFT

This version of the Parsifal Automatic Large Date and Power Reserve Indicator is classically elegant with its steel bracelet, coordinated gray sunburst dial and burgundy power-reserve indicator.

## CHRONOLOGY

**1976** Raymond Weil creates RAYMOND WEIL S.A. in Geneva, at a time when the watch market is suffering a severe recession.

**1982** Olivier Bernheim, Raymond Weil's son-in-law, joins the company. He will become President and CEO.

**1983** RAYMOND WEIL introduces the Amadeus collection. The names of all RAYMOND WEIL leading collections will be drawn from classical and operatic music.

**1986** RAYMOND WEIL celebrates its 10th anniversary and launches the Othello collection, combining avant-garde technology (the ultra-flat movement is just 1.2mm thick) with sophisticated aesthetic design.

**1991** The luxury watch segment is growing. RAYMOND WEIL launches the Parsifal collection, the brand's first in stainless steel and 18-karat gold.

**1994** RAYMOND WEIL adopts a new image and chooses the world of dance for its new advertising campaign entitled "Precision Movement." The company also launches mechanical models in the Tradition collection.

**1995** RAYMOND WEIL adds a cinema and television advertising film to its media campaign and launches the Tango and Toccata collections—steel watches with youthful, sporty lines.

**1996** For its 20th anniversary, RAYMOND WEIL creates the Duo Jubilé limited edition, a men's watch with a dual-time-zone display and a solid steel, oblong case hugging the curve of the wrist. Introduction of the W1, an avant-garde collection in steel and carbon fiber.

**1998** Launching of three new product lines: Don Giovanni, rectangular and steel; Tema, available in ladies' size or mini version; and Allegro, a trendy watch in steel or yellow gold-plated.

**2001-2002** RAYMOND WEIL gives the Othello collection a new lease on life and launches, after the dark blue Othello, the yellow- and pink-gold models. To crown its efforts, the company also launches the new Don Giovanni Così Grande, an unusual version with out-of-the-ordinary dimensions.

**2003** RAYMOND WEIL begins repositioning the brand in the luxury industry with complications and materials in addition to overhauling almost all ofits collections by reinforcing their stylistic cohesion and giving each one its own aesthetic appearance. RAYMOND WEIL also pays special attention to the re-conceptualization of its legendary Parsifal collection.

**2004** RAYMOND WEIL focuses on offering mechanical movements in its signature Parsifal collection and in its Don Giovanni line while solidifying its position in the luxury timepiece segment.

TOP

The Parsifal Diamonds is crafted in steel and set with 48 full-cut Top Wesselton VS diamonds.

BOTTOM

Don Giovanni Così Grande Diamonds.

# RGM

RGM is definitively a rare breed of watch. Entirely handcrafted in house by Roland G. Murphy, RGM watches are made in America.

Indeed, for just over a decade, Murphy has been creating his own timepiece collection according to old-world techniques and turns out mechanical masterpieces that easily compare to Switzerland's finest.

A Swiss-trained watchmaker residing in Lancaster, Pennsylvania, Murphy has been creating watches since the mid 1980s, when he worked for one of Switzerland's large watch companies. It was his dream to build his own timepieces and to make his mark in America's watchmaking history—a dream he first fulfilled in 1993 when he introduced his RGM line.

All RGM timepieces are assembled in Lancaster using Swiss or American movements as their bases, and each demonstrates Murphy's stringent attention to detail. All watches are created of only the finest materials: platinum, 18-karat gold and high-grade steel. Cases are unique, designed by Murphy and produced in Switzerland exclusively for him. RGM dials are also incredibly exquisite, as the brand preserves centuries-old methodology.

Indeed, engine turning (the act of cutting geometric patterns in a rotating metal dial with a stationary cutting tool called a rose engine) is an art at RGM, where the delicate work is carried out with reverence. To execute the process properly, the guillochéur must mount the piece to be decorated on his machine and ensure that all components are properly aligned, and then he must carve the pattern line by line being careful not to carve too deeply and to apply consistent force throughout the entire time-consuming process. It is a point of honor for RGM to design its dials in such a way. It can take an expert craftsman up to three hours to create a single engine-turned guilloché dial by hand. While RGM does not use this process for every watch it creates, it has exclusively utilized authentic guilloché on watches in its Classic and William Penn collections.

RGM's collections feature sublime technical complications that include minute repeaters, tourbillons, chronographs, perpetual calendars, moonphases and power-reserve indicator models. The brand creates just about 500 watches per year—a testament to the time and effort of one man. Indeed, Murphy creates his timepieces with true passion, and shares his love with a select global audience that has the same appreciation for fine craftsmanship.

THIS PAGE

ABOVE

The RGM 151E is a Classic automatic watch with hour, minute, second and date. It is crafted of solid 18-karat rose gold with a sapphire crystal and caseback and features a solid silver, hand-engraved dial. This Classis is also available in steel and houses a modified ETA 2892-A2 movement with 21 jewels and solid 18-karat gold rotor.

FACING PAGE

A special new project by RGM, this Vintage American Movement has been refinished and modified completely by Roland Murphy. It is a stainless steel 41mm manual-winding movement.

THREADED
U.S.A.
ADJUSTED
5 POSITIONS

Along with his unique collection of fine watches, Murphy also insists on offering custom watches. RGM will build a particular watch to suit any customer's needs—a service that only a few select brands in the world offer today. The customization of a watch can be simple or complex, ranging from a specially engraved rotor, to a unique dial or a complete watch with a rare vintage movement. RGM can accommodate any request, including creating a timepiece with a personalized complication. RGM's custom-built watches are assembled by hand and feature decorative elements that honor the old masters of dying arts.

**ABOVE**

This array of timepieces demonstrates RGM's multiple talents in the world of watchmaking.
From left to right:

RGM 175 Minute Repeater Tourbillon

RGM 170 Tall Ships Series featuring the USS Constellation

Custom RGM DaVinci Universal Man

RGM 151E Classic date watch

RGM 161 Master Chronograph with a Valjoux 72 movement

**LEFT**

A custom project by RGM, this stunning watch features Da Vinci's Universal Man, hand-engraved on a solid gold dial.

## CHRONOLOGY

**1980s** Roland Murphy, a Swiss-trained watchmaker, begins creating watches for one of Switzerland's large watch companies.

**Late 1980s** Murphy returns to America and settles in Lancaster, PA, once known for watchmaking.

**1990s** Murphy follows his quest and begins designing and producing his own timepieces.

**1993** The first RGM watches are unveiled. They are mechanical masterpieces crafted in exclusive, limited editions. These timepieces are received by collectors and connoisseurs with great enthusiasm. Over the ensuing decade, RGM continues to create superb timepieces based on old-world traditions and craftsmanship. RGM adds custom watchmaking to its repertoire.

**2000** RGM unveils its Pilots Professional Automatic series of watches.

**2002** RGM creates its Tall Ships collection of watches with hand-engraved dials.

ABOVE

The RGM 151P is a Pilots Professional Automatic watch, crafted in steel with luminous markers. It houses a modified ETA 2892-A2 automatic-winding movement with 21 jewels.

RIGHT

Roland Murphy.

Personal attention is also important to Murphy, who insists on being easy to reach for his clientele and followers. It is not unusual to call RGM and be greeted by Roland at the other end of the line within minutes. This approachability is a tradition Murphy intends to preserve so that RGM watch owners can speak directly to the man who created their timepieces. It is this attention to the needs and desires of the consumer, along with executing the most intricate details of watchmaking, that have made Murphy an icon of America's watchmaking future.

# RICHARD MILLE

Richard Mille has deftly blended high-performance, advanced technology and bold styling to achieve some of the most complicated watchmaking feats in unique timepieces.

THIS PAGE

ABPVE

A view of the RM 009 caseback.

FACING PAGE

The revolutionary RM 009 tourbillon features a bottom plate in aluminum-lithium. The case is made of Aluminum AS7G-Silicium-Carbon (ALUSIC), an extremely exclusive material reserved solely for use in satellites, due to its enormous cost. Its main characteritics are a superior level of rigidity, a high resistance to wear. Its density of 2.95 allows the total watch head (case and movement) to weight less than 30 grams, making it by far the lightest mechanical watch ever made.

To house—and present—the incredible complications in Richard Mille timepieces, the design and appearance of each model had to be totally original. The results of a talented team of engineers working in an ultra-modern production workshop, Richard Mille watches offer a strong 21st century concept.

All of the components of Richard Mille watches are manufactured from scratch, and many are totally integrated. It requires more than 20,000 mechanical operations to produce the 267 components that comprise each RM 002 movement. Even the tiny titanium screws undergo 20-plus operations before meeting Mille's approval.

The research and development processes employed at Richard Mille's workshops are geared toward achieving remarkable performance in a wristwatch. The main elements of the movement—including the flexible tourbillon and barrel bridges—have been specially studied and tested to achieve a high level of shock resistance. Mille has developed a special, rapidly rotating spring barrel designed to ensure a smooth power flow by reducing the slippage between turns. Additionally, the brand has created a extraordinary escapement to reduce friction. Many of the numerous developments represent a new turn in watch making history. All functions serve a purpose. The pursuit of perfection can be seen in any tiny details and it is for this reason that each model requires so much time in development. For example, the RM 004 and RM 008 demanded tens of thousands of hours of study and six years of research and development.

The materials used for Richard Mille watches are high-tech, including carbon fiber, aluminium-lithium, aluminium-silicium-carbon, titanium, ceramic (for the cap jewel on the tourbillon) and ARCAP (an alloy with superb mechanical properties of endurance and resistance to distortion). Cases are luxuriously hand milled of 18-karat gold or platinum, and no casing ring is required in the integrated production of the watch. In terms of design, comfort is key. The watch has an ergonomically curved case and lateral ribs for extra strength. The RM 009 and the ladies' model RM 007 are the latest to appear in the Richard Mille range.

The RM 007, a ladies' watch, is an uncompromising and undiluted version of Richard Mille's men's watch. The complications and techniques one expects of a Richard Mille timepiece remain, with only a few concessions toward a more glamorous and feminine styling.

The RM 009 is an ultra-light tourbillon, which pushes the boundaries of watchmaking. It has been developed through cutting-edge materials, for example aluminium-lithium and aluminium AS7G-silicium-carbon. When unveiled, it will be the lightest mechanical watch ever made.

RICHARD MILLE
RM009
SWISS
MADE

RICHARD MILLE
SWISS MADE

FACING PAGE

Caliber RM 007-1 Automatic Lady's watch. Bi-directional automatic winding 18k gold rotor 100 micro balls in 18k gold Tooth system of barrel with corrected involute profile V VS F/C diamond setting Folding buckle Available in platinum, white gold and red gold.

THIS PAGE

Rear view of RM 007-1.

When Mille entered the master watchmaking sector, it was with a relentless attitude that he should produce a watch that pushed all the boundaries of existing techniques. His first timepiece was followed by others, with each as impressive as its predecessor and all remarkable for their innovation and cutting-edge techniques.

It was at the insistence of his brand's authorized dealers that Mille decided to create a watch for women. However, it would have to be a ladies' watch without compromise and with as much importance given to technique and originality as its masculine counterpart. The mechanical automatic RM 007 does indeed reflect the same detailed attention found in the gentleman's watch—the titanium bottom plate, bridges and screws for example. The caliber also incorporates a good number of new innovations such as a self-winding process with a forward and reverse capacity, a tooth-system with central involute profile as well as an impressive rotor. In order to increase inertia and to optimize the barrel-spring winding action, a container has been designed in which more than hundred 18-karat micro-balls move freely. In the event of a knock or a jolt, the energy at the point of impact is dispersed, thus reducing the shock wave and safe guarding the mechanical integrity. However, despite these advanced developments, the RM 007 remains an uncomplicated and reliable watch for everyday wear, with the date at 6:00, linked to a quick-change mechanism.

From the aesthetic point of view, the model has vigorous lines, its length equals that of the men's watch but the width has been slimmed down. The ergonomics have been handled sensitively and can be adapted easily for any wrist. The RM 007 will be launched only in its VVS F/G diamond set version and will be available with various dial options and straps.

## CHRONOLOGY

**1974** Richard Mille begins his 20-year career as a commercial director for one of the world's largest watch companies.

**1994** Mille joins the renowned house of Mauboussin and rises to the position of President and CEO of the watch division.

**1998** Mille resigns from Mauboussin and strikes out on his own as a watch-development consultant to a number of companies, including Audemars Piguet, Repossi and Baccarat. (He helped create the Baccarat watch, launched in late 2002.)

**1999** Mille begins developing his own timepieces in a joint venture with his old Swiss friend Dominique Guenat, whose watch factory is based in Les Breuleux, Swiss Jura. Inspired by the perfection and precision in the automotive and aviation industries, and impressed with high-tech mechanical items, Mille vows to create a performance timepiece. His designs are incomparable in standards and incorporate a specially developed tourbillon escapement. The level of technology Mille employs in his sophicticated watch designs require thousands of hours to develop. For more than two years, Mille designs and redesigns his watch until he achieves perfection.

**2000** Mille subjects his timepieces to rigorous testing and fine-tuning to ensure precision and reliability.

**2001** Mille unveils his collection. The first watch is the RM 001 Tourbillon, followed by the RM 002 Tourbillon—an evolution of the RM 001 but now featuring a titanium plate and function indicator.

**2002** Mille unveils the RM 003 Tourbillon with dual-time indication, and the RM 004 split second chronograph, developed in 1999 and finally will be released in 2004.

**2003** Mille unveils the RM 008 Tourbillon Chronograph with 70 hours of power reserve, a new escapement and function indicator.

**2004** Mille unveils the RM 006 tourbillon with a carbon fiber movement plate, and the RM 005, an automatic watch retaining many of the properties and technologies of its predecessors, introducing a spectacular variable inertia rotor.

## TOURBILLON RM 002-V2

**Movement:** mechanical, manual winding with tourbillon device; Richard Mille RM 002-V2 Caliber; movement plate in carbon fiber; 70-hour power reserve; variable inertia balance; fast-rotating barrel; barrel pawl with progressive recoil; ceramic counter-pivot; central bridge in rigidified ARCAP; splined screws in Grade 5 titanium for the bridges and case; tooth system of barrel and third-pinion with central module.

**Functions:** hour, minute; torque indicator; power reserve indicator; function indicator.

**Case:** three-piece case; assembled with 12 spline screws in Grade 5 titanium; sapphire crystal bezel side and caseback with double-sided anti-glare treatment; water resistant to 50 meters.

**Dial:** in sapphire with double-sided anti-glare treatment; protected by 8 silicone braces inserted into the upper and lower grooves.

**Strap:** leather or crocodile with through reinforcement fastened by the case screws; titanium, white- or pink-gold tongue buckle.

**Versions:** titanium, white or pink gold, platinum (all with strap).

## TOURBILLON RM 002-V2

The back of the RM 002-V2 shows some very innovative and specific devices: Time-setting mechanism fitted against the caseback with module. The advantages of this development: mounting and dismantling of this module form the back without removing the hands and the dial; mounting of this component outside the movement: in the event of a defect, this time-setting assembly can be changes without affecting the integrity of the bottom plate. Positioning of the time-setting lever by means of a small wheel: improves the time-setting functions by eliminating engaging friction, which is replaced by rolling frictions. The more rigid stem body reduces slack during winding. Central bridge in rigidified ARCAP: The ribs ensure better rigidity for the bottom plate/bridge assembly.

**Other features:** 21,600 vph; tourbillon size: Ø 12.3mm; balance wheel: Ø 10mm; 23 jewels; Glucydur balance with 2 arms, 4 setting screws, inertia moment: 10mg cm2—angle of lift 53°; Elinvar balance spring, alloy by Nivarox; torque indicator: a strengthened spring—reference measurement dN-mm; anti-shock system: Kif Elastor KE 160 B28; ceramic endstone for the tourbillon cage; stone setting in white gold; barrel shaft in nickel-free chronifer (DIN x 46 Cr 13 + S).

## TOURBILLON DOUBLE FUSEAU RM 003-V2

**Movement:** mechanical, manual winding with tourbillon device; Richard Mille RM 003-V2 Caliber; movement plate in carbon fiber; 70-hour power reserve; variable inertia balance; fast-rotating barrel; barrel pawl with progressive recoil; ceramic counter-pivot; central bridge in rigidified ARCAP; splined screws in Grade 5 titanium for the bridges and case; tooth system of barrel and third-pinion with central module.

**Functions:** hour, minute; second time-zone display; torque indicator; power reserve indicator; function indicator.

**Case:** three-piece case; assembled with 12 spline screws in Grade 5 titanium; sapphire crystal bezel side and caseback with double-sided anti-glare treatment; water resistant to 50 meters.

**Dial:** in sapphire with double-sided anti-glare treatment; protected by 8 silicone braces inserted into the upper and lower grooves.

**Strap:** leather or crocodile with through reinforcement fastened by the case screws; titanium, white- or pink-gold tongue buckle.

**Versions:** titanium, white or pink gold, platinum (all with strap).

## TOURBILLON DOUBLE FUSEAU RM 003-V2

The back of the RM 003-V2 shows some very innovative and specific devices: Time-setting mechanism fitted against the caseback with module. The advantages of this development: Mounting and dismantling of this module form the back without removing the hands and the dial; Mounting of this component outside the movement: in the event of a defect, this time-setting assembly can be changes without affecting the integrity of the bottom plate. Positioning of the time-setting lever by means of a small wheel: improves the time-setting functions by eliminating engaging friction, which is replaced by rolling frictions. The more rigid stem body reduces slack during winding. Central bridge in rigidified ARCAP: The ribs ensure better rigidity for the bottom plate/bridge assembly.

**Other features:** 21,600 vph; tourbillon size: Ø 12.3mm; balance wheel: Ø 10mm; 23 jewels; Glucydur balance with 2 arms, 4 setting screws, inertia moment: 10mg cm2—angle of lift 53°; Elinvar balance spring, alloy by Nivarox; Torque indicator: a strengthened spring—reference measurement dN-mm; anti-shock system: Kif Elastor KE 160 B28; ceramic endstone for the tourbillon cage; stone setting in white gold; barrel shaft in nickel-free chronfier (DIN x 46 Cr 13 + S).

## CHRONOGRAPH RM 004-V2

**Movement:** mechanical, manual winding; Richard Mille RM 004-V2 Caliber; movement plate in carbon fiber; 70-hour power reserve; titanium column wheel, gear wheels and lever; split-second mechanism with improved function; reduced friction on the spindle; balance wheel with variable inertia; fast-rotating barrel; barrel pawl with progressive recoil, special curve of the hairsping; new in-line escapement, hand-setting mechanism at bottom and the modular; closure of the barrel using off-center screws, Grade 5 titanium spline screws for the bridges and case; tooth system of barrel and third-wheel pinion with central involute profile. **Functions:** hour, minute, second; chronograph; split seconds; torque indicator; power reserve indicator; function indicator.
**Case:** three-piece case assembled with 20 spline screws in Grade 5 titanium; sapphire crystal bezel side and caseback with double-sided anti-glare treatment; water resistant to 50 meters.
**Dial:** in sapphire with double-sided anti-glare treatment; protected by 8 silicone braces inserted into the upper and lower grooves.
**Strap:** leather or crocodile with through reinforcement fastened by the case screws; titanium, white- or pink-gold tongue buckle.
**Versions:** titanium, white or pink gold, platinum (all with strap).

## CHRONOGRAPH RM 004-V2

The back of the RM 004-V2 features innovative and specific devices. The modern architecture of this movement has allowed the consistent and rational arrangement of its constituent parts, avoiding unnecessary superimposition and permitting the best possible use of the functions and technical solutions. Another characteristic of the RM 004-V2 is the virtually complete elimination of jumping second hands, with gear wheels and lever in titanium, thus reducing inertia. Energy consumption has been reduced by approximately 50% by reducing friction on the spindle. Another innovation is the hand-setting mechanism located at the bottom.
**Other features:** 21,600 vph; balance wheel: Ø 10mm; 37 jewels; Glucydur balance wheel with 2 arms, 4 adjusting screws; inertia moment: 10mg cm2; lever angle: 53°; Elinvar balance spring, alloy by Nivarox; torque indicator: spring reinforced standard; reference measure dN-mm; anti-shock system: Kif Elastor KE 160 B28; barrel shaft in nickel-free chronifer (DIN 46 x Cr 13 + S).

## AUTOMATIC RM 005-1

**Movement:** mechanical, self winding; Richard Mille RM 005-1 Caliber; rotor with variable geometry; bottom plate; combined bridges and titanium balance cock; double-spring barrel; Grade 5 titanium spline screws.
**Functions:** hour, minute, second; date.
**Case:** three-piece case assembled with 12 spline screws in Grade 5 titanium; sapphire crystal bezel side and caseback with double-sided anti-glare treatment; water resistant to 50 meters.
**Dial:** calendar disc in sapphire crystal with double-sided anti-glare treatment; semi-instantaneous date display; sapphire crystal protected by 8 silicone braces inserted into the upper and lower grooves.
**Strap:** leather or crocodile with through reinforcement fastened by the case screws.
**Buckle:** double deploying; titanium blades; safety catch; screw-secured caps in titanium, pink or white gold (for watches in white gold or platinum).
**Versions:** titanium, pink or white gold, platinum (all with straps).

## AUTOMATIC RM 005-1

The back of the RM 005-1 shows its own innovative device:
Rotor with variable geometry: arm in Grade 2 titanium; flange in Grade 2 titanium; adjustment with Grade 5 titanium screws; 18K gray-gold ribs; weight segment in tungsten/colbalt alloy; ceramic ball bearing; unidirectional rewinding (counterclockwise).
This exclusive Richard Mille design allows the rewinding of the mainspring to be adapted most effectively to the user's activity (golf, tennis, etc.). As a result, this invention allows the movement's motion to be optimized and personalized.
**Other features:** 28,800 vph; 31 jewels; angle lift: 53°; balance spring in Nivarox alloy; 55-hour power reserve; inertia moment: 4.8mg cm2; monocrystal ruby pallet stone; pallet wheel with 20 teeth; Incabloc for bottom plate and cock; Glucydur balance wheel with 3 arms; bottom plate and bridges in hand-ground titanium; wet sandblasted; PVD treated; barrel-arbor: in AP 20 steel; hand-fitting: height 5; index assembly: triovis N° 2 on the left.

## TOURBILLON CHRONOGRAPH — RM 008-V2

**Movement:** mechanical, manual winding with tourbillon device; Richard Mille RM 008-V2 Caliber; movement plate in carbon fiber; 70-hour power reserve; column wheel, gear wheels and lever in titanium; reduced friction on the spindle; balance wheel with variable inertia; fast-rotating barrel; barrel pawl with progressive recoil, special curve of the hairspring; new in-line escapement; hand-setting mechanism located at the bottom and modular; closure of the barrel via off-center screws; Grad 5 titanium spline screws for the bridges and case; tooth system of barrel and third-wheel pinion with central involute profile.

**Functions:** hour, minute, second; chronograph; split seconds with improved function; torque indicator; power reserve; function indicator. **Case:** three-piece case assembled by 20 spline screws in Grad 5 titanium; sapphire crystal bezel side and caseback with double-sided anti-glare treatment; water resistant to 50 meters.

**Dial:** in sapphire with double-sided anti-glare treatment; protected by 8 silicone braces inserted into the upper and lower grooves.

**Strap:** leather or crocodile with through reinforcement fastened by the case screws; titanium, white- or pink-gold tongue buckle.

**Versions:** titanium, white or pink gold (all with straps).

## TOURBILLON CHRONOGRAPH — RM 008-V2

The architecture of the RM 008-V2 movement accommodates the precise arrangement of all its parts, avoiding unnecessary superimposition and permitting the best possible use of the functions and technical solutions. Another characteristic of the RM 008-1 is the virtually complete elimination of jumping second hands, with gear wheels and lever in titanium, thus reducing inertia. Energy consumption has been reduced by approximately 50% by reducing friction on the spindle. Another innovation is the hand-setting mechanism located at the bottom.

**Other features:** 21,600 vph; tourbillon size: Ø 12.3mm; balance wheel: Ø 10mm; 38 jewels; Glucydur balance wheel with 2 arms, 4 adjusting screws; inertia moment: 10mg cm2; lever angle: 53°; Elinvar balance spring, alloy by Niravox; torque indicator: spring reinforced standard; reference measure dNmm; anti-shock system: Kif Elastor KE 160 B28; barrel shaft in nickel-free chronifer (DIN 46 x Cr 13 + S).

## CALIBER RM 002-V2

**Movement:** manual winding; 12.3mm tourbillon; 23 jewels; 70-hour power reserve; 21,600 vph; Elinvar balance spring, alloy by Nivarox; Glucydur balance with 2 arms, 4 setting screws; variable inertia balance; inertia: 10mg/cm2, 53° angle lift; 10mm balance wheel; KIF Elastor KE 160 B28 shock absorber; torque with strengthened spring, reference measurement dNmm; quick-rotating barrel (6 hours) with progressive recoil; nickel-free barrel shaft (DINx46 Cr13+S), stainless steel, antimagnetic and suitable for tempering; central bridge in rigidified ARCAP; bridges beveled and polished by hand; hand-polished locking section; sapphire-blasted milled sections; steel parts: hand polished chamfers; PVD coating; ceramic endstone for tourbillon cage; ceramic counter pivot; gear wheels: concave chamfered with diamond tool, circular-smoothed faces, gilded; Grade 5 titanium splined screws for bridges and case.

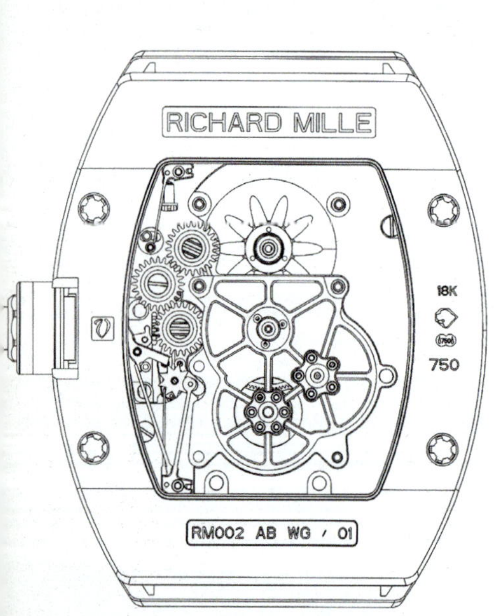


**Functions:** hour, minute; power-reserve and torque indicators; function selector; time-setting mechanism fitted against the case back with module.

## CALIBER RM 003-V2

**Movement:** manual winding; 12.3mm tourbillon; 23 jewels; 70-hour power reserve; 21,600 vph; Elinvar balance spring, alloy by Nivarox; Glucydur balance with 2 arms, 4 setting screws; variable inertia balance; inertia: 10mg/cm2, 53° angle lift; 10mm balance wheel; KIF Elastor KE 160 B28 shock absorber; torque with strengthened spring, reference measurement dNmm; quick-rotating barrel (6 hours) with progressive recoil; nickel-free barrel shaft (DINx46 Cr13+S), stainless steel, antimagnetic and suitable for tempering; central bridge in rigidified ARCAP; Bridges: beveled and polished by hand, hand-polished locking section, sapphire-blasted milled sections, PVD coating; Steel parts: hand-polished chamfers, bevels, sapphire-blasted surfaces; ceramic endstone for tourbillon cage; ceramic counter pivot; Gear wheels: concave chamfered with diamond tool, circular-smoothed faces, gilded; Grade 5 titanium splined screws for bridges and case.

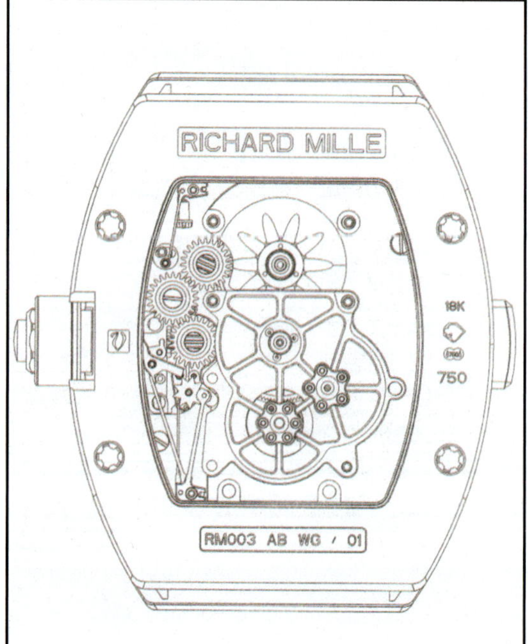


**Functions:** hour, minute; power-reserve and torque indicators; second time zone; function selector; time-setting mechanism fitted against the caseback with module.

## CALIBER RM 004-V2

**Movement:** manual winding; chronograph; titanium column wheel; new inline escapement; 37 jewels; 70-hour power reserve; 21,600 vph; Elinvar balance spring with specially curved hairspring, alloy by Nivarox; Glucydur balance with 2 arms, 4 adjusting screws; variable inertia balance; inertia: 10mg/cm2, 53° angle lift; 10mm balance wheel; KIF Elastor KE 160 B28 shock absorber; torque with reinforced standard, reference measurement dNmm; quick-rotating barrel (6 hours) with progressive recoil; nickel-free barrel shaft (DINx46 Cr13+S), non-oxidized, antimagnetic and hardened; central bridge in rigidified ARCAP; Bridges: beveled and polished by hand, hand-polished locking section, sapphire-blasted milled sections, PVD coating; Steel parts: hand-polished chamfers, bevels; sapphire-blasted surfaces; satin-finished surfaces; Gear wheels: concave chamfered with diamond tool, circular-smoothed faces, gilded; Grade 5 titanium splined screws for bridges and case; carbon fiber bottom plate.

**Functions:** hour, minute; power-reserve and torque indicators; chronograph; split-second mechanism; function indicator; hand-setting mechanism located at bottom and modular.

## CALIBER RM 005-1

**Movement:** automatic winding; 28,800 vph; 55-hour power reserve; 31 jewels; rotor with variable geometry; arm and flange in Grade 2 titanium; Grade 5 titanium adjustment screws; 18-karat gray-gold ribs (alloyed with palladium); weight segment in tungsten-cobalt alloy; ceramic ball bearing; unidirectional, counterclockwise rewinding; PVD-treated titanium bottom plate, bridges and balance cock, sandblasted; balance wheel pallet pin angle: 53°; Glucydur balance with 3 arms; inertia: 4.8mg/cm2; monocrystal ruby pallet stone; pallet wheel with 20 teeth; flat Nivarox balance spring; double-spring barrel; barrel-arbor in AP 20 steel; Incabloc shock absorbers for bottom plate and cock; Index assembly: Triovis N°2 on left; Grade 5 titanium spline screws; Steel parts: hand-polished bevels, drawn tops and sides; Gear trains: sandblasted rhodium-plates wheels; beveled and hooped wheels, diamond-polished shinks on the bridge side; pinions with undercuts; Pallet bridge: drawn top and side, diamond-cut shells and edge.

**Functions:** hour, minute, second; semi-instantaneous date; stem with 3 positions: manual rewinding, manual setting with stop, date adjustment.

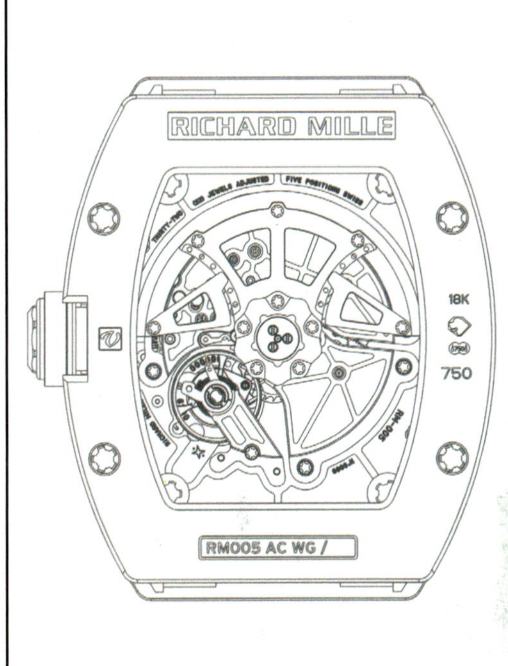


## CALIBER RM 008-V2

**Movement:** manual winding; 12.3mm tourbillon; chronograph; titanium column wheel; new inline escapement; 38 jewels; 70-hour power reserve; 21,600 vph; Elinvar balance spring with specially curved hairspring, alloy by Nivarox; Glucydur balance with 2 arms, 4 adjusting screws; variable inertia balance; inertia: 10mg/2cm, 53° angle lift; 10mm balance wheel; KIF Elastor KE 160 B28 shock absorber; torque with reinforced standard, reference measurement dNmm; quick-rotating barrel (6 hours) with progressive recoil; nickel-free barrel shaft (DINx46 Cr13+S), non-oxidized, antimagnetic and hardened; central bridge in rigidified ARCAP; Bridges: beveled and polished by hand, hand-polished locking section, sapphire-blasted milled sections, PVD coating; Steel parts: hand-polished chamfers, bevels; sapphire-blasted surfaces; satin-finished surfaces; Gear wheels: concave chamfered with diamond tool, circular-smoothed faces, gilded; Grade 5 titanium splined screws for bridges; carbon fiber bottom plate.

**Functions:** hour, minute; power-reserve and torque indicators; tourbillon; chronograph; split-second mechanism; function indicator; hand-setting mechanism located at bottom and modular.

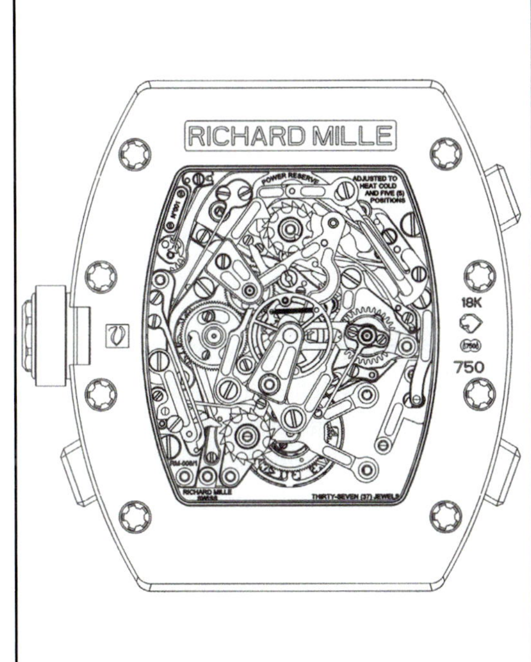


## RICHARD MILLE CALIBER RM 009-1

This Richard Mille tourbillon watch has been produced in a limited edition of 25 numbered watches and by way of an experiment. In fact, for the first time in the history of horology, it has been possible to manufacture a movement plate in aluminium-lithium*, after years of research and development.

**Movement:** manual winding; 10.9mm tourbillon; 48-hour power reserve; 21,200 vph; 19 jewels; 10mm Glucydur balance wheel with 2 arms; inertia: 10mg/cm2, lever angle: 53°; Elinvar balance spring, alloy by Nivarox; KIF Elastor KE 160 B28 shock absorber; nickel-free barrel shaft (DINx46 Cr13+S), non-oxidized, antimagnetic and hardened; winding-stem joint: 100g/mm; beveled and polished by hand; hand-polished locking section and chamfers; sapphire-blasted milled sections; satin-finished steel surfaces; Gear wheels: concave chamfered with diamond tool, circular-smoothed faces, gilded; bottom plate made of aluminum-lithium alloy.

* This alloy normally restricted to the aviation industry, and notably to the new AIRBUS A 380, is made of lithium, aluminium, titanium, zirconium, chrome-silicium, zinc, manganese. Lithium improves resistance and the elasticity module, amongst other characteristics, but paradoxically reduces density: aluminium-lithium is 2.6, while titanium is 4.9. Aluminium-lithium was selected from the aluminium alloys because of its high resistance to corrosion.

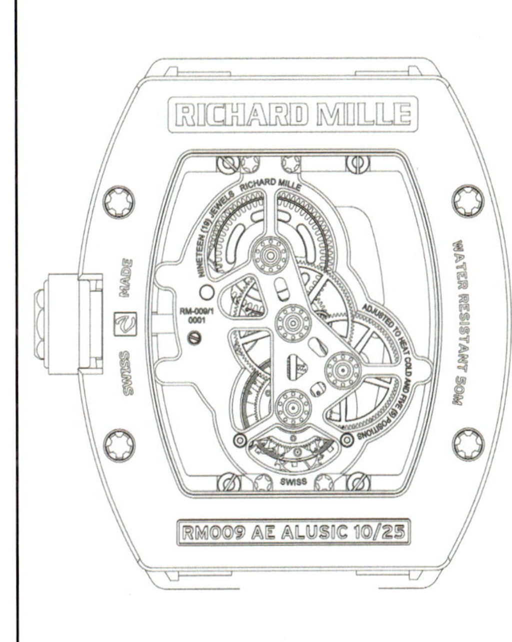

# Roger Dubuis

Bold and different are defining words for the Roger Dubuis brand. Not even a decade old, this company has made distinguishing strides in the watch world and has been credited—and praised—for breaking traditional design rules on a regular basis.

The newest introductions from Roger Dubuis this year encompass several main themes. Venturing in a big way into the world of sports watches for the first time, the brand unveils the Sports Activity Watch (SAW) Collection. The SAW Collection and its nuances are the brainchild of CEO and founder, Carlos Dias. Within this series are three separate watch models: EasyDiver, AcquaMare, and SeaMore.

The EasyDiver watch is a bold 46mm and houses a tourbillon escapement as well as a mechanical chronograph with screw-in pushers. Underscoring the rugged durability of this watch, Roger Dubuis's watchmakers have equipped it with a vulcanized rubber strap and a galvanized metal dial. In contrast to the round EasyDiver, the SeaMore series is a rectangular watch with a classically elegant, satin-finished, sun-ray galvanized metal dial and gold applied numerals. The even more avant-garde AcquaMare is a square version with raised numerals on the bezel and a satin-finished dial.

Each SAW model is created in three different metals: 28 in 18-karat gold, 280 in steel-and-gold, and 888 in steel. Additionally, every SAW is water resistant to 300 meters and all are stamped with the Geneva Seal. Each watch in the collection features a caseback engraving reading "Just for Friends" to establish a relationship between the brand and the customer.

Love is also an important theme in the Roger Dubuis lines as the brand unveils playful, whimsical watches. In the FollowMe Collection, a stunning mother-of-pearl dial sports a diamond heart of rubies, along with the words Love and Amore. The same theme rings in the TooMuch Collection and the Golden-Square Collection where the word Love mingles with diamond accents and well placed hearts.

THIS PAGE

TOP

This EasyDiver watch is crafted in 18-karat white gold and houses an automatic chronograph movement.

BOTTOM LEFT

Part of the EasyDiver series, this bold 48mm mechanical watch is crafted in 18-karat gold and features the flying tourbillon, caliber RD02.

BOTTOM RIGHT

Part of the new Sports Activity Watch Collection, the AcquaMare is created in steel, or steel and 18-karat white gold.

FACING PAGE

TOP LEFT

This GoldenSquare features a flying tourbillon with instantaneous large date and power resreve indicator.

TOP RIGHT

This MuchMore watch houses the RD 57 movement with 25 jewels and perpetual calendar with moonphase.

**ABOVE LEFT**

This MuchMore watch houses the RD 28 caliber mono-push chronograph with coaxial crown.

**ABOVE RIGHT**

This GoldenSquare watch features sailboats on the hand-enameled dial. Its mechanical self-winding movement has 25 jewels.

**CENTER**

The FollowMe's case is set beautifully with 210 diamonds and sapphires, and the silver dial is set with 54 rubies. The movement features 19 jewels.

**RIGHT**

In 18-karat gold, this MuchMore is set with 56 diamonds on the case and another 338 diamonds on the bracelet. It houses the manually wound RD 54 movement.

**FAR RIGHT**

From the GoldenSquare series this 18-karat gold watch is set with 96 diamonds and houses the RD 98 mechanical movement.

For men, exact timing is important, as Roger Dubuis releases the TooMuch and the MuchMore with single-pusher chronographs. Both watches house RD 28 movements with 25 jewels. Manually wound, each watch is made in just 28 pieces. Holding to its tradition of uniqueness, Roger Dubuis also unveils a hand-enameled GoldenSquare watch dipicting a miniature sailing scene. The watch houses a mechanical self-winding movement with 25 jewels and is crafted in 18-karat rose gold. Each of these watches is created in limited editions of 28 pieces.

## CHRONOLOGY

**1995** A partnership is formed between entrepreneur Carlos Dias and watchmaker Roger Dubuis, wherein Sogem SA is created to produce timepieces under the Roger Dubuis brand name.

**1996** The first Roger Dubuis collections are unveiled: Hommage (a classically round case) and Sympathie (an unusual scalloped-case design). Both offer bi-retrograde perpetual calendar functions and are created in the Dubuis signature production number of 28 pieces.

**1998** Roger Dubuis unveils new calibers, and the MuchMore Collection of large rectangular watches.

**1999** The TooMuch is unveiled—a series of rectangular watches with double leather straps on each side.

**2000** Roger Dubuis releases complications including a minute repeater and tourbillon.

**2001** Roger Dubuis determines to open a new atelier in a small province of Geneva to bring all its watchmaking processes under one roof to become a fully integrated manufacture.

**2002** Roger Dubuis inaugurates its state-of-the-art 10,000-square-foot manufacturing facility in Geneva. The three-floored facility houses everything from the tooling and heavy machinery to the gemsetting and watchmaking stations.

**2003** Roger Dubuis releases the cross-shaped FollowMe Collection, which gains immediate acclaim.

## FollowMe REF. F18 54 0-FDR 33R/LO

**Movement:** mechanical manual-winding caliber RD 54; 8'''; 19 jewels; rhodium plated; decorated with Côtes de Genève pattern; fine adjustment in five positions; marked with the Geneva Quality Hallmark.
**Functions:** hours, minutes.
**Case:** 18K white gold, polished and satiny; cross-cambered; set with 210 diamonds and sapphires; solid back; water resistant to 3atm.
**Dial:** silver; set with 54 rubies; satin-finished letters; blued steel hands.
**Strap:** hand-sewn calfskin; 18K white-gold buckle set with 52 diamonds.
**Production:** 28 pieces.

##  GoldenSquare REF. G34 98 0-SDC GCN1 7A

**Movement:** mechanical manual-winding caliber RD 98; 10 3/4'''; 19 jewels; rhodium plated; decorated with Côtes de Genève pattern; fine adjustment in five positions; marked with the Geneva Quality Hallmark.
**Functions:** hours, minutes.
**Case:** 18K white gold, polished and satiny; square-curved; set with 96 diamonds; sapphire back; water-resistant to 3atm.

**Dial:** white mother-of-pearl dial; guilloché; painted Arabic numerals; blued steel hands.
**Strap:** hand-sewn crocodile leather; 18K white-gold buckle set with 31 diamonds.
**Production:** 28 pieces.

## GoldenSquare REF. G40 03 5 GN1 7A

**Movement:** mechanical manual-winding caliber RD 03; 15'''; 27 jewels; rhodium plated; decorated with Côtes de Genève pattern; fine adjustment in five positions; marked with the Geneva Quality Hallmark.
**Case:** 40mm; 18K rose gold, polished and satiny; square-curved; sapphire back; water resistant to 3atm.
**Dial:** white mother-of-pearl dial; painted Roman numerals; rose-gold and blued steel hands.

**Strap:** hand-sewn crocodile leather; 18K rose-gold folding buckle.
**Indications:** center hour, minute; power-reserve indication between 4 and 5; tourbillon carriage at 7; date at 12.
**Special Features:** flying tourbillon with instantaneous large date and power-reserve indication.
**Production:** 28 pieces.

## GoldenSquare REF. G40 57 5 CBO/COW

**Movement:** mechanical self-winding caliber RD 57; 11 1/2'''; 25 jewels; rhodium plated; decorated with Côtes de Genève pattern, fine adjustment in five positions; marked with the Geneva Quality Hallmark.
**Functions:** hours, minutes.
**Case:** 40 mm; 18K rose gold, polished and satiny; square-curved; sapphire back; water resistant to 3atm.

**Dial:** miniature painting on enamel (Cowes ship); blued steel hands.
**Strap:** hand-sewn crocodile leather; 18K rose-gold buckle.
**Production:** 28 pieces

## MuchMore — REF. M22 54 0-SD 3 7A/20-P8

**Movement:** mechanical manual-winding caliber RD 54; 8'''; 19 jewels; rhodium plated; decorated with Côtes de Genève pattern; fine adjustment in five positions; marked with the Geneva Quality Hallmark.
**Functions:** hours, minutes.
**Case:** 18K white gold, polished and satiny; rectangular-cambered; set with 56 diamonds; sapphire back; water-resistant to 3atm.
**Dial:** silver; satin-finished; painted Roman and Arabic numerals; blued steel hands.
**Bracelet:** 18K white gold set with 338 diamonds.
**Production:** 28 pieces.

## MuchMore — REF. M32 28 0 G33 7C

**Movement:** mechanical manual-winding caliber RD 28; 10 3/4'''; 25 jewels; rhodium plated; decorated with Côtes de Genève pattern; fine adjustment in five positions; marked with the Geneva Quality Hallmark.
**Functions:** hour; 30-minute counter at 3; small second at 9; central chronograph second. Special Features: mono-push chronograph with coaxial crown.
**Case:** 18K white gold, polished and satiny; rectangular-cambered; sapphire back; water resistant to 3atm.
**Dial:** silver; guilloche; painted Roman numerals; blued steel hands.
**Strap:** hand-sewn crocodile leather; white-gold buckle.
**Production:** 28 pieces.

## MuchMore — REF. M34 5739 0 9 7A

**Movement:** mechanical self-winding caliber RD 57; 11'''; 25 jewels; rhodium plated; decorated with Côtes de Genève pattern; fine adjustment in five positions; marked with the Geneva Quality Hallmark.
**Functions:** hour, minute; window perpetual calendar (day and month at 12, leap year at 3); date, moonphase.
**Case:** 18K white gold, polished and satiny; rectangular-cambered; sapphire back; water resistant to 3atm.
**Dial:** black; painted Roman numerals; white-gold hands.
**Strap:** hand-sewn crocodile leather; 18K white-gold buckle.
**Production:** 28 pieces.

## TooMuch — REF. T 22 54 0-FD-23RD/SM

**Movement:** mechanical manual-winding RD54 caliber; 8'''; 19 jewels; rhodium-plated; decorated with Côtes de Genève and circular graining patterns and beveled; hallmarked with the Geneva Seal and the Bulletin de l'Observatoire.
**Functions:** hour, minute.
**Case:** 18K white-gold two-piece case; anatomically curved rectangular shape; 22x30mm, thickness: 7.8mm; set brilliants on bezel, lugs and middle; curved sapphire crystal, antireflective on both sides; bezel and lugs with set brilliants; white-gold crown; back fastened by 8 screws, displaying the movement through a sapphire crystal; water resistant to 3atm.
**Dial:** entirely brilliant and ruby pavé lips; blued steel Poire hands.
**Strap:** hand-stitched crocodile leather; threefold screwed attachment; white-gold clasp with brilliants.

## EasyDiver — REF. SE46 57 9 K9 53

**Movement:** mechanical automatic caliber RD 57; 11'''; 25 jewels; rhodium plated; decorated with Côtes de Genève pattern; fine adjustment in five positions; marked with the Geneva Quality Hallmark.
**Functions:** hours, minutes.
**Case:** 46mm; steel; round-cambered; screw-down sapphire back; pushpiece and crown; unidirectional turning bezel; water resistant to 30atm/990ft.
**Dial:** carbon, galvanized metal; Super-LumiNova appliques and index; sun satin-finish.
**Strap:** black vulcanized rubber.
**Production:** 888 pieces.

## EasyDiver Chronograph — REF. SE46 56 9 12 53

**Movement:** mechanical manual-winding caliber RD 56 with column wheel; 12'''; 21 jewels; rhodium plated; decorated with Côtes de Genève pattern; fine adjustment in five positions; marked with the Geneva Quality Hallmark.
**Functions:** hour; 30-minute counter at 3; small second at 9; center chronograph hands.

**Case:** Ø 46mm; steel; round-cambered in steel; screw-down sapphire back; pushpiece and crown; unidirectional turning bezel; water resistant to 30atm/990ft.
**Dial:** champagne-color galvanized metal; Super-LumiNova appliques and index; sun satin-finish.
**Strap:** black vulcanized rubber.
**Production:** 888 pieces.

## EasyDiver Flying Tourbillon — REF. SE48 02 9/0 3 53

**Movement:** mechanical caliber RD 02; 15'''; flying tourbillon; 19 jewels; fine adjustment in five positions; marked with the Geneva Quality Hallmark.
**Functions:** hour, minute, second by the index of the tourbillon.
**Case:** Ø 48mm; steel and 18K white gold; round-cambered; bezel; screw-down sapphire back; pushpiece and crown; unidirectional turning bezel; water resistant to 30atm/990ft.

**Dial:** rhodium-color galvanized metal; Super-LumiNova appliques and index; sun satin-finish.
**Strap:** black vulcanized rubber.
**Production:** 288 pieces.

## AquaMare — REF. G41 57 9 12 53

**Movement:** mechanical automatic caliber RD 57; 11'''; 25 jewels; rhodium plated; decorated with Côtes de Genève pattern; fine adjustment in five positions; marked with the Geneva Quality Hallmark.
**Functions:** hours, minutes.
**Case:** 41mm; steel; square-curved; double-sided antireflective sapphire crystal; screw-down sapphire back; pushpiece, crown, crown protector; water resistant to 30atm/990ft.

**Dial:** champagne-colored galvanized metal; Super-LumiNova appliques and index; sun satin-finish.
**Strap:** black vulcanized rubber; adjustable folding buckle.
**Production:** 888 pieces.

## Sympathie Chrono Perpetual Calendar Bi-Retrograde REF. SY43 56 10 5

**Movement:** mechanical manual-winding RD5610 cal. (Lemania 2320 base + Roger Dubuis calendar module); 21 jewels; rhodium-plated; decorated with Côtes de Genève and circular graining patterns and beveled; hallmarked with the Geneva Seal and the Bulletin de l'Observatoire. **Functions:** hour, minute, small second; perpetual calendar (date, day, month, year, week, moonphase); chronograph with 2 counters. **Case:** 18K pink gold; carré galbé; 43x43mm, thickness: 15.5mm; polished and brushed finish; curved sapphire crystal, antireflective on both sides; polished embossed bezel; 4 correctors on the middle; semi-recessed crown and pushers with case protections, all in pink gold; back fastened by 8 screws, displaying the movement through a sapphire crystal and engraved logo; water resistant to 3atm. **Dial:** silvered and brushed with a sunray pattern; black subdials decorated with circular beads; black outer ring; applied pink-gold triangular marker at 12; skeletonized pink-gold leaf-style hands.
**Indications:** day of the week and date with retrograde Cathédrale hands at 3 and at 9; minute counter at 3; month and four-year cycle at 6; small second at 9; moonphase at 12; week with a center hand with a red tip.
**Strap:** hand-stitched crocodile leather; screwed attachment; pink-gold fold-over safety clasp.
**Also available:** white gold; platinum on request. Small size (40x40mm): pink or white gold; platinum on request.

## Hommage Chronograph, Perpetual Calendar Bi-Retrograde REF. H43 5632 5

**Movement:** mechanical manual-winding RD5632 cal. (Lemania 2320 base + Roger Dubuis calendar module); 12'''; 21 jewels; rhodium-plated; decorated with Côtes de Genève and circular graining patterns and beveled; hallmarked with the Geneva Seal and the Bulletin de l'Observatoire.
**Functions:** hour, minute, small second; perpetual calendar (date, day, month, year, week, moonphase); chronograph with 2 counters. **Case:** 18K pink-gold three-piece case; Ø 43mm, thickness: 15.75mm; curved sapphire crystal, antireflective on both sides; hollowed bezel; 4 correctors on the middle; semi-recessed crown and pushers with case protections, all in pink gold; two screwed-on backs: a closed one and the other displaying the movement through a sapphire crystal and with an engraved logo; water resistant to 5atm.
**Dial:** silvered; brushed; subdials decorated with circular beads; painted Roman numerals; skeletonized pink-gold leaf-style hands.
**Indications:** day of the week and date with retrograde hands at 3 and at 9; minute counter at 3; moonphase at 6; small second at 9; month and four-year cycle at 12; center second; minute track with divisions for 1/5 second.
**Strap:** hand-stitched crocodile leather; pink-gold fold-over clasp.

## Hommage Chronograph, Perpetual Calendar Bi-Retrograde REF. H43 5610 0

**Movement:** mechanical manual-winding RD5610 caliber (Lemania 2320 base + Roger Dubuis calendar module); 21 jewels; rhodium-plated; decorated with Côtes de Genève and circular graining patterns and beveled; hallmarked with the Geneva Seal and the Bulletin de l'Observatoire. **Functions:** hour, minute, small second; perpetual calendar (date, day, month, year, week, moonphase); chronograph with 2 counters. **Case:** 18K white-gold three-piece case; Ø 43mm, thickness: 15.25mm; curved sapphire crystal, antireflective on both sides; 4 correctors on the middle; semi-recessed crown and pushers with case protections, all in white gold; back fastened by 6 screws, displaying the movement through a sapphire crystal and with an engraved logo; water resistant to 5atm.
**Dial:** silvered; brushed; applied white-gold triangular marker at 12; painted railway minute track; skeletonized white-gold leaf-style hands.
**Indications:** day of the week and date with retrograde Cathédrale hands at 3 and at 9; minute counter at 3; month and four-year cycle with digital display at 6; small second at 9; moonphase at 12; week via a center hand with a red tip.
**Strap:** hand-stitched crocodile leather; screwed attachment; white-gold fold-over safety clasp.
**Also available:** pink gold.

## Hommage Flying Tourbillon REF. HO43 03 0

**Movement:** mechanical manual-winding RD03 caliber 15'''; with a tourbillon volant device; 27 jewels; rhodium-plated; decorated with Côtes de Genève and circular graining patterns and beveled; hallmarked with the Geneva Seal and the Bulletin de l'Observatoire. **Functions:** hour, minute, small second; date; power reserve.
**Case:** 18K white-gold three-piece case; Ø 43mm, thickness: 13.35mm; polished and brushed finish; curved sapphire crystal, antireflective on both sides; hollowed bezel; white-gold crown with a coaxial pusher for date correction; two screwed-on backs: a closed one and the other displaying the movement through a sapphire crystal and with an engraved logo; water resistant to 5atm.
**Dial:** white mother-of-pearl dial; aperture on the tourbillon; painted Roman numerals and railway minute track; white-gold Poire hands with skeletonized luminescent ends.
**Indications:** power reserve between 4 and 5 bordered in white gold; small second at 7 integral with the tourbillon carriage; oversized date with two coaxial and complanar discs at 12 bordered in white gold.
**Strap:** hand-stitched crocodile leather; white-gold fold-over safety clasp.

# ROLEX

A legend in the Swiss watch industry, Rolex has earned a reputation for consistency and reliability in all it creates.

With many great collections under its brand umbrella, Rolex is unveiling new and improved models. Of particular note is the attention given to the exterior of some of its lines. For instance, the Oyster Turn-O-Graph with a black dial and luminous markers and hands now is equipped with a solid Oyster bracelet and features a bi-directional bezel for measuring short periods of elapsed time. Also new in the Oyster family is the 18-karat yellow-gold Datejust for men on a tan crocodile strap with white detailed stitching.

In the Daytona line, the brand offers an 18-karat white-gold Cosmograph Daytona on solid link bracelet. This chronograph watch houses the 4130 caliber movement and features a tachometric bezel and improved legibility. Gemstones join the Cosmograph Daytona line on several versions. The various models include a watch with a bezel of trapezoid diamonds and a diamond pavé dial, a version with either red or blue sapphires on the bezel and diamond pavé dial, and an all-diamond version with 32 baguettes on the bezel.

Also new from Rolex is a fun departure from its usual style: the 18-karat gold Cosmograph with leopard motif. Diamonds and 36 yellow sapphires to emulate the elegance and extravagance of the daring cat.

As always, Rolex continues to create new models in its coveted Cellini line, as well, such as the striking two-toned Cellini Danaos that recalls a retro style with its elegant case and pink- and white-gold motif.

THIS PAGE

**ABOVE**

The Oyster Datejust Turn-O-Graph is equipped with a solid Oyster bracelet and features a bi-directional bezel for measuring short periods of elapsed time.

**BOTTOM LEFT**

The Oyster Datejust is crafted in 18-karat gold and features a hand-stitched crocodile strap.

**BOTTOM RIGHT**

Created in 18-karat white gold, this Cosmograph Daytona houses the 4130 caliber movement and features a tachometric bezel and improved legibility.

FACING PAGE

**TOP**

These gemstone-adorned Cosmograph Daytona watches are crafted with diamonds and rubies or sapphires.

## CHRONOLOGY

**1905** Hans Wilsdorf establishes a London-based firm and creates timepieces of technical ingenuity and advancement.

**1908** Wilsdorf coins the name Rolex for his timepieces.

**1910** Rolex obtains the first official chronometer certification ever awarded to a wristwatch.

**1914** The Kew Observatory in Great Britain awards the Rolex wristwatch a Class A precision certificate, a distinction previously reserved for marine chronometers.

**1926** Rolex develops and patents the Oyster watch, deemed to be the first truly water-resistant, airtight timepiece.

**1927** The Rolex Oyster crosses the English Channel on the wrist of swimmer Mercedes Gleitze. This event marks the first of a long list of testimonials to the superior quality of Rolex timepieces.

**1931** This is the year of Rolex's Perpetual Rotor, a self-winding mechanism that runs continuously with the flick of the wrist.

**1945** The company invents the Oyster Datejust, the first watch to display the date automatically via an aperture at 3:00.

**1947** Rolex is on the wrist of Chuck Yeager when he defies the speed of sound.

**1953** Sir Edmund Hillary wears a Rolex to the top of Mt. Everest. Rolex also unveils the Submariner, the first diving watch water resistant to 100 meters.

**1960** The Bathyscaphe is created. With reinforced build, crystal and winding crown, it plunges 35,787 feet into the Mariana Trench in the Pacific Ocean on the outer hull of the Trieste Bathyscaphe.

**1971** The Oyster Explorer II is launched, with an orange hand that indicates day/night orientation.

**1988** The Oyster Cosmograph Daytona chronometer with perpetual rotor is launched.

**2001** Rolex unveils the Oyster Lady-Datejust in 18-karat yellow, pink or white gold on the Oyster bracelet and housing the newest self-winding mechanisms.

**2002** Rolex puts renewed emphasis on its Cellini collection of classic, elegant timepieces. Top among them is the Cellinium. Crafted in platinum, this exclusive timepiece is fitted with a black crocodile strap and a mother-of-pearl guilloché dial with small seconds at 6:00.

**ABOVE**

The Cosmograph Daytona is set with diamonds and 36 yellow sapphires to enhance its stunning leopard motif.

**RIGHT**

The Cellini Danaos is crafted of 18-karat pink and white gold.

## CELLINI DANAOS — REF. 4233/9 BIC

**Movement:** mechanical manual-winding Rolex 1602 caliber.
**Functions:** hour, minute.
**Case:** 18K white- and pink-gold three-piece case, in carré galbé shape; sapphire crystal; pink-gold crown; snap-on back; water resistant to 3atm. **Dial:** black; tone on tone; printed Arabic numerals; applied 6 and logo at 12 in pink gold; pink-gold Régate hands. **Strap:** crocodile leather; pink-gold clasp.
**Also available:** in white or yellow gold; with leather straps in different colors.
**Below:** Cellini Basket Ref. 5320/9, in white gold with mother-of-pearl dial, white-gold markers; ostrich skin strap (on request).

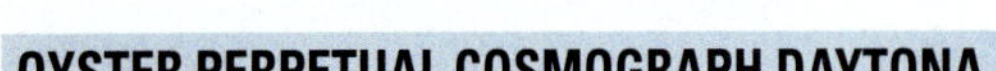

## OYSTER PERPETUAL AIR-KING — REF. 14010M

**Movement:** mechanical automatic-winding Rolex 3000 caliber.
**Functions:** hour, minute, second.
**Case:** stainless steel three-piece case (Ø 34mm, thickness: 11.5mm); polished and brushed finish; sapphire crystal; fixed knurled bezel and polished, embossed hour markers; screw-down crown with double gasket; screw-on back; water resistant to 10atm.
**Dial:** blue soleil; applied bâton markers in white gold; printed minute track with luminescent dots; luminescent bâton hands in white gold.
**Bracelet:** Oyster in steel, brushed; fold-over clasp.
**Also available:** with white enameled dial, printed Roman numerals; with silvered dial, smooth bezel Ref. 14000M.

## OYSTER PERPETUAL COSMOGRAPH DAYTONA — REF. 116518

**Movement:** mechanical automatic-winding Rolex 4130 manufacture caliber; 72-hours autonomy; Glucydur balance with Micro-star micrometer-screw regulation; 44 jewels; 28,800 vph; Breguet balance-spring; COSC-certified chronometer.
**Functions:** hour, minute, small seconds; chronograph with 3 counters.
**Case:** 18K yellow-gold three-piece case (Ø 40mm, thickness: 12.5mm); polished and brushed finish; sapphire crystal; fixed bezel with engraved tachometer scale; white-gold screw-down crown with threefold gasket and case protection; screw-down pushers; screw-on back; water resistant to 10atm.
**Dial:** natural black mother-of-pearl; subdial crowns with gold rims; applied gold Roman numerals; gold bâton hands.
**Indications:** minute counter at 3; small seconds at 6; hour counter at 9; center second; minute track with divisions for 1/5 of a second.
**Strap:** crocodile leather; gold fold-over clasp.

## CALIBER 4130

Automatic-winding movement, with 72-hour autonomy; two-piece rotor mounted on a ball bearing.
**Shape:** round. **Jewels:** 44.
**Balance:** in Glucydur with four arms, a Micro-star micrometer regulation device, four elements screwed on the balance ring.
**Frequency:** 28,800 vph. **Balance-spring:** Breguet, first quality, antimagnetic.
**Shock-absorber system:** Kif. **Notes:** COSC-certified chronometer. The pillar-plate is decorated with a circular graining pattern; the bridges and chronograph levers are brushed and beveled; the rotor is decorated with a concentric-circle pattern.
As a result of a project developed entirely inside the manufacture, the 4130 automatic caliber is now mounted on all Daytona chronographs. This movement is different from the former version (derived from El Primero) by the position of the permanent second counter at 6 (previously at 9) and hour counter at 9 (previously at 6). It features all of the technical prerogatives typical of Rolex, among which is the Micro-star balance adopted on a chronometer.

## OYSTER PERPETUAL DATE GMT MASTER II REF. 16713

**Movement:** automatic Rolex 3185 caliber; COSC-certified chronometer.
**Functions:** hour, minute, second; date; three time zones, 24-hour.
**Case:** stainless steel and 18K yellow-gold three-piece case (Ø 40mm, thickness: 12mm); polished and brushed finish; sapphire crystal with Cyclope magnifying lens on the date; bi-directional turning ring with black ring for the 24-hour reading of home time and two additional time zones; screw-down crown with double gasket and case protection; screw-on back; water resistant to 10atm.
**Dial:** black enameled; luminescent applied gold round and bâton markers; printed minute track; luminescent gold Mercedes hands.
**Indications:** date at 3; 24-hour home time and second time zone (by independent adjusting of the single main hour hand) or third time zone via an arrow-shaped center hand (by turning the ring and matching positioning of third time zone and arrow-shaped hand).
**Bracelet:** Oysterlock steel and gold, polished and brushed finish; fold-over clasp.
**Also available:** with Jubilé bracelet; with bronze dial and two-color ring; in stainless steel with black dial and red-black ring Ref. 16710, Oysterlock or Jubilé bracelet.

## OYSTER PERPETUAL DATE GMT MASTER II REF. 16718

The typical Oyster case and the Jubilé bracelet characterize the essential aesthetics of the Rolex GMT as a perfect synthesis of outstanding class and sportsmanlike aspect. The abbreviation GMT (Greenwich Mean Time) was used for the first time by Rolex in the 1960s for a watch featuring two time-zone indications. The GMT Master allows reading the time of three different time zones thanks to the independent adjusting of the main hour hand with respect to the arrow-shaped GMT hand indicating home time. To know the time of a third zone, one must turn the ring until the time of the selected town coincides with the GMT hand. To return to the previously set time zone, one must move the triangular marker of the bezel to the position of 12 on the dial. The photograph shows the yellow-gold version with a champagne dial and brilliants and rubies as markers.
**Also available:** without precious stones, with black or bronze dial and ring, Oysterlock, Jubilé or Superjubilé bracelet.

## OYSTER PERPETUAL DATE EXPLORER II REF. 16570

**Movement:** mechanical automatic-winding Rolex 3185 caliber; COSC-certified chronometer.
**Functions:** hour, minute, second; date; second time zone, 24-hour.
**Case:** stainless steel three-piece case (Ø 40mm, thickness: 12.5mm); polished and brushed finish; sapphire crystal with Cyclope magnifying lens on the date; fixed brushed bezel with engraved 24-hours for the reading of an additional time zone; screw-down crown with double gasket and case protection; screw-on back; water resistant to 10atm.
**Dial:** white enameled; luminescent applied round and bâton markers in black enameled gold; printed minute track; luminescent Mercedes hands in black enameled gold (independent adjusting of the hour hand by pulling the crown).
**Indications:** date at 3; 24-hour second time zone via a red arrow-shaped center hand.
**Bracelet:** Oysterlock steel, brushed; fold-over clasp.

## OYSTER PERPETUAL DATE SEA-DWELLER 4000 REF. 16600

**Movement:** mechanical automatic-winding Rolex 3185 caliber; COSC-certified chronometer.
**Functions:** hour, minute, second; date.
**Case:** stainless steel three-piece case (Ø 40mm, thickness: 15mm); polished and brushed finish; thick sapphire crystal (3mm) resisting high pressure; pressure compensating valve for helium release; counterclockwise-turning ring with black ring and graduated scale for the calculation of diving times; screw-down crown with threefold gasket and case protection; screw-on back; water resistant to 122atm.
**Dial:** black enameled; luminescent applied round and bâton markers in white gold; printed minute track; luminescent Mercedes hands in white gold.
**Indications:** date at 3.
**Bracelet:** Oysterlock in steel, brushed; fold-over clasp with Fliplock safety stop. Comes with an additional link, an extension plate of the clasp and a screwdriver to allow extending it to wear over a diver's suit.

# ROTARY

With 110 years of history, Rotary has the distinction of remaining a family-owned and operated watch business—one that thrives on its heritage and deftly blends its art into appealing avant-garde timepieces.

Having remained a family business for four generations, Rotary purports the privileges of private ownership—namely, the ability to create innovative timepieces without corporate restraints.

Perhaps most impressive in the Rotary collection is the Rotary Revelation™ watch. Recently unveiled, this timepiece is the brand's crown jewel. Its creative design incorporates technology and aesthetics within a case that swivels to totally reverse itself. Created in a men's version and a ladies' version, with or without gemstones, the watch houses two movements and incorporates two faces—giving the wearer a different look with the flip of a case. Additionally, because the watch has two movements and two dials, it can be set to two different times.

The Rotary Revelation™ fashionably fuses style and practicality. On each watch, one dial offers a date aperture, while the reverse dial offers a second hand. A sapphire crystal adds to the overall appeal of the watch. The men's model is available in five contemporary designs with either black or brown leather straps, or stainless steel bracelets. The Rotary Revelation™ is available with several reversible-dial combinations for men, including black and white; black and

THIS PAGE

TOP

Wearers can turn day into night with this stone-set steel Rotary Revelation™.

BOTTOM

These Rotary Revelation™ watches offer Roman numerals on one dial side; the flip side features a seconds hand.

FACING PAGE

This gents' Rotary Revelation™ with black leather strap features one black dial with indexes and one white dial with Roman numerals.

ROTARY
ROTARY
SWISS MADE
SWISS

silver; chocolate-brown and ivory; blue and slate-gray. There is also a model with one black dial and one mother-of-pearl dial. Each watch features Roman numerals on one dial and Arabic numerals or indexes on the other.

Similarly, the ladies' watches come in a variety of colors and styles falling within three main designs. Among them: a steel case with black leather strap and Arabic-numeraled black dial; a gold-plated case with retro-styled dial; a steel case with mother-of-pearl dial.

Encouraged by the attention given to the Rotary Revelation™, the brand recently unveiled the stunning Sofia watch—a versatile beauty with new technology. The patented design of the Sofia enables the wearers to choose whether they want to wear their watches with stones or without stones. By simply squeezing the retractable stone-set bars on each side of the watch face, the wearer changes the look of the timepiece as the stones "disappear." A simple push on two buttons on the caseback "pops" the stone-set bars out again. The Sofia is available in titanium or rose-gold-plated stainless steel.

Additionally, Rotary has unveiled a Limited Edition collection. The series is restricted to 500 pieces of each model. Each watch has its own serial number on the caseback and houses an automatic movement. The self-winding caliber is visible through a transparent caseback and each watch is water resistant to 30 meters. Every Rotary watch is backed by an international two-year guarantee.

THIS PAGE

TOP LEFT

The Sofia watch, with retractable stone-set bars, gives the option of a look with or without stones.

TOP RIGHT

The dials of these Rotary Revelation™ models for women are either mother of pearl or painted black.

FACING PAGE

TOP

These versions of Rotary Revelation™ feature sapphire crystals, leather straps and slimmer appeal.

BOTTOM

This steel Limited Edition automatic watch houses a self-winding movement and is accompanied by an authenticity certificate.

## CHRONOLOGY

**1895** Moise Dreyfuss opens his factory in La Chaux-de-Fonds, naming the brand Rotary. It is his goal to offer value and quality in every timepiece.

**Early 1900s** Dreyfuss's sons, Georges and Sylvain, join the company.

**1907** The Dreyfuss sons open an office in Britain to import the family watches.

**1925** The Dreyfusses introduce the Rotary winged-wheel logo.

**1940** Rotary becomes an official watch supplier to the British Army.

**1987** Fourth-generation Robert Dreyfuss joins the company. He moves the Rotary head office to new premises on Regent Street, London, and the Swiss offices to Neuchâtel.

**1997** Rotary's 200 models are sold in more than 35 countries.

**2002** Rotary is voted Supplier of the Year at the UK Jewelry Awards, the first of two back-to-back titles.

**2003** Rotary launches a range of Limited Edition watches, each with its own serial number engraved on the caseback and each design limited to 500 pieces.

**2004** Rotary unveils its third Limited Edition model—a gents' automatic with transparent caseback.

# S. COIFMAN

Honoring the tradition of Swiss hand craftsmanship and detail, S. Coifman watches are classic, elegant timepieces created according to designs of a century ago. Indeed, in the 1900s, S. Coifman timepieces were especially appreciated by craftsmen who applied the same meticulous attention to details in their own trades.

Since 1906, the watches of Simon Coifman have been a personal tribute to science and design. Originally created as homages to fine artists, each S. Coifman piece is an expression of its maker, not of a manufacturing process. It's the difference between mass production and sixty hours spent hand engraving a skeleton movement. It's not about commerce. It's about art.

There have been a small number of S. Coifman timepieces introduced over the last century. From the days when Coifman worked in the back room of a tiny music box workshop to the modest studio in which the company resides today, there has always been a strong belief in the adage "quality, not quantity." The Gentlemen's Stainless Steel Mechanical is a perfect example of that creed. Classically designed, this watch is one of the purest pieces in the collection. The modest presentation and diminutive details enhance the simple elegance of the solid stainless steel bezel and case.

Simon Coifman

THIS PAGE

**TOP**
The Swiss-made S. Coifman Flyback with Big Date complication.

**BOTTOM LEFT**
Simon Coifman.

**BOTTOM RIGHT**
Each part of the movement for the 1950s 18-karat Gold Red-12 Mechanical was completely hand engraved with all of the steel edges beveled by hand.

FACING PAGE

Each Swiss-made S. Coifman Grand Exhibition case is solid 18-karat gold, numbered individually and houses a 1950s Val de Joux 22 mechanical movement that has been hand decorated extensively. White enamel dials and sapphire crystals complete each gorgeous piece.

S. Coifman
S. Coifman

The refined silver dial features an intricate guilloché pattern, finely hand-applied single minute markers, black Roman numerals, Breguet hands, and a silver subdial at 6:00 in a concentric circle pattern. All features are protected by a sapphire crystal and accented with a push/pull pumpkin crown, a favorite of Coifman. Even more spectacular is what this slender piece conceals beneath its steely surface: a mechanical manual-winding INCABLOC© Unitas 7046 Swiss movement.

Then there is the S. Coifman Hebdomas 8-Day. Particularly enamored with this design, which traces back to 1888, Coifman would often tell friends it reminded him of the pocket watches he admired as a budding young horologist. The word Hebdomas finds its origins in the word Hebdomandaire, which indicates that a watch should be wound once a week, on the seventh day, hence the 8-day functionality of this unique achievement. The S. Coifman Hebdomas presents a small ceramic dial with an off-center time indication with Arabic numerals, Breguet hands, and an exposed balance wheel mounted on a beautifully hand-engraved bridge with a pattern of Coifman's creation. The handmade mechanical movement is a vintage Hebdomas 15-A with an 8-day power reserve when fully wound. It is guilded in gold.

In 2003, S. Coifman was acquired by the Invicta Watch Group. Together, they will be able to create a number of groundbreaking timepieces that combine the unique assets and expertise of each brand. In an age that yields to mechanical fabrication and mass production, S. Coifman continues to pay homage to the time-honored tradition of hand craftsmanship. Created in limited numbers, each piece is hand tooled according to the original material specifications and Simon Coifman's vintage 1906 designs. From the rare metals to the precision movements, everything is as it was.

LEFT

The stately Gentlemen's Stainless Steel Mechanical is powered by a mechanical manual-winding INCABLOC© Unitas 7046 Swiss movement. The shock-absorbing system protects the most sensitive pivot point of the movement, increasing shock-resistance considerably.

**RIGHT**

The three-piece case of the Hebdomas 8-Day is solid stainless steel plated in 18K gold with an oversized push/pull pumpkin crown, domed sapphire crystal, and an engraved SC escutcheon on the rounded back.

## CHRONOLOGY

**Late 1800s** Simon Coifman grows up in Chiasso, a Swiss hamlet near the Italian boarder. He is inspired by physics and fascinated with mechanics as a young man. He not only studies the greats such as Newton and DaVinci, but also becomes enamored with mechanical timepieces.

**Early 1900s** Coifman apprentices in a music box shop by day and analyzes mechanical watches by night.

**1906** Coifman perfects his first watch movement, a complicated timepiece with 17 jewels. Soon after, he crafts his first S. Coifman timepiece, and is quickly recognized for the detail and perfection of his work.

**1907** Coifman begins building timepieces for the town's masons, metal workers, cooper smiths and other artisans. He admires their ability to transform stone into monuments and metal into machines. In little time, S. Coifman timepieces become known as the "craftsman watches."

**1911** Like many horologists influenced by Abraham-Louis Breguet, Coifman perfects his own tourbillon movement. He is quickly commissioned to create a tourbillon watch, the first of five one-of-a-kind S. Coifman tourbillons, each commissioned for untold sums.

**1953** S. Coifman is commissioned to create the 18-karat Gold Red-12 Mechanical for a select few collectors. Each individually numbered piece houses a limited production Valjoux hand-winding chronograph movement with two counters. Each part is completely hand engraved with all of the steel edges beveled by hand. A polished 18-karat yellow-gold case is constructed with a sapphire crystal, push/pull pumpkin crown and bezel measuring 1.5 inches in diameter. The 1920s enamel dial features a prominent, eye-catching red numeral 12. Even more unusual are the offset red Arabic numbers that count military time.

**2002** S. Coifman Timepieces is reestablished and the watches it produces in Chiasso pay homage to the time honored tradition of hand craftsmanship. The company's creed is quality not quantity.

**2003** After decades of dormancy, S. Coifman is acquired by the Invicta Watch Group and joins the company's successful Invicta and Activa brands. S. Coifman still calls Chiasso home, nearly a century after Simon Coifman created his first timepiece there. Each watch is still painstakingly crafted by hand in limited numbers, and each carries with it the influences and inspirations of the brand's creator.

# SCATOLA DEL TEMPO

Arguably the benchmark by which other watch-winding box companies set their standards, Scatola del Tempo creates the most luxurious, advanced pieces of equipment in which to protect and preserve timepiece heirlooms.

THIS PAGE

TOP

Sandro Colarieti *(center)* and his family.

BOTTOM

All the mechanical parts are produced in St.Imier, as well as the motors of the rotors. Final assembling, internal and external finishing of the boxes, as well as final testing and quality control, all take place in Italy.

FACING PAGE

Unveiled at BaselWorld 2005, the spectacular 1 RTM Diamonds is crafted of solid brass and leather. It is covered with 1,428 Top Wesselton VVS-quality diamonds with an astonishing total weight of 90 carats.

Established in the 1980s by Sandro Colarieti, Scatola del Tempo is the result of the will and initiative of a collector who wanted a watch holder suitable for the quality of the models he owned. Finding none that matched his needs, Colarieti resolved to construct his own box using only the finest high-quality materials. It was the start of a dynasty of an all-new types of boxes in a centuries-old jewelry world.

Inspired by Colarieti's dedication and his belief in luxury and excellence, the family continues to carry on in the creation of the world's most coveted watch boxes. This classic Italian product is loved and appreciated on five continents, in all of Europe's capital cities, and on the islands of the Pacific Ocean.

R.W. SYSTEM

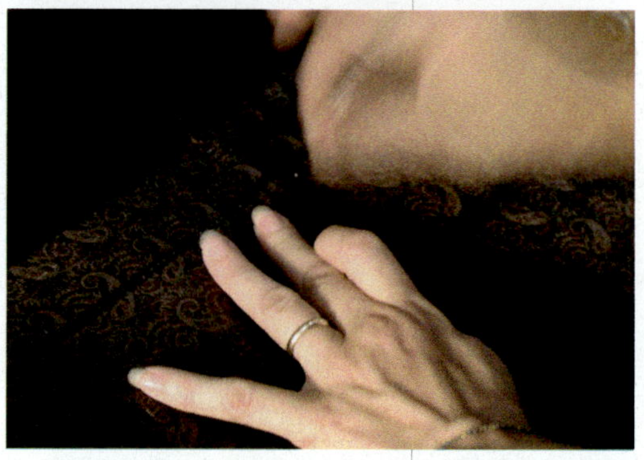

The reasons for such success are simple, but not taken for granted. Scatola del Tempo is based on an essential principle: none of its constructive details can be left to chance or be underestimated. From the ergonomic boxes to the exquisite silk linings to the mechanics of fastenings and the outer leather finish, each element is chosen with deliberate precision and finely finished. Scatola del Tempo—always on the cutting edge—was the first manufacture to create and produce boxes with internal rotors for winding watch movements.

The realization of Scatola del Tempo's rotors was achieved by cooperating directly with some of the most famous houses of Swiss horology (including Patek Philippe, which uses these for its perpetual calendars) and by focusing essentially on the following four basic parameters: rotational speed; turning direction of the rotor; number of revolutions per hour; and time interval of functioning of the rotor in one day.

LEFT

One of the brand's most recent creations is the prestigious 32RT model, designed for great collections or specialty shops.

**TOP AND BOTTOM**

The new 18RT-RA is provided with a patented opening device. Details of the box include the exceptional level of finishes and the sophisticated engineering of electronic and mechanical elements.

These guidelines are essential due to the fact that the watch must be wound but not overwound, i.e. it must work in optimal conditions and no organ must be stressed needlessly. Furthermore, the choice of the motor is also based on its reduced magnetic field, in such a way as to not jeopardize the functioning of the balance-spring. Finally, all of the mechanical components are tested for accuracy.

All of them are produced in Switzerland by adopting the same tolerance standards and machines used to produce tourbillon carriages or the pillar-plates of minute repeaters. Scatola del Tempo watch boxes are exquisite objects of unmatched detail.

**ABOVE AND LEFT**

The rotor of the La Scatola del Tempo, in the Squelette model (3RTM), combines extreme mechanical perfection with a design of great impact.

**ABOVE**

First-quality materials and skillfully hand-manufactured parts are used throughout the entire production cycle. (7RT)

## The boxes with Rotory Mechanism

These devices, designed for automatic movement wristwatches (particularly useful for perpetual calendars) substitute the wrist's movement to keep the watches wound regularly. Scatola del Tempo has, for several years, produced special containers with one or more rotating supports run by an electronic micro-motor that supplies the movement with ideal winding. The traditional models offer ten different rewinding programs, making it possible to simulate one's own activity level through a program selector placed inside the battery holder. Each program specifies a set schedule (considering the natural habits of people who wear the watches by day and set them down at night) of so many hours of rotations in both directions. Starting from the setting "0" there is a gradual lessening in the number of running hours but an increase in the number of rotations. The indications show, besides on-off, the state of the batteries (via both an automatic LED signal on the exterior, and a dial indicator on the back activated by a button) and the stand-by power. By using a 6-volt transformer in the jack, one may eliminate the use of batteries. However, rotors using alkaline batteries will work for more than one year for all models.

## The "SdT" Watch

The name of this chronograph refers to the name of this Italian company, a leader in the production of precious leather cases for watches, considering taste and quality that are particularly modern as well as formal and functional choices of definite class.

Chronograph with automatic movement (Valjoux cal. 7750) with three counters and date. Steel case with screw-down crown and screw-on caseback, water resistant to 10atm. Dial with Arabic numerals and sword-style hands with red/sky-blue "SdT" logo, counters and flange with tachymeter scale contrasting the black background. Calfskin strap and case with electronic rotational winding system programmed at 1,200 revolutions in 24 hours, the basic piece of Scatola del Tempo in Barzanò, an old hamlet in the Province of Lecco in Northwest Italy.

**TOP RIGHT**

The meticulous care put into Scatola del Tempo's finishing processes guarantees a very high standard of quality, known and appreciated all over the world. (9RTRA)

TOP LEFT

Box for keeping three automatic watches wound, in black, leather, red (3RT). It is available in the Squelette version with briarwood base and the motor gears are visible in black polished brass.

FAR RIGHT

Box for keeping one automatic watch wound, in black (1RTSL). Made of nylon and black leather with an opening with a metal ring making the watch visible.

CENTER

Trousse tool box with utensils produced by Bergeon, a Swiss company, for the care of one's watches.

Box for keeping one automatic watch wound. (1RT) In the single-watch box, the selection of the rotation direction (clockwise, suitable for almost all automatics, or counterclockwise) can be made by using a selection-slide on the front of the rotor.

BELOW

Box for two watches with leather straps or flexible bracelets. (2A)

Men's jewelry box (1P) for travel, black with space for one watch and accessories (cuff links, rings, lighters, pens, etc.).

Box for one watch with leather strap or flexible bracelet. (1A)

## Technical specifications

Exterior structure: Evaporated beech wood covered in natural organic tanned leather.

Interior: Flexible polyurethane resin, differentiated density, covered in jacquard silk in paisley design or in leather. The internal structure can hold perfectly the specified number and size of watches. Each place provides the necessary space for the winding crown and pushpieces.

Clasp: Gilded brass, marked and numbered by hand.

Each piece is entirely handmade by craftsmen; the hardware has received antimagnetic treatments.

# TB Buti

A young brand, TB Buti deftly blends the tradition of watch-making with chic Italian styling and bold oversized designs.

The TB Buti watch brand is the result of an encounter between Tommaso Buti and a leading Tuscan watchmaker who has been creating timepieces for decades. The two joined forces and introduced a bold new brand created in Florence, Italy.

The case of the TB Buti watches was developed and designed by Buti, a keen watch collector. It is a striking, oversized case that incorporates the circle and the tonneau in its design. In creating this line, it was Buti's goal to develop a exceptional collection designed and produced entirely in Florence. Naturally, he turned to Swiss parts for his watches, combining Italian sophistication with Swiss knowledge. The entire production cycle of the TB Buti collection takes place in Florence, where the ancient tradition of watchmaking combines with some of the best state-of-the art computerization in a precise melding of tradition and technology.

The TB Buti watch collection is comprised of a variety of complex functioning timepieces. One such series is the Galileo—a line of Rattrapante Dual Time GMT watches. This line houses the automatic Jacquet 8171 chronograph movement modified by Maison Jacquet SA on a Valjoux 7750 base. The watch features a chronograph rattrapante function and offers 40 hours of power reserve and a dual time readout at 3:00. Crafted in 18-karat gold the watch is water resistant to 20atm and comes in a variety of dial choices with color-coordinated alligator straps.

Similarly the Giotto Flyback GMT watch line houses the automatic Jacquet 8112 chronograph movement that has been modified. The rotor is engraved with the TB Buti logo. This elegant watch offers hours, minutes and seconds at 9:00, with the chronograph seconds in the center. The chronograph rattrapante, with flyback function, offers 30-minute and 12-hour totalizers and the GMT readout is in the center of the watch.

THIS PAGE

ABOVE

The Giotto GMT Crono Flyback is crafted in titanium and rose gold. It houses the automatic Jacquet 8112 chronograph movement and offers flyback function. Water resistant to 20atm, it features a sapphire caseback.

LEFT

The Galileo Split Second GMT is crafted in 18-karat white gold. It houses an automatic Jacquet 8171 chronograph movement with split seconds chronograph function and 40 hours of power reserve. The rotor is engraved with the TB logo. This model is water resistant to 20atm.

FACING PAGE

The Giotto GMT, referred to as The Black, houses the automatic Jacquet 8112 chronograph movement with flyback function. It is water resistant to 20atm and features a sapphire caseback. This case is crafted in 18-karat gold.

# TB Buti

TB Buti's Yanick Series is quite diverse. The debut model is the Yanick II Chronograph, with an automatic movement and 40 hours of power reserve. It offers date, hours, minutes and seconds, as well as chronograph seconds and minutes. The case is created in gold with a screw-locked bezel and back plate. The watch features a screw-down crown and pressure pushers, and is available in white gold with natural diamonds on the dial. In addition to this model, there is the Yanick II Tricompax Chronograph, Yanick II Bicompax Titan Chronograph, Yanick II Tricompax Titan Chronograph, and the Yanick II Special Chronograph with black bezel.

**ABOVE**

This Giotto GMT is crafted in stainless steel and offers chronograph functions and GMT readout.

**LEFT**

The Yanick II Bicompax Chronograph is crafted in 18-karat gold and houses the automatic Jacquet 8147 chronograph with date.

## CHRONOLOGY

**2000** In Florence, Tommaso Buti begins designing a new watch collection that houses Swiss movements.

**2002** TB Buti makes its debut at the Basel Fair with a collection of strikingly bold watches with complexities. Among the initial watches unveiled are several chronograph rattrapante styles and GMTS.

**2003** TB Buti introduces the LuLu collection.

**2004** TB Buti begins working in black gold.

**ABOVE**

Crafted in steel, this LuLu watch houses the automatic Candino 28362-1 on ETA base with seconds subdial. The 36mm case features a screw-locked bezel set with 8 diamonds.

**RIGHT**

The Michelangelo Grand Data watch houses an automatic Dubois Dépraz movement on an ETA 2892-2 base that is modified with the addition of a separate disc for the big-date function at 12:00 and the seconds subdial at 6:00.

The Michelangelo is a Grand Date is powered by the automatic Dubois Dépraz caliber on ETA 2692-2 base, modified with the addition of an upper plate with separate disc for big-date function and subdial for the seconds. The watch offers 40 hours of power reserve and a case made of three pieces of stainless steel and machine carved from a solid black. A total of 16 screws lock down the bezel and back plate. The watch is water resistant to 2atm. A bit bolder is the Shark Underwater watch with automatic Valjoux 7750 chronograph movement and three subdials. Also crafted in steel, it is 42mm in diameter and offers striking legibility under water.

Offering a somewhat softer side, TB Buti reveals the LuLu Automatic with subseconds offset at 8:00. It is available in a variety of dial colors with color-coordinated straps and diamonds on the bezel. A certificate of authenticity accompanies every TB Buti watch.

# TAG HEUER

A unique pioneering legacy—from the Monaco V4 concept watch to the Monaco Sixty Nine to the Golf watch—TAG Heuer's innovative spirit is stronger than ever. It fuels the brand's uncompromising campaign to drive the frontiers of watchmaking forward and fulfill the philosophy expressed in the motto, "Swiss Avant-Garde Since 1860."

Founded by Edouard Heuer in 1860, the TAG Heuer brand holds an impressive number of patents, starting with its winding crown mechanism patented in 1869. The oscillating pinion, invented by TAG Heuer in 1887, is still an essential component in today's mechanical chronographs. In 1916, TAG Heuer's Mikrograph stopwatch was the first to achieve 1/100th of a second accuracy. In 1966, TAG Heuer's Microtimer was the first miniaturized timekeeping instrument to achieve accuracy to 1/1,000th of a second. In 2003, TAG Heuer unveiled the Microtimer timepiece, the first prestigious Swiss wristwatch accurate to 1/1,000th of a second and winner of the Best Design award at the Grand Prixd'Horlogerie de Genève in 2002. TAG Heuer received the same award in 2004 for the Monaco Sixty Nine.

THIS PAGE

TAG Heuer Microtimer, the first prestigious Swiss wristwatch accurate to 1/1,000th of a second and winner of the Best Design prize at the Grand Prix d'Horlogerie de Genève in 2002.

FACING PAGE

TAG Heuer ambassador and actress Uma Thurman wears the Microtimer Denim diamonds for evening soirées for its glamour and trend-setting appeal.

ABOVE

The TAG Heuer Monaco Steve McQueen, worn by the actor in *Le Mans*.

## The Monaco Sixty Nine

The Monaco Sixty Nine: Symbolizing TAG Heuer's dual commitment to tradition and the avant-garde, this new legendary timepiece is a fusion of 19th and 21st century watchmaking, housed in a pivoting case inspired by the famous Monaco worn by Steve McQueen.

The major innovation of the Monaco Sixty Nine lies in the extraordinary technical feat that it represents: two timepieces with radically different movements are united in a single case—the result of 144 years of TAG Heuer expertise and patents in the field of mechanical and digital movements.

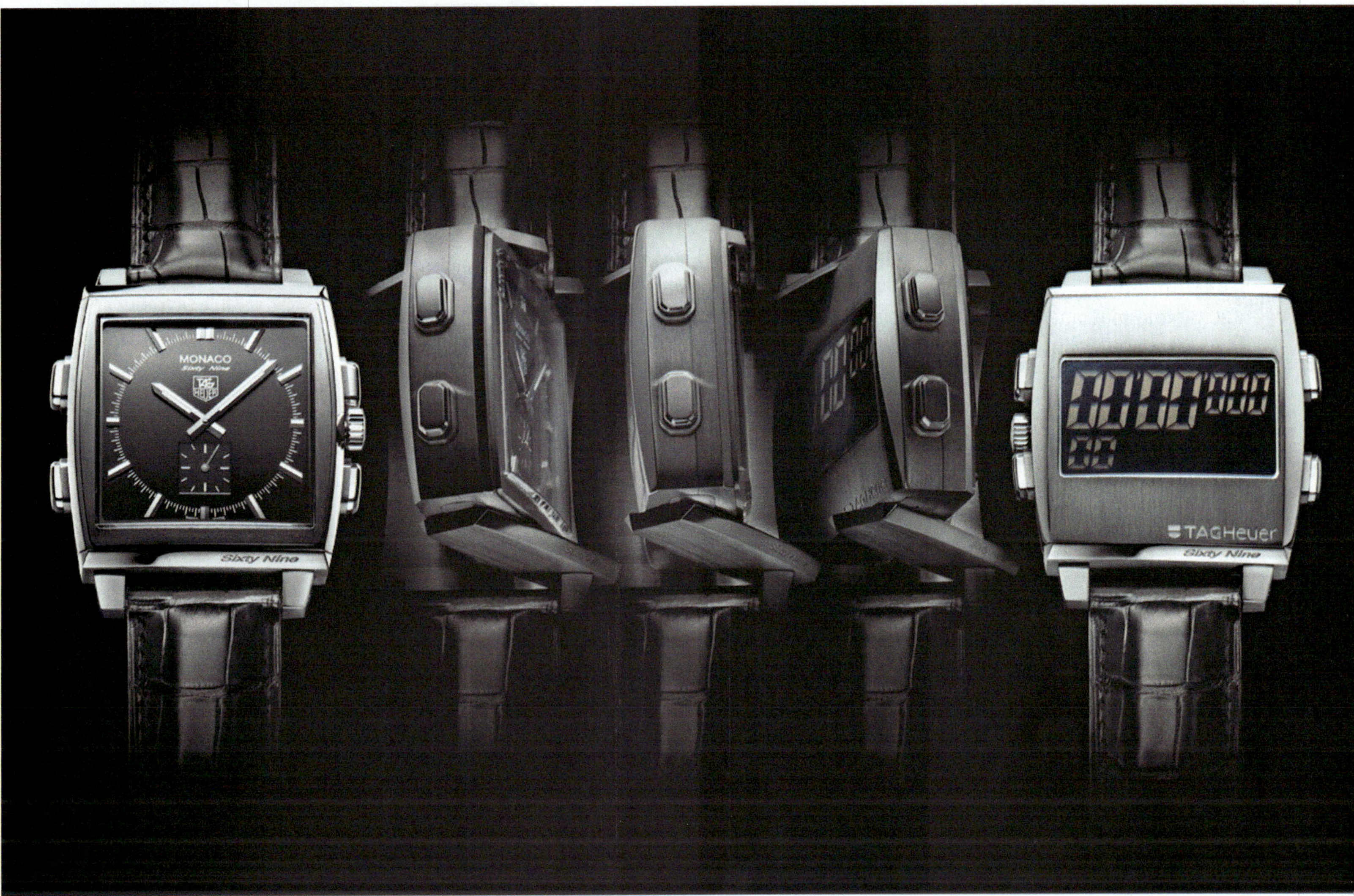


**ABOVE**

TAG Heuer Monaco Sixty Nine, the first watch to offer both mechanical and digital displays by merely pivoting the case. It was named Best Design at the Grand Prix d'Horlogerie de Genève in 2004.

The Monaco Sixty Nine is the first watch to offer both mechanical and digital displays with the turn of the case and TAG Heuer has been awarded a patent for this new pivoting system. The strikingly bold model combines tradition and the avant-garde in a way never before seen. On one side, there's the mythical, uncompromising look and square case of the initial 1969 Monaco—the model preferred by Steve McQueen and worn by the actor in *Le Mans*; on the other, the unique, ultramodern digital face of the Microtimer, the first Swiss wristwatch accurate to 1/1,000$^{th}$ of a second, invented by TAG Heuer just 18 months ago. The two timepieces signify the company's evolution since 1860: a digital chronograph that features unbeatable precision and contemporary functions presents a vision of the 21$^{st}$ century while the traditional mechanical watch, powered by 19$^{th}$ century wheel and pinion technology, displays the local time with classic, understated appeal—all enclosed in a single case boasting exceptional character.

# TAG Heuer

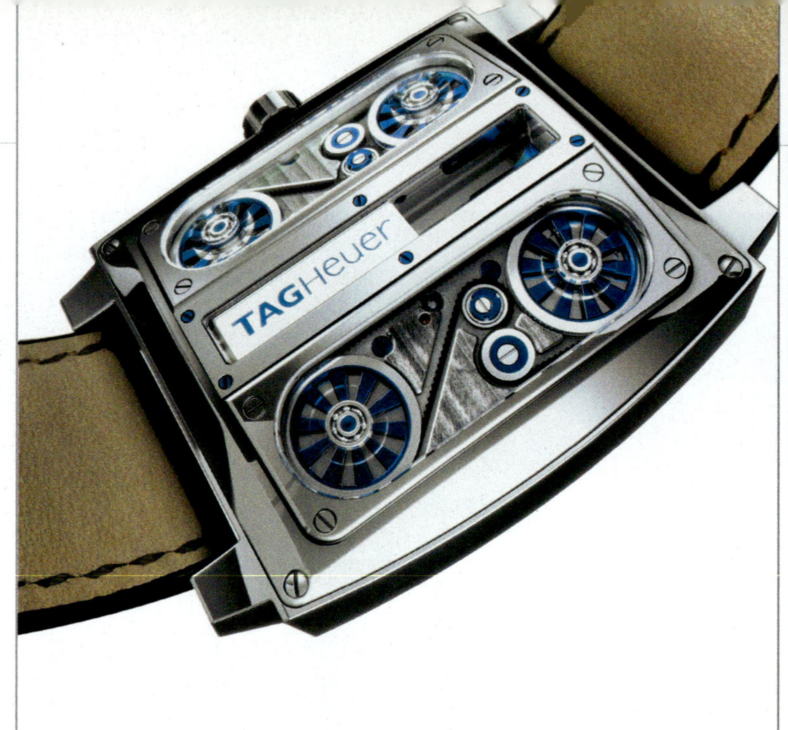


## The Monaco V4 Concept Watch

The TAG Heuer Monaco V4 Concept Watch, unveiled at BaselWorld 2004, represents a stunning technological breakthrough. At its heart is an advanced integrated mechanical movement, encased upside down in a high-design evolution of the classic TAG Heuer Monaco. The name V4 derives from the movement's four barrels, which are mounted in a V shape like cylinders in a supercharged motor-racing engine. It also pays tribute to the movement's genesis: while the V4 draws from the newest concepts in industrial technology, its true inspiration comes from the world of high-tech, high-performance race-car engines. The Monaco V4 marks a total reinvention of the mechanical movement. This timepiece has been recognized by the international press and watchmaking world as the star of the BaselWorld 2004.

**ABOVE**

TAG Heuer Monaco V4 concept watch associates an avant-garde movement and a classic icon among timepieces.

**LEFT**

TAG Heuer Monaco V4 concept watch's movement's four barrels are mounted like cylinders.

## Professional Golf Watch

This timepiece originated from one assessment: virtually no golfers wore watches while playing. Tiger Woods, TAG Heuer ambassador, was no exception. To enable him to wear a timepiece during tournaments, TAG Heuer developed with Tiger Woods a professional golf watch to meet the unique ergonomics demand of golfers.

So as not cause the golfer discomfort when the wrist is bent, the crown had to be located at 9:00. As the clasp and folding buckle of a regular watch hurts the wrist while playing golf, the TAG Heuer Professional Golf watch has a patented integrated unfolding system. This exclusive super elastic rubber strap adapts length at anytime to any wrist diameter and holds the watch in place—always away from the glove. The entire watch is made out of ultra-light materials (titanium, rubber, etc). During the product development, Tiger Woods confirmed that he does not feel the watch on his wrist while playing. The challenge has been responded to and, during the 2004 Boston PGA, Tiger Woods wore the TAG Heuer Professional Golf watch while competing.

THIS PAGE

ABOVE

TAG Heuer Professional Golf watch: an innovative timepiece born thanks to the brand's collaboration with the world's most legendary golfer.

BOTTOM

TAG Heuer Professional Golf watch's integrated unfolding system: eliminates clasp that hurt golfers' wrists.

FOLLOWING PAGE

Tiger Woods wearing the TAG Heuer Professional Golf watch during the 2004 Boston PGA.

## CHRONOLOGY

**1860** The TAG Heuer watchmaking company is founded in Saint-Imier, Switzerland, by Edouard Heuer.

**1869** TAG Heuer registers one of the first crown-winding mechanism for pocket watches.

**1886** Major improvement in the chronograph industry: TAG Heuer invents the famous "oscillating pinion" for mechanical chronographs.

**1889** The TAG Heuer chronograph collection wins a silver medal when presented at the World Exhibition in Paris.

**1911** TAG Heuer presents the first watch for automotive instrument panels, featuring a trip-duration indicator.

**1916** The firm tests the Micrograph, the first stopwatch capable of measuring time with a precision to 1/100th of a second.

**1920s** TAG Heuer is appointed official timekeeper of the 1924 Olympic Games in Antwerp and Paris in 1928.

**1933** TAG Heuer produces the first dashboard stopwatch for racing cars, the Autavia.

**1950** In the house's workshops the extraordinary Mareograph chronograph is developed; it indicates the state of tides. A patent is obtained the same year.

**1964** First Carrera chronograph with a hand winding movement.

**1966** The Microtimer is patented as the first electronic miniaturized sports chronometer capable of readings up to 1/1,000th of a second.

**1971** TAG Heuer becomes the official timekeeper of Ferrari; the partnership will last until 1979.

**1975** The new Microsplit chronometer is presented with an LCD (liquid-crystal display).

**1980s** TAG Heuer is appointed the official timekeeper of the Olympic Games in Moscow and at the Winter Games in Lake Placid, New York.

**1986** TAG Heuer launches the sports watch Formula 1 in stainless steel and fiberglass. Driver Alain Prost emphasizes the house's return to Formula 1 racing by winning the World Championship.

**1987** The TAG Heuer S/El (sport/elegance) collection is created, with a bracelet that will become a brand emblem.

**1989** TAG Heuer is appointed official timekeeper of the F.I.S. Alpine Ski World Cup.

**1992–2003** TAG Heuer is the official timekeeper of the Formula 1 World Championship.

**1997** TAG Heuer launches the Kirium Series, a watch combining technology with avant-garde design.

**1998** The TAG Classic collection is enriched with a new edition of the Monaco, the square chronograph worn by actor Steve McQueen in the 1971 film *Le Mans*.

**2000** TAG Heuer creates its first ladies-only model, the Alter Ego.

**2002** TAG Heuer wins the 2002 Best Design award at the Grand Prix d'Horlogerie de Genève with the Microtimer, and signs on a new ambassador, golf champion Tiger Woods.

**2003** TAG Heuer introduces a line of timepieces dedicated to Tiger Woods and becomes a key sponsor of the newest PGA tour, the Deutsche Bank Championships.

**2004** TAG Heuer introduces the Monaco V4 concept watch at BaselWorld. TAG Heuer wins the 2002 Best Design prize at the Grand Prix d'Horlogerie de Genève with the Monaco Sixty Nine. TAG Heuer becomes official timekeeper and chronograph of the Indy Racing League (IRL) / IndyCar Series (accuracy: 1/1,0 000th of a second)

**2005** 45 years after Steve McQueen, new star ambassadors join TAG Heuer team. Launch of the Professional Golf watch, developed in close partnership with Tiger Woods.

## NEW 2000 AQUARACER AUTOMATIC REF. WAF2110.BA0806

**Movement:** mechanical automatic-winding TAG Heuer Calibre 5.
**Functions:** hour, minute, second; date.
**Case:** fine-brushed stainless steel three-piece case with polished edges; Ø 38.4mm, thickness: 10.9mm; sapphire crystal with inner antireflective treatment; fully polished unidirectional turning bezel with Super-LumiNova dot at 12 and engraved numerals on the base; polished screw-in crown; screw-in caseback with stamped diver decoration; water resistant to 300m.
**Dial:** black with Clous de Paris pattern; hand-applied indexes and numerals; diamond shaped hands with polished facets; luminescent markers on hands and indexes; monochromatic TAG Heuer logo.
**Indications:** date at 3.
**Bracelet:** 5-row steel bracelet with double-safety clasp and diving extension system; alternate polished and fine-brushed steel with polished edges.
**Also available:** silver dial; blue dial.

## NEW 2000 AQUARACER AUTOMATIC REF. WAF2111.BA0806

**Movement:** mechanical automatic-winding TAG Heuer Calibre 5.
**Functions:** hour, minute, second; date.
**Case:** fine-brushed stainless steel three-piece case with polished edges; Ø 38.4mm, thickness: 10.9mm; sapphire crystal with antireflective inner side; unidirectional turning bezel completely polished with Super-LumiNova dot at 12 and engraved numerals on the base; polished screw-in crown; screw-in caseback with stamped diver decoration; water resistant to 300m.

**Dial:** silver with Clous de Paris pattern; hand-applied indexes and numerals; diamond-shaped hands with polished facets; luminescent markers on hands and indexes; monochromatic TAG Heuer logo.
**Indications:** date at 3.
**Bracelet:** 5-row steel bracelet with double-safety clasp and diving extension system; alternate polished and fine-brushed steel with polished edges.
**Also available:** black dial; blue dial.

## NEW 2000 AQUARACER CHRONOGRAPH REF. CAF2110.BA0809

**Movement:** mechanical automatic-winding TAG Heuer Calibre 16.
**Functions:** hour, minute, second; date; chronograph with 3 counters.
**Case:** fine-brushed stainless steel three-piece case with polished edges; Ø 41mm, thickness: 14.9mm; sapphire crystal; unidirectional turning bezel with fixed central aluminum ring, fine-brushed turning base and polished studs; engraved numerals with black varnish on the turning base; Super-LumiNova dot at 12; polished screw-in crown; screw-in caseback with stamped diver decoration; water resistant to 300m.

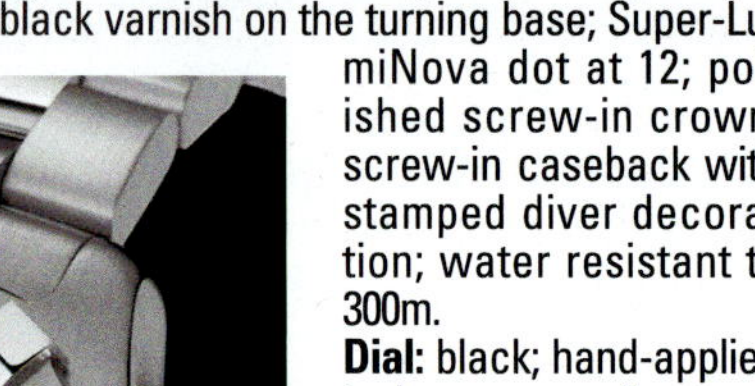

**Dial:** black; hand-applied indexes; diamond shaped hands with polished facets; luminescent markers on hands and indexes; monochromatic TAG Heuer logo.
**Indications:** small second at 9; hour counter at 6; minute counter at 12; date at 3.
**Bracelet:** 3-row steel bracelet with double safety-clasp and diving extension system; alternate polished and fine-brushed steel with polished edges.
**Also available:** with silver aluminum dial and fixed silver ring; blue dial and fixed blue aluminum ring.

## NEW 2000 AQUARACER CHRONOGRAPH REF. CAF1112.BA0803

**Movement:** quartz. **Functions:** hour, minute, second; date; chronograph with 3 counters. **Case:** fine-brushed stainless steel three-piece case; Ø 41mm, thickness: 12.15mm; sapphire crystal; unidirectional turning bezel; polished "chimney" with engraved minute scale with black varnish; fine-brushed base with engraved numerals with black varnish and polished studs; Super-LumiNova dot at 12; polished screw-in crown; screw-in caseback with stamped diver decoration; water resistant to 300m. **Dial:** blue with sunray effect and silver counters; hand-applied indexes and numerals; diamond shaped hands and indexes; colored TAG Heuer logo.
**Indications:** minute counter at 6; hour counter at 10; 1/10th of a second counter at 2; date at 4.
**Bracelet:** 3-row steel bracelet with double-safety clasp and diving extension system; alternate polished and fine-brushed steel with fine-brushed edges.
**Also available:** black dial and silver counters; silver dial and blue counters.

## 2000 AQUARACER AUTOMATIC REF. WAB2011.BA0803

**Movement:** mechanical automatic-winding TAG Heuer Calibre 5.
**Functions:** hour, minute, second; date.
**Case:** fine-brushed stainless steel three-piece case with polished edges; Ø 41mm, thickness: 11.24mm; sapphire crystal; unidirectional turning bezel with blue aluminum ring matching the color of the dial and contrasted numerals; Super-LumiNova dot at 12; polished screw-in crown; screw-in caseback with stamped diver decoration; water resistant to 300m.
**Dial:** blue; hand applied indexes; luminescent markers on hands and indexes; second hand with red arrow; monochromatic TAG Heuer logo.
**Indications:** date at 3.
**Bracelet:** 3-row steel bracelet; double-safety clasp and diving extension system; alternate polished central row and fine-brushed lateral rows with fine-brushed edges.
**Also available:** with black dial and black aluminum ring.

## 2000 AQUARACER AUTOMATIC REF. WAB2010.BA0804

**Movement:** mechanical automatic-winding TAG Heuer Calibre 5.
**Functions:** hour, minute, second; date.
**Case:** fine-brushed stainless steel three-piece case with polished edges; Ø 41mm, thickness: 11.24mm; sapphire crystal; unidirectional turning bezel with black aluminum ring matching the color of the dial and contrasted numerals; Super-LumiNova dot at 12; polished screw-in crown; screw-in caseback with stamped diver decoration; water resistant to 300m.
**Dial:** black; hand applied indexes; luminescent markers on hands and indexes; second hand with red arrow; monochromatic TAG Heuer logo.
**Indications:** date at 3.
**Bracelet:** 3-row, fine-brushed steel bracelet; double-safety clasp and diving extension system.
**Also available:** blue dial and blue aluminum ring.

## 2000 AQUARACER QUARTZ REF. WAB1111.BA0801

**Movement:** quartz.
**Functions:** hour, minute, second; date.
**Case:** fine-brushed stainless steel three-piece case; Ø 38.2mm, thickness: 9.4mm; sapphire crystal; unidirectional turning bezel with polished steel ring matching the color of the dial and contrasted numerals; Super-LumiNova dot at 12; polished screw-in crown; screw-in caseback with stamped diver decoration; water resistant to 300m.
**Dial:** silver; hand-applied indexes; luminescent markers on hands and indexes; yellow second hand; colored TAG Heuer logo.
**Indications:** date at 3.
**Bracelet:** 3-row steel bracelet; double-safety clasp and diving extension system; alternate polished central row and fine-brushed lateral rows with fine-brushed edges.
**Also available:** black dial and black aluminum ring; blue dial and blue aluminum ring.

## 2000 AQUARACER QUARTZ REF. WAB1112.BA0801

**Movement:** quartz.
**Functions:** hour, minute, second; date.
**Case:** fine-brushed stainless steel three-piece case; Ø 38.2mm, thickness: 9.4mm; sapphire crystal; unidirectional turning bezel with polished steel ring matching the color of the dial and contrasted numerals; Super-LumiNova dot at 12; polished screw-in crown; screw-in caseback with stamped diver decoration; water resistant to 300m.
**Dial:** blue; hand-applied indexes; luminescent markers on hands and indexes; yellow second hand; colored TAG Heuer logo.
**Indications:** date at 3.
**Bracelet:** 3-row steel bracelet with double-safety clasp and diving extension system; alternated, polished central row and fine-brushed lateral rows with fine-brushed edges.
**Also available:** black dial and black aluminum ring; silver dial and silver polished steel ring.

## 2000 AQUAGRAPH AUTOMATIC CHRONOGRAPH REF. CN211A.BA0353

**Movement:** mechanical automatic-winding TAG Heuer Calibre 60.
**Functions:** hour, minute, second; date; chronograph with 3 counters.
**Case:** fine-brushed stainless steel three-piece case; Ø 41mm, thickness: 15.9mm; scratch-resistant sapphire crystal; unidirectional patented auto-lock turning dodecagonal bezel; luminescent markers each 5 minutes for optimal reading of diving times; screw-in crown with screw-in crown indicator; automatic helium valve; screw-on caseback with stamped diver decoration; water resistant to 500m.
**Dial:** black; applied rhodium-plated dot markers; with luminescent hour markers; printed minute track; luminescent rhodium-plated hour and minute hands; yellow second hand; oversized chronograph minute hand in luminescent yellow.
**Indications:** small second counter at 3; hour counter at 6; 24-hour display at 9.
**Bracelet:** 3-row fine brushed steel bracelet; pushbutton safety clasp and diving extension system.
**Also available:** with rubber strap.

## CALIBRE 60

The Calibre 60, specially developed for TAG Heuer, is the only automatic movement with the minutes of the chronograph displayed in the center of the dial rather than on a small register, thus making it quicker and easier to see the time elapsed, especially when making decompression level in diving.

## LINK CALIBRE 36 AUTOMATIC CHRONOGRAPH REF. CT511B.BA0564

**Movement:** mechanical automatic-winding TAG Heuer Calibre 36; 1/10th of a second precision guaranteed by high frequency vibrations of the movement: 36,000 vph; the oscillating weight is decorated with a Côtes de Genève (Geneva Waves) vertically striped pattern; power reserve of 50 hours minimum; COSC-certified chronometer.
**Functions:** hour, minute, second; date; chronograph with 3 counters. **Case:** stainless steel, three-piece polished and fine-brushed case (Ø 42mm, thickness: 14.48mm); scratch-resistant sapphire crystal, with anti-reflective treatment on both sides; glare-proof on both sides; polished fixed bezel; shaped pushbuttons; transparent caseback in scratch-resistant sapphire crystal; water resistant to 200m. **Dial:** opalescent silver dial; sand-blasted faceted indexes; spiral-decorated applied counters; monochrome logo; faceted skeleton hands; luminescent markers on hands and beside indexes; Link Calibre 36 printed below the monochrome TAG Heuer logo. **Indications:** date at 4:30; hour counter at 6; small seconds at 9; minute counter at 3.
**Bracelet:** Link S-shape fine-brushed stainless steel bracelet with double safety-clasp folding buckle with incorporated pushbuttons.
**Also available:** black dial with fine-brushed fixed bezel.

## CALIBRE 36

This exceptional automatic movement has been specially developed by TAG Heuer to permit time measurement to an accuracy of 1/10th of a second. It is the ultimate in precision; no other automatic movement in the world is more accurate today. This performance is made possible by the high frequency of the movement, 36,000 vibrations an hour. The caseback has a transparent sapphire crystal through which the movement and gear train may be admired.

## LINK AUTOMATIC CHRONOGRAPH REF. CJF2114.BA0576

**Movement:** mechanical automatic-winding TAG Heuer Calibre 16.
**Functions:** hour, minute, second; date; chronograph with 3 counters.
**Case:** fine-brushed stainless steel case; Ø 42mm, thickness: 15.5mm; curved scratch-resistant sapphire crystal; polished fixed bezel with tachometer scale; screw-fitted crown; screw-in caseback; water resistant to 200m.
**Dial:** dual-zone blue dial with a central zone decorated with 4 zones of "45° streaks"; hand-applied faceted indexes; faceted hands; luminescent markers on hands and beside indexes; minute circle flange; monochrome TAG Heuer logo.
**Indications:** small seconds at 9; hour counter at 6; minute counter at 12; date at 3.
**Bracelet:** Link S-shape fine-brushed stainless steel bracelet with double safety-clasp folding buckle.
**Also available:** gray dial.

## LINK QUARTZ CHRONOGRAPH REF. CJ1110.BA0576

**Movement:** quartz.
**Functions:** hour, minute, second; date; chronograph with 3 counters.
**Case:** fine-brushed stainless steel case; Ø 42mm, thickness: 13mm; curved scratch-resistant sapphire crystal; fine-brushed unidirectional turning bezel; screw-in crown, screw-fitted caseback; water resistant to 200m.
**Dial:** black dial; hand-applied faceted indexes; faceted hands; luminescent markers on hands and beside indexes; luminescent red arrow minute hand; monochrome TAG Heuer logo.
**Indications:** small seconds at 6; hour counter at 10; 1/10th of a second at 2; date at 4.30.
**Bracelet:** Link S-shape fine-brushed stainless steel bracelet with double safety-clasp folding buckle.
**Also available:** silver dial with polished turning bezel; blue dial with polished turning bezel.

## LINK LADIES QUARTZ CHRONOGRAPH REF. CJF1310.FC6189

**Movement:** quartz.
**Functions:** hour, minute, second; date; chronograph with 3 counters.
**Case:** polished stainless steel, polished case; Ø 33mm, thickness: 11.5mm; curved scratch-resistant sapphire crystal; polished fixed bezel; screw-in crown, screw-fitted caseback; water resistant to 200m.
**Dial:** white mother-of-pearl dial; hand-applied faceted indexes; faceted hands; lumine-scent markers on hands; minute circle flange; monochrome TAG Heuer logo.
**Indications:** small seconds at 6; minute counter at 10; 1/10th of a second at 2; date at 4:30.
**Strap:** white enamel calf leather.
**Also available:** pink mother-of-pearl dial with pink enamel calf leather strap; white mother-of-pearl dial with 12 diamonds on white enamel calf leather strap; pink mother-of-pearl dial with 12 diamonds on pink enamel calf leather strap.

## LINK AUTOMATIC REF. WJF2111.BA0570

**Movement:** mechanical automatic-winding, TAG Heuer Calibre 7.
**Functions:** hour, minute, second; date.
**Case:** fine-brushed stainless steel case; Ø 39mm, thickness: 10.5mm; curved scratch-resistant sapphire crystal; polished fixed bezel; screw-in crown; screw-fitted caseback; water resistant to 200m.
**Dial:** dual-zone silver dial with a central zone decorated with 4 zones of "45° streaks"; hand-applied faceted indexes; faceted hands; luminescent markers on hands and beside indexes; minute circle flange; monochrome TAG Heuer logo.
**Indications:** date at 3.
**Bracelet:** Link S-shape fine-brushed stainless steel bracelet with double safety-clasp folding buckle.
**Also available:** black dial with fine-brushed fixed bezel; blue dial with polished fixed bezel.

## LINK QUARTZ — REF. WJ1110.BA0570

**Movement:** quartz.
**Functions:** hour, minute, second; date.
**Case:** fine-brushed stainless steel case; Ø 39mm, thickness: 10.5mm; curved scratch-resistant sapphire crystal; polished unidirectional turning bezel; screw-in crown; screw-fitted caseback; water resistant to 200m.
**Dial:** black dial with 2 zones; hand-applied faceted indexes; faceted hands; luminescent markers on hands and beside indexes; monochrome TAG Heuer logo.
**Indications:** date at 3.
**Bracelet:** Link S-shape fine-brushed stainless steel double safety-clasp folding buckle.
**Also available:** black dial with fine-brushed unidirectional turning bezel; silver dial with polished unidirectional turning bezel; blue dial with polished unidirectional turning bezel.

## LINK LADIES QUARTZ — REF. WJF1318.BA0572

**Movement:** quartz.
**Functions:** hour, minute, second; date.
**Case:** polished stainless steel case; Ø 27mm, thickness: 9mm; curved scratch-resistant sapphire crystal; polished fixed bezel set with 52 diamonds (0.385 carat); screw-in crown; screw-fitted caseback; water resistant to 200m.
**Dial:** white mother-of-pearl dial; 8 hand-applied faceted indexes and 3 diamonds (0.022 carat); faceted hands; luminescent markers on hands; minute circle flange; monochromatic TAG Heuer logo.
**Indications:** date at 3.
**Bracelet:** Link S-shape polished stainless steel bracelet with double-safety-clasp folding buckle.

## PROFESSIONAL GOLF QUARTZ — REF. WAE1110.FT6004

The first ever Professional Golf Watch developed and worn by Tiger Woods—to meet the unique ergonomics demands of golfers.

**Movement:** flat line quartz movement.
**Functions:** hour, minute, second; date at 3.
**Case:** stainless steel and titanium (55 gr); 37.5x36.7mm, thickness: 10.5mm; crown at 9; massive stainless steel 316L folding buckle incorporated in the case with safety pushbuttons at 10 and 2; lettering: TAG Heuer at 12; water resistant to 50m.
**Dial:** hand-applied indexes; luminous markers (Super-LumiNova C3 GL) on hands and beside indexes.
**Strap:** black silicon elastic strap.
**Note:** Professional Golf Watch by Tiger Woods. Limited edition of 4,000 pieces.

## MICROTIMER QUARTZ CHRONOGRAPH — REF. CS111C.FT6003

Digital chronograph:
T1 mode: main time and date.
AL mode: alarm clock.
F1 mode: displays the timing of an event (typically a lap time in a circuit race) in minutes, seconds, and thousands of a second plus the main time while timing continues; can time up to 80 laps.
BEST LP mode: best lap. The wearer can consult the laps in the memory, find the best lap, and rank each lap by lap number.
Standard Chronograph mode (Start, Stop, Split).
T2 mode: second time zone.
Stand by mode (black display).
Digital display with white backlight.
**Case:** polished stainless steel 316L; 38x 42.7mm, thickness: 12mm; 4 pushbuttons; sapphire crystal with antireflective coating; water resistant to 100m.
**Strap:** vulcanized rubber strap with massive folding buckle with double-safety pushbuttons.

## CARRERA AUTOMATIC CHRONOGRAPH REF. CV2010.BA0786

**Movement:** mechanical automatic-winding TAG Heuer Calibre 16.
**Functions:** hour, minute, second; date; chronograph with 3 counters.
**Case:** stainless steel three-piece polished case; Ø 41mm, thickness: 16.1mm; scratch-resistant sapphire crystal; polished fluted crown; screw-on caseback with scratch-resistant sapphire crystal; black tachymeter scale on the fixed bezel; water resistant to 50m.
**Dial:** black; hand-applied rhodium-plated indexes, luminescent hour markers; silver-ringed hour and minute counter; luminescent rhodium-plated hour and minute hands; monochrome TAG Heuer logo.
**Indications:** hour counter at 6; small second counter at 9; minute counter at 12; date at 3.
**Bracelet:** 5-row steel bracelet; solid steel folding clasp with safety pushbuttons; alternated fine-brushed central and lateral rows with polished edges and small polished rows in between.
**Also available:** silver dial with anthracite hour and minute counters and anthracite tachymeter scale on the fixed bezel.

## CARRERA AUTOMATIC REF. WV211A.BA0787

**Movement:** mechanical automatic-winding TAG Heuer Calibre 5.
**Functions:** hour, minute, second; date.
**Case:** polished stainless steel three-piece case; Ø 39mm, thickness: 12.1mm; scratch-resistant sapphire crystal; polished fluted crown; screw-on caseback with scratch-resistant sapphire crystal; water resistant to 50m.
**Dial:** silver with sunray effect; hand-applied rhodium-plated indexes and Arabic numerals; luminescent hour markers; luminescent rhodium-plated hour and minute hands; monochrome TAG Heuer logo.
**Indications:** date at 3.
**Bracelet:** 5-row steel bracelet; solid steel folding clasp with safety pushbuttons; alternate fine-brushed central and lateral rows with polished edges and small polished rows in between.
**Also available:** with black dial.

## CARRERA RACING AUTOMATIC CHRONOGRAPH REF. CV2113.FC6182

**Movement:** mechanical automatic-winding; TAG Heuer Calibre 17.
**Functions:** hour, minute, second; date; chronograph with 3 counters.
**Case:** stainless steel three-piece polished and fine-brushed case; Ø 39mm, thickness 13.5mm; scratch-resistant sapphire crystal; fluted crown; screw-on caseback; water resistant to 50m.
**Dial:** black dial with three silver-ringed counters; applied faceted rhodium-plated baton markers; with luminescent hour markers; printed railway minute track; luminescent rhodium-plated baton hour and minute hands.
**Indications:** small second at 3; date at 4; hour counter at 6; minute register at 9.
**Strap:** black calfskin perforated leather, polished steel folding clasp with safety pushbuttons.
**Also available:** with black or silvered dial and/or black or brown calfskin leather strap.

## CARRERA TWIN TIME AUTOMATIC REF. WV2116.FC6181

**Movement:** mechanical automatic-winding TAG Heuer Calibre 7.
**Functions:** hour, minute, second; date; second time zone.
**Case:** polished and fine-brushed, stainless steel three-piece case; Ø 39mm, thickness: 11.9mm; scratch-resistant sapphire crystal; fluted crown; screw-on caseback; water resistant to 50m.
**Dial:** silver dial; hand-applied faceted rhodium-plated indexes with luminescent markers; luminescent rhodium-plated hour and minute hands; blue arrow with Super-LumiNova on second time-zone hand; monochrome TAG Heuer logo.
**Indications:** second time zone; date at 3.
**Strap:** brown alligator strap; polished steel folding clasp with safety pushbuttons.
**Also available:** black dial with black or brown alligator.

## TAG HEUER FORMULA 1 QUARTZ CHRONOGRAPH REF. CAC1112.BA0850

**Movement:** quartz.
**Functions:** hour, minute, second; date; chronograph with 3 counters.
**Case:** fine-brushed stainless steel case; Ø 41mm, thickness: 12mm; scratch-resistant sapphire crystal; unidirectional turning bezel in stainless steel with titanium anthracite treatment; "easy grip" system screw-in crown; screw-fitted caseback; polyurethane "bumpers"; water resistant to 200m.
**Dial:** red dial; hand-applied indexes; faceted hands; luminescent markers on hands and beside indexes; 5-color TAG Heuer logo.
**Indications:** small seconds at 6; minute counter at 10; 1/10th of a second at 2; date at 4:30.
**Bracelet:** fine-brushed stainless steel double-safety clasp with extension system.
**Also available:** red dial on rubber strap and white dial, black dial available on rubber strap and stainless steel double-safety clasp with extension-system bracelet.

## TAG HEUER FORMULA 1 CHRONOTIMER QUARTZ REF. CAC111D.BT0705

**Movement:** quartz, digital and analog movement.
**Functions:** analog hour, minute and second; LCD digital display hour, minute, second and date; 1/100th of a second chronograph; countdown; alarm; second time zone; perpetual calendar.
**Case:** fine-brushed stainless steel case; Ø 41mm, thickness: 12mm; scratch-resistant sapphire crystal; unidirectional turning bezel in stainless steel with titanium anthracite treatment; "easy grip" crown; screw-fitted caseback; polyurethane "bumpers"; water resistant to 200m.
**Dial:** black dial with LCD digital display; skeletonized hands; luminescent markers on hands; minute circle flange; monochrome TAG Heuer logo.
**Strap:** rubber strap with pin buckle.
**Also available:** fine-brushed stainless steel double-safety clasp with extension-system bracelet.

## TAG HEUER FORMULA 1 QUARTZ REF. WAC1110.BA0850

**Movement:** quartz.
**Functions:** hour, minute, second; date.
**Case:** fine-brushed stainless steel case; Ø 41mm, thickness: 12mm; scratch-resistant sapphire crystal; unidirectional turning bezel in stainless steel with titanium anthracite treatment; "easy grip" system screw-in crown; screw-fitted caseback; polyurethane "bumpers"; water resistant to 200m.
**Dial:** black dial; hand-applied indexes; faceted hands; luminescent markers on hands and beside indexes; 5-color TAG Heuer logo.
**Indications:** date at 4:30.
**Bracelet:** fine-brushed stainless steel double-safety clasp with extension system.
**Also available:** black and red dial on fine-brushed stainless steel double-safety clasp with extension-system bracelet and rubber strap; white dial and red dial on metal bracelet and rubber strap; blue dial on metal bracelet.

## TAG HEUER FORMULA 1 QUARTZ REF. WAC1212.BA0851

**Movement:** quartz.
**Functions:** hour, minute, second; date.
**Case:** fine-brushed stainless steel case; Ø 37mm, thickness: 9.5mm; scratch-resistant sapphire crystal; unidirectional turning bezel in stainless steel with titanium anthracite treatment; "easy grip" screw-in crown; screw-fitted caseback; polyurethane "bumpers"; water resistant to 200m.
**Dial:** blue dial; hand-applied indexes; faceted hands; luminescent markers on hands and beside indexes; 5-color TAG Heuer logo.
**Indications:** date at 4:30.
**Bracelet:** fine-brushed stainless steel double-safety clasp with extension system.
**Also available:** black dial, white dial or orange dial on fine-brushed stainless steel double-safety clasp with extension-system bracelet and rubber strap.

## MONACO SIXTY NINE (DIAL 1) REF. CW9110.FC6177

First mechanical watch with 1/1000th second chronograph
**Movement:** mechanical manual-winding movement; 21,600 vibrations per hour; 17 jewels; 42-hour power reserve. **Functions:** hour, minute, second; small second register at 6. **Case:** fine-brushed and polished stainless steel 316L; 39.5 x41mm, thickness: 18mm; 4 push-buttons designed in the Monaco spirit; sapphire crystal on both sides (with antireflective coating on the digital side); water resistant to 50m.
**Dial 1:** 2-level black dial with sun effect; 13 hand-applied indexes.
**Dial 2:** Digital chronograph:
T1 mode: main time and date.
AL mode: alarm clock.
F1 mode: displays the timing of an event (typically a lap time in a circuit race) in minutes, seconds, and thousandths of a second plus the main time while timing continues. Enables timing up to 80 laps.
BEST LP mode: best lap. The wearer can consult the laps in the memory : find the best lap, then rank each lap by lap number
Standard Chronograph mode (Start, Stop, Split).
T2 mode: 2nd time zone.
Stand by mode (black display).
Display: digital display with white backlight.
**Strap:** Classic Monaco alligator strap; massive folding buckle with double-safety pushbuttons.

## MONACO SIXTY NINE (DIAL 2) REF. CW9110.FC6177

**Patented system:** Using a simple and intuitive system designed and patented by TAG Heuer, the Monaco Sixty Nine is the first reversible watch alternating between a traditional dial and a high-tech digital display. Designed to make the operation as simple as possible, the system allows the case to be raised vertically on two systematically opposed arms so that it can rotate on its axis. After turning it over, simply replace the watch case on its base.

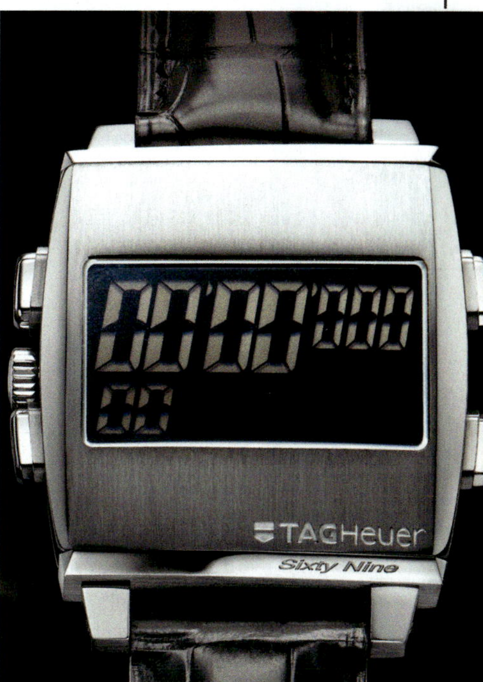


## MONACO AUTOMATIC CHRONOGRAPH REF. CW2113.FC6183

**Movement:** mechanical automatic-winding TAG Heuer Calibre 17.
**Functions:** hour, minute, second; date; chronograph with 2 counters.
**Case:** stainless steel three-piece polished and fine-brushed case; 40.4 x 38.5mm, thickness 13mm; curved Plexiglas; semi-recessed crown; protected elliptical pushers with 8 facets; caseback fixed with 4 screws; water resistant to 30m.
**Dial:** metallic-blue dial with sun pattern; applied faceted rhodium-plated baton markers with luminescent dots; 2 square silvered registers; printed minute track; luminescent rhodium-plated baton hour and minute hands; red chronograph hands.
**Indications:** small second at 3; date at 6; minute register at 9.
**Strap:** blue genuine crocodile leather strap with polished steel folding clasp with safety pushbuttons.
**Also available:** with blue dial and steel bracelet; with black dial and black alligator strap, black calfskin strap or steel bracelet.

## MONACO ABSOLUTE WHITE AUTOMATIC CHRONOGRAPH REF. CW2117.FC6198

**Movement:** mechanical automatic-winding TAG Heuer Calibre 17.
**Functions:** hour, minute, second; date; chronograph with 3 counters.
**Case:** polished and fine-brushed, stainless steel three-piece case; 40.4x38.5mm, thickness: 13mm; curved Plexiglas; semi-recessed crown; protected elliptical pushbuttons with 8 facets; caseback fixed with 4 screws; water resistant to 30m.
**Dial:** white dial; hand-applied faceted rhodium-plated indexes with luminescent markers; 3 counters; printed minute track; luminescent rhodium-plated hour and minute hands; monochrome TAG Heuer logo.
**Indications:** small second at 3; hour counter at 12; minute counter at 9; date at 6.
**Strap:** white perforated calfskin strap; polished steel folding clasp with safety pushbuttons.

# TUTIMA

Satisfying the most exacting demands at all times has always been an essential part of the corporate tradition at Tutima. The brand's yardstick is the watch connoisseur who sets meticulous standards.

—*Dieter Delecate, owner and president.*

Since 1927, Tutima has been crafting some of the finest wristwatches in Glashütte, Germany. By 1941, the brand was creating sophisticated Flieger Chronographs—a tradition it continues today.

In fact, the year 2005 marks the 20th anniversary of the Tutima Military Air Force Chronograph (also known as the NATO Chronograph). The Tutima Military Air Force Chronograph is a precision wristwatch designed for split-second decision-making above the clouds. A true precision instrument, the watch was developed in response to a request by the German Armed Forces in 1983 to develop a chronograph with integrated pushbuttons. Tutima rose to the challenge and manufactured the Military Air Force Chronograph, which is water resistant to 20 bar and features widely spaced, integrated pushers. A masterpiece of German engineering, the watch required two years of development and was the brainchild of Tutima owner and president Dieter Delecate. Today, Tutima continues to create this authentic aviation watch.

In addition to its incredibly coveted Military series of watches, Tutima offers new timepieces in its successful FX series: the FX Automatic and the FX UTC Chronograph with three time zones. Not only does this series use the highest quality materials, the entire range offers a perfect blend of precise workmanship and maximum functionality. All versions feature self-winding mechanical movements.

The Tutima FX UTC Chronograph is created in steel and features a rotating 24-hour or 60-minute bezel depending on the model. The watch offers universal time via a central 24-hour readout for the second time zone with a large hour hand for easy reading.

**TOP**

The Tutima NATO chronograph is part of the Military Air Force series that was first developed in 1983 in response to a request by the German Armed Forces. The watch, unveiled in series production in 1985, features integrated pushbuttons and is water resistant to 20 bar.

**BOTTOM LEFT**

The Tutima FX UTC Chronograph offers a 24-hour rotating bezel.

**BOTTOM RIGHT**

Part of a new series, this FX UTC Chronograph offers three time zones and houses a self-winding mechanical movement.

The version with the 24-hour rotating bezel allows the wearer to keep track of a third time zone by setting the bezel to the appropriate position. The chronograph can measure time from an eighth of a second up to 12 hours and is water resistant to 100 meters.

There is also a classic FX UTC Automatic timepiece with 60-minute scale bi-directional rotating bezel to track intervals of up to one hour. The watch beats at 28,800 vibrations per hour.

Recently, Tutima unveiled an all-new watch to its renowned Flieger collection: the Flieger Chronograph F2 PR. The F2 PR is a self-winding watch with a power-reserve display and a modified Valjoux 7750 chronograph movement. Crafted in stainless steel, the watch is water resistant to 10 bar and offers eight displays on the elegant dial. Several variations exist, including a blue and white dial. Both versions are offered with either alligator strap or bracelet, and are available in 18-karat gold.

**TOP**

The FX UTC Automatic watch is a classic automatic timepiece with bi-directional rotating bezel to track intervals of up to one hour.

**BOTTOM**

Part of the Flieger series, the Flieger Chronograph F2 PR is a self-winding Valjoux 7750 chronograph movement that has been modified to show the power reserve on the dial next to the date.

## CHRONOLOGY

**1926** A new group of companies was founded, Uhren-Rohwerke-Fabrik Glashütte AG—UROFA and Uhrenfabrik Glashütte AG—UFAG, set up and headed by Dr. Ernst Kurtz.

**1927** The companies start to develop and produce their own German ebauches for wristwatches. The top-quality models are named Tutima. This quality and its exclusive distribution earns Tutima an excellent reputation.

**1941** UROFA-UFAG have developed and completed the Tutima Flieger, Germany's first two-pusher-flyback chronograph.

**1945** Glashütte is bombed and the watch factories are merged into a state-owned combine. Kurtz leaves and sets up a new factory in the South of Germany: Uhrenfabrik Kurtz.

**1951** Uhrenfabrik Kurtz moves to lower Saxony and picks up previous developments of movements.

**1956** Operation of the brand turns over to Glashütte colleague Werner Pohlan. Approximately 70,000 ebauches are produced in the ensuing two years.

**1959** Dr. Kurtz resumes management of the ebauche factory, again giving it the name UROFA.

**1960** Dieter Delecate takes over the Tutima Uhren branch of the business and continues the watch production. He sets his sights on success and founds Tutima Uhrenfabrik GmbH.

**1985** Tutima launches the mechanical Military Chronograph 798, specially developed for the German Army and becomes standard equipment for the German Air Force and NATO pilots.

**1994** Tutima produces the authentic replica of its famous classic 1941 chronograph.

**1997** Tutima sponsors Sean D. Tucker of the power aerobatic team USA. The brand becomes the official sponsor of several international aerobatic shows.

**1999** The Tutima Mega Banner—a world record for the largest advertisement ever to be pulled behind an aircraft—is 25 meters high and 60 meters long.

First Trophée Volez! de la Montre d'aviation presented in Paris to Tutima. The Experienced French jury of professional pilots, editors of *Volez*! magazine and *La Revue des Montres* choose Tutima as the winners of the coveted Trophée Volez! award.

**2000** The FX-line: Tutima develops and debuts the FX Chronograph UTC with a central 24 UTC on a chronograph.

**2003** The Classic Flieger Chronograph is worn by Al Pacino in the movie *The Recruit*. One million DVDs are produced with the first crossmarketing campaign of Tutima and Al Pacino.

Tutima Chronographs are awarded to the German Handball Champions of TBV Lemgo in recognition of their outstanding achievements.

The Tutima Yacht crosses the Atlantic in the Daimler Chrysler North Atlantic Challenge.

**2004** Tutima becomes official main sponsor of German engine-powered-flight national teams of the DAeC, Deutscher Aero Club e.V.

## TUTIMA DI 300 — REF. 629-12

**Movement:** mechanical Swiss automatic movement Caliber ETA 2836-2; 25 jewels; 38-hour power reserve.
**Functions:** hour, minute, second; day and date.
**Case:** titanium case (Ø 43.2mm (without crown), thickness: 11.8mm); double-sealed screw-in crown; counterclockwise-rotating titanium bezel with 60-minute diver's scale; antireflective scratchproof sapphire crystal; water resistant to 1,000 feet.
**Dial:** orange dial; black seconds hand.
**Indications:** day and date at 3; all markers and hands made with extensive after-glow non-tritium luminous compound.
**Bracelet:** adjustable solid titanium with safety extension clasp.
**Also available:** matte black dial; on strap.
**Price:** available upon request.

## TUTIMA FX AUTOMATIC UTC — REF. 632-04

**Movement:** mechanical Swiss automatic movement Caliber ETA 2893-2; 21 jewels; 42-hour power reserve.
**Functions:** hour, minute, second; date; Universal Time Coordinated (UTC) second 24-hour time zone.
**Case:** stainless steel case (Ø 38.5mm (without crown), thickness: 10.9mm); double-sealed screw-in crown; plain fixed bezel (second time zone); scratchproof convex sapphire crystal; scratchproof sapphire crystal caseback; water resistant to 100 meters.
**Dial:** matte black; permanent seconds hand.
**Indications:** date at 3; inner 24-hour dial for second time zone; all markers and hands made with extensive afterglow non-tritium luminous compound.
**Bracelet:** adjustable solid stainless steel with quick release clasp.
**Also available:** white dial; polish finish; bi-directional 24 hours (third time zone); bi-directional 60-minutes (second time zone); water-resistant leather strap.
**Price:** available upon request.

## TUTIMA FX CHRONOGRAPH UTC — REF. 740-74

**Movement:** mechanical automatic movement Caliber Valjoux 7750/Tutima; 25 jewels; 42-hour power reserve; high-precision regulating; shock resistant.
**Functions:** hours, minute, second; date; chronograph with 3 counters; second 24-hour time zone.
**Case:** stainless steel case (Ø 38.5mm (without crown), thickness: 15.5mm); double-sealed screw-in crown; bi-directional 24 hours (third time zone); antireflective, scratch-proof convex sapphire crystal; water resistant to 100 meters.
**Dial:** matte white.
**Indications:** date at 3; 12-hour counter at 6; second at 9; 30-minute counter at 12; second 24-hour time zone; markers and hands made with extensive afterglow non-tritium luminous compound.
**Bracelet:** adjustable solid stainless steel with quick release clasp.
**Also available:** black dial; polished finish; plain fixed bezel (second time zone); bi-directional 60-minutes (second time zone); water-resistant leather strap; exhibition case-back.
**Price:** available upon request.

## TUTIMA MILITARY CHRONOGRAPH TL — REF. 750-02

**Movement:** mechanical automatic movement Caliber Lemania 5100; 17 jewels; 28,800 semi-oscillations/hour; 45-hour power reserve; high-precision regulating; antimagnetic; shock and vibration resistant at an acceleration of 7 g in all directions or vibrations of 4Hz and 20mm amplitude. **Functions:** hour, minute, second; day and date; chronograph with 3 counters. **Case:** solid titanium (Ø 43.2mm (without crown); thickness: 14.6mm); rounded corners; compression-resistant for usage up to 15,000 m above M.S.L.; bi-directional rotating bezel with ratchet; screw-in crown; pushbuttons widely spaced and case integrated (safe and functional); double-sided antireflective scratchproof sapphire crystal; water resistant to 200 meters. **Dial:** black.
**Indications:** date and day at 3; 12-hour at 6; small second at 9; red-tipped arrow 60-minute hand; red center-second hand; a.m./p.m. military-time indicator at 12; all markers and hands made with extensive after-glow non-tritium luminous compound.
**Bracelet:** adjustable solid bracelet with safety clasp.
**Also available:** in two-tone solid titanium and 18K gold case and bracelet; water-resistant leather strap.
**Price:** available upon request.

## TUTIMA FLIEGER CHRONOGRAPH F3 REF. 758-01

**Movement:** mechanical automatic movement Caliber Lemania 5100; 17 jewels; 28,800 semi-oscillations/hour; 45-hour power reserve; high-precision regulating; antimagnetic; shock and vibration resistant at an acceleration of 7 g in all directions or vibrations of 4Hz and 20mm amplitude.
**Functions:** hour, minute, second, small second; day and date; military time; chronograph with 3 counters. **Case:** stainless steel (Ø 38.7mm (without crown), thickness: 15.5mm); double-sealed screw-in crown; bi-directional rotating coin-edge bezel; antireflective scratchproof convex sapphire crystal; water resistant to 100 meters.
**Dial:** matte black.
**Indications:** day and date at 3; 12-hour counter at 6; small second at 9; a.m./p.m. military-time indicator at 12; white-tipped arrow 60-minute hand; white center-second hand; all markers and hands made with extensive after-glow non-tritium luminous compound.
**Strap:** water-resistant leather strap.
**Also available:** stainless steel bracelet (Ref. 758-02).
**Price:** available upon request.

## TUTIMA FLIEGER CHRONOGRAPH F2 UTC REF. 780-72

**Movement:** mechanical automatic movement Caliber Valjoux 7750/Tutima; 25 jewels; 42-hour power reserve; high-precision regulating; shock resistant.
**Functions:** hour, minute, second; date; chronograph with 3 counters.
**Case:** stainless steel case (Ø 38.5mm (without crown), thickness: 15.5mm); double-sealed screw-in crown; bi-directional rotating coin-edge 24-hour bezel; antireflective scratchproof convex sapphire crystal; water resistant to 100 meters.
**Dial:** matte white.
**Indications:** date at 3; 12-hour counter at 6; small second at 9; 30-minutes at 12; central 24-hour second time zone; all markers and hands made with extensive after-glow non-tritium luminous compound.
**Bracelet:** adjustable solid stainless steel with butterfly clasp.
**Also available:** black dial; water-resistant crocodile leather strap (brown); exhibition back.
**Price:** available upon request.

## TUTIMA FLIEGER CHRONOGRAPH F2 PR REF. 780-84

**Movement:** mechanical automatic movement, modified Caliber Valjoux 7750; pearl and striped brush finish; 48-hour power reserve; high-precision regulating.
**Functions:** center hour, minute, second; date; power reserve; chronograph with 3 counters (hour, minute, second).
**Case:** stainless steel case; convex sapphire crystal; screw-down crown and sapphire crystal caseback; screws blued to match dial color; pressure- and water resistant up to 10 bar.
**Dial:** blue; raised white numerals and markers with glossy finish; white subdials with raised blued numerals and markers; markers and hands coated with luminous compound.
**Indications:** date at 3; power reserve display at 3 on a glossy finish; 12-hour counter at 6; 60-second counter at 9; 30-minute counter at 12.
**Bracelet:** stainless steel; stainless steel folding clasp.
**Also available:** alligator leather strap with folding clasp (Ref. 780-83).
**Price:** available upon request.

## TUTIMA FLIEGER CHRONOGRAPH F2 PR REF. 780-82

**Movement:** mechanical automatic movement, modified Caliber Valjoux 7750; pearl and striped brush finish; 48-hour power reserve; high-precision regulating.
**Functions:** center hour, minute, second; date; power reserve; chronograph with 3 counters (hour, minute, second).
**Case:** stainless steel case; convex sapphire crystal; screw-down crown and sapphire crystal caseback; pressure- and water resistant up to 10 bar.
**Dial:** white; raised blue numerals and markers with glossy finish; white subdials with raised blued numerals and markers; markers and hands coated with luminous compound.
**Indications:** date at 3; power reserve display at 3 on a glossy finish; 12-hour counter at 6; 60-second counter at 9; 30-minute counter at 12.
**Bracelet:** stainless steel; stainless steel folding clasp.
**Also available:** alligator leather strap with folding clasp (Ref. 780-81).
**Price:** available upon request.

# URWERK

Urwerk® is a young Geneva-based team of creative artisans and watchmakers who have joined forces to create a series of unusual timepieces. Their belief: Small, independent watchmakers are original thinkers who can pursue the creation of time in new venues.

Since banding together, the watchmakers that comprise Urwerk remain true to the guiding principle of creating quality, precision mechanical watches in a revolutionary design shaped by the spirit of our times. Their goal is to create a new version of time that expands our borders and offers a new experience.

The founding team consists of watchmaking brothers Thomas and Felix Baumgartner and designer Martin Frei. The name Urwerk is derived from several inspirations. Ur in the German language represents something ancient or original and its roots go back to the city of Ur, the first city of mankind, founded circa 4000 BC. This highly advanced civilization invented the calendar, almost as we know it today. The Sumerians celebrated numerous annual and monthly festivals, including a feast to celebrate the sighting of the New Moon.

The Baumgartners felt these references to something ancient, original, creative and passionate made a strong basis for their company.

The goal of the newly formed brand was to create a special way to tell time. In fact, through his research, Thomas Baumgartner uncovered a clock from 1656 that displayed time in a manner similar to the way he wanted to execute it. Made by the Campanus brothers, it was an unconventional night clock that used rotating discs to tell time.

The Campanus clock inspired the Baumgartners to design Urwerk's first wristwatch, the UR-101, wherein time is displayed on a solid gold "dial" via an arc aperture with a single aperture inside to announce the hours. Each sweep of the display arc represents a one-hour period and the digital readout changes to indicate the hour. To create the watch, Felix Baumgartner had to develop a new Maltese cross system to track time to their specifications.

ABOVE

The Urwerk UR-101 was the first model created and has been sold out entirely.

FACING PAGE

The Urwerk UR-103 is futuristic in design and emulates the cross-section of a jet's wing.

URWERK
15
10
5
min
60
40
103 EW
60
45
30
min
URWERK
15
0

The movement consists of a rotating bridge instead of an hour-hand system. At both ends there is a rotating hour disc for the odd and even hour figures. The two discs perform one complete revolution every two hours and alternate every 60 minutes to appear in the window—displaying the proper hour through a visible traveling indicator of the time.

The Urwerk UR-101 was created in a solid 18-karat gold round case. The Urwerk UR-102 was available in gold or in steel and features an unusual case-to-bracelet attachment inspired by the Sputnik. Both models are sold out entirely.

Now Urwerk unveils the UR-103—a futuristic watch somewhat rectangular in shape and extremely aerodynamic. Inspired by Marcel Duchamp and executed by Martin Frei and Felix Baumgartner, the watch is a futuristic symbiosis of time and space and is designed to emulate a cross-section of a wing. The crown is positioned at 12:00, offering a streamlined look. The 103's inner mechanics are "different." The creation of the UR-103 required an all-new movement, the UR03-1 caliber. Felix Baumgartner invented a rotating element which keeps and guides the four cone shaped hour discs. This arrangement insures absolute synchronism. The platins for the complications are crafted in PVD blackened arcap P40, a new material ensuring stability, precision and no tensions.

The reverse side of the watch, known as the Control Center, depicts a 42-hour power-reserve indicator and 15-minute and 60-second dials, as well as a precision adjustment function. This is an all-time first. Next to the seconds display is a regulating screw with finely engraved subdivisions. This will tweak the watch forward or back 30 seconds in a 24-hour period. The manually wound caliber features a four-Maltese-cross base and offers 42 hours of power reserve.

Available in 18-karat rose or white gold, the UR-103 comes with either a highly polished surface or an engraved gadrooned surface. The polished surface is an ideal canvas for creating unique special pieces, such as the Dragon Watch, unveiled in Singapore.

**TOP LEFT**

The Urwerk UR-102 featured a case-to-bracelet attachment that was inspired by the Sputnik.

**TOP RIGHT**

The UR-101/Star Diamond is a one-of-a-kind piece that is hand-engraved and adorned with 142 Top Wesselton diamonds.

## CHRONOLOGY

**1996** The Baumgartner brothers and Martin Frei join in business to open a new chapter in chronometry.

**1997** The Baumgartners unveil the first prototypes of the UR-101 in three versions of solid 18-karat gold at the Basel Fair.

**1998** The UR-101 makes its production debut. Only 50 pieces are being made. Urwerk joins the Académie Horlogère des Créateurs Indépendants (AHCI) association of independent watchmakers.

**1999** The UR-102 is released to the public. Seventy-five pieces are created.

**2000** A variant of the UR-102 called the Nightwatch is released with a black ceramic anodized aluminum case with platinum back and luminous hour markers. The 20 pieces made are sold out within a year.

**2002** Various special editions and unique pieces are being produced. Urwerk works on the development of the highly complicated UR-103.

**2003** The UR-103 is unveiled and welcomed with acclaims at the Basel Fair.

**2004** The production of the UR-103 is ready and 70 pieces are created.

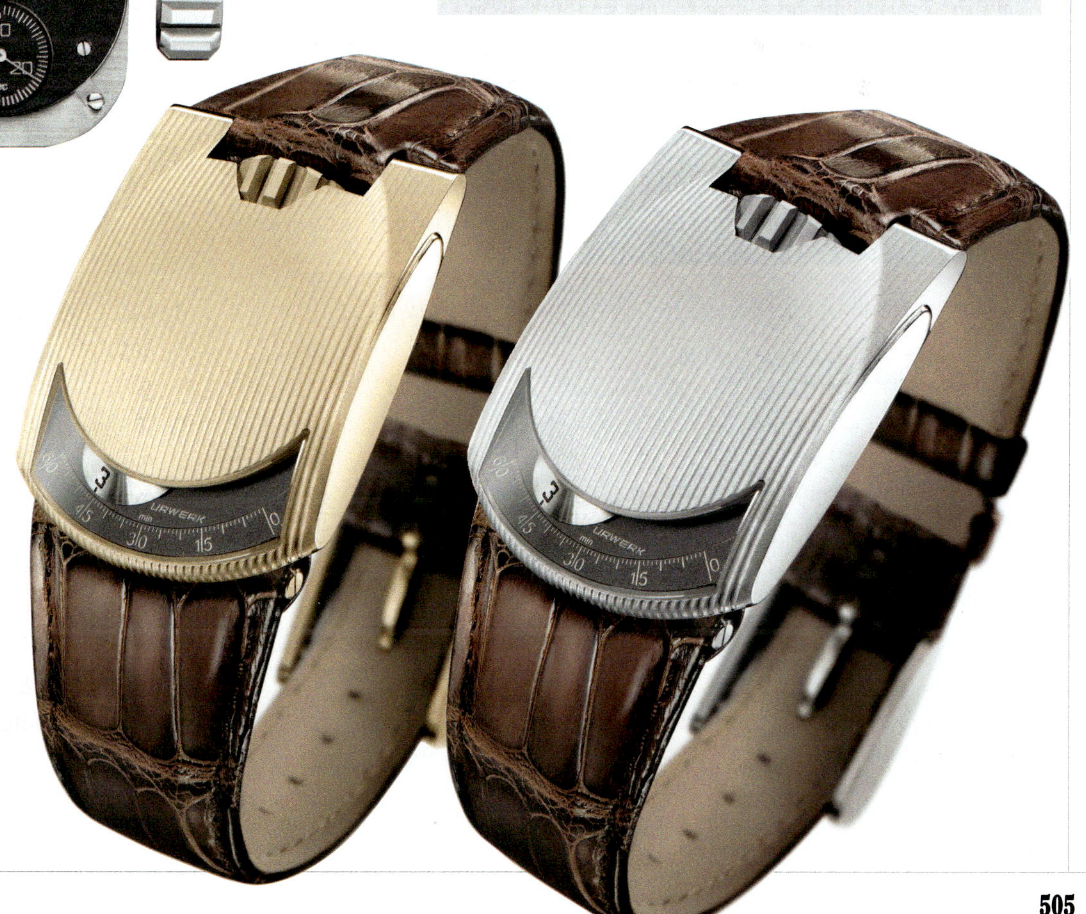

**TOP LEFT**

The reverse side of the UR-103 features three apertures depicting the power-reserve indicator, minutes and seconds.

**CENTER**

The movement of the UR-103 is the caliber UR03-1 with a four-Maltese-cross base.

**BOTTOM**

The UR-103 is created in 18-karat rose or white gold with either an engraved or high-polished surface.

# VACHERON CONSTANTIN

Heralded as a creator of technical watches of complexity and beauty, Vacheron Constantin consistently has been creating watches of distinction for an amazing 250 years.

Busy creating not only new timepieces but also a new venue to build those watches, Vacheron Constantin ushers in 2005 with the implementation of a state-of-the-art factory, le Maison Vacheron Constantin museum and boutique, and the recognition of the Geneva Hallmark. In celebration of these achievements, the brand ushers in a limited-edition series of incredible timepieces that salute the famous explorers in history and display the excellent craftsmanship of the brand.

Called Tribute to the Great Explorers, the new series is both a mechanical and artistic feat. In all, there will be four Tribute to the Great Explorers models created—each paying homage to a special explorer in history, and each released in a limited edition of 60 pieces. The first watches unveiled pay tribute to Ferdinand de Magellan and Chinese mariner Zheng He.

The Tribute to the Great Explorers watches are powered by a patented mechanism that provides an original display of hours and minutes on a hand-enameled set of dials. The design of the Tribute to the Great Explorers line incorporates Vacheron Constantin's famous Maltese Cross logo into the movement. Building on the Vacheron Constantin caliber 1126AT self-winding movement, this watch design houses a series of original devices.

THIS PAGE

ABOVE

From the Tribute to the Great Explorers line, this model houses a patented mechanism, and offers an original display of hours and minutes on the hand-enameled dial.

LEFT

Depicting the Asian portion of the world, this Tribute to the Great Explorers is created in honor of Chinese mariner Zheng He.

FACING PAGE

This Tribute to the Great Explorers timepiece is dedicated to Ferdinand de Magellan.

VACHERON CONSTANTIN
GENEVE
TIERRA
S. Julian
PATAGONES
Cabo
EL
MAR PACIFICO
Estrecho
de
El Oceano
Atlantico
Cabo de Hornos

Three of the four crosses in the movement act as the driving devices for the three pivoting hour-bearing satellites. With this ingenious system, the display of time on the dial is always moving—traveling over the land and sea that have been hand-painted exquisitely on the two-disc dial.

The main enamel dial depicts the area on earth that is associated with the explorer's travels. The second, lower dial forms the bottom arc of the watch face and bears the minute track. The case of each Patrimony watch is crafted in 18-karat gold. Each watch is delivered in a solid wood presentation case—complete with a magnifying glass to view the delicate enamel work.

Elegance reigns supreme in the new 1972 Grand Modele Cambré—a beautiful elongated asymmetrical watch that depicts true charm and grace. Based on a model from the 1970s, the watch demonstrate the brand's free spirit and daring soul. The newest models are crafted in 18-karat white or pink gold and are set with varying degrees of diamonds. One model features a bezel set with 2.71 carats of brilliant-cut diamonds.

Other elegant new timepieces include the Malte Chronograph with the caliber 114 hand-wound mechanical movement that is engraved with the Côtes de Genève decorative graining pattern. The column-wheel construction of this watch is elaborately decorated and offers a 30-minute totalizer. The Malte Chronograph is a certified chronometer that offers 48 hours of power reserve and an exhibition sapphire case-back. It is crafted in either 18-karat white or pink gold and features a stunning bracelet.

ABOVE LEFT

The Patrimony Grande Taille is a large round watch that features a minimalist design reminiscent of the brand's early days. The ultra-slim watch houses Vacheron Constantin's caliber 1400 hand-wound mechanical movement with the Geneva hallmark.

ABOVE RIGHT

The Malte Chronograph houses Vacheron Constantin's caliber 114 with a hand-wound mechanical column-wheel construction.

A B O V E

These 1972 Grand Modele Cambres reflect the strong design heritage of Vacheron Constantin.

R I G H T

This 1972 Grand Modele Cambré is set meticulously with 2.71 carats of brilliant-cut diamonds.

## C H R O N O L O G Y

**1755** Jean-Marc Vacheron establishes his workshop in the heart of Geneva.

**1819** Vacheron enters a partnership with François Constantin to create the Vacheron & Constantin company. Sales are big in the Italian and Turkish markets.

**1821** First Grande Complication striking automatically on request is produced.

**1840** A year after joining Vacheron Constantin, George-Auguste Leschot upgrades all the tools required for the production of a caliber whose parts are all interchangeable. This is the beginning of the so-called industrial era of horology and the end of pure artisan-like watchmaking.

**1880** The famous Malta Cross is registered as a trademark for Vacheron Constantin.

**1915** While Europe is involved in World War I, a special series of pocket chonographs is realized for the American expeditionary force.

**1939** At the beginning of World War II, the house produces a series of watches with aluminum cases.

**1953** The new Chronomètre Royal is born; it is hallmarked for the first time with the Geneva Seal.

**1955** To commemorate Vacheron Constantin's $200^{th}$ anniversay, the world's thinnest mechanical movement is introduced.

**1996** Vacheron Constantin is incorporated into the Vendôme Luxury Group, which later becomes The Richemont Group. The Overseas collection of luxury sports watches is developed and the premiere diving watch holds a patent for technology ensuring water-resistance even if the crown is not screwed down completely.

**1997** The Kalla Amalfi men's watch is unveiled with 148 baguette-cut and trapezoidal diamonds.

**1999** The manufacture's movements are entrusted to its new factory in Le Sentier. This year's star is the 1972—an asymmetric watch inspired by the archives.

**2000** The Medicus chronograph equipped with a pulsometer scale and inspired by a 1930s model is reproduced with a pillow-shaped case. The Malte collection is also released.

**2001** The Malte collection is enriched by the addition of the caliber 1400 movement, manufactured and finished in Vacheron Constantin's workshop and hallmarked with the Geneva Seal.

**2002** The company unveils the To-and-Fro Calendar in honor of the brand's $247^{th}$ anniversary.

**2004** The brand opens an all-new manufacture in Plan-les-Ouates.

## TRIBUTE TO THE GREAT EXPLORERS — REF. 47070/000J-9076

**Movement:** patented Vacheron Constantin automatic movement.
**Functions:** hour, minute.
**Case:** 18K yellow gold.
**Dial:** detail of Magellan Expedition (1519-1522) with map of the straight that bears his name.
**Indication:** hour numeral moves from right to left in the lower part of the dial.
**Strap:** brown alligator strap.
**Also available:** dial detailing Zheng He Expedition (1371-1434) in honor of the Chinese admiral.

## MALTE MANUAL CHRONOGRAPH — REF. 47120/000G-9098

**Movement:** manual-winding movement.
**Functions:** hour, minute, second; chronograph with column wheel, 30-minutes counter at 3.
**Case:** 18K white gold.
**Dial:** light silver; hand-guillochéd pattern; 18K gold applied numerals.
**Strap:** black alligator strap.
**Also available:** rose gold.

## PATRIMONY SEMI-FLAT — REF. 81160/000R-9102

**Movement:** manual-winding movement; Seal of Geneva.
**Functions:** hour, minute, second at 6.
**Case:** 18K rose gold.
**Dial:** light silver; opaline center; circular satin-finished external zone; 18K gold applied numerals and indexes.
**Strap:** black alligator strap.
**Also available:** yellow gold and white gold.

## PATRIMONY GRAND TAILLE — REF. 81180/000G-9117

**Movement:** manual-winding movement; Seal of Geneva.
**Functions:** hour, minute.
**Case:** 18K white gold.
**Dial:** light silver opaline, external zone domed; 18K gold applied indexes.
**Strap:** black alligator strap.
**Also available:** yellow gold.

## MALTE SKELETON — REF. 43080/000G

**Movement:** mechanical self-winding Caliber 1120SQ; Ø 28mm, thickness: 2.45mm; 19,800 vph; 36 rubies; entirely skeletonized, decorated, chased by hand; provided with the Geneva Hallmark.
**Functions:** hour, minute.
**Case:** round; light fan-shaped lugs; entirely polished bezel; movement visible through two sapphire crystals: one on the dial side, one on the bridge side.
**Dial:** No dial—it is a completely skeletonized movement. Bluish steel fan-shaped hands.
**Strap:** alligator leather strap; 18K white-gold buckle.
**Also available:** in 18K yellow gold; with diamond bezel on strap or diamond bezel on bracelet.

## 1972 GRAND CURVE WITH PAVE DIAMONDS — REF. 25510/000G-9119

**Movement:** quartz.
**Functions:** hour, minute.
**Case:** 18K white-gold case with 2.71 carats of pave diamonds.
**Dial:** light silvered; vertically satin-finished; asymmetric and curved with mirrored Roman numerals.
**Strap:** purple alligator strap.
**Also available:** blue dial.

## 1972 GRAND CURVE — REF. 25010/000R-9122

**Movement:** quartz.
**Functions:** hour, minute.
**Case:** 18K rose gold.
**Dial:** pink; vertically satin-finished; asymmetric and curved.
**Strap:** black alligator strap.
**Also available:** silvered dial.

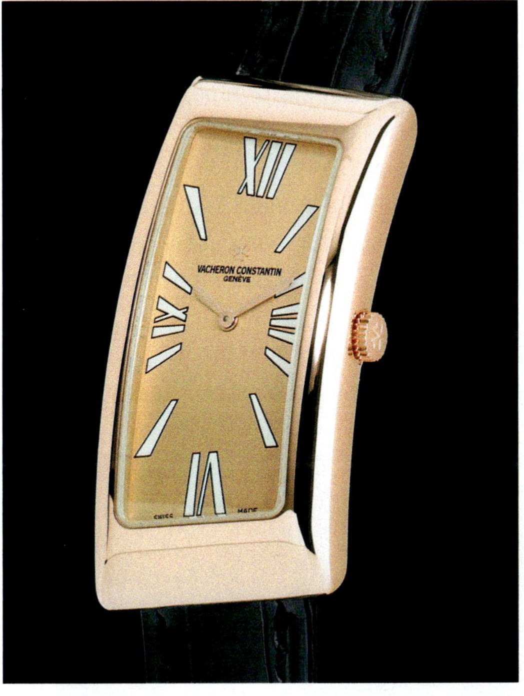


## 1972 MEDIUM MODEL — REF. 25021/000R-9115

**Movement:** quartz.
**Functions:** hour, minute.
**Case:** 18K rose gold.
**Dial:** white mother of pearl; painted Roman numerals.
**Strap:** dark blue alligator.
**Also available:** 18K white gold.

# ZANNETTI

Each Riccardo Zannetti design is a work of art with a personality entirely its own, from its intricate movement and elaborate functions to the finishing touches of color splashed onto its dials and cases via enamel or jewels.

Some watches make your heart beat faster while others make it race...but only a few make it fly high.

The power to fully express fantasy and imagination are the ingredients that this professional Italian watchmaker relies upon to transform an ultra-flat automatic Squelette movement in a golden Arabian-style caliber.

Few people have inherited the art of enameling luminous miniature pocket watches. Without hesitating, the engravers cut and carve delicate designs in memory of a long tradition that takes us back to the first watches made during the Renaissance era, while gem- and stone-setters give us a taste of what jewelry and gorgeous jewel watches are like.

In his atelier on the banks of the Tiber, Riccardo Zannetti's team creates and produces more than 1,000 exceptional hand-finished watches per year. Zannetti's models are subject to the same intense processes which transform them from primary matter into magnificent keepers of time, where designs and mechanics become one. The house of Zannetti is now increasing its product line, rendering itself more accessible to its faithful clients in the beautiful world of horology.

Steel is an ideal material when it comes to the fabrication of watches. Its contact with the skin is pleasant, it has beautiful aesthetic qualities, and is very strong and suitable for many uses. From the Pegaso to the Squelette, from the Montgolfier to the traditional Impero, Zannetti has many versions crafted of steel.

All series are numbered progressively and in limited editions. The case, back and the precious dials are refined by hand and house Swiss-quality movements, personalized by the house of Zannetti.

THIS PAGE

TOP

Zannetti's quarter-repeater mechanism now is housed in a honeycomb engraved case.

BOTTOM

This Brain Orgy adds to the Regent collection an erotic theme, which can be appreciated with a magnifying lens.

FACING PAGE

TOP

The solid silver dials of the new Sailing collection are individually engraved and enameled by hand.

BOTTOM

This Time of Drivers is dedicated to Ascari and, for the first time, the dial is designed with the micro-mosaic technique.

## CHRONOLOGY

**1982** The working life of Riccardo Zannetti, founder of the Italian house, begins. His first original models are realized.

**1986** Zannetti designs and produces watches for some big contemporary companies as well as private customers.

**1987** The first Zannetti collection is born: the Stradivarius. It will remain in production until 2003.

**1989** The Zannetti style will be strongly characterized with the Impero collection, and Zannetti begins filling orders from other European countries. A regular distribution is established in Italy.

**1990** The opening of the first Zannetti boutique in Rome.

**1992** Daphne, a watch dedicated to women, is unveiled. The brand's first jewel watches are realized and personalized models are made upon request of some customers.

**1994** Zannetti participates at its first International Salon of Horology in Basel.

**1995** This year's Frog Line is destined to become a long-lasting success. The model will evolve into various versions including one with a cover to hide the dial. Some models will be set with precious pavés of rubies, emeralds or diamonds.

**1996** This is the year dedicated to technique. The first movements are made and the first prestigious 5-minute Repeaters are developed.

**1998** Zannetti's headquarters in Rome are renovated. Important production units and laboratories are added.

**1999** The Mongolfier is introduced. It is a prestigious GMT characterized by an original engraved gold rotor and from a multicolored base-relief dial.

**2000** The Squelette is released. By its distinctive characteristics, it is the first squelette movement in the world that has been treated with blue PVD.

**2001** The first two models in the Time of Drivers collection, Ascari and Fangio, are created.

**2002** A new line of jewels with precious stones is unveiled.

**2003** A new steel collection, in line with the actual trends but perfectly adapted with the characteristics of the house, is presented.

**2004** The Regent collection is extended with the Brain Orgy and a second line of Sailing dials, both hand engraved and enameled. The micro-mosaic series explores new materials and themes.

## IMPERO AUTOMATIC SPECIAL EDITION

**Movement:** mechanical automatic-winding ETA 2892A2 caliber; gold-plated rotor.
**Functions:** hour, minute, second.
**Case:** palladium-plated (thickness: 10 micron), three-piece case (Ø 38.2mm, thickness: 11.7mm); jointed central attachment; curved sapphire crystal, antireflective, with secret logo; hexagonal crown; back fastened by 8 screws; engraved and enameled by hand with themes inspired by the Roman Empire, with logo and individual number engraved on a small medallion; water resistant to 3atm.
**Dial:** blue opal mosaic; yellow-gold and luminescent Alpha hands.
**Indications:** date at 3.
**Strap:** crocodile leather; palladium- plated clasp (10 micron) with hand-engraved Greek fret design.
**Also available:** pink, yellow or white gold; engraved bracelet; with personalized mosaic or miniatures.

## IMPERO AUTOMATIC REF. IPA115N

**Movement:** automatic-winding ETA 2892A2 caliber; gold-plated rotor.
**Functions:** hour, minute, second; date.
**Case:** yellow-gold three-piece case (Ø 38.2, thickness: 11.7mm); engraved totally by hand; jointed central attachment; curved sapphire crystal, antireflective, with secret logo; hexagonal crown; back fastened by 8 screws; enameled by hand with themes inspired by the Roman Empire, with logo and individual number engraved on a small medallion; water resistant to 3atm.
**Dial:** natural mother-of-pearl dial with spike-shaped engraving and black Greek fret design, engraved and enameled; white Roman numerals at quarters; enameled, and small triangles in yellow gold, applied on the printed minute track; luminescent yellow-gold enameled Alpha hands.
**Indications:** date at 4.
**Strap:** crocodile leather; yellow-goldclasp with hand-engraved Greek fret design.
**Also available:** back without drawing; palladium-plated or pink or white gold; engraved bracelet; black dial with white enamels.

## IMPERO AUTOMATIC ARLECCHINO

**Movement:** mechanical automatic-winding ETA 2892A2 caliber; gold-plated rotor.
**Functions:** hour, minute, second.
**Case:** palladium-plated (thickness: 10 micron), three-piece case (Ø 38.2mm, thickness: 11.7mm); engraved totally by hand; jointed central attachment; curved sapphire crystal, antireflective, with secret logo; hexagonal crown; back fastened by 8 screws; enameled by hand with themes inspired by the Roman Empire, with logo and individual number engraved on a small medallion; water resistant to 3atm.
**Dial:** multicolored sliced glass mosaic; yellow-gold applied markers at quarters set with brilliants; yellow-gold luminescent Alpha hands.
**Strap:** crocodile leather; palladium-plated clasp (10 micron) with hand-engraved Greek fret design.
**Also available:** pink, yellow or white gold; engraved bracelet; with personalized mosaic or miniatures on request.

## IMPERO AUTOMATIC REF. IPAM05

**Movement:** mechanical automatic-winding ETA 2892A2 caliber; gold-plated rotor.
**Functions:** hour, minute, second.
**Case:** palladium-plated (thickness: 10 micron), three-piece case (Ø 38.2mm, thickness: 11.7mm); engraved totally by hand; jointed central attachment; curved sapphire crystal, antireflective, with secret logo; hexagonal crown; back fastened by 8 screws; enameled by hand with themes inspired by the Roman Empire, with logo and individual number engraved on a small medallion; water resistant to 3atm.
**Dial:** opal mosaic in gradation from black to white; applied cabochon markers in yellow gold, 12 with set brilliant; luminescent black enameled Alpha hands.
**Strap:** crocodile leather; palladium-plated clasp (10 micron) with hand-engraved Greek fret design.
**Also available:** pink, yellow or white gold; blue or black dial, engraved bracelet; with personalized mosaic or miniatures.

## AUTOMATIC REF. ACA322

**Movement:** mechanical automatic-winding ETA 2892A2 caliber; gold-plated rotor.
**Functions:** hour, minute, second; date.
**Case:** stainless steel three-piece case (Ø 39.2mm, thickness: 9.3mm); jointed central attachment; curved sapphire crystal, antireflective, with secret logo; screw-down crown, with engraved logo; numbered middle; bezel with Roman numerals engraved; back fastened by 5 screws, displaying the movement through a sapphire crystal; water resistant to 10atm.
**Dial:** bordeaux red; soleil; yellow gold- plated markers applied on the printed minute track; luminescent gold-plated sword-style hands.
**Indications:** date at 3.
**Strap:** hand-sewn crocodile leather; steel fold-over clasp with hand-engraved logo.
**Also available:** yellow gold; with bracelet; blue or green dial.

## SQUELETTE REF. QGE1123

**Movement:** mechanical automatic-winding ETA 2892A2 caliber base, personalized for Zannetti; movement and rotor totally skeletonized and hand engraved; with blue PVD treatment.
**Functions:** hour, minute, second.
**Case:** 18K yellow-gold three-piece case (Ø 38mm, thickness: 11.4mm); jointed central attachment; flat sapphire crystal, antireflective, with secret logo; bezel with engraved Arabic numerals; yellow-gold crown; back fastened by 8 screws; numbered; displaying the movement through a sapphire crystal; water resistant to 5atm.
**Dial:** hand-engraved gold flange; 4 round applied gold markers; luminescent enameled leaf-style hands.
**Strap:** alligator leather; fold-over clasp in yellow and white gold.
**Note:** produced as a limited edition.
**Also available:** white gold, stainless steel (water resistant to 10atm).

## PEGASO GMT AUTOMATIC

**Movement:** mechanical automatic-winding ETA 2893-2 caliber base; modified by Dubois Dépraz. **Functions:** hour, minute, second; date; second time zone; 24 hour; power reserve. **Case:** 18K yellow-gold three-piece case (Ø 38.2mm, thickness: 11.6mm); jointed central attachment; curved sapphire crystal, antireflective, with secret logo; model name engraved on the middle; bezel with Arabic numerals engraved (1-12 AM); yellow-gold screw-down crown with engraved logo; back fastened by 8 screws; numbered; displaying the movement through a sapphire crystal; water resistant to 3atm. **Dial:** solid silver; center decorated with a circular graining pattern; brushed hour ring; guilloché soleil subdials; applied yellow-gold cabochon markers; black enameled Arabic numerals (1-12PM) and minute track; luminescent black enameled leaf-style hands. **Indica-tions:** date at 3; power reserve at 6; 24-hour second time zone at 12. **Strap:** crocodile leather; hand-engraved fold-over clasp. **Also available:** stainless steel; with bracelet.

## TIME OF DRIVER "FANGIO" CHRONOGRAPH DIAMONDS

**Movement:** mechanical automatic-winding Valjoux 7750 caliber base; rotor hand-engraved with a representation of checked flags. **Functions:** hour, minute; date; chronograph with 3 counters. **Case:** 18K yellow-gold two-piece case (Ø 38mm, thickness: 14.4mm); bezel with fire-enameled markers; curved sapphire crystal, antireflective, with secret logo; gold pushers and crown; hand-engraved; egraved wheel on the lugs; back fastened by 8 screws; numbered; movement visible via a sapphire crystal; water resistant to 3atm. **Dial:** solid yellow gold with rhodium-plated zone; hand-engraved representing an old-fashioned racing car "flying" around a racetrack; signed and numbered; applied yellow-gold cabochon markers; luminescent sword-style hands; red enameled chronograph hands. **Indications:** date at 1:30; hour counter at 6; minute counter at 12; center seconds. **Strap:** ostrich leather; fold-over clasp in yellow gold with logo. **Note:** limited edition of 20 pieces; comes in a motorized Scatola del Tempo box. **Also available:** red, blue or green car.

# ZENITH

With true cutting-edge design and technology, Zenith still continues to craft according to a centuries-old art that is dictated by exquisite, intricate workmanship.

Zenith is a brand run by passion—the passion of its executives, its watchmakers and its followers. At the heart of all Zenith timepieces are proprietary movements comprised of hundreds of parts and Zenith has unveiled some stunning complicated watches for men, and now the brand expands its women's collection, offering delightfully dramatic timepieces.

Balance, harmony and detail are the critical driving forces behind the designs, powered by advanced technology and precise movements—most recently evidenced in the ChronoMaster Open for Men, Star Open for Women and the new Grande ChronoMaster XXT Tourbillon.

After three years of research and development, Zenith releases the Grande ChronoMaster XXT Tourbillon. Housing the famed El Primero movement (the new caliber 4005) with chronograph that beats at a record 36,000 vibrations per hour, the watch also features a patented calendar disc that is inserted between the bridge and the tourbillon carriage, turning in the opposite direction. That means the date changes at midnight in the opposite direction. The dial is clean despite the abundance of functions the watch has to offer and the tourbillon carriage is set slightly to the left of 11:00 to allow ample room for all the readouts.

THIS PAGE

ABOVE

From the Grande Chrono-Master Open series, these three watches depict the available dial choices for the Grande ChronoMaster Open with power reserve.

BOTTOM LEFT

The Queen of Hearts Star Open is crafted in steel.

BOTTOM RIGHT

The Star Open is offered with a white dial and red or black sculpted Arabic numerals.

FACING PAGE

Shown here in rose gold with a silver guilloché dial, the spectacular Grande ChronoMaster XXT Tourbillon is powered by the El Primero 4005 automatic movement and boasts a tourbillon at 11, date around the carriage and is water resistant to 30 meters.

ZENITH
El Primero
TOURBILLON
DATE

Other new timepieces have been added to the Grande ChronoMaster Open series for men. First unveiled in 2003, the Grande ChronoMaster Open houses the El Primero movement. The bold, elegant watch features a triple-circle aperture on the dial to allow for viewing of the elegantly finished movement's balance, escape wheel, pallets and seconds wheel. Originally unveiled in 18-karat yellow gold, this chronograph timepiece is now created in steel and in pink gold, and features stunning silver guilloché or black dial options.

**TOP LEFT**

The Open Men in black, cobalt and white, colors of the Grande ChronoMaster Open dials.

**TOP RIGHT**

With a dial aperture revealing the movement, this Grande ChronoMaster Réserve de Marche is created in steel.

**BOTTOM LEFT**

A close-up view of the Grande ChronoMaster Réserve de Marche aperture.

**TOP**

The Grande Class Rattrapante Grande Date watch houses the El Primero movement and features the split-second chronograph function and big date at 6:00.

**FAR RIGHT**

The Grande Class Grande Date on rubber strap.

**BOTTOM RIGHT**

Zenith's Grande Class II collection is an expression of luxurious living.

Also new is the Grande Class II Collection with a superb Grande Date and Grande Date Rattrapante timepieces. Both models house the brand's Grande Date double window at 6:00. The Grande Class II Grande Date Rattrapante also offers the split-second chronograph function for timing mutlitple intervals. All of the Grande Class II watches house the El Primero movement, and are at once discreet and sophisticated—a signature mark of all Zenith watches.

In its new Star and Star Open collections for women, both of which house the famed El Primero COSC-certified chronometer movement, the brand unveiled stunning cuff-strap watches in all hues of pastels, gray and gold. These Baby Doll watches feature a wide band of leather with the removable leather-strapped timepiece looped onto it. The watch can be worn with or without the outer cuff. There is also a stunning Glam Rock version of the Star with black lizard strap. The Baby Star, with the Elite movement, features a new supple and chic steel bracelet.

Zenith also unveils the scintillating Queen of Hearts Star Open watch. Housing the El Primero movement, this watch features a heart-shaped aperture on the dial revealing the elegant movement. It is created in several versions, including one with red numerals and red strap. There are also gemstone-adorned versions of this stunning chronograph watch.

THIS PAGE

TOP LEFT

For a Glam Rock look, this stunning Star is produced with a silvered black dial and curved numerals.

TOP RIGHT

This Baby Star cuff watch has a shimmering gold lizard strap that attaches to a wider outer strap.

BOTTOM LEFT

The Baby Star is delightfully dramatic.

FACING PAGE

The Star Open is created in a wealth of colors. Housing the El Primero COSC-certified chronometer movement, the striking timepiece features a heart-shaped aperture on the dial.

# CHRONOLOGY

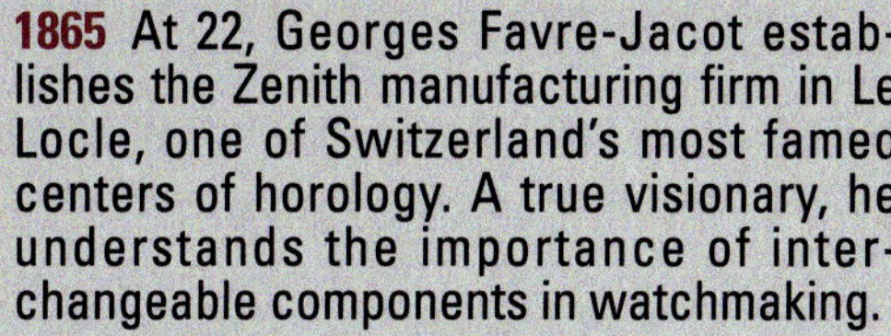

**1865** At 22, Georges Favre-Jacot establishes the Zenith manufacturing firm in Le Locle, one of Switzerland's most famed centers of horology. A true visionary, he understands the importance of interchangeable components in watchmaking.

**1875** Numerous innovations contribute to the evolution of Zenith and the entire watchmaking industry. Just ten years old, the company employs thirty percent of Le Locle's population.

**1900** Favre-Jacot wins First Prize at the Grand Prix de Paris.

**1911** The brand's official name is changed to Fabrique des Montres Zenith S.A. By now, the company has accumulated 1,565 first prizes from the Universal Exhibitions in Paris, Milan, Barcelona and Montreal, as well as the Diamond International in New York. At the Mercurio d'oro in Rome, Zenith places first and is awarded by the chronometer observatories.

**1954** Zenith sets the new record in the wrist chronometer category at the Observatory of Neuchâtel.

**1969** A legend is born: the El Primero chronograph caliber, the first integrated automatic watch with 36,000 vph.

**1975** The production of mechanical movements yields to the rise of quartz.

**1984** With the strong revival of mechanical horology, Zenith is ready to reclaim its status at the top. It relaunches its proprietary El Primero movement.

**1994** The new automatic extra-flat movement Élite is presented and voted Best Mechanical Movement by the International Professional Press.

**1997** Two important novelties are developed: the sports chronograph Rainbow Fly-back and the ChronoMaster Élite featuring a power-reserve display.

**1999** Luxury-conglomerate LVMH acquires Zenith.

**2003** Zenith produces 17 movements for 25 new models. The manufacture distributes these great timepieces through 15 branches around the world.

**2004** The brand launches an incredible collection of ladies' mechanical timepieces, including the Baby Star Élite with stunning colors and gemstone accents.

## GRANDE CHRONOMASTER XXT TOURBILLON REF. 65.1260.4005/21.C505

**Movement:** El Primero 4005 automatic movement with chronograph, visible through dial.
**Functions:** tourbillon at 11; date around carriage;
**Case:** white gold; water resistant to 30 meters.
**Dial:** black; three-dimensional gold indexes in progressive sizes.
**Strap:** black alligator leather; triple-folding clasp.

**Approx. retail price:** $7,600.
**Note:** limited editions.
**18.1260.4005/01.C505:** rose-gold case, silver guilloché dial, black alligator leather strap.

## GRANDE CHRONOMASTER XXT QUANTIÈME PERPÉTUEL REF. 65.1260.4003/21.C505

**Movement:** automatic El Primero 4003; COSC-certified chronometer.
**Functions:** moonphase; chronograph; perpetual calendar (date, day, month and year).
**Case:** white gold; water resistant to 30 meters.
**Dial:** black.
**Strap:** black alligator leather; triple-folding clasp.

**Also available:** rose-gold case, silver guilloché dial, black alligator leather strap.

## GRAND CHRONOMASTER XXT OPEN REF. 03.1260.4021/73.C505

**Movement:** mechanical automatic-winding Zenith El Primero caliber 4021; rotor, decorated with Côtes de Genève; official COSC-certified chronometer.
**Functions:** hour, minute, small second; power reserve; chronograph with 3 counters.
**Case:** stainless steel three-piece case (Ø 45mm, thickness 14.6mm); domed sapphire crystal, antireflective on both sides; steel oval pushers and crown; back fastened by 8 screws, displaying the movement through a sapphire crystal; water resistant to 30 meters.

**Dial:** aperture with movement at 10; rhodium-plated triangular markers and Roman numerals applied by hand; rhodium-plated Régate hands.
**Indications:** minute counter at 3; power reserve between 5 and 7 with a center hand; small second at 9 with a three-arm hand, center second.
**Strap:** alligator leather; double fold-over steel clasp.

## CHRONOMASTER OPEN REF. 03.0240.4021/02.C495

**Movement:** mechanical automatic-winding Zenith El Primero caliber 4021; 22K pink-gold rotor; guilloché grain d'orge; official COSC-certified chronometer.
**Functions:** hour, minute, small second; power reserve; chronograph with 2 counters.
**Case:** stainless steel three-piece case (Ø 40mm, thickness 14.1mm); domed sapphire crystal, antireflective on both sides; stainless steel oval pushers and crown; back fastened by 8 screws, displaying the movement through a sapphire crystal; water resistant to 30 meters.

**Dial:** silver guilloché; brushed hour ring and subdial crown; rosé-bordered aperture with movement at 10; arrow-shaped markers applied by hand; Régate hands.
**Indications:** minute counter at 3; power reserve between 5 and 7 with a center hand; small second at 9 with a three-arm hand; center second.
**Strap:** alligator leather; steel double fold-over clasp.

## GRAND CLASS RATTRAPANTE GRANDE DATE REF. 65.0520.4026/73.C492

**Movement:** El Primero 4026 automatic movement; COSC-certified chronometer.
**Functions:** split second; big date at 6; 2 counters.
**Case:** white gold; water resistant to 20 meters.
**Dial:** cobalt blue.
**Strap:** black alligator leather; triple-folding clasp.

## GRAND CLASS GRANDE DATE REF. 03.0520.4010/21.R511

**Movement:** El Primero 4010 automatic movement with chronograph; COSC-certified chronometer.
**Functions:** chronograph; date.
**Case:** stainless steel; water resistant to 50 meters.
**Dial:** black dial; silver counters.
**Strap:** black rubber; triple-folding clasp.
**03.0520.4010/21.C492:** stainless steel case, black dial with silver counters, black alligator leather strap.
**03.0520.4010/21.M520:** stainless steel case and bracelet, black dial with silver counters.

## GRANDE CLASS EL PRIMERO REF. 03.0520.4002/01 C492

**Movement:** automatic El Primero 4002; COSC-certified chronometer.
**Functions:** chronograph; date.
**Case:** stainless steel; water resistant to 50 meters.
**Dial:** silver.
**Strap:** black alligator leather; triple-folding clasp.
**Also available:** silver or black dial, black rubber strap or stainless bracelet; red-gold case, silver or black guilloché dial, black alligator leather strap; white-gold case, silver or black guilloché dial, black alligator leather strap.

## CLASS EL PRIMERO REF. 03.0510.4002/21.C492

**Movement:** automatic El Primero 4002 with chronograph; COSC-certified chronometer.
**Functions:** date; chronograph.
**Case:** stainless steel; water resistant to 50 meters.
**Dial:** black dial.
**Strap:** black leather; triple-folding clasp.
**03.0510.4002/01.C492:** stainless steel case, silver dial, black leather strap.
**03.0510.4002/01.M510:** stainless steel case and bracelet, silver dial.
**03.0510.4002/21.M510:** stainless steel case and bracelet, black dial.

## GRANDE CLASS RÉSERVE DE MARCHE & DUAL TIME REF. 03.0520.683/01.C492

**Movement:** automatic Élite 683.
**Functions:** date; power-reserve indicator; second time zone.
**Case:** stainless steel; water resistant to 50 meters.
**Dial:** silver guilloché.
**Strap:** black alligator leather; triple-folding clasp.
**Also available:** stainless steel bracelet, silver guilloché dial; yellow-, rose- or white-gold case with silver guilloché dial, black alligator leather strap.

## GRANDE CLASS RÉSERVE DE MARCHE REF. 03.0520.685/01.C492

**Movement:** automatic Élite 685.
**Functions:** power-reserve indicator.
**Case:** stainless steel; water-resistant to 50 meters.
**Dial:** silver dial.
**Strap:** black alligator leather; triple-folding clasp.
**Also available:** black rubber strap; stainless steel bracelet; black dial.

## GRANDE PORT ROYAL GRANDE DATE REF. 03.0550.4010/21.C503

**Movement:** El Primero 4010 automatic movement with chronograph; COSC-certified chronometer.
**Functions:** big date; chronograph with counters.
**Case:** stainless steel; water resistant to 50 meters.
**Dial:** anthracite dial.
**Strap:** black alligator leather; triple-folding clasp.

**03.0550.4010/01.C507:** stainless steel case, sand dial, black alligator leather strap.
**03.0550.4010/21.M550:** stainless steel case and bracelet, anthracite dial.
**03.0550.4010/01.M550:** stainless steel case and bracelet, sand dial.
**03.0550.4010/21.R512:** stainless steel case, anthracite dial, black rubber strap.
**03.0550.4010/01.R513:** stainless steel case, sand dial, brown rubber strap.

## GRANDE PORT-ROYAL EL PRIMERO REF. 03.0550.400/02.C507

**Movement:** automatic El Primero400.
**Functions:** chronograph; date.
**Case:** stainless steel case; triple-folding clasp.
**Dial:** silver guilloché dial.
**Strap:** Zenith-brown alligator leather.
**Also available:** Zenith-brown rubber strap; stainless steel bracelet; black guilloché dial, black alligator leather strap or black rubber strap; rose-gold case, silver guilloché dial, black alligator leather strap or black rubber strap.

## GRANDE PORT-ROYAL RÉSERVE DE MARCHE REF. 03.0550.685/01.C507

**Movement:** automatic Élite 685.
**Functions:** power-reserve indicator; date.
**Case:** stainless steel; water resistant to 50 meters.
**Dial:** silver guilloché.
**Strap:** Zenith-brown alligator leather; triple-folding clasp.
**Also available:** Zenith-brown rubber strap; or stainless steel bracelet; black guilloché dial, black alligator leather strap; black rubber strap or stainless steel bracelet.

## PORT-ROYAL ELITE RECTANGLE REF. 01.0251.684/02.C504

**Movement:** automatic Élite 684.
**Functions:** date.
**Case:** stainless steel; water resistant to 50 meters.
**Dial:** silver guilloché.
**Strap:** Zenith-brown alligator leather; triple-folding clasp.
**Also available:** stainless steel bracelet or black alligator leather strap; guilloché dial.

## NEW VINTAGE 1965 REF. 35.1965.670/01.C506

**Movement:** automatic Élite 670.
**Functions:** date; central second hand.
**Case:** rose-gold; water resistant to 30 meters.
**Dial:** silver sun-effect; standard buckle.
**Strap:** black alligator leather.

## GRANDE CHRONOMASTER XT

El Primero 4009 automatic movement with fly-back chronograph; date, day, month; moonphase; COSC-certified chronometer; water resistant to 30 meters; triple-folding clasp.

**03.1250.4009/01.C495:** stainless steel, silver guilloché dial, black alligator leather strap.
**03.1250.4009/01.C496:** stainless steel, silver guilloché dial, Zenith-brown alligator leather strap.
**03.1250.4009/01.M1250:** stainless steel case and bracelet, silver guilloché dial.
**35.1250.4009/01.C495:** yellow-gold, silver guilloché dial, black alligator leather strap.
**35.1250.4009/01.C496:** yellow-gold, silver guilloché dial, Zenith-brown alligator leather strap.
**35.1250.4009/01.M1250:** yellow-gold case and bracelet, silver guilloché dial.
**35.1250.4009/01.C495:** rose-gold, silver guilloché dial, black alligator leather strap.
**35.1250.4009/01.C496:** rose-gold, silver guilloché dial, Zenith-brown alligator leather strap.
**35.1250.4009/01.M1250:** rose-gold case and bracelet, silver guilloché dial.
**35.1250.4009/01.C495:** white-gold, silver guilloché dial, black alligator leather strap.
**35.1250.4009/01.C496:** white-gold, silver guilloché dial, Zenith-brown alligator leather strap.
**35.1250.4009/01.M1250:** white-gold case and bracelet, silver guilloché dial.

## GRANDE CHRONOMASTER GT

El Primero 4001 automatic with fly-back chronograph; date, day, month; moonphase; COSC-certified chronometer; water resistant to 30 meters; triple-folding clasp.

**03.1240.4001/01.C495:** stainless steel case, silver guilloché dial, black alligator leather strap.
**03.1240.4001/01.C496:** stainless steel case, silver guilloché dial, Zenith-brown alligator leather strap.
**03.1240.4001/01.M1240:** stainless steel case and bracelet, silver guilloché dial.
**03.1240.4001/01.C495:** yellow–gold case, silver guilloché dial, black alligator leather strap.
**03.1240.4001/01.C496:** yellow–gold case, silver guilloché dial, Zenith-brown alligator leather strap.
**03.1240.4001/01.M1240:** yellow-gold case and bracelet, silver guilloché dial.
**03.1240.4001/01.C495:** rose-gold case, silver guilloché dial, black alligator leather strap.
**03.1240.4001/01.C496:** rose-gold case, silver guilloché dial, Zenith-brown alligator leather strap.
**03.1240.4001/01.M1240:** rose-gold case and bracelet, silver guilloché dial.
**03.1240.4001/01.C495:** white-gold case, silver guilloché dial, black alligator leather strap.
**03.1240.4001/01.C496:** white-gold case, silver guilloché dial, Zenith-brown alligator leather strap.
**03.1240.4001/01.M1240:** white-gold case and bracelet, silver guilloché dial.

## CHRONOMASTER T

El Primero 410 automatic movement with chronograph; date, day, month; moonphase; COSC-certified chronometer; water resistant to 30 meters; triple-folding clasp.

**01.0240.410:** stainless steel case, silver dial, black alligator leather strap.
**01.0240.410/02.C495:** stainless steel case, silver guilloché dial, black alligator leather strap.
**01.0240.410/02.C496:** stainless steel case, silver guilloché dial, Zenith-brown, alligator leather strap.
**02.0240.410/01:** stainless steel case and bracelet, silver dial.
**02.0240.410/02.M241:** stainless steel case and bracelet, silver guilloché dial.
**01.0240.410/21:** stainless steel case, black dial, black alligator leather strap.
**01.0240.410/23.C495:** stainless steel case, black silver, black alligator leather strap.
**02.0240.410/21:** stainless steel case and bracelet, black dial.
**02.0240.410/23.M241:** stainless steel case and bracelet, black guilloché dial.
**30.0243.410/01.C495:** yellow-gold case, silver guilloché dial, black alligator leather strap.
**30.0243.410/01.C496:** yellow-gold case, silver guilloché dial, Zenith-brown, alligator leather strap.
**60.0240.410/01.M240:** yellow gold case and bracelet, silver guilloché dial.
**17.0240.410/01:** rose-gold case, silver guilloché dial, black alligator leather strap.
**62.0240.410/01:** rose-gold case and bracelet, silver guilloché dial.
**39.0240.410/01:** platinum case, silver guilloché dial, blue-black alligator leather strap.
**39.0241.410/01.C494:** platinum case with a secret sapphire crystal caseback, silver guilloché dial.

## CLASS SPORT

El Primero 400 automatic movement with chronograph; date; water resistant to 50 meters; triple-folding clasp.

**03.0510.400/04.C491:** stainless steel case, silver dial, Zenith-brown alligator leather strap.
**03.0510.400/04.M510:** stainless steel case and bracelet, silver dial.
**03.0510.400/24.C492:** stainless steel case, black dial, black alligator leather strap.
**03.0510.400/24.M510:** stainless steel case and bracelet, black dial.

## CHRONOMASTER STAR — REF. 03.1230.4002/21.C509

**Movement:** automatic El Primero 4002; COSC-certified chronometer.
**Functions:** chronograph; date.
**Case:** stainless steel; water resistant to 30 meters.
**Dial:** black guilloché.
**Strap:** black lizard; triple-folding clasp.
**Also available:** stainless steel case, silver guilloché dial, silver lizard leather strap; yellow-gold case, beige guilloché dial, Zenith-brown lizard leather strap; rose-gold case, black guilloché dial, black lizard leather strap.

## STAR OPEN — REF. 03.1230.4021/01.C538

**Movement:** automatic chronograph Zenith El Primero 4021; 13'''; Ø 30mm, thickness: 7.75mm; 39 jewels; 36,000 vph; 50-hour power reserve; measures to a 10th of a second; central rotor on ball bearings; bi-metallic oscillating weight with Côtes de Genève pattern; 249 components.
**Functions:** center hour, minute, second; 30-minute counter at 3; small second at 9; power-reserve indicator from hour axis.
**Case:** stainless steel; Ø 37.5 (opening: Ø 28mm); curved, double-sided antireflective sapphire glass; transparent sapphire caseback engraved with Zenith stars; water resistant to 3atm.
**Dial:** silver, white or black dial; open dial at 10 displaying El Primero heart; sanded rhodium or painted hands; power-reserve indicated with Cupid's arrow; small second hand is a rotating heart.
**Strap:** black, white, red, orange, pink or blue satin strap; stainless steel triple-folding buckle.

## BABY STAR — REF. 03.1220.67/21.C531

**Movement:** mechanical automatic-winding Zenith Élite 67 caliber; 11'''1/2; Ø 25.6mm, thickness: 3.81mm; 27 jewels; 28,000 vph; more than 50 hours' power reserve; central rotor on ball bearings; 22K yellow or rose gold, or heavy metal oscillating weight, stamped with Zenith numerals and stars.
**Functions:** hour, minute, second.
**Case:** 18K rose or yellow gold, or stainless steel three-piece case; Ø 32mm (opening: Ø 22mm); curved, double-sided antireflective sapphire crystal; steel crown; transparent sapphire caseback displaying the movement through star-shaped aperture; water resistant to 3atm.
**Dial:** silver; beige, black, pink, green or blue dial with guilloché wave pattern; powdered Arabic numerals; beveled window; 18K rose or yellow gold, or sanded rhodium leaf-style hands.
**Strap:** black, silver, pastel pink, blue or green pumiced lizard leather strap, lined with silky Alzavel calf leather; removable wrist protection; steel tongue buckle.
**Also available:** 18K rose- or yellow-gold bracelet; stainless steel bracelet.
**Diamond version:** set with 56 full-cut Top Wesselton VVS1 diamonds, approx. 0.53 carat.

## CALIBER EL PRIMERO 4021

Caliber 13'''; 249 parts. **Diameter:** 30mm. **Thickness:** 7.75mm. **Jewels:** 39. **Frequency:** 36,000 vph. **Power reserve:** over 50 hours.

Measures short time intervals to a 10th of a second.
Automatic winding in both directions.

Mechanical movement manufactured, assembled and decorated by hand.

Chronograph functions coordinated by the column-wheel.
Open plate showing the escapement mechanism through the dial.

**Functions:** hour, minute, small seconds; power-reserve indication; 30-minute counter; sweep second hand.

## CALIBER ÉLITE 683

Caliber 11'''; 192 parts. **Diameter:** 25.60mm. **Thickness:** 4.95mm. **Jewels:** 36. **Frequency:** 28,800 vph. **Power reserve:** over 50 hours.

Extra-flat movement; automatic winding in both directions.

Mechanical movement manufactured, assembled and decorated by hand.

**Functions:** hour, minute, small seconds; date; power-reserve indication; second time zone.

# GLOSSARY

ACCURACY s. Precision

ALARM WATCH (image 1)
A watch provided with a movement capable of releasing an acoustic sound at the time set. A second crown is dedicated to the winding, setting and release of the striking-work; an additional center hand indicates the time set. The section of the movement dedicated to the alarm device is made up by a series of wheels linked with the barrel, an escapement and a hammer (s.) striking a gong (s.) or bell (s.). Works much like a normal alarm clock.

AMPLITUDE
Maximum angle by which a balance or pendulum wings from its rest position.

ANALOG or ANALOGUE
A watch displaying time indications by means of hands.

ANTIMAGNETIC
Said of a watch whose movement is not influenced by electromagnetic fields that could cause two or more windings of the balance-spring to stick to each other, consequently accelerating the rate of the watch. This effect is obtained by adopting metal alloys (e.g. Nivarox) resisting magnetization.

ANTIREFLECTION, ANTIREFLECTIVE
Superficial glass treatment assuring the dispersion of reflected light. Better results are obtained if both sides are treated, but in order to avoid scratches on the upper layer, the treatment of the inner surface is preferred.

ARBOR
Bearing element of a gear (s.) or balance, whose ends—called pivots (s.)—run in jewel (s.) holes or brass bushings.

AUTOMATIC (image 2)
A watch whose mechanical movement (s.) is wound automatically. A rotor makes short oscillations due to the movements of the wrist. Through a series of gears, oscillations transmit motion to the barrel (s.), thus winding the mainspring progressively.

1

AUTOMATON
Figures, placed on the dial or case of watches, provided with parts of the body or other elements moving at the same time as the sonnerie (s.) strikes. The moving parts are linked, through an aperture on the dial or caseback, with the sonnerie hammers (s.) striking a gong.

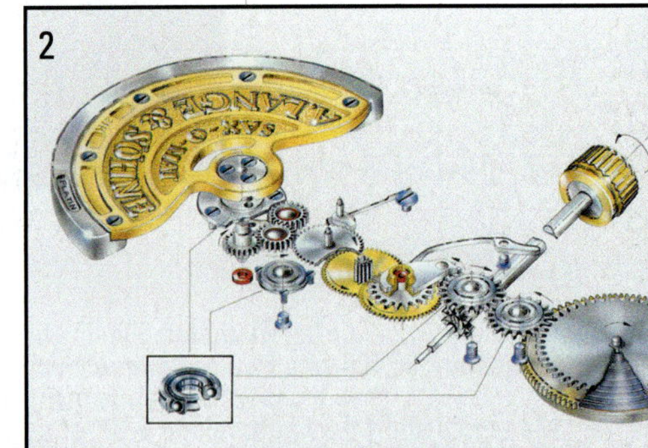
2

BALANCE (image 3)
Oscillating device that, together with the balance spring (s.), makes up the movement's heart inasmuch as its oscillations determine the frequency of its functioning and precision.

BALANCE SPRING (image 3)
Component of the regulating organ (s.) that, together with the balance (s.), determines the movement's precision. The material used is mostly a steel alloy (e.g. Nivarox, s.), an extremely stable metal compound. In order to prevent the system's center of gravity from continuous shifts, hence differences in rate due to the watch's position, some modifications were adopted. These modifications included Breguet's overcoil (closing the terminal part of the spring partly on itself, so as to assure an almost perfect centering) and Philips curve (helping to eliminate the lateral pressure of the balance-staff pivots against their bearings). Today, thanks to the quality of materials, it is possible to assure an excellent precision of movement working even with a flat spring.

3

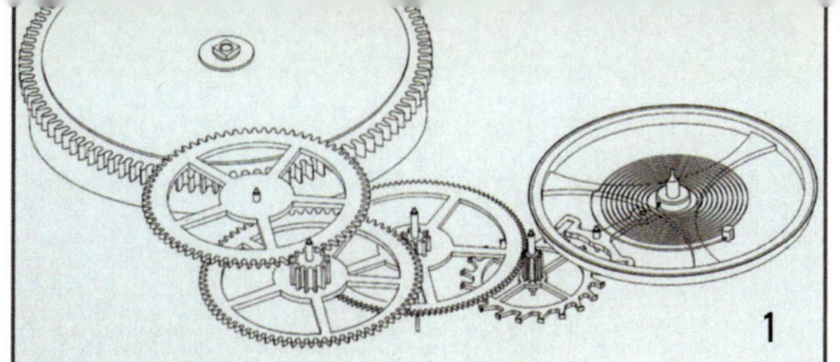

1

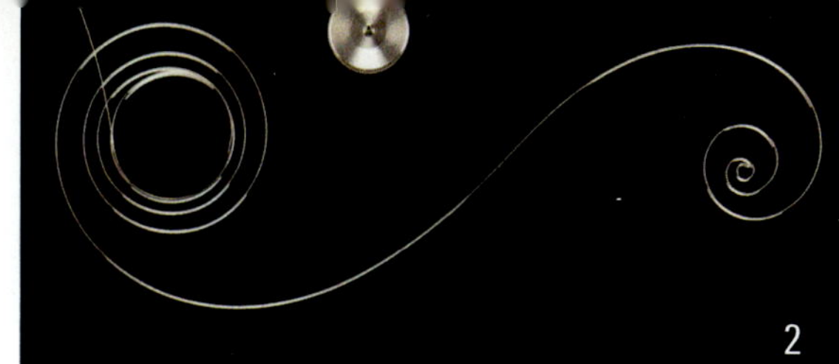

2

BARREL (image 1-2)
Component of the movement containing the mainspring (s.), whose toothed rim meshes with the pinion of the first gear of the train (s.). Due to the fact that the whole—made up of barrel and mainspring—transmits the motive force, it is also considered to be the very motor. Inside the barrel, the mainspring is wound around an arbor (s.) turned by the winding crown or, in the case of automatic movements, also by the gear powered by the rotor (s.).

BEARING
Part on which a pivot turns, in watches mostly a jewels (s.).

3

BEVELING (image 3)
Chamfering of edges of levers, bridges and other elements of a movement by 45∞, a treatment typically found in high-grade movements.

BEZEL
Top part of case (s.), sometimes holds the crystal. It may be integrated with the case middle (s.) or a separate element. It is snapped or screwed on to the middle.

BOTTOM PLATE s. Pillar-plate

BRACELET
A metal band attached to the case. It is called integral if there is no apparent discontinuity between case and bracelet and the profile of attachments is similar to the first link.

4

BRIDGE (image 4)
Structural metal element of a movement (s.)—sometimes called cock or bar—supporting the wheel train (s.), balance (s.), escapement (s.) and barrel (s.). Each bridge is fastened to the plate (s.) by means of screws and locked in a specific position by pins. In high-quality movements the sight surface is finished with various types of decoration.

BREGUET HANDS (image 5)
A particular type of hands in a traditional elegant shape.

BRUSHED, BRUSHING
Topical finishing giving metals a line finish, a clean and uniform look.

5

CABOCHON (image 6)
Any kind of precious stone, such as sapphire, ruby or emerald, uncut and only polished, generally of a half-spherical shape, mainly used as an ornament of the winding crown (s.) or certain elements of the case.

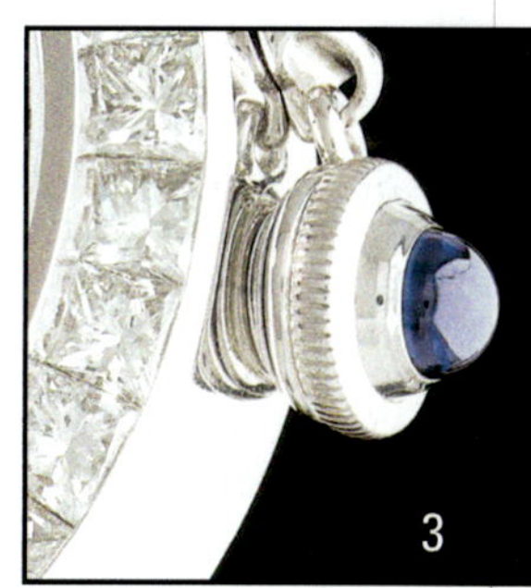

3

CALENDAR, ANNUAL
An intermediate complication between a simple calendar and a perpetual calendar. This feature displays all the months with 30 or 31 days correctly, but needs a manual correction at the end of February. Generally, date, day of the week and month, or only day and month are displayed on the dial.

CALENDAR, GREGORIAN
With respect to the Julian Calendar (s. Calendar, Julian), the calendar reform introduced by Pope Gregory XIII in 1582 corrected the slight error of the former calendar by suppressing a leap year every hundred years, except for years whose

numbers are divisible by 400 (this entailed the elimination of the leap years in 1700, 1800 and 1900, but not in 2000 and 2400). In non-Catholic countries this reform was introduced after 1700.

CALENDAR, FULL
Displaying date, day of the week and month on the dial, but needing a manual correction at the end of a month with less than 31 days. It is often combined with the moonphase (s).

CALENDAR, JULIAN
The calendar established by Julius Caesar was based on the year duration of 365.25 days with a leap year with 366 days every 4 years. In 325 AD, this calendar was adopted by the Church. Due to the slight error (0.0078 day) implied in this time count, the Julian Calendar was later replaced by the Gregorian Calendar (s. Calendar, Gregorian).

CALENDAR, PERPETUAL (image 1)
This is the most complex horology complication related to the calendar feature, as it indicates the date, day, month and leap year and does not need manual corrections until the year 2100 (when the leap year will be ignored).

1

2

CALIBER (image 2)
Originally it indicated only the size (in lines, "') of a movement (s.), but now this indication defines a specific movement type and combines it with the constructor's name and identification number. Therefore the caliber identifies the movement.

CANNON
An element in the shape of a hollow cylinder, sometimes also called pipe or bush, for instance the pipe of the hour wheel bearing the hour hand.

CHAPTER-RING
Hour-circle, i.e. the hour numerals arranged on a dial.

Carousel
Device similar to the tourbillon (s.), but with the carriage not driven by the fourth wheel, but by the third wheel.

CARRIAGE or TOURBILLON CARRIAGE (image 3)
Rotating frame of a tourbillon (s.) device, carrying the balance and escapement (s.). This structural element is essential for a perfect balance of the whole system and its stability, in spite of its reduced weight. As today's tourbillon carriages make a rotation per minute, errors of rate in the vertical position are eliminated. Because of the widespread use of transparent dials, carriages became elements of aesthetic attractiveness.

3

CASE (image 1, next page)
Container housing and protecting the movement (s.), usually made up of three parts: middle, bezel, and back.

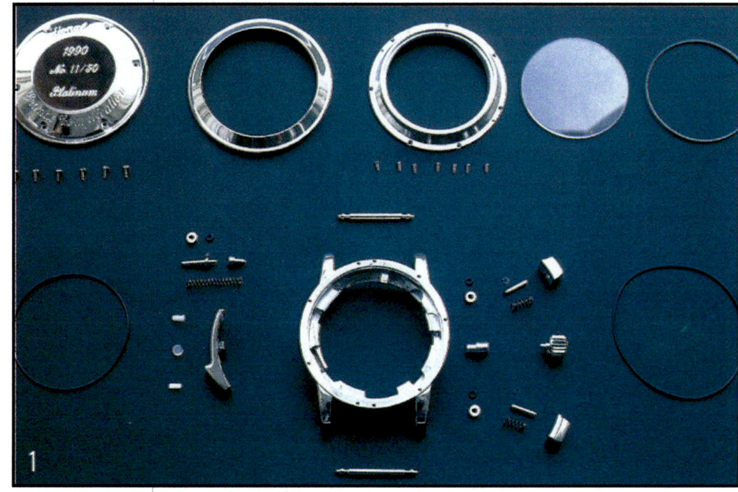

1

2

CENTER SECOND HAND, s. Sweep second hand.

CENTER-WHEEL
The minute wheel in a going-train.

CHAMPLEVÉ (image 2)
Hand-made treatment of the dial or case surface. The pattern is obtained by hollowing a metal sheet with a graver and subsequently filling the hollows with enamel.

CHIME
Striking-work equipped with a set of bells that may be capable of playing a complete melody. A watch provided with such a feature is called chiming watch.

3

CHRONOGRAPH (image 3)
A watch that includes a built-in stopwatch function, i.e. a timer that can be started and stopped to time an event. There are many variations of the chronograph.

CHRONOMETER
A high-precision watch. According to the Swiss law, a manufacture may put the word "chronometer" on a model only after each individual piece has passed a series of tests and obtained a running bulletin and a chronometer certificate by an acknowledged Swiss control authority, such as the COSC (s.).

CIRCULAR GRAINING (image 4)
Superficial decoration applied to bridges, rotors and pillar-plates in the shape of numerous slightly superposed small grains, obtained by using a plain cutter and abrasives. Also called Pearlage or Pearling.

CLICK s. Pawl

CLOISONNÉ (image 5)
A kind of enamel work— mainly used for the decoration of dials—in which the outlines of the drawing are formed by thin metal wires. The colored enamel fills the hollows formed in this way. After oven firing, the surface is smoothed until the gold threads appear again.

4

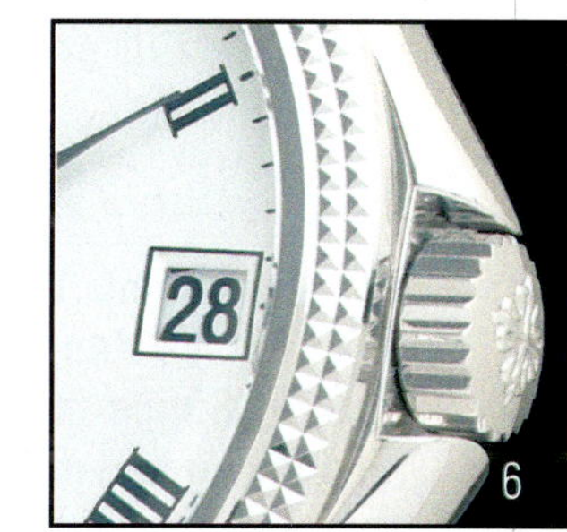


6

CLOUS DE PARIS (image 6)
Decoration of metal parts characterized by numerous small pyramids.

COCK, s. Bridge.

COLIMAÇONNAGE (image 1 next page), s. Snailing.

5

COLUMN-WHEEL (image 2)
Part of chronograph movements, governing the functions of various levers and parts of the chronograph operation, in the shape of a small-toothed steel cylinder. It is controlled by pushers through levers that hold and release it. It is a very precise and usually preferred type of chronograph operation.

1

2

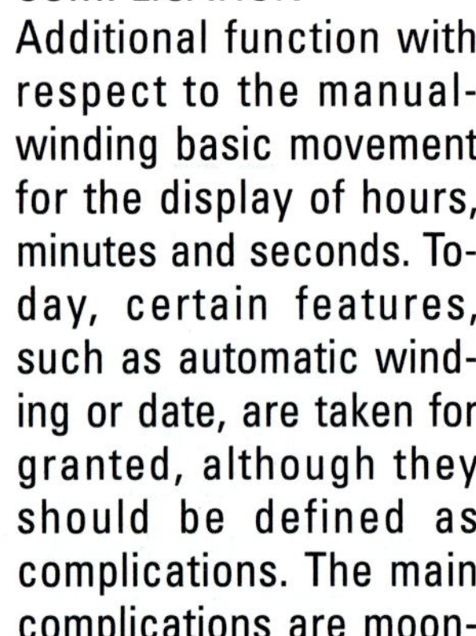

COMPLICATION
Additional function with respect to the manual-winding basic movement for the display of hours, minutes and seconds. Today, certain features, such as automatic winding or date, are taken for granted, although they should be defined as complications. The main complications are moonphase (s.), power reserve (s.), GMT (s.), and full calendar (s.). Further functions are performed by the so-called great complications, such as split-second (s.) chronograph, perpetual calendar (s.), tourbilon (s.) device, and minute repeater (s.).

CORRECTOR
Pusher (s.) positioned on the case side that is normally actuated by a special tool for the quick setting of different indications, such as date, GMT (s.), full or perpetual calendar (s.).

COSC
Abbreviation of "Contrôle Officiel Suisse des Chronomètres," the most important Swiss institution responsible for the functioning and precision tests of movements of chronometers (s.). Tests are performed on each individual watch at different temperatures and in different positions before a functioning bulletin and a chronometer certificate are issued, for which a maximum gap of -4/+4 seconds per day is tolerated.

3

CÔTES CIRCULAIRES (image 3)
Decoration of rotors and bridges of movements, whose pattern consists of a series of concentric ribs.

CÔTES DE GENÈVE (image 4)
Decoration applied mainly to high-quality movements, appearing as a series of parallel ribs, realized by repeated cuts of a cutter leaving thin stripes.

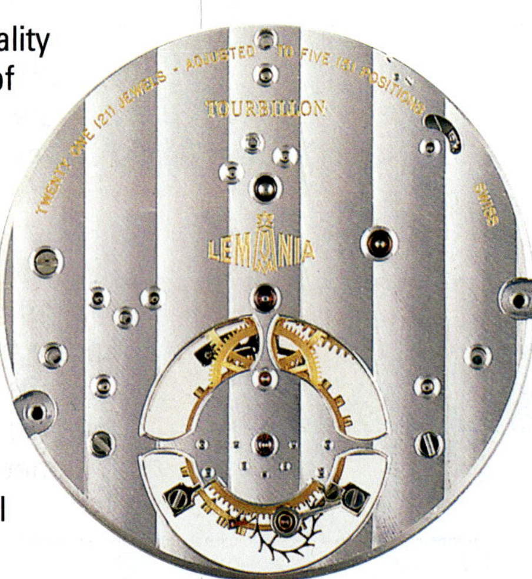


4

COUNTER (image 5)
Additional hand on a chronograph (s.), indicating the time elapsed since the beginning of the measuring. On modern watches the second counter is placed at the center, while minute and hour counters have off-center hands in special zones (s.), also called subdials.

CROWN
Usually positioned on the case middle (s.) and allows winding, hand setting and often date or GMT hand setting. As it is linked to the movement through the winding stem (s.) passing through a hole in the case. For waterproofing purposes, simple gaskets are used in water-resistant watches, while diving watches adopt screwing systems (screw-down crowns).

5

CROWN-WHEEL
Wheel meshing with the winding pinion and with the ratchet wheel on the barrel-arbor.

DECK WATCH
A large-sized ship's chronometer.

DEVIATION
A progressive natural change of a watch's rate with respect to objective time. In case of a watch's faster rate, the deviation is defined positive, in the opposite case negative.

1

DIAL (image 1)
Face of a watch, on which time and further functions are displayed by markers (s.), hands (s.), discs or through windows (s.). Normally it is made of a brass—sometimes silver or gold.

DIGITAL
Said of watches whose indications are displayed mostly inside an aperture or window (s.) on the dial.

EBAUCHE (image 2)
Incomplete (jeweled or non-jeweled) watch movement without regulating organs, mainspring, dial and hands.

ENDSTONE (image 3)
Undrilled jewel, placed on the balance jewel with the tip of the balance-staff pivot resting against its flat surface, to reduce pivot friction. Sometimes used also for pallet staffs and escape wheels.

2

3

ENGINE-TURNED, s. Guilloché.

EQUINOX (image 4)
The time when day and night are of equal length, when the sun is on the plane of the equator. Such times occur twice in a year: the vernal equinox on March 21st-22nd and the autumnal equinox on September 22nd-23rd.

4

EQUATION OF TIME (image 4)
Indication of the difference, expressed in minutes, between conventional mean time and real solar time. This difference varies from -16 to +16 seconds between one day and the other.

ESCAPE WHEEL (image 5)
A wheel belonging to the mechanism called escapement (s.).

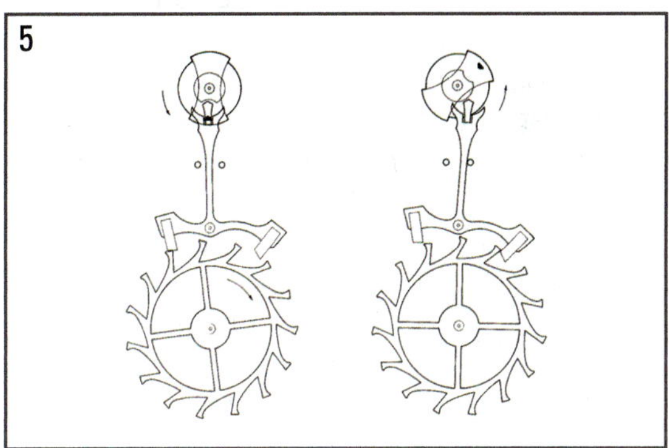
5

ESCAPEMENT (image 5)
Positioned between the train (s.) and the balance wheel and governing the rotation speed of the wheel-train wheels. In today's horology the most widespread escapement type is the lever escapement. In the past, numerous types of escapements were realized, such as: verge, cylinder, pin-pallet, detent and duplex escapements. Recently, George Daniels developed a so-called "coaxial" escapement.

6

FLINQUÉ (image 6)
Engraving on the dial or case of a watch, covered with an enamel layer.

FLUTED (image 1)
Said of surfaces worked with thin parallel grooves, mostly on dials or case bezels.

FLY-BACK (image 2)
Feature combined with chronograph (s.) functions, that allows a new measurement starting from zero (and interrupting a measuring already under way) by pressing down a single pusher, i.e. without stopping, zeroing and restarting the whole mechanism. Originally, this function was developed to meet the needs of air forces.

FOLD-OVER CLASP (image 3)
Hinged and jointed element, normally of the same material as the one used for the case. It allows easy fastening of the bracelet on the wrist. Often provided with a snap-in locking device, sometimes with an additional clip or push-piece.

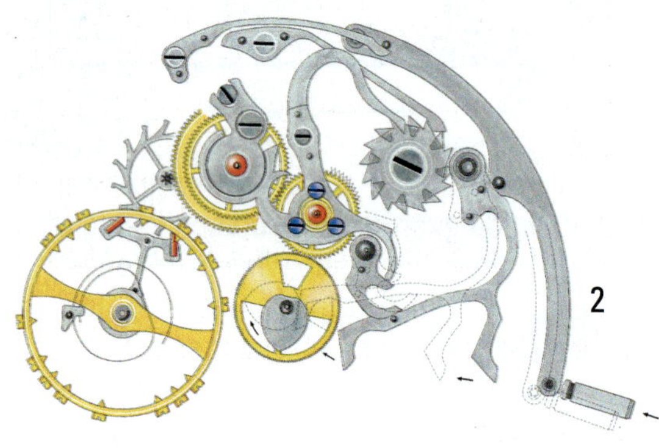


FOURTH-WHEEL
The seconds wheel in a going-train.

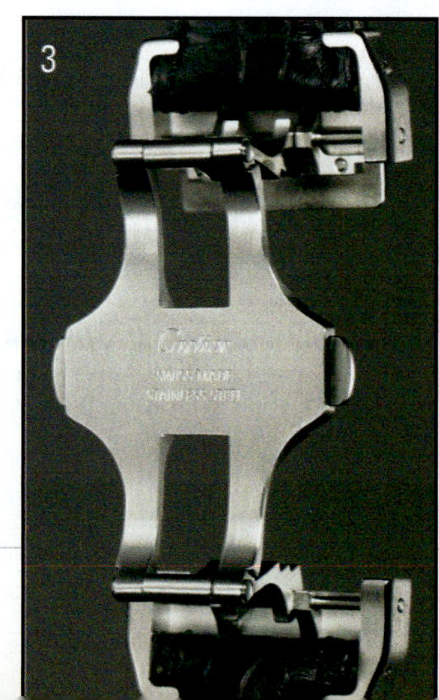


FREQUENCY, s. Vibration
Generally defined as the number of cycles per time unit; in horology it is the number of oscillations of a balance every two seconds or of its vibrations per second. For practical purposes, frequency is expressed in vibrations per hour (vph).

FUSEE
A conical part with a spiral groove on which a chain or cord attached to the barrel (s.) is wound. Its purpose is to equalize the driving power transmitted to the train.

GENEVA SEAL, s. Poinçon de Genève.

GLUCYDUR
Bronze and beryllium alloy used for high-quality balances (s.). This alloy assures high elasticity and hardness values; it is non-magnetic, rust-proof and has a very reduced dilatation coefficient, which makes the balance very stable and assures high accuracy of the movement.

GMT (image 4)
Abbreviation for Greenwich Mean Time. As a feature of watches, it means that two or more time zones are displayed. In this case, the second time may be read from a hand making a full rotation in a 24-hour ring (thereby also indicating whether it is a.m. or p.m. in that zone).

GOING TRAIN s. Train.

GONG (image 1, next page)
Harmonic flattened bell in a steel alloy, generally positioned along the circumference of the movement and struck by hammers (s.) to indicate time by sounds. Size and thickness determine the resulting note and tone. In watches provided with minute-repeaters (s.), there are often two gongs and the hammers strike one note to indicate hours, both notes together to indicate quarters and the other note for the remaining minutes. In more complex models, equipped also with en-passant sonnerie (s.) devices, there may be up to

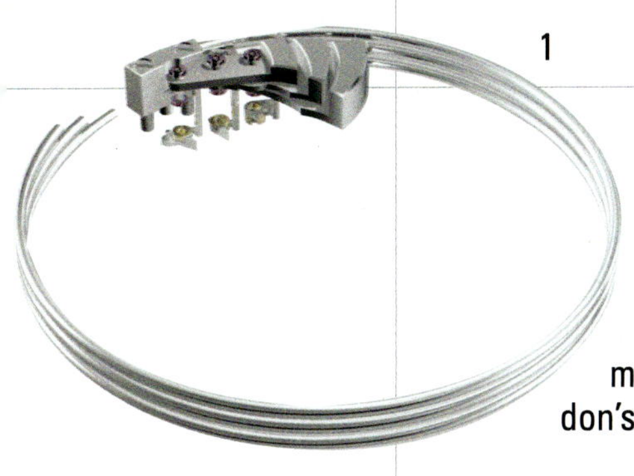

1

four gongs producing different notes and playing even simple melodies (such as the chime of London's Big Ben).

GRAND (or GREAT) COMPLICATIONS s. Complication

2

GUILLOCHé (image 2)
Decoration of dials, rotors or case parts consisting of patterns made by hand or engine-turned. By the thin pattern of the resulting engravings—consisting of crossing or interlaced lines—it is possible to realize even complex drawings. Dials and rotors decorated in this way are generally in gold or in solid silver.

HAMMER
Steel or brass element used in movements provided with a repeater or alarm sonnerie (s.). It strikes a gong (s.) or bell (s).

HAND (image 3)
Indicator for the analogue visualization of hours, minutes and seconds as well as other functions. Normally made of brass (rhodium-plated, gilded or treated otherwise), but also steel or gold. Hands are available in different shapes and take part in the aesthetic result of the whole watch.

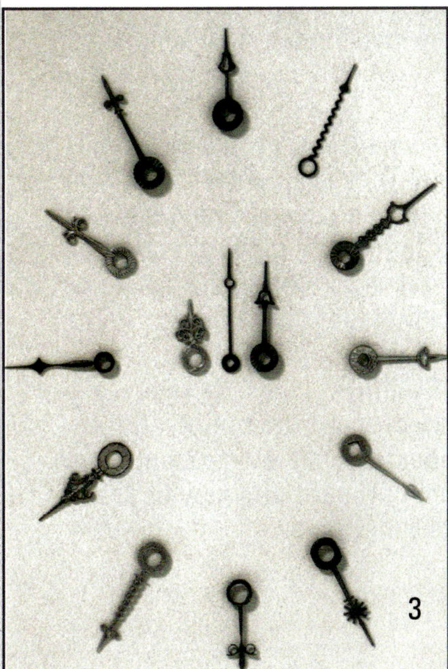

3

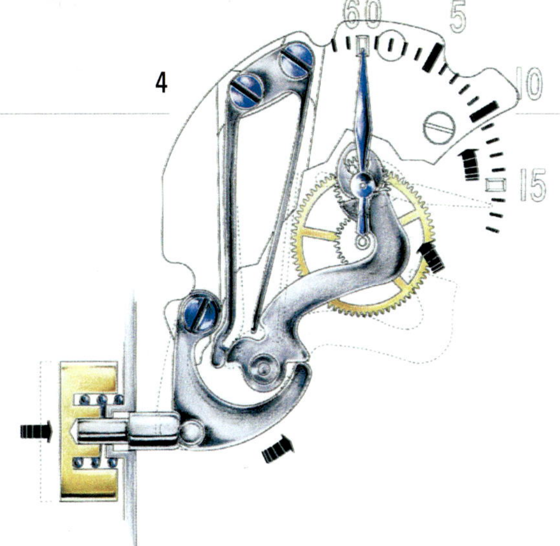

4

HEART-PIECE (image 4)
Heart-shaped cam generally used to realign the hands of chronograph counters.

HELIUM VALVE (image 5)
Valve inserted in the case of some professional diving watches to discharge the helium contained in the air mixture inhaled by divers.

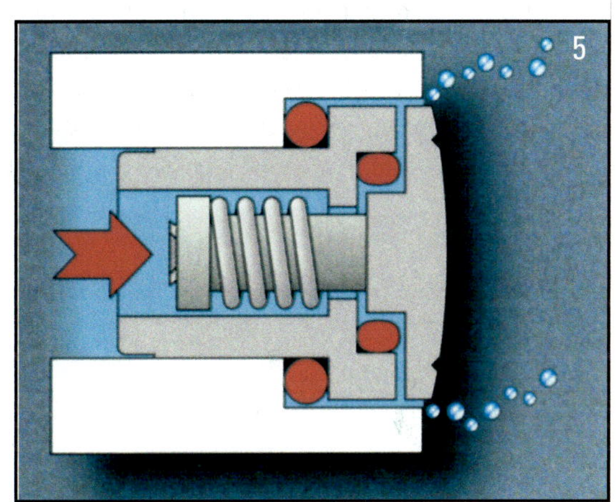

5

HEXALITE
An artificial glass made of a plastic resin.

HUNTER CALIBER
A caliber (s.) characterized by the seconds hand fitted on an axis perpendicular to the one of the winding-stem (s.).

IMPULSE
In a lever escapement (s.) the action of the escape-wheel tooth on the impulse face of the pallet; in the Swiss lever escapement it is produced by the impulse face of the wheel tooth and that of the pallet.

INCABLOC, s. Shockproof.

1

INDEX s. Regulator

JEWEL (image 1)
Precious stone used in movements as a bearing surface. Generally speaking, the steel pivots (s.) of wheels in movements turn inside synthetic jewels (mostly rubies) lubricated with a drop of oil. The jewel's hardness reduces wear to a minimum even over long periods of time (50 to 100 years). The quality of watches is determined mainly by the shape and finishing of jewels rather than by their number (the most refined jewels have rounded holes and walls to greatly reduce the contact between pivot and stone).

JUMPING HOUR (image 2)
Feature concerning the digital display of time in a window. The indication changes almost instantaneously at every hour.

2

LEAP-YEAR CYCLE
Leap or bissextile years have 366 days and occur every 4 years (with some exceptions, s. Calendar, Gregorian). Some watches display this datum.

LÉPINE CALIBER
A caliber (s.) typical for pocket-watches, characterized by the seconds hand fitted in the axis of the winding-stem (s.)

LIGNE s. Line.

LINE
Ancient French measuring unit maintained in horology to indicate the diameter of a movement (s.). A line (expressed by the symbol ''') equals 2.255mm. Lines are not divided into decimals; therefore, to indicate measures inferior to the unit, fractions are used (e.g. movements of 13'''3/4 or 10'''1/2).

LUBRICATION
To reduce friction caused by the running of wheels and other parts. There are points to be lubricated with specific low-density oils such as the pivots (s.) turning inside jewels (s.), the sliding areas between levers, and the spring inside the barrel (requiring a special grease), as well as numerous other parts of a movement.

LUG
Double extension of the case middle (s.) by which a strap or bracelet is attached. Normally, straps and bracelets are attached with removable spring bars.

LUMINESCENT
Said of materials applied on markers (s.) and/or hands (s.), emitting the luminous energy previously absorbed as electromagnetic light rays. Tritium is no longer used and was replaced by other substances having the same emitting powers, but with virtually zero radioactivity, such as Super-LumiNova and Lumibrite.

MAINSPRING
This and the barrel (s.) make up the driving element of a movement (s.). It stores and transmits the power force needed for its functioning.

MANUAL
A mechanical movement (v.) in which winding is performed by hand. The motion transmitted from the user's fingers to the crown is forwarded to the movement through the winding stem (s.), from this to the barrel (s.) through a series of gears (s.) and finally to the mainspring (s.).

MARINE CHRONOMETER
A large-sized watch enclosed in a box (therefore also called box chronometer) mounted on gimbals and used, on board of ships, to determine the respective longitude.

MARKERS
Elements printed or applied on the dial, sometimes they are luminescent (s.), used as reference points for the hands to indicate hours and fifteen- or five-minute intervals.

MEAN TIME
The mean time of the meridian of the Greenwich Observatory, considered the universal meridian, is used as a standard of the civil time system, counted from midnight to midnight.

1

MICROMETER SCREW (image 1)
Element positioned on the regulator, allowing to shift it by minimal and perfectly gauged ranges so as to obtain accurate regulations of the movement.

MICRO-ROTOR, s. Rotor. (image 2)

2

MINUTE REPEATER, s. Repeater.

MODULE (image 3)
Self-contained mechanism, independent of the basic caliber (s.), added to the movement (s.) to make an additional function available: chronograph (s.), power reserve (s.), GMT (s.), perpetual or full calendar (s).

MOONPHASE (image 3)
A function available in many watches, usually combined with calendar-related features. The moonphase disc advances one tooth every 24 hours. Normally, this wheel has 59 teeth and assures an almost perfect synchronization with the lunation period, i.e. 29.53 days (in fact, the disc shows the moonphases twice during a single revolution). However, the difference of 0.03 days, i.e. 44 minutes each month, implies the need for a manual adjustment every two and a half years to recover one day lost with respect to the real state of moonphase. In some rare case, the transmission ratio between the gears controlling the moonphase are calculated with extreme accuracy so as to require manual correction only once in 100 years.

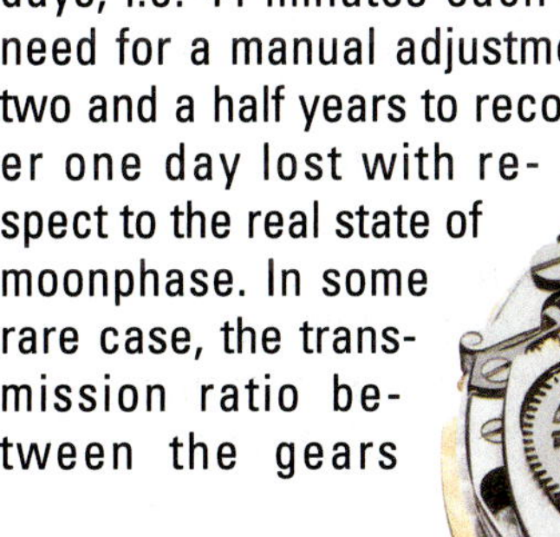

MOVEMENT
The entire mechanism of a watch. Movements are divided into two great families: quartz and mechanical; the latter are available with manual (s.) or automatic (s.) winding devices.

MOVEMENT-BLANK s. Ebauche

NIVAROX
Trade name (from the producer's name) of a steel alloy, resisting magnetization, used for modern self-compensating balance springs (s.). The quality level of this material is indicated by the numeral following the name in decreasing value from 1 to 5.

OBSERVATORY CHRONOMETER
An observatory-tested precision watch that obtained the relevant rating certificate.

OPEN-FACE CALIBER s. Lépine Caliber.

OSCILLATION
Complete oscillation or rotation movement of the balance (s.), formed by two vibrations (s.).

OVERCOIL s. Balance spring.

PALLETS
Device of the escapement (s.) transmitting part of the motive force to the balance (s.), in order to maintain the amplitude of oscillations unchanged by freeing a tooth of the escape wheel at one time.

PAWL
Lever with a beak that engages in the teeth of a wheel under the action of a spring.

PILLAR-PLATE OR MAIN PLATE
Supporting element of bridges (s.) and other parts of a movement (s).

3

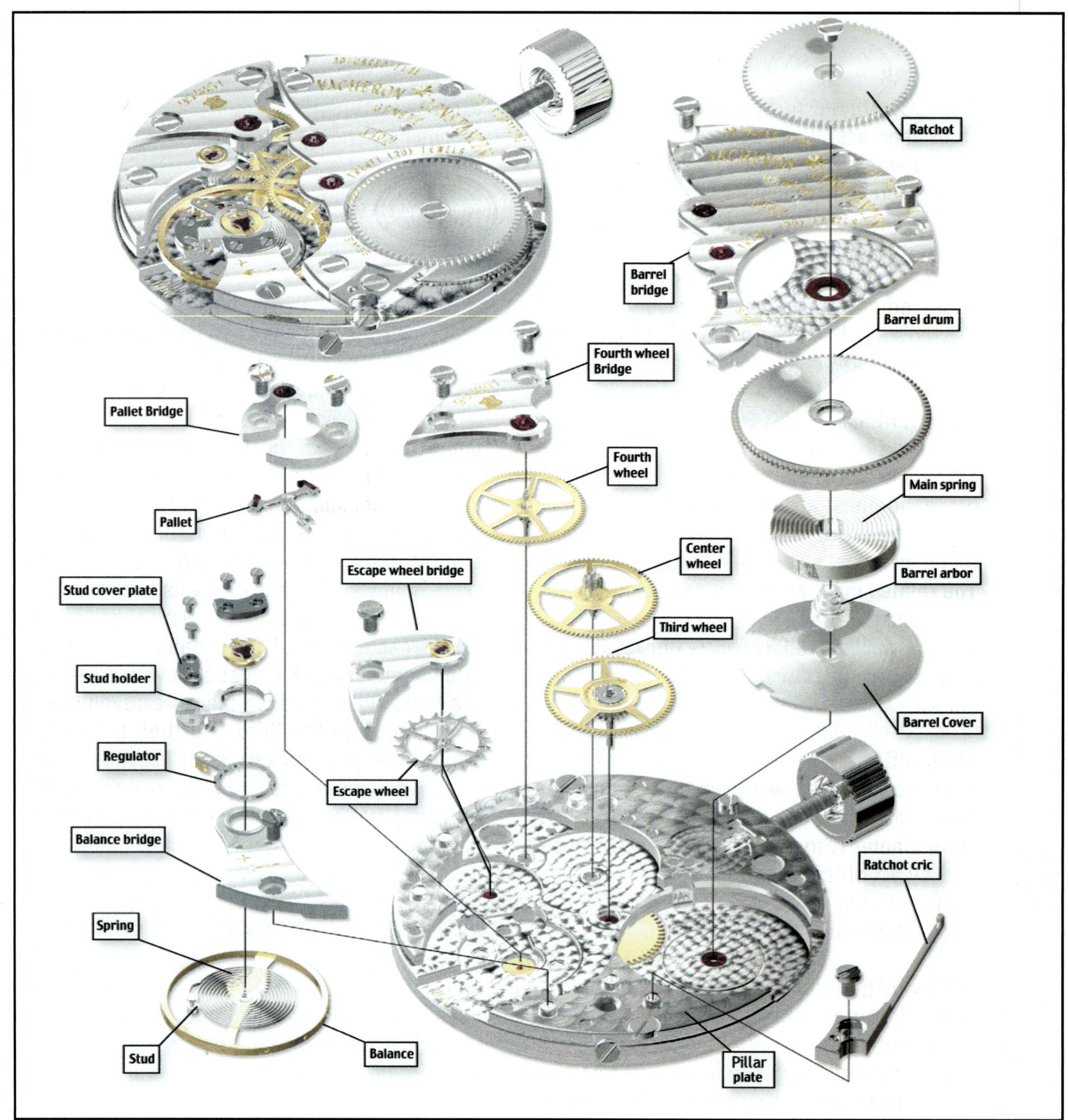


PINION
Combines with a wheel and an arbor (s.) to form a gear (s.). A pinion has less teeth than a wheel and transmits motive force to a wheel. Pinion teeth (normally 6 to 14) are highly polished to reduce friction to a minimum.

PIVOT
End of an arbor (s.) turning on a jewel (s.) support. As their shape and size can influence friction, the pivots of the balance-staff are particularly thin and, hence, fragile, so they are protected by a shockproof (s.) system.

PLATE s. Pillar-plate.

PLATED
Said of a metal treated by a galvanizing procedure in order to apply a slight layer of gold or another precious metal (silver, chromium, rhodium or palladium) on a brass or steel base.

PLEXIGLAS
A synthetic resin used for watch crystal.

POINÇON DE GENÈVE (image 1)
Distinction assigned by the Canton of Geneva to movements produced by watchmaker firms of the Region and complying with all the standards of high horology with respect to craftsmanship, small-scale production, working quality, accurate assembly and setting. The Geneva Seal is engraved on at least one bridge and shows the Canton's symbol, i.e. a two-field shield with an eagle and a key respectively in each field.

POWER RESERVE (image 2)
Duration (in hours) of the residual functioning autonomy of a movement after it has reached the winding peak. The duration value is displayed by an instantaneous indicator: analog (hand on a sector) or digital (through a window). The related mechanism is made up of a series of gears linking the winding barrel and hand. Recently, specific modules were introduced which may be combined with the most popular movements.

1

2

PRECISION
Accuracy rate of a watch, a term difficult to define exactly. Usually, a precision watch is a chronometer whose accuracy-standard is certified by an official watch-rating bureau, and a high-precision watch is a chronometer certified by an observatory.

PULSIMETER CHRONOGRAPH
The pulsimeter scale shows, at a glance, the number of pulse beats per minute. The observer releases the chronograph hand when starting to count the beats and stops at the 30th, the 20th or the 15th beat according to the basis of calibration indicated on the dial.

PUSHER, PUSH-PIECE or PUSH-BUTTON
Mechanical element mounted on a case (s.) for the control of specific functions. Generally, pushers are used in chronographs (s.), but also with other functions.

PVD
Abbreviation of Physical Vapor Deposition, a plating process consisting of the physical transfer of substance by bombardment of electrons.

RATCHET (WHEEL)
Toothed wheel prevented from moving by a click pressed down by a spring.

RATING CERTIFICATES s. Chronometer and COSC.

REGULATING UNIT (image 3)
Made up by balance (s.) and balance spring (s.), governing the division of time within the mechanical movement, assuring its regular running and accuracy. As the balance works like a pendulum, the balance spring's function consists of its elastic return and starting of a new oscillation. This combined action determines the frequency, i.e. the number of vibrations per hour, and affects the rotation speed of the different wheels. In fact the balance, by its oscillations, at every vibration (through the action of the pallets), frees a tooth of the escape wheel (s. Escapement). From this, motion is transmitted to the fourth wheel, which makes a revolution in one minute, to the third and then the center wheel, the latter making a full rotation in one hour. However, everything is determined by the correct time interval of the oscillations of the balance.

3

REGULATOR (image 3)
Regulating the functioning of a movement by lengthening and shortening the active section of the balance spring (s.). It is positioned on the balance-bridge and encompasses the balance spring with its two pins near its fixing point on the bridge itself. By shifting the index, the pins also are moved and, by consequence, the portion of the balance spring capable of bringing

the balance back is lengthened or shortened by its elastic force. The shorter it is, the more reactive it tends to be and the more rapidly it brings the balance back and makes the movement run faster. The contrary happens when the active portion of the balance spring is lengthened. Given today's high frequencies of functioning, even slight index shifts entail daily variations of minutes. Recently, even more refined index-regulation systems were adopted (from eccentric (s.) to micrometer screws (s.)) to limit error margins to very few seconds per day.

REMONTOIR, CONSTANT-FORCE
Old term used to denote any mechanism assuring a constant transmission of the driving power to the escape wheel.

REPEATER (image 1)
Mechanism indicating time by acoustic sounds. Contrary to the watches provided with en-passant sonnerie (s.) devices, that strike the number of hours automatically, repeaters work on demand by actuating a slide (s.) or pusher (s.) positioned on the case side. Repeaters are normally provided with two hammers and two gongs: one gong for the minutes and one for the hours. The quarters are obtained by the almost simultaneous strike of both hammers. The mechanism of the striking work is among the most complex complications.

1

RETROGRADE (image 2)
Said of a hand (s.) that, instead of making a revolution of 360 before starting a new measurement, moves on an arc scale (generally of 90 to 180) and at the end of its trip comes back instantaneously. Normally, retrograde hands are used to indicate date, day or month in perpetual calendars, but there are also cases of retrograde hours, minutes or seconds. Unlike the case of the classical indication over 360, the retrograde system requires a special mechanism to be inserted into the basic movement.

2

ROLLER TABLE or ROLLER
Part of the escapement in the shape of a disc fitted to the balance staff and carrying the impulse pin that transmits the impulses given by the pallets to the balance.

ROTOR (image 3)
In automatic-winding mechanical movements the rotor is the part that, by its complete or partial revolutions and the movements of human arm, allows winding of the mainspring (s.).

3

SCALE (image 4)
Graduation on a measuring instrument, showing the divisions of a whole of values, especially on a dial, bezel. The scales mostly used in horology are related to the following measuring devices: tachometer (s.) (indicating the average speed), telemeter (s.) (indicating the distance of a simultaneously luminous and acoustic source, e.g. a cannon-shot or a thunder and related lightning), pulsometer (to calculate the total number of heartbeats per minute by counting only a certain quantity of them). For all of these scales, measuring starts at the beginning of the event concerned and stops at its end; the reading refers directly to the chronograph second hand, without requiring further calculations.

4

SECOND TIME-ZONE INDICATOR, s. GMT and World Time.

SECTOR, s. Rotor.

SELF-WINDING, s. Automatic.

SHOCKPROOF or SHOCK-RESISTANT (image 1)
Watches provided with shock-absorber systems (e.g. Incabloc) help prevent damage from shocks to the balance pivots. Thanks to a retaining spring system, it assures an elastic play of both jewels, thus absorbing the movements of the balance-staff pivots when the watch receives strong shocks. The return to the previous position is due to the return effect of the spring. If such a system is lacking, the shock forces exert an impact on the balance-staff pivots, often causing bending or even breakage.

SIDEREAL TIME
The conventional time standard refers to the sidereal year (defined in terms of an average of 365.25636 days) considered to be perfectly regular until very recently, but – even though this is not true – the difference is so slight that it is virtually neglected. As a unit of time, the sidereal day is used mainly by astronomers to define the interval between two upper transits of the vernal point in the plane of the meridian.

SKELETON, SKELETONIZED (image 2)
Watches whose bridges and pillar-plates are cut out in a decorative manner, thus revealing all the parts of the movement.

2

SLIDE
Part of a mechanism moving with friction on a slide-bar or guide.

SMALL SECOND
Time display in which the second hand is placed in a small subdial.

SNAILING (image 3)
Decoration with a spiral pattern, mainly used on the barrel wheel or on big-sized full wheels.

SOLAR TIME
Generally speaking, the time standard referred to the relative motion of the Earth and the Sun governing the length of day and night. The true solar day is the period measured after the Sun appears again in the same position from our point of observation. Due to the non-uniform rotation of the Earth around the Sun, this measure is not regular. As an invariable measure unit, the mean solar day corresponds to the average duration of all the days of the year.

SOLSTICE
The time when the sun is farthest from the equator, i.e. on June 21st (Summer solstice) and December 21st (Winter solstice).

SONNERIE (EN PASSANT)
Function consisting of an acoustic sound, obtained by a striking work made up of two hammers (s.) striking gongs (s.) at set hours, quarter- and half-hours. Some devices can emit a chime (with three or even four hammers and gongs). By a slide (s.) or an additional pusher (s.) it is possible to exclude the sonnerie device and to select a so-called grande sonnerie.

SPLIT-SECOND CHRONOGRAPH (image 4)
Chronographs with split-second mechanisms are particularly useful for timing simultaneous phenomena which begin at the same time, but end at different times, such as sporting events in which several competitors are taking part. In chronographs of this type, an additional hand is superimposed on the chronograph hand. Pressure on the pusher starts both hands, which remain superimposed as long as the split-second mechanism is not blocked. This is achieved when the split-second hand is stopped while the chronograph hand continues to move. After recording, the same pusher is pressed a second time, releasing the split-second hand, which instantly joins the still-moving chronograph hand,

4

synchronizing with it, and is thus ready for another recording. Pressure on the return pusher brings the hands back to zero simultaneously, provided the split-second hand is not blocked. Pressure on the split pusher releases the split-second hand, which instantly joins the chronograph hand if the split-second hand happens to be blocked.

STAFF or STEM, s. Arbor.

STOPWORK
Traditional device (now obsolete) provided with a finger piece fixed to the barrel arbor and a small wheel in the shape of a Maltese cross mounted on the barrel cover, limiting the extent to which the barrel (s.) can be wound.

STRIKING WORK, s. Sonnerie and Repeater.

SUBDIAL, s. Zone.

SUPER-LUMINOVA, s. Luminescent.

SWEEP SECOND HAND
A center second hand, i.e. a second hand mounted on the center of the main dial.

TACHOMETER or TACHYMETER (image 1)
Function measuring the speed at which the wearer runs over a given distance. The tachometer scale is calibrated to show the speed of a moving object, such as a vehicle, over a known distance. The standard length on which the calibration is based is always shown on the dial, e.g. 1,000, 200 or 100 meters, or—in some cases—one mile. As the moving vehicle, for instance, passes the starting-point of the measured course whose length corresponds to that used as the basis of calibration, the observer releases the chronograph hand and stops it as the vehicle passes the finishing point. The figure indicated by the hand on the tachometer scale represents the speed in kilometers or miles per hour.

TELEMETER (image 1)
By means of the telemeter scale, it is possible to measure the distance of a phenomenon that is both visible and audible. The chronograph hand is released at the instant the phenomenon is seen; it is stopped when the sound is heard, and its position on the scale shows, at a glance, the distance in kilometers or miles separating the phenomenon from the observer. Calibration is based upon the speed at which sound travels through the air, viz. approximately 340 meters or 1,115 feet per second. During a thunderstorm, the time that has elapsed between the flash of lightning and the sound of the thunder is registered on the chronograph scale.

THIRD WHEEL
Wheel positioned between the minutes and seconds wheels.

TIME ZONES
The 24 equal spherical lunes unto which the surface of the Earth is conventionally divided, each limited by two meridians. The distance between two adjacent zones is 15° or 1 hour.
Each country adopts the time of its zone, except for countries with more than one zone. The universal standard time is that of the zero zone whose axis is the Greenwich meridian.

TONNEAU (image 2)
Particular shape of a watchcase, imitating the profile of a barrel, i.e. with straight, shorter, horizontal sides and curved, longer, vertical sides.

TOURBILLON (image 1, facing page)
Device invented in 1801 by A. L. Breguet. This function equalizes po-

1

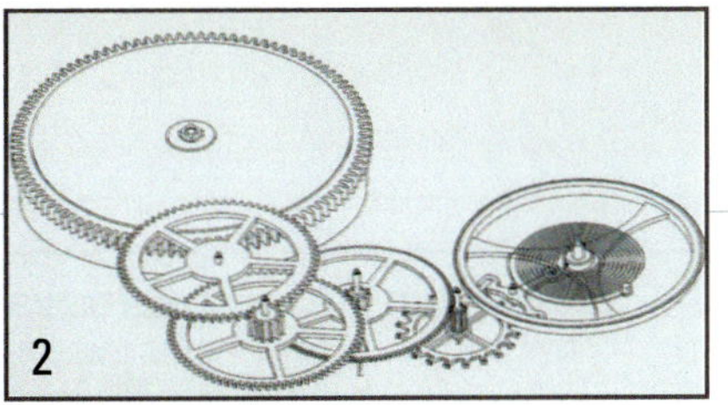

2

sition errors due to changing positions of a watch and related effects of gravity. Balance, balance spring and escapement are housed inside a carriage (s.), also called a cage, rotating by one revolution per minute, thus compensating for all the possible errors over 360. Although this device is not absolutely necessary for accuracy purposes today, it is still appreciated as a complication of high-quality watches.

TRAIN (image 2)
All the wheels between barrel (s.) and escapement (s.).

TRANSMISSION WHEEL s. Crown-wheel

UNIVERSAL TIME
The mean solar time (s.) of the Greenwich meridian, counted from noon to noon, Often confused with the mean time (s.) notion.

VARIATION
In horology the term is usually referred to the variation of the daily rate, i.e. the difference between two daily rates specified by a time interval.

WINDING, AUTOMATIC s. Automatic

VIBRATION
Movement of a pendulum or other oscillating bodies, limited by two consecutive extreme positions. In an alternate (pendulum or balance) movement, a vibration is a half of an oscillation (s.). The number of hourly vibrations corresponds to the frequency of a watch movement, determined by the mass and diameter of a balance (s.) and the elastic force of the balance spring. The number of vibrations per hour (vph) determines the breaking up of time (the "steps" of a second hand). For instance, 18,000 vph equals a vibration duration of 1/5 second; in the same way 21,600 vph = 1/6 second; 28,800 vph = 1/8 second; 36,000 vph = 1/10 second. Until the 1950s, wristwatches worked mostly at a frequency of 18,000 vph; later, higher frequencies were adopted to produce a lower percentage of irregularities to the rate. Today, the most common frequency adopted is 28,800 vph, which assures a good precision standard and less lubrication problems than extremely high frequencies, such as 36,000 vph.

3

WATER RESISTANT or WATERPROOF (image 1)
A watch whose case (s.) is designed in such a way as to resist infiltration by water (3 atmospheres, corresponding to a conventional depth of 30 meters; 5 atmospheres, corresponding to a conventional depth of 50 meters.)

WHEEL
Circular element, mostly toothed, combines with an arbor (s.) and a pinion (s.) to make up a gear (s.). Wheels are normally made of brass, while arbors and pinions are made of steel. The wheels between barrel (s.) and escapement (s.) make up the so-called train (s.).

WINDING STEM
Element transmitting motion from the crown (s.) to the gears governing manual winding and setting.

WINDOW
Aperture in the dial, that allows reading the underlying indication, mainly the date, but also indications concerning a second zone's time or jumping hour (s.).

WORLD TIME (image 3)
Additional feature of watches provided with a GMT (s.) function, displaying the 24 time zones on the dial or bezel, each zone referenced by a city name, providing instantaneous reading of the time of any country.

ZODIAC
Circular belt with the ecliptic in the middle containing the twelve constellations through which the sun seems to pass in the course of a year.

ZONE
Small additional dial or indicator that may be positioned, or placed off-center on the main dial, used for the display of various functions (e.g. second counters).

# BRAND DIRECTORY

**A. LANGE & SÖHNE**
Altenberger Strasse 15
D-01768 Glashütte, Germany
Tel: 49 (0) 35053 440
USA: 1 310 317 9852

**ANONIMO FIRENZE**
85 Hazel Road
San Francisco CA 94705 USA
Tel: 1 510 649 9844

**ARMAND NICOLET**
590 Fifth Avenue, 2nd Fl.
New York NY 10036 USA
Tel: 1 800 988 3254

**ARNOLD & SON**
Avenue Leopold-Robert 23
2300 La Chaux-de-Fonds
Switzerland
Tel: 41 32 910 90 62
USA: 1 212 688 4550

**AUDEMARS PIGUET**
CH-1348 Le Brassus
Switzerland
Tel: 41 21 845 14 00
USA: 1 212 688 6644

**BAUME & MERCIER**
Route de Chêne 61
1211 Geneva 29, Switzerland
Tel: 41 22 707 31 31
USA: 1 212 909 6385

**BLANCPAIN**
Chemin de l'Etang 6
1094 Paudex, Switzerland
Tel: 41 21 796 36 36
USA: 1 201 271 1400

**BOVET FLEURIER SA**
9 Rue Ami-Lévrier
CH 1207 Geneve, Switzerland
Tel: 41 21 731 46 38
USA: 1 212 869 1888

**BREGUET**
1344 L'Abbaye
Switzerland
Tel: 41 21 841 90 90
USA: 1 800 897 9477

**BREITLING**
Case Postale 1132
2540 Grenchen
Switzerland
Tel: 41 32 654 54 54
USA: 1 203 762 1180

**BVLGARI**
34 Rue de Monruz
2008 Neuchâtel, Switzerland
Tel: 41 32 722 78 78
USA: 1 212 315 9700

**CARTIER INTERNATIONAL**
51 Rue Pierre Charron
75008 Paris, France
Tel: 33 1 4218 4383
USA: 1 800 227 8437

**CHANEL**
25 Place du Marché St Honoré
75001 Paris, France
Tel: 33 1 55 35 50 00
USA: 1 212 688 5055

**CHARLES OUDIN**
8 Place Vendôme
75001 Paris, France
Tel: 33 1 40 15 99 00

**CHAUMET**
12 Place Vendôme
75001 Paris, France
Tel: 33 1 44 77 24 00

**CHOPARD**
Rue de Veyrot 8
1217 Meyrin-Geneva 2
Switzerland
Tel: 41 22 719 31 31
USA: 1 800 821 0300

**CLERC SA**
Rue Charles Bonnet 2
1206 Geneva, Switzerland
Tel: 41 22 731 79 31

**CONCORD**
650 From Road
Paramus NJ 07652 USA
Tel: 1 888 812 6626

**CORUM SA**
Rue du petit Château
2300 La Chaux-de-Fonds
Switzerland
Tel: 41 32 967 06 70
USA: 1 949 788 6200

**CUERVO Y SOBRINOS**
8000 N Federal Highway, Ste: 220
Boca Raton FL 33487 USA
Tel: 1 877 283 7869

**DAVID YURMAN USA**
24 Vestry Street
New York NY 10013 USA
Tel: 1 212 896 1550

**DE BETHUNE**
6 Granges-Jaccard
1454 La Chaux L'Auberson
Switzerland
Tel: 41 24 454 22 81
USA: 1 305 695 1435

**de GRISOGONO**
Route de St. Julien 176
1228 Plan-les-Ouates
Switzerland
Tel: 41 22 817 81 00
USA: 1 212 821 0280

**DEWITT**
28, Route de Pressy
1253 Vandoeuvres
Switzerland
Tel: 41 22 750 82 13
USA: 1 305 531 6004

**DIOR WATCHES**
8 Rue Fourcroy
75017 Paris, France
Tel: 33 1 44 29 36 36
USA: 1 973 467 1890

**DUBEY & SCHALDENBRAND**
Industrie 7
2316 Les Ponts-de-Martel
Switzerland
Tel: 41 32 937 14 30
USA: 1 888 919 8463

**EBEL**
113 Rue de la Paix
2301 La Chaux-de-Fonds
Switzerland
Tel: 41 32 912 31 23
USA: 1 201 267 8000

**EBERHARD & CO**
Riva Paradiso 12
6900 Lugano, Switzerland
Tel: 41 91 993 26 01

**F. P. JOURNE**
Rue de l'Arquebuse 17
1204 Geneva, Switzerland
Tel: 41 22 322 09 09
USA: 1 305 531 2600

**FRANCK MULLER**
Rue de Malagny 22
1294 Genthod
Switzerland
Tel: 41 22 959 88 88
USA: 1 212 463 8898

**GEVRIL**
23 Dover Terrace
Monsey NY 10952 USA
Tel: 1 845 425 9882

**GIRARD-PERREGAUX**
Place Girardet 1
2301 La Chaux-de-Fonds
Switzerland
Tel: 41 32 911 33 33
USA: 1 201 804 1978

**GLASHÜTTE ORIGINAL**
Altenberger Strasse 1
D-01768 Glashütte in Sachsen
Germany
Tel: 49 (0) 35034 6231

**GRAHAM**
Avenue Leopold-Robert 23
2300 La Chaux-de-Fonds
Switzerland
Tel: 41 32 910 90 62
USA: 1 212 688 4550

**GREUBEL FORSEY**
19-21 Rue du Manège
2300 La Chaux-de-Fonds
Switzerland
Tel: 41 32 751 71 76
USA: 1 310 205 5555

**GUY ELLIA**
21 Rue de la Paix
Paris 75002 France
Tel: 33 1 53 30 25 25

**HARRY WINSTON**
Rue de Lausanne 82
1202 Geneva
Switzerland
Tel: 41 22 716 29 00
USA: 1 212 245 2000

**HERMÈS**
Erlenstrasse 31A
2555 Brügg-Bienne
Switzerland
Tel: 41 32 366 70 50
USA: 1 212 759 7585

**HOUSE OF EIGHT**
10800 West Pico Boulevard, #197
Los Angeles CA 90064 USA
Tel: 41 21 862 18 41
USA: 1 310 470 1388

**HUBLOT**
44 Route de Divonne
CH 1260 Nyon 2
Switzerland
Tel: 41 22 990 90 00
USA: 1 800 536 0636

**INVICTA**
3069 Taft Street
Hollywood FL 33021 USA
Tel: 1 954 921 2444

**IWC**
Baumgarten Strasse15
8201 Schaffhausen
Switzerland
Tel: 41 52 635 65 90
USA: 1 212 891 2460

**JACOB & CO**
48 East 57th Street
New York NY 10022 USA
Tel: 1 212 719 5887

**JAEGER-LECOULTRE**
Rue de la Golisse 8
1347 Le Sentier, Switzerland
Tel: 41 21 845 02 02
USA: 1 212 308 2525

**JAQUET DROZ**
Rue Jaquet Droz 5
2300 La Chaux-de-Fonds
Switzerland
Tel: 41 32 911 28 88

**JEAN-MAIRET & GILLMAN**
11 Chemin du Petray
1222 Visenaz
Switzerland
Tel: 41 22 703 40 20
USA: 1 561 651 7272

**JEANRICHARD**
129 Rue de progrès
2301 La Chaux-de-Fonds
Switzerland
Tel: 41 32 911 36 36
USA: 1 201 804 1978

**LOCMAN**
Piazza G. da Verranzzano, 7
57034 Marina di Campo (LI)
Italy
Tel: 39 05 6597 90 02
USA: 1 212 371 1888

**LONGINES**
2610 Saint-Imier
Switzerland
Tel: 41 32 942 52 25
USA: 1 201 271 4630

**MAURICE LACROIX**
Brandschenkestrasse 2
8039 Zurich, Switzerland
Tel: 41 1 209 11 11
USA: 1 800 794 7736

**MEYERS WATCHES**
8 Rue de la Paix
75002 Paris, France
Tel: 33 1 4770 03 09
USA: 1 866 463 9377

**MICHELE WATCHES**
20201 NE 16th Place
Miami FL 33179 USA
Tel: 1 305 650 9771

**MOVADO**
650 From Road
Paramus NJ 07652 USA
Tel: 1 800 810 2211

**OMEGA**
Rue Jakob Stämpfli 96
2500 Bienne 4, Switzerland
Tel: 41 32 343 92 11
USA: 1 717 394 7252

**OFFICINA DEL TEMPO**
1784 West Avenue, Bay 3
Miami Beach FL 33139 USA
Tel: 1 305 538 9300

**PANERAI**
Via Ludovico di Breme, 44/45
20156 Milan, Italy
Tel: 39 02 30261
USA: 1 212 888 8788

**PARMIGIANI FLEURIER**
Rue du Temple 11
2114 Fleurier, Switzerland
Tel: 41 32 862 66 30
USA: 1 949 489 2885

**PATEK PHILIPPE**
Chemin du Pont du Centenaire 141
1228 Plan-les-Ouates
Switzerland
Tel: 41 22 884 20 20
USA: 1 212 218 1240

**PAUL PICOT**
2346 Le Noirmont Jura
Switzerland
Tel: 41 32 953 15 31
USA: 1 561 241 3599

**PIAGET**
Route du Chêne 61
1228 Plan-les-Ouates, Switzerland
Tel: 41 22 707 32 32
USA: 1 212 355 6444

**RAYMOND WEIL S.A.**
Avenue Eugène-Lance 36-38
1211 Geneva 26, Switzerland
Tel: 41 22 884 00 55
USA: 1 212 355 3350

**RGM**
801 West Main Street
Mount Joy PA 17552 USA
Tel: 1 717 653 9799

**RICHARD MILLE**
11 Rue du Jura
2345 Les Breuleux Jura
Switzerland
Tel: 41 32 959 43 53
USA: 1 310 205 5555

**ROGER DUBUIS**
Rue André-de-Garrini 2
CH-1217 Meyrin-Geneva
Switzerland
Tel: 41 22 783 28 28
USA: 1 570 970 8888

**ROLEX**
Rue François Dussaud 3-7
1211 Geneva 24, Switzerland
Tel: 41 22 302 22 00
USA: 1 212 758 7700

**ROTARY WATCH LTD**
8486 Regent Street
London W 1 B 5 RR
England
Tel: 44 207 434 5541

**S.COIFMAN**
3069 Taft Street
Hollywood FL 33021 USA
Tel: 1 954 921 2444

**SCATOLA DEL TEMPO**
Via del Mille, 17
23891 Barzanò, Italy
Tel: 39 03 921 14 81
USA: 1 800 988 3254

**TAG HEUER**
Avenue des Champs-Montants 14A
2074 Marin, Switzerland
Tel: 41 32 755 60 00
USA: 1 973 467 1890

**TB BUTI**
1784 West Avenue, Bay 3
Miami Beach FL 33139 USA
Tel: 1 305 538 9300

**TUTIMA**
Trendelbuscher Weg 16-18
D-27777 Ganderkesee
Germany
Tel: 49 422198 830
USA: 1 310 378 78520

**URWERK**
34 Rue des Noirettes
CH- 1227 Carouge-Genève
Tel: 41 21 900 20 25
USA: 1 310 205 5555

**VACHERON CONSTANTIN**
Rue des Moulins 1
1204 Geneva
Switzerland
Tel: 41 22 9302005
USA: 1 212 713 0707

**ZANNETTI**
Via Monte d'Oro
00186 Rome, Italy
Tel: 39 06 687 6651

**ZENITH**
2400 Le Locle
Switzerland
Tel: 41 32 930 62 62
USA: 1 973 467 1890